DALE L. MORGAN

Dale L. Morgan

MORMON AND WESTERN HISTORIES IN TRANSITION

Richard L. Saunders

THE UNIVERSITY OF UTAH PRESS
Salt Lake City

The Defiance House Man colophon is a registered trademark of The
University of Utah Press. It is based on a four-foot-tall Ancient Puebloan
pictograph (late PIII) near Glen Canyon, Utah.

LIBRARY OF CONGRESS CATALOGING-IN-PUBLICATION DATA
Names: Saunders, Richard L., 1963– author.
Title: Dale L. Morgan : Mormon and Western Histories in Transition / Richard
   L. Saunders. Description: Salt Lake City : The University of Utah Press, [2023] |
   Includes bibliographical references and index. | Summary: "This is the first biography
   of Dale L. Morgan, preeminent historian of the Latter Day Saints, the fur trade,
   and the trails of the American West. The book explores how, despite personal
   struggles, Morgan remained committed to interpreting the past on the strength
   of documentary evidence, leaving a legacy to inspire contemporary historians.
   Connecting Morgan's life with some of the broad cultural changes that shaped his
   experiences, this book engages with the methodological shifts that coincided with
   his career: the mid-twentieth-century collision of interpretations within Latter
   Day Saint history and the development of a descriptive, scholarly approach to that
   history. Morgan's work signaled the start of new ways of understanding, studying,
   and retelling history, and he motivated a generation of historians from the 1930s
   to the 1970s to transform their historical approaches. Sounding board, mentor,
   and close friend to Nels Anderson, Leonard Arrington, Fawn Brodie, Juanita
   Brooks, Bernard DeVoto, and Wallace Stegner, Dale Morgan is the common factor
   linking this influential generation of mid-twentieth-century historians of western
   America"—Provided by publisher.
Identifiers: LCCN 2023005958 | ISBN 9781647691202 (hardback) |
   ISBN 9781647691219 (paperback) | ISBN 9781647691226 (ebook)
Subjects: LCSH: Morgan, Dale L. (Dale Lowell), 1914-1971. | Church of Jesus Christ
   of Latter-day Saints—Historiography. | Mormon Church—Historiography. |
   Historians—United States—Biography. | Mormons—United States—Biography. |
   West (U.S.)—Historiography. | BISAC: BIOGRAPHY & AUTOBIOGRAPHY /
   Historical | HISTORY / United States / State & Local / West (AK, CA, CO, HI,
   ID, MT, NV, UT, WY) | LCGFT: Biographies.
Classification: LCC E175.5.M65 S28 2023 | DDC 289.3/32092 [B]—dc23/eng/
   20230221
LC record available at https://lccn.loc.gov/2023005958

Frontispiece photo of Dale L. Morgan used by permission,
Utah State Historical Society.

Printed and bound in the United States of America.

Errata and further information on this and other titles
available online at UofUpress.com

to all those who, like Dale Morgan, work as they must
so as to write of the past as they choose

Conflict makes news, and news makes history, yet men live rich and quiet lives outside the boiling currents of their times, and who shall say whether the thousand existences in quiet do not more nearly express the shape of human experience than the fiercely spotlighted existence that survives as history.

—Dale L. Morgan, *The Great Salt Lake*

Beneath every history, there is another history—there is, at least, the life of the historian.

—Hilary Mantel, *The Reith Lectures*, 2017

Contents

PART II: AN UNCOMFORTABLE INTERLUDE

PART III: WESTERN AMERICAN HISTORIAN

Photographs follow page 254.

Foreword

My relationship with Dale L. Morgan was twofold. Most obviously, he was a prominent American historian of the generation preceding my own. Of more significance in my life, however, he was an example and mentor to me when I was growing up. Dale (I always called him by his first name even when I was a child) was a good friend and historical collaborator of my father, Maurice L. Howe. A Utah newspaper reporter, my father was also an amateur Utah historian at a time in the early twentieth century when Utah history was often pursued by amateurs. He coauthored a biography of the early Utah settler Miles Goodyear, a "gentile" (i.e., non-Mormon) whom Brigham Young's followers bought out when they established their own settlement on the shores of Great Salt Lake.[1] Dale Morgan and my father got to know each other when both of them worked on the Utah state guidebook created by the Federal Writers' Project of the Works Progress Administration (WPA) during the Great Depression. Their friendship continued enduringly thereafter.

My father had a weak heart left from a childhood bout with rheumatic fever. Nowadays such a condition could be treated medically and the patient could live a long life, but not in 1945, when my father died at the age of 42. I was then eight years old. Dale Morgan continued his friendship with my mother and visited us occasionally. I grew up loving history, inspired by my father and Dale.

Neither Dale nor my father pursued a PhD in history as I did. Nor did either of them become a college history teacher as I did. Dale's deafness impaired his speaking ability and would have posed a significant challenge to a teaching career at that time. My father taught junior high school briefly after losing his job as a newspaper reporter during the Great Depression, but did not specialize in teaching history. My years in graduate school at the University of California, Berkeley, 1962–66, occurred during the time when Dale was working there in the Bancroft Library, and my mother and I would see him frequently there. But when he died in 1971, I had gone to teach at Yale University; I did not return to teach at UC Berkeley until 1973. I am glad Dale Morgan's own story, through which my father's life weaves in and out, is at last before a new generation of readers. Dale has remained an inspiration to me all my life.

—Daniel Walker Howe
Rhodes Professor Emeritus, American History, Oxford University, and Professor Emeritus, History, University of California, Los Angeles

Acknowledgments

No one writes in a vacuum, particularly not when one writes biography. Writing history is, as Gary Topping once noted, both an intensely individual and an essentially communal activity. The atmosphere of biography insures that any writer relies heavily upon others in the prosecution of his craft. Gary, perhaps my first and certainly best critic, is the most insightful reviewer I've ever met. He grasps themes, unmasks errors, and offers praise with equal parts surgical precision and generosity. Every scholar should have such a resource!

I must express particular appreciation to various members of the extended Morgan family—various Morgans, Holmes, Hardys, Bleaks, and Ostlers—for their kind assistance with family and personal information across more than thirty years. Of especial kindness were the members of Dale's late immediate family I knew personally, brother James S. and wife Mary Beth Morgan, and Robert H. Morgan and wife Audry (who found it difficult or impossible to communicate in the aftermath of a massive stroke by the time I knew them). That list also includes Dale's cousins T. Gerald (Jerry) Bleak, Norma Bleak Engen, and Clyde Hardy. Since his father's death nearly in the middle of this project, Jim Morgan Jr., has been the custodian of his uncle's legacy. I am similarly grateful to nieces and nephews Jim Barton, Susan Morgan Todd, and to Lynn and Lisa North. Many interviewees, identified individually in the notes, shared personal reminiscences and knowledge of Dale.

The support and encouragement of some friends can only be expressed posthumously, and for that I am deeply sorry. Such thanks are due to the late booksellers Curt Bench and Kent Walgren, both of whom set their hooks on this fish more firmly than they understood, and to Chad Flake of Brigham Young University (BYU). Brighter, happier thanks are due to the living: Bill Slaughter and Mike Landon, both formerly of the

Church History Library; Dr. Gregory C. Thompson, Roy W. Webb, and Nancy V. Young, all now formerly of the J. Willard Marriott Library's Special Collections department at the University of Utah, and the staff there now, particularly Todd Victor Samuelson and Rachel Ernst; booksellers Chris Bench, Kent Tschanz, and Ken Sanders; the successions of special collections librarians at Brigham Young University (BYU) who followed Chad, including Larry Draper, and now Greg Seppi and Cindy Brightenburg; and former Bancroft Library deputy director and friend Peter Hanff, as well as photo curator Jack von Euw and Kathryn Neal at the UC Berkeley Archives.

I have read hundreds of biographies, looking for models and inspiration. Among them, the work of three authors stand out: A. Scott Berg, D. Michael Quinn, and David L. Roll, whose smooth but forthright, masterful biographies of Charles Lindbergh, J. Reuben Clark, and George C. Marshall impressed me deeply.

Part of the research was underwritten by several Faculty Research Grants made by the University of Tennessee at Martin while I was employed there. The work further profited from a research fellowship at the Harry Ransom Center at the University of Texas at Austin in 2002, as well as faculty travel support from Southern Utah University. The comments and criticism of readers Jim Barton, Brian Cannon, Dan Howe, Leo Lyman, Patrick Mason, Jim McConkey, Jim Morgan, Jr., and Gary Topping were of material help in revision. Tom Krause championed this work at University of Utah Press, and Glenda Cotter saw it through to fruition. Copyeditor Anya Martin slew the run-on sentences and drove spikes through far too many grammatical, factual, and citational errors.

Finally, those who materially made this book possible at various evolutionary stages across this excessively long arc: longtime friends Scott and Megan Christensen, hosts to innumerable research trips in the early years, and my long-suffering, altruistic wife Carrie, with the Saunders hooligans in tow: AnnMarie, Stephen, Heidi, David, Pinkie (Rebecca), Dan, Missy, and Nathan. And Jiuye (Joy). A bit of autobiographical context for this project is merited: my research for the biography began when AnnMarie was a preschooler; it now comes to fruition only after completion of her second graduate degree, and four subsequent weddings among her then-unborn siblings. Yes, it has taken that long.

* * * * *

Let me say a bit about the project in terms of two friends. This book progressed formally in fits and starts through two of my three graduate degrees, the first one of them taken directly under Chas Peterson. I think I may have been his last grad student at Utah State University. In 1985, the year my wife and I married, I did a readings course with Chas on the fur trade. Sitting behind the oak desk that had been Frederick Jackson Turner's during his summer as visiting faculty member, I remember Chas pulling a copy of the paperback edition of *Jedediah Smith and the Opening of the West* from his shelf and explaining that it was one of the key books in the literature. He also helped me understand that no book, no research is ever complete or definitive, showing me Morgan's update to his own work in *Jedediah Smith and His Maps of the American West*.

I was trying to decide then if I wanted to pursue the West and fur trade specifically as a study topic. With more insight than I had at the time, Chas discouraged me. It was exciting, he admitted, but this field of study had been transcended by other subjects and approaches. As a callow college student, I didn't understand, but a couple years later in one of my first graduate seminars, Chas had us read Patricia Nelson Limerick's *The Legacy of Conquest* when it was published. That book finally began to reify what he was trying to help me understand about history: as a discipline, history is less a study of the past than it is a conversation in the present. Perhaps I owe Chas Peterson the most because he introduced me to Hiram Martin Chittenden, Frederick Jackson Turner, and a score of other important writers, but particularly to Dale Morgan. He never intended to hand me a life's work. Better than thirty years down the river, long after retiring from USU and as we reconnected at his retirement home in St. George, Utah, Chas still remembered I was working on a biography of Morgan, and each time we met, he asked how I was doing. Rarely have I been so flattered.

Will Bagley, independent researcher and the most recent significant historian without portfolio, and I never really disconnected. We met sometime around 1994, maybe earlier. He asked for a bit of help (just a bit) with his first book. Thereafter we shared notes and questions back and forth from the beginnings of email. Lots else could be said about our relationship (beyond the fact that I remained a Latter-day Saint and he did not), but the truest point hurts the most—though Will read the finished manuscript, it breaks my heart that submission to the publisher was made only the day after he died. He will not see (with mortal eyes at least) the finished work he poked and prodded me to complete for so long.

"History itself," observed the subject of this biography, "is simply a sum total of personal experience."[2] At least once every time I sit down and turn on the lamp, I recall some insight, fact, or connection one or more of those friends told me about the fur trade, or Dale Morgan the historian, or the writing of history. I can never pay back what they gave me, but I can pay it forward in their honor.

A Note on Sources

The single most useful source of material on Dale Morgan's life and work is unquestionably his massive collection of papers (BANC MSS 71/161c) and photographs (BANC PIC 1971.121) at the Bancroft Library, University of California, Berkeley. The Dale L. Morgan Papers are generally available on microfilm there, with a duplicate at the University of Utah Manuscripts Division (Mfilm 560). Since the 80-reel microfilm set is the point of contact for the Dale L. Morgan Papers, notes in this biography cite Morgan's correspondence by *date, [reel]:[frame]* without citing which location holds the microfilm—Bancroft Library, Marriott Library, or my bedroom. To convert the microfilm locations to box and folder numbers for the actual letter, consult the Bancroft's finding aid to the collection. Where an item from a source other than the Morgan Papers is cited, individual items are listed by institutional manuscript number and box:folder number.

This biography required thirty years of my own lifetime because comprehending Morgan's papers required looking at virtually everything in them. The direct result of that process is my corpus of notes, essentially a calendar to the collection, describing at an item level the collection's contents. This multivolume document will be published separately with an eye toward facilitating scholarly access to Morgan's amassed material. Those interested in Morgan, his circle of acquaintances, or in mid-century Western American history are referred to that resource. The calendar also includes citations to hundreds of other Morgan materials scattered among manuscript collections other than his papers. The work of the Utah Historical Records Survey (HRS) and Writers' Project is divided between the Morgan Papers and the records of the Utah Historical Records Survey, MS B 114, Utah State Historical Society, Salt Lake City. These files tend to be the functional working files of both the HRS and the Writers' Project, which were given to the Utah State Historical Society and then, to a greater or lesser extent, comingled. Most of the documentary transcripts collected by both units are catalogued individually in the institution's general small-manuscript or MS A holdings.

Sometime about 1938, Dale Morgan began an autobiographical essay in which his hearing loss figured prominently. He proceeded through several drafts, probably intending it as literary or personal-experience comment. Later in the year he confided to Emily Morgan that he intended one day to write a novel about the social challenges he faced as a person with complete hearing loss. Textual comparison of the essay drafts show that they served as the foundations for the novel's opening, the writing of which progressed as far as his collegiate career in a corrected second draft. The novel manuscript remained incomplete and untitled when the project was dropped in early 1940. The untitled personal essay drafts are filed among his papers in the section of autobiographical writings (reel 25, frames 1709–1772); with some unused first draft material, the novel is today filed among surviving drafts of Morgan's short fiction on reels 54 and 55 (the connection was unrecognized by the processors).

Although Morgan wrote the UAN as a creative work, this topic of sensory loss and social isolation was emotionally a part of him, so the novel was a disingenuously drafted *roman à clef*. All personal names were fictionalized, but events, emotions, and details mentioned therein were lifted directly from his experience, and many can be collaborated by other independent sources. On the strength of those ratifications, and since Morgan's later historical work is characterized by such scrupulous dedication to factual accuracy and interpretive validity, as a biographer I am willing to accept this writing as genuine albeit disguised autobiography rather than a straightforward fictional work. I have relied upon it as an accurate rendition of Morgan's early life and familial realities. It is referred to in the notes as the "untitled autobiographical novel" (UAN). The respective second and additional draft typescripts of the novel are cited as such. Where possible, the factual authority of the autobiographical essay drafts has been cited over that of the UAN. Significant details differ somewhat between the drafts.

Abbreviations

The following abbreviations are used consistently throughout the notes.

[c]	Photocopy
CK	Charles Kelly
CU-Banc	Bancroft Library, University of California, Berkeley
DLM	Dale L. Morgan
DMEM	*Dale Morgan on Early Mormonism: Correspondence and a New History*, ed. John Phillip Walker (Salt Lake City: Signature Books, 1986).
EHM	Emily Holmes Morgan
ETH	Eleanor Towles Harris
FMB	Fawn M. Brodie
GPH	George P. Hammond
JB	Juanita Brooks
LJAHA	Leonard J. Arrington Historical Archive, Utah State University Special Collections and Archives, Logan
LN	Louise North
MoInRC	Reorganized Church of Jesus Christ of Latter Day Saints Library and Archives (now Community of Christ Library and Archives), Independence, MO
MRM	Madeline Reeder (Thurston) McQuown
MSR	Marguerite Sinclair Reusser
RKG	Robert K. Greenwood, Talisman Press
TxU-Hu	Harry Ransom Center, University of Texas at Austin.
UAN	Untitled autobiographical novel, edited revised typescript, DLM Papers, 54:1087–1262, *and* earlier draft typescripts, 54:1264–1330.
UHi	Utah Division of State History library, Salt Lake City.

ULA   Utah State University Special Collections and
          Archives, Logan
UPB   Brigham Young University, Provo, Utah.
USlC   Church History Library, Salt Lake City, Utah.
UU-Ms   Manuscripts Division, Special Collections, J. Willard Mar-
          riott Library, University of Utah, Salt Lake City.

"A Thousand Utterly Trivial Things"[1]

Books, I find, have a way of establishing their own internal imperatives.[2]
—Dale Morgan

DALE L. MORGAN WAS a mid-twentieth-century historian of the Latter Day Saints, of the fur trade, and the trails of the American West. As a historian of the latter, he was a figure of note, comfortable among the academic historians who knew him and his work well. Morgan was also a transitional figure whose career bridged changes in the way history was told and studied in America. Among the former, he was the linchpin figure linking a circle of Utah-involved writers who came to history in the 1930s and practiced between the 1940s and 1970s. No less an icon than Juanita Brooks acknowledged Morgan as a mentor, and he was a reader and advisor to fellow Utahns Nels Anderson, Fawn M. Brodie, Bernard DeVoto, and Wallace Stegner, as well as one of Leonard J. Arrington's earliest sounding boards. In sum, Dale Morgan was the common link binding Utah's influential mid-twentieth-century historians, encouraging their reconstructions of Western and of Mormon history. Even though he barely began and never finished a single major work of history in the field, his reputation as a researcher was so influential in Mormon history of the time that the two largest churches, long at odds with each other, joined forces to wheedle out of him a private review of what he was writing.

Morgan was a key figure in shifting the Latter Day Saint tradition of history from focusing on moralism, to documentation and explanation. It is only a bit of a reach to say that Dale Morgan has the distinction of being among the first significant historians of the Latter Day Saint tradition outside the churches themselves. Even after his career followed a different subject, Latter Day Saint history developed as a field of study during his lifetime, partly in direct response to his writing, even though he sat outside of its practice through most of his professional life.

* * * * *

With the utter naiveté of youth, I energetically decided to pursue this biography in 1991, just as the microfilmed Dale L. Morgan papers became available. Having written one biography as a graduate thesis (though with a completely different problem—virtually no source material), I thought I knew what would be involved. How wrong I was, and this book is the better for the three-decade delay. Over that long time span, I learned that there were no shortcuts. Early in my research, I read Morgan's own comment to Juanita Brooks that "any historian is only a joke without his files" and another comment asserted to a librarian that "there is no substitute, ever, for going to the ultimate sources when you are doing a job in history."[3] That experience made me think about the nature of biography itself. "To try to understand the experience of another," John Berger wrote:

> it is necessary to dismantle the world as seen from one's own place within it, and to reassemble it as seen from his. For example, to understand a given choice another makes, one must face in imagination the lack of choices which may confront and deny him. The world has to be dismantled and reassembled in order to be able to grasp, however clumsily, the experience of another. To talk of entering the other's subjectivity is misleading. The subjectivity of another does not simply constitute a different interior attitude to the same exterior facts. The constellation of facts, of which he is the center, is different.[4]

This was wise counsel for a biographer. I soon came to see that neither Morgan nor his work could be adequately comprehended without first comprehending his correspondence. The challenge was that there are over twenty-two *thousand* letters in his papers. I had not gotten far through them when Gary F. Novak published his critique of Morgan's approach to Latter Day Saint history. Novak assumed that Morgan's voluminous correspondence files were complete and thus offer a clear window into his historical thinking.[5] I had already found that his files provide nowhere near a complete record.

Perhaps between two-thirds and three-quarters of Dale Morgan's correspondence survived him. Regrettably, the missing quarter to third are the really important ones. If this biography lacks much of an interpersonal dimension, it is because its subject self-censored the record he left to history. To his mind, personal relations were precisely that—personal. Fortunately, family members and friends held onto scores of personal letters from Dale that he himself never retained as carbons. Those sheets provide contexts unavailable in any other source. For instance, while he kept over 900 letters from Madeline McQuown, his papers contain fewer than twenty-five carbons of his letters to her. Another twenty-five or so are found among her papers, but her letters refer directly to at least 229 now-missing letters and postcards from him, and evidence supports that she destroyed the vast majority of his letters to her. Of what does survive, Madeline censored many heavily—literally tore them into pieces—before her own papers became part of an institutional collection. I must observe parenthetically here that a biographer faces the danger of falling in love with one's subject when pursuing biography. However, villainizing those who opposed them is also a coincident danger. One of Morgan's foils was unquestionably McQuown, who must figure prominently in any consideration of him or his work.

I found it indispensably necessary to read the Morgan letters—all of them. So, legwork in the correspondence began and progressed sporadically between 1997 and 2012. It occupied consistent, almost daily effort between 2013 and 2019. The result of this staggering volume of material is that I have fought the factor plaguing Morgan himself: "there seems to be some inner compulsion," he observed while drafting his Jedediah Smith biography, "that requires one to put into a book all that is theoretically desirable, whether or not space limits and the internal necessities of a narrative will permit it to remain there!"[6]

The effort at basic research has exacted its price, however. Dale Morgan was more relevant in the 1990s. Senior scholars of Morgan's generation who had known and worked with him just two decades earlier were still listed in departmental and local telephone directories and were making the transition from activity into scholarly and regional immortality. That generational evolution added new layers of research. Then everything changed within a decade. Stegner sustained fatal injuries in an automobile accident. Juanita Brooks expired at ninety from age and under the soul-crushing weight of dementia. Historical interest was shifting generationally—and I was not yet ready to write, raising yet more new problems.

Avery Craven observed about historians that "those who were hailed as profound scholars in their day become objects of pity in the next. They are either revised, rejected, or ignored." H. J. Jackson was absolutely correct when he stated that "No dead author's work can be sustained without a convergence of audiences." In other words, a figure from the past must become relevant in the present. Jackson also noted that "revival of a once-celebrated name is a harder sell than rediscovery of an unknown one."[7]

Half a century after his passing, Dale Morgan is not a recognized name like DeVoto, Stegner, or Brooks, so his first biography needs to be less about the details of life and work than a contextualization of his life and his career. Morgan did exactly that in *Jedediah Smith and the Opening of the West*, as did Stegner in his biography of John Wesley Powell in *Beyond the Hundredth Meridian*. For Morgan again to become significant to history requires that he and his work be relevant to readers of a different, present generation.

* * * * *

I began this project in the 1990s because I considered Morgan to be ripe for a biography. I thought he was impressive—my own indulgent bit of antiquarianism. I complete the work in the 2020s, having crafted the biography as an unquestionable exercise in *synecdoche,* using Morgan and his career to represent broader changes his time and field. I have been a bit more explicit than synecdoche employed in other works, perhaps the best known of which is DeVoto's *The Year of Decision: 1846* (1943). The chapters of *Dale L. Morgan: Mormon and Western Histories in Transition* often step far beyond Morgan's life to explore some of the broad cultural changes that shaped his experience. The book is laced together around the broad shift coinciding with his career: the mid-twentieth century collision of interpretations within Latter Day Saint history and the development of a descriptive, detached, scholarly approach to that history. Of all his work, Morgan's efforts within Latter Day Saint history have greatest relevance to today's readers, and I elected to make this context the biography's unifying element.

Concentrating on one theme necessarily leaves less room for others, in this case, Morgan's career in the context of Western American history. Western history had already buried its pioneers by the time Morgan came to history, but it was emerging as an academic specialty at the same time and for the same reasons as Latter Day Saint history. Dale Morgan came to history and practiced his craft as, arguably, one of the last of the

American West's "citizen historians," great amateurs in the tradition of William H. Prescott, Reuben Gold Thwaites, Hiram Martin Chittenden, and Hubert Howe Bancroft. Morgan earned no advanced academic degrees and was decidedly looked down upon by some academics of his time, yet he enjoyed a respected reputation—though sometimes grudgingly given—as a researcher and writer. Morgan and fellow "amateur" Alvin M. Josephy, Jr. (whose historical calling was the West's Native Americans), fell into their research specialty entirely by accident toward the closing of the era of the great amateur. Many historical writers before both men had come late and largely untrained to their calling, qualified mainly by their skill in writing or an unflagging interest in their topic. Over and over through his professional career, Morgan echoed what military historian John Toland said of his own: "I have no academic credentials as an historian. So I must let my work speak for me."[8]

A tell-all or "unauthorized" biographer typically remains free of positive attachment to the subject and writes with a negativity often approaching animus. A scholarly biographer is different. All of us have lived things we would prefer to leave unmentioned—most of them so minor as to be more personally embarrassing than damaging to ourselves or to others. Yet frequently the things we most desire to push out of memory have shaped character and weighted decisions most tellingly. All that has actually happened is a proverbial "matter of record" that has all happened, for good, ill, or indifference. As a believer in postmortal existence, I fully expect to face Dale Morgan some day and be required to justify to him every conclusion I reach. He will challenge every error and misstated fact, each inference and interpretation.

It is difficult to live another's life vicariously without trivializing the substantive or overemphasizing the meaningless. How does one choose the moments, decisions, feelings, and relationships that are important to another person? Summarizing an entire life in a few hundred pages is an act of remarkable arrogance, but the biographer's task is to condense the slow development of thought, to summarize agony, to distill time itself, to cast aside whole days in a well-lived life—in short, to abbreviate the passage of years into what will be for the reader a few hours of quiet occupation. But just as the hottest coal reveals an unattractive coat of dead gray ash when painted by a flashlight's bright beam, the risks of biographical scrutiny threaten to reveal more than we ourselves perceived.

Despite any best effort, biography is a type of voyeurism, albeit one cloaked in cultural acceptance. Carl Rollyson even called biography, not entirely irreverently, "a higher form of cannibalism."[9] In biography, the responsibility of determining what is emphasized and what is ignored, what is documentable and what is outright guessed, falls upon the writer, not the subject. George Marsden observed wisely that "individual lives do not fit a single neat story line. Many things happen at once."[10] That statement is never truer than of Dale L. Morgan, and I have thus taken (or tried to take) David Herbert Donald's approach to his subjects (both Abraham Lincoln and biography generally) as a model: "I have asked at every stage of his career what he knew when he had to take critical actions, how he evaluated the evidence before him, and why he reached his decisions. It is, then a biography written from Lincoln's point of view, using the information and ideas available to him. It seeks to explain rather than to judge."[11] An honest biographer walks in the narrow margins between ignoring his subject's human failings as irrelevant and overlooking them in a form of censorship, and between discussing his subject's foibles fairly and emphasizing them as sensationalism. History, of which biography is one form, is the pursuit of contemporary context. Still, even biographies require some sort of thematic coherence or they devolve into mere antiquarian chronologies.

Beyond simply chronicle, however, biographers are also interpreters, and that interpretation must be based on actuality. Morgan himself wrote to Juanita Brooks:

> The writing of any biography, I think, is attended by a certain empathetic response in the writer. If one wasn't interested in the first place, he would not normally be writing the fellow's story; and it is the business of a writer to "understand" his subject better than other people have. Whether the man himself or in his behavior is admirable or not, to understand why he is or how he is motivated in anything he does tends to give one a certain sympathy for him.[12]

Thus, this biography is partially my answer to earlier works using Dale Morgan as a launching point in opposite directions. In 1991, I attended as John Phillip Walker discussed his experience editing *Dale Morgan on Early Mormonism* (1986) at the First Unitarian Church in Salt Lake City. Walker admitted to his audience that compiling the book was cathartic for his personal disbelief and departure from the Church of Jesus Christ of Latter-day Saints: if a researcher as careful as Morgan dismissed Latter-day Saint claims, then certainly there was no reason for Walker to believe.

Dale Morgan had been deceased for less than fifteen years at the time Walker's book appeared. His reputation as a historically informed skeptic of Latter-day Saint origins, a standing given new life by Walker's work, was still influential enough to merit a head-on challenge. Part of that task came a decade later in the second work of influence on this biography, Gary F. Novak's lengthy *FARMS Review of Books* critique of Morgan's empiricism in 1996. Novak pointed to holes in Morgan's empiricism to demonstrate that he wrote with an anti-church agenda.[13]

Both writers produced insightful works, but both also are flawed. Walker's position seems like nonsense to me for the simple reason that he (like Morgan) incorrectly conflated historical evidence with faith, but more importantly because he accepted a lack of evidence as proof of an assertion. Morgan himself noted that a scholar never possesses all relevant facts. While I happen to agree with Novak and disagree with Morgan on the faith thing, Novak's work is similarly polemical, trying to cut both mortal and eternal truth from same cloth. Both Walker and Novak invoke Morgan's reputation as their authority, vindicating either positively or negatively their own perspective. Both justify themselves in their critique, using Dale Morgan in a motivating, ethical, or utilitarian fashion, the very perspective Morgan himself challenged. Neither looks at Morgan in his own context—as a pioneer, yes, and perhaps possessing a pioneer's zeal, but also possessing the pioneer's line-of-site limitations to their discoveries. Morgan had new facts, but he never had all the facts, and he dismissed the veracity of LDS claims to revelation well before embarking on his histories.

My biography adopts a historicist's view of Dale Morgan but at the philosophical price of historicism as well: all I do is describe and contextualize, leaving readers no basis to *do* anything because of Morgan. Perhaps the best I can hope for is that by better understanding the man and his work, we allow him to *be* a man, a man of his time: one piece within this mortal puzzle of context, neither Walker's unimpeachable saint of factualism nor Novak's naive devil of skepticism. But there is more. In teasing out that context, I hope to provide not only a long-overdue biography of one of Utah and the West's great nonfiction writers, but also an exploration of Mormon history's transitional writers, those who existed between the polemics of the nineteenth century and the detached scholasticism of the late twentieth. Hopefully one may see not merely who the actors were as perspectives changed, but *why* the generational change was meaningful.

This work will not please every reader. A good biography never will, for by their choices of theme and selection of evidence the biographer must foster coherence, and life lived is anything but coherent. The best I can hope for is to clear and outline a temporal path for Dale Morgan's subsequent biographers who will craft their works around different themes. There are plenty from which to choose. Morgan's career and his ocean of correspondence are threaded by currents and crosscurrents, obstacles, and new channels. Conflicting actions, unrealized intents, hundreds of friends and acquaintances, dozens of significant writing projects, and scores of opportunities both seized and untaken make up the man. Hopefully the bibliography at the end of this volume will help remedy the omissions, for out of a sense of obligation to comparative brevity, the biography callously omits discussing even briefly projects that may have consumed Morgan's attention for years.

In 1964, to a graduate student who wanted to generate a bibliography of his work, Morgan commented that he had never studied under a scholar or had a class in his professional field. He had instead, he wrote, "gone my own way, following and developing my own interests, and learning what I needed to know to do what I wanted to do. All the rest has followed from a desire to understand some things about the [W]est."[14]

PART I

Mormon, Historian

CHAPTER I

"Under the Shadow of Her Love"[1]

Family and a Salt Lake City Childhood, 1914–1929

No one should take up history who has not also the capacity for taking infinite pains.[2]
—Dale Morgan

ON A CLEAR ATLANTIC-SEABOARD DAY, early in the spring of 1971, Jim Holliday of Lafayette, California, and a few friends repaired to a spot in Louise North's garden south of Washington, DC. The April day was cool. The first budding green was beginning to tint the spindly undergrowth. Beneath the rattling, upswept boughs of an enormous tulip poplar, someone produced a spade. The group was subdued as they excavated a small hole between the tree's roots. Into it was gently poured a powdery, granular ash—the cremated remains of historian, long-time friend, and possibly the man who might have been North's future husband, Dale L. Morgan.

Six months earlier Louise and Dale had visited the same spot. Though nothing had been overtly discussed, Dale continued gently to press his suit. His visit to her home in Accokeek, Maryland, was the most recent in a long, happy series of encounters which had begun with both her and her late husband Max in the early 1940s. Since Max's death in 1964, Dale's occasional visits to Maryland had taken a more intimate turn. In October 1970, Dale left Louise to return to Berkeley, California, and his work as a research historian at the Bancroft Library, fully intent on formally proposing marriage to her—again—the following spring. That trip, just the previous October, as pleasant as it was, wrung him out physically. In November, symptoms finally tipped off his physician to look for the metastatic colon cancer that had quietly, insidiously ravaged his body and left him merely a few months of uneasy mortality.

Privately secreting a small pile of ash in the Maryland countryside may have marked the finality of a man's death. It did not carry the commemorative solemnity nor pay the formal homage that another memorial service did, held nearly half a continent away in Salt Lake City. Morgan would have appreciated the private act in the Maryland woods; the memorial service doubtless would have irked him as a cultural formality which met the needs of the living rather than the dead. The staid ceremony of best dress, song, and memorial reminiscence, undergirded by veiled appeals to a faith he did not share with his family, was held in the church building of the Canyon Rim Second Ward, a local congregation of the Church of Jesus Christ of Latter-day Saints, still commonly known as Mormons. If Dale Morgan was not already dead, the unapologetic agnostic might have resented the family dragging his memory back into church.[3]

* * * * *

Life is made of chances missed and taken. Had not an itinerant preacher chanced across a peculiar new book late in the summer of 1830, then Dale L. Morgan might not have embarked on a career to become one of the great historians of the American West a little more than a hundred years later. Parley Parker Pratt regarded his happenstance discovery of the Book of Mormon as nothing less than divine providence. Believing in neither divinity nor fate of any sort, Pratt's great-grandnephew Dale Morgan certainly would have disagreed but probably appreciated the historical significance of the event anyway.

Pratt's itinerant travels took him east from his home in northern Ohio to Buffalo, New York, and eastward along the Erie Canal. Leaving his wife in Rochester and continuing alone on foot, Pratt left the canal and walked inland, preaching as he found opportunity. Travelling through the neighborhood of Newark, inviting residents to attend his meetings, he was introduced to a local Baptist deacon, Squire Wells. Mr. Wells found Pratt's religious ideas intriguing and mentioned that he had acquired a well-travelled copy of a curious new book published a few miles away in Palmyra. The Book of Mormon purported to have come from an angel and was offered as a book of revelation. Early the next day Pratt called on Wells to see the book, and began reading. The narrative related the arrival, faith, and eventual downfall of a primitive Christian people in the New World. Pratt remained with the Wells through the day, into the night, and on till morning to consume most of its 588 pages in a single sitting. Its contents impressed him deeply enough that he walked a few more miles to Manchester to meet the book's "author and proprietor," one Joseph Smith, Jr. Smith was not at home, but after a few short days of intense discussion with Smith's family, Pratt was baptized by Oliver Cowdery into the small sect known then as the "Church of Christ." Cowdery had written out the book's text at Smith's dictation. Hyrum Smith, Joseph's older brother, presented Pratt with a copy of the Book of Mormon. Two weeks later, with his copy of the book in hand, Pratt set out to rejoin his wife.[4]

Meanwhile, Orson Pratt, Parley's younger brother, was off at college. Orson was fourth of the five sons born to Jared and Charity Pratt, junior to Parley by five years. While his older brother was striding about the countryside on his religious mission, nineteen-year-old Orson was at school in Canaan, New York. Parley arrived unannounced in Canaan in mid-September 1830 with news for the family and Orson of the new sect to which he now belonged. This small group stood firmly on Biblical scripture but also accepted the Book of Mormon as both a companion volume to the Bible and as irrefutable evidence that God had reopened the heavens to mankind. The church, derisively labeled *Mormonites* by critics, accepted and practiced the gifts of the Spirit and advocated Christian principles, but they also denied the authority of other Christian sects and the validity of their ordinances, claiming instead to be a complete restoration of priesthood authority under the hands of the original apostles. Orson immediately accepted the invitation to baptism on the strength of Parley's word, and in October 1830, left Canaan for Fayette on his own effort to meet Joseph Smith.

Thus began Parley and Orson Pratt's tenure in what became known a few years later as the Church of Jesus Christ of Latter-day Saints. The brothers gave themselves to their newfound faith in careers that revolved around lifetimes of service as missionaries and, more importantly, as prolific and influential writers. In a church dominated by a hierarchical structure but conducted by a lay priesthood, other than the founder Joseph Smith, the Pratt brothers produced the most important written doctrinal works of the church's first and second generations. A committee comprised of Martin Harris, Oliver Cowdery, and David Whitmer (all important early converts) appointed both Parley and Orson to the newly organized Quorum of Twelve Apostles in 1835. Orson, at 23, was the youngest person ever to serve in that body. A little more than a decade later, Orson Pratt was among the members of the Pioneer Company as the largest segment of a divided church moved to the Great Basin in 1847.

With George A. Smith, Orson Pratt was the first of the saints to stride into the Salt Lake Valley, several days before the body of the camp arrived. A week later, he offered the dedicatory prayer in the valley as the party began to lay the first foundations for the Mormons' new home. As did the other apostles, he served many proselyting missions abroad, several of which were to Great Britain, where he was editor of the *Latter-day Saints' Millennial Star* from 1848 to 1850, and again from 1856 through 1857. A collection of his pamphlet treatises, *Orson Pratt's Works,* was a key book of doctrine and theology in England for decades.

Though his older brother and fellow apostle Parley Pratt made a reputation for himself as a foreign missionary and as the church's greatest early pamphleteer, it was Orson who came to be regarded as the closest thing to a systematic theologian the church produced after the death of Joseph Smith. Orson possessed a keen analytical mind that bordered on brilliance. His hobbies were mathematics and astronomy, both of which he studied as a young man. He published in the field, including a book, *A New and Easy Method of Solution of the Cubic and Biquadratic Equations,* and eventually compiled an extensive manuscript on differential calculus that remained unpublished.[5] Orson Pratt maintained an astronomical observatory for decades on the Temple Block in Salt Lake City. Recognizing Pratt's gift for rationality and deductive logic, Brigham Young delegated to Orson the responsibility for making the official announcement and argument for the practice of "plural marriage" in 1852.[6]

Like most of the church's apostles of the time, Orson Pratt became a polygamist during the 1840s. Over the next forty years, despite his travels abroad, Pratt presided over and provided for a family that eventually consisted of ten wives and their families, forty-five children in all. Pearl Pratt was one of fifty-seven-year-old Orson's youngest children from his ninth marriage to Margaret Graham. Pearl was born in 1872, Margaret's second child and only daughter, a few years before her father died in 1881 as the last of the original apostolic quorum members in Utah. Margaret remarried, though her oldest children were raised in Salt Lake City by her aunt, Pratt's sixth wife Marion Ross Pratt. In 1893, at age sixteen, Pearl Pratt married James Samuel Morgan.

James S. Morgan, called Samuel or Sam throughout his life, was born the fourth child and third son of English converts and emigrants Joseph R. and Mary Morgan. Joseph served for many years as bishop of the Salt Lake City Fifteenth Ward. Following their marriage, James and Pearl Morgan settled their new family a few blocks to the north of downtown in a newer neighborhood of comfortable if close-set brick homes favored by many of the city's skilled workers. Their first child, James Lowell Morgan (called Lowell), was born the next year. Lowell was followed by four brothers and finally a sister: Orson Joseph, known always as OJ; Harold, known as Hal; Ralph; Alan Dale; and Carolyn. None of the Morgans left comments about their upbringing, but the memories slipped occasionally into family letters that suggested a household environment of competitive mischief and activity.

Lowell Morgan grew into a round-faced, energetic young man with a natural gift for music. While still in high school, Lowell and a group of friends at West High School formed a dance band, the Eolians. Lowell played piano. The Eolians filled dance dates across the city. In the summer they and their instruments (minus Lowell's piano) rode the Bamberger Interurban rail line north from Salt Lake City into Davis County to play in one of the promenades at Lagoon, a resort on the eastern shore of the Great Salt Lake. Lowell's self-taught piano skills were impressive and his taste decidedly ran to popular music. When travelling on the road as a salesman a few years later, Lowell Morgan often returned to his hotel after a day of making sales contacts and played the lobby piano for a couple hours to kill time and relax.[7] At a time when community events like dances were predominant forms of entertainment, the Eolians' style of popular dance music could be learned and improvised from the blizzard of sheet music blanketing the country from the creative storm centered in New York City's Tin Pan Alley. While still in high school, Lowell fell hard for a neighborhood girl, Emily Holmes, a schoolmate and the youngest of Samuel and Mary Deeks Holmes' quartet of close-knit daughters.

* * * * *

Dale Morgan's maternal relatives included no such notables as the Pratts. His great-grandparents, Samuel and Agnes Holmes, joined the Mormons in London during the 1850s. They eventually emigrated to Utah with their family, as did thousands of other British citizens who joined the church between 1837 and the turn of the twentieth century. Samuel and Agnes Holmes waited longer than most, bearing a family and remaining in England for over two decades after their conversion and marriage. Samuel was a gunsmith. By 1875 he had worked at the Royal Small Arms Factory in Enfield for nineteen years. What prompted their emigration has not come down through the family, but the couple and their seven surviving children departed London in January 1876, bound for the American West.

Within a year, the Holmes family settled into a house on 300 North Street, between 500 and 600 West. By this time railroad spurs crosscut the western half of the city, which was the heart of its industry and manufacturing. One spur line delivered the massive stone blocks from the mountains south of the valley through the gated adobe wall directly to the downtown Salt Lake Temple site. A year after he arrived, Samuel Holmes was walking home from downtown, cutting through the Utah Central Railway yard when he stumbled and fell across the rails beneath a backing locomotive. The heedless iron wheels cut him quite literally in half. Agnes, his wife, expecting her husband home for lunch that afternoon, heard steps on the porch and went to greet him at the door. She was instead met by men bearing into the kitchen a plank on which lay her husband's severed remains, the unannounced shock untempered even by a sheet covering the gore. The man sent ahead to inform her before the body arrived had stopped to fortify himself with a drink and never made it to the house.[8]

Samuel and Agnes Holmes' son, also Samuel Holmes, became the family breadwinner by necessity at age eighteen. The Utah Central offered him employment in their repair shop, perhaps as compensation for the family's loss, which he accepted. A few months later, Mary Louise Deeks, whom the Holmeses had known in London, moved into the Holmes's household. She arrived in Salt Lake City only a few months after them as an unaccompanied immigrant. The rest of the Deeks family remained in England.

Samuel and Mary married in 1880. By 1882, he was a skilled boiler-maker. Seven years later, Samuel borrowed $600 and formed the Garrick & Holmes Boiler Shop in a partnership with former coworker Alexander Garrick. Like the Morgans, Samuel Holmes was financially stable but definitely circulated on the lower end of Salt Lake City's middle-class economy. Garrick was twenty years older than his young partner, but the men's reputations guaranteed them business so long as steam remained the main power source in industry and transportation. Samuel became politically active and participated in the Twenty-second Ward congregation, serving as elder's quorum president and then as its bishop.

Samuel and Mary Holmes raised a tight-knit family. Their first child, Ernest, born in 1881, was followed by four girls and a second son, who died in infancy. The four sisters grew up virtually inseparable. Every family photo showing one of the Holmes girls shows the other three as well.

Inevitably, however, each of the girls found beaux and eventually married. Ernest Holmes, older than his four sisters and the sole male in that generation of the family, married and became actively involved in the state Democratic Party. The party championed organized labor, which populated the West's coal, copper, and silver mines, its smelters and railroad crews with a stream of Central and Eastern European immigrants. For the first half of the twentieth century, Democrats controlled the Utah legislature, and frequently held the governor's office. Clara, the oldest Holmes girl and senior to the youngest sister by ten years, married William Hardy. Annie, Clara's junior by five years, married Thomas N. Bleak (pronounced *blake*), a descendant of southern-Utah pioneer James Godson Bleak. Ada, two years younger than Annie, married Frank Ostler. Emily Holmes, the youngest, was born in 1894. In the early 1910s, she fell for classmate J. Lowell Morgan, six months her junior.

After high school graduation, Lowell Morgan began working as a bank teller and playing dance dates on weekends with his band. While she was dating Lowell, Emily determined to attend college. In fall 1912, she registered for a qualifying "normal" or teacher-training course at the University of Utah, which sat high on the alluvial bench above the city. In the 1910s, the country was in the middle of a nationwide drive to upgrade public schools and qualify teaching staff. Commuting the four miles on the city's streetcar lines, the seventeen-year-old doubled her class load each term and completed the two-year course in a single year. In her fall term she took classes in Educational Psychology, Nature Study, Training, Elementary Education, Manual Training, Physical Education, and Hygiene; she substituted electives in art with five core classes through the spring term to qualify for a normal certificate.[9] Emily Holmes was awarded her normal degree at commencement ceremonies on June 4, 1913.

A little more than a year later, nineteen-year-old Emily May Holmes married her youthful sweetheart, James Lowell Morgan, in a civil ceremony across the county line just to the north of Salt Lake City. The couple moved in with her parents, either to their small yellow-brick house in the north end of Salt Lake City at 418 West 400 (or Fourth) North Street, or perhaps into the detached cottage behind the house, both within the boundaries of the Salt Lake Twenty-second Ward. Given their mutual feelings, both families were probably not surprised by the match. A few months later in August, Lowell Morgan received the Melchizedek priesthood and was ordained an Elder, perhaps a step towards a Latter-day Saint temple ceremony "sealing" their civil marriage.[10]

Lowell and Emily Morgan were dedicated to each other and undoubtedly a happy couple. Emily delivered the couple's first child, a boy,
on December 18, 1914.[11] She and Lowell chose to name their son *Lowell* for his father and *Dale* for Lowell Morgan's youngest (and favorite)
brother, Alan Dale Morgan.[12] Two months later, on the first Sunday of
the following February in the Salt Lake Twenty-second Ward, Lowell
Dale Morgan was given the Latter-day Saint equivalent of a Christian
christening. Standing in front of the congregation holding his son, Lowell offered a prayer in his son's behalf. In it, Lowell formally specified his
son's full name, by which the baby would be known on the records of
the church, and asked God for specific blessings on the infant's behalf.[13]
Until he attended college, Dale was recorded as "Lowell D" or just "Lowell" on both church records and legal documents, but following family
practice the baby boy was called by his middle name—Dale—and was
never known publicly as anything else. By the time he was in high school
the young man was signing his name "Dale L. Morgan" and eventually
convention simply won out over legality.

* * * * *

Dale Morgan was born into a Latter-day Saint family in the heart of Zion.
Salt Lake City reclined contentedly on the northern slope of a broad
mountain valley. Its settlers did not think in small terms. The initial plat
of Salt Lake City was laid off in a four-square grid of identical blocks. Its
streets measured a uniform 164-feet wide, planned to be sufficient to turn
a wagon and double yoke of oxen without backing. For three decades the
Mormons exercised, or tried to exercise, an uneasy independence from
the world. The transcontinental railroad, completed in 1869, tied the
Wasatch Front (so named for the range of mountains forming its eastern
boundary, dividing the Great Basin from the Colorado Plateau) to the rest
of the American nation, but statehood for Utah was still years off. Though
the Mormons accommodated to Victorian sentiments and eventually surrendered the practice of polygamy, the functional independence provided
by statehood was delayed until 1896.

Neither Utah nor the Mormons were well received by the young twentieth century. Apostle Reed Smoot's election to the U.S. Senate in 1902
reignited a firestorm against the church and its religious practices in the
American press. The 1910s saw popular anti-Mormon agitation in Britain. State economics were no better than Utah's cultural ostracism. The

collapse of farm-commodity prices following World War I, compounded by a decade-long drought, complicated by high unemployment as mining and smelting industries adopted mechanization, simply meant that the Intermountain West had already practiced depression living for a decade when the Great Depression hit.[14] The state voted Democratic, thanks to a high population of laboring voters scattered throughout its mines and farms in rural counties. Most of the Wasatch Front did as well, but much of the population in Utah's largest city was stolidly Republican.

The city in which Dale Morgan was born occupied a fraction of the geography over which it would later sprawl. Cities and towns between Draper in the south and the Wasatch Hot Springs on the north were still widely separated by the last vestiges of local agriculture, but the fields were filling rapidly with new developments. Salt Lake City effectively ended at 2100 South or Twenty-first South Street. Between that and the smelter town of Murray lay worked fields of hay, grain, and sugar beets, as well as pasturage for cattle and horses. The space was what urban geographer Carl Abbott called "superficially rural": open land transportationally adjacent to urban concentrations all around it. With railroads bringing far cheaper foodstuffs from larger fields and urban centers abroad, the floor of the Salt Lake valley merely waited to be developed over the succeeding two generations into the Wasatch megapolitan.[15] In the 1920s, however, the state capital was still the gravitational center in the valley's constellation of small towns.

Dale Morgan grew into a fair-faced baby boy with an unruly shock of strikingly blonde hair. Like many first-time parents, Lowell and Emily spent a good deal of money on camera film and took dozens of pictures of their boy in the bath, in the yard, and posed or playing with one or the other of them. On a whim Emily entered Dale in Salt Lake City's annual "Beautiful Baby" contest in 1915. Her son carried off first prize and ten dollars in gold as "prettiest baby" from among more than a thousand entrants, and his photo was published in the *Salt Lake Herald*.[16] Lowell Morgan worked frantically to keep the family financially afloat. In the mornings he carried a newspaper route for one of the city's dailies before heading to his bank job. During the 1915 Christmas holidays Emily got pregnant again, and while President Woodrow Wilson was busily keeping the U.S. out of European war, Dale's sister Ruth was born on August 12, 1916.

Emily's mother died suddenly from an undiagnosed ailment in the first week of January 1917.[17] James Samuel Morgan, Lowell and Emily's third child, was born on February 4, 1918, a year after the country finally leapt headlong "over there" and into the mechanized nightmare of Flanders' fields and the Great War. Now with three children, Lowell needed a better income. Building on his experience at the bank, Lowell made a transition to sales, becoming the northern Utah and Idaho representative for the Burroughs Adding Machine Company, headquartered in Salt Lake City. Lowell's younger brother Hal settled into insurance. The brothers had separate offices in the Walker Bank building downtown.[18] It was a smart career move for both young men. Hal remained with insurance into the 1950s, but his career was built on pure office work. Lowell's choice seemed more exciting. Across the country the metallic ticks and chatters of mechanical office machines were beginning to replace the papery scratching by clerks who tallied and checked columns of ledger figures. Even rural banks were beginning to use the tabulating calculators, and hundreds of rural banks and credit-fueled local businesses were scattered in small towns in the still-rural valleys—rich opportunity for an energetic extrovert like Lowell Morgan. Lowell was on the road through fall 1918 but probably came home as the Spanish Flu epidemic began laying waste to the country. For a year the life of many, perhaps most families seemed to exist on borrowed time. By 1919 the epidemic was clearly in decline, and the streets became populated again.

With their young family expanding quickly, Lowell and Emily moved away from both extended families in northern Salt Lake City to the new suburban neighborhood being built in the open fields on the city's south side. There they settled the children into a rented house on Redondo Avenue. In 1919 Hal Morgan loaned his older brother a Ford Model T automobile, probably to help his new career as a salesman. Lowell liked it well enough that several months later he bought one of his own. One of Dale's earliest memories was of playing outside when his father rolled up in the car and called to him from the driver's seat. Five-year-old Dale stood proudly on the running board as Lowell slowly drove the chuttering automobile the remaining few hundred feet down Redondo Avenue to the house.[19] Perhaps in the relief of being spared by the Spanish Flu epidemic, Emily became pregnant again. The last of J. Lowell and Emily Morgan's children, Robert Holmes Morgan, was born September 25, 1919. The only public record recording the entire family is the 1920 US Census.[20]

Lowell Morgan's business as an office machine salesman took him away from home on some circuit of his sales route quite often and for weeks at a time. During the last week of February or the first days of March 1920, Lowell cut short a trip to Boise, Idaho, and arrived home without much prior notice. The children's joyful welcome-home was soured by his severe stomach pains. One of Dale's last memories of his father was of Lowell standing in his bathrobe, framed by the kitchen doorway, suffering with "indigestion." He phoned his mother for advice, who told him to get some rest and prescribed "a good dose of salts," a common home-remedy but the worst possible treatment for the acute appendicitis festering inside him. By morning Lowell was in agony. With help from nearby family members, Emily got her husband to LDS Hospital, which sat on the opposite side of the city high in the Avenues.

Here Lowell got medical attention but no real help. Doctors quickly gave him a sedative, diagnosing the pain as a severely infected appendix. Lowell was rushed into surgery almost immediately. By this time, however, the inflamed tissue had held in the putrid rot as long as it could. During surgery Lowell's appendix ruptured, spewing bacteria into his abdominal cavity and the surgical incision as well. Today the implications of such a complication would have been controlled simply and effectively by antibiotic drugs, but in 1920 even sulfa drugs were still decades in the future. Despite surgical sterilization, hospitals lacked the means to control postoperative infections. The best that the surgeon could do was to cut out the infected organ, clean out Lowell's innards as well as possible, and close the wound. Peritonitis set in immediately.

Through the next week, the young father remained hospitalized, failing visibly toward a lingering, inevitable end. Lowell Morgan took twelve days to die. Even then he put on a brave face for the family. "A few days before he died," Hal Morgan wrote Dale in 1956, "I went up to see him and he said he at last had religion. I asked him what he meant and he said he was holy. Of course, he was kidding about the incision but he was a good sport till the end."[21] A cheery disposition did not change the stark reality facing his young wife. Emily's daily visits became a deathwatch. Haggard and grim-faced, she left their children with a neighbor or family member to ride the trolley, or saved a nickel and walked the three miles through the city's raw March mornings to sit through the day with her dying husband. On March 10, 1920, James Lowell Morgan succumbed to his disease and died of complications due to infection from a ruptured appendix.[22] He was twenty-five.

Years later Dale drafted a short story about a young boy being told of his father's death. It might have been pure invention, but the story probably included elements dredged from his own early memories. Morgan wrote about a five-year-old boy playing in the low-ceilinged concrete basement of his grandmother's home with his brother and sister. The mother returns home and gathers the children to tell them that their father is gone. Face flushed from their chase, still breathing heavily, too young to comprehend the meaning of this loss, the boy in the story wiggles free and bounds after his younger brother, finding naïve pleasure in the simple noise and alliteration of bawling "Daddy's dead! Daddy's dead!"[23]

Lowell's death left his twenty-five-year-old widow to provide for four children under five with no means of support. Robert, the baby, was not yet a year old. Dale, at five, was spared the scarring emotion of witnessing Lowell's agonized death by his youth and his father's hospitalization. Of the Morgan children, only he had dim recollections of his father; the other children remembered nothing at all. For more than forty years, on the rare times that Dale Morgan referred to his father in correspondence or conversation it was impersonally as "Lowell." Only after Emily died and Dale became gripped with a passion to know the man he had never really known, did he ever refer to Lowell Morgan as "my father."

* * * * *

Emily nursed her grief alone in the quiet hours while the children slept. Even without a father they needed care, and once funeral expenses were retired by the small life insurance policy Lowell carried, Emily had to face the fact that she was a single mother with virtually no assets, no savings, and no income. Records and family memory conflict about how she managed in those early months. According to family memory, despite her situation, Emily shouldered responsibility along with her grief and determinedly faced the future. The independent young widow took matters into her own hands and set about arranging her family's affairs. Initially her plan was to maintain her family independently, relying upon the families for emotional support but accepting their offered financial support only in desperation. She sold the car. In this version, Emily was able to maintain a family home on Fourth North for about a year, but hired day help to watch the children.[24] During the day, her domestic watched the children and kept house while Emily looked for work. Where she worked in the summer and autumn of 1920, any financial help she received from the family and her immediate plans were never recorded and are not remembered.

Eventually, however, the financial strain of maintaining a house and family while providing for domestic help, streetcar fare, and school expenses became too much for her. At the end of 1920, Emily finally decided she was desperate enough to ask her family for help, and she moved herself and the four children back into her father's home. A complication to the family memory is provided by two points of contemporary documentation. First, in fall 1920, six months after his father died, Lowell Dale Morgan began kindergarten in Marie Fox Felt's class at the Washington Elementary School on 400 N and 200 W.[25] The alternate version of events, recorded in her father's diary, was that Emily and the children moved from Redondo Avenue back home with her father two weeks after Lowell's death.[26]

Emily Morgan's family living arrangements on Fourth North lasted for about a year and a half. As close as the family was, and as much as Samuel Holmes loved his daughter, living back in his home proved awkward. A year after Emily's mother died, 59-year-old Samuel Holmes married 40-year-old Lucy Annie Widdison. By 1920 and before Emily and her children moved home, Lucy had a baby of her own to care for, Emily's half-sister Lucile. Accommodations, both emotional and physical, were made.

For Emily to maintain her family independently, she clearly needed a career and the stability provided by a contract and salary, not merely a job as a wage-earning worker. That reality brought her back to teaching. The decision was not a light one. Secure in her husband's reasonably stable career, she had allowed her teacher's certificate to lapse. She now needed to complete enough classroom credit hours to renew the credential, another tremendous sacrifice of time and resources. In summer 1921 Emily enrolled again at the University of Utah's Normal Department for a full load of three classes: Music, Hygiene and Sanitation, and Literature for Children. From 400 North and 200 West Emily boarded the downtown trolley to catch a connecting car up North Temple Street or Broadway Street (300 South) to the university, reversing the route for the trip home. In late summer Emily negotiated an employment contract with the Salt Lake City School District to teach first grade at the Edison School on 800 South and 1400 West Streets. She taught grade school in Salt Lake City for 35 years, until her retirement in 1955. Emily commuted between home and school on the city's trolley lines, a long trip, better than seven miles, and she was glad to be done with it when a school year ended.

At the conclusion of her first contract year, Emily Morgan was finally in a position financially and emotionally to strike out on her own. Late the next summer, during the first year of Emily's teaching, Dale began first grade at Washington Elementary School. Three weeks later, perhaps on the strength of her employment, perhaps with family help, Emily paid $3,000 for a small, new bungalow of maroon brick at 364 Hollywood Avenue. The tract house was located about a block from 500 East Street and one street north of the city's southern boundary at 2100 South. In the first week of October 1921, the Morgans moved into the new house, and Dale was forced to change schools. Since Emily had to get to her own Edison School job before Dale was in class, she could only give her six-year-old son some basic instructions and leave him to follow LeRoy Phillips, who lived across the street, to Whittier Elementary.

Years later Dale recalled clearly how he "arrived at the school in the afternoon, kids all around at lunch hour, the bell ringing, and all of them purposefully disappearing into the building, leaving me stranded in a wide expanse of cement out in front. I did not know where to go or what to do, so I did what comes naturally to a six-year-old in those circumstances: I began to cry. In a few minutes, out came a teacher to salvage me."[27]

In Rae Woodcock's class Dale met and quickly became friends with classmates Albert Heiner and John Silver. Heiner lived a few blocks away. His family were Wells Ward members too, so Dale and Ab (as he was known) were thrown together on weekends as well. Both were bright, capable students, but Heiner had an affinity for head-to-head competition that fueled something of an annual contest between the boys. "One year I would be named class president, next year he would," Dale recalled for Eleanor Harris years later. "He was a much better athlete than I (class A, let us say, while I was maybe B-minus or C-plus), and also much more gifted at arithmetic. But I had a slight edge on nearly everywhere else, reading, history, geography, and especially art, for which he had no gift at all."[28]

* * * * *

Until the late 1910s the neighborhood between Hollywood Avenue and 2100 South Street had been rural pastureland at the southern edge of Salt Lake City. The Wells Addition would today be considered a subdivision. It repeated the four-square street pattern of the old Mormon city, but the modern urban lots were designed for suburban residences and were not the ten-acre, self-sufficient homesteads of the original community, nor the narrow but deep lots surveyed for city expansion during the late Victorian decades. Hollywood Avenue split a city block and ran east–west through the middle of the Wells Addition, two half-blocks north of the busy thoroughfare of 2100 South Street, the direct route to the mills sitting on the gravel bench above the new construction.

The streets were newly paved, shaded only by the thin whips of maple, box elder, and green ash saplings. Lining the north side of the street were late Victorian homes, built a few decades earlier. Facing them on the south side, in what was once hay fields or pasture, stood boxy bungalows, uniformly of brick but varying across a wide color range from sandy yellow to almost purple. The bungalows were built on one of two mirror-image floor plans with a small back porch notched out of one corner. Set back only a few feet from the sidewalk, a visitor took three or four steps up the short front walk and up three steps to the concrete porch. Each house was built with a large front window overlooking the concrete porch that stretched across the front of the house. The houses were inexpensively constructed, what today would be considered "starter homes." Behind a few houses hunkered detached frame garages with dirt floors and open-studded, clapboard-sided walls. Odd patchworks of power poles and vegetable gardens interrupted the otherwise level playing field of the block's unfenced backyards. Most houses on the north side of the street had a bit more lawn in front, and their mature trees stood along old pasture and yard fencerows.

Dale Morgan and his siblings inhabited perfectly ordinary, middle-class childhoods. Everyone in the Morgans' circle of friends was hovering just above or right on the margin of solvency, dipping below it for a time when an unforeseen expense hit. Clothes were handed down and traded between cousins and neighbors, or made over from an aunt or grandfather. Anything bought new was an occasion. The luxurious indulgences that characterize stereotypical images of the Roaring Twenties were few in this neighborhood and in Utah generally.

The family shopped at Dunn's Grocery, a small neighborhood store on 500 East and 2100 South, where the butcher was one of Emily's cousins, a Beasley, from one of Grandmother Holmes' half-brother's sons. Emily charged groceries on account. She paid a collector who circulated monthly through the neighborhood and also brought small sacks of hard candy when a household account was paid fully.[29] The dairy's horse-drawn delivery wagon usually came too early in the morning to interrupt play. A quart or two of bottled milk was whisked from a morning-cooled front porch into the house for breakfast. Domestic refrigeration was still waiting to be invented, and ice boxes on the screened back porches held any perishable leftovers not eaten within a day or two. Hygeia Ice Company's horse-drawn wagon delivered twice weekly. Invariably on summer days the iceman's wagon would be surrounded by a pack of hot children, all trying to sneak from the back a chip shattered from the massive ice blocks as they were split. If a kid was quick and lucky, he could burrow a hand through the wet sawdust packing and snatch a good-sized ice chip to suck on before the iceman returned to the wagon.

For the children, poverty was the mother of inventive diversion. Few families could afford the luxury of bicycles or the steel-wheeled roller skates that strapped onto one's shoes, though most boys could boast a baseball mitt or football. After-school hours were full of physical activity, and summers were a kid's glory. Fun was cheap even before the Depression, and plenty of other kids lived in the Wells neighborhood. The detached garages served an informal function as hideouts and clubhouses, bases for games of tag, cops-and-robbers, and hide-and-seek. Find a couple of empty Sego Milk cans from someone's garbage, lay them on their sides and stomp one's feet onto them till the ends clamped your shoes, and a kid could clatter down the pavement. Use a can opener to punch a pair of triangular holes across the tops instead, tie a loop of twine or kitchen string through holes, and instantly one had a pair of tin-can stilts. A baseball or tennis ball and someone's house were pressed into service as an "Annie-Aye-Over" court: someone on one side of the house threw the ball over the roof, and those on the other side would catch it; with a holler of "Annie-Aye-Over," the horde came streaming around the house, dodging each other to get into the other yard before the ball carrier was caught and tagged to become a member for the other team. "Run-Sheepy-Run" or tag could fill up any afternoon that sandlot baseball or football didn't.

The streets themselves also provided diversions. In the 1920s, Salt Lake City neighborhoods were threaded by a network of ditches that ran irrigation water from the canyons to flood thirsty city lawns, gardens, and outlying fields in the summer. Where they did not flow in culverts under the streets, boats of all varieties were launched and chased downstream. In the evenings after dinner, visitors simply walked up to the porch to say hello and start up a conversation as families sat on steps outside in the evening. After the Columbia Broadcasting System (CBS) and National Broadcasting Corporation (NBC) launched network radio in 1924, the new invention began pouring music and narrated entertainment into living rooms and front porches up and down the block.

* * * * *

Despite the absence of a father, Dale's childhood on Hollywood Avenue was largely a normal one. Morgan's single-parent childhood did not seem to shape him hardly at all, save in one respect: his sense of responsibility matured rapidly. As the oldest child, Dale Morgan commonly assumed charge of his younger siblings. By the time Robert started kindergarten in 1926, twelve-year-old Dale was already practiced at getting the family dispatched in the morning.

Getting Mother off to school entailed a familial production that bordered on slapstick. Emily typically rode the 400 East electric trolley to work, a line that crossed Hollywood Avenue and ended on 2100 South Street. That placed the nearest trolley stop about half a block east and two half-blocks south from the Morgan home.[30] Since Emily had to be at school before her students began arriving, she was the first to leave the house. Drivers on the line knew she was pressed for time in the mornings. When they passed Hollywood Avenue on the last reach of the outbound trip, the driver would clang the trolley bell. As Dale and Emily shared or split last-minute tasks in the kitchen, confirming homework was in hand and tying shoes, one of the younger Morgan children was assigned to wait on the porch, listening for the bell. The posted kid hollered an alert to Emily when the second end-of-the-line bell sounded distantly through the neighborhood. At their shouted warning, Emily dropped whatever preparations she was making for the day, snatched up her handbag, and bolted out the front door, racing up the street to the corner. By the time she had gathered herself and traversed the half block to 400 East, the car had hit the end of the line on 2100 South, reversed its path, and was approaching the intersection where she would climb aboard.[31] Dale's younger brother Jim recalled with a laugh that "she'd always make it because I think [the trolley drivers] got to where [they'd] look for her [to] be sprinting up the street."[32] Dale would then bustle the other children off to school before catching his own trolley.

If Emily wanted to gather the family for an after-school activity, Dale was responsible for rounding up the three younger kids, with Ruth's help insuring that they were all presentable, getting them on the trolley with fares, and making the necessary connections to arrive at their destination.[33] Eventually Emily gave up the morning sprint, instead catching a ride to school with Helen Sanders, another teacher at Edison, who was her closest friend and whom the family adopted as an informal aunt. At about the time Dale began college (1934), Helen moved into the Morgan home, since she had a car but no house, and Emily a house but no vehicle.

Within a few years of Emily's widowing, her sisters' families followed her to the south end of the city. By 1930 most of the family lived within walking distance of each other, and none were more than a tram-ride away. Aunt Clara's family, the Hardys, lived half a mile north of the Morgans on Emerson Avenue, and Aunt Annie Ostler's family lived slightly closer on Logan Avenue. The Bleaks lived on Formosa Place. Only Uncle Ern's family remained in the old neighborhood, north of downtown on Pugsley Street, just past West High School. There was less interaction with the Morgan side of the family. Emily Morgan's brothers-in-law—OJ, Ralph, and Hal—had all gone to California (though OJ returned to Utah ten years later), Alan went to Colorado, and Carolyn and her husband Ralph Peterson did not start their family until after Dale had graduated from high school.

Bound by the close ties of the Holmes sisters and their older brother, the adults of the various families opted to spend most holidays together with the entire family at various city parks for picnics and recreation, and attending fireworks displays, parades, and other special events. At least once each summer the entire group retreated up Little Cottonwood Canyon, in the mountains east and south of Salt Lake City, to stay at Grandfather Holmes's summer house at Wasatch Cabins. Here they burned bonfires and roasted marshmallows, sang, and fished in the creek. Dale cultivated an early love of fishing on these outings. During the year if one of the uncles decided to spend an afternoon fishing on the Jordan River or one of the mountain streams, Dale generally was the one invited along. For Emily Morgan's four children, summers were filled with family activity. The various Holmes cousins congregated and interacted in age-delimited cousin pairs, trios, or quartets. The constellations of children among the five tight-knit families were forever hosting or being hosted by someone for dinner or a weekend. Several times during the summer the cousins would scramble the extended family's sleeping arrangements. The boys might be relegated to a pile on the Hardys' screened porch at the back of the house and their beds commandeered if a few of the girls were staying over there, too. More often, if the girls were at one home, the boys were off sleeping somewhere else.

Dale's Holmes-cousin coalition was a trio that included Jerry Bleak, older than Dale by a year and a half, and Clyde Hardy, eight months older. During their late childhoods and into their teen years the three were little short of inseparable. Like many kids of the time, they invented their own entertainment. Clyde, Jerry, and Dale improvised track and field venues in an alley behind the Hardys' house. They stretched string or rope across the alley for hurdles, pressing a hefty rock into service for a shotput. The long jump could be held anywhere, judged by marks on the ground chalked with a scrap begged or appropriated from Emily's school supplies. With a little effort, the boys could get a bamboo pole from a carpet core, serving both as a pole for the vault and as a high jump bar. The sidewalk around the block itself constituted their track. Being the youngest of his companions, Dale was not as physically developed nor inclined to this activity. Still, he was a good sport and an active participant.

Life was good.

* * * * *

As Dale grew older, Emily loosened her emotional grip on her son and he was allowed to ride the north-south trolley with Jerry and Clyde along 400 East. The trolley provided a tangible connection to the busy downtown and its attractions. The trio took in minor league baseball games of the city's Pacific Coast League team, the Salt Lake Bees. They travelled to ice and roller rinks, spent afternoons swimming either at Fairmont Pool or the one at Warm Springs up on Beck Street in Grandpa Holmes's neighborhood, or whacked at tennis balls at the school courts. They discovered the Salt Lake City Public Library. Clyde was not one for much reading, but Jerry and Dale quickly began making a biweekly pilgrimage uptown. Each would check out the limit of four books and begin reading on the tram home. After a week they met to exchange their books with the other boy, doubling the dose of available reading material. As a result, Dale was exposed to a wide variety of authors and many forms of literature.

Morgan's introduction to letters in the 1920s was made during the high point of American commercial publishing and the industry's coming-of-age in the following decade. Max Brand's western novels became favorite reading, as did the pulp fiction magazines of the period, particularly *Argosy*. Twice a month in the 1920s *Argosy* delivered over 120 pages of some of America's best short and serial fiction writing into the hands of eager readers across the country. It was the leading title among the industry's general-story publications, not thematic like *True Romance*, *Western Story*, or *Detective Fiction Weekly*. A single issue of *Argosy* could include science fiction, an adventure set in Africa, a detective mystery, and a fortune story. Entries could stretch from a fifteen-page short story, to a forty-five-page novelette, to a ninety-page novella.

Reading shaped Dale Morgan far more than he would have recognized as a youth. The 1920s has been called the age of the short story partly because recreational reading was a major form of in-home entertainment that crossed American social classes and its national geography. Popular fiction provided Dale Morgan's entrée to the world of writing and letters.

Though Emily Morgan and her late husband had been members of the state's predominant Church of Jesus Christ of Latter-day Saints, in Dale's young years the Morgans were not ardent churchgoers. Like most families at the time, even most Mormons, the Morgan family attended church two or three times each month rather than with weekly regularity. The Morgans were members of the Wells Ward, and the church building or "ward house" sat a block east of their home like a bookend to the blocks of homes between Hollywood and Redondo avenues. The structure and order of Latter-day Saint worship services remain essentially unchanged from the church that Dale and his family knew in the 1920s, but participation has changed dramatically since then. As was expected of members, Dale was baptized as an eight-year-old. Since Dale lacked a priesthood-holding father, another Wells Ward member William C. Wardell baptized him, and he was confirmed as a member of the church a few days later by William Vankirk.[34] Dale Morgan would find services held today reasonably familiar if he had a mind to attend, but the weekly activity meetings and habits of church members are very different. Neighborhood activities then were dominated by the Wells Ward building, which had a cultural hall large enough for movies, dances, and parties and activities of all kinds. Ward members were always invited, but everyone in the neighborhood, church member or not, was welcome.

In his adult life, Morgan was a thoroughgoing agnostic; yet through his childhood and into his teen years he was just as thoroughly a believing, participating Latter-day Saint. His few bits of autobiographical writing suggest that he harbored a callow but genuine belief in the church and its scripture, albeit one borne more of family tradition and social participation than study and faith, but nonetheless real for its juvenile intensity. His father's death complicated his understanding of religion to some extent. Dale crafted a mental image of God or a "Father in Heaven" with Lowell rather than Jesus Christ as an intercessor.[35] That small personal heresy was straightened out sufficiently at some point in his youth.

Enough young men lived in the still-new neighborhood that by the time Dale was twelve, the Wells Ward organized three quorums or classes of deacons, the first office in the church's Aaronic priesthood. When Dale turned twelve, like most young men he was ordained a deacon by the ward bishop, Francis D. Higginbotham, and assigned to the ward's second quorum of Deacons.[36] Within a year Dale was asked to serve as a counselor or assistant to another boy serving as the quorum president. The following year (1928) Dale was sustained or accepted by the boys and young men of the ward as president of the second quorum of Deacons.[37] The responsibility was not a recognition of popularity or reward, but such a calling tended to reflect his standing among his peers. The charge put him at the forefront of about a dozen boys his age and provided him with practical lessons in social leadership and motivation. That status must have been personally rewarding. Under adult leadership he would routinely have conducted church meetings in their class, made service assignments and accepted reports from the boys, and made quorum service, activity, and participation reports to the ward bishop. Years later Bob wrote to his older brother of that idyllic summer when Dale sat confidently atop a young teenager's social world. "I recall," his brother Bob wrote in a personal letter years later, "walking home from the ward show with you and the rest of the family and looking up into the clear starry summer sky and hearing you sing 'In a Little Spanish Town.'"[38]

The soft summer days of the Morgan children's childhood had a few hard edges, however. Emily's career as a teacher left her without an income during the summer months. One reason Emily's older brother, Ernest (or *Uncle Ern* within the family), remained in the old north-side neighborhood was because he had assumed management of the family boiler-making business. His star was rising in Utah's Democratic political administration, and by the mid-1920s he was manager for the Utah State Fair. After Lowell's death, Ern pulled some political strings and secured his youngest sister a summer clerical position in the city's Water Department, an arrangement she maintained for years. While she was gone during the day, the younger children were left under the care of an aunt or a part-time sitter/housekeeper.

As soon as Dale was old enough to recognize the effort Emily put into providing for the family fiscally and emotionally, he began looking for personal opportunities to supplement the family income. In summer 1928 and again in 1929, Dale jumped at an opportunity to make money as a delivery carrier for a local direct-advertising service. A handful of young teenage boys crowded into the bed of the owner's pickup truck, each with a canvas satchel crammed with printed handbills and flyers for local businesses. Pairing off and working opposite sides of the street, they would disperse to stuff the papers into neighborhood screen doors and mailboxes. The boys were dropped off on specific delivery routes, picked up for a quick lunch, and then scattered out through the neighborhoods a second time for afternoon deliveries.[39]

Dale started eighth grade in fall 1928, his last year at South Junior High School. In December Uncle Ern's family suffered a tragedy: Dale's strapping, handsome oldest cousin, Ernest Eldredge Holmes, known as Eldredge or Edge, came home with a raging fever and wracking cough. In two days, the sixteen-year-old high school senior was dead. A lab test diagnosed an "epidemic cerebrospinal meningitis" infection complicated by influenza.[40] The tragedy affected the Holmes cousins deeply, but it would not be the only time that meningitis would claim a victim in the Holmes-Morgan family.

* * * * *

Sometime in early August 1929, Dale sustained a personal blow when his well-paying direct-mail summer job expired just before school started. Being jobless, however, left Dale with more time on his hands, enough to enjoy a brief revel before his ninth-grade school year started. Dale and some friends caught the trolley on one of their pilgrimages. Years later Jim remembered this as a trip to the outdoor Fairmont Pool up a few blocks east in the Sugar House neighborhood. Still damp from the swim, jostling each other noisily as they rode the trolley back down the hill that evening, Dale began feeling ill. He was running a temperature by the time he arrived home. Ever-protective Emily immediately put him to bed. All the pleasure of a late-summer Saturday was erased by morning as Dale began vomiting violently and became almost delirious with a spiraling fever. This illness was clearly serious. Emily moved Jim and Bob into the living room and installed herself on a pallet beside Dale's bed. With his mother frantically helpless at the bedside, Dale tossed in delirium.[41]

The boy slept fitfully, partially waking before again lapsing into an uneasy sleep. Late that night Dale became suddenly aware that he was fully conscious, but floating upward in what he described later as "a still, immense, and depthless darkness; a vast, quiet, starless, blackness." Below him he sensed the familiar things of home and of family; above him, out of sight in the inky black, was another world of light and immense presence. That he was dead came as an obvious but unexpected thought, and he called out the idea to no one in particular. Emily startled awake to find her son absolutely still in bed. Above her, unseen in the blackness, Dale could hear her ask if he was all right with the whispered intensity of a concerned mother. Her voice, he wrote later in a third-person narrative, "seemed like a thread which held him weightlessly poised in that strange black immensity of death, holding him to earth; and then it seemed to draw him down from that dark unguessable height, down through space and darkness, down to the warm summer earth of walls and lights and beds." A moment of sensing the proximity of earth, a sensation of dizzy vertigo, and the boy became aware that it was night and that his mother was leaning over him. That he had had a dream "at once seemed no clear explanation." Dale reassured her he was fine, but as she settled back into sleep, he began hearing a train bell clanging ceaselessly in the distance.[42]

The sun rose and set. A hot summer breeze worried the curtains listlessly while Dale Morgan remained in bed, still feverish, for a week. As he napped and tossed fitfully over the next few days, the bedroom began changing audibly. The train bell he had "heard" distantly the night of his illness became irritatingly constant. A day or two later the bell faded, only to be replaced by louder and more frequent sounds. The only words a young teenager could assign to the experience later were "whistles" and "howls." They were the last sounds he would ever hear. Eventually these irritating, mindless noises faded: from a roar to a murmur, from a murmur to a whisper, and then to nothing at all. Something had happened, clearly; no one knew what, only that it had inconveniently plugged his ears.

By the time Dale's fever left and his condition began to improve, the damage was done. The silence was absolute. As he returned to consciousness he began to notice that he could not hear the family in the house. No one expected this complication. The doctor who made the house call was not a specialist. Dale's illness was something outside of the general practice of irritating coughs, rashes, and occasional broken limbs. Talking with an understandably anxious Emily before he left, the physician prescribed strict bed rest for the young patient, hoping that rest would allow Dale's body to throw off the infection by itself. "Probably" that rest would let the "congestion" in his ears clear as well. As the days came and went, his fever lessened but the ears did not clear and Dale's hearing did not return.

As the fever dissipated and Dale returned to normal patterns of sleep and wakefulness, Emily took to writing him notes as instructions. Despite his enforced rest regimen, Dale's hearing did not return. Puzzled, on a return visit the doctor had to admit he did not know what Dale might have suffered but counseled the family to make sure he rested from it. Dale was confident that his strength would be back and he would be ready for school, which started in a few days—and of course his hearing would be back soon, too. Wouldn't it?

CHAPTER 2

"A Sense of Being Socially Maimed"[1]

Salt Lake City's West High School, 1929–1933

I am cut off from many of the nuances of social life so I depend upon an introspective analysis of observation.[2]

—Dale Morgan

AS SOUTH JUNIOR HIGH SCHOOL dismissed its students in late spring 1929, Dale Morgan burst from its doors an average, fourteen-year-old kid inhabiting the small, casual world of summer-vacation activities and the Wells Ward deacons' quorum. He was self-assured, popular, talented, well-liked. Four months later, by the time students began ninth grade in autumn, Dale Morgan was a trembling, wrung-out shadow who could barely stand on his own and hardly communicate with visitors. Despite desperate hoping it would not be so, it seemed that he was facing a new normal. The weakness would pass as his body recovered strength, but Morgan's hearing was gone completely. He was totally deaf.

No clinical diagnosis of the episode was ever made. Long after the danger was past, late that winter the family doctor finally put a tentative name to what had happened: *meningisimus.* Since he had no good explanation, Morgan's physician coined the new word based solely on the case history—sort of, but not quite the well-known meningitis, the disease which had claimed Uncle Ern's boy three years earlier. Meningitis is an infection of nerve tissue, typically in the brain or spinal cord, but Morgan's symptoms did not match the common pathology, which is why medical staff were confused. The doctor could only conclude that in Dale's case the infection's swelling had occurred in the inner ears and around the auditory nerves rather than in the spinal column.

Most commonly, meningitis is viral. Occasionally, however, meningitis may result from an opportunistic bacterial infection. Morgan's symptoms point toward bacterial meningitis, which can progress with astonishing rapidity and be dramatically more severe than the viral form. It remains a serious fatality risk today, even when treated with modern antibiotics. This form of the disease was less well known at the time Morgan contracted it, probably due to the likelihood that most patients who contracted a bacterial form either recovered entirely or died quickly. Dale Morgan's case history was a comparatively rare one. If Morgan's infection was bacterial rather than viral, then a likely source may have been tainted water entering through his throat or ears in an unchlorinated swimming pool. Oddly, however, no meningitis outbreak was tracked or reported by the county at that time, so Morgan might have contracted the infection elsewhere.

Morgan's delirium had likely been caused by intracranial pressure, a side effect of the infection. As the bacteria attacked the soft tissue surrounding his brain, the infection triggered increased phagocyte production to contain the bacterial population explosion. Infection spread. Swelling in the *dura mater,* the cranial lining, squeezed everything mercilessly inside the brain cavity and probably in the surrounding bony structures. The cochlear nerve passes up the auditory canal and through the base of the modiolus to branch into the hair cells of the inner ear. Swelling reduced the already slender space for the blood vessels and nerves passing from the cranial cavity to the *cochlea* or inner ear. Eventually swelling in the soft tissue restricted blood flow to the cochlear hair cells.

Tossing fitfully with a high fever during the acute phase of his illness, Dale mentioned enduring endless head noises: bells, whistles, howls. The sounds were caused by his own blood coursing through the vessels in and around the cochlea. The regular tolling of "bells" was due to his ear registering the systolic pressure of his heartbeat as it worked ever harder to circulate blood through increasingly swollen tissue. Eventually as the tissue swelled, the pressure on the arteries would have been great enough to squeeze off the increased pressure wave of blood pushed by the heart, leaving the starving nerve to register only the whooshing "howl" of the blood's diastolic pressure—the pressure of the bloodstream itself with the heart at rest. Eventually the infection swelled the tissue sufficiently to pinch off the blood supply to the delicate cochlea, his inner ear where sound waves were translated into electrochemical impulses. The minute hair cells translated the audible world into neural impulses for transmission to the auditory centers of the brain cortex, just above and behind the ear, but without blood flow oxygenating the tissue of the ear, these fragile cells died from oxygen starvation. In 1929, a precise diagnosis was impossible.

His tympanic membrane seemed fine, and no one could guess whether or not the boy's inner ear alone or the brain's auditory center as well were affected. Perhaps today physicians could make a more accurate conjecture: medically, the auditory nerve tissue was likely dead. By the time he began recovering, there was probably nothing of Dale's sense of hearing left to recover.

Dale Morgan joined an elite number of deafened Americans. Qualifying hearing loss and defining deafness remained difficult in the 1920s. In its own statistical summary of deaf Americans, the U.S. Census Bureau admitted frankly that "no high degree of accuracy is to be expected in the census." Its 1930 figure of 57,089 deaf-mute Americans was a severe underreporting, since the Bureau collected and reported only the data collected from state educational institutions, so the total for Utah was an undercount by at least one. The report indicated 87 "deaf-mute" people for Salt Lake City. Using numbers compiled years later, an estimate of population that included hard of hearing suggests that deafness in the national population in 1930 might total as much as 270,000 people. If the ratios in the population had not changed much, then more than half of those with acquired deafness (i.e., not born congenitally deaf) were over 65; fewer than 4 percent of those deafened were younger than eighteen.[3] Given his unusual experience, Dale Morgan likely had few or no postlingual deafened peers within Utah's small deaf population.

* * * * *

After a few days, though, the symptomatic aches and fever left. Besides the irritating side-effect that made conversation difficult, the illness had left a second side effect: Dale was now a pale husk of a teenager, his physical condition wrecked. Already lanky and thin, he was now too weak to get himself out of bed and across the floor. His balance was off entirely. Though he did not understand why, with a damaged inner ear Morgan had difficulty standing upright as the room whirled around him. By the end of a week, he could at least sit up without falling over but could not walk unaided. Dale slept through much of those first days as his body tried to regenerate itself and fight off the physical cost of his illness. When it was evident that her son's worst danger had passed, Emily departed to finish her summer job at the city's Water Department offices, relying on one of her sisters to stay with the shut-in while the rest of the Morgan children played outside. Dale spent his days in bed, still too weak to move around much, but his long stretches of daytime sleep were at least uninterrupted by noisy outside disruptions—a pitifully small consolation.

As the recovery progressed, the doctor's well-intentioned instructions for strict rest quickly became a regimen of insufferable tedium. Though Dale had countless hours on his hands, he was not allowed to read, his favorite pastime and almost the only thing he could do while confined. He spent hours in bed, which stretched into days in the bedroom, which lengthened into weeks in the house. While a few weeks or days of summer vacation yet remained, cousins Jerry and Clyde and neighborhood friend Clinton McDaniel came to sit with him. Visits were awkward since conversation was pointless. The quartet would typically play cards: gin, rummy, or bridge. With most of his days spent in uninterrupted isolation, Dale learned to play solitaire exceedingly well. He was impatient to be well again and for his existence to return to its cyclical normalcies. With the money earned from his advertising job he planned to repair the bicycle that had been his father's, and he was eager for his ninth-grade school year to begin. Learning came easily for Dale, and high grades were a source of personal pride. Given his social standing among his classmates the previous year he half-expected to be elected president of his homeroom and thus have a seat on the student council. He was looking forward to the city's Jaycee speech competition, in which he expected to carry away the first-place position. He trusted firmly that his ears would open and he would hear normally.

None of that happened.

Within two weeks, Dale was fully alert but physically weak and still unable to hear anything. For a while, the deafness seemed like an inconvenient but temporary side effect for a boy still physically drained, feverish, and unsteady from his ordeal. The family expected the impairment would dissipate as he gathered strength. Dale himself believed that suddenly his hearing would return—perhaps right now, or maybe the next instant, but sometime soon, surely.

The tangle with some microbe left Dale Morgan *perceptively deaf* or *nerve deaf,* biologically incapable of registering sound waves. Someone who is not deaf rarely appreciates how dependent humans are on hearing, and hearing people may find it difficult to imagine total soundlessness. Sound is invisible but real. The senses of sight, smell, and hearing are the body's early warning system. Together they allow us to triangulate and judge potential threats and opportunities beyond the direct intimacies of touch and taste. Hearing is also the chief sensory platform for interspecies communication. What happens to one's perception of surroundings and conceptions of "reality" when a disproportionately large portion of one's sensory cues are no longer present? When the wind and the odors it carries can be felt and smelled, but its rush and gust streaming past makes no noise? If no audible clues are present before crossing a street, does doing so become an exercise of strictly line-of-sight perceptions of potential danger? Conversation retains the expressive cues of a face, but the interaction is stripped of symbolic basis—language. Discussion suddenly becomes a silent view of a face and moving mouth. Soon casual conversations disappear. Despite their best intentions, friends' attentions drift elsewhere, to those who respond. Confronted by these almost instantaneous transformations, Dale developed an awareness of his disability that stood like walls between him and his acquaintances, cutting him off from the easy participation in all the things he had known: school, home, friends, church, family.

* * * * *

Shortly after Dale was out of immediate danger, Emily invited Bishop Francis D. Higginbotham of the Wells Ward and his two counselors to the house to administer a priesthood blessing to her son. Dale recalled the weight of their hands on his head, the solemnity of the occasion, and his unwavering belief and will that something would change—must change. When the press of the hands was lifted off and he opened his eyes, there was no difference in his hearing. Neither Dale nor Emily's trust in the healing power of priesthood administrations was rewarded. No miracle. Her request was based on a foundation of faith in God, not medical evidence. Nevertheless, she was willing to explore any avenue to explain or remediate her son's stunning loss. She began taking him to hearing specialists throughout the city, first looking for hope of a complete recovery, then to determine the possibility of how much hearing he might partially regain, and ultimately to confirm her worst fear that his ability to hear would not return.

Deafness was not the only aftereffect. The inner ear not only translates sound vibrations into nerve impulses, which is how we hear, but its semicircular canals in the bracketing bone also function as the body's gyroscope, allowing us to recognize up from down and regulating balance. Though his ears remained "plugged," Dale discovered that the illness had left another mark: his equilibrium was gone as well. He could barely stand.

Initially the family thought their oldest brother teetered and stumbled because he was weak. Days and weeks passed with Dale still unable to stand without support and certainly unable to walk unaided. While lying down, he was fine. After a week or so, sitting was not much of a problem, but in standing up, the room would sway, the floor would turn and buckle, and Dale would pitch over, off-balance. Always anxious about Emily's compulsion to care for him, and fearing that it was given at the expense of the needs of Ruth, Jim, and Bob, Dale soon began testing his strength. He later recalled one attempt made just before school began in late August 1929. While the family was eating in the kitchen one evening, Dale carefully levered himself to his feet from a chair in the living room. Bracing himself with both hands, he shuffled along the walls to the door and shuddered haltingly across the few remaining feet to the door frame. There he halted triumphantly, fearing to let go. His mother was not amused by this show of recovered ability and shooed him back before vertigo leveled him. He turned and made his way haltingly on soda-straw legs back to the chair, Emily giving him the scolding of a relieved but still anxious mother, warning him against trying a similar stunt. She was thinking about his physical safety; Dale was thinking about school, but until whatever was affecting his sense of balance was physically resolved, there was no question of him returning to school. Though his fever was gone, his physical recovery was otherwise excruciatingly slow. Expectations were beginning to bump uncomfortably against realities, threatening the young man's sense of worth, grounded, as it was, in uninterrupted social involvement.

It took more than a month of practice, but by the middle days of September, Dale had more or less relearned to walk. Mostly. Yet he found the experience frightening. To the sense of moving forward across the two-dimensional plane of the floor was added a third dimension of up-and-down motion, and he had to recalibrate his spatial awareness after every jarring step before taking another. With his mother's help, Dale staggered about the house until his strength and balance returned sufficiently to keep himself upright. After a long stretch of weeks and practice, he recovered enough to move about the house without aid. When he fell, there was no sensation of falling, only the visible world's impossible tilt and an inevitable jarring crash against the earth or floor. Eventually Emily allowed Dale outdoors, but the problems continued. For a while he could not walk a straight course and despite the concentrated effort he put into it and to his great embarrassment, he wandered from side to side down a sidewalk like a drunk.

Morgan eventually reconquered the simple activity of walking only by developing a visual sense of balance to replace the sense of equilibrium that had been lost with his hearing. Dale eventually learned to use his eyes to compensate for the innate balance he could no longer sense clearly. Thereafter, even into late adulthood, the associated vertigo was never completely gone. For years, he could not move about in the dark. Stairs were a terror. Morgan rarely talked about these personal challenges, but even as an adult, periodically something of his visual sense would betray him, and without warning he would pitch headlong to the floor or the ground.[4]

Only as he was forced to relearn an ability as simple as walking upright did Dale realize that life had fundamentally changed. He had been the man of the house since his father's death, the big brother who was Mother's right hand in caring for the younger children. No longer—or at least, not yet. In the wake of his illness Dale was weak, making him feel like he was not an asset to the family and, in fact, a burden. The emotional security of his place in the world he had previously known and in which he had once taken comfort could not possibly outweigh the new immediacy of his self-perceived weakness.

* * * * *

The summer of 1929 slipped past while the neighborhood children waited wistfully for the end of summer vacation, begging to stretch their play into the shadows of summer twilight. As the first day of the new school year approached, Dale's painfully slow recovery became a major family concern. In light of his weakened ability, Emily worried about what a school schedule might do to Dale's compromised constitution. She could not stay home to nursemaid Dale once school began, since the family finances depended almost entirely upon her modest salary as an elementary school teacher. By the middle of August 1929, a month after his fevered week, Emily needed to return to prepare her classroom for the year. A school schedule would pull herself and all three younger children into the classroom and leave Dale at home alone. During the late summer and as she readied her classroom, responsibility fell to the younger children to take care of their older brother during the day. While playing outside, Ruth or one of the boys could look in on Dale occasionally to see if he needed anything.

School changed that. Shortly before Emily's students returned to school, Dale's lack of improvement required a decision. Ultimately, her fear of losing Dale because of undue haste for normalcy won out over the other concerns. Because of his delicate health, she determined to hold Dale out of at least the first few weeks of the 1929–1930 school term, his ninth-grade year.

For a boy who had thrived in school, isolation from the energy and social scrum at the beginning of a school year levied another share of disappointment, but Dale and his mother both harbored hope that after a couple additional weeks of recovery he would regain his strength and begin classes as well. He emotionally settled for a return after a few weeks. Catching up would not require too much effort, and everything would be back to its past routine. He had to give up the hope for the class presidency of the ninth grade, but that setback was not a major one. Curiously, the inability to hear was not his biggest worry. When his physical strength returned, he was confident his hearing would return as well. Writing years later of his experience with the newness of absolute deafness, Morgan later recalled that "it was as though there were a reservoir laid out within, and when this reservoir were [*sic*] filled to the brim and began to flood over, his hearing would return. By the time he was up and around and ready to go back to school, automatically he would be able to hear."[5] Hearing didn't just *quit;* it might go for a time, but was one of the fundamental elements of life that could be depended upon.

Labor Day came, and the neighborhood streets emptied as his friends returned to school, leaving Dale young and alone in a profound social stillness. Ruth and Jim began their classes, even Bob was gone half-days for kindergarten, and Dale was left to watch them walk anxiously down the street, excitedly and a little expectantly conversing among themselves about what the coming year would be like. For Dale, who loved school, it must have been terrible. Edna Sullivan, one of his eighth-grade teachers from the previous year, was aware of Dale's emotionally needy circumstance and took the time to write him reassuringly that he hadn't been forgotten and filling him in with beginning-of-the-year news about classes and new teachers.[6] In its way, to Dale, loneliness was even less tolerable than the impenetrable, surreal silence that was now his constant companion.

For a few weeks after school began, Aunt Clara Hardy or grandmother Morgan came to stay with Dale through the day. Within a few weeks and as his strength mended, the travel was reversed. On Tuesdays, Dale would take the streetcar across town to the Morgans' house for the day; on Thursdays if the weather was good, he would shakily walk the half mile to Hardy's, working to build his strength but now all the time avoiding contact with friends going off to school. On Mondays, Wednesdays, and Fridays he remained alone at home, and soon after that, most every weekday. He spent the rest of the 1929–1930 school year at home, alone. There was no reason to dress in the morning. In pajamas, he sat at the table by the coal-fired kitchen stove, reading, the one activity he enjoyed that could continue uninterrupted. Most days he would dress some time into the afternoon, just before the family returned from school, and then only to avoid a scolding. Even after school as the kids returned home, Dale could only watch the front-yard football matches, pom-pom-pull-away, and before-bed kick-the-can battles, his lungs weary of shallow breaths and aching for the deep heaving draws and adrenaline rush of good physical exertion.

By now, a sense of being maimed began growing like a prickly weed in his consciousness. On the streetcar Dale occasionally encountered friends or schoolmates off to their classes, and the weed would intrude into his social interactions. He could make out what people were saying only as they spoke directly to him with exaggerated slowness. Following group conversation was impossible, especially the rapid-fire, omnidirectional adolescent chatter. Unable to communicate, existing beyond the social pale, the fourteen-year-old boy began planning carefully to avoid chance encounters. A year earlier, the self-awareness of his own scholastic abilities had given him a sense of beneficent superiority. From Dale's writings about this early experience in acquired deafness, he clearly felt that to be now the overlooked object of pity by those of lesser ability whom *he* had once pitied—that bitterness was more than could be borne.[7] While Dale sat at home or was at a family member's house, he could be quietly himself. Beyond that, he no longer wanted to talk to people he had known because it emphasized how different he had become. He later described the circumstance as "a bright familiar world [that] went on without him, and he could not enter it." Dale Morgan was slowly, almost methodically, deconstructing the world he had known and grown up in—but did not yet have anything to replace it.

It is reasonable to wonder why Emily Morgan did not take a firmer hand in her son's education during his year at home. Possibly she did not understand what resources were available to her, or maybe no mechanism existed locally for educating an at-home student. So, Dale Morgan spent days, weeks, and then months at home, mostly alone and massively bored. Christmas vacation passed. He could no longer bellow carols. He could not follow the half-stated, implicit communication chatter as the younger children opened their gifts. Nevertheless, Morgan tried to maintain an upbeat perspective. After all, he had regained most of his strength, and staying home from school was a break anyone his age would have envied. Right? Still, with his physical abilities limited, being home became a ceaseless regimen of torture by boredom. He began reading the dictionary, an attempt to compensate for his absence from school.

To provide Dale with a flash of novelty amidst his endless days and a break from endless reading, Emily scraped together enough money to buy Dale a chemistry set. The gift was an unanticipated luxury—something new *and* a creative outlet. He spent hours using and learning from the simple formulae. Before very long, however, the supplies included in the set were exhausted. In the days before chemical toxicity was feared publicly and the availability of chemicals became tightly controlled, many basic solutions could be purchased over the counter at drugstores and hobby shops. That fact was not lost on Dale. Once during the year, Emily left him carfare and a quarter to have his hair cut, but Dale had other plans. With the haircut money, he refilled his chemical stocks and returned home to face his mother. She was obviously unhappy with his choice of purchases after she had specifically told him to use the money for a haircut. His response to maternal ire was a risk at tongue-in-cheek humor: "well, *I* didn't hear you!"[8]

Dale Morgan passed his fifteenth birthday in December, 1929. Around that time, his place in the "normal" world of the family suffered another personally devastating setback: Emily at last bought the family a radio. This cutting-edge technology of the 1920s fascinated Dale. Salt Lake City acquired its first radio station, KDYL, in 1924, the same year that the National Broadcasting Company initiated a national network to distribute program content. The LDS church opened a commercial radio station in 1925 (which allowed General Conference proceedings to be accessible beyond Temple Square for the first time). Part of the delight Dale had enjoyed about Sunday family visits only a few months earlier was popular music, radio programs, and sports broadcasts on the Hardys' radio set. Prior to losing his hearing, Dale quickly grasped the principles of AM radio tuning, turning the dial back and forth to tune the frequency.

The new acquisition was a cheap cabinet model, large enough to require its own space standing to one side among the living-room furniture. The family could listen to the radio, sharing in what was heard, but Dale existed beyond that activity, fiddling with the dial until the vibrations in the cabinet told him that he had reached a station. "What's happening now?" he asked constantly, eager to exercise the sense of control that a radio tuner bestowed. Deafness left him only the ability to watch for clues about the content on the gathered faces. Years later he recalled being disheartened by "the absorption in their faces, a blankness to him in the room, so that if he said something they would hush him unthinkingly before they remembered to smile apologetically and say 'Just a minute, there something on that's interesting.'" With the radio on and the family gathered, faces would again turn blank and unknowable to him as they listened raptly to what he could not sense.[9]

* * * * *

As snow began falling in Salt Lake City, Dale's hearing had still not returned and Emily was getting worried. Someone mentioned to her a local chiropractor that had once had rather spectacularly restored sight to a blinded man. Emily bundled Dale off to see him. Dale submitted with some anxious trepidation. He had begun expecting that his hearing would return only if prefaced by the same sort of pain that had preceded its disappearance. Pain he could tolerate, he could even welcome, *if* it guaranteed his hearing would return. His fears were fruitless. After an exam, the chiropractor suggested that the boy's malady was probably beyond his help.

Emily then took her son to an ear specialist. This office was more clinical. Its soulless, polished nickel and blank, staring walls reawakened Dale's deepest-kept inner fear of doctors and hospitals and the pain they represented. He tended to avoid medical attention throughout the rest of his life when he could. In fact, the otolaryngologist merely looked in Dale's ears and used mirrors and lights to examine his throat. Emily was told that Dale's ears were physically intact, which was good, and that the damage left by the disease was evidently restricted to the ears' innermost nerve structure. That, he explained, was beyond medical attention. Perhaps the nerve was undamaged enough to regenerate itself, or perhaps not. Hearing might return slowly or all at once, but the doctor did not hold out much hope for that. The possibility of recovering his hearing was unthinkable to modern science of the time. Once physicians had exhausted their educated guesses, nothing could be done. If it was only the inner ear that was affected and his brain's auditory center was still viable, then had Morgan lived into his 70s, the first generation of cochlear implants might have bypassed his inner ear to stimulate his brain's auditory cortex directly, perhaps restoring part of his hearing. Such a medical marvel could not even be dreamed in the pre-Depression years.

Upon turning fifteen, Dale was considered old enough to be advanced in the Aaronic priesthood like other boys his age. In January 1930, he was ordained to the priesthood office of Teacher by Bishop Higginbotham.[10] Once he was walking again, Dale continued attending church with the family as if nothing had changed. Though he could not hear the music, the speakers, announcements, or the friends he met there, initially he welcomed the calm, solemn patterns of worship that became evident to one reliant wholly on his eyes for understanding. In Sunday school classes, participants studied the printed lessons from scriptures, stories from the Bible, Book of Mormon, or faith-promoting stories from church history. He quickly began to feel, however, that an ability to hear was key to participating in Latter-day Saint worship services. The ward sacrament meetings, Sunday school classes, and priesthood meetings, all of the ward's sermons, lessons, and discussions, were verbal. He could follow nothing sung, taught, or discussed. Meetings simply became so many more hours of bored isolation as others bantered around him. In a day when disabilities were still regarded as "handicaps," the church made no local provisions for those thus afflicted.

Within a few months of resuming his church activity, Dale decided that his inability to hear left him virtually no reason to attend the full schedule of meetings. First he quit attending priesthood quorum meetings (which were held separately from Sunday school). Soon thereafter he began leaving at the break between Sunday school's opening exercises and classes. The family walked home after the morning meetings for dinner. Usually one or more of Emily's sister's families would arrive late that afternoon and visit until dark, so the Morgan family rarely returned to the afternoon sacrament meeting. Within a year Dale went to church services merely for the sake of appearing on the roll. Finally, he concluded that even attending ward church services was pointless, and he quit attending altogether. Emily could not argue with his reasoning. Dale began staying home to read scriptures by himself, eventually setting those aside just to follow his own interests on days while the rest of the family was at church. By the beginning of 1932 Dale Morgan's experiences with his family's church were essentially over. Another decade would pass before the church began to wrestle publicly over the participation of deaf and deafened members.[11]

Within a year, Dale also gave up participating in the ward Boy Scout troop. Dale had previously completed the activity requirements for his

First Class rank. While he was convalescing, he wrote up the required report of his hike and service project. Yet, the games which once had been so easy were now physically dangerous for him because of his poor balance. At one meeting, he crashed to the floor with momentary vertigo and lay looking up at the ceiling as concerned faces peered down at him inquiringly. He did not go to many more Scout meetings after that. Other losses included his former pleasure in singing and burgeoning interest in popular music.

More than anything, deafness cut off Dale absolutely and irrevocably from the casual interpersonal social interactions that had been the center of his youthful existence. He could speak, but could not converse. He could participate in a social group, but could not follow the drifting currents of freewheeling conversation. He had things to say, but no longer had a sense of conversational timing nor was he able to assess his words' effect on listeners. "They did not rebuff him. They tolerated him," he recalled of his interactions with high school classmates, "but they ignored him."[12] He was a social outcast by fact if not by choice. Slowly Dale withdrew from the routine social interactions he had loved and once lead. He simply dropped out of social circulation, unwilling to be sidelined or ignored or be thought an inconvenience.

To an unknown conversant a few years later in college, probably a professor, Morgan scribbled a comment on the back of one of his story drafts about how he handled story composition. "In my serious writing I am cut off from many of the nuances of social life so I depend upon an introspective analysis of observation. In other words[,] I translate objective observations to subjective action—I put myself in the place of the character and give many of my own reactions. Of course, this is tempered by an adaptation of myself to the peculiar quality of the character I attempt to depict."[13] To another friend he put it more plainly: "I don't become casually acquainted as most people do, and thus am left to my own fantasies to explain things people customarily pick up by a kind of social osmosis."[14] Dale Morgan began inhabiting a social world he had to imagine and construct around a population of one, having had little or no experience in early adulthood with establishing or working out complex interpersonal relationships. His world became one of assumptions, observation, and ideals, reinforced by a personal sense of loyalty. Where his family and friends interacted and learned with as much thought as breathing, Dale studied, analyzed, and interpreted by his own understanding, trying to fit in. Deafness reinforced and magnified his innate and unexpressed fear of being different from those with whom he spoke—or worse, being misunderstood and dismissed in frustration over some simple point. The isolation piled its own weight atop normal adolescent angst.

* * * * *

During this uncommitted, unstructured time, Dale discovered the pictorial representation of women in motion pictures and the fan magazines the industry spawned. He began to search newspapers, magazines, and various posters, for pictures or descriptions that revealed or even suggested an intimate revealing, hoarding what he discovered in an immature, disjointed intellectual fashion. Where once he had clipped and saved thousands of pictures of baseball players, Dale now tore images of women out of fan magazines and newspaper advertisements. Some days he would stagger or slowly walk the dozen blocks east along 2100 South to the library branch in Sugarhouse. Alert to this new aspect of life, at the library Dale was pleased to discover erotic innuendo throughout Western literature. His disease had struck inopportunely at virtually the onset of puberty and the biological changes it forces on one's perceptions and interests. All of this in his developing character he kept buried deeply from his family and friends, and an adolescent Dale Morgan found himself on his own to comprehend and interpret the biological changes to which he was subjected by being a pubescent teen. On one hand, he was abnormally shy about social interactions with girls, while on the other he was fascinated by the allure and secrets of female flesh. And still he read.

In his desperation to stave off mind-numbing boredom at home, Dale reread all of the story magazines that he had not already read from cover to cover, that had accumulated for years in the basement. Like a scavenger, he went looking for more. He read a neighbor's discarded outdoor magazines. He read science fiction, Westerns, romance—especially romance—action stories, fortune stories, nonfiction, and everything else he could find. Dale "read foolishly and dangerously," he remembered, ignoring eye strain, beating back the exhaustion of physical inaction.

That first year of loss and isolation was hard and lonely. Deeply grieving his sensory loss and wrenched out of the society he knew, Dale harbored what he later called "a deep-running, unreasonable feeling that if [I] did not admit to any change in things as they had been, change was denied: it did not exist."[15] Yet, one by one, the things that Dale Morgan had done in his previous, what he dubbed "real," life were cut away from him, and nothing comparable took their places. For months, Dale held in his frustration, confusion, and imbalance, but the brew corroded his self-image and confidence. He did not admit it, even to himself, he later admitted. On top of this, by the time Emily felt Dale was strong enough to attend school, the school year ended. Late in spring 1930, he wrote a friend reminiscently: "One night some trivial conflict with one of my younger brothers led Mother to bawl me out, unjustly, as I then felt, and that blew [the] top, emotionally, off the whole thing. I was in a semi-hysterical state for a couple of hours, and during the course of it for the first time admitted to my mother as well as to myself the state of my feelings about the world I was having to make for myself." The outburst was an important turning point for the adolescent. By his own account the process of rebuilding himself required another eight years, but nine months after losing his hearing, "that night I reached bottom. I began to face the future instead of wasting myself in bitter regret over a past that was beyond my reach."[16]

While Dale Morgan's coping mechanism was grounded on denial, unable to control the circumstances of her son's deafness, Emily's coping mechanism was to become emotionally invested about her son learning speech reading. She was determined to help him adjust to a life that may have been alien to most in his society but was beginning to look wholly inescapable. When school let out for summer vacation in 1930, Emily enrolled Dale in a lip-reading class, the first of several. Dale resented spending $10 of the family's badly needed funds on a registration fee to teach him something he was certain he could not learn. The course gave him his first positive step back into a classroom environment. The class was an age- and gender-mixed group, taught by a teacher who was herself totally deaf. Dale was amazed at the facility with which she read speech, but he found it difficult to force himself to shift from watching a speaker's eyes and face, as happens in oral-aural conversation, to watching a mouth and throat. Two younger girls caught on quickly, but Dale concentrated so much on catching specific words that he missed the strings of collective meaning that made up sentences. He strove for precision but missed context. It was frustrating, maddening, and he resented not only the effort involved, but having to work to re-learn something he already understood.

Over several summers, he attended separate classes downtown. At these classes he often was joined by his aunt, Annie Bleak, who struggled with the loss of much of her own hearing.[17] He attended speech-reading classes to please his mother but did not want to admit to himself that he was as his fellow classmates—part of what he termed the "un-normal, the not-like-other-people."[18]

Once the speech reading class concluded, beginning in the summer of 1930 and continuing well into his late teens, Emily insisted that Dale devote part of each day practicing lip reading. Ruth, Jim, and Bob were each assessed blocks of time to model and tutor Dale on textbook speech-reading drills. The youngest of the children, Robert, remembered sitting with his brother on opposite ends of the wooden front porch swing through many summers, endlessly saying words and drilling Dale on the facial shapes and motions of speech that he now could not hear. Dale often stormed off in frustration, entirely aware of the aural subtleties of spoken language but unable to differentiate between the visual intricacies of spoken sound. "The lip reader goes 'by guess and by God,'" he wrote later, "and must try to gather what is meant by the context: whether, in a given case, the speaker is talking, say, about a pad, pat, pan, bad, bat, ban, mad, mat, man, pant, or band."[19] In his later years the native quickness of Dale's mind gave him the capacity to mentally configure the "context" of a conversation and therefore anticipate questions and comments from family and close friends. He did learn to follow speech well enough to carry on a semblance of normal conversation, but those closest to him agree that despite his native intelligence and the effort devoted to the drills, Morgan was never truly able to conquer speech reading for people much beyond his immediate family and closest friends. An inborn drive for accuracy made speech reading a welter of maddening supposition that he tended to avoid when possible.

To compensate, Dale formed his own faculty for recognizing others' speech entirely independently and by trial and error. That development was hard, lonely, and painful. For the rest of his life, his comprehension of face-to-face communication depended largely on the context of the topic, an incredibly quick mind, the rudiments of speech reading, and words, phrases, and sentences sketched with a finger in the palm of a hand or jotted quickly onto whatever paper might be on hand.[20]

Dale became an observer and analyzer. Because he could not hear to orient himself physically or socially in the space around him, he leaned toward his other senses, making him hyperaware of what normal exchanges between people and within society looked and felt like. Questioning what one knows is entirely typical for someone his age; what was not typical was the degree of self-actuated thought he had to give to trivial interactions.

Isolation and introspection magnified and reinforced both doubt and fear. He became a teen riddled with more than the usual allotment of angst.

* * * * *

The summer of 1930 brought Dale's cousin trio of Jerry Bleak, Clyde Hardy, and Dale back together. For a while, they were all a little unsure of how to handle Dale's deafness. They were too good of friends to simply leave Dale out of physical activities, but Dale now also had to cope with imbalance due to his inner ear issue. Jerry and Clyde had played a lot of tennis during Dale's recuperation, but many of the trio's traditional activities—the ersatz track meets, tennis matches, and swimming excursions—became things of the past partly because of Dale's disability but also due to each of the boys' changing interests. Dale and Jerry still hit the public library and traded their stacks of books every other week. If anything, Dale's reading broadened and increased to fill the time once spent with neighborhood friends and cousins in social activities.

Sometime during the summer Jerry brought down a chessboard and showed his younger cousins the moves of the various pieces. Besides cards, chess was something they could do together without having to talk (or hear). Dale and Clyde picked up the moves quickly, and the trio set to work on each other. Their first games were slugging matches as both became familiar with the board, but within a few weeks Dale was holding his own against Jerry's head start. The game quickly became a fad among the neighborhood boys near his age. Chess was an intense and time-consuming pastime. Jerry would bring the board and play Dale, the winner might play neighbor Clinton McDaniel, that winner would play Jerry again, and if someone else showed up, they would work into the rotation. Soon Dale discovered books of chess strategy and began working his way through them, trying to improve his skill and better his game. Within a year he could beat Jerry consistently.

In August 1930, Ruth turned fourteen and Emily authorized a party at their house. This event was more than the usual Morgan/Bleak/Ostler/Hardy-cousins gathering; Ruth and Dale were growing beyond those. Friends from school and church were invited this time. Dale knew almost everyone who came and for a while lost his self-consciousness in the crowd. He was once again the big brother. During the evening, Emily allowed the living room rug to be rolled back, and the kids turned on the new radio for dancing. Despite knowing nothing about dancing and unable to hear whatever was on the set, Dale put an arm around his cousin June Bleak. While she followed as best she could to the radio, Dale hopped and bobbed along, following her lead. The moment of youthful informality and excitement fit neatly together, as normally as could be. Glancing up after a few minutes, Dale noticed Aunt Clara and his mother watching them through the half-open kitchen door. Instantly the sharp realization came that Emily was watching him, not the party. Dale wrote in third person years later of the change that single look wrought in him: "He had almost forgotten his deafness. But [his mother's] approving look, her gratification at seeing him, had said freezingly to him that she was glad to see him being like other people. And this very pleasure at him being the same made him not the same." The reaction was that of an unsteady, acutely self-conscious boy, but her concern made the unintended wound no less real.[21]

* * * * *

By June 1930 Dale had missed the entire year of ninth grade. Emily felt he could not lose another year of school. As the summer waned and the beginning of the 1930–1931 school grew closer, Dale faced an unspoken nightmare that loomed ever larger. Unable to interact in the same way he had as a hearing student, school no longer represented security to him. By his own admission and still grieving deeply for the loss of the comfortable life he had enjoyed, Dale "had no conception of any future, no conviction that with his own hands and will he could make a sound and solid life."[22] Enlightenment writer Samuel Johnson called deafness, "the most desperate of human calamities," though his words reflect the perspective of a hearing viewpoint rather than the Deaf community. There is no question that deafness isolates a person more or less from hearing culture, but even within Deaf culture there are shades of accommodation and experience.

In the 1930s a strong pull existed to integrate Deaf people within the larger hearing community. Today Deaf advocates point out that integration is never equality. It is pursued and accomplished only on the terms comfortable to its hearing participants. With the development of dry-cell batteries, portable electronic sound amplification became an accepted mediation to reconnect the hard-of-hearing with the hearing world.[23] A generation later the development and integration of cochlear implants provided an intervention or remediation whose effectiveness or challenges could be measured objectively, but again, only in terms of defining hearing as a normal sensory function rather than accepting deafness as a different experience within "normal." Culture and even humor can and does evolve among Deaf people, and it is not necessarily the same culture or on the same terms expressed by those who hear.

There are other complications as well. If one looks only at scholarly, scientific, and educational research available even today, it becomes quite clear that a sizable chunk of the American deaf population were ignored, even by experts, educators, and the larger congenitally Deaf community. Generally, the experiences and challenges of speech acquisition, acculturation within a hearing world, and employment of those *born* deaf take precedence. The fears and experiences of youth and adults with acquired deafness has not been understood as effectively, despite being a fairly large segment of the American deaf population.[24] One of the best summaries of the social challenges of acquired deafness, Ethel B. Warfield's "Problems of Deafness," was published while Morgan was still pursuing his basic education.[25] Many of those post-lingually deafened remain within or at the fringes of the oral world and do not effectively integrate with the Deaf community.

Dale Morgan's experience certainly reflected that outcome. Finding or making Dale Morgan an opportunity to transition out of the world he had known and integrate into a Deaf community was therefore never considered, for either reason, which imposed on the young man a decision grounded partly in the sharp and vigorous professional disagreements about Deaf education. One side argued strenuously for relying solely on instructional *oralism,* the other advancing the merits of adopting a newly emerging manual sign language for Deaf education. Both sides were in full cry in the 1930s, and the disagreement over method was described by one teacher as "the rock upon which the [Deaf-education] profession splits."[26] Nothing among the papers of either Dale or Emily Morgan suggests that the family gave the slightest thought to enrolling him at the Utah School for the Deaf and Dumb, the state's residential facility in Ogden, an hour's drive from where the Morgans lived.

From our comfortable present, weighing the safely abstract opportunity costs, it is easy to recommend that the Morgans should have taken the hardest option for Dale. In Ogden he would certainly have had peers. He would have made new friends, been in a better position to learn sign language to communicate, and undoubtedly eased into a new culture—a different culture and very nearly a different world—that eventually would have supplanted the one in which he had grown up as a typical, hearing teen; but opportunities remain mere abstractions when harsh realities bode large and stare directly in your face, demanding action. Neither could the family afford daily transportation back and forth from Ogden for Dale, so whether to enroll him as a resident at the school or to give up Deaf culture entirely (which they did not know existed) was the only choice to make. Not until 1959 would the School create an extension division allowing deaf students elsewhere along the Wasatch Front to pursue schooling closer to home.[27]

Going to Ogden for an education essentially meant life as Dale knew it was over. His accomplishments in speech competitions and at school would be meaningless. He would begin entirely anew. Going to school elsewhere in the state threatened to eject him permanently from his shrinking circle of remaining acquaintances, which he both feared and clung to desperately. Coming from a close-knit family of her own, plus having lost a husband and mother and clinging to her children as the center of her barely stable world, Emily Morgan had difficulty imagining her oldest son drifting away from the family and toward anywhere else. If residential oralism was the basis of his re-education in Ogden, then the family probably saw no reason that Dale could not remain at home and under his mother's protective shadow for a while longer.

Perhaps another concern also lurked around his awareness. The teen-aged Dale Morgan may have harbored a bias against what his options offered, perceiving the Deaf school essentially as a job training curriculum rather than a conditioning of the mind—as technical training rather than an education (however, the latter was essentially what a high school curriculum of the day provided).[28] The school option available to mediate his deafness seemed to impose on a youthful Dale Morgan a deep and nameless fear of being unable to function in the "regular" world. In the depressed world of work, those who were deaf had a dramatically harder time finding employment. Though there was agitation nationally for labor bureaus to help deaf people find jobs, on the ground in Salt Lake City, Dale feared being *placed* because he was deaf rather than being *hired* because he was competitively competent. Yes, there were still career options to be managed, most of which involved skill sets that did not appeal to his interests. In fact, newspapers across the country favored hiring deaf employees as typesetters, since they could work without distraction in the constant roar and clatter of the Linotype or Intertype machines in a composition room. Having drunk deeply from literature, Morgan was more interested in design and writing than the technology of printing. Whether because of his mother's anxiety or his own, having turned down his entry into Deaf culture as a teen, thereafter Dale Morgan actively shunned opportunities to enter the Deaf community. As an adult he chose specifically to function within the hearing world, a reality he forever after inhabited without apology or accommodation.

* * * * *

Despite sitting out a year from school Morgan was evidently capable (or desperate) enough to skip the missing grade; he entered Salt Lake City's West High School as a tenth-grade student in fall 1930. On the first day of classes, Dale walked into West with some acquaintances, but felt alone in the group. He sat through the opening assembly entirely unable to follow what was transpiring, and as the crowd drained out of the auditorium to their room assignments, Dale stopped the principal as he walked up the aisle. Could he please attend classes at West High School? He could not hear, he explained, and therefore could not participate in discussions, but he could read assignments and write reports. The principal shook his head, saying something that Dale could not decipher. *I cannot hear you at all. I do not know what you are saying,* he wanted to shout but could not admit aloud. The head shook again and the principal walked off, followed by the remaining students. Dale Morgan stood numbly as icy fear trickled over him and pooled in his stomach.

That afternoon Emily returned home from her own class to find her eldest son reading on the front porch. Dale could not volunteer the story of failure at school, but she gently pulled out of him the basic facts and promised that she would take time to go with him herself and straighten things out the next day. Emily argued her point while Dale stood uncomprehendingly beside her. The principal, probably distracted by the noise of the crowd around him and other pressing matters of the day, said he had misunderstood Dale's request. Of course, he was welcome at West High. Weak with relief that his tenuous grip on a meaningful life had not shattered, Dale began classes on the second day. Part of Dale's lifelong solicitude for his mother stemmed from this event and others like it; forever after he credited Emily with his redemption.[29]

Dale quickly realized that his deafness had one minor positive side to it—he could not hear his teachers' voices, which he had once perceived as shrill and critical. Based now strictly on the person-to-person communication his handicap required, he found that he got along rather well with virtually all of his instructors. The major problem he now faced was that he was merely the deaf kid; his prior accomplishments in school now counted for nothing in the eyes of his new classmates. Besides the obvious complications of being deaf in a school system grounded on the ability to hear, returning to high school represented one more wrenching social experience for Dale. Turning sixteen in December, he was now in class among a group of students a full year younger than himself. It galled him to compete against kids younger than him, and at a comparative disadvantage because of his hearing loss. As someone who hungered for success, his classmates' ignorance of his previous competence was a bitter pill, and his deafness made him a nonentity as well. Two years earlier Dale had known many of his peers and enjoyed a degree of popularity; this year he knew virtually no one and was further isolated from casual acquaintance and conversation by his hearing loss.

A year later the high school district was divided. The newly constructed South High School was ready for occupancy, only a few blocks from their house. Over the summer Emily arranged for Dale to avoid transferring from West High School. Both of his brothers and cousin Jerry all reported years later that the reason Dale did not leave was that West had a speech-reading class, but it is at least as likely that Emily Morgan realized her son needed the emotional support of continuity.

Morgan did well in history and English as a high school student, but geometric lines and planes became prison bars he could not understand, and in physical education class he felt clownish in his tottering, residual imbalance. Dale tried reaching out in other ways, carefully calculating how to use humor to ease into whatever small groups he managed to find. He was usually welcomed, but was often thereafter ignored. Dale could walk down a hall in a group and be entirely alone, unable to hear the context of conversations while he concentrated on staying upright and putting one foot in front of another—*what are we talking about, who has the upper hand, is it light or serious?* His attempt to time the use of a witty observation was like target-shooting in a crosswind while blindfolded. Worse, it made Dale into little more than a tolerated fool. Others would look at him and then glance away, sometimes embarrassed by his out-of-context jokes. At the same time, Jerry was getting more interested in their church, while Dale was becoming less interested; and although bespectacled and acne-prone Dale was painfully self-conscious around the opposite sex, handsome Jerry was suavely comfortable.[30] As a whole, attending high school took on the grimy quality of an endurance race rather than the glories of a sprint.

Through the rest of his high school years Dale also maintained acquaintances with the neighborhood kids his age, and these relationships suffered less from the dissociation he felt with others at school. He participated with them when he could in after-school games, running as hard as his ungainly balance allowed. One afternoon they were playing touch football in the street in front of the house. On one play, complicated by repeated hand-offs and feints, Dale hurled hopefully down field as a receiver. He snagged the ball from the air, tucked and swung around for the goal—and sprinted into the grille of an oncoming car. Dale crashed headlong into the hood and fell to the street in front of the wheels. For a blissful moment he may have felt himself back in "real life," but because he did not hear the car, he did not look for it either. Emily raced from the house, ashen-faced and her worst fears realized. Thankfully, the driver, having seen the game, allowed the car to creep along and stopped without hitting the boy. Dale's world instantly constricted further; Emily would have no more of him playing sandlot ball in what now represented another needless risk. His mother's previous solicitude gelled into fear, fear that her son again might not see a car when crossing a street, fear that he might turn in front of one.[31]

Adolescent hormones were behind the final blows to his self-esteem— within a few short weeks of school beginning in the fall of 1930, Dale's eyesight degenerated to the point that he required glasses. They were another expense to the family that he resented bitterly. And yet, more pieces of his protective world continued falling away. Within a few months of his hearing loss the hormonal changes in a fourteen-year-old boy caught Dale literally around the throat—his voice began to change. For someone who can hear, a vocal change is merely a temporary and sometimes entertaining inconvenience. For someone used to speaking but suddenly unable to hear, it means that one must accommodate to changes without knowing the results. Though deafened, Dale remembered the voice he had had; but with this new voice, he could only guess how to make it behave. Could he be heard? Was it too loud? Too shrill? Too nasal? Too fast? He could only estimate by the strain on his neck and rely on the graces of others to tell him gently when he needed to moderate volume or tone or rate.

"Stated quite simply," he later wrote, "I had no mental background for a reliable method of expressiveness within the lower registers . . . The throat-strain attendant on high tones served to inform me that my voice was out of step, I naturally attempted to restrain my voice; a degree of monotone has quite inevitably followed in my speech."[32] In addition, because he had no aural benchmark against which to compare his vocal expression, Dale's speaking voice became rather loud. Acquaintances often discretely waved a hand to communicate that he needed to modify his volume. Generally, reticence caused him to be rather shy about his vocal quality to the point that he did not actually speak except among family and close friends.

Over the years, as familiarity with his voice and the sounds it made receded ever more dimly behind him, the quality of Dale's speech deteriorated. He began slurring words and missing pronunciations, adding to the complications of conversing with him. "It's one of the more unfortunate disabilities of my inability to hear that it has limited me in my adult conversations with people," he once wrote to an aunt. "To talk with people very intimately or at very great length involves a certain amount of labor, both for me and for the person I'm talking to."[33] "I had always to fear that my voice was playing grotesque tricks with me, and fear of making myself ridiculous was powerful incentive toward taciturnity in public." Though sophisticatedly literate and possessing a quick mind, Dale never quite overcame the need for that labor and never did become comfortable speaking conversationally with those with whom he was not well acquainted. For instance, despite lengthy contacts with Morgan (including a three-day marathon compiling the *Overland in 1846* index), Talisman Press publisher Robert Greenwood was unaware that Dale could even speak until they met over lunch to discuss his third book for the press.[34] At school as a young man and with casual acquaintances as an adult, Morgan often communicated back and forth in longhand only.

* * * * *

Dale's microcosm of personal angst was compounded by larger worries. He was nearly through high school and was beginning to think about an adult life, but bank and business closures were at their most alarming frequency in 1932. The Hoover administration's fiscal measures and assurances failed and the year saw a record number of bank failures, which affected households across the nation. Within a short time that failure was reflected on Hollywood Avenue as about a third of the homes in the Morgans' neighborhood between 300 and 400 East were back on the market without buyers after foreclosures. Emily's lender made a deal not to fore-close if she would pay down the interest. She managed to hold onto the house—barely. The Depression forced accommodations on much more than just banks and stores. Employment in Utah stagnated like other areas of the country. At the hard heart of the Depression, Will Hardy lost his business. The family moved from Salt Lake City to Seattle, taking one of the "three amigos" of Dale's cousins.

By then even the family ritual was changing. Both Jerry and Clyde were out of high school and developing interests beyond the family. They came to family gatherings only infrequently. Jerry, who graduated in 1932, a year older and grade ahead of Dale, was allowed a year of "postgraduate" study at West High School for the 1932–1933 school year, Dale's senior year. West offered a half-dozen postgraduate training options for students who could not enter the depressed job market. As uncertain as it was, life continued. On June 2, 1933, Dale L. Morgan graduated from high school, having completed the school's "Elective Course."[35]

Now what?

CHAPTER 3

"The Strange Mixture of Emotion and Intellect"[1]

The University of Utah, Salt Lake City, 1933–1938

I never looked forward to what I might be in the future, only backward at what I had been.[2]

—Dale Morgan

DALE MORGAN'S HIGH SCHOOL GRADUATION coincided with the black heart of the Depression and he faced a future colored only in dust-bowl greys. "Nobody knew what would happen," remembered Bruce Bliven of the *New Republic*. The Great Depression "was like being on a falling elevator when you don't know how far it is to the bottom— or what you will find there." Worse than the remorseless economics of hunger and idleness that afflicted many lives was the sense of direction-lessness and instability that seemed to grip everyone. Unemployment in Utah was nearly 35 percent.[3] Utahns wanted to work, but precious few paying jobs were available. Between August 1932 and March 1933, the number of Utahns receiving public income assistance climbed from 29,206 to 161,506—nearly a third of the state's adult population and the highest figure of any state outside the deep South. Four years later Utah ranked in the top five US states providing public old-age assistance.[4] Dale's personal writings validate that he was understandably worried about his chances in the world, uneasy about the prospect of finding work as a deaf participant in an economy which lacked jobs for even its hearing citizens.

With the country's free-market solutions piled in jittery economic wreckage, voters welcomed a new economic model proposed by the gov-ernor of New York and Democratic presidential candidate, Franklin D. Roosevelt. Business leaders were unwilling to jeopardize capital to finance the investments needed to restart the stalled economy, so if the private business sector abdicated its position as the national economic engine and states individually were not equal to the task, something else would have to replace it. The only entity large enough was the federal government. Historian Michael Barone pointed out that in 1930 the federal government as a whole consumed less than four percent of the value of the gross national product. Six years later the figure was nine percent, a 125 percent increase. In addition, federal back-to-work programs accounted for seven percent of the national workforce.[5] Utah's business owners (and church leaders), however, mistrusted public programs of any sort, especially fiscal ones. Nevertheless, despite First Presidency members' frequent denunciations of politically liberal social and economic measures in speech and print, the state's Latter-day Saint population welcomed the federal relief and work programs.[6]

With no other prospects at hand, Jerry Bleak joined the Civilian Conservation Corps (CCC), a federal work-relief project focused on recreational infrastructure and natural-resource conservation established as part of the New Deal.[7] In midsummer of 1933, Jerry received his CCC assignment and left the south Salt Lake City neighborhood for company 961, two hundred miles away at camp F-16 on Duck Creek, high in the mountains east of Cedar City.[8] With Clyde and the Hardys now in Seattle and Jerry in southern Utah, Dale was deprived of his boon companions of the Bleak/Hardy/Holmes/Morgan cousin-pairings. Dale's closest relationships dispersed completely. Graduating from high school piled on an added expectation and fear to the expectation and anxiety facing a young man with limited choices, along with a surplus of unstructured time through the summer of 1933. With no chance of participating in any of the relief work beginning under Roosevelt's first administration, Dale occupied his summer primarily by reading, following sports reported in the newspaper, participating in family activities, and writing monthly to Jerry (when he could afford paper, envelopes, and stamps). Dale's letters to Jerry, written in longhand, were chatty and filled with news of mutual interest: the Washington Senators had lost to the Yankees; he had been beaten at chess once by Clinton McDaniel but had since recovered his honor; the U.S. tennis team was trounced by the British team in the International Lawn Tennis Challenge; a mutual friend was critically injured in a Provo Canyon automobile accident.[9] He wrote in less detail of the bridge games played with his mother and aunts.

Above all, Dale passed along reports of the stories in the fiction magazines that both young men loved. In fact, Dale was forced to construct long shelves in the basement merely to hold his growing collection of *Argosy* issues. The weekly short-fiction story publication was a perennial favorite shared by both boys, and Dale kept Jerry closely apprised of its contents, as he did of all his reading. He outlined one week's literary diet as seven to nine Western novels, as many novelettes in half a dozen magazines, plus whatever else might be sandwiched between the covers.[10]

On August 23, 1933, Morgan passed another of the small landmarks that seem to divide circumstances in regular life: sitting down at grandmother Morgan's typewriter, Dale typed out a letter to Jerry, the first instance in a lifetime of involvement with what became his mechanical voice. The typewriter was much faster than handwriting, and in years to come it became his primary means of communication. "He wrote magnificent detailed letters," remembered a colleague decades later, "but when you talked to him, why, it was kind of excruciating to get any information across both ways."[11]

Dale's pastime of voracious and omnivorous reading was perfectly suited to his disability. At this period particularly he began to stretch his capacity for concentration and his innate gift for comprehension and recall. It was also probably now that he began to accelerate his reading speed that would in later life allow him, when he needed to, to devour books at a rate of about two to three seconds per page without compromising his remarkable comprehension.[12] Morgan also discovered chess played by mail, a pastime that allowed him to play Jerry in addition to the half-dozen friends he played weekly in person.[13]

Still, reading and chess provided escapes from the world around him, not substitutes for it. Emily Morgan sat down to speak with her son about a means of supporting himself. She encouraged him to do something toward a career, one of the matters that frightened him most. Years later he confessed that the conversation affected him deeply "because it touched so peculiarly upon my early distortion, upon my fear and belief that I was so maimed that I could not take care of myself if my family were to be taken away. The damning helplessness of that feeling which I had for so many years was pretty hard to bear."[14]

* * * * *

In the depths of the Depression, the Morgans would not have recognized it, but they were among the millions of Americans who nonetheless improved their standing across the arc of their existence. Dale Morgan's lifetime corresponds almost precisely with the period in recorded history that has been called *the great leveling,* one of the very few times in human history when social and economic mobility upward was possible and real for large numbers of people.[15] Dale Morgan was one for whom opportunities for education, employment, and the tremendous growth in infrastructure were the basis for their general rise in condition and status, all of which began, thankfully, with a rescue line thrown his direction just before his West High School graduation. Due to his scholastic record and his handicap, Morgan qualified for a probationary full-tuition scholarship to the University of Utah provided by the Utah State Rehabilitation Department.[16] That he attended college is quite remarkable in itself, as the rate of college attendance among the lower middle-class demographic group to which his family belonged was vanishingly small.

Nonetheless, Morgan began a freshman's load of classes at the University of Utah in fall 1933, as soon as possible after his high school graduation. The U, as it was and is still known, was a regional college at the time, with a student body of fewer than 3,500 students. Throughout his collegiate career, Dale lived at home on Hollywood Avenue, commuting to and from the university by streetcar and on foot.

As an incoming freshman, Dale was more conscious than ever of the challenges posed by his hearing loss and could not maintain the exemplary grades of his high school days. The then-prevalent collegiate lecture system meant larger classrooms, some with auditorium-style seating, putting him far enough away from professors that he could not easily see a face well enough to follow what was said in class. Dale was overwhelmed, but not undone. He describes improvising for what instruction he could glean from the notes of neighbors to his right and left, as well as trying to decipher whatever was committed to the chalkboards at the front. People generally accommodated his glances. The method was not without drawbacks, however. "There was [a] memorable class where my only neighbor, a Japanese student," he recalled, "wrote his notes in a combination of English, shorthand, and Japanese."[17] For at least one of his classes, the professor engaged him in individual tutorials grounded on long handwritten discussions.[18]

Despite the challenges class lectures provided, so long as Dale worked carefully through the textbooks and completed assignments, by and large he fared well enough. Morgan qualified in Latin as the foreign-language requirement for his Bachelor of Arts degree. If it seems odd to pursue a collegiate language requirement when one cannot hear at all, consider that if one wants to graduate with a bachelor of arts degree, it might as well involve a language *nobody* will be using conversationally.

Morgan's first two years of college were a steeplechase through self-doubt, a race of dogged determination not to fall behind. Like any college student, Morgan was required to take scientific classes, but despite a youthful interest in chemistry, they did not hold the fascination for him that the humanities did. As he continued through college, Dale gravitated toward fields in which he felt he could study and perform well as an individual with total hearing loss: English (specifically writing), sociology, psychology, and art. Each of them in turn shaped his perception of himself and provided important footings for his opinion of Mormonism and his relationship to it. As disciplines, both art and writing had the feature of being self-generative, while psychology classes demanded pedagogical (and for Morgan, introspective) study.

Dale decided to pursue an art major with an eye toward working in an advertising agency. He possessed some natural talent for drawing and layout, and his posters in high school had regularly won student awards. However, he really wanted to write "copy"—promotional text for printed advertisements. Art classes offered him a formal opportunity to train his eye and hand, but of more personal importance, they offered the opportunity to draw from life. "Drawing" for Morgan, was life drawing, not still life or landscape. Until he left Salt Lake in 1942, life drawing became one of his favorite pastimes and apparently came to provide a modicum of vicarious satisfaction for the intimacy Morgan felt he lacked.[19] Just as importantly, introductory classes in psychology and sociology affected him deeply. Psychology provided the first opportunity and intelligible structures to analyze himself and his drives and to come to terms at least scientifically and quite matter-of-factly with what he had missed or not understood when developing as an adolescent.

By this time he may have no longer felt himself to be a believer in Mormonism, but by reading Havelock Ellis's philosophy and sexual psychology, and Freudian developmental psychology, he was able to distance himself from his family's and cultures' mores. An introspective psychological critique of himself soon turned outward to hold at arm's length the Utah/Mormon culture of which he was emotionally still very much a part.

Continuing the social-accommodation methods he had begun after being deafened, Dale watched others closely. He knew *how* friends acted because of what they said they felt and believed, but he could not really grasp *why* they acted or believed that way. He had little opportunity to discuss the nuances of personal feelings or philosophy. In college, introspection and personal perspective measured what he could see in others, and it eventually took the place of religious faith.[20] Dale later claimed that his faith was in "the decency of human relationships," an existential position characterized by loyalty and personal integrity. What remained of his perception of religion became no longer something he experienced personally but rather a lens through which he could interpret how others acted. Dale began to feel that for someone to "be" a believer was not enough of a qualification to justify one's belief or actions. While Dale mixed with many people of differing perspectives and beliefs, he no longer held to even the possibility of metaphysics. This self-defined moralism he projected onto the Latter-day Saint community around him. In a community dominated by religion, Morgan dismissed faith, defining metaphysics and religious faith out of life's observable realities. With his intellectual development complicated by an inability to communicate easily, profound religious skepticism was reinforced by a self-reinforcing echo chamber or feedback loop of his own perspectives, insular thinking, and reasoning.

However much art pleased Dale and psychology stimulated him, writing was where Dale Morgan finally found not only an outlet for his creativity but also some of the expressive freedom for which he longed. Years later he confessed to his mother that until his third year of college, "I never looked forward to what I might be in the future, only backward at what I had been."[21] His attempts at serious fiction began with introductory writing classes at the University of Utah around 1935 and concluded in crescendo after graduation with a never-completed autobiographical novel in late 1939. His reading habits as a teenager provided a solid foundation in good writing, narrative, and writing style. College offered both a workshop and an outlet for his first serious efforts in literary creativity.

Also in 1935, Morgan was accepted as a staff writer on the university's student newspaper, the *Utah Chronicle,* where he was introduced to and worked under the nominal tutelage of advisor Wallace Stegner, also a University of Utah graduate and now a young faculty member with a new PhD from the University of Iowa.[22] Dale worked at the *Chronicle* with a group of would-be writers and journalists gaining experience on the student newspaper: editor Charlie Wood, news editor Dwight Jones, and sports writer Jack Thornley.[23] As an "editorial assistant," Dale's participation eventually devolved into a role as an informal copyeditor for the rest of the staff, only occasionally publishing an article under his own name. When he did write, his articles covered virtually everything at the university, occasionally under a byline. Journalistic work, however, was a diversion and training ground for his interest in fiction.

* * * * *

During his college years Morgan collected early notice for his developing ability as a writer. Guided by his study in psychology, and square in the midst of his intellectual coming of age, in 1935, Morgan wrote and submitted to the *Salt Lake Tribune* a short story called "The Atheist." Carefully constructed in the language of the eight-year-old character, a boy discovers through personal tragedy that "there is no God!" The story won its author a $5 first prize in the *Salt Lake Tribune's* freelance competition for short fiction.[24] Part way through the year Dale also was enlisted as the associate editor of the campus literary magazine, *The University Pen,* and in 1936, one of his stories took the university's prize for short fiction.[25] To someone who felt incapable of interacting meaningfully with the world, these small successes encouraged Morgan the college student to pursue writing actively. Morgan published eight times in the quarterly student literary magazine, *The University Pen,* and not only fiction either. Four of his published works were insightful critical essays on the collegiate experience.[26]

For three years, until he joined the Utah Writers' Project in 1938, Morgan constantly wrote and revised short stories, and produced outlines and plot sketches for longer works.[27] Fiction provided a path to discuss himself and personal concerns that he felt uncomfortable expressing to his Latter-day Saint mother and family; consequently Morgan's fiction is strongly autobiographical. The bulk of Morgan's own literary explorations fell into the realm of collegiate juvenilia and, like much collegiate work, tended to be rather existential, with characters portrayed from intensely personal perspectives. Disability, social or interpersonal awkwardness, and poverty were prominent themes in his stories.[28] In "The Business Man," a local-award short story, he spills out the frustration of a disabled person (blind, in this case) seeking to be considered an equal in society. "Twenty-nine Dollars", "Eve," "For the Sun Will Be Always Bright," and surviving drafts of plots and story outlines hint at the weight that sexual awareness played in his own coping with social mores and adjustment in society. Death and emotional loss also figured prominently. In another of his autobiographical tales, Morgan's character "had gone through the four years [of college] without ever speaking to any girl on a plane of intimacy. He had never taken a girl out."[29]

To an unknown conversant, scribbled on the back of one of his story drafts Dale wrote about how he handled composition: "In my serious writing I am cut off from many of the nuances of social life so I depend upon an introspective analysis of observation. In other words I translate objective observations to subjective action—I put myself in the place of the character and give many of my own reactions. Of course, this is tempered by an adaptation of myself to the peculiar quality of the character I attempt to depict."[30] In other words, finding a voice as a creative writer began thawing the cold fear he faced making his way in a hearing world, a bone-deep anxiety that had seized and roiled his insides for nearly six years and which he could not bring himself to express to anyone but himself.

Some of Morgan's most telling documents at this time are several surviving "discussions" with either a writing or psychology professor about composition and his concept of self. These and other long conversations with instructors from his days at the University of Utah exist in his papers and provide an unparalleled view into his schooling and thought processes. "Originality and genuineness," he wrote in one discussion, "are liberated only within narrow limits; the strange mixture of emotion and intellect which make up my character is forcibly subdued . . . [and is revealed] only [as] a shadow of the real self, which would emerge if I were liberated from all social, intellectual, and moral restraints."[31]

Morgan appeared to be drinking in some of the radical individuality—and hubris—that seems to characterize those seeking to understand themselves analytically. The restraint he felt was not specifically Mormonism, but unnamed (perhaps unknown) forces of social mores and self-controls accentuated by his deafness. His fiction, particularly the unpublished drafts, reveals the ambivalence of someone who wants to seek absolute freedom but yearns for the security of predictable and comfortable social institutions. What liberating diversion that reading had brought to a precollegiate Dale Morgan, now art, psychology, and writing served that purpose. "Perspective on Platitude," written during his junior year, is a surprisingly mature comment on the role of education in fostering social thought. His later accounts of the challenge of being a deaf student in the hearing-dependent world of higher education, "Social Experience Minus a Sense" and "To Those with Ears," are balanced and insightful but remained unpublished.[32]

At the same time, the physical scars of his bout with meningitis left hidden marks. Well into his twenties Dale found he was still plagued by balance problems from damage to his inner ear. Fortunately these challenges were uncommon, but they were entirely unpredictable and serious enough to threaten disaster. Once while visiting an uncle in the hospital, he became momentarily dizzy and suddenly found himself on the floor with the frames of his eyeglasses broken.[33] No amount of talent with writing could compensate adequately for these sudden and destabilizing incidents.

Like many young adults, Dale Morgan crafted a personal identity during college. Cut off from casual discussion, course work especially in basic sociology and psychology provided a set of tools Morgan felt he could use to good effect in understanding his friends, family, and church on a more vital level than others could. To govern his own conduct in relationships, Morgan replaced moral strictures imposed by a system of beliefs with a carefully garnered code of individuality of his own construction. Dale explained to chess partner Richards Durham and later to other friends that he no longer felt bound by social conventions of morality but rather by his "belief in the decency of human relationships." To be sure, it was a high moral code, but one of near-absolute individualism. Like many focused on a panoramic view, Morgan acknowledged but generally tended to overlook the deficiency in his perspective. "I admit," he wrote Durham, "and I don't say this with conceit, that such a philosophy is not for everyone. It is too easily bastardized."[34]

His personal philosophy recalled an ideal attributed to Joseph Smith when once asked how the Saints were governed: "I teach them correct principles *and they govern themselves*."[35] In both cases, as long as relationships were an interaction of rational, like-minded, committed equals, relationships would work smoothly. But Morgan's faith in the "decency of human relationships" was objectively lacking in any relationship with someone willing to exploit others for personal ends. In fact, even as Morgan was discoursing to his friends about his egalitarian philosophy, he established a relationship with an individual who would exploit his decency and loyalty almost for the rest of his life.

One result of his first publication in the *University Pen* was that late in the 1934 school year Dale was invited to a meeting of Sigma Upsilon, an honorary literary club at the university. Here he met Jarvis Thurston, an Ogden native a year ahead of him in class standing. Thurston became a good friend but graduated the following year and accepted a position teaching mathematics at Ogden Junior High School. Jarvis introduced Dale to Madeline Reeder, who was several years older than either Morgan or Thurston and also from Ogden. Jarvis had met Madeline at the Ogden Public Library while he was in college, where she worked and he studied regularly. Madeline occasionally travelled to Salt Lake City to visit Thurston on campus. She and Thurston married shortly after he graduated in 1935.[36] The next year she spent the summer as a fellow at the prestigious Bread Loaf Writers' Conference and returned with a personal acquaintance of Ogden's most famous native son, Utah expatriate and *Saturday Review of Literature* editor Bernard DeVoto.

Morgan was captivated. "Honest," he wrote to Jerry Bleak, "she is 'more fun than a picnic,' because she has a brain like a razor, very penetrating wit, and a remarkable literary background." Dale's hunger for literary success elevated Madeline Thurston and her writing experience to a high pedestal. In her letters to Dale, she carefully referred to DeVoto the novelist, essayist, and Harvard professor as "Benny" (though name-dropping, she really was on a first-name basis with him). Discussions of literary criticism between Dale and Madeline resulted in soul-baring analysis for the two writers that drew them closely together.[37] For her, the relationship with this younger man, eight years her junior, may have been limited to intellectual intimacy; for Morgan, the emerging relationship was one of near-captive devotion lasting almost thirty years. The summer after Dale graduated from the University of Utah in May 1937, he and an unidentified "friend" had a long, intense discussion about human sexuality. This conversation seems to have provided for Morgan the catharsis of sexual identity that had been the focus of his collegiate fiction, and Dale himself acknowledged the lasting effect that this exchange had on his psyche.[38] As he had few intimates, that friend was most likely Madeline Thurston.

By the time Morgan graduated from college, self-directed study following his one class each in sociology and psychology had awakened a critical vein of thought that surgically cauterized his severed emotional ties to the Church of Jesus Christ of Latter-day Saints, though less so to the broader Latter Day Saint culture. Intellectual ties and what spiritual ties he may once have harbored, dissolved years earlier. Though Dale continued to draw recreationally for five more years, the studio was also largely left behind. After graduating with a BA and an art emphasis in June that year, Morgan was left with writing. As he had four years before, he faced the prospect of being unemployed. This time, however, he was becoming reconciled to the concept of human sexuality and to his deafness, emotionally able to face the situation with increased confidence. Not that confidence mattered much. Despite federal work-relief programs, Utah reported nearly 24,000 adult citizens out of work in the spring of 1937.[39] White-collar jobs for college graduates were scarce in Depression-era Utah, especially if the one looking for work also carried the added challenge of deafness.

* * * * *

After he graduated and while unemployed, a socially hungry Dale plunged into a deeper personal study of social psychology. Beyond the work of British social philosopher Havelock Ellis, Morgan left little record of how broad or deep his exploration ran. If nothing else, he had discovered in college and was drawn toward the perceived certainties of describing and cataloging human behavior through observation. It fit him well. The language and inherent certainty of scientific observation flowed together, and he seemed to have absorbed the categories and many of the assumptions of the subject.

Meanwhile, the summer and fall involved a fruitless job search. Almost immediately upon graduating, twenty-three-year-old Dale Morgan approached the *Salt Lake Tribune*'s Literature and Art Department with a suggestion that he be hired to write a daily book review. In the midst of the summer slow season the section editor did not feel that a column was warranted but offered Morgan the opportunity to write a regular Sunday review.[40] He accepted the compromise and wrote for the paper until 1939.

Dale also pondered how he would land the job he really wanted in advertising. In August, he drafted a pair of sample ad campaigns for two of the best customers of Gillham Advertising, Salt Lake City's largest advertising firm. Initially he was encouraged by their interest and waited anxiously to hear more from them. Nothing came. In October, however, he learned from an acquaintance who worked for Gillham that his appointment was virtually certain until a staid vice president concluded not to interview him because of his deafness.

Through the rest of the fall of 1937, Morgan played chess, read, worked around the Hollywood Avenue house, and wrote to Salt Lake City's department stores and advertising companies, unsuccessfully seeking work on advertising and art staffs. The newspapers also had no interest, and Dale finally wrote Jerry, by now serving an LDS proselyting mission in Samoa, he had "about given up the idea of a local journalistic career for the present."[41] Near the first of October, the State Rehabilitation Department wrote offering to help him in his job search. Dale was reluctant to accept the proffered assistance, preferring to have choice in employment rather than being placed. Dale travelled to Ogden and stayed with the Thurstons for two weeks through the middle of October, perhaps a platform for extending the job search to Utah's second-largest city and unquestionably its transportation hub. Not only did he unsuccessfully continue his search for a job in advertising, he also played an exhibition chess match against the entire Ogden chess club simultaneously with white pieces on alternate boards. He carried the match by winning ten and drawing one of the fourteen games.[42]

After returning to Salt Lake City in mid-October, Dale essentially dropped job-hunting through the holiday season to concentrate on personal study and writing. Through January, 1938, he put four hours daily into studying advertising until he set it aside, consumed by a flash of literary inspiration. Dale began a novel of contemporary Utah, alternating as inspiration struck him with shorter fiction. "I am in the very middle of the most fertile period I have experienced in over two years of writing," he confessed to Jerry. "I begrudge almost every minute stolen from that writing, whether to eat, sleep, read, play chess, bathe, or keep up with my correspondence." Dale wrote feverishly for several months. Before May he had composed what he felt was his best short fiction and submitted several short pieces to magazines.[43] From the turn of the 1938 new year until July, Morgan alternated between writing his Utah novel and short fiction at home in Salt Lake City, and assisting Madeline Thurston to rewrite her own novel at her home in Ogden, with chess matches scattered irregularly around the calendar. Thirty years after Morgan's death I asked Jarvis if he thought Dale had the capacity to be a successful fiction writer. Thurston—who had taught creative writing for more than half a century by then—said no, Dale didn't grasp the importance and use of metaphor. In other words, he had fine technical capability and a good grasp of literature, but probably could not have cut it as a fiction writer.[44] Magazine editors uniformly agreed; what responses Dale received to his fiction manuscripts across his career (other than from his college professors) were scribbled dismissals.[45]

* * * * *

Morgan played chess at lunch and in the evenings, one of the few interactive recreations he could pursue with people whose speech patterns he did not know well. He helped organize the Utah Chess Federation's first formal competition in 1937. In the last two days of May 1938, the UCF held a two-day match at the downtown Alta Club between club members from across the Wasatch Front and scattered invitees from Idaho and Arizona. Morgan arranged to record moves of each match. Someone took photos. From the two Dale wrote up an account of the meet. Ray Kooyman volunteered to duplicate the booklet for distribution to the twenty-three participants. It is unlikely that anyone else was interested.

During the last week of July, as Kooyman was busily mailing out copies of the commemorative 1938 chess book, Dale once again packed his bags and took the train to Ogden, this time to accompany the Thurstons on a trip to Yellowstone National Park. Dale arrived at their apartment to find that Jarvis had an intriguing suggestion. A few days before Dale arrived, Thurston had been approached by Maurice L. Howe, a former *Ogden Standard-Examiner* writer. Howe now directed the Utah branch of the Historical Records Survey (HRS), a federal white-collar relief project in the state, but also a cultural project which attempted to replicate at a local level what the still-new National Archives had done for identifying public records at a federal level. The HRS was looking for an editor—and the position was not a welfare placement. The vacancy was a professional one, Thurston explained. Howe was looking for a competent editor, a specialized skill, which meant that those not on public relief roles could apply. The HRS needed someone with practical writing experience who could smooth out choppy wording produced by the less-experienced staff writers. Thurston declined the offer in favor of continuing his teaching contract in the Ogden public school district but suggested Dale Morgan's name as an alternate. While Jarvis and Madeline finished last-minute preparations for the Yellowstone trip, Jarvis directed Dale to the WPA office on Ogden's 24th Street to inquire into the position.

Morgan caught a streetcar to the office, completed an application, and was given an immediate interview on the strength of Thurston's recommendation. The staff interviewer was concerned about his lack of hearing, yet with suitable experience in writing and aims at a career in advertising, Morgan and his qualifications were clearly impressive. Dale was tentatively hired for a junior position in the Historical Records Survey.[46] Having a solid job prospect in writing and editing, two functions he could do quite well (and without hearing) must have provided a rush of relief. The Morgan-Thurston trio cut short the trip to Yellowstone. Their early return allowed Dale a second opportunity to interview, this time with

Ogden-office superintendent Hugh F. O'Neil, then with state Writers' Project director Maurice L. Howe, and finally approval by the Utah WPA board, all of which required added time. All Dale could do was to sit on his hands and wait.

Meanwhile, Emily was planning for a before-school excursion to see her sister-in-law Ida's family in California. Anxiously anticipating a job at last, Dale declined the opportunity to accompany her. Instead, he moved temporarily to the Thurston's home in Ogden. There he waited through the first week of August, probably a bit anxiously, for his hire to be finalized. In the second week of August 1938, Dale received final employment clearance from the state WPA board. At last he had a job.

CHAPTER 4

Digression

Telling the Past in Latter-day Saint Utah, 1930s Style

> *We Utahns certainly like to read about Utah history—provided it reads*
> *like we think it should.*[1]
> —Darrell Greenwell

EVERY BOOK HAS A RATIONALE behind its writing; every author, a motivation. Part of my reason for writing a biography of this particular Utah/Western historian (besides that no one else yet has) has been to explain what I see as a significant series of shifts in the way the past was understood and related within Dale Morgan's community. His career coincides with changes between "seasons" within Latter Day Saint and Latter-day Saint history. These shifts are not in perspective or interpretive lenses (although that was involved), but something much deeper, involving a change in philosophy or *historiology*. A biography does not provide enough space to fully explore this broad transformation, so I will substitute at least a summary foray into *historiography,* or the way in which history has been presented. Most readers will find it less intimidating to think of historiography as *the story of storytelling,* but on a community level.

Before exploring Morgan and his introduction to history, one needs to grasp what history, historical writing, and the politics of history involved in 1930s Utah. Understanding Utah and the politics of public memory are important to understanding Morgan and his choices, since it is at this point that Morgan is introduced to the cultural history of the locale and region. In this book, the story of history among the Latter Day Saint traditions (mostly the Utah-based Church of Jesus Christ of Latter-day Saints) and about the western United States will be woven into the narrative. Neither historiography is comprehensive. As befitting a generalization, it blurs many crosscurrents within historiography to illustrate trends rather than details, but the trends are worth considering in a Utah context. In the 1930s, few outside Utah were especially interested in Mormons beyond literature or sensationalism, certainly not historically, but the Latter-day Saints were eager participants in commemorative history, and their perspectives reflected broader American sentiments.[2]

* * * * *

By the time Dale Morgan came to history in the late 1930s America was seventy-five years or so into a national strain of historical *antiquarianism*. Antiquarianism is an approach to the past implying attention to the past divorced from its contemporary relevance or from contextual significance. Antiquarianism eagerly corrects or adds detail to what is already known of the past. Initiative, sequence, and participative details are important to antiquarians, who preserve and correct a knowledge of the past merely for the sake of doing so. Comprehension of the past itself became a significant artifact.[3] Across the country, and in the American West more recently, popular desire to memorialize the founders of any state consumed the public. Eagerness for commemoration fueled interest in the adventures of town, county, and state founders. Historical organizations of all sorts cropped up. State and local historical journals presented the edited records of a rapidly dwindling pioneer population for the sake of preserving the local past—and for a chance for readers to imagine the romance of local origins disappearing under the pressures of Modernity. Publication of diaries and letters was a means of textual preservation. Journals often reprint primary works without explanatory notes or comment.

Utah's manifestation of this drive was the founding of the Utah State Historical Society in 1895, and the *Utah Historical Quarterly* in 1928. A small but thriving culture of local and family history publications, especially with the church and state's pioneer founders a generation gone and their children aging quickly, documented family and community history. "With the rapid decline in numbers of those who have actually experienced pioneer life," wrote one *Deseret News* columnist, "their stories are becoming more interesting and important even though they may not reach as high a literary standard as we could desire."[4] Within Utah, antiquarianism sparked many family publications claiming a place for their grandfather or grandmother within the founding stories of the church, the settlement of Utah, or of a particular locality.

Not that commemorative memory was strictly accurate. Without the inconvenient complications of a "special institution" like slavery, it was easy to glide over the racial omissions involved in Utah's past. Exhibiting a marked antebellum sympathy for "states' rights" doctrine and despite being nominally a slave territory, Utah's early immigrants were virtually all white Europeans. Even late immigrants who arrived to work its coal, silver, and copper mines were white. Native people were crowded aside not only from valleys, but also from a serious position in the region's story, relegated to being the antagonistic backdrop against which to memorialize "Indian war" veterans. The Chinese who built the rail lines were ignored. Without being overtly racist, Utah's story was so by its omissions.[5]

Beside antiquarianism stood a related approach, a moral imperative for recalling the past. Two generations earlier, Mason Weems compiled his inspiring but fanciful biography of George Washington to encourage the nation's emerging civic religion of patriotic nationalism. Within Morgan's state, the motivation to instruct and inspire Utah's rising generation grew as strongly. This desire became entangled with the religious sentiment of Utah's mainstream culture. Local history in the 1930s, any local history, tended to be an expression of *memory* into which flowed tributaries of warmly held faith, mainstream politics, and selective recollection. Folklorist William A. "Bert" Wilson noted that "memory usually does at least two things. It selectively chooses to remember those happenings that have special significance to an individual [or society]; and, through the years, it often embellishes these happenings, making them larger than life. As a result, storytelling often becomes an attempt by the teller to characterize the past in terms meaningful to him in the present."[6] From either side of Utah's polemic divide, history in the state involved storytelling, and local stories were often treated as proprietary.

Those values give a name to *presentism, patriotic history,* or more pejoratively, *ethicism* or *utilitarianism.* Presentist history has a persuasive, instructional, motivational purpose, using the past as a lesson manual to foster or encourage some quality, idea, or attitudes among readers. It works by selecting stories illustrating some inspirational quality or action and then often explicitly encourages readers to believe, follow, or act similarly. In doing so the story often works by setting aside complications to the main theme. No bright, clear line separates antiquarianism and ethicism/presentism. Within Dale Morgan's Utah, other than textbooks, the major publication of this memorial ethicism were the Daughters of Utah Pioneers lesson series.

Besides antiquarianism and ethicism, a third factor complicating Utah's storytelling was Church of Jesus Christ of Latter-day Saints members' feelings about the Restoration. This stream of social discourse had its own division. During Morgan's lifetime, Utah's written history was essentially a binary. On one side, history was almost an outgrowth of LDS church authority, the venue of encyclopedists like Andrew Jenson, romantic compilers and analysts like B. H. Roberts or Preston Nibley, and particularly doctrinarians like Joseph Fielding Smith. Other than school texts, comparatively little unofficial Utah or Mormon history was written or marketed. As late as the 1920s, key writers among the Latter-day Saints were used to thinking of history and the understanding of the past as a mortal manifestation and enactment of revealed truth. History became a form of uncanonized scripture, proof of God's guidance of the church. Challenging accepted history was an assault on God's word and church leaders' testimony. In fact, within the HRS itself a memo came to Morgan from someone in the office (perhaps Howe) with an instruction to document carefully and rely little or not at all on current histories for "there can be no cleancut [*sic*] distinction between Mormon history and doctrine because of a Mormon tendency to see their history as proof of their doctrine."

As a result, works like the seven-volume semiofficial *History of the Church of Jesus Christ of Latter-day Saints* (1902–1932) were both source material and explanation. B. H. Roberts' "History of the 'Mormon' Church," published serially in *Americana* magazine and later compiled into the six-volume *A Comprehensive History of the Church of Jesus Christ of Latter-day Saints* (1930), was essentially romantic. Studies like Joseph Fielding Smith Jr.'s *Origin of the Reorganized Church* (1907) and *Essentials in Church History* (1922) were openly polemic. Their author was an ardent proponent of a Latter-day Saint version of *monism,* as well, the perspective that "Truth" and reality existed solely within the bounds of the church and its revealed perspectives; differing ideas or conflicting views were incorrect by definition and could be dismissed. Because these writers tended to write *both* doctrine and history and argued about doctrine from a historical perspective, neither works nor writers separated the assertive claims of doctrine from the common temporal realities that were merely factual. "For the same reason," the note warned Morgan, "all accounts of Mormon history, gentile and Mormon alike, have been violently partisan, and not reliable."[7]

Add to these factors the challenge of what the church, the state, and their history represented to the mature generation of the 1930s. To this second generation of Latter-day Saints, history rested chiefly on faith-promoting stories. Latter-day Saint doctrine was not content to retreat within the believers and accept the status quo of occasional growth. Both Morgan and Latter-day Saint culture reflected a much-later observation by theologian Ingolf Dalferth of Christianity generally, that "if we view ourselves as created beings, we see God everywhere; if not, then we see God nowhere."[8] Latter-day Saints saw God everywhere among his mortal agents in the last-days Restoration. Many, like Joseph Fielding Smith, made a logical leap concluding that God's hand therefore shadowed *every* action of the saints, and that their hard-bitten opponents pushing against the church therefore pushed against God. That perspective saw history as moving forward along a divinely predetermined path. No step, no decision was an error for the church.

The church was the leading force in this making of history, carrying forward, preparing the saints, and warning the world of the impending Second Coming of Jesus Christ. In this sense, the road through history and the present was linear, predetermined, and could be marked off. If progress wavered slightly, it was only slight. The sense of mission and ordination left little space for individual choices or real setbacks of any sort. History was less a set of circumstances than it was a matter of progressing along a straight and narrow line leading directly from 1820 to the dawning millennial day. Each day brought believers and the world around them closer to the inevitable. This generalization was not a carefully thought-out rationalization, visible in the writings of contemporaries. It was rather a perspective and set of assumptions that allowed the saints to look at themselves and the world around them and see things in a certain way.

By the 1930s, whether or not intended, telling the Latter-day Saint story had become closely entangled with church doctrine in the minds of key writers of Utah's story. An attack on one was, by point of argument, necessarily an attack on the other. Drawing on antiquarianism but also a strong strain of ethicism, histories touching on the state tended to be produced in terms of church leaders' lives and their agency in the past, often written by well-placed younger leaders. The generation of firsthand witnesses to the church's founding and the state's settlement was long gone, and access to firsthand written source material was dramatically limited. Latter-day Saint culture held clearly established ideas about how the past should be regarded and how it was appropriately used within the church's culture of belief and participation. Within their sphere of interest, the saints operated with an internal historical consciousness of the sense that Paul Ricoeur identified (and *not* as cultural pejorative) as *primitive naiveté,* meaning they tended to accept uncritically what was presented by authorities as it fit their expectations.[9]

Antiquarianism, ethicism, and the Restoration combined to form a cultural "master narrative" of the state's mainstream culture. By the 1930s Utah's master narrative was a romantic, patriotic, inspirational, culturally affirming view of the state's past not much different than similar stories told about Massachusetts Puritans or Virginia Baptists or land-bounty claimants in a dozen Midwestern states. The difference was that with few exceptions, Mormon history was generally written by Mormons for Mormons. Writ large within the master narrative was the Pioneer myth (that is, *myth* as *founding story,* not falsehood). The Pioneer myth focused on prominent figures and political institutions, relying heavily on scriptural interpretation, inspirational story, and personal testimony: stories told and books written to congratulate the living on their heritage, partly to gild the founders, and certainly to reinforce values and views.[10] The important point in all this is that the state's history (except for outright polemic) was generally written by Utah's Latter-day Saints for Utah's Latter-day Saints (or by those outside the church, specifically to challenge or document a competing narrative).

From the inside, by the 1930s, Mormon history had a well-developed message and a means of self-fulfillment. Even its few moderates, such as B. H. Roberts, did not question the fundamental triumphalism of the historical message and its written expressions.[11] In short, both writing and reading history until the 1930s (at least in and around the Mormons and Utah) tended to be an exercise of encouraging commemoration and values. Those who wrote history tended to do so to emphasize a point or teach a lesson or to inspire.

The Mormons' "ethical history" encouraged allegiance to central moral authority. In order to move forward, modern people almost always look back. Invoking or at least consulting the past is critical to creating cultural authority. For those inside the church, history tended to demonstrate how God had guided and upheld them in their trials, affirming their status and standing as the chosen modern Israel, their forebears heroic and ordained by God, worthy of emulation. This perspective of a morally useful history was illustrated in 1947 as floats and decorations of the Pioneer

Centennial. That same year Daughters of Utah Pioneers president Kate Carter addressed a Brigham Young University faculty group on the subject of source material. When asked what she considered "editing," Carter announced that "I never allow anything to go into print that I think will be injurious to my church, or that will in any way reflect discredit upon our pioneers."[12]

Carter's approach was largely nostalgic, but a nostalgia still filtered by bowdlerizing expedience. Dale Morgan and others sharing his approach to history, disagreed vehemently. "In the long run, such writing is worthless, it has neither historical nor biographical validity," Morgan gave as an opinion several years later.[13] On the heels of the 1930 Latter Day Saint centennial and in the march up to the 1947 Utah Pioneer centennial, history "reading the way it should" meant that history about the church or the state was uplifting or promotional. Most Utah history was written either for schoolchildren, for local citizens and family descendants, or for those interested in preserving the past for its own noble sake.

* * * * *

Of course, the master narrative faced an opposing side: writers aspiring to tell the Mormon/Utah story from very different perspectives. To the Mormon majority, those who wrote about the Mormons or the state from the outside were either scurrilous detractors, lying malcontents, and/or grasping opportunists. A Utahn's list of historical undesirables included a small but committed group of cultural gadflies, writers or works such as memoirs (or purported memoirs) by R. N. Baskin and C. C. Goodwin, and histories or biographies by E. L. T. Harrison, Frank J. Cannon, J. H. Beadle, Thomas B. H. Stenhouse, William A. Linn, or Ruth and Reginald Kauffman.[14] Strongly, sometimes vitriolically partisan, these works carried Mormonism to national and international audiences, and not kindly. For those writing from the outside, the value they espoused tended toward emphasizing the Mormons' political duplicity, antidemocratic theocracy, lack of Christian values (particularly regarding polygamy), and general wrongheadedness. In the note to Morgan about distrusting LDS histories, cited earlier, was he also warned about the questionable merits of these works as well. The conflicting expectations are important because the two sides made Utah and Latter-day Saint history into polemical binary, with not much in the "interactive and dialogic" middle besides a few travel narratives by curiosity-fueled tourists, such as

Horace Greeley, Jules Remy, John W. Gunnison, Elizabeth Kane, or Sir Richard F. Burton.[15]

American culture had stewed in antiquarianism, but for about the same amount of time its tiny clutch of colleges and university scholars were integrating a new perspective to history as well. Building on the work of German historian Leopold von Ranke, scholars were beginning to look for paths around both antiquarianism and ethicism (and polemic), seeking a perspective that looked at the past dispassionately on the past's own terms.[16] An objectified quest for actuality and context rather than inspiration is broadly grouped under the idea of *historicism*. Historicism became the perspective of emerging generations of academic scholars, those who might look in on the past from the outside either culturally or temporally. Historicism aimed more at description and explanation, context and critique, without attempting to take sides. Even so, scholarly training alone was not an objective inoculation against cultural ethicism.

The experience of the first two generations of Latter-day Saints with graduate education is addressed in a recent study by Thomas W. Simpson. Focusing on acquiring credentials in medicine and the sciences, there were very few humanities scholars among Mormons who went east seeking professional training. The exception was the half-dozen attendees of the University of Chicago Divinity School: Sidney Sperry, Russel Swensen, Daryl Chase, George Tanner, T. Edgar Lyon, and Carl J. Furr.[17] These men had a terrific influence on Brigham Young University, church education, and historiography, but almost no effect on LDS historiology. Nels Anderson also earned a University of Chicago doctorate, but in sociology. Utah's trained historical scholars of the time—Joel E. Ricks, Andrew Neff, Leland Creer, Milton R. Hunter, and others (including by avocation and activity, chemist John A. Widtsoe and geologist James E. Talmage)—were decidedly and contentedly within the master-narrative camp, despite their training.

In the opposing camp, scholarship could be used on the Mormons like a polemic stick in the hands of scholars like I. Woodbridge Riley in, *The Founder of Mormonism: A Psychological Study of Joseph Smith Jr.* (1903), or George B. Arbaugh, *Revelation in Mormonism: Its Character and Changing Form* (1932). From beyond Utah and Latter-day Saint culture, actual scholarship was a minor theme dribbling into the milieu. In the early twentieth century, scholarship was far less significant to the collective sense of LDS history than it is today. Academic scholarship involving the Mormons cropped up occasionally, but mostly in the form of masters' theses and dissertations read by few besides the candidate's graduate committee. Fewer of these made it to print, including Ephraim E. Eriksen's *Psychological and Ethical Aspects of Mormon Group Life* (1922), Joseph A. Geddes, *The United Order among the Mormons (Missouri Phase): An Unfinished Experiment in Economic Organization* (1922), or Lowry Nelson's *The Mormon Village: A Study in Social Origins* (1930). The truth is, few people read scholarship; such work written about the Mormons was generally unread even among Mormon academics.[18]

Almost as soon as he began working for the HRS, Morgan heaped imprecations on Utah's academic historians who by virtue of professional training should have been generating more objective, more accurate, more interpretively critical work. He knew the state's trained historians from their published work alone, having taken no history classes in college beyond the required undergraduate survey. At the time, the list of scholars was not long and most of the state's academics did not teach or write much about Utah or the American West, but of those who did Morgan held similar opinions. In his eyes, if Utah's academic historians of the day were any measure, then professional training was a liability rather than an asset. Leland Creer may have impressed University of Utah students with engaging classroom lectures, but Morgan considered his editing of colleague Andrew Neff's book on Utah's founding "absolutely incompetent."[19] Creer wasn't a lone figure in Morgan's low estimation. Morgan dismissed Milton R. Hunter's and Levi Edgar Young's work on the state and its people as fatally compromised by cultural ethicism.[20] He later interacted directly with Utah State Agricultural College (later Utah State University) professor Joel E. Ricks as the latter chaired the Utah State Historical Society board of control. There would be no institutional improvement under Ricks, Morgan concluded.[21]

From Morgan's emerging perspective two problems plagued the work by the academically trained writers of his generation. First, despite their methodological training they tended to concentrate on broad, mainstream, culturally triumphant "master narrative" subjects: they were Latter-day Saints first and scholars second. Secondly, these historians tended to accept colleagues' secondary studies uncritically rather than getting into the weeds of actual documentation to identify and resolve discrepancies. Morgan came to regard both as cardinal sins.

* * * * *

As a newly appointed editor Morgan discovered that WPA writers faced a suite of problems in writing about Utah at every level, because the story of the state—even of *which* story of the state—was loaded with values carried by the teller. Because of its religious and therefore political demographics, treatments of Utah's past tended to divide over confrontations about values. In Utah, cultural entities like the Church Historian's Office of the Church of Jesus Christ of Latter-day Saints and newly emerging heritage organizations like the Daughters of Utah Pioneers expected the state's history to reflect the heroic past they chose to remember and memorialize. In light of the anti-church polemics of an earlier generation (church historian Joseph Fielding Smith had personally seen the publication of many), and given the open antipathy to the WPA stated by church president Heber J. Grant and counselor J. Reuben Clark, the Historian's Office was wary of extending wholehearted cooperation and access to the HRS. Nevertheless its holdings retained the only substantial primary-document collection in the state. The federally sponsored program's determination to adopt an objectified, outsider focus on fact and documentation, write without taking sides in the polemic struggle, or adopt the state's "master narrative," all proved to be a challenge.

The WPA's Historical Records Survey and Utah Writers' Project also struggled in Utah partly because in the 1930s the single library in Utah with a substantive, publicly available local-history book collection was the Salt Lake Public Library.[22] The chief source for information on the state was the Church Historian's Office. The presence of WPA research workers there was a new experience for the church, awakening its staff to the fact that its collection of books and documents was of interest to researchers tracing non-church, non-genealogical subjects. This secular interest was new territory, and CHO staff addressed it with an air of uncomfortable uncertainty over exactly how to accommodate the research use and what it might yield. Add to this the fact that HRS workers tended to prefer documents—which generally they could not see—to the compiled and published encyclopedic histories and biographies which the Office had churned out over decades for public consumption. Merely asking to see the originals may have been taken by the CHO staff as a tacit expression of distrust of their work.

To complicate matters, the CHO staff felt very much that they were the custodians of the church's records by virtue of ecclesiastical appointment and proven loyalty to the church (Smith was an apostle; Roberts one of seven presidents of the First Council of Seventy). Thus they served as guardians of their collective reputation within memory, the only appropriate interpreters of the church and its members' past. Maurice Howe wrote a friend about his experience starting Utah's branch of the Historical Records Survey in 1935 that "LDS historians were jealous of our work at first because they thought we were trespassing in their fields."[23] The Mormon past, and by extension, the settlement-of-Utah past, was a nearly exclusive preserve to which an outsider must be admitted and generate what was expected (laudatory praise, or at least not challenge assumptions), or be considered a poacher.

Largely because history was couched in stories rather than evidence, the CHO countered writers whose work it did not approve by the simple expedient of controlling access to its collections, based on whether or not one's topic seemed unflattering. The federal projects in Salt Lake City experienced gatekeeping firsthand. As the Historical Records Survey began poking around uncomfortably in the state's past, new sources and questions surfaced, making some people uncomfortable. WPA researchers were shut out of the CHO in August 1939 after A. William Lund disagreed with an interpretation made publicly in some HRS publication.[24] Access was reopened a week later, but the closure drove home the point that the Historian's Office collection and staff cooperation was a beneficence and not a right.

With academic institutions barely beginning to establish research collections of rare books (primary material generally came later), a proprietary attitude was not unique to the Mormons. On a trip to Berkeley, California, a bit later in the year Morgan requested research access to the Bancroft Library manuscript holdings, nominally a public research collection. He was denied, partly because he made the mistake of mentioning that he was a Writers' Project employee (and thus historically unqualified), and partly because his letter of introduction from nonacademic Maurice Howe held no weight with director Herbert I. Priestley.[25] Such attitudes were changing—slowly—but a commitment to "access" appeared in no institutional or professional code of ethics, leaving the use of institutional collections rather less a matter of scholarly credentials than an acknowledgment of one's relationship with a suitable patron. Research material could be denied almost arbitrarily.

* * * * *

Dale Morgan's introduction to history in the 1930s came at the beginning of a long, slow collision between Mormonism's inspirational, ethical narrative with this new style of objectified historical study and the new strains of inquiry that the federal projects represented. Exemplified by HRS historical work, and its commitment to source material as a basis for history, inspirationalism was simply bypassed. As young and inexperienced as he was, Dale L. Morgan was among a new generation of historical writers emerging from beyond Utah's cultural organizations. This group tended not to accept common master-narrative stories at face value, preferring to hunt down contemporary records to see what *was* experienced. Relying on documents and context brought to light new sources and new facts. A graduate student facing a similar circumstance years later captured the conflict Latter Day Saint history encountered in the 1930s. These new thinkers didn't change the facts of history. Instead, "we discovered a history that the old facts could not explain. We did not invent new facts, either; they had always existed. But, through education, we had been trained not to see them, for they contradicted the assumptions that most historians held."[26] Within Mormon history, some rediscovered facts similarly seemed to contradict or question the stories established and accepted tradition. Newly uncovered realities complicated the traditional and triumphal "master narrative" forms of Utah and Mormon history, threatening to displace myth—or perhaps more accurately, a new myth threatened to displace an older one.

Utah and its culture suffered somewhat less from the collision than did other areas of the country, but the Depression generally discredited the focus on industrial and political barons of the Gilded Age, motivating a quest for a different and more inclusive approach to the nation's history. The WPA projects introduced an external purpose to local history. Outsiders, who didn't necessarily share community sensibilities, risked pulling skeletons out of closets. Stirring around in the attics and closets of local cultures is precisely why Congress mandated external reviews for WPA cultural program publications. Whether in Utah, Michigan, or Alabama, the WPA projects wrote history not merely to laud the founders and congratulate the city fathers, but to meaningfully and carefully inform people.

The federal culture projects found their new approach to the understanding and relating the past in an investigative, narrative style from Britain: *documentary*. The term was coined in 1926 by British writer and filmmaker John Grierson. He settled on a new word to describe this method of storytelling because he felt it stood apart and beyond values, allowing the visual or written record to provide convincing evidence on its own. The cultural programs of the New Deal adopted documentary intentionally, sidestepping the "great man" history championed by the nation's elite culture, to focus on common citizens, routine activity, and community progress through joint action.[27] "Documentary," wrote historian William Stott, "deals with people 'a damn sight realer' than the celebrities that crowd the media." Influenced by the work of photographers Lewis Hine and Jacob Riis, and by the Progressive "muckraker" journalism of writers like Lincoln Steffens, Ida Tarbell, and Upton Sinclair, visual and narrative documentary focused on the experiences and records of non-elite populations. Early forms of documentary emphasized common people, work routines, and daily life, requiring an entirely new set of source materials. The previously available memoirs and writings of community political, social, and business leaders—the basis of traditional mainstream history— became only marginally significant compared to the diaries, letters, and memoirs of those who had been on-the-ground followers and common citizens. This approach to history broadened the perspective about "what really happened" away from elite figures and onto the often-conflicting experiences of everyone else.

Morgan's chief complaint about Latter-day Saint stories was that both writers and readers expected their progenitors to be heroes first and people only secondarily. "Let your people be human first," Dale later counseled Juanita Brooks, "people second, and only then Mormons."[28] Standing outside, looking in on the participants and their choices, objectified the nature of Latter-day Saint history.

In fact, the HRS insistence on "fact," and that fact was somehow beyond challenge by values, was a much newer factor further complicating Utah's sometimes-combative argument over history and the state's master-narrative Pioneer myth. Historian William Stott's examination of the documentary style helps to explain what seemed like a maniacal drive for fact among WPA projects. "All facts *are* created equal," Stott summarized, "all must be taken into account; all are potentially important, and any, however banal, may prove crucial."[29] Back in Utah, the cultural projects were confident that *documentary evidence* was a basis for a documentary-style approach to the state's history that could not be compromised by faith or tradition. When once challenged over details in a county history draft, Morgan asserted that "we are making every effort to establish the validity of any statements we use in our histories."[30]

The new documentary approach to history which Morgan was practicing rejected historical narratives either compiled or presented as moral, political, or religious instruction—master-narrative ethicism. Morgan

especially stood against inspirational narratives by what one LDS historian later derisively called "Holy Ghosters," people whose philosophical
monism asserted the Spirit and its representatives as the sole source of
knowable truth.[31] Any such utilitarian approach, a historicist like Morgan
would charge, is too willing to oversimplify story for the sake of singular
clarity, and too willing to put factual contradictions out of sight in favor
of message. Against the perceived façade of "faithful history" and upon
the rock-solid foundation of historicism, the WPA culture projects and
eventually Dale Morgan attempted to build their house. "When religion
removes from the metaphysical to the physical plane ... it subjects itself
to material criteria," he wrote assertively to a challenger. "As it lays claim to
'facts,' so it becomes embodied in 'facts,' and those facts may be taken up
and individually evaluated by even the most materialistic of historians
without legitimate objection."[32] Factual, evidence-based history could
not be subject to the assertions of faith and "character," just as history
should not be expected either to dismiss or reinforce religious belief.
Morgan understood that simply because no record existed did not necessarily imply that a historic event, like the First Vision, did not happen.
In his writing, however, he would not assume that it *had* happened simply
because people believed it had.[33]

This new approach held tradition and testimony to historical, documentable account—both as the basis for Latter Day Saint origins and
for Utah's master narrative of its Pioneer myth. From the perspective of
federally backed writers, little or no effort was made outside project offices
to be either inclusively complete or objective. Because Utah's and Mormonism's writers and its Latter-day Saint and Latter Day Saint readers
shared cultural perspectives, implicit assumptions of what needed to be
said, how stories were related, and what was *not* subject to critical study,
the faith's historical writing tended to strengthen the cultural perceptions
of its readers. One could say that its storytelling had evolved to meet its
needs. Latter-day Saint history was not so much inaccurate or falsified
as it was simply insular. In the 1930s and 1940s, the demands made of
Mormonism's stories began shifting.

Morgan was affected deeply by documentary philosophy and its
approach, not by affinity but by persuasion of its human power. It clearly
influenced his telling of Utah/Mormon history. His rendition of the past
weighed the Mormons strictly as an American social phenomenon and
not as agents of divinity. "Mormonism really was compounded out of the
lives of hundreds and thousands," Morgan wrote to Bernard DeVoto in

1942, referring to the diary of a man otherwise unknown to Mormon or to Utah history. "There is more to Mormonism than the lives of Brigham Young and Joseph Smith."[34]

Importantly, bringing up the differing perspectives of documentary often challenged or at least complicated official stories all across the country, not just in Utah or among the Mormons.[35] But within Utah, dredging up from trunks and closets new records documenting very different and sometimes conflicting experiences challenged the inspirational Pioneer myth of Latter-day Saint culture's master narrative.[36] By the end of the Second World War, the combination of historicism and the documentary approach proved powerful enough to begin reshaping American national memory and itself merit a reaction. Within Mormon culture, the large-scale collision between these conflicting perspectives did not occur until the mid-1940s, but the trajectories pointing both sides toward that collision were drawn by the frontline WPA projects of the 1930s, and by then Dale L. Morgan was well-known among its chief proponents.

CHAPTER 5

"One of Those Minds Which Dwell in a Typewriter"[1]

The Historical Records Survey, Ogden, Utah, 1938–1940

Just to give you an idea, all at the same time now I am winding up the Tooele history, directing the research on Washington County (which will be next), directing special research by workers in every county on towns and settlements, digesting of county court minutes, and preparing of special abstracts on the United Order, Polygamy, Political Parties, Irrigation, Education, and a flock of other things, on which I will one day write some essays for special publication by the Survey; I have just finished writing a 2,500 word introduction to the Ordinances of the State of Deseret . . . and I have indexed every paper in every folder in the whole historical files, the preliminary indexing now being complete so that, when I get the time, I can draw up the final indexes with hundreds of entries for all the existing and extinct counties; and I am doing the publicity for the Survey, not to mention a thousand odd jobs and assisting [Leonard] Hart in the bibliographical research program. I think quite seriously that I ought to be quintuplets.[2]

—Dale Morgan

ON MAY 23, 1934, with nearly a fifth of Utah's adult citizens unemployed, state officials eagerly filed a Federal Emergency Relief Act (FERA) application for a state public records survey. Its local sponsor was the one state agency that dealt with records (sort of), the Utah State Historical Society. The Society was more impressive in name than in fact. It occupied one small room in the state capitol building, with a Board of Control appointed by the governor, a few hundred dollars in an annual appropriation, a thousand books or so, and a part-time secretary-treasurer-librarian who doubled as a volunteer editor keeping the *Utah Historical Quarterly* afloat by sheer force of will. Despite that tenuous support, or maybe because of it, the antiquarian publication of "old diaries, journals, letters and other writings of the pioneers" had lapsed the previous year.[3] Noting that state, county, and municipal records had not been maintained appropriately, the proposal pledged "a state-wide [*sic*] survey of the whereabouts and condition of public documents in state, county, city, and town depositories." The application read: "The importance of collecting and assembling this historical data in public places cannot be too strongly emphasized . . . Utah is willing to be judged by its records. Therefore, the records must not be allowed to perish."[4] Two days after filing the request, the National Archive Survey Commission appointed a six-member Utah Archive Committee, but that was about the only progress made. Nothing else was done, and Utah's state record project was folded into the Historical Records Survey (HRS) when the national project was established the next year.

Five projects made up the cultural arm of the federal Works Progress Administration (WPA) program, each in a field identified as arts or humanities: Writers, Theatre, and Art projects, the American Imprints Inventory, and the Historical Records Survey. To WPA administrator Harry Hopkins, HRS represented an historic opportunity to throw a net of modern attention and documentation over the nation's public records for the first time in history, an attempt to replicate at the local level the success of the newly established National Archives.[5]

As the state cultural projects were being set up, in Washington DC, Federal Writers' Project director Henry Alsberg asked Civil Works Administration official and Ogden native Dean R. Brimhall if he could name anyone in Utah capable of directing the Writers' Project and its documentary branch, the HRS. Brimhall immediately recommended Maurice L. Howe, a well-traveled history buff and staff writer with the *Ogden Standard-Examiner*. Howe had compiled a popular series of interviews with surviving local pioneers and had cowritten *Salt Desert Trails* with Salt Lake City printer and fellow buff Charles Kelly, a book describing the 1846 Donner party's crossing the Salt Desert, and documenting the remains of their stranded wagons. Howe got the job.[6]

While Dale Morgan was slowly picking his way through the University of Utah, cribbing lecture notes from seat-mates and "talking" back and forth with professors in longhand, Howe began hiring staff and establishing an office in half of one floor in the Village Building on 24th Street and Lincoln Avenue in Ogden, at the eastern end of the viaduct over the Denver & Rio Grande Western Railroad yard, and with a branch office in the Chamber of Commerce building in Salt Lake City. Three years after its founding, in July 1938, the Historical Records Survey (HRS) divided from the Federal Writers' Project and was created as an independent project under the direction of Dr. Luther Evans. At the division, Howe, Utah's founding project director, was summoned eastward and reassigned to an administrative post within the federal offices in Washington, DC, but retained responsibility for supervising both state projects from afar.[7] Another *Standard-Examiner* writer, Hugh F. O'Neil, took over the HRS, and Charles K. Madsen headed the Utah Writers' Project (UWP). To produce meaningful writing on a suitable scale using unemployed (and, detractors argued, unemployable) white-collar workers required a managerial and editorial staff capable of ensuring a measure of stylistic consistency and content quality. Dale Morgan's hire as a part-time professional editor, three years after the Survey office was established in Utah, was a step toward that larger goal.

* * * * *

Dale moved from his childhood house in Salt Lake City to the Thurstons' home in Ogden. There he waited through the first week of August 1938, probably a bit anxiously, for his hire to be finalized. Office bureaucracy delayed the appointment, but it did finally come. On August 13, 1938, Dale Morgan climbed the stairs at the Village Building, perhaps straightened his tie at the door, and began employment with the Utah Historical Records Survey. Utah's HRS office employed about thirty people around the state when Dale Morgan arrived and was assigned a desk. About a third held part-time, non-relief professional appointments like Morgan.

The Historical Records Survey (HRS) and Writers' Project (WP) produced useful public-interest writing in the way the Civilian Conservation Corps built public infrastructure. With the WPA projects, the federal government crafted an employment-based alternative to a straightforward public-relief dole. Despite critics' loud denunciations, WPA work was not meaningless. Hallie Flanagan, director of the Federal Theatre Project, noted that "for the first time in the relief experiments of this country the preservation of the skill of the worker, and hence the preservation of his self-respect, became important."[8] Sociologist Robert Leighninger later observed, "work relief was preferred [by the unemployed] over public assistance (the dole) because it maintained self-respect, reinforced the work ethic, and kept [marketable] skills sharp."[9]

The Historical Records Survey wasted no time putting its new editor to work. Employment energized Morgan with purpose. "My work is somewhat diverse in character," Dale reported to Jerry, "but I will handle all the publicity for the Survey in Utah, do general rewriting and editing work on the inventories . . . and in general make myself useful."[10] There was plenty to do, and a friend later described Dale Morgan's integration to history and office work to be "one of the shortest success stories I know."[11] The Survey's pattern for writing followed the "corporate journalism" model of contributive authorship and editing pioneered by the enormously popular *Life* and *Time* magazines. There were no bylines. While individual state offices generated research files and drafted the written work, the regional and then national offices reviewed, revised, and occasionally approved material for publication and distribution. In July 1938, the federal office directed that the standard two- to three-page historical sketches prefacing county records inventories should be expanded into pieces of greater detail and historical value. Morgan's boss, Hugh F. O'Neil, explained to him that improving the content of the historical sketches had definite priority over HRS publicity.[12]

Despite her son's newfound security, Emily Morgan missed having her eldest at home. Her letters to him encouraged him to eat well and to avoid too many complicating activities. His to her assured that he was eating well and often provided menus as evidence. After a couple of weeks of gainful employment, on the second of September, Dale sat down and wrote Emily a long, self-revelatory letter explaining how much a job meant to him and his sense of self-worth. Reading it now, one gets the sense that this letter was, perhaps, the first time he had attempted to explain to his mother the fearful weight he felt becoming deaf in a hearing world, and how her motherly attempts at support unintentionally reinforced his fears of being unfit for it—particularly in the depths of the Depression. "I wondered if you sometimes conceived of me as being particularly helpless in some ways," he wondered. "From the time I lost my hearing I had something of a sense of being socially maimed—that is, cut off from many opportunities readily available to the average person."

He continued: "my sense of being crippled in a way in a world where even men with all their physical capacities unmarred could hardly get along was very difficult for me. I felt completely cut adrift from life, outside it almost[.]" The independence he found in college ironically did not help him learn, he said, it only postponed an inevitable confrontation with the world at large. Only after beginning to write fiction seriously, did he begin feeling a sense of capability and value. More than anything, being employed crystalized in Morgan a change in his social outlook and self-awareness that had begun only shortly before, instilling in its catharsis a real vitality. Lack of employment over the prior year had depressed him; life at home confined him (for instance, he was concerned that writing late into the night would disturb the family with his typewriter clacking, and as a result felt literarily hampered):

> I wanted the sense of paying for my own way in life, of living on my own terms, being my own master, responsible to myself, under-standing just how and in what ways taking care of myself consists in.... Do you understand me a little better now, mother, I don't want you to feel hurt by what I say, or to feel that I am ungrateful and unmindful of all that you and the family have done for me, but I have achieved something in my life which means very much to me, much more than it could mean to a person outside the peculiar facts of my own life, and this feeling of achievement has come at the very time when it could mean most to me.[13]

Emily, a concerned and protective mother, was watching her beloved, disabled eldest son strike out on his own. Dale, eager but genuinely solic-itous of his mother's feelings, was trying to do so gently.

With physical and psychological needs stabilized by employment, Dale Morgan was in a stronger emotional position to turn outward the results of his self-examination of the previous two years, essentially to evangelize his friends into his brand of naturalism. Even before leaving Utah for the East four years later, the remaining strands connecting the deaf young man with Latter-day Saint culture quietly dissolved. After high school those outside the family perceived that he did not consider himself a believer in the LDS church but also not out of it.[14] Grounded by his self-proclaimed ability—or at least a stated desire—to "think as freely and objectively as any subject might require, free of the local taboos," in a long letter to former chess partner Rich Durham, who was proselyting as an LDS missionary in South Carolina, Dale issued a challenge to step outside the bounds of Mormonism to discuss "things" openly, without prejudice.

The letter to Durham states the crux of Morgan's twofold argument with Utah's Latter-day Saint culture and with religion in general: inconsis-tencies between the professed belief and actions of adherents, and "the com-placence, the self-righteousness, and the 'holiness' with which [religion] surrounds itself." He disliked and disapproved of the pressure that tradition and assumption enforced upon adherents, crowding their inquiry with pre-determined expectations. "This is, in fact, my verdict on all religions, and does not apply exclusively to Mormonism," he asserted."[15] Personal read-ings in psychoanalysis reduced Latter-day Saint faith structures to simple psychological dependence and group sociology, Dale concluded. Primarily, however, Morgan was critical of the casual hypocrisy that he felt character-ized the lives of many Latter-day Saints and Utahns generally. Shaped by these earlier readings, Dale Morgan continued turning a critical eye on the church and religion generally, complaining that "Mormonism is for many here simply a kind of social habit, not a vital ethic in their living." He had settled on a perspective: "Maybe I'd better just tell you that I see Mormon-ism in terms of its social history, and I see its social history in terms of its context in human behavior and social forces of its period."[16]

To Juanita Brooks later, Dale Morgan reflected that "if I have a reli-gion, it is a belief in what I call 'the decency of human relationships.' I live life as I see it from day to day." Dale's respect for a religious believer seemed to be based on an appreciation of critical, thoughtful belief. Morgan did not care for doctrine and pointedly did not reject Mormon beliefs, but rather he was critical of the thoughtless disregard that individuals paid to their own religious participation and the casualness with which Latter-day Saint ethical strictures were held in its social culture. Though, as an unbeliever, he dismissed the doctrines of his family's faith, he did not reject them as an apostate.

Instead he seemed to place himself within the larger context of Mor-monism that encompassed all groups claiming a heritage from the follow-ing of Joseph Smith. Responding pointedly to a later criticism from RLDS librarian Samuel A. Burgess, Morgan wrote that he "[did] not subscribe to the doctrinal contentions of any of the several Mormon churches," yet he continued to be intrigued by the Latter-day Saints and Latter Day Saints. For Dale Morgan, Mormonism remained alive and vital, but only as a cultural vitality, not as a faith.[17] Having broken his dependence upon home, he was now breaking formally with its culture.

* * * * *

The Historical Records Survey introduced twenty-three-year-old Dale Morgan to a broad and compelling new field of writing. Morgan's ado-lescent and collegiate sense of language had been cultivated across the colorful breadth of fiction and literature and in the focused precision of advertisement writing; he was now tossed into nonfiction and regional history. Though historical writing was something new, it was rich with detail, captivating inference, and had tantalizing gaps. The stuff of history existed in different forms, as well: primary sources like letters, diary transcripts, and reminiscence; and in secondary sources such as biographies, county histories, and books of all sorts. Morgan immediately began to see that the two did not always agree. Secondary sources made errors in chronology, sequence, and location. Both types of writing were also shaped by perception and the bugaboos Morgan always suspected—bias and assumption. The historical sketches destined to preface county records inventories focused heavily on the sort of precise chronology and geography that appealed to his regional identity as a Utahn, cultural Mormon, and his innate sense of precision. Within a short time, he found it profitable in his position as editor to check notes himself, not merely confirming facts but challenging inferences and documenting actual errors. He also quickly learned to confirm facts by checking the earliest contemporary form of a document available. One could track specific details and challenge memory or interpretation in one source by referring to another.

Dale's deafness-imposed ability to concentrate in a busy office and his personal attention to detail quickly distinguished him among the project staff. Morgan's penchant for good writing and memory for detail prompted him to suggest heavy revision to draft after draft of county historical sketches, newspaper releases, and eventually radio scripts. However, like any office, there was politics. In Morgan's case, the politics came in the person of E. Geoffrey Circuit, a fellow University of Utah alumnus with whom Morgan had worked on the *Utah Chronicle* and as officers in the University of Utah's writing club, the Scribblers. Circuit headed the HRS final drafts division, the entity charged with producing the publishable versions of the materials issued from the Survey.[18] Since the writing staff had been recently expanded, Circuit seems to have held staff seniority but, in Morgan's opinion, was an inadequate writer with a tendency to revise good writing into bad. As editor for the Survey's public interest writing, his position made Morgan a middle man in the process, not the final authority. Morgan's desk edited initial drafts of material before forwarding revisions for rewriting by Circuit's division. In October 1938, Circuit made a move to draw Morgan under his direction.

Attempting to push back against the obligation to submit carefully researched and edited work for rehashing through Jeff Circuit, Morgan and bibliographer Leonard Hart submitted a joint proposal to establish an independent "historical department" within the Survey, answering directly to O'Neil as the state HRS supervisor. This move would separate straightforward historical writing from other writing produced by the Survey. O'Neil agreed on the first of November. Morgan's new duties involved a pay raise to $77 per month, a new job title as "Historian," and being sent back to work. Two and a half months after being hired, the change left Morgan in charge of virtually the entire HRS research, transcription, and files program, as well as the research correspondence with counties and research workers, including directing research in published secondary sources conducted in libraries, all this in addition to continuing to write HRS publicity for newspapers and magazines which emanated from the office. "I was practically a babe in arms when I started," he wrote Maurice Howe, "and while I do not yet claim to be an authority, I have learned a great deal and talk intelligently on the subject of Utah history."[19]

Hart and Morgan's suggestion for an independent History division turned out to be Opportunity, knocking. Research for Historical Records Survey productions threw Morgan into contact with all the primary and secondary history of the state and the Mormons that had been written to date, and with the state's nineteenth-century diaries and autobiographies, both those already published and others transcribed as file material by the HRS and its predecessor.[20] With the former, he was not impressed. His foray into the histories and documents of Utah's past was disconcerting. To his mind, they did not match—the history books did not report precisely what the documents documented. In a pique, Dale wrote Jerry Bleak a week after his promotion to Historian that "practically nothing really worthwhile touching upon Utah and Mormonism, what they have been, and what they have become, is worth one single damn, and that goes not only for non-Mormon writing but for Mormon writing. There is a golden opportunity for some gifted writer," Dale argued to his cousin, "to produce the first extensive, penetrating work on the whole amazing phenomena of Utah, the West, and the Mormon relation to itself and both."[21] This statement was bold and somewhat reckless for someone with merely three months of informal personal study in a field.

To be fair, even as a still-callow youth, Morgan would not likely have been arrogant enough to make such an unqualified statement on his own authority. As widely read as the college graduate was, Morgan's remarkable assertion likely rested on a firmer foundation. Eight years earlier, Bernard DeVoto, an Ogden expatriate teaching at Harvard University and a significant American literary light on the East Coast, said essentially the same thing. "There is no really adequate study of Mormonism," DeVoto pronounced from Cambridge. "No Mormon has ever written an accurate account of his church, and all but one of those written by apostates are untrustworthy."

After naming William Alexander Linn's *The Story of the Mormons* from 1902 as the sole reasonably credible work available to date, DeVoto's observation continued: Linn's book still "studies Mormonism in a vacuum, quite without relation to American life and thought. No professional historian, theologian, economist, or sociologist has ever treated the Saints at any length; in particular, the historians have neglected the job."[22] Morgan's brash comment to Jerry Bleak makes much more sense if seen as a restatement of a more informed view. DeVoto's sentiment may have alerted Dale Morgan to challenges of the field, which were then confirmed by his early reading in the HRS. That assessment identified a hole, a vacancy, a void to be eventually filled. Morgan did not comprehend at the time he wrote Jerry Bleak just how prophetic his own words were, nor the wrenching effect they would have on his life in little more than a decade. He also did not yet comprehend that he was standing at the cusp of a revision to Mormon culture, literature, and history, nor that he himself would be one of several personalities driving that revision.

The Historical Records Survey itself was merely the most recent, organized foray in a much broader drive to collect historical documentation that had begun stirring nationally during the 1870s. In Utah, HRS efforts at cataloging public records was supplemented by locating, collecting, and transcribing nineteenth century diaries and autobiographies, and conducting oral histories with Utah's oldest surviving emigrants. Dale Morgan landed in a support position as new troves of material pulled from trunks, drawers, and attics were being seen for the first time and as the broad discipline of history itself was in flux.[23]

* * * * *

Before the end of 1938 and six months into his introduction to history and historical method, Dale set aside chess for several months as he began work for the HRS. In mid-October he returned to local chess competition, showing off a bit by playing three members of the Ogden Chess Club simultaneously, winning five games from the three players, without losing any. The following December came a twenty-board match.[24]

By policy, the HRS output was reviewed by knowledgeable local people, a natural extension of corporate journalism and a critical review intended to minimize the prospective backlash for "objective" misstatements made by mere outsiders. Besides Maurice Howe, during his first year at the HRS Morgan made the written and personal acquaintance of people across the state, including three who would figure large in his later career: St. George housewife and educator Juanita Brooks, Salt Lake City printer and historical writer Charles Kelly, and warehouse owner/operator J. Roderic Korns. Neither of the men were Latter-day Saints. Kelly owned and operated the Western Printing Company on Pierpont Avenue. He published *Salt Desert Trails* jointly with Maurice Howe in 1930 and a biography of fur trapper and overland guide Caleb Greenwood the next year on his own, and he had just produced an edited version of John D. Lee's available diaries.[25] Letters exchanged between the two led Morgan to J. Roderic Korns, who owned and operated a family warehouse business on 400 South, what was then the edge of downtown Salt Lake City. Both Kelly and Korns were passionately committed to Utah's pre-Mormon history and captivated by the trails and people which had crossed Utah, most before Mormon settlement. Korns and his pursuit of trail-related material was well known in the Church Historian's Office; no matter what sources were available at the CHO, the antagonistically irreligious Kelly patently refused even to darken its door.

Juanita Brooks, whom Morgan wrote in relation to a Washington County history, needs little introduction, but in 1938 her notable career had not yet launched. She was a busy housewife and junior college instructor in an isolated, red-rock desert town in the extreme southwestern corner of the state. A year earlier rediscovery of two firsthand accounts pulled her attention toward the infamous Mountain Meadows Massacre. Polite official correspondence between Morgan and Brooks about FERA-project typescripts sometime in 1939 began a close personal affinity and three-decade literary friendship. Within a few months, they dropped formalities and operated forever after on a first-name basis. For more than a decade they wrote each other frequently as confidantes and as a private mutual-support group.[26] Juanita's youngest daughter, Willa Dean, recalled years later that a letter from Dale provided the family a bit of an occasion as her mother read his letters aloud to the family at the dinner table.[27]

Morgan contributed greatly to Brooks' development as a writer. "Juanita", wrote her biographer Levi S. Peterson, "accepted Morgan as her mentor in scholarly and literary matters.... his editorial and technical advice profoundly influenced the form and content of her major writings."[28] Brooks herself admitted frankly that Morgan "more than any other person influenced my work and my thinking."[29] From her, Morgan gained not only a disciple but also a personal connection to what he felt was the last living pioneer blood. Their common ground was less Utah than it was Mormonism, though the pair found themselves on opposing sides when it came to spiritual belief. Brooks and Morgan grew to trust each other implicitly.

Morgan brought to his new correspondents a zeal and an emerging awareness. The varied demands of his job as an editor and eventually a writer in the HRS tossed Morgan bodily into a new corpus of writing as well. Collating histories of Utah's counties required at least passing familiarity with Euro-American discovery of the region in the years preceding settlement. Morgan's writing assignments coincided with a geographic region also of interest to the "mountain men" fur trappers of the 1820s and 1830s, and to emigrant trails across the state in the 1840s and later explorers. Before he was a year on the job, Morgan had consumed the basic works on exploration and the fur trade, as well as what Maurice Howe could recommend. They were a revelation. Here he found a source-based challenge to the state's cultural hegemony. In writing the short historical essays, Morgan's attention was seized by the exhilarating challenge of discovering, collating, and confirming detail in ways that *belle lettres* and popular fiction never affected in him. Morgan's rapid, expansive learning curve can be traced across the drafts for county histories in his papers.[30] For Morgan's part, work in the Historical Records Survey, despite its imposed limit of ninety hours of paying work monthly, and perhaps because of it, became a training regimen for intense research, requiring unanswered questions to be identified and responses integrated in the process of composition or revision, and writing efficiency.

By the turn of 1939, Maurice Howe was confident that in Morgan he had found an exceptional asset. Project administrators reviewed and approved each piece of writing prior to its publication, and both Howe and O'Neil corresponded regularly with Morgan by interoffice memorandum, partly a convenience because of his deafness, partly because Howe was in Washington, DC. Howe quickly developed confidence in Morgan's skills, and in January 1939, he asked his HRS historian confidentially for help with the main task of the Writers' Project. Like every state project across the country, the UWP was charged specifically with producing a state guidebook, a description of the state combining topical essays with tourist information, photographs, and maps. The first guide had been issued by Idaho in 1937; in 1939, many of the projects completed and released their guide publications. Utah would not. The drafts produced so far, particularly the centerpiece state history essay, were tangled in the politics of language and of the state's cultural memory, leaving the guidebook's publication stalled because of it.

* * * * *

For his part, by early experience in the public history of the HRS, Morgan formed and settled into a set of research and writing habits that he relied on through the rest of his career. The HRS expectations and procedures presented Dale Morgan with the first codified statement of appropriate perspective for a historian. An unknown writer (probably Circuit) noted that "our enterprise being a cooperative one should show evidence of thorough research on all debatable points of history and should discuss all sides of such questions to avoid showing partiality."[31] Building on this perspective, Morgan never believed in or asserted an abstract, absolute objectivity as a researcher or writer, but he became supremely confident that balancing the tensions involved in writing history in Utah was excellent training in grounding historical narrative and conclusions on documents—in other words, to hunt down and stand firmly on evidence. Morgan also developed elements of his research and writing style during his HRS service. He was forever systematically culling large sources: runs of newspapers, specific record series, scores of published primary sources, and an endless succession of books. Second, since his work was done at a time when reproduction was difficult, he relied heavily on making and collecting transcriptions. He began to realize his work in the county histories was good largely because he did not accept formal histories uncritically, and because of the effort he personally expended on confirming details in independent research.[32] His personal source files eventually bulged with reams of typed abstracts, extracts, and transcripts of books, letters, documents, and articles.

Third, unlike writers who produced then revised a draft *after* concluding their research, the need to write quickly from what sources were at hand also imposed far-reaching consequences. During his introduction to historical enterprise in the HRS, Morgan developed a lifelong habit of sending out scores of queries, chasing specific details and new sources even as he drafted and revised his conclusions from what resource material he had on hand. His writing process integrated a form of cyclical query resolution. Since Morgan worked at a time before text could be stored and revised endlessly in a single digital file, he drafted at the typewriter and edited manually with a pencil before retyping.

Morgan's research habits were time- and labor-intensive and led to a fourth practice that governed his actual writing practices, a practice that proved problematic; in fact, though he was remarkably productive, his writing process also tended to plague him throughout his career: Morgan became accustomed to writing under pressure, close to a deadline, to leave as much time for broad research and exploration as possible. "Except for the nervous tension involved," he wrote Fawn Brodie, while hammering away on *The Great Salt Lake* a few years later, "there is a novelty and interest to working under pressure and finding out things under pressure." The challenge growing out of the writing process he preferred was that it left him chronically behind and never able to give up a project until no more avenues were left to be explored or until an editor unequivocally demanded the manuscript. By the time he was composing *The Great Salt Lake*, Morgan was convinced that pressure made him a better writer and asserted naively that if he lived through the immediate obligation to the lake book, "I should be equal to any other strain on my mind during the rest of my life."[33]

* * * * *

Despite the heady, energizing interest in the past, not all in Morgan's life was going so evenly. Dale related to his mother a confrontation with a local gossip over rumors the woman had been spreading about his relationship with the Thurstons. In truth, Dale, Jarvis, and Madeline spent a good deal of time together on a level of intimacy that, viewed from the outside, might raise eyebrows. Most of their time together was constructive. Besides the days that Dale spent working over Madeline's novel and story manuscripts, Dale would sometimes play chess with Jarvis while "discussing" literature with Madeline. Quickly glancing over the board and moving a chess piece, Morgan would turn to Madeline and pose a literary question of some sort. "Then you would have to reply by writing it all down," Jarvis Thurston remembered years later, speaking of these multifaceted sessions, "and these questions were [questions] like: 'what do you think of Flaubert's *Madame Bovary*' or something; then you'd have to write four pages in order to explain about it." With the two simultaneously busy at their respective tasks, Morgan would read a book.[34]

Part of the gossip was grounded in an emerging renegotiation of reality. By spring 1939 Jarvis and Madeline Thurston's three-year marriage seemed to be deteriorating subtly, and then not so subtly. She began shifting her attention elsewhere. Madeline captivated and energized Dale, and as he watched the couple's relationship raveling, he seemed quietly eager to pick up for her what pieces there may have been. Emily Morgan, Dale's mother, looked past her son's intellectual stimulations and disliked Madeline intensely as a crass opportunist, but Dale's equally intense loyalty to his friends defended the older woman from any ridicule from whatever source, even if from his revered mother.[35]

Despite their deepening friendship, Dale was acutely aware that Madeline did not accord him the same emotion that he held for her. At this time Dale briefly kept a diary, recording in it his frustrated longings. "Came home to find a letter from Madeline," he wrote in an undated diary entry from the period. "I was greatly disappointed; it was so chill and remote for all the surface warmth. Again I had the wretched feeling of being only of intellectual interest." Events later suggested that there was much truth to his despondent guess. In fact, Madeline told him plainly of her feelings a few weeks later. "Would you be happier if I said I loved you when you know I don't?" she asked pointedly, adding later in the letter: "I want to be [a] friend unto you—I admire and like you and understand you and like you, but I cannot live with you."[36] Ever the optimist, Dale seemed confident a tiny spark existed between them that could be fanned to flame in the tinder of truthfulness, confidence, and emotional intimacy. Morgan confided to himself his determination to "enter her life energetically for her benefit . . . [I]f I possibly can, I'm going to make her life what she wants it, and if then everything goes to pieces as I somehow feel it will, at least some finality will have been achieved, in her life and mind. I wonder how the hell all this will work out, finally." Their relationship did eventually work itself out, but not as he expected, and only twenty years later.[37]

Despite the complication that the Thurstons represented, Morgan liked them both and enjoyed his work for the HRS. All of his letters to friends and family breathe energy and recount the incredible scope of his activity. Dale could not help but remember that his promotion to Historian was at best an indeterminate job, sure to end no later than with the project's conclusion. In late March, he visited HRS administrator Dee Bramwell's office. Dale had already prepared a letter laying out his willingness to remain with the HRS for at least another year "if it could be made worth my while." Between interruptions, Morgan explained himself. Bramwell asked immediately what salary he considered worth-while. Morgan may have been surprised to learn that Bramwell's subordinate, Ruby Garrett, was already working on a substantial pay raise for him, and that Bramwell planned to bring up retaining Morgan when he visited the regional WPA administrator in Denver. He promised an answer in April.[38]

Within a few months of being introduced to historical writing, Dale Morgan's attention was captured. He gave himself to research and writing with the same zeal and energy he had given to learning chess strategy. In the second week of May 1939, Morgan felt confident enough with what he had learned that he opened up to HRS director Maurice Howe in a private letter, sending Howe transcripts of sources that could be used to update his 1925 book *Miles Goodyear*. Other HRS staff were pursuing history as a mere job; Howe, Morgan felt, was the only person he had thus far encountered who shared his growing sense of "historical enthusiasm."

Dale still thought of advertising as his career path, though, given his awakening to history, he first planned to write a novel about the current generations of Utahns, those living at a time when "the old beliefs and values which sustained previous generations here (in the infallibility of the land, the church, and the state) have broken down, and from turning to group values the present generation is turning to individual values."[39] Explaining his Latter-day Saint background and personal skepticism, Morgan confided an awakened interest in also writing a social history of Utah, and how his work at HRS was changing his outlook. "I think if any really authoritative history of Utah and the Mormons is ever written, it will have to be from a viewpoint somewhat approximating mine," he asserted of his newfound but unnamed faith of historicism. "The entirely orthodox Mormon is quite incapable of bringing to his study the necessary detachment."

Howe responded with encouragement. HRS certainly profited from Morgan's involvement, and Howe agreed that the alternative form of historical inquiry, academic history, was not worth pursuing. "Your worth will be tried out more in the crucibles of life than in the classroom," he wrote back to Morgan. "Keep plugging along. I think you have a real aptitude for research."[40] Morgan responded a week later, confirming that he liked nothing better than the thought "to be able to give myself to history," but that the realities of earning a living could not be ignored entirely. With a trace of humor Dale observed that he was working full-time at a half-time rate because of his passion for the newly discovered subject, but he wanted to draw an income sufficient to begin paying back his mother for the sacrifices she had personally made for her family. "So if an opportunity [came up] for me to leave the state for an excellent job," he admitted, "I think I would accept it, particularly since I would like to get out of state for awhile, to view it and its people and its culture with the perspective of distance."[41] The exchange drew the two men from professional acquaintance into a close personal friendship.[42]

Howe's perspective on graduate training reinforced counsel Dale received from New York advertising executive George Burton Hotchkiss, who worked with his own profound hearing loss. Morgan had written Hotchkiss asking for career advice. The executive brushed graduate training aside, at least in advertising, suggesting instead that Morgan get something into publication, not only to demonstrate an ability to write but also to "prove your ability to please editors and the public."[43] Whether in advertising or in history, an advanced degree seemed to offer nothing constructive besides a credential, Morgan eventually told Howe, and he did not need that to further either his interest or proficiency to write history. "I can do the same work without any specific correlation to a degree; the work itself seems sufficient as an end."[44] Such an assertion this early in his career invites a biographer's analytical digression.

Morgan's emerging approach is much closer to the academic historicism or ".objectivity" that was something of a mantra to some branches of American scholarship.[45] Two decades later and after he was a well-known name in his field, Dale expressed surprise over Bernard DeVoto's challenge to history:

> I guess when you come right down to it, the term "history" had better be redefined to mean, "a species of writing produced by or enroute to a PhD." I have had enough troubles trying to break a path alongside this main-traveled road to know something of the snobberies at work here, and the ways in which the academic world and even the world of learning are geared to these attitudes. Yet I think it would be instructive to make a survey of every field of American history and note how many of the major works in those fields have been produced by mavericks, or someone working outside his formal specialization.

"One might as well face the fact," he wrote DeVoto, "if he is going to be a maverick and write history outside the well-beaten roads under academic control, he will have to do it the hard way." In 1939, Morgan was becoming confident that he had the mental equipment to do history "the hard way" from outside academia, yet Morgan's career eventually fulfilled the older man's hard-nosed secular prophecy. Partly because he lacked academic credentials Dale also resigned himself that he would, however, "have to get where I am going by dint of much scraping and scratching, and more slowly than might otherwise have been the case, but I'll get there in the end."[46]

As his interests turned slowly from advertising toward history, if he knew writing independently and without a credential would be difficult, why didn't Morgan pursue a graduate degree? The answer is one of those simple choices around which human existence turns: he was convinced he didn't need it. Morgan's native competence and disdain for the few academics whose work he knew in Utah during the 1940s—coupled to the still reasonably informal nature of history writing nationally, and counsel from two men he respected—fed his sense that academia was both too narrow and insular. Related to his reticence is the fact that admission to the upper reaches of academia has never been purely a meritocracy. In the 1940s, it was less so, arguably second only to politics as the oldest of the old-boy networks of relationships and interactions. Since undergraduate work in art pushed him in an entirely different direction from history, Dale Morgan lacked an academic mentor or any other academic connections to make his introduction and smooth his admission to a graduate program.

Another major factor in his choice was certainly his deafness. Dale scraped through college but may have feared the collegial challenges that a graduate program would require. Graduate education was built around not only research but grounded in the collegial experience of the seminar—a roundtable discussion rather than a lecture, led but (ideally) not dominated by the faculty member. Certainly pursuing an advanced degree in the 1940s without being able to hear would be extremely difficult. Even in beginning his professional life, Dale Morgan still avoided most conversation with all but the closest friends. Morgan was intensely frustrated by the imprecision of spoken communication. Perhaps in his deep fear of deafness-imposed dependence, he saw imprecise speech as a personal vulnerability. Madeline Thurston incisively described his speech-related habits directly to Morgan thus: "you have been content in your isolated world with the most limited contacts, usually satisfying yourself with the physical presence of people, afraid of attacking your fundamental problems, waiting for someone else to do it for you."[47]

Finally, there was the issue of jobs. In the early 1940s the only purpose to graduate study was to secure a teaching position in another academic program. Sensitive about his vocal decline, Morgan could not have been comfortable teaching academically. Years later, Doyce Nunis, a long-time professor at the University of Southern California, confirmed Dale's bias: "The academic world is far from an ivory tower," he wrote Morgan, "Teachers are paid to do all things except have the time, energy, and money to research quietly, uninterruptedly, and consistently"—precisely the tasks Morgan valued most highly.[48] Being uncomfortable with the prospects of educational administrivia would have only added weight to his dismissal of written work by academic writers he knew. Confident that he could get by well enough as a historian without academic credentials, Morgan felt he could do so by mastering written sources. These possessed their own shortcomings but at least did not change in the moment.[49]

At the time, the work of most historians was written for nonacademic readers anyway, published and disseminated by the country's commercial-trade book houses. Morgan was interested in writing history, not studying history, and certainly not pursuing it as an academic hothouse plant. Morgan saw academic training as little more than reinforcing the principles of evidence and argument he had already learned on his own. By regarding graduate school as a series of hoops to a mere credential, however, Morgan missed a third element to academic training: developing a reflective etiology—exploring the philosophical limits of evidence and how a historian *knows* about what they write, and how they identify and compensate for a point of view. Morgan believed his reliance on documentary sources compensated fully for any bias he brought to the study (factors which he essentially denied, anyway). Dale Morgan's later comment about disinterest in graduate education echoed Walter Prescott Webb's not quite tongue-in-cheek observation about writing on the American West that "I was excellently prepared because I had never had a course in that field, and therefore could view it without preconceived notions or borrowed points of view."[50] In the end, both men crafted defining contributions within their regional specializations.

To the end of his life, Dale Morgan was content to let his published work stand as his credentials and remain Dale L. Morgan, BA. Like many of the self-taught, self-assured in the "objective" world they have comfortably created, Morgan missed perceiving many of his own limitations. He remained exceptionally well-read, but once his perspective on history had been set, he remained confident and uncritical of his own interpretive biases or methods of interpretation. The expedient decision not to chase a PhD credential would later prove an unfortunate limit on professional opportunities, but obviously not one he could foresee.

Anyway, such a step was unnecessary in 1939; Dale still focused on a professional career in advertising, not history. The Ogden HRS research office closed in the fall of 1939; its staff and files were consolidated with the Salt Lake City office. Hugh O'Neil returned to private employment with a railroad when the Ogden HRS office closed, and he was replaced by Dee Bramwell. For the moment Bramwell insisted on retaining Morgan on the HRS staff.[51] In the midst of the office move, Morgan began establishing contacts with ad agencies in San Francisco.[52]

* * * * *

Perhaps motivated by Bramwell's uncertainty about his position and certainly by Madeline's "chill," Dale decided to make another attempt at pursuing a career in advertising. He immediately wrote his namesake uncle, Alan Dale Morgan in Denver, who in turn confidentially contacted a friend of his at the Gillham Advertising Agency in Salt Lake City. Word came back that timing was good, but that Dale should take the opportunity to demonstrate his advertising skills by selling the firm on himself and his skills. Alan warned his nephew that Gillham's president, Marion C. Nelson, was sharp, but that the hiring decision would ultimately be made by vice president J. Y. Tipton.[53]

Dale devoted time to outlining ad presentations for various prospective employers and drafted an ad campaign for Vico Motor Oil from the Utah Oil Company, one of Gillham's major accounts. Writing to Nelson again and reminding him of the firm's prior interest, Dale pointed to his current office experience. Along went his ad roughs as proof of his skills and ideas, and Dale was again invited for an interview. When he arrived at the Gillham office in the Continental Bank Building on a warm mid-May afternoon, there is a good chance that he was guided though the office by Marion Nelson's teenaged son, Russell M. Nelson, who worked there as general office and errand help. Gillham was interested, but again the interest cooled quickly. Later he learned from the inside source that once again Tipton nixed hiring Morgan, this time on the premise of the growing place of radio advertising in the firm's business.

So Dale turned his attention outside Utah. By the end of May 1939, he was making plans for a job search on the West Coast, but it required some advance work. He wrote up a list of possible openings in Salt Lake City and San Francisco. He typed out "things to know" about advertising for various industries and business and dived into *How to Write Advertisements* and *Layout Techniques in Advertising.* Dale approached four different businesses in Salt Lake City and Ogden, offering a trade: Morgan would produce ad campaigns for Anderson Jewelry, Boyle Furniture Company, the Hotel Ben Lomond, and Minnoch Glass & Paint Company, if they would provide him solid answers to his questions and allow him to use the ad work in his portfolio. After brushing up with several weeks of careful reading and by working at night, Dale drafted the sample campaigns to introduce himself and his skills by mail to prospective employers.[54] The timing was good, since political pressure from Republicans against the Democratic social programs was building at the national level, and it looked as if the entire HRS risked being defunded.[55] Morgan's plan to look for work beyond the HRS solidified in early June when word was received that the HRS staff in Utah would be cut from eighty to thirty-two—the level at which it stood when he had been hired.[56] Howe recommended Morgan apply to the UWP, which had slightly better political support, and pledged to support Morgan to its director, Charles Madsen.[57]

Into the summer of 1939, Dale continued hammering out revisions to the Ogden city history and forwarding query after query to local sources about county histories, even as he worked on ad ideas and sketches for his portfolio. Occasionally Dale kept his artistic skills fresh by sketching figures when he had the opportunity—always women. He might employ a model for a private session as well, one of whom was Muriel Taylor, the wife of a friend; more than once he mused to himself that all the models were married.[58] Just before leaving on the job-hunting trip to the Coast, Morgan received a letter from Howe, who proposed the pair of them cooperate on a book documenting the annual fur-trade rendezvous of the 1820s and 1830s. Despite his plans, Morgan fired back an enthusiastic acceptance immediately, pledging to begin a bibliographic search for source material when he got back from California. The invitation forged the first formal link tying Morgan to the study of the American fur trade. He also visited Dee Bramwell's office in the Newhouse Building to talk about the trip. Bramwell agreed to retain Morgan in the Survey if the San Francisco expedition produced no job offers.[59]

On Sunday July 2, the carload of three Morgan boys, their mother, and friend Helen Sanders drove north along US 30 out of Salt Lake City.

Stopping overnight in Boise, Idaho with one of Dale's chess acquaintances, they continued through Portland, Oregon, then Seattle, across the Canadian border into Vancouver and Victoria, British Columbia before turning south across the Olympic Peninsula down US 101 south to San Francisco. The family took an apartment on Sacramento Street.[60] Dale planned to remain in San Francisco and took a studio apartment on Taylor Street for a week. The family wandered about San Francisco, which Dale compared to "a slightly shop-worn courtesan," and he began working his list of advertising-agency and newspaper contacts. He got interviews and encouragement. Morgan's contacts took every opportunity to praise his creativity, cleverness, and imagination, but none was willing to hire him. He had nothing else to do but head home.

Though entertaining, the trip was unproductive. The only job that resulted from it was a commission from former HRS regional supervisor Col. J. M. Scammell (who had lost his position in the federal reductions) to design a prospectus brochure for a silver-lead mine; Morgan's payment was to be in the mine's stock.[61] The only other bright spot was that while on a day trip working in the Bancroft Library collections, Dale met Helen Harding, who became an important contact and took a personal interest in his work. On July 21, Dale sent a telegram to Dee Bramwell that he was coming back to Salt Lake City. The next day Morgan checked out of his hotel and caught a Burlington Line bus for Utah. Dale returned to find that during his absence Gillham had produced ads for their Fisher Brewing Company account based on the roughs Dale had submitted in his sample portfolio a year earlier—his ideas were good enough, it seems; he was not.[62] Worse, he found himself out of a job at the Survey. Due to a federal employment rule, employees voluntarily absent from work more than five days were subject to dismissal. Administrative tangles between the WPA and the Salt Lake office of the National Re-employment Service were ironed out, allowing him to be rehired, but Dale idled at home for nearly a month.

Not only this, but after an openly tense year, the Thurstons were clearly heading toward a separation. Dale wrote Madeline in frustration about the trip, with the hollow knowledge that writing would do no good:

> I would give a very great deal to talk to you. But even here there is a kind of paralyzing sense of futility. I have about 62 cents in my purse, and not another damned cent. I would come up to Ogden anyway—hitch a ride or walk if I had to, if only I truly could come

home to you, come home to all I know and believe in you. But what would be more empty than to come up and see you and have you indifferent to my coming, not wanting me to come or embarrassed because I am such a damned fool as not to know when I am not wanted.[63]

In the end, however, the futility Dale felt was itself futile. He never sent the letter. With Madeline determinedly holding him at arm's length, Dale used the downtime of temporary unemployment to clean up some details in Survey writing, particularly to critique for Howe the latest version of the Utah guidebook history essay. He found the current draft worse than any preceding draft he had seen and tore it to shreds with criticism. "I know exactly what should be done, and if I could spare the time, I would take on the job," he wrote Howe, "but I cannot donate so much time as this job would involve."[64]

* * * * *

Dale's monthly letter to elder Jerry Bleak back in May had assumed a more serious aspect and revealed deeper issues that he was not comfortable expressing to his immediate family. "I have written you letters which had hardly more of me than of the man in the moon in them—they could have been written by any of six thousand people on this earth—and your letters have been much of the same sort . . . I have been possessed, up to now, with a thousand utterly trivial things. I am now undergoing a wholesale revision of all my beliefs and habits and methods of living. . . ."[65] This "revision" was not broadcast beyond his most intimate acquaintances. "There are no more than about four more persons to whom I am saying this—and you are the only one among my relatives to whom I so express myself." In coming months, he continued to plead with Jerry to approach their relationship seriously and not merely as a superficial friendship. "I am simply driven now by a desire to establish my life on a more vital basis," he explained.[66]

Otherwise Dale used this enforced free time after returning from the Coast to return to creative writing. Having reviewed Thomas Wolfe's novel *The Web and the Rock* for the *Salt Lake Tribune*'s book review page, Wolfe's autobiographical work finally crystalized for Dale the approach he wanted to take in the novel he had promised Howe earlier in the year. On Saturday August 5, Dale sat down and began typing. A draft came as a slow trickle at first, then as a steady stream, and finally began flooding out of him through the keys of the typewriter.

Initially he wrote in straight autobiography. After several drafts, he changed perspectives, adhering to autobiography but shading it behind third-person narration and changing the names involved. The main character was himself, thinly disguised as Ed Garnett, a boy deafened at fourteen by meningitis. Summoning all of his creative energy and passion for writing and expression, Morgan spilled the lonely, silent frustration of ten years onto page after page of self-revelation. For weeks, between August 1939 and about May 1940, Dale wrote of the confused disbelief over losing his hearing and of the several attempts to explain and then cure the problem, the agony of being thrust beyond society, the inability to understand or meaningfully communicate the biology of puberty, the fascination and the repulsion of sexuality, the challenges of school, and all the hard, or sharp, or weak, or fearful things with which experience could hurt or confuse or alienate him. Setting down the novel manuscript was cathartic, not exactly what he set out to write but what he needed to write. Dale pushed the manuscript as far as a cleanly-typed revision edited from his first (and possibly second) drafts, telling Jerry that it would hopefully be ready by the time he returned from Samoa in October.[67]

As early as 1937, Dale toyed with the idea of beginning a novel about "the Utah generation now coming of age—the generation for whom the frontier no longer exists in the land but in the minds of men."[68] The theme was a logical extension of a novel Madeline Thurston said she had completed and was busily revising,[69] suggesting how closely he identified with the older woman. The stated theme of Morgan's novel (which was never written in the form he first imagined it) fits cleanly within a genre that was poised to emerge from the Mormon heartland the same year. Trade publishers were beginning to publish the earliest volumes of what would become a regional literary movement. Drawing upon the popular film genre that had begun mythologizing the violent yet romantic distinctness of the American West, in the late 1930s, Western writers—as opposed to writers of Westerns—were maturing to a point where they were attracting attention from national publishers. The Mormons and Utah fell into a subset of the new regionalism, which was maturing and ready for serious literary picking. This new cultural literary focus which rose during the hard-hearted late years of the Depression was generated by a group of writers later called by a critic "Mormondom's Lost Generation," a name reminiscent of the bleak, introspective literary nihilism in American literature immediately following the end of World War I.[70] For the Lost Generation writers—among whom were counted Sinclair Lewis, Thomas Hornsby Ferril, Ezra Pound, and particularly F. Scott Fitzgerald and Ernest Hemingway—the desolation of war provided the stress needed to reappraise the shallow selfishness of Gilded Age culture and mores preceding it. Mormon Utah of the 1930s was in a similar social upheaval, its founding generation gone, its current generation scoured by depression, urban growth, and Modernism, poised to create its own literary reappraisal of a culture that was merely a shadow of the state's and Mormon culture's pioneer generations.

The loosely affiliated members of Mormonism's "Lost Generation" were a diverse lot of academics and writers with familial roots in Utah but who almost always circulated outside of the state's boundaries. Bernard DeVoto, Fawn Brodie, and Nels Anderson were three from the social sciences who in the mid-half of the 20th century bolted or drifted away from the Utah or LDS church but never really left behind ties to the state or the tensions of its overwhelmingly Mormon/Gentile culture. Others included novelists Virginia Sorensen, Jonreed Lauritzen, and Morgan's collegiate peer, Richard Scowcroft. Along with Brodie, Dale L. Morgan has come to popularly symbolize the Latter-day Saint Lost Generation. They were among the first generation of "modern" Utahns with emotional or temporal roots not directly in the Pioneer past of Mormonism in the American West.

A literary upwelling within Mormonism at this moment was no accident. In the early 1870s the beginnings of federal prosecutions for polygamy and the Mormons' insular culture coincided with the rise of a "home literature" movement while the Saints weathered the outside attacks from muckrakers' yellow journalism and the purple prose of sensationalists. Federal prosecutions ended after the seating of Senator Reed Smoot in 1904. By the late 1930s, Utah's dominant culture was beginning to stir somewhat uncomfortably, wriggling within itself in a cultural reappraisal with the passing of one era and the emergence of another. The last of the Pioneer generation, faithful American and European converts to Mormonism, those who had sacrificed almost everything for the chance to walk to Utah in the mid-1800s, had aged and were dying away. The stories of their tragedies and sacrifices made in behalf of their raw desert settlements were punctuated by the faith that they were establishing the kingdom of God in the Great Basin. Their experiences generated and defined LDS culture for three quarters of a century; their passing left something of a cultural vacuum waiting to be filled. When they were gone, when that type of sacrifice was unnecessary, what would sustain their grandchildren's faith and identity? The question was not merely an academic one. Utah's capital, like most of the country, was losing regional distinctiveness and quickly becoming homogeneously urban.

As he worked in the HRS office, Dale was aware of the region's emerging literary trend and firmly intended on joining in it himself. Between graduation in 1937 and 1939, Morgan submitted several short stories to magazines like *Argosy* and even *Harper's* without having his work accepted for publication. After committing to write the fur trade book with Maurice Howe, fiction became only an interesting diversion. Upon shelving the incomplete novel manuscript to concentrate on historical writing, much of the pain of Dale Morgan's shortchanged youth apparently dissipated. With only isolated exceptions, Dale Morgan's literary career ended upon shelving his untitled autobiographical novel in May 1940, receding irretrievably into his past; though he dabbled with a few sections until the following year, he never really returned to the manuscript.[71]

As the pages of his novel and its revisions cycled through his typewriter, Morgan occasionally checked in with Bramwell, eager about his reemployment status. In mid-August, Morgan learned that the appointment file had been lost between the WPA office and the National Reemployment Service office, despite WPA administrator Darrell J. Greenwell's prior authorization for the action. Several days later Dale got a note from Greenwell telling him to come in. Morgan went downtown and completed the required paperwork. His rehire was at last approved on August 15, 1939, and he returned to work.[72]

* * * * *

Once back on the HRS staff, Dale returned to drafting and revising histories for the county records inventories. Some of his free time was given to reinvestigating advertising, but before the end of the year, he abandoned the idea of advertising as a career and did not return to California in the fall of 1939 to continue the job hunt as planned. Instead, Morgan made his first step toward a full commitment to history, prodded to action by announcement of Julian Dana's book *The Sacramento*. The volume was the first on a western river to appear in the Rivers of America series published by the New York firm of Farrar & Rinehart. Farrar & Rinehart's "Rivers" series was quite successful and produced very competent, pleasurably readable regional histories. In 1939, the series included fewer than half a dozen titles but attracted critical acclaim. Most of the books in the Rivers of America series were about large eastern rivers, the blood of commerce and settlement in some of the most populated areas of the United States. Dana's book set Morgan thinking, and in October 1939, he wrote the publishers proposing a second book on a western river. It was a cold call, made solely on the merit of the idea itself, without prior introduction or intervention. His inquiry became the second hinge pin around which his entire future turned.[73]

Morgan proposed (there was no manuscript at this point) a book on the Mary's or Humboldt River, a vital ribbon of brackish water crawling resentfully across northern Nevada, but which defined an important stretch of the California Trail. The Humboldt boasted no industry, no population, and had neither a real headwater nor mouth, simply sinking sullenly into the desert floor before reaching the ocean, a larger river, or even a lake.

"Publishing is no ordinary trade," wrote English playwright George Bernard Shaw, "It is gambling. The publisher bets the cost of manufacturing, advertising and circulating a book, plus the over head of his establishment, against every book he publishes exactly as a turf bookmaker bets against every horse in the race. The author, with his one book, is an owner backing his favorite at the best odds he can get from the competing publishers. Both are gamblers."[74] On nothing more than the decent success of their own book series and the sales pitch in Morgan's proposal, Farrar & Rinehart took the gamble against possible competition, accepting the Humboldt River proposal almost at once (after a second query on the author's part). At the close of 1939, Morgan returned a signed contract, obligating him to produce the book.[75] Other than that, in fall 1939 Morgan was already buried deeply in his first major work of history, one that ultimately forged his career as a writer and was the first published work in the collision between Latter-day Saint historical ethicism and historicism.

In early 1939, Morgan had been assigned to generate an introduction to the ordinances of the State of Deseret. It was conceived as merely a "historical sketch" introduction to a mimeographed reprinting of the ordinances. Under Morgan's hands the work expanded far beyond conception. The "provisional state" of Deseret was the Mormons' earliest secular government, organized and functioning independently in Great Salt Lake City before territorial status was granted to Utah in 1850. Its ordinances existed in a small printed collection of barely half a dozen widely scattered copies. By the time Morgan was comfortable with contemporary sources and had produced a draft, the "sketch" had grown substantially beyond the size of a typical introduction. With this work the Utah HRS was in a position to make an original contribution to state history. Morgan floated the idea to Dee Bramwell, then a law student and the HRS administrator who had started the Ordinances project. As the HRS office moved, Bramwell approached Howe, convinced that the project should publish Morgan's work.

By this point the ordinance text had become essentially an appendix to Morgan's history of it, but clearly the monograph was one of the most significant statements on the state made in years. Maurice Howe read a carbon sent to him in Washington and passed it on to sociologist Nels Anderson, the WPA personnel director and a BYU graduate with a PhD in sociology from the University of Chicago, who was thinking about writing a sociological study on the Mormons and Utah. By grounding the narrative on contemporary documents rather than traditional published church sources, Morgan told a complicated and not very heroic story that was nonetheless difficult to criticize. Anderson was impressed and wrote Morgan directly that he had "done a job that many an aspirant for a PhD would be proud to claim." The federal HRS approved publication virtually without changes the next month. Rather than a HRS-published booklet, Morgan's monograph was a local-history godsend and the *Utah Historical Quarterly* editor, J. Cecil Alter, leapt at the chance to get the *Quarterly* back in print.[76]

Per federal requirements, the manuscript was subject to review by a local authority, which in this case was CHO assistant historian A. William Lund. Dale walked through the manuscript with Lund in a series of conversations. "I was amused by him," Morgan reported privately to Howe. "He pointed out a couple of distinct errors ... but most of the conversation revolved around certain of the interpretations. He was 'reasonable' enough, not assertive—but quietly insistent on his point of view (I should say more accurately, unconscious of any other point of view.)"[77] Lund's views exemplified the church's approach to its past, another reason Morgan thought little of the church's written history. After many delays, in October 1940, the entire work was released in three combined issues of the newly revived but struggling *Utah Historical Quarterly.*[78]

Morgan's production of *The State of Deseret* was important to his development as a writer for several reasons. The writing and approval of *The State of Deseret* became not only Morgan's main introduction to the potential pitfalls of Latter-day Saint history, but also demonstrated the value of original documentation in establishing historical fact. Since he knew their work was a touchy subject for the CHO staff, who were already wary of outsiders, he anticipated challenges by grounding every claim and interpretation in contemporary documentation drawn mostly from their own library resources. While writing in the HRS had introduced him to the importance of primary sources, this high-visibility project cemented his perspective of the value of source material, and of shaping assertion and interpretation to fit the evidence. Mastery of sources forestalled counterarguments and provided a firm position to fend off criticism. In this way, Morgan's experience with *The State of Deseret* shaped the way he approached history and historical writing forever after.

Morgan's twenty-fifth birthday and the New Year turning from 1939 to 1940 both carried a bright outlook. His first major work, *The State of Deseret* manuscript was slated for publication. He also had a contract for a book independent of his federal service. He was secure in his job, and it looked like both would open up new opportunities. Survey work for Dale in 1940 involved a continuous round of manuscripts, proofreading, corrections, galleys, and correspondence. For the next year or two, chess and a few sputtering attempts at fiction were relegated to back seats as he pursued historical writing and his personal life, though he still found time for occasional chess games and for dropping in to life-drawing studios at the community arts center.[79] Due to the new Farrar & Rinehart contract for *Humboldt*, he shelved the autobiographical novel and determined to clean up his writing projects in progress at work. By February 1940, Dale was putting a finish to the manuscript for *The State of Deseret*; was writing the Carbon and Utah county histories; and had begun work expanding the initial draft on Ogden's founding into a genuine municipal history. In the evenings and on weekends, he pursued *Humboldt* research.

* * * * *

The cycling warm–cold relationship with the CHO dumped the UWP's central task, to publish a guidebook to the state, into a tangle of personal relationships, formal and informal approvals (and disapprovals), and the politics of public memory. The Writers' Project was not precisely stuck, but progress was limited and that attracted attention in the federal offices.

Intransigence of the CHO was not the only problem completing the Utah guidebook; administrative boondoggles were also an issue. The former project director, Maurice Howe, searched the federal project files for draft carbons which had been received from Utah and filed, ignored. That effort helped, but with the state guidebook stalled, Howe alerted UWP director Charles Madsen in late 1939 that the national office was dispatching one of its field editors to help resolve what they perceived as an editorial impasse with the Utah Guide. Darel McConkey was expected in Salt Lake City by mid-February 1940. McConkey also needed a competent local writer on the ground, and Howe privately told his man to hunt up Morgan. Howe asked Dale to look through the critical essay on state history ahead of McConkey's arrival since, he said bluntly, "you have a better command of Utah history than anyone in the state."[80] Unaware that Howe had gone around him and already approached the editor, Madsen showed up at the HRS office and asked Morgan for the same favor.[81]

Setting aside a revision to the State of Deseret study, after three days of work the Historical Records Survey Historian returned a thirteen-page, single-spaced critique of the guidebook's state-history essay. "I have only been able to check out of personal knowledge," Morgan wrote Madsen officially, "I have not had time to check the material against sources." A duplicate of the letter went to Howe in Washington. "Do I sound like an unbearable know it all?" he penned on the carbon sent to Howe.[82] A week later Princeton University Press solicited a publication review for Nels Anderson's manuscript that would become *Desert Saints*. Dale was little less than stunned. "I don't know how the hell I came to be an authority on Utah history," he observed to his friend in Washington.[83] The answer was quite simple, the older man explained: Howe and Anderson were actively promoting Morgan as the best living authority on the state's history. "We mean it," Howe told Dale bluntly. "There simply is no person with the command of knowledge of detail, the power of interpretation, and the objective viewpoint as concerns Utah history that can even come close."[84] Dale Morgan was becoming an authority mostly because he was becoming known for his grasp of documentable facts.

* * * * *

Federal Writers' Project field editor Darel McConkey, trailed by his wife, Anna, arrived in Salt Lake City late in January 1940. After reviewing the draft essays of the state guidebook, appraising the staff situation, and talking selectively with state WPA staff, McConkey took less than two weeks to decide that a major problem stalling Utah's guidebook was administrative and that likely only one person could get the book moving and finished on time—HRS editor/historian Dale Morgan.[85] Howe agreed. HRS director Dee Bramwell panicked. State administrator Darrell Greenwell consented reluctantly to loan Morgan to the Writers' Project to write the state history essay and several others for the volume. Morgan's work in Utah was well-known from the clean editorial reviews it received in the HRS office in Washington, DC, and transfer approvals happened quickly. Bramwell finally took Dale to lunch and explained that the two projects agreed to an accommodation: Dale would work in the mornings for the Writers' Project, his research supported by a staff of three, and in the afternoons for the Historical Records Survey. His part-time calendar in the latter was already fully committed through July to the Deseret study, Ogden city history, and six county histories.[86] At home Morgan was still retyping the last revised pages of his autobiographical novel, though it would be shelved this same month.

Part of the reason for McConkey's recommendation was that he and Morgan became fast friends almost immediately. By the middle of March, a month after the former's arrival, Dale was confidentially coaching McConkey on how to approach the state's WPA administrators.[87] *The State of Deseret* final manuscript was handed to Bramwell for review on the first of April, in the midst of the machinations that were drawing ever more of the project programs into its maw. A few days later, Morgan entrusted his incomplete and untitled autobiographical novel manuscript to McConkey, the only person to whom he is known to have shown it, a sign of the intimate trust they built in a short time.[88] McConkey praised the draft highly in terms that characterized its literary use of documentary style: "your emotional approach makes the reader forget plot, plan, method, and of the conscious strivings for effect. This lives, glows, breathes, is light and shadow and chiaroscuro and mountain and valley."[89] Praise for Morgan's writing came from Howe as well, who read the guidebook's re-drafted "Contemporary Scene" manuscript with delight and was placed well enough in Washington to bring Morgan and his writing to the attention of national HRS director Dr. Luther Evans.[90]

In the midst of discussion and before a decision about his future employment was made in the late spring of 1940, Dale began hunting seriously for information on the Humboldt River region. Fortunately, Dale's friend Dwight Jones was a native of Metropolis, Nevada, a desert boom town of the 1910s that had busted even before the bust of the early 1930s. Dale wanted to see the ground along the California branch of the historic overland trail, which ran along the river. He did not drive, but Jones agreed to take him and act as guide. The pair left Salt Lake City on June 20, 1940. Driving north along the eastern shore of the Great Salt Lake, they crossed the old graded road across the Promontory, site of the 1869 "Wedding of the Rails" which completed the transcontinental railroad, crossing north of the lake to Kelton, Goose Creek Canyon, and into Oakley, Idaho. The pair bivouacked three miles outside City of Rocks, the isolated boulder field where the overland trail branched north to the Oregon country or south toward the California gold fields. The next day they entered the empty quarter of northeastern Nevada.

That evening from Wells, Dale posted a long, descriptive letter to McConkey, mustering the observations and language that later found expression in his book about the region. "Yesterday we rode for endless miles through the vastest emptiness imaginable," he wrote McConkey, the West-by-God Virginian for whom the arid American West was a land of brown and gray strangeness. "It is not merely 'desolate'; I got rather a feeling of total emptiness, a sort of limp unbeing." The pair followed roads through canyons not appearing on any map. This was the deep desert.

Sometimes the hills roll out for miles on east and west, not mountains of the kind you are accustomed to see in the Wasatch Mountains—just one rolling range of hills after another, dry and husky grey-green and blue, deepening in the distance to dry flat masses lying low against the horizon. It makes you wonder what the California emigrants must have thought, because if anything ever seemed endless, these rolling hills do.

There is a kind of arid toughness, a dry, tough beauty which has its appeal. . . . These seem irreclaimable forever and ever, a desert spirit inviolate of man's endeavor. There is not even the strange beauty of the desert here, because the sagebrush, even, is too scattered to make velvety the rolling flanks of the hills. In some places the hillsides look scarred as by waves, the sagebrush seeming planted in serrated rows.[91]

The pair chased the horizon into Wells, Nevada, stopped for a soda, and then drove toward Jones' former home in the ruins of Metropolis. Virtually nothing was left of the community among the sagebrush but a single brick and concrete building, the former city hall. They hiked Bishop Creek and slid for an afternoon soak into the containment pond. Back in

Wells for a second time, Dale stopped at the post office. A letter in general delivery was waiting for him from McConkey.

The day after Morgan and Jones had driven northward, McConkey wrote Dale that "You're IT[sic]!" At McConkey's prompting, the state WPA office reorganized Utah's cultural projects. Former journalist Gail Martin assumed direction of three projects: the HRS, UWP, and Art Project. HRS offices consolidated in Salt Lake City under Cleon Harding, and HRS editor Dale Morgan was instructed to give up his editing and writing position, having been named director of the UWP.[92] Dale was pleased, of course, having only half-expected McConkey to pull off something so bold. Personally, if it accomplished nothing else, Morgan's appointment to the UWP directorship sealed in his mind that he was a competent adult and not merely a deaf charity case with an uncertain future.

Jones drove them into the Sierras as far as Donner Lake and Lake Tahoe. On the way back, Dale accidentally knocked his glasses to the ground in the Carson City tourist camp, shattering one of the lenses. There was nothing to do but cement the major pieces together, hoping the repair would hold together long enough to get home. The pair arrived back in Salt Lake City, dusty and tired, on the morning of June 29 after an all-night drive. Dale got cleaned up, found his old pair of glasses, and went in to work.[93]

CHAPTER 6

"This May Not Last, but It's Fine While It Does"[1]

The Utah Writers' Project, Salt Lake City, 1940–1942

I find the more I find out, the more I need to find out.[2]
—Dale Morgan

DAREL MCCONKEY DEPARTED UTAH for Washington, DC, after announcing the administrative changes to both the Utah Historical Records Survey (HRS) and Utah Writers' Project (UWP) offices, two days before the new director returned home. Both staffs were buzzing like hornets, particularly because despite his transfer to the UWP, Dale retained authority over the final form of HRS writing prior to publication. UWP Director Dale L. Morgan entered the front door of the Utah Institute of Fine Arts building in the old brick Elks Lodge on Main Street in Salt Lake City on the morning of July 8, 1940. He would not officially assume his duties for a few days, but he was in the office ostensibly for orientation and to smooth the transfer from Madsen's direction. At the time Morgan took over the UWP, its staff stood at thirty-six, including two other people partially or profoundly deaf.[3] In less than a week, Dale was feeling the irony of an executive position and his age: "I had a sense of being two persons, a guy who was sitting in a chair behind a desk talking to people like God, and another guy who was standing somewhat incredulously by, asking what the hell this fellow was doing here." Yet, there he was. "This may not last," Dale observed privately to McConkey, "but it's fine while it does."[4]

Morgan's first and chief responsibility at the UWP was staff morale. The disposition of his predecessor had set staff against each other, drawing hard walls around responsibilities which created tension over job duties and accountability. Aware that most were uncertain of him and his abilities, Dale asked each to write him a letter with a bit of autobiography and a summary of their defined responsibilities. Though Morgan continued corresponding widely, he also talked frequently with his staff, carefully watching faces and learning to follow their conversation patterns. Deafness undoubtedly complicated his interpersonal communication, but the need to be precise and clarify twice or three times what had been said did not lessen his zeal for his job or seem to compromise his performance. By all accounts available to a biographer, he was an effective and engaged supervisor, an active participant in office social circles, and enormously dedicated to his staff and the work that they did.

As Morgan became familiar with his staff, to McConkey and Howe he also identified three administrative priorities: to complete a source-file reorganization (rows of filing cabinets filled with carbons of transcripts), to increase the actual writing output of the staff, and to secure the local sponsorships now required by federal mandate for any new writing projects.[5] The file reorganization required merely time and effort. Morgan's second major responsibility centered on the stalled Utah state WPA guidebook, managing final revisions and then coordinating publication. Though a manuscript for the Utah guidebook had been submitted and approved, its commercial publisher, Hastings House, reordered priorities to push the guide to Louisiana ahead of Utah's, hoping to have the Southern volume out in time to capitalize on sales at Mardi Gras.[6] That bought Utah's WP office time to return to revision.

The other challenge was sponsorships. Unwilling to allow federal largess to fund local writing—and deeply concerned about outsiders digging up local skeletons or dismissing the honored traditions and views of city fathers—Congress mandated that WPA projects create partnerships with a local organization, which had to support as well as approve the final content of any project. One of Morgan's chief duties as project director was to secure partnerships that would result in writing commissions and supportive contributions or funding. During his tenure, Dale pursued a dozen or more sponsorships, projects, and publication proposals. He met with people between Logan at the north end of the state, to Provo at the south end of the Wasatch Front. Morgan immediately secured support for the grazing history from the U.S. Forest Service office, which created a policy conflict since one federal agency could not contribute funding to the work of another. In place of a cash sponsorship, Morgan successfully renegotiated for an in-kind contribution of typing and carbon paper, typewriter ribbons, and the like. A proposal for a guide to Provo City became one of the UWP's most notable publications. Dale drove the forty miles south of Salt Lake City and returned late the same evening with commitments from the Provo mayor, the president of Brigham Young University, and the secretary of the city's chamber of commerce.[7]

Successful activity as an executive came at a cost. In August, 1940, Dale confessed to John Farrar of Farrar & Rinehart that he had not touched *Humboldt* yet, due to the push of compiling the Utah *Guide*. By his own account, Morgan expended much of the summer to "40,000 words to the Utah guide, including the 20,000 word history of the state." In the process, he told Howe, he "found several errors in the fur trade history, especially with respect to Jedediah Smith." He might also have added that within the past month he had taken over the UWP with responsibility not only for the history he was writing but also overall editorial responsibility for all work produced by the project; and still he continued doing the press releases and project publicity. He promised Farrar to begin writing in November, over a year after his letter proposing the book. His burden was eased considerably by completing the *History of Ogden* and the historical sketch for the Uintah County inventory in October and November respectively, by returning the corrected galleys for the *Guide* in February 1941, and finishing the Emery County historical sketch in March.[8] One of Morgan's new office staff noted that "the work is in your blood, it is all of you, your heart's in it."[9]

On July 19, *The State of Deseret* was mailed to *Utah Historical Quarterly* subscribers.[10] The study garnered praise immediately. Even the irascible Charles Kelly had to admit that Morgan successfully avoided controversy without ignoring the inconvenient facts involved in the Provisional State of Deseret.[11] *Deseret* is Dale Morgan's first important work as a historian. His 155-page historical introduction, addressing Utah's earliest settlement and first local attempt at political organization, provides the first half of the publication, with the second half occupied by a republication of the "state's" printed ordinances. *The State of Deseret* allowed Morgan the room to bring his rapidly growing talent to bear on a large issue. On one level, the work is straightforwardly historical, addressing a history both tangled and conflicted, and in places intentionally obfuscated.

Before too much time passed, the year that began with such a bright outlook for Dale Morgan also held an important and unpleasant personal rift that affected much of his later life. Jarvis and Madeline Thurston's marriage had frayed further. Their relationship was now to a point of constant and uneasy tension. Dale asked his mother if she could again put up Madeline for a couple nights and Emily did so grudgingly. He watched the Thurstons from the sidelines, unwilling to step in to see the marriage preserved in any case. Perhaps unknown to Morgan, Madeline had formed an attachment to Tom McQuown, a chess partner of both Jarvis and Dale. Late in autumn 1940, McQuown finally persuaded Madeline to leave Jarvis and establish residency in Nevada preliminary to seeking a divorce. Madeline left a brief note at home for her husband and without a hint of her destination or intent, caught a train out of the Ogden passenger rail yards.

Jarvis was thunderstruck but surmised the purpose. He rightly supposed that Dale would know her whereabouts and went to see him. Madeline and Dale apparently had a discussion before she left, but perhaps in a thin hope that he could talk Madeline into marrying him once the divorce was completed, Morgan was unwilling to tell his friend and chess partner anything. Jarvis Thurston left angrily. The two former friends never spoke directly to each other again. On his own, Jarvis eventually traced Madeline to Las Vegas and talked her out of pursuing the legal action, but Tom McQuown continued prompting and she completed the proceedings. Dale probably never understood and certainly did not accept that Madeline had no romantic interest in him. His mournful longing was confided to a brief series of undated diaries entries. The previous March he had written Madeline a pleading letter seeking the emotional intimacy that leads to affection. Madeline folded it and on the back over Morgan's signature doodled Tom McQuown's name dozens of times. She ignored Dale's affections and married McQuown in late January 1941.[12]

Meanwhile, in October or November 1940, Dale was confident enough with his senses of balance and sight that he finally learned to drive an automobile. Fifty years later Dale's youngest brother Bob, who taught him, recalled that teaching his older brother was a positively harrowing experience. Unable to hear, Dale could not get a sense of the motor's effort as the transmission meshed the engine's output with the drive train. As a result, Dale had a difficulty understanding the timing necessary to shift gears manually. He was forced to rely on the tachometer, the gauge of engine speed, to make sense of the timing needed to shift a manual transmission reasonably smoothly. Unfortunately, watching the dashboard tachometer took his eyes from the road and caused him to drift across traffic lanes and toward obstacles like trees, parked vehicles, oncoming cars, lampposts, Post Office drop boxes, and virtually anything else that would not get out of the way on its own.

Bob recalled one time when Dale drove Bob and a girl he was dating on a practice run down 2100 South to 300 West. Though still somewhat on the edge of the city, the streets were paved and not heavily travelled. Early in the process Bob got Dale's attention and told him to practice turning off the wide 300 West onto a narrow side street. Without stepping on the brake to reduce speed or even pulling his foot from the accelerator, Dale simply pulled the steering wheel in the direction of the cross street, moving much too fast to make the corner. The car leaned dangerously toward the outside of the curve, its tires screaming in protest as it swung close to the deep irrigation ditch on the side of the street opposite to where they should have been. Dale narrowly missed dropping into the ditch and rolling the car. Once Dale straightened out and glanced at his instructor, he had a good laugh at the panic on both passengers' faces.[13] Shortly after his birthday in December, Dale qualified for a driver's license; around the middle of following January he bought his first car from his younger brother Jim, a 1934 Chevrolet sedan.

Dale continued working doggedly on research for his pending book on the Humboldt, but other projects kept nagging at his attention. Three years earlier he had asserted boldly to his cousin Jerry that little in Latter-day Saint history was reliable. Clearly he was beginning to think of writing (and correcting) that history himself. "I want to get Mormon history damned well written up," he wrote McConkey in frustration. "I want to write all those things about Mormonism that haven't been written, how and why everything went as it did, in terms both of its relation to itself and its relation to American life." A month after apologizing to John Farrar for not having written anything on his river book, he wrote again saying that he planned to begin writing some "tentative chapters" on the Humboldt by the turn of October.[14] The federal office returned the lead "Contemporary Scene" essay for the Utah guidebook at almost the same time, unwilling to let it see publication in its current form. Recalling his delight with Morgan's history essay, Howe suggested the state project director take it on himself, the fifth writer to attempt a manuscript in four years. Morgan's draft was the version finally approved for publication.

January 1941 had hardly passed before Morgan and the UWP staff were buried in galley and then page proofs for the guide. Dale had the authors of the various chapters, sections, and tours check proofs if they were available, and evidently he read everything himself as well. Corrected proofs were dispatched back to the publisher as quickly as copymarks could be collated. Then it was a waiting game. At exactly the same time, the upswing in military preparations beneath the brooding clouds of war in Europe began enticing employees out of the WPA and local businesses.

A single copy of *Utah: A Guide to the State* in its bright yellow and blue jacket arrived at the UWP on March 28. The staff gingerly handed the book around the office. The next day Ruby Garrett, Gail Martin, and Morgan ceremonially presented the first copy to Utah Governor Herbert Maw.[15] Early guidebook shipments began arriving the next week, and distribution began. Unfortunately, Hastings House failed to market or advertise the book even within the state it described. Unwilling to see their work wasted, Morgan mustered the UWP into gear as its own marketing agency. Through the spring, the staff generated ads, made sales calls to department stores, wrote radio spots, and hawked the book energetically. The staff managed to get half of the press run sold within a year of publication.[16]

Though Utah's volume was one of the last WPA guidebooks released, the UWP found the major purpose of its existence accomplished. Thankfully, the Provo guidebook also was moving along. Dale continued prodding for writing and sponsorship opportunities around the state. The office and its massive vertical files of notes, transcriptions, summaries, and pamphlets were also a quasi-public resource.

One afternoon a tall, tanned man walked in off the street. He stopped to visit with Jack Thornley. After a few minutes the pair came to Dale's desk asking for material on several subjects. Morgan recognized but could not mentally place the newcomer, but dug out the material from the files and set him to work at one of the office desks. After an hour the man left, and Morgan asked Thornley who it was. "My God, Dale," Thornley replied, "that's Wally Stegner." Morgan had met the older man a few times while he was a student at the University of Utah. Stegner, himself a U graduate, returned to Salt Lake City in fall 1934 fresh from completing his PhD at the University of Iowa. Stegner had been the faculty advisor to the *Utah Chronicle,* but as a low-level student writer, Morgan had had little or no interaction with him. Stegner left his faculty appointment in a huff the same quarter that Dale graduated in 1937, a casualty of Depression finances and a stiffly conservative department chair who would not promote him. Now five years later Stegner was back in town doing research on a book eventually published in the American Folkways series by Duell, Sloan, and Pearce, titled *Mormon Country.*

After his first visit to the UWP office, Stegner visited again over several more days. He and Morgan took to each other quickly. After returning to his teaching post in Wisconsin, Stegner continued writing to Morgan to resolve questions.[17] These early contacts were the basis for an easy, timeless familiarity between the two men, born of early adult acquaintance and mutual respect, a friendship that was never forgotten but did not require constant cultivation or long correspondence. It could be picked up unimpaired at the drop of a stamp. Long after they were both in California, Morgan at Berkeley and Stegner at Stanford, the men remained correspondents and trusted each other's professional talents.

In July, Morgan took a week off to undergo a tonsillectomy. If the motivation was the constant series of sinus infections and colds which plagued him, the surgical procedure did not work. To the end of his life Dale seemed to suffer sinusitis at least annually. He returned to work in time to reorganize the office in response to a deep staffing cut mandated by the federal and regional project offices. With Japan expanding across the Pacific basin and the Nazis moving almost unopposed through Poland, "defense has all priority," wrote Darrell Greenwell, the state WPA administrator. The percentage of regular or non-relief employees of WPA projects was capped at five percent of the total project allotment and was rumored to soon be reduced to four percent.[18] The UWP, which had nearly doubled its staff during the short time Morgan directed it, was due for deep cuts. Dale lost other staff to employment in private business, and at least one to isolation in a tuberculosis sanitarium. Ironically, Morgan himself was given a raise.

* * * * *

The second half of 1941 served as a watershed or tipping point that determined Dale Morgan's writing career—or attempts at a career. A litany of small accomplishments, activities, decisions, and connections led from his bold quip to cousin Jerry about the value of Latter-day Saint history in 1938, to his stated plans for "a Mormon book" in 1941. Now, events between July and December 1941 committed him firmly to the project. Each had a long-term effect on his career or on the world in which he moved.

The first broad development was that Morgan committed himself to a historical study of Utah's founders and still-dominant culture, the Church of Jesus Christ of Latter-day Saints (his interests were not yet the broader Latter Day Saint tradition). Morgan was working on the Humboldt manuscript in 1941, but he was also planning ahead. For months, Dale walked the block and a half from his office to the Church Administration Building on South Temple Street to spend an hour in personal research in the third-floor Historian's Office. On August 14, though he had not set a single sentence to paper and had barely begun the research he felt the book needed, Dale wrote bracingly to Darel McConkey that his book on the Latter-day Saints "is pretty close to maturation." It was a mental construct only, however. The first book—one of several, he told McConkey—would explain the Mormons and their church "as a people set in the environment of their time, with especial reference to their ideas, where they came from and how they evolved in Mormon society." Later in the letter, Dale added, "I would begin work on it tomorrow if I didn't have Humboldt on my hands." [19]

But he did have *The Humboldt* on his hands, and lacked both the unencumbered time and the financial stability to write without interruption. In his regular apology to John Farrar about slow progress on the book manuscript, Dale told his publisher that the Mormon book would require a year of research in Utah and two more outside of the state before he would be in a sufficient position to begin writing. [20] He considered the merits of applying for the Alfred A. Knopf Fellowship in history being offered by the publisher in 1942. However, Juanita Brooks asked for Morgan's support in her application for the Knopf Fellowship in Biography, and he gave up making his own proposal to support her application.

The letters between Morgan and Brooks took on a more focused theme as she confided her interest in writing about one of the dark moments of the state's history, the 1857 massacre of 120 emigrants at Mountain Meadows. The next week Morgan responded by posting a package to Brooks—everything he had collected on Southern Utah and the Mountain Meadows Massacre, and mentally added Jacob Hamblin and Mountain Meadows to the list of subjects on which he made notes and transcriptions in lunchtime forays to the CHO. [21] These went south to Brooks as well, who was among the first of many scholars, writers, and curious inquirers who profited from Morgan's scholarly generosity. "I do not feel that I have ever lost anything by lending whatever helping hand I could," he explained to a correspondent later that month. That attitude was a characteristic generosity for which Dale Morgan became noted throughout his career. [22] This exchange with Brooks was the beginning of a silent partnership resulting in her landmark *Mountain Meadows Massacre* published in 1950 by Stanford University Press.

The publication of two minor but personally significant essays, both appearing in a local literary magazine, also contributed to Morgan's decision to write a history of Mormonism. The first was a comment on the state's contemporary culture. A year later he tested the water again, publishing an assessment of contemporary Mormon literature.[23] Neither provoked any outrage or reaction as Bernard DeVoto's opinionated blasts had attracted in 1930. Alongside *State of Deseret,* the Ogden history, and various published and unpublished county histories, these publications were significant. Morgan later claimed that "I demonstrated to WPA in Utah that you can say almost anything you like about Utah and the Mormons if you say it within the framework of a responsible scholarship."[24]

A third major development tying Morgan to the Mormons was an informal connection to the Utah State Historical Society. During his years in the WPA programs, Morgan became intimately familiar with the cramped basement room of the Utah State Capitol occupied by the Utah State Historical Society. J. Cecil Alter's employment transfer to Cincinnati, Ohio, in August 1941 upset the small organization and left Marguerite Sinclair, its clerical assistant, without guidance. With Alter all but out the door, she approached Morgan asking for help.[25] Alter independently asked Morgan to consider the same step. "I could hope for no better fortune for the Society than that you could become even more closely connected with and interested in its aims and projects," he wrote Dale.[26]

Their entreaties would have been mere flattery had not Juanita Brooks given him the same compliment less than a week later, referring to the mass of historical files becoming increasingly accessible at the UWP office. "More and more I appreciate what you are doing. I doubt that any other single person is making so great a contribution to the permanent good of this state. Not only are you to become Utah's top historian, but you are to leave the state a collection of records that will be priceless." Morgan demurred, noting that Brooks had been among the first collecting manuscript material. He was glad that the collection was being built, for a state library would be "permanently accessible to all, unlike too many historical collections in this state." Even if the Society was unable to pay for his involvement, Morgan agreed to an unofficial role as mentor and sounding board, willing to help occasionally with editing material for its publications as well.[27] His involvement and influence as the Society's unofficial director grew quietly for a decade, ending only at the hiring of a genuine full-time professional in 1950.

By the end of 1941, Morgan had committed to himself and to several of his key correspondents that once *Humboldt* was finished, he was prepared to take on a revisionist history of Mormonism. Of course he still had much research to do, but he was firmly committed. He would be a historian.

* * * * *

As Great Britain and the Soviet Union stood alone against Nazi Germany in Europe, and as the empire of Japan secretly finalized its preemptive strike on the U.S. Pacific Fleet, Dale drove south on another business excursion near the first of May 1942. This trip went into the state's coal country and then east into the red-rock landscape around Moab before turning around at Blanding in the state's southeast corner. He was back five days later to pluck his draft notice from the mail. The Selective Training and Service Act of 1940 mandated men between 18 and 45 register for future military service. Dale and millions of other American men presented themselves to their local draft boards. Draftees were inducted into military service beginning in October 1940, though without a sense of hearing, Morgan would be neither conscripted by the draft nor allowed to volunteer. Classification as IV-F or "unacceptable for military service" by reason of "physical, mental, or moral reasons" insured that Morgan's writing on *Humboldt* or for the UWP would not be interrupted by military service.[28] At the end of August, Dale also overcame a point deficit to take a consecutive city chess title.[29] The in-person game was an exception. His letters hint that he was by now so busy that the only chess games he played regularly were by correspondence.

The force reduction in the federal work programs took effect at the end of September. The HRS statewide staff of 109 lost 73 of its workers to various causes and discontinued its county record surveys because no workers were available.[30] Despite deep cuts to UWP staffing, or perhaps because of it, Morgan successfully arranged to employ Madeline McQuown as a noncertified writer.[31] Well-intentioned though her hire was, the move created for Morgan one more complication. Through the fall, the UWP limped on with its reduced staff, generating brochures, historical-play radio scripts, and a series of Utah history article releases for newspapers around the state. By this time the Humboldt River manuscript for Farrar & Rinehart had been completed, but Morgan wanted to cut the book by a fifth before submitting the manuscript. Though he self-imposed a deadline of the New Year, which would push delivery only a couple of months beyond the contract date, the deadline was merely a pleasant dream; the manuscript required of him nearly another full year of work.

On December 7, 1941, Dale was dusting and cleaning his bedroom after a paperhanger had refreshed the space a couple of days earlier. Bob touched him on the arm to get his attention and relayed the radio news about the bombing of Pearl Harbor. Dale dismissed the story as improbable, but his mother Emily sat by the radio the entire day. In the UWP office the next day Dale recorded his impressions and activities in one of the occasional diary entries. He had remained at work until the evening newspapers were issued, went home for supper, and then returned to the Art Center to draw model LaPriel Flora in a life-drawing class, wondering to himself what her husband thought of his wife posing nude.[32] Morgan was like many Americans, who simply went about their routines as the already-spread net of the Second World War finally drew the United States into its gaping red maw.

Within a few days, Howe wrote that the Federal Writers' Project administration was telling state projects to make no more commitments, anticipating a move to war-production activities.[33] The UWP office was nearly at a standstill, the staff certain that they would be mobilized as an information service, which did not happen. The Federal Writers' Project had too many powerful political enemies who wanted the offices dismantled, dispersed, and utterly forgotten. On Christmas Eve, Dale decided to take the interurban line to Ogden and visit Tom and Madeline McQuown. Unfortunately, she had exactly the same idea, and somewhere along the line their trains passed each other. "You are probably blaming me bitterly as usual," she wrote.[34]

The daily news at the turn towards 1942 was generally not good. The *Arizona* and a dozen other warships still lay as tangled, smoking hulks in the water at Pearl Harbor Naval Base, wreckage and oil littering the shallow bay. General Douglas MacArthur's entire air force had been destroyed on the ground in the Philippines, despite advance warning of likely attack. The Japanese fleet was sweeping American and British naval forces across the Pacific, from Guam to Sri Lanka. Even as his fleet logged victory after victory, former Harvard University student Isoroku Yamamoto, who had reluctantly masterminded the strike at Hawaii, quietly observed to his staff that Japan had accomplished nothing with the attack beyond awakening a sleeping giant.

In January 1942 the United States was awake and stirring. Despite years of ardent isolationism, the country was now resolved to fight a war on two fronts; yet the U.S. first had to recover its naval losses and convert its production capacity from consumer goods to war materiel. No one knew where cultural writing fit, other than it wasn't war production. Among the workers and administrators of the state WPA offices, no one was precisely sure what would happen. Rumor ruled. One of the national editors told a friend that the Federal Writers' Project staff was individually ready to go job hunting as the country mobilized, but were waiting to see whether the office would be absorbed into a government or civilian defense agency.

In one western state, having celebrated his twenty-seventh birthday weeks earlier, the project director wasted no time in rumor or fear. He was too busy laying plans and considering options that would create a secure future for his staff. The crisis of war time galvanized Dale Morgan, who perceived in it an opportunity to put the UWP, or at least its staff and functions, onto permanent footing. In May 1941, Morgan considered the merits of proposing the State of Utah absorb its office as a state information and development bureau.[35] Dale was confident—for the moment— that the UWP could function as a ready-made public relations office. By 1942 the war offered opportunities for public relations commissions to generate public-instruction material from government offices which had no information infrastructure. In Washington, DC, Howe wrote that the federal Community Service Division project offices (parent of the late-term WPA projects) were to be restructured into the War Service Division and folded into one of the secretary-level Departments. No one was sure what was going to happen or when, but Federal Writers' Project staff were now leaving in droves for employment elsewhere.

While Morgan was pouring hours into the UWP, he was spending long hours drafting historical work of his own. In the spare time he could free up, he also took on another major project, for the first time helping the *Utah Historical Quarterly* compile its 1941 volume as a single monograph around the theme of medicine in early Utah. Over the next decade Morgan would be involved to a greater or lesser extent with every issue the journal published.

Not everything else was going so well. Between his noontime research and personal writing, his time sketching at the Art Center, and the day-long work schedule, Dale's relationship with Madeline McQuown was rocky, seeming to revolve around her commitment to Tom McQuown and Dale's open distrust and growing dislike of him. Despite carefully phrased insights into problems she faced, despite his reasoning, despite Dale's analysis of both her and their fraught situation, in the few letters of his that survive Morgan it is clear that he could not persuade her that McQuown was an unsuitable match nor that her anxiety and medical troubles were chiefly in her mind. His occasional diary entries were bleak and morose. Dale was utterly devoted to Madeline; he just as utterly failed to accept that she had no romantic interest in him and intentionally held him at arm's length. "I behave as a friend; you try to behave as a lover," she wrote him at about this time. "There *can* be no common ground and so you are right when you say that trouble lies ahead."[36]

So, through the beginning of 1942, Morgan seemed to have been balancing with one foot on an emotional seesaw and the other on a professional one. He remained, however, supremely confident about the practical education in historical research and writing the WPA had given him and the range of opportunities that that lay before him. "I don't worry especially," he wrote to his editor, "since I have capabilities and enough imagination to enable me to get them employed."[37] Despite his effort and commitment to the UWP, the programmatic axe finally fell on state WPA projects in March 1942. On about the tenth, Morgan wrote his office manager to schedule the staff for as many hours as they could work before the terminal April 1 date reduced the entire office to fifteen, a skeleton crew that thereafter could anticipate only future reductions toward eventual closure.[38] One of those terminated was Madeline McQuown, though for "illness."

The pending end of the UWP gave Morgan the opportunity— or push—he needed as well, solidifying his personal post-WPA plans, which he had been mulling over for weeks or months. To Juanita Brooks at the other end of the state, he observed that the UWP job "has been in large part a means to an end; it has been financing my leisure hours."[39] Dale decided not to wait out its demise. He would leave Salt Lake City and go east, partly for the obvious opportunities that Washington, DC, offered. In a letter to Missouri Historical Society manuscripts librarian Stella Drumm, Morgan laid out the plan in one sentence: "For some four years past I have been gathering everything about the Mormons on which I could lay my hands, with a view to attempting, presently, a book which will have serious claims to definitiveness." A much longer letter, with the same message but more explanation, went to Juanita Brooks.[40] "I am not yet ready to write it," he explained to her, and there was much left to do, "but I believe that I am fortunate enough to have the equipment. I have an emotional understanding of Mormonism, and also an intellectual detachment essential to the critical appraisal of it; my work for the [HRS and UWP] during the past four years, has been, in effect, a fellowship in the history of this state; I have a pretty good educational background, and I have sunk enough time in research to have a pretty extensive command of resources."[41]

Today such a pronouncement would be dismissed as naive or more than a little arrogant; in the context of the early 1940s, it was undeniably ambitious but almost reasonable. Morgan made his commitment to history in the middle of the period that Ian Tyrrell proposes represents the high point of American historians' involvement and attraction to public engagement and readership.[42] Besides, the Humboldt manuscript was nearly done, and would be done by the time he travelled eastward. Morgan cited these reasons publicly, but he decided to leave Utah primarily, he admitted in a private letter to Madeline, because he was unable to work out satisfactorily with her a trust-based relationship.[43] Toward the beginning of April, he wrote Darel McConkey that he planned to come to wartime Washington to look for employment. At the end of May Morgan informed his supervisor, Ruby Garrett, that he would leave UWP within two months and asked for a letter of recommendation.

* * * * *

Dale Morgan worked for three and a half years in the Utah HRS and UWP initiatives with the certain knowledge that he would ultimately leave Utah.[44] Doing so he felt was merely a matter of timing. In 1938 he had been convinced that his departure would be to pursue a career in advertising; by spring 1942 he was turning toward historical writing as a profession. At the end of his tenure directing the UWP, Morgan made about $2,000 annually; in 1940, he estimated that royalties from the sale of 15,000 copies of *Humboldt,* a then-realistic national sales figure for a nonfiction work in a popular book series, might net him about the same amount.[45] Setting himself up to publish a book a year looked like a decent career move. Any way he looked at the numbers, historical writing looked like it could provide him enough to live on, but to meaningfully pursue a career as a writer of history, Dale felt that he had to be near the greatest concentration of source material. Boston or New York offered perhaps as many work options as any other location, "but apart from my private historical interests, Washington seems, from this distance, to offer a more significant field for service."[46] Friends Darel McConkey, Nels Anderson, and Maurice Howe were there already, as well as the large research libraries, notably the Library of Congress and the still-new National Archives. By late spring 1942 Dale Morgan finally and permanently abandoned advertising to commit himself to history.

Morgan began to wrap up his WPA activities through early summer and made plans to leave. In June 1942, with the U.S. up to its elbows in the carnage of a new world war, Dale received a further draft board classification as "Scientific and Specialized Personnel," a rating that allowed him to work permanently in the private sector throughout the war effort.[47] He hosted Juanita Brooks on a tour of the city libraries and archives in Salt Lake City during one of her trips to the capital. Before the summer closed he also read and critiqued the galleys for Wallace Stegner's *Mormon Country*, worked furiously to complete a manuscript for the *Humboldt*, and wrapped up what work remained for him at the UWP. Practically his final act in Salt Lake City, prior to turning over the directorship to Grace Winkelman in October 1942, was to write to Farrar & Rinehart, notifying them that the manuscript for *The Humboldt: Highroad of the West* would be delivered to him from the typist the following morning and then mailed to the publisher "one year late, almost to the day."[48]

Dale applied for a civil service rating in May but had heard nothing by July. He still planned the move east, confident that the wartime economy in the capital and his classification guaranteed him a position of some sort. With this slim certainty for the future, he boarded an eastbound train from Ogden in mid-October 1942 that would take him out of Utah. With the train lurching beneath him, Dale installed his portable typewriter in the club car, otherwise crowded with draftees. He tapped out a poignant letter to his mother that was also very much a goodbye to Utah, Mormonism, and the insecurities of his youth. "I want to get outside the world I have lived in for so long," he wrote Emily:

> to get a new perspective on this world and upon myself. I want to see what the Mormon people, and Utah, look like from the vantage point of another culture in another environment. And I want to see how I fit into the world, where I belong in this world. I have always had the sense of dependencies: people have had to do things for me. Of course, that is true of everyone in life, but it means something to me to take hold of my life with both hands

and do with it something affirmative. I think going away in this manner will give me a little better idea of where I fit into the world and what is to come of me hereafter.... For my own good, I want whatever come of my life to be of my choice.[49]

Perhaps gently appropriate, he was riding on the Union Pacific's passenger train named the *Challenger*.

The Dale Morgan who traveled eastward in October 1942, had intellectually matured, but more importantly had reached a point of self-reconciliation. Born of successful work in the HRS and UWP, Morgan's self-confidence was a far cry from the fearful high school student's prospects about finding employment as a deaf man. The angst of his post-deafness youth was conquered. He found in writing an identity and competence, and he had proven to himself that he was capable of succeeding on the merits of his own skills. Unlike Fawn Brodie wrenching herself out of Mormonism, unlike Bernard DeVoto disgustedly dismissing Utah's parochialism, unlike Wallace Stegner's fond but nostalgic bemusement with the state's dominant culture, Morgan was not escaping from Utah or from Mormons literally or figuratively. In moving east, he was making a calculated investment in self-development, finding greener pastures. Through the coming decades, if he intended to return frequently to Salt Lake's Hollywood Avenue, it would be only as a guest. Dale Morgan was riding off into the sunrise.

CHAPTER 7

"Not So Dull as It Sounds"[1]

Office of Price Administration, Washington, DC, 1942–1947

> *I resigned my job with the Writers' Project because I wanted to complete in the Library of Congress and the National Archives the research job on the West and the Mormons that has principally occupied my private energies during the last four years. . . . and I wanted to enter upon some work centrally connected with the prosecution of the War, for until that war is won, history cannot have quite the meaning it should for those who are its devotees.*[2]
>
> —Dale Morgan

DALE WAS CERTAIN that a IV-F draft board rating ("rejected for military service: physical, mental, or moral reasons"), a classification on the national register of "Scientific and Scholarly Personnel," and his demonstrated qualifications as a writer virtually guaranteed him a job in wartime Washington, DC. By the middle of 1942, with the U.S. Navy positioning itself for a strike at the Japanese-held islands in the Pacific and the Allies preparing to challenge the Nazis in North Africa, voluntary enlistments and the draft of qualified young men to active military service had drained the federal workforce. Government office and clerical ranks were re-filled by tens of thousands of young women, many entering the workforce for the first time, and by men like Dale Morgan, ineligible for military service. Still, Morgan had to find employment in a strange city and nail down a position that did not rely too much on such aural interactions as face-to-face discussions or telephone use.

Issued by the Civil Service Commission in summer 1942, the *Tips to Newcomers to Washington, DC,* brochure suggested pointedly: "Don't come to Washington to look for a job."[3] Not that the advice stopped anyone. Wartime Washington was in constant motion. Many offices staffed double and sometimes triple shifts to coordinate and sustain the war effort. Even offices that dealt with civilian or "home front" issues rattled with activity. Five-day work weeks were uncommon; weekend hours were expected of everyone. Republicans had grumped for nearly a decade that the New Deal bloated the federal bureaucracy unnecessarily, yet those who were not outright isolationists quietly supported Chairman of the Joint Chiefs of Staff George C. Marshall's systematic military expansion beginning in 1940. Even when New Deal offices were repurposed for the war effort or reassigned, the national mechanism found itself entirely under-equipped to staff, direct, or sustain a global war. More people were needed in government service, just as they were needed to staff factories. "Everything here is defense," wrote former WPA administrator Nels Anderson, now an administrator for the National Labor Relations Board, "and ordinary people doing other work have to more or less apologize for their existence."[4] The WPA agencies at the federal level were losing staff to war work possibly more quickly than even the state offices.

Married and with a problematic heart (thus ineligible for the draft), Maurice Howe left the FWP for a position with the new Social Security Administration. Well before the *Challenger* chuffed with its human load from Salt Lake City in October 1942, Maurice and Lucie Howe invited Dale to stay with them in the capital as long as he desired or found necessary. Maurice was at Union Station, north of the Capitol Building, to meet Dale's train after his five-day trip from Ogden.

Besides Washington's attractive research opportunities, Morgan was looking for a way to contribute to the war effort. Darel McConkey began pulling strings even before Morgan arrived. He arranged for Dale to meet with former national Historical Records Survey (HRS) director, Dr. Luther Evans, on the morning after arriving. Now the Librarian of Congress, Evans reviewed and openly praised Morgan's historical writing while both worked in the HRS. The Library of Congress employed a large staff and, as one of the country's major research institutions, was high on Morgan's list of prospective employers. One of the Library's reference staff expected his draft notice imminently; someone thought Morgan might take that position. Despite his position, Evans was not the hiring authority, but he fulfilled Dale's more immediate desire by introducing him to the Reading Room superintendent, who at the Librarian's prompting assigned Morgan a vacant office as a research and writing space. A week later Dale spent half a day registering as a researcher at the National Archives.[5]

Settled into the McConkeys' spare bedroom, Morgan began a less-than-systematic job hunt. Darel first took him to the Civil Service division itself, but there were no vacancies. McConkey also enlisted the informal network of former FWP staff, who occasionally gathered for lunch, on the premise that sooner or later somebody would hear of an open position.[6] Everyone Morgan talked to "seems impressed that I have a book coming up, and that Farrar is interested in a Mormon book when I have one."[7] He was sure the right job would certainly come in time.

A greater concern was the more difficult matter of finding a place to live. Growth in personnel meant growth in the accommodations needed to employ and house them. The buildup in federal offices to support two combat fronts and domestic mobilization for war production created a clamor for space in the capital. Following the attack on Pearl Harbor, housing, office, and street construction in Washington, DC, became very nearly explosive, spilling into emerging Maryland and Virginia suburbs. Even with new construction everywhere, the huge influx of new government employees meant that housing existed as a landlord's market. Ideal locations close to the Library or Archives were filled or cost-prohibitive. Finally, Morgan found a vacant apartment in a newly constructed complex on Key Boulevard in Arlington, Virginia, situated on a hill overlooking the Potomac River. Three years earlier the street had been a hillside pasture, overhung with trees lining its fence rows; now Arlington was a suburban hotspot. The place was a one-room studio with a kitchenette, a tiny private bath, and a Murphy bed that folded off the floor into a cupboard. On October 22, the Howes helped Dale move in.

The next day Dale's final paycheck from the Utah Writers' Project (UWP) arrived in the mail, closing that episode of his life. He immediately spent part of the money on wood planks and bricks to begin putting up bookshelves. He eventually acquired a couch, but his writing workspace was limited to a card table beneath the window, which was quickly buried beneath strata of jumbled notes, resource files, drafts, and typing supplies. The apartment came just in time. In the first week of November, the Social Security Administration suddenly transferred Maurice Howe to Denver. He and wife Lucie quickly packed, and with their young son Danny, bid goodbye to Dale and the McConkeys, leaving Washington on the run for the West once again.[8]

By the end of October 1942, having settled into a routine of research and transcription at National Archives, Dale was ready to begin seriously looking for a job. Through the last two months of the year Dale wrote letters sparkling with originality to virtually every government department with a public-information section: the Office of Defense Health

and Welfare Services, the News Division of the Social Security Administration, and both the Office of War Information and the War Information Service. He submitted queries to the Natural Resources Planning
Board, the Federal Housing Authority, and the Office of Reports within
the War Relocation Authority. At the latter, Dale was told that he needed
to submit Civil Service forms. He had, but as had happened with his
rehire to the HRS in 1939, the Civil Service office had lost them. A friend
who had job-hunted in Washington the previous year warned Dale that
"bureaucratic hiring is a lumbering process—and utterly indifferent to
pin pricking."[9] When his federal documents still had not been found a
month later (and it would not be the last time), Dale wrote his mother:
"The moral to be read from this is that it is always well to do your own
job-hunting without leaving it to Civil Service to do it for you."[10]

Dale brought with him to Washington an intense research regimen
to fill his unoccupied time. Having once lamented the malnutrition of
Utah's libraries, now he chafed at being hedged about by restrictive rules
in federal institutions. The National Archives and the Library of Congress
were his main venues. With *Humboldt* complete, the Mormon history
had priority, and in fall 1942, he set about reading *Niles Weekly Register*
page by page, extracting every mention of the Latter Day Saints. *Niles*
was the equivalent of an eighteenth and nineteenth century news feed,
a digest and reprint of information gleaned and republished from dozens
of local newspapers across the country. Because many of the country's
early newspapers had never been preserved, the digest was an invaluable
window into the happenings of the nation.

Morgan's job queries continued to issue forth but received surprisingly few positive responses. Undoubtedly he failed to realize that despite
the huge expansion in employment, by the turn of 1943 the federal war
bureaucracy was already essentially mature and the explosive hiring that
had been done in the run-up to war had largely stabilized. Its major task
was now coordination.[11] His first preference, the pending vacancy at the
Library of Congress, evaporated when the draft board decided not to
accept the Library employee.

Through one of his contacts Dale decided to pick up an opportunity
for freelance work from the American Council on Public Affairs, editing
doctoral dissertations being readied for publication. By the end of November, Morgan completed copyediting a University of Minnesota study of
messiah figures by Wilson Wallis. Working with the book seems to have
reified and grounded his interpretive position about Joseph Smith.[12] The

latter was about the only benefit realized from this freelance work which netted him merely $35, a third of his starting salary at the HRS four years earlier. The Council could not pay what Morgan felt his time was worth, and Dale decided that freelance work was an insufficient foundation for a career. "There are a couple of possibilities for jobs, but they are not more than tentative," he grumbled to John Farrar, "and 'tentative' jobs never supported anyone."[13]

Also in the first week of November, Howe and McConkey began reading carbons of the *Humboldt* draft. Louise North, a new acquaintance working for the Technical Services branch within the Office of Price Administration, corrected the manuscript's technical structure. Howe confessed that he read late into the night, unable to set the copy aside. "Funny, everybody so far has a higher opinion of the book than I have," Dale wrote to his mother.[14] John Farrar returned his assessment with publisher's internal-review comments early in the second week of November. Morgan set aside job-hunting immediately for several intense days of cutting and revising the manuscript and nailing down permissions for quotes. The revision complete, Dale sent the final manuscript back to Farrar & Rinehart on November 16 with a query about the status of the advance on royalties as specified by the contract. "I'm not broke—yet," he admitted to Farrar, "but a bank account is often conducive to better sleep at night." Dale also brought up the planned Mormon book, telling Farrar that "I believe I can write a book that will not only be sound history of Mormon beginnings, but an exciting exploration of American society. You wait and see!"[15]

Unfortunately, the Farrar & Rinehart editor quickly alerted Dale to the uncomfortable news that the *Humboldt* manuscript required still further trimming. In early December the firm sent a request to cut about forty pages. After two weeks of intense effort, Morgan resubmitted the revised manuscript a few days before Christmas. "For the first time I feel really happy myself about the book," he told his editor. "First I read each chapter, cutting what I could, then I went back over the chapter, page by page, counting the words on each page and seeing what more could be cut."[16] The once-neat typed pages were a bit of a mess with no time for retyping, but this version satisfied the publisher, and the book went into production.

The holidays brought a flurry of invitations. Dale had Thanksgiving dinner with Nels Anderson's family and spent Christmas with the McConkeys. Two days later, Dale typed out a long letter to John Farrar looking ahead to his next major writing project and outlining the background study he was considering prior to writing his Mormon history books. "I intend to interpret the Mormons in terms of the social forces and ideas operating in American life during the origin and growth of Mormonism.... What I expect this book actually to be is a picture of what was going on in America between 1800 and 1870—the folk beliefs and folkways of the people, and all the extraordinary pageantry. I propose to show where the Mormons got their ideas."[17]

By January 1943, after three months and when Dale still had no job, Emily Morgan began openly expressing worry about the career risk her son had taken. Dale responded kindly but firmly: "I know, of course, that you would like to have me around, and of course also I miss you all. But I came here to get a job done, and while that job is unfinished, I'll stick here, you may be sure. It will probably take me at least two years to finish the research." "In the meantime, however," he asserted, "I have this personal job to do, and for the furtherance of this job, I require a wage-earning job here in DC." He pointed out that whether living in Salt Lake City or in Washington, the employment challenges he faced would be the same, but that Washington, DC, was a much larger and more fertile field both for employment and for research. Dale was certain wartime government service ultimately would give him the edge he needed to build a competitive career: "After the war, with all the boys home from overseas again, and once more out of the army, I'll ask only for a free field and no favor."[18]

On December 18, 1942, Dale Morgan passed another milestone—his twenty-eighth birthday. Still young, full of plans and expectations, confident in his ability, he could not know the significant watershed that this birthday represented: before he had even begun the serious pursuit of a career writing history, he crossed the temporal midpoint of a too-short mortal existence.

* * * * *

In the second week of January, the job-hunting effort finally returned a result. Dale was invited to a series of interviews at the Office of Price Administration (OPA), the agency directing domestic consumer policy during the war: commodity rationing, wholesaling, and retail pricing. Morgan interviewed in the OPA branch that functioned essentially as a public relations office, charged with explaining and motivating public commitment to wartime consumer-market controls. Attracted by Dale's training in advertising and copy-writing, despite his obvious disability, Leigh Plummer's Press and Campaigns Division was short-staffed. "As I talked pretty straight to him, I evidently convinced him," Dale wrote his mother in a letter the next evening.[19] Plummer headed off to a meeting but sent Dale upstairs, and while no one else in the office was quite certain exactly where Morgan would land, only formalities remained to complete the hire.

On January 14, Dale returned to the OPA office and was introduced to Robert Kaye, supervisor in the Trade Services subunit of the Press and Campaigns Division, itself part of OPA's Information Department. Morgan explained to Charlie Kelly back in Salt Lake City that the work in that branch of the OPA office consisted primarily of writing "for retailers, wholesalers, and the trade services bulletins" concerning federal war-time pricing policies and American industry. The division did not set commodity prices but generated information to help industry officials and consumers understand national pricing policies. Their output might be reports, summaries, or press releases concerning topics such as manufacturers' reactions to pricing policy, savings made towards the war effort from imposed price ceilings, explaining the value or savings from rationing, countering black-market trading, or to answer public general pricing concerns. Translated into terms of daily activity, the job meant making editorial reviews, distilling information summaries, and abstracting consumer price policy both for industry executives and other government agencies.[20]

As Dale began working in the Information Services Division through the spring, his specific duties were largely editorial, reviewing the output of several other writers. As had happened in Ogden half a decade earlier, Morgan's assignment changed as he demonstrated just how good, dependable, and quick a writer he was. Despite his early assertion to Kelly that the work "was not as dull as it sounds," Dale's description in fact did make the job sound more interesting and his position more responsible than it actually was. Though he had been state director of the UWP with a staff ranging between twenty-six and seventy-seven, in the OPA's central Washington, DC, offices Morgan was merely a low-level editorial functionary. Dale knew that an OPA position would not be a glamorous war job when he accepted it, but remaining in this high-pressure, low-reward appointment became Morgan's opportunity to serve his country and his personal contribution to the war effort. Men his age were being assigned to battlefields they would rather avoid; the OPA was service on a more personal battlefield.

Still, despite his patriotic dedication, Dale's responsibilities did not provide the professional challenges he had met as a member of the Writers' Project, and he felt that absence most keenly. He certainly would have looked elsewhere for more rewarding work had it not been a time of sacrifice for the entire country. Years later Morgan mused to a friend that his service in the OPA used only about forty percent of his abilities. Why did he stay? Having once led the UWP, he was "determined to show that I could be a good private in the ranks as well as a general of the armies."[21] Later he regretted the choice, but during the war he stuck with it.

If the OPA job was not particularly rewarding, Morgan did enjoy OPA's location on the corner of Second and D streets, about four blocks away from both the Library of Congress and the National Archives. A year earlier, Howe forwarded to Morgan a letter of W. J. Ghent, a writer of early history of the American West, which reinforced both Howe's and Morgan's views about the primacy of documentary research for historical writing. Ghent wrote Howe that "more and more I am persuaded that much of what has been printed and circulated is at least uncertain, and some of it preposterous."[22] Morgan had already stated a low opinion of Latter-day Saint writing, but Ghent's letter helped shape his ideas about the status of scholarship on the broader American West and committed him still more deeply to primary documentation. Primary-source research snatched in bits on lunch hours, weekends, and after work, was a blessed escape from fifty- and sixty-hour work weeks at the office. Immediately after beginning at OPA, Dale continued his pattern of lunchtime research begun in the Church Historian's Office in Salt Lake City, walking quickly to one or the other repositories and poking his head into in the public reading rooms to read a few feet of newspaper microfilm or leaf through a few files of government records.

Morgan's research effort involved locating and then typing out ream after ream of transcriptions: notices, letters, reports, and articles mentioning the Mormons. While he was looking, he decided he might as well copy similar material documenting the early fur trade and exploration of the American West. With his little portable typewriter skewed on a desk beside him or perched with a wobble on his knees, or by copying them out longhand and then transcribing at home, Morgan's wartime service was the fountain for a dry river of paper rustling like the liquid sound of water. Tens of thousands of pages of transcriptions included material from War Department records about Indians and their agents, the Interior Department's territorial records series, the U.S. Geological Survey about early exploration, and General Accounting Office records about survey employees and expenses. In the evenings he retyped transcriptions and bobbed, sometimes helplessly, in another river of correspondence. Over the five years Morgan lived in Washington, he may have produced as much as 20,000 pages of transcribed matter on his lunchtime and after-hour forays. Never had federal records been canvassed so completely for information on the fur trade or exploration, and not until the Joseph Smith Papers project began in the early 2000s was such a careful, methodical search made for the contemporary records of Mormonism—and significantly it was done by one man, not by an army of volunteers nor a professional staff.

A crate of *The Humboldt: Highroad to the West* was sitting on his doorstep in the first week of May. Dale wrestled it into his apartment. The first copy out of the box was inscribed and mailed immediately to Madeline, to whom the book was dedicated. Morgan's first book was an evocation of landscape using the medium of historical essay, rather than a straightforward work of history. Grounded on an admirable grasp of source material, virtually none of which is cited directly, it was one of the few volumes in the series to have a bibliography. The book ranges widely, from the scarcity of water in a chapter titled "Rain," to the vainly, almost criminally optimistic policy of western land schemes exemplified by the deep-desert boom town of Metropolis, Nevada. For the first time, Morgan introduces readers to fur-trade explorer Jedediah Smith, who traced the river eastward across the Great Basin desert, not once, but twice in the mid-1820s. The Humboldt also provides an arc for the California trail and to address Mormon settlement of Utah Territory's western reaches.

The book's style leans strongly toward popular readers, colored with descriptive fact and detail, set down in shades of simile and metaphor. Every page is unquestionably a work of historical research but is crafted as a work of literature. Even now, decades after its writing, the book reads with a truth and timelessness that makes the brackish stretch of water and dust and sagebrush real to readers. Sadly, the relative success of this first book—the only one of his works to ever go into reprint—gave its author the confidence and expectations that he could ground a writing career in regional history on book sales alone. That goal proved to be as chimerical as the dreams that fueled those who followed the river named in the title.

On June 15, 1943, Morgan received a letter from a woman he did not know. She was also a Utahn, living in Washington while her husband worked as a naval strategist in the War Department. "I have had four people within the last fortnight," Fawn Brodie wrote Morgan, "tell me that I should by all means meet you and draw upon your phenomenal knowledge of Mormon source materials before I proceed any further with my own study."[23] A year earlier Brodie captured the fellowship offered by publisher Alfred A. Knopf for which Dale had recommended Juanita Brooks. Now Brodie was at work on her first book, a biography of Joseph Smith. She invited Dale to dinner with her family, and the pair hit it off immediately. Within weeks, they were sharing information and source material on early Mormon history between them, just as Morgan and Brooks were sharing material on the Mountain Meadows Massacre.

Eventually Dale connected his two friends as well, and introduced Brodie to Bernard DeVoto. In doing so, Dale Morgan became the central figure linking the loose group of influential literary acquaintances and friendships identified a generation later as "Mormondom's Lost Generation."[24] For Morgan, letters from this circle of distant friends offered a fulfilling after-hours distraction from his stringy, unfulfilling diet of price policy and trade-journal editorials.

Late in the summer, Morgan made a trip to New York City. A friend at OPA learned of a visiting French ear specialist who had found some success restoring hearing to deaf adults. An initial consultation suggested that Dale's auditory nerves might not have been completely dead. Morgan returned to New York in mid-November for a series of injections to stimulate the tissue sufficiently to perhaps restore some of his hearing. Both physician and patient knew the treatment was a longshot but worth the effort, though neither was surprised when it had no effect. "My ears work perfectly in all respects that I can see," he wrote his mother, "except that I don't hear with them."[25] This attempt was the only one Morgan ever personally made toward restoring his lost sense.

* * * * *

Dale's relationship with Madeline McQuown continued through the mails during Morgan's tenure in Washington, DC. The rift between Dale and Jarvis Thurston was left deep and unbridged in the two years following the divorce. Dale listened to only one side of the matter, and Madeline lost no opportunity to reshape Dale's memory of the past. She vilified Jarvis as domineering and damned him with the faintest praise, asserting that his growing body of successful publications were stolen and reworked from her poetry or story manuscripts. She also claimed he was so jealous of her talent that he tried to kill her. Dale seemed to have forgotten that Madeline's physicians in Salt Lake City had long before concluded she was a hypochondriac, that Jarvis actively protected his wife from demands throughout their marriage, and Madeline had been the one who had walked out. A year after their divorce and probably unaware that she had married Tom McQuown, Thurston wrote Madeline late in 1943, having concluded she was disinterested in repairing their relationship, and told her he had married a fellow graduate student. "I think I could draw her portrait beforehand," Madeline fumed to Dale early the next year, "All I am not—someone of no character, definitely."[26]

About a month after the OPA reorganization, Dale was asked to take on two new projects. One was a short-term assignment to produce a "general—but very complete" history of the national Home Front Pledge campaign. The history of the Home Front Pledge was not only a report but also served as a piece of subtle economic propaganda. The campaign was conducted by appealing to citizens' patriotic support for the war effort and personal ties to American servicemen in combat. The drive was widely successful. As badly as rationing and price controls were despised, federal consumer rationing successfully prevented the kind of widespread black markets and overt price gouging that plagued the country during the First World War. As he did with other routine assignments, Dale knocked off the piece from first draft to finished report in less than a month.[27]

The second project was more substantial, a weekly compilation of positive and negative industry reactions to OPA pricing policies extracted from trade journal editorials. This internal war-effort publication occupied Morgan's time for the rest of his service. In his duties as general manager of the Office of Price Administration, Chester Bowles needed to be aware of both the praise and criticisms made of his governmental charge and its policies. OPA's constituency was largely the individually committed but unorganized American consumer, but public criticism of the agency came mostly from business and industry.[28] Bowles wanted to be able to respond to industry opinions accurately and directly. To do that effectively, agency administrators needed to know what was being said.

Bowles' request for a regular summary of the trade-editorial comments made about OPA activities was routed to the Information Division at large, handed to the Trade Services Branch, and ultimately assigned to Dale. Kaye approached Morgan with the problem. In a day of strong unions and newsprint communication, data sources would be industrial newsletters and trade journals. They discussed creating some kind of digest, drawn directly from industrial publications, that was complete,

up-to-date, accurate, and short enough to be easily read and comprehended. While Morgan was given some ideas for desirable formats, the
compilation and structure of the report was left up to him. Looking at
examples of similar compilations, Dale decided against compiling time-
consuming abstracts or summaries in favor of simply copying short
extracts mentioning OPA or its policies. *What's Going On in the Business
Press* became both the title and description. To be of any value, the new
periodical had to be compiled weekly, which added enormous strain to
Dale's already substantial workload.

Though it was essentially an informal internal publication, *What's
Going On in the Business Press* provided an important barometer of
economic-sector opinion, war-production effectiveness, and consumer
pricing policy for OPA section heads; its creative young compiler found
it nothing beyond unimaginative drudge work. The time investment
proved substantial. Since his other duties now were seriously squeezed,
Dale approached his supervisors about the structure of his work. Having
put the publication on its feet, Morgan asked that, since the report was to
constitute an ongoing project, would it not be better to staff adequately at
its beginning? The administration responded by hiring an assistant, Naomi
Peres, to do much of the preliminary weekly groundwork, sifting union and
trade publication editorials and identifying OPA-related comments. Dale
was still responsible for typing the final form of the summary compilation.

Naomi's hire freed Dale to accept other short-term assignments.
Through spring 1944, he produced an extensive revision of a pamphlet
on the nature and reasons of production subsidies; an article for the trade
press on the need for enforcing price regulations through record-keeping
and about specific records to be retained for wholesale furnishings, house-
wares, hand tools, and floor covering sales; and a draft of an official "price
debate" article.[29] To complicate things, Dale's supervisor Robert Kaye
transferred out of OPA to another department in February 1944. In light
of this departure, Kaye's own supervisor in the Information Division,
Elliot Marple, asked Dale to "keep [an] eye out for Information Department copy that seems off-base." From that point *all* departmental writing
was routed through Morgan for editorial review.[30] This activity was in
addition to his regular responsibilities for the ebb and flow of specific
writing projects.

In autumn 1944, however, Peres took sick and was confined at home.
Morgan was asked to again assume her responsibilities. Naomi's absence,
however, lengthened from days to weeks, and from weeks to months.

While Dale was willing to shoulder the extra responsibility for a short time, he was unhappy with having to concentrate on the ceaseless routine of compiling *What's Going On* at the expense of being pulled from other writing jobs. As small as they were, they at least demanded some creativity. The assignment was particularly difficult to accept when Naomi finally returned to work around the turn of 1945, not to her former responsibilities, but to an assignment elsewhere in the office.

With *Humboldt* done and not yet ready to begin the "Mormon book," Morgan chafed to begin another large-scale writing project, preferably one that could be managed from his body of extant notes. An invitation and opportunity landed in his lap, unannounced. Mimicking Farrar & Rinehart's popular Rivers of America series, the Bobbs-Merrill Company initiated an American Lakes Series. By April 1944, books on the Great Lakes were already complete, and the series' scope was broadening. The publisher anticipated Utah's state centennial in 1947 and wrote Dale looking for an author to address the Great Salt Lake. Initially Dale directed the firm to Jack Thornley, who had planned to write a book on the lake for the UWP. Thornley was not in a position to do so and gave his blessing for Dale to pursue the subject if he was interested. In November the firm offered Morgan the volume.[31]

On January 15, 1945, Dale received a memorandum from his supervisor Del Beman permanently assigning him to compile and produce the weekly *What's Going On in the Business Press*. Morgan, never one himself to begrudge someone their successes or advancements, wrote a memo to Beman, explaining his frustration with the work, not "a very adequate long-time outlet for my abilities." Beman, who had replaced Robert Kaye the previous fall, was genuinely sympathetic, but his answer was that with the Trade Services Branch and the larger Editorial Services section shorthanded, and given the importance of the weekly summary to the conduct of OPA officials generally, it was important that Morgan continue to work on it. "This assignment . . . is strictly dictated by the necessity of a lack of manpower in our Division," Beman wrote back. "It does not cast any reflections upon your ability as a writer; therefore, I hope you will accept it in that spirit."[32] Dale dutifully continued reading trade editorials and producing the extractive summary every week.

Fortunately, the drudgery ended with the close of the workday and was something Dale was quite happy to leave behind him at the office. He did not, however, leave at the office either reading or his typewriter. Soon after arriving in Washington, Dale joined the city chess club, the Washington

Chess Divan. Here, for perhaps the first time in his life, Dale faced competition well above his considerable abilities at the game. While he often
placed in the top ten and occasionally in the top five players' match play,
Dale never took home a first-place finish during all the years he spent in
the city. Competitors played at a level that made an absurdity of the multi-
board stunt matches Dale had routinely won in Ogden. Chess, however,
was only an occasional diversion. Dale eventually wrote his former chess
partner Richards Durham that eventually his participation declined to
the point of managing to find time for the game as "a kind of tournament
dilettante," playing in competitions without practice or analysis. While
he had been a top-ranked player in the intermountain west, entering the
Federal Chess Club championships, he placed no better than third—and
only once, the best showing he ever managed while living in the East.[33]

* * * * *

At the turn of the 1945 New Year, the war in Europe was clearly pressing
to an inevitable Allied victory, and the Pacific Theatre was hopefully not
far behind. Dale knew his job was tied to the war, but had no real plan for
what employment would look like after the war. Should he find a permanent job now? Should he write the Mormon book first? Could he split
the difference and take a leave of absence to write as much as he could?
Lots of options were available but no real answers. Like much of what
would happen after the war, his next move could be approached only as a
calculated risk. In December 1944, Morgan finally hardened his resolve
and wrote to Milo Quaife, John Farrar, Wally Stegner, Dean Brimhall, and
Bernard DeVoto—each of them an acquaintance with a national reputation or notable position—asking them to serve as references for a John
Simon Guggenheim Memorial Foundation fellowship application. A year
earlier the foundation temporarily changed its grant terms to accommodate scholars engaged in the war effort, offering a "post-service" option
available to recipients any time after separation from war service. In late
January 1945, Dale forwarded his fat application package to the foundation's offices in New York City.

Morgan's four-and-a-half-page "Plan for Work" in the fellowship
proposal was confident and assertive. His project was not small: "The
preparation of a history of Mormonism and the Mormons with particular
reference to the influence of the Mormons upon American life since 1830,
and to the significance of the Mormons as a product and exemplar of

American ideas and social forces during that time." Upon Joseph Smith's death nearly a century earlier, an Illinois correspondent had written a New York newspaper that the Latter Day Saint prophet "was one of the most remarkable men of the age. The time for writing his history has not arrived. Men who have known him long and well, differ in their estimate of his character; the future historian alone can reconcile the contradictory statements of his friends and enemies to place him in his true position."[34] Brodie's biography of Smith was nearly complete, but Dale Morgan was convinced he was the one to fulfill that letter-writer's century-old challenge. "I am engaged," he wrote boldly to the Guggenheim Foundation committee, "with what I believe will have claims to be considered the definitive history of the Mormons."

Morgan's proposal set the religion convincingly within the broad social and geographical contexts of nineteenth-century America, pointing out that Latter-day Saints had settled not only Utah, but also contributed to the settlement of Minnesota, Wisconsin, Michigan, Iowa, Texas, and New Mexico, and played a part in the early history of South Dakota, Nebraska, Oklahoma, Idaho, California, Arizona, and Nevada. He argued—correctly, in the context of his time—that a polemic binary existed in writing about the Mormons, pointing out that it had been infected by a partisan view of the church, its people, and their past. Years later one scholar noted that studies of that era on the Latter Day Saints (and Latter-day Saints) tended to be, on one hand "designed to maintain the status quo by fostering an environment of spirituality and orthodoxy without tackling the difficult matters affecting faith," and on the other, a determined effort to expose Smith and his successors as a set of duplicitous rouges, a reality whitewashed by a later generation of culpable apologists.[35] There was not much else between the poles.

Morgan continued his proposal by asserting that two chief challenges had to be overcome when writing about the Mormons: first, the general lack of an external perspective (by which he meant one that accepted neither polarity as an interpretive basis); and second, the relative scarcity and inaccessibility of contemporary records. Morgan explained that he had addressed these problems by cultivating a meaningful interpretive position avoiding both poles of the binary and going directly to source materials. He pointed to seven years of prior research, tens of thousands of pages of compiled notes and transcripts gleaned from not only Mormon sources but also newspapers and books in the Library of Congress and previously unexplored government records in National Archives. The plan presented to complete the work seemed reasonable and manageable: a road trip between local government institutions and libraries to see the original records and manuscripts that did not exist in national or state institutions. He stated up-front that he was angling for a two-year project: six months of research, another six of intense writing, and a year—perhaps granted as a renewal—of additional effort on second and third volumes for a series of three.[36]

The undertaking was huge, sprawling, and complicated. He was, Dale later confided to Fawn Brodie, "appalled by the extent of my own ignorance, yet I have practically no time to repair it."[37] Morgan was convinced that an abstractly objective reliance on documentary resources could stake out a real, defensible middle ground, but one resting firmly on naturalistic perspective. The problem was, that by privately dismissing the motivations of faith and reality of Divinity, he set himself up on the "detractors" side of the 1940s binary. His action was, however, an important early step toward a modern scholarly view of Latter Day Saint experience.

With the fellowship application submitted, Morgan continued his OPA office slog through the rest of the spring, interspersed with letters to dozens of correspondents and chatty round-robin letters about overland travel across Utah between correspondents Rod Korns and Charlie Kelly. The three men independently discovered that the pre-Mormon history of the region was badly understood. Their shared letters were a step toward teasing out the intricacies of movement and geography. Each was convinced the historical record could and should be corrected and refined. In February, Morgan wrote to both friends that "I may ultimately write an article on the parties going east and west along the Oregon and California trails in 1846, trying to work out some chronologies and so on."[38] He would do so in years to come, though in a much larger work than a mere journal article.

A letter from the Guggenheim Foundation arrived on April 7, 1945. Tearing open the envelope and unfolding the sheet within, Morgan was relieved to read "I have the honor to inform you that the Trustees of the Foundation today, upon the nomination of the Committee of Selection, have approved your appointment to a post-Service Fellowship" with its award of a $2,000 stipend supporting his research, equivalent to nearly a year of his OPA salary.[39] He was in good company, ranked among forty-four post-service fellows for 1945, including the likes of composer Samuel Barber, historian C. Vann Woodward, and sound researcher Leo L. Beranek (whose company would build the first routing switches making up the Internet two decades later). This list complemented a longer list of fellows for the year who were not post-service awards, including intellectual historian Jacques Barzun, mathematician Paul Erdös, and composer Lukas Foss. The awards lists were published in the foundation's printed announcement. Within weeks, Morgan began receiving letters from publishers soliciting submission of the work he would produce on the fellowship. The interest was flattering, but the book was committed morally if not contractually to Farrar & Rinehart. "My postwar future has become a little clearer," Dale wrote when reporting the good fortune to his mother. "After all this works out, what kind of existence I'll lead I dunno [*sic*]; but I'll leave that to its own time. Maybe I'll then be able to live by my own writing; or maybe if I want to work for a salary, some library or institution will want to 'buy' the kind of authority I can expect to be by that time."[40]

The "post-service" Guggenheim Fellowship was good news and could be activated any time in the next several years, but at closer range, the Great Salt Lake book had to be completed before launching the Mormon project. Based on his memory of the outline he had produced for a prospective UWP book on the lake in September 1940, Morgan sent Bobbs-Merrill and Detroit-based series editor Milo Quaife an outline for the chapter divisions.

Dale made a rail trip home to Salt Lake City late in April 1945. Emily Morgan was thrilled to have her eldest home to fuss over. Still, the vacation was a working one, an opportunity to look at the lake and reconnect with the salty wetness of its shores and the bordering communities that largely ignored it. He also wrote encouragement to Brooks on her Mountain Meadows Massacre research and its writing, suggesting that the Huntington Library might publish such a work. Before she finished, Dale recommended Juanita approach First Presidency counselor David O. McKay about access to church sources on the premise "that such a book *is* going to be written regardless of how the Church feels about it, and by no friendly critic."[41] Less than a month later, Heber J. Grant passed away, and Morgan revised his suggestion. The book by McKay's niece, Fawn Brodie, was by this time in production with a publication date close to the end of the year. Whether Latter-day Saints were comfortable with it or not, the landscape of Latter Day Saint history was about to change.

Dale spent two days with Korns and Kelly scouting Emigration and Weber Canyons to pick out the precise routes followed by pre-Mormon emigrants. He spent another day with Maurice Howe, who was passing through town on Social Security Administration business and was invited to dinner at the Morgans. Always glad to see his friend, Dale was neverthe-less alarmed to see that Howe was gaining weight, tired easily, and looked unnaturally pale, slack, and lethargic. A trip to the increasingly cramped Utah State Historical Society room in the Capitol, his first since leaving Salt Lake City three years earlier, extracted from him a pledge to generate a series of formal suggestions to direct and reinforce Marguerite Sinclair's effort to build the institution. In all, the trip was pleasant, if busy.

Returning to Washington, DC, during the second week of May, Morgan first wrote out the promised series of programmatic recommen-dations, concrete steps the Utah Historical Society could take toward reorganizing as Utah's modern research institution. Notably, he stated, the society needed a real director, the state needed an actual archive for its records, and the *Utah Historical Quarterly* needed to be resurrected to catch up its numbering and begin publication as a genuine journal.[42]

V-E Day in May brought relief from war-borne anxiety to millions of families. Dale's younger male cousins soon began returning from overseas postings. At the end of the first full week of June, Dale was handed a note at work. His mother was on the telephone for him. Her calls were infre-quent, marking the occasion as something serious. Someone in the office acted as intermediary as Emily told Dale that Maurice Howe had died at home in Denver earlier in the week. Lucie's brother had telephoned Emily with the news to pass along to Dale. Dale acknowledged the per-sonal debt he owed Howe for developing his interest into a career as an historian. "[M]ore than any other single person, perhaps, he contributed to my professional growth."[43]

By July, Dale and Darel McConkey still lunched more or less regularly, but the Great Salt Lake book had become all-consuming. Dale left his apartment for work before 8 a.m. and worked until returning home just before 7 p.m. After a quick supper he typically hammered on the text or correspondence queries until turning in around midnight.

Relief and some extra free time came for Dale in the first week of August as OPA employees were no longer *required* to work Saturdays. Government workers in Washington huddled closely around office radios the next week after a pair of atomic blasts incinerated the Japanese cities of Hiroshima and Nagasaki, and expectations of an end to war heightened. Dale went to visit Anna McConkey, who was in the hospital having just delivered the McConkeys' fourth child, Thomas. While they visited, the friends became aware of a growing racket in the street. News of Japan's unconditional surrender had broken on news wires, and the national capital went wild. Dale walked out of the hospital to push his way to the streetcar through crowds cheering madly in relief. "I didn't myself exactly feel like a wild celebration," he wrote his mother with a note of personal introspection. "This war has cost us and the world too much, and my principal reaction was one of profound gratitude that the killing was over, that my brothers and cousins and friends have come safely through, and that now we can make a beginning on the very hard work of creating a peace and a new world that can endure."[44]

Government offices closed in celebration on August 15 and 16, the first workday closures since 1942. Dale spent both days fact-checking data for his lake book, though he took some time outdoors to sketch for the first time in several years. With national fuel rationing finally over, Darel McConkey picked up Dale for lunch on August 20 after filling the gas tank of the family car for the first time since the war began.

The watchwords in the country became *reversion* and *reconversion*—a return to social and economic normalcy. Four days after V-J Day the business-dominated War Production Board (WPB) revoked nearly a third of federal restrictions on production of high-price durable consumer goods. The action set up an inevitable policy conflict between the industrial/manufacturing-advocacy perspective of WPB administrator Julius Krug and the small-business/consumer-protection strategy OPA administrator Chester Bowles preferred. Bowles recommended keeping price controls in place long enough for production to meet public demand for consumer goods and wait for demand to decline. Doing so would head off runaway inflation, but the economic-policy fight was one in which Bowles was outmaneuvered and inevitably lost.[45]

The federal workweek also was officially cut back from six days to five days and to a standard forty hours beginning September 1, 1945. The new schedule left Morgan free on Saturdays for the first time since entering federal employment three years earlier, but the extra time off was a foretaste of things to come. Shortly before the former combatants officially signed the surrender documents aboard the *USS Missouri,* Dale mused to Fawn Brodie that the end of the war "merely armed the time bomb which has been in place in my life since April."[46] Fully immersed in the Great Salt Lake book, he now had to begin thinking and planning toward the Mormon book as well. Any plan involving the Guggenheim Fellowship now hinged directly on his employment and eventual termination from the Office of Price Administration. As ever, Dale's attention to enticing future projects was dragged back to present realities by the commitment at hand. Drafts for *The Great Salt Lake*'s first chapters were handed to Darel McConkey for critique in August. After he and Anna had both read them through, McConkey helped Morgan shape the work into something more evocative and less straightforwardly factual.[47]

Fawn Brodie's book was not yet out, slated for publication in November, when she wrote Dale late in the month that the RLDS church had acquired a set of galleys for her biography, *No Man Knows My History*, from a Knopf employee. The church was "yelping" about the book but made no rebuttal. Brodie felt it boded ominously of the reaction in Utah once the book was on store shelves. Engaged in preparing an edited version of the Howard Stansbury/John W. Gunnison exploration diaries, that sort of concern did not worry Morgan—much. By concentrating on Western geographic exploration the Mormons faded somewhat into the background.

Needing to clear his commitments and get to work on the Great Salt Lake book, in mid-October Dale asked Marguerite Sinclair for a commitment on the *Utah Historical Quarterly*'s publication for the Stansbury/Gunnison work. The Society's secretary was not in a position to promise anything. Board of Control chair Herbert Auerbach's death in March 1945 threw the state's historical society into a simmering conflict over priorities and control. She could not publish anything without the Board's approval, and the Board refused to provide Sinclair any help with functions. Morgan abandoned further work on the Stansbury/Gunnison diaries and never had the time or inclination to find another publication venue. This work was not the first of his to be abandoned, partially finished, beside the trail and certainly would not be the last.

Two books published by Alfred A. Knopf arrived in Morgan's mail toward the end of October and sparked in him completely different reactions. The first was Maurine Whipple's *This is the Place: Utah!*, for which the *Saturday Review of Literature* commissioned Morgan as a reviewer. He was not complimentary. In fact, Dale pointed out that passages in the book bore a striking and unattributed resemblance to sections of a 1941 work, *Utah: A Guide to the State*. The other book was a pre-publication copy of *No Man Knows My History*, Fawn Brodie's biography of Joseph Smith. "From 11 a.m. to midnight I accomplished absolutely nothing except a visit to the grocery store," Dale wrote Fawn. "I think that is a sufficient summation of your book, that on the third reading in three years, and after all that has gone into it, I can be spellbound by it still, and read in it with absolute fascination."[48]

Readers elsewhere were not as complimentary. The Church Historian's Office staff had struggled when confronted with the WPA's insistence on direct, uninspiring versions of history. In Brodie's book, Latter Day Saint culture experienced essentially the same disjunction faced by Christians when Christianity's *primitive naiveté* and utilitarian approach to church history collided with historicism. Facts kept surfacing for which tradition did not account, and church tradition could not muster supportive evidence for itself. Believing scholars eventually came to understand that history does not invalidate belief, but it does challenge belief to provide evidential bases for its assumptions.[49]

Brodie's biography was a naturalistic explanation of Smith and his religious career. That wasn't the problem. The great challenge to Latter Day Saint psyche posed by *No Man Knows My History*—and the potential threat Morgan's own work represented—was less in Brodie's interpretations (which Hugh Nibley challenged in the contemporary *No Ma'am, That's Not History* [Bookcraft, 1946]) than the body of unimpeachable documentation on which its conclusions were based—and they were not church sources. As she was beginning her research, determined to get away from faith-promoting secondary works and into sources contemporary to Smith, she found a sympathetic ear in M. Wilford Poulson of Brigham Young University. "I am astonished," Poulson wrote her encouragingly, "that both Mormon and non-M[ormon] students and writers have so very seldom felt the need of delving energetically and long into all possible source materials to find out as much of the truth [i.e., historical facts] as possible."[50]

The 1930s had kicked off a new era of archival spadework by Brodie, Morgan, Stanley S. Ivins, and their contemporaries, which brought to light many new sources and a determination to fit explanations to the evidence. Once the issue of a contradictory historicism was in the open, it could not be tucked back where it came from. "I agree with you that a definitive biography of Joseph Smith can hardly be written without access to the original material in the LDS Church library," Ivins later wrote to a colleague, "but as one who has tried to work there, I cannot share your optimism in regard to the availability of this material to researchers. I'm afraid we will wait a long time for a better biography than the one Mrs. Brodie has written."[51] Juanita Brooks wrote Dale that "if Mormon laiety [sic] will not read it, Mormon scholars should. Some of them will. And the book cannot but have its effect, and in the long run, a very profound effect."[52]

Most stores in Utah's urban centers sold but did not advertise "the Brodie book" publicly, and church-related stores like the ZCMI department store and Deseret Book, both owned by the church, did not stock the volume at all.[53] Nevertheless the book was available and discussed far more widely in Utah and Missouri than church officials liked. Book groups reviewed and discussed it (often negatively), but copies quietly passed hand to hand in Utah, and in the rest of the country, the book sold. Officially, Brodie's *No Man Knows My History* was publicly decried, but both churches failed to put out a credible counterweight to the new set of facts and the interpretation that accompanied them. After the initial outcry, stony silence ensued, but the book continued to sell, reprinted a second time in January 1946 and a third time the following June. Later in the year the church's publisher rushed a reprint of John Henry Evans' popular 1933 biography *Joseph Smith: An American Prophet*.[54] "The controversy stirred up has accentuated the division of the Mormons into orthodox, less orthodox and still less orthodox groups," Stan Ivins reported.[55]

Morgan's firm hold on naturalistic interpretations reflected the influence of secondary material as well. For instance, his 1943 editing of Wilson Wallis's dissertation on messiah figures seems to have reinforced this view, arriving at the point that religious figures are pretentious poseurs and often "pathologic" or intentionally deceptive. "In all ages," wrote Wallis, beginning his second chapter, "the messiah [figure] has been a divine apostle of hope."[56] Morgan perceived the generalized yearning for hope Wallis describes in the fear and escapist theologies of the Burned-Over District. Wallis never described the historical figures as charlatans, but the way he handled the fantastic claims and stories left little room for other characterizations. Though avoiding prejudicial language, Wallis painted these religious figures as self-deluded wishers or self-interested charlatans and mountebanks. Followers, the author treated as credulous naïfs. For Morgan, it was a simple step to add Joseph Smith Jr. to the litany of Wallis's descriptively explained figures like the Leatherwood God, the Bedford church in Jamaica, and dozens of other Christian-based self-proclaimed prophets, selfish deliverers, and would-be millennial heralds. Joseph Smith's call to renewed faith and personal commitment to God got buried in recounting his fantastic claims of angels, visitations, gold plates, and stones in hats that marked him, to Morgan's mind, with the others which Wallis described. Beyond the assertions of believers and scripture, which had its own host of historical problems, religion offered for its central tenets none of the empirical evidence Morgan craved. It was non-evidentiary. Conversely, though Dale later read John M. Mecklin's *The Story of American Dissent,* he could not fit Joseph Smith's angels, visitations, gold plates, disgruntled apostates, and failed business ventures into the principled, ethical, and genuinely religious perspective on American religious dissent that Mecklin portrayed. The Mormons as principled believers simply did not match the story Morgan perceived in the documents he found.[57]

Why was Brodie's and Morgan's historical naturalism—which might be considered *scientism*—so threatening? Partly because of a historical assertion that believers had made for decades. The Book of Mormon had been cited as convincing evidence that Joseph Smith was a prophet. But focusing attention on the book itself (and by implication, the reality of divine authority and revelation) left open a deficit regarding the mechanism and process of the book's production. For three generations Mormons had *asserted* revelation; content in their own beliefs and assumptions they had failed to *define* what revelation was or how it worked in terms that explain the book. For many believers, revelation needed to be understood as something apart from common experience so it would not be mistaken for something else, but that left a descriptive vacuum. By digging into the objective verity of the book's production itself, Brodie and Morgan challenged the validity of the assertion, and by implication, of divine revelation itself.

The inevitable negative reaction to Brodie's book among all his Latter Day Saint contacts was a warning claxon for Morgan. Even his mother was concerned about the prospective reception his own history would receive, writing Dale that she "wonder[ed] about the close association you had with [Fawn Brodie] on it and if you also will come in for a share of the criticism. Perhaps you, yourself, are unconcerned about it but I always have so many people ask me about you and your feelings." "To you facts are facts," she worried, "but there are some things that I am sensitive about and it is rather hard to explain."[58] Her concern flooded his resolve. His work, which took an interpretive position similar to *No Man Knows My History* but was of a far broader scope, would elicit similar criticism.

Morgan calculated correctly. Defenders among the Latter Day Saints in the 1940s knew how to handle detractors and sensationalists. They had done so effectively for two generations, but they were unprepared for the new perceived assault of historicism. This contribution made Brodie's biography arguably the most significant study of Latter Day Saint history published during the twentieth century. How did one argue against a factual context? For those who accept an ethical or utilitarian view of history, the most suitable means was straightforward denial and denunciation. The Latter Day Saints of both traditions reacted to Brodie's biography by retrenchment. Rather than make available primary source material from church holdings to counter her conclusions, access to the Church Historian's Office in Salt Lake City was restricted even further, seemingly on the idea that without sources no more inconvenient histories could be written.

Dale complained to Jerry Bleak that Latter-day Saint officialdom's response to Brodie's biography amounted to "a sort of ostrich-like burial of the collective Utah head in the sand, and what good did it do, when all is said and done? Everybody heard about it, and everybody who troubles to read books or keep up with what's going on in the world of books read it anyhow."[59] Unfortunately, for the churches, the action came just at a time that at least the large research institutions were actively building substantial Mormon collections. Unless the churches were willing to discuss interpretations of their history other than as faith-promoting triumphalism, they could not propose a reasonable alternative account.

* * * * *

Despite working furiously on the lake book, Morgan's correspondence with Bernard DeVoto picked up, resulting in a series of long letters back and forth between Washington and Boston, each defending or challenging the interpretation of Joseph Smith as a paranoid personality. The round-robin flow of trail-related information about emigration across Utah between Kelly, Korns, and Morgan continued unabated. Korns, however, was trying to manage blood pressure and heart problems. Kelly encouraged Morgan to write something about fur trader and explorer Jedediah Smith. Dale brushed him off. Months earlier he had queried the Hudson's Bay Record Society for data from the seminal but tightly controlled Peter Skene Ogden journal of 1824–1825. A reply came months later declining to supply data since the society slated the volume for future publication in its records series. "Some day I may attempt a really ambitious study of Jedediah Smith's life," Morgan told Kelly, "but it won't be until the [Peter Skene] Ogden journal of 1824–25 has been published."[60]

With OPA office work, his constant correspondence, and the vagaries of daily life, Dale finally wrote Bobbs-Merrill president D. L. Chambers that it was unlikely he would be able to complete and submit the *Great Salt Lake* manuscript by its December 31, 1945 due date. The delay created for him an uncomfortable situation, he noted, because he had planned to spend most of 1946 concentrating on the Mormon book. He would, instead, deal with the lake. The month between the holidays was devoted to ever-increasing numbers of letters to and from historical societies, researchers, scholars, and those with a family interest in the lake, exploring details as minor as the number of sailboats in the Great Salt Lake Yacht Club. Through January, Morgan ground away on the *Great Salt Lake* manuscript, falling further and further behind on personal goals for his writing pace. "Authoring is a tough racket, but there is nothing better for a writer's ego than to have his book moving along," he told his mother, "just as there is nothing more corroding than to be stalled."[61]

Dale drafted the *Great Salt Lake* manuscript between assignments at work and every evening until midnight. Saturdays and Sundays were given wholly to the task. He recruited and paid one of the typists at work, Mary Gaither, to produce a clean typescript for Milo Quaife to review as series editor. In the middle of the month, a letter from IBM's *Think* magazine editor offered Dale the then-substantial sum of $200 for a 2,000-word article on the Great Salt Lake—equivalent to nearly $3,000 presently. Rather than take time to write out a reply, Morgan simply sat down and typed out the article, sending it to the company as his acceptance.[62] Something in his schedule had to give, and the weak link again was chess. After his third-place finish, Dale now limited his playing to correspondence games only, and once he embarked on the Guggenheim Fellowship travel and for the rest of his life, he played rarely.

While Dale wrestled the Great Salt Lake manuscript, Congress wrestled with loosening the statutory holds imposed on consumer goods during the war. By necessity, the Office of Price Administration and the latter's hold on consumer regulations were a major topic of concern. During the war, production of consumer goods like washing machines and homes was limited in favor of production of guns, uniforms, war planes, and ships. Now in the middle of 1946, the situation Chester Bowles feared a year earlier stared Congressmen squarely in the face. Corporations had been willing to endure a planned economy during the war, but with the dismantling of the War Production Board, business leaders were chafing to have free hands in not only open production but in open consumer markets again. Civilian bank accounts were fat with unspent wages from war-production jobs and military service. Manufacturers wanted the money that had piled, unspent, into savings accounts. Consumer goods had not been produced in substantive quantity since 1942 and Americans were eager for new cars, new fashions, conveniences, and appliances for new suburban homes. New legislation in Congress directly targeted the activities and power of the Office of Price Administration and the price ceilings which could be charged for goods available during the war. Under the pressure of business interests, Congress eventually repealed price controls and OPA's neck was slated for the chopping block.[63]

After much cajoling on Dale's part, Madeline McQuown arrived in late June to pursue research for her Brigham Young biography while Dale still had a place in Washington to house her. She lasted less than two weeks in the summer heat before bolting for Maine. Once there, after dropping Morgan a postcard that things were "somewhat awq" for her and that she was thinking of returning, Dale took her to task for leaving without notice or an explanation. Madeline wrote again from New York blasting her friend for an "inhuman lack of understanding" and archly citing her physical inability to endure high temperatures. She took a train home to Utah from New York City.[64]

Meanwhile, congressional wrangling about pricing sidelined most OPA employees until either a funding or decommissioning bill was passed. Not Morgan. As the editor of the department's digest, his workload increased tremendously as industry publications increased editorial pressure to end price controls. The work left him less time to write the Great Salt Lake book. Whether or not OPA was decommissioned did not trouble Dale, who was eager to complete the book so that he could take up the Guggenheim fellowship. Morgan accomplished virtually nothing on the manuscript or research for a month, then completed the *Great Salt Lake* manuscript during weeks of late-night work, sending it to Indianapolis in late October. The result was presented in not only evocative writing, but also extraordinarily well-documented by standards of the time. "Many a scholarly book of the 1940s contained less unpublished information, and was based on far fewer hours of research, than *The Great Salt Lake*," Ray Allen Billington later observed.[65]

By the time the manuscript was in, Congress finally killed the Office of Price Administration. For his part, Dale was scrimping for the coming adventure. Ironically, just as he was mentally preparing for the cross-country drive (though he did not yet have a car; they were unobtainable in the East and Madeline was looking for a used one for him in Utah), two job opportunities arrived within days of each other. The first was from former OPA supervisor Bob Kaye, who asked if Dale would be interested in a temporary editorial position in New York City. The other came from Marguerite Sinclair. J. Cecil Alter was resigning as editor of the *Utah Historical Quarterly*.

As Utah Historical Society secretary, she offered Morgan the position on a salary. Either would have taken him in directions toward which he would have jumped a few years earlier. Eager to embark on his masterwork and wary of distraction from his goal, Morgan declined both.[66]

After nearly a year's negotiation, Madeline found Dale a car, a Hudson dealer's personal vehicle. After wrangling over payment options, taxes, insurance, and license, Madeline completed the purchase in late 1946. She agreed to drive the car to Dale in Washington, DC, also an opportunity to complete the research she had begun in July. He at last had a firm travel option. On the day before Thanksgiving, which he spent with friends Max and Louise North, Morgan received his OPA furlough letter. He would separate from federal employment in thirty days from its post-dated delivery of November 30, pending recall if a transfer to the History section was enacted, after which accrued leave would be paid him until February 26, 1947.[67]

While he waited through the holidays, Dale began planning a ten-hour daily research regimen for the two months of paid leave available to him. Too much remained to be done in various federal archives to justify a March 1 departure, so Dale planned to leave Washington on May 1. "Without a tear," he quipped to Juanita Brooks in mid-December, "I am bidding farewell to the government, and come the first of the year, I shall be exclusively in the Dale L. Morgan business, for as long as I can yield a living from it."[68] Just before Christmas he turned down an offer to remain an extra month with OPA. Freedom was too enticing. But then Bobbs-Merrill's castoff of the *Great Salt Lake* manuscript put its estimated length far above what the firm calculated as a retail price for the book. To meet the production schedule required Morgan to cut dozens of pages from his labor, a task which had to be completed in just one week.

With the newly tailored manuscript in production a month later, the publisher wrote asking innocently whether the Church of Jesus Christ of Latter-day Saints had approved the book and asking the author's opinion about sending a carbon there for review. Dale fired back a response that "only over my dead body" would he agree to give the church an advance look at his work. Planning to eventually write several books on the Mormons and with Utah's Pioneer centennial coming up, he wanted no precedent established that would give the church reason to think that publication of anything relating to the state hung on their approval.[69] The Bobbs-Merrill's salesman, however, was not done. After talking with bookstores in Utah, he balked at allowing Morgan's characterization of Brodie's

No Man Knows My History as "brilliant" to stand in the end-matter, fearing it would compromise sales in the church's headquarters. Morgan refused to be baited or to change a word in his book, willing to let the work's quality (and an unexpectedly positive review from apostle John A. Widtsoe) answer complaints raised by marketing. "Even with Dr. Widtsoe's review," he wrote Juanita with a touch of disdain, Salt Lake City booksellers were "lying low till they got a better idea of the Church reaction."[70]

Galleys consumed Morgan's attention through the first week of January 1947. Thereafter he plunged back into his intense daily schedule of research, beginning in the Library of Congress newspaper collection, interspersed with map proofs, and photo captions.[71] Morgan bumped into another Guggenheim Fellow while working at National Archives, Carlos Bosch García, a Mexican diplomatic historian. Bosch García's wife, Concepción, was the daughter of José Giral, head of the Spanish Republican government in exile. The trio immediately struck up a friendship, based partly on Dale's fascination with the striking, dark-eyed woman.

The first royalty check for *The Great Salt Lake* was not due until April, but Dale was able to squeak by on OPA leave and a commission to write an essay on the character of Utah's capital for a forthcoming book on western cities.[72] The rest of January was devoted to page proofs, and completing an index dribbled into February. In the middle of February, Morgan wrote to the Guggenheim Foundation, activating his fellowship effective March 15. "It is an exhilarating thing to enter upon a fellowship of this kind and be freed, after a fashion, to create the best book that it is in me to write," he told the foundation's officer, "I expect this year to come, notwithstanding the worries that are sure to attend it, to be one of the most stimulating of my life."[73] Within days he had his fellowship recommendation letter and a check covering the first installment on the grant.

By then however, the stress of his intense research began to take a toll on his eyes. Dale noticed he was having trouble focusing, even with his glasses. He planned to cut back from fourteen-hour days reading newspapers and microfilm to something much more manageable. And to get new glasses. Madeline sent Dale a bill for repairs to the Hudson, which she had been driving for four months, and together they began planning for her eastward trip with the vehicle. Not knowing exactly how much the journey would cost, she wanted *carte blanche*. Dale responded that he was saving for the trip and offered her a specific figure. "It shocks me to think that you stick so rigidly to a budget that you would ruin [a trip] for me just to stay on it," she responded caustically.[74]

On the last day of March, Dale returned home to find a box of *The Great Salt Lake* waiting on his doorstep. He inscribed the first copy out of it to Madeline, as the book had arrived on her birthday. Out on bookseller shelves in time for sales at the church spring General Conference and the state centennial, the book was praised highly. Arthur L. Crawford of the University of Utah wrote the author directly, noting that "as a citizen of Utah, I am proud that we have at last produced an historian with the stability of purpose and the breadth of understanding, coupled with the artistry of a master of literature that is necessary to make an author rate as an historian of the first rank."[75]

The twenty chapters carefully cited specific data on geology, bird life, salt mining, sailing, and racing, but the heart of the story, as in *Humboldt,* was the people who explored and even settled on the lake: Jim Bridger's purported discovery, Jedediah Smith and John C. Frémont's near disasters, the Howard Stansbury survey, exile John Baptiste, and the Wenner family. More importantly the author provided a foretaste of how Mormon history would be treated. *The Great Salt Lake* turned out unwittingly to be Morgan's only published comment on Latter-day Saint history outside *The State of Deseret.* In the book he cataloged the roisterous relationships between Mormons, non-Mormons, and ex-Mormons. Less combative than it could have been, Morgan's choice of conflicts still made Pioneer-era Utah seem slightly less inspiring and more conflicted than the master narrative expected it to be, yet far more believably human.

The book also was strongly geographical, with the lake serving as a reckoning point for the stories which crawl around its shores and occasionally creep across its surface. But since Salt Lake City sits hard against the lake, separated from its peripatetic shores by a few miles of salt marsh and marl, the lake provides a foil for the characters that goaded each other in political and economic intrigue, vying for dominance in the City of the Saints and the territory and state which surround it. The saga was good history and better storytelling, but not inspirational. Morgan was flattered by the praise but pointed out that like *Humboldt, The Great Salt Lake* was "merely a by-product" of his major work. Eventually he expected to "tackle the farther West, in a series of books beginning with Lewis and Clark, continuing through the era of the mountain men and that of the occupation of the West, its exploitation, and so on down."[76] Dale Morgan was thinking well beyond the Mormons.

* * * * *

In early April Madeline alerted Dale that she had left Salt Lake City in the Hudson, without providing advance notice or an itinerary. She wrote again from Omaha upon receiving word that her mother's blood pressure was bad. In Chicago she dashed off a note that she dropped the Hudson in a local AAA garage and was taking a train back to Salt Lake City immediately; her mother lay dying. Dale would have to retrieve the car himself.[77] Under the circumstances Morgan could do nothing but drop everything, but was not happy about doing so. "It is as much for [your own] psychological reasons as for your mother's sake that you are returning to Utah," he wrote from the train west as it passed through Harrisburg, Pennsylvania, "in this respect I am again sorry that you would not come psychologically half way to meet me."[78] "The whole trouble has seemed to originate with you," she fired back bluntly in August. "What you want of me is marriage . . . nothing else will satisfy you. Am I right? You have asked me to marry you often enough."[79] The Morgan-McQuown relationship, now solely a correspondence, remained stormy, with Dale bluntly analytical and craving her "intimacy" and Madeline platonically needy, both of them certain in their emotions and unwilling to give an inch to the other.

But Dale at last had the car. The 1942 Hudson Commodore Eight was neither sleek nor sporty. Like most cars of the time the sedan was a squat, bulky room on wheels. Dale had no time to admire his purchase. In mid-June he took the car on a road test to visit the McConkeys in West Virginia. Rather than return to Washington, DC, Dale drove to New York for a month of sleeping in his sister's spare bedroom in a spacious Brooklyn apartment, where one of the neighbors was New York Philharmonic maestro Arturo Toscanini. The accommodation allowed him to cull the New York Public Library's collections, sparing him a future detour. A huge order for microfilm allowed him to take some source material away with him, but nearly bankrupted his account. Then brother-in-law Doug Barton received a transfer from the Army, ordering him and the family from Brooklyn to Fort Leavenworth, Kansas. Dale helped the family pack hurriedly as the movers arrived. Things worked out. By September the Bartons were settled and had space for him also in their barracks accommodations, a far cry from the comforts of Brooklyn but a base of operations reasonably close to another major destination in Independence, Missouri.

Dale was home again in Washington, DC, by the middle of July. In addition to last-minute research, Morgan's pending departure periodically required him to squat and pivot in his one-room apartment, hands filled with jumbled stacks of paper, trying to sort three years of an enormous and growing accumulation of incoming and outgoing letters, transcripts, and notes littering every available surface. Packing had to happen before he could leave, and some semblance of organization had to be imposed before packing.

Time compressed as the calendar fell away. In early August 1946, Dale wrote Fawn Brodie that in the Library of Congress he had read every available newspaper from Ohio, Illinois, Missouri, and Iowa published prior to 1849; "there is hardly a phase of trans-Mississippi history for that period that I could not rewrite."[80] Most of the late summer was devoted to more newspaper reading, which stretched daily until the Library closed at 10 p.m. Other than a day trip to Baltimore and the Enoch Pratt Free Library, he was too broke to travel further.

As travel plans and an itinerary were finalized for his cross-country research expedition, Stan Ivins noted a number of Mormon-related publications to which he had found references but could not locate copies. Dale checked the titles in the Library of Congress's National Union Catalog without finding them listed there either. He decided to keep the citations as notes to look for on his coming travel and began dispatching letters to librarians across the country to expect him during the coming year. Morgan handed notice of his plan to vacate his apartment to Maud Hildreth, his landlord, on September 1. Later that day he drove Carlos and Concepción Bosch García south along the Potomac River to visit Max and Louise North, who were busily building a house on twelve acres of an old farmstead outside Accokeek, Maryland. Also in September, Madeline McQuown finally completed a cross-country drive, this time with husband Tom in tow. They arrived mid-month on their own circuitous research trip, remaining as guests at Dale's apartment until the day before he left himself on October 1.

Dale Morgan's stay in wartime Washington was a personal odyssey, a patriotic commitment to the nation. It provided him a convenient opportunity to launch himself seriously into primary source material, federal records being a historical resource not yet adequately tapped by predecessors or contemporaries. He was both committed and prepared. By the time he was ready to depart, Dale Morgan had embarked on a writing career.

CHAPTER 8

"It Is Best to Make the Most of My Opportunities"[1]

The Guggenheim Fellowship Travel and Salt Lake City, 1947–1949

> *If we wait for that theoretically "normal" time to come around before doing anything, we never will get it done. The only system that works is to superimpose . . . things on the general disorder and live happily in the state of confusion.*[2]
>
> —Dale Morgan

DALE DROVE THE LOADED HUDSON down Key Boulevard on October 1, 1947, made a left, and then a right turn across the Francis Scott Key Bridge. US 1 led him north out of Washington, DC. He was, finally, setting out to live as he had long hoped: "on my wits and my typewriter."[3] Dale pulled away relying on the kindness of his apartment manager to superintend shipping 22 crates of his books, another nine of miscellaneous files and papers, and two four-drawer steel filing cabinets bulging with transcripts—three-quarters of a ton of material requiring nearly a month's salary to transport across the country to his mother's home on Hollywood Drive.[4]

"I am glad at last to have reached the payoff point on all these years of research," he wrote his publisher and fellowship reference, Stanley Rinehart, a few days later when announcing his embarkation, "and from now on books are going to issue from my typewriter with some frequency— we hope. So far they have been byproducts; now I get to grips with the books I hope to be remembered by."[5]

Through the late autumn mists and remaining days of October and into November Dale trailed between Mormon sites and library collections in

Vermont and New Hampshire. The late-fall landscape that had flamed in oranges, reds, and yellows was dying to the duns and grays of skeletal trees standing in heaps like cold ashes on the slopes. The ancient, weathered, rolling hills posed a stark contrast to the vertical angularities Dale knew in the Wasatch and the Rocky Mountains.

For the next several months Morgan travelled New England, to the birthplace of Mormonism in upstate New York, then to Ohio, Michigan, Illinois, and on to Missouri. His Thanksgiving holiday was a hasty meal in a roadside diner, but he was at the home of Ruth and Doug in Fort Leavenworth for Christmas. Despite the fellowship's financial support, money was short, and his travel itinerary was repeatedly but irregularly compromised by the Hudson. As the trip wore into its fourth week, the car became hard to start, and curiously, especially with the engine warm. It was an ill omen. Over the several months of the rest of the trip, travel was marred by three blown tires and plagued by inexplicable mechanical malfunctions no one seemed able to identify and even less able to fix. Dale was forced into a series of shops for repairs both minor and major, car trouble eating insatiably into his fellowship funding. The trip was otherwise largely uneventful, except for the troublesome automobile.

In Detroit, Milo Quaife's collection on James J. Strang and his following contained a trove of incredibly rare printed material, much of which was known from only two or three copies, and many of which had not been described in any library. As Dale worked, he slowly began to realize that the published record of Mormonism itself was a topic worth studying, and that asking about printed material opened doors to manuscript material. Dale began writing queries to the scattered members of other branches of Mormonism, seeking information and confirming details on printed works. From Chicago, he finally gave form to an idea as he wrote ahead to Israel A. Smith, president of the Reorganized Church of Jesus Christ of Latter Day Saints, that "it is my expectation to publish in advance of my history a critical bibliography of every title and edition of works by or about the Mormons printed down to 1849."[6] A distraction? Maybe, but not long thereafter he expressed a truism of the time, observing to a friend that "anyone who works in the field of Mormonism must do everything himself. The tools of the trade are simply nill."[7]

Spending the Christmas holidays with his sister's family in Fort Leavenworth, Kansas, put Morgan within an hour's driving distance of the Reorganized Church of Jesus Christ of Latter Day Saints' library collection in Independence, Missouri. Here he had access to primary material on early Mormonism of the sort that was securely locked away from view or inquiry in Salt Lake City: letters from Joseph Smith to his wife and family, early church histories, memoirs and financial records of early members, manuscript versions of published revelation texts. The longer he worked in the Reorganized Church library, the more material seemed to emanate from file drawers, cabinets, boxes, shelves, rooms, and memory. One afternoon librarian Samuel A. Burgess brought out Hiram Page's seer stone. "Burgess peered through the stone at me, then said facetiously that he couldn't make it work—lack of faith!"[8]

Levity aside, Morgan decided to grab as much transcribed material and make as many notes as he could manage. "As long as the [RLDS library] keeps pulling important material out of its files," he confided to his mother, "I should keep my nose to the grindstone, for of course this is a private rather than a public library, and research in such a library is always at the caprice of its owners. So it is best to make the most of my opportunities."[9] That final sentence stood like a revolving beacon at the beginning of one of the busiest yet least productive periods of his adult life.

Morgan's experience with the sheer volume of unique material in Quaife's collection and the RLDS library was evidence that not all documentation of the Mormon experience existed in Salt Lake City. Everything needed to be understood if he was to include the entire spectrum of Latter Day Saint experience in what he was now calling "the Mormon book." Israel A. Smith felt his denomination's founder (his grandfather) had been treated unfairly in Fawn Brodie's biography. Neither his demeanor nor comments suggested he would welcome her back. The same was certainly true in Salt Lake City. Brodie had washed her hands of Mormons and moved on to other fields, but Dale Morgan planned to write three books about church history, not one. If the Latter Day Saint churches reacted to his first book as they had to hers, he worried about their level of cooperation when it came time to continue research for the second and third volumes. Morgan began to realize how much his project rested on the cooperation of private libraries. Writing from Ruth's house soon after the New Year, Dale typed a formal request to the Guggenheim Foundation for an extension to his Fellowship.[10]

Leaving western Missouri, Dale tacked back across the state to St. Louis, a target for more than the Fellowship research on the Mormons. The private Missouri Historical Society's stellar collection of fur trade material proved to be the trove he expected: a William Sublette diary (which did not look quite right), the 1826 agreement between William H. Ashley and the partners of Smith, Jackson & Sublette; Harrison G. Rogers' journal. "I went through the Ashley papers with some care also, fulfilling a very old ambition of mine," Dale wrote Harvey Tobie. "For some years past I have wanted to write a critical article of Smith, Jackson & Sublette, for the period 1826–1830 is really the unknown period in the fur trade.[11]

From St. Louis, a drive made upriver to Nauvoo was little more than a whistle-stop detour, barely long enough to take photographs. He shot two rolls of film, taking in the departure point where the Mormons crossed the frozen Mississippi River early in the bitter winter of 1846. He could not resist snapping a photo of the "Mormon Cocktail Bar" on the bluff a block east of the temple site, but was too broke to step in and have a drink for the sake of the novelty. By mid-February, Dale was back at Fort Leavenworth with Ruth and Doug and their family. After a few days to relax and play with Anne and Jimmy, he set out on the long drive westward across the plains. The Interstate Highway System was not yet built in 1948. The driving route along US 24 and then KS-18 followed roughly the overland trail route before turning southwest toward Great Bend, Kansas, and then across the open plains along the Santa Fe Trail: Dodge City, Garden City, Trinidad, Colorado, and finally Santa Fe, New Mexico, often gliding on ice from a persistent freezing rain.

The mail caught up with Morgan occasionally, including a plea from Madeline probing to see "if we could find some place cheap, somewhere in the West to stay for a month? I don't want to cook, wash dishes, or do anything but write and rest," she proposed. "Maybe you will understand. Could you meet me at Las Vegas, or should I try to get to Los Angeles itself.... Can you manage your end of it—or raise some money somehow?"[12] No, in fact, Dale couldn't; to replace one of the car's problem tires, Emily was already cashing Dale's dwindling number of war bonds. Helen Sanders sent a personal check for another $40 as a loan to cover incidental travel expenses.

Despite what had been spent in the first half of the trip on distributor points, an oil pump, blown tires, and an accelerator linkage, car trouble pushed Morgan into debt financing while he worked in the Bancroft Library at the University of California, Berkeley. There Helen Harding, a bright young woman who worked as reference staff, made a point of introducing Dale to the Bancroft Library's director, George P. Hammond, whom he already knew from correspondence. After hours, he visited with aunt Ida Holmes and his Holmes cousins, Uncle Ern and Ida's Laurine, June, Sam, and Gordon, who all lived east of Oakland.

As the month of March wound to a close, Dale took an expeditious measure of his finances and decided to drive straight home from Berkeley across the Sierras and Nevada desert, with no return to Los Angeles, no side trips, nor unnecessary stops to break up the daylong drive. On March 28, 1948, the Hudson turned onto Hollywood Avenue, rocked its bulk across the curb cutout, gliding to a stop in his mother's driveway. Dale arrived home from his travels, he explained to a correspondent, "a good deal worse than broke"—in fact, he had spent the $2,000 fellowship, all of his personal savings and war bonds, and arrived nearly $300 in debt to family members and friends.[13] He was ready, eager to begin writing seriously, but also facing the uncomfortable possibility of having to return to salaried work if he could not make a living writing the kind of books he wanted to write.

The Guggenheim Fellowship-funded travel was a defining experience for Dale. It reinforced both his assumptions and commitments made previously, providing a broader basis for not only the contemplated "Mormon book" but also his later career as a historian within the American West. Beyond learning a tremendous amount, Morgan gained a broader understanding of what he was undertaking with his work on the Mormons. He learned firsthand that there was much more to Mormonism and its past than merely the Utah tradition in which he had grown up. A broad and complex history existed beyond Brigham Young and the heroic settlement of the far west.

What grew out of his fellowship study was an awareness of just how little he or anyone actually knew about the documentary sources of Mormonism. That imposed tangential choices. First, he solidified his commitment to locate and comprehend Mormon source material and to write about the faith inclusively rather than limiting his work to the Utah branch of the church. Second, he recognized the potential value that bibliography—even a mere list of the printed works of Mormonism—represented to the larger history project. By the time he returned to Salt Lake City, Dale clearly appreciated the significance of bibliography as fundamental research. Until he had a grasp of Mormonism's published past, he would not be able to write authoritatively about the culture at all.

Most importantly, his first tentative steps to his "Mormon book" resulted in a concern that research access to the holdings of the churches' private libraries, large and small, rested on their church gatekeepers' regard for the cultural utility they would see in his work. "If I accept any part of what one of these [churchmen] says, I am immediately challenged by some other among them," Dale wrote Samuel Burgess in Independence, and "whether one is regarded as 'friendly' or not by one of these men depends upon the extent to which one accepts his views."[14] Simply, if what he wrote did not fit the churches' values, then he risked finding the doors to its archives closed, and quite possibly subject to other forms of quiet pressure. "Some if not all of these churches will close up on me like so many clams once my first book is in print," he wrote Fawn Brodie. "To that end if I do not get the information I need out of them beforehand, I never will."[15] Nels Anderson had precisely that experience when writing *Desert Saints* several years earlier.[16]

The Guggenheim Fellowship had been granted for a study of the Mormons, but it contributed to Morgan's parallel field of choice, the fur trade and early exploration of the American West. Though he spent much more time on the Mormons, the discoveries made in Missouri and California collections also solidified his commitment to the fur trade as a subject ripe for a major update—perhaps a complete restructuring—on the strength of new research and information. Morgan's grasp of fur-trade documentary history strengthened materially. He not only gained firsthand research in the manuscripts held by library collections, particularly at the Missouri Historical Society, but more importantly, he formed personal connections to the staff servicing those collections. They became his eyes as collections expanded; these personal relationships and friendships existed beyond the cycle of query-and-answer correspondence. All of these factors shaped his choices in the coming months and years, giving unintended direction to his career as a writer of the history of the American West.

* * * * *

The day after arriving home from his transcontinental research trip, Dale typed and mailed a formal request to Church of Jesus Christ of Latter-day Saints President George Albert Smith seeking access to the Church Historian's Office collections. The choice of words in the request reflected earlier correspondence with apostle and former University of Utah President John A. Widtsoe. Widtsoe had written Morgan two years earlier, praising *The Great Salt Lake* from galley proofs and encouraging Morgan in his writing. "When you consult President Smith, I think you will find that if you are not writing an anti-Mormon book, as so many do who receive privileges of the Church, you will be given all possible help from the archives of the Church."[17] Dale was clearly aware that the Church

Historian's Office held documentary sources beyond the material transcribed and abstracted in the scrapbook *Journal History of the Church*. Invoking his prior relations with academically-minded Widtsoe and Levi Edgar Young of the church's First Council of the Seventy, Dale asked specifically for permission to dive into the manuscript holdings and for help checking the library's holdings for his growing bibliography of Mormonism. "I believe this is the first time the opportunity has offered for the history of the Church to be examined by a qualified scholar," he asserted boldly, "with full assurance that the fruits of the work will be objective and in accordance with the highest principles of scholarship.... The Church itself has not lacked scholars, but a question has always remained, and always will remain until an outside scholar has been accorded every facility for research, whether all the facts have been developed and whether they have been impartially treated by the Church historians."[18]

Within the church, challenges to the Latter-day Saint narrative in the work of writers like Brodie and Morgan were looked on as merely the latest iterations of nineteenth-century polemic anti-Mormonism. Yet appeals like Morgan's were not the only ones that regarded a grasp of source material to be fundamentally desirable. An internal wrestle about its own history and sources was already in process. Grounded in his training as a scientist, John A. Widtsoe fully expected to muster science and inquiry in advancing the church's mission, as well as encouraging scholarly explorations of its past, such as the effort undertaken by Dale Morgan. Morgan's query would have profited from the advice elder Widtsoe tendered to a young doctoral student at the University of North Carolina, who wrote him a few years earlier about research in the Church Historian's Office. "They're very hesitant about sharing the abundant resources they have," Leonard Arrington recalled of Widtsoe's response. "So you must build up their confidence by beginning to use printed material, then asking for theses and dissertations, then the Journal History, and eventually you'll be able to see anything because you will have built up their confidence."[19]

Widtsoe, not Church Historian Joseph Fielding Smith, wrote a column in LDS magazine *The Improvement Era* exploring church history. A few years earlier, church educator Daryl Chase published a commemorative volume about Joseph Smith which obliquely but pointedly anticipated a day in which "access to *all* the manuscript materials which are now gathered in American libraries and archives dealing with Joseph Smith and the rise of Mormonism" was available.[20] When Francis Kirkham compiled his *New Witness for God in America*, he was convinced as much as Widtsoe that mustering primary documentation would vindicate the Book of Mormon as divine revelation and put detractors to silence. Even apostle Richard L. Evans noted in a Mormon Tabernacle Choir broadcast that "Truth can be very inconvenient at times. And so we try to talk ourselves into what we wish were true, or out of what we wish weren't true, by admitting all the evidence that will take us where we want to go, and excluding all the evidence that would take us where we don't want to go. In other words, we sometimes decide what we would like the answers to be, and then work back to make them seem to be what we would like."[21]

Morgan's query was made with confidence in the perspective Widtsoe had expressed privately and others within the church were beginning to voice. Ultimately, however, a study "objective and in accordance with the highest principles of scholarship" did not interest the church's historical staff or its leadership, and access to the private reserve was not Widtsoe's to grant nor to encourage. George Albert Smith was out of town, so Morgan's query may have been routed to Church Historian Joseph Fielding Smith for an opinion. If it was, then Smith, who likely did not know Historian's Office research patrons personally, undoubtedly asked A. William Lund, who did know them, what he thought. Lund was still chafing over Fawn Brodie's *No Man Knows My History*. Despite his own good relations with Dale during the HRS and UWP, Lund never forgot nor forgave Morgan's prominent mention among Brodie's acknowledgements.

Morgan's request, however, probably did not get as far as the CHO staff for consideration. Two weeks after Morgan's letter, First Presidency Secretary Joseph Anderson responded, which means Morgan's request to the church president had likely been routed to Smith's counselor, J. Reuben Clark. Clark had also read Brodie's biography with meticulous care, and like Lund, he would have noticed Morgan's name in the acknowledgements. A lawyer by profession and former State Department official, Clark's greatest personal concern was disloyalty to authority, whether secular or sacred. Failing to affirm official answers, more than asking questions about the past, was a form of disloyalty. No hard evidence confirms that Clark was the official who gave instructions for Anderson's response to Morgan's letter, but the secretary wrote mildly that the Church Historian's Office "is not a research library," adding that "experience running over several years has persuaded us of the unwisdom of giving access to our manuscript records to people writing books, because that same experience has shown that people writing such books are rarely qualified to appraise accurately what they read, and too frequently, whether consciously or unconsciously, they misrepresent what they find." The church did agree, however, to cooperate on his bibliography.[22]

Dale waited for months without another word from CHO staff. Finally a year later, after spending a week in the Church Historian's Office working with Will Lund to check his bibliography against the informal holdings catalog maintained there, he understood why the church had not replied. "Nobody can find anything in it, and how much stuff they have uncataloged they don't know themselves," he groused to Juanita Brooks.[23]

The day Anderson's letter was delivered to Hollywood Avenue, Morgan formulated a responding comment. "So long as the Church permits access to its archives only when it can control the fruits of the scholarship, so long must it be content to be misrepresented and misunderstood," he asserted archly.[24] No matter; the church was content to limit access to its archival holding only to those it deemed appropriate, for the remainder of Morgan's lifetime.[25]

In retrospect, Anderson's response to Dale Morgan's request was not just a matter of being upset over bad press, or a matter of the church's leadership whitewashing its past. During this generation, history—represented by the church's past and the lives, choices, and experiences of its leaders and members—was tightly bound up with its truth claim. With notable exceptions, like Widtsoe, church leaders expected to control its historical message in the way it controlled the gospel message delivered by missionaries. After the passing of its founder, Mormon culture had not distinguished prophetic status from personal agency. A question about the latter was a challenge to the former. The church had official accounts of its history; merely asking questions outside of the official explanations of historical realities was evidence that a person rejected the church and its mission. Accepting the church meant accepting Truth, while questioning the church meant rejecting Truth and espousing Error. Morgan didn't buy that argument. "Some day the Church will become smart enough to realize that every time it involves itself in a suppression of some kind, the reaction does it more damage in a public relations sense than could ever be done by letting the chips fall as they might fly," he commented privately to Fawn.[26] Several months later Dale wrote Utah folklorist Austin Fife that he wondered "when and if the Church will ever reconcile itself to the fact that it is a social and cultural phenomenon which is liable to study just like the Hottentots or Kiwanis and Rotary."[27]

Dale probably expected the answer Anderson delivered; this blow, however, was merely a second one to his research. A few days before

Anderson's letter arrived, another letter finally caught up with Morgan. Henry Allen Moe, the Guggenheim Memorial Foundation's secretary-general, informed him that the foundation had decided to favor funding new fellowship requests over renewals and declined Morgan's request to extend his fellowship.[28] Only after the year's fellowship list was published did Dale notice that the only extensions granted were to Fellows holding doctoral degrees. In short, he might have been talented with a compelling project, but credentials now counted for much more than he anticipated.

Denials from both the church and the Guggenheim Memorial Foundation left Morgan without an occupation, but at least he could hole up temporarily at his mother's house and launch into the Mormon book without distraction. "I've had enough of this business of working all day and writing all night, and I mean to spend all my working time writing for a few years," he informed Juanita Brooks.[29] On the other hand, he still needed an income of some sort. Dale's immediate plan was to pursue work as a freelance magazine writer, preferably on a commission basis rather than writing on speculation, "and if worst comes to worst, I will contract for my Mormon books and get some kind of advance to help underwrite their production."[30]

By late April, a lack of paying work in the city left Morgan few options. Fortunately, Marguerite Sinclair of the Utah State Historical Society provided a lifeline. Though Dale had previously turned down her offer of the *Utah Historical Quarterly* editorship, she had committed to publishing William Culp Darrah's edited versions of the diaries from John W. Powell's exploration of the Colorado River. She asked if Morgan would get Darrah's transcriptions into editorial shape for the *UHQ*, informally and on merely a part-time basis. He agreed. It was something, at least.

Rooming and boarding with his mother meant no rent but committed Dale to a daily regimen of dishes, cleaning, and yard work. He was dutiful, but Emily was at school most of the day, which left Dale free to pursue other activities. In early May, he made a trip upstate to Logan to survey the holdings of the Utah Agricultural State College library there. He also hammered out a revision to "The Administration of Indian Affairs in Utah" manuscript drafted four years earlier, sending the sheets to John Caughey, managing editor at the *Pacific Historical Review*.[31] Dale also made time to wander through the Salt Lake Valley watersheds and canyons with friends. On May 10, Dale and Rod Korns cruised the streets of Salt Lake City, trying to pin down the route of the California-bound 1846 Russell-Bryant emigrant party across the valley.

Juanita Brooks arrived in town on May 15, bringing with her the manuscript for what at Dale's prompting over the past several years had grown
into a book-length study of the Mountain Meadows Massacre, and which
she offered rather timidly to her mentor for critique.[32] The two of them
picked up friend Vesta Crawford and made a day trip driving Parley's Canyon and Emigration Canyon, picking out the routes into the valley of the
1846 and 1847 emigrations. The next week Morgan was back with Korns
in the mountains east of Ogden, following geographic clues about the
1841 Bartleson-Bidwell party route in the James Clyman diary.

Organizing his own notes and papers from the cross-country trip, also
ate into his days, as well as unpacking and shelving books. A stream of
correspondence required nearly daily attention to some matter: Mormon-
related book holdings at Bethany College library in West Virginia, dimen-
sions of individual publications at the New York Public Library, queries
about the availability of specific titles to libraries across the country, and
supplying notes and suggestions to others' queries. Novelist Virginia
Sorensen appreciated Morgan's response to her questions about Nauvoo
and the early move west. "Thank you for all this," she wrote. "You never
fail to amaze me with what you know about practically everything."[33]

No matter how much time he spent in writing, housework, local travel,
or correspondence, Dale continued to read widely. He devoured new novels and made time to keep abreast of relevant new historical works at the
University of Utah library. By this time, he was well-read enough to comment substantively on both the literary quality and the historical accuracy
of nearly any work that involved the Mormons, the fur trade, or the exploration of the American West. If Dale Morgan did not like a work, he could
generally explain why in specific detail, whether in reviews or informally
in letters to friends. Some, however, were beneath mention. New books
published for the state centennial by Milton R. Hunter reinforced Morgan's low opinion of Hunter's competence generally, and Morgan's earlier
low opinion of University of Utah historian Leland Hargrove Creer's professional ability declined still further after release of *The Founding of an
Empire* (1947). Both were professionally credentialed historians, but after
reading the work of both men, Morgan deemed their work as nothing but
"the shoddiest kind of historical workmanship."[34]

By May 22, Dale had to admit to Fawn Brodie that "I've been so busy
with miscellaneous matters that I haven't even remotely got started on the
Mormon job yet."[35] Unfortunately, other than the work on the *Quarterly*,
none of Morgan's "miscellaneous matters" was paying him anything. The

personal time Morgan had available for research and writing was devoted to extending and organizing his handwritten "slips" of publication information into a massive checklist of Latter Day Saint-related publications for a bibliography of Mormonism. By the end of April, the newly typed author-title checklist (backed by three carbons) ran to something over six hundred entries, all dating prior to 1850. Dale dispatched carbons to institutions in the mail and carried a carbon to the Church Historian's Office, requesting that institution make good on the promise to cooperate on the bibliography. The church staff was slack-jawed at the title-list's length, able to tally in their holdings fewer than a third of Morgan's checklisted items.

Ralph V. Chamberlin at the University of Utah volunteered to see if the university would publish the finished list, but Morgan was not content with its state of completion and began reaching out to non-institutional collectors as well. Chicago collector Everett D. Graff (to whom Morgan had been introduced by Wright Howes) and New Jersey collector Thomas W. Streeter were delighted to compare Morgan's list against their collections, as was Morgan's friend and rare-book dealer Charles Eberstadt in New York. Over the next several months the carbons circulated in and out of the mail to the owners of these collections and to historical societies in California, Wisconsin, Illinois, Iowa, and the Library of Congress.

By late May 1948, Morgan's finances were in complete shambles, and he felt under immediate pressure to find paying work. Despite his pinched standing, Dale agreed to serve as managing editor for a *Utah Historical Quarterly* publication of the diaries of the 1869 Powell expedition as its fifteenth volume essentially for free, accepting as compensation only enough to cover a dental bill. The work required much more than either Morgan or Marguerite Sinclair expected. She offered Dale a permanent half-time position working for the Historical Society as the journal's managing editor. He liked the idea, but wanted full-time work in history. Had Dale accepted, his career might have unfolded much differently. Over the three years he served as the journal's ghost editor, Morgan discovered problem after problem with Darrah's notes and even with the document transcriptions themselves, all of which he patiently corrected and forwarded to Darrah, who lived in Massachusetts. By the time the text went to press in September, the resulting volume was probably as much or more Dale Morgan's work as it was the cited editor's.

One summer afternoon while Morgan was uptown and quite by accident, he bumped into former WPA supervisor Gail Martin. Martin was working as marketing and publications manager for Capitol Publishing, which was producing a biographical and community reference guide to cities and towns in Utah to appeal to the nation's postwar upswing in self-guided tourism. Given Dale's background in the UWP, Martin hired Morgan on a project basis to assist with writing and editorial work. Through the first half of June, Dale worked three days a week in the Capitol Publishing office. As he had at the HRS, Morgan's first act was to review the source material the company already had in its files. He found a messy and irregular patchwork of notes and publications. Some major communities had no documentation at all, leaving Morgan with the added responsibility of researching essential facts on the towns he was to write about. The project had a July 15 deadline for draft text.

Morgan turned in several sections of draft material, but no payment was approved. An unidentified coworker (perhaps Martin) wrote Dale about having approached Capitol Publishing's owner Carl J. Brown and asking why Morgan's payment had not cleared. Brown asserted that he had committed to publish drafts by city chambers of commerce. The individual reported pointing out flaws in Brown's assertions, concluding that the owner was essentially a racketeer who planned to have Morgan do basic writing then edit and take credit for the work himself, and that he probably would not pay for Morgan's work.[36] On July 13, Gail Martin telephoned Morgan at home to report that he was quitting Capitol Publishing because of Brown's capriciousness and advised Morgan to present an itemized bill for his services immediately. Dale had taken in half of his manuscript for retyping the day before. On the fourteenth, Morgan went in to the Capitol offices and spent the day correcting and revising, then corrected galleys while waiting to talk with Brown. He eventually got into the office, but Brown stalled about committing to use Morgan's writing. Three days later Morgan returned for payment; this time Brown was openly evasive. On August 2, Morgan arrived in the office without announcement and demanded payment on his work. Brown had planned ahead, for he handed Morgan a backdated letter refusing payment on the work as unacceptable. Two days later, Dale hammered out his account of the impasse and filed a formal complaint for nonpayment of wages with the Utah Industrial Commission.[37]

Despite the mess with Capitol Publishing, Dale busily chased other freelance opportunities. In early June he floated a proposal to produce a promotional map illustrating Utah's historical trails and projected onto a modern road map of the state, to fellow trails buff Arthur L. Crawford, director of the Utah Department of Publicity and Industrial Development and husband of acquaintance Vesta Crawford.[38] The proposal may have provided the spark for an article on Morgan appearing in a *Deseret News* series on modern Utahns.[39] Two weeks later, Rulon S. Howells reported that the department agreed to commission a map and text from Morgan for $500.[40] On August 2, the day Dale confronted Carl Brown of Capitol Publishing, he visited at length with Howells about arrangements and content for the map. There Dale discovered that the commission expected him to deliver a camera-ready map ready for printing and not merely a manuscript. Dale still readily agreed, writing to his mother who was visiting family in California that he had done so "since of course I was more in need of the money than the Commission was of the map."[41]

In the middle of this frenetic summer, John Selby, editor in chief at Farrar & Rinehart, wrote Dale asking how much draft manuscript of the Mormon book he had ready to show the publisher. Dale returned a letter admitting that since April he had resorted to "sundry kinds of hack work" to stay afloat. He continued: "within a few weeks, I expect to launch upon this work with or without any outside help, and at whatever cost; I have been living too long with this work to be able to rest until I finish it." Without asking outright, if, he wrote, "a substantial royalty advance can be made of the first book to enable me to give all my time to it, we will make a deal on this basis." No matter what his intentions or his plans were, writing this book would be nothing like writing *The Humboldt* or *Great Salt Lake*. While completing both prior books, Morgan was supported by the solid foundation of a regular income, though *The Humboldt* advance had been his financial ace in the hole while job-hunting in Washington, DC. Asking for an advance to subsidize a book's writing was a risky proposition, and Dale knew it. "I prefer not to spend a book before it has been written, and am only getting involved in such a proposition now because it seems the best of the several expedients open to me," he admitted to Selby.[42] In a later exchange, the pair agreed on a $1,000 advance, paid in installments on request, and on August 31, Dale signed and returned duplicate contracts obligating him to a three-book series on Mormon history, with manuscript due dates annually on September 1, 1949, 1950, and 1951.[43]

Between necessities and distractions, Dale carefully read and commented on Juanita Brooks' revised manuscript on the Mountain Meadows Massacre. He returned it in mid-August with a long letter, making editorial suggestions about the appendices and pointing out several discrepancies between sources she had cited. He also wrote Wally Stegner, who had recently founded with Morgan's classmate, Richard Scowcroft, the writing program at Stanford University and now headed the program. Juanita's manuscript was well crafted, Morgan opined, but more of an academic volume than a trade book. He felt strongly that it should be published in the west, which required finding a university publisher with enough gravitas to be immune to possible complaints or pressure from the church. Dale recommended Juanita submit the manuscript to Stanford University Press and asked Stegner to prod the Press on Juanita's behalf.[44]

In the middle of August, after the Hudson's motor was completely overhauled and Dale paid to have four cracked pistons replaced, he and Rod Korns piled in the car to drive up Parley's Canyon into southwestern Wyoming as far as the Bear River headwaters, hunting trail geography. Dale snapped photos at every stop. Dale could not watch Korns's face while he drove, and Korns could not drive and write notes for Dale to read, so Korns sat in the passenger seat and Dale did the driving.

Following Dale's return from Washington, Madeline McQuown continued to hold Dale at arm's length while simultaneously complaining of his neglect. The fact that he would not drop everything of his own to fulfill her whims rankled her. "I will, in fact, be lucky to have car fare, so if you would rather not see me in such a pathetic financial state, let me know that, too. . . . Anyway, you have proved very stubborn about seeing me the times when I could come down by myself so I have given up trying to arrange such times now." She was still at work on the Brigham Young biography, she assured him, though she asserted that she would be "glad to have this book done so that I can get more rest on which my very life depends."[45]

Complications continued multiplying. On one hand, the trails-map research was moving forward. From September 10 through 12, Dale drove to the Uinta Basin in eastern Utah for field research on the trails map, by sheer chance missing Stegner by a few hours at Dinosaur National Monument. A few weeks later, Dale took Will Lund into the Wasatch canyons in the mountains rimming the Salt Lake valley on other excursions. Fortuitously, in the first week of October, out of the blue Dale received an offer from former FWP director Henry Alsberg asking for a set of descriptive automobile tours of Utah's major highways for a forthcoming national guidebook.[46] Having just tramped the state for the trails map, this commission amounted to an outright gift. The rush job was due 15 November, but paid $200.

In the meantime, Dale contracted with the *Utah Historical Quarterly*'s artist, Herbert Fehmel, to produce the drawn map of the trails.

In mid-October he submitted the descriptive texts for the map to the Utah Department of Publicity and Industrial Development. The Powell proof began arriving from the printer, but Marguerite Sinclair, having married secretly earlier in the year, suddenly announced her new family was moving to California. The Utah Historical Society's Board of Control extracted from her a promise to push the second volume of Powell diaries through the press, as well as to return to Utah during the legislative session to lobby for an increased appropriation.[47] Of course, nothing went as planned. On November 25, ten days after the date he had promised the manuscript, Morgan wrote Alsberg that he planned to send the guide text that day. He borrowed heavily from *Utah: A Guide to the State,* updating information where needed and matching it to the current state highway map.[48] That paid work meant Dale was unable to get to work on the Mormon book before Thanksgiving.

The year's freelance work, while frustrating and anything but stable, provided enough income that Dale felt he could finally afford a place of his own. After the Thanksgiving holiday he found an apartment on Allen Park Drive, four blocks north of where Rod and Sara Korns lived. Making the move required a week and with all his books and papers, the place was cramped, but it was his, even if "too little space for the money I have to pay for it."[49] Commissioned book reviews for the *Saturday Review of Literature* helped to pay the rent, but routine expenses required more. Dale began sending article proposals to publications all over the country: "The Mormons and the Forty-niners" to the *California Historical Society Quarterly*; a series on "little-known episodes in the history of Utah and the West" to the *Salt Lake Tribune*; an article on Forty-niners in Salt Lake City to the *Utah Humanities Review*. In response, he received nibbles but no bites.

Dale returned to typing up a final checklist of his Mormon bibliography, but by the end of December 1948, he finally decided that his apartment was too small and too expensive and began looking again. He settled on a converted basement unit in a house several blocks north on 1000 East and 1000 South, below and a bit south of the University of Utah. Another weeklong move, complicated by heavy snow blanketing the city and slowing traffic to a crawl, ate into his available writing time. Still, letters of thanks for the recently published "Administration of Indian Affairs in Utah" article offprint began sifting into the mailbox. One of them, from John A. Widtsoe, complimented Morgan on the article. Clearly, the apostle thought, non-Mormons who came into Utah Territory found it difficult to understand the motives of the Latter-day Saints, and therefore, "in their conclusions were many personal interpolations." As a trained scientist, Widtsoe pointed out diplomatically that what one expected to find shaped the interpretation of evidence as much as evidence shaped interpretation.[50] Morgan didn't think so, writing back: "don't you think we have had enough books about the Mormons which started with the conclusions and worked around to the facts?... I think it is time that we tried another angle of approach, marshalling all the available facts, and then going on from there."[51] Widtsoe's knowledge that Morgan was writing a history of the Latter Day Saints with the support of a Guggenheim Fellowship would take on great relevance to the church in another year.

* * * * *

By the late 1940s Dale Morgan remained convinced that circumscribing and organizing historical facts would lead inevitably to a correct interpretation of them. In his view, the pursuit of history was strictly a quest for objective empiricism—either an event happened, or it did not. He completely dismissed claims of Mormonism's revealed origins. His perspective left him to pursue the history of a people who looked to issues beyond daily existence in faith, by studying almost solely their footprints. In a December 1945 letter, Bernard DeVoto had pinned Morgan like a butterfly, saying that "when you have found an environmental explanation of something you are content, you feel you have settled matters"[52] By focusing on sources and fact, Dale Morgan pointed out the trap of patriotic tradition the Latter-day Saints had created for themselves. "So long had factual accuracy been submerged in Utah historiography by faith-promoting legends," Gary Topping observed decades later, writing about Morgan and his generation, "that they considered it a daunting enough task merely to establish what those facts were, while letting the less-tangible aspects of personality and motivation take care of themselves."[53]

Morgan's later work demonstrates his mastery of detail in tracking the movements and interactions of fur traders and overland companies. When tracking the geography of westward movement, the travelers' motivations were unimportant to Dale, but when seeking to understand their personal faith and commitment, he relied on little more than Freudian psychology and the observations and assertions of Havelock Ellis, both of whom he had encountered on his own in college. Reflecting his own daily wrestle as a social analyst, his personal compensation for deafness, Morgan assumed that studying facts allowed him to see into hearts and minds. In other words, Dale approached history the way he approached life, operating with a high degree of analysis.

However, Morgan was also correct. He was locating historical facts which supported a different version of Latter Day Saint history than the churches were comfortable acknowledging. Tradition and personal witness were not always as neat as official histories presented them to be. Sources differed and occasionally conflicted. Personal testimony was still regarded as the most reliable form of evidence, though the effectiveness of perception and memory were not questioned to the extent that they would be in the 1990s and 2000s, long after Morgan's passing. The problem was, that the passion for printed and manuscript Americana which fueled antiquarian collecting in the last third of the nineteenth and first two-thirds of the twentieth century, brought into the open neglected or overlooked source material that often challenged the founding stories told by heritage groups. Another writer recalled of this revolution "we discovered a history that the old facts could not explain. We did not invent new facts, either; they had always existed. But, through education, we had been trained not to see them, for they contradicted the assumptions that most historians held."[54]

It would be incorrect to say that in 1949 the Latter Day Saints of any tradition were "reeling" from the new facts and stories of the first studies. Nels Anderson's sociological *Desert Saints* had made Utahns uncomfortable in 1942 because it told the story of settlement and expansion without resorting to prophetic direction. Stegner's *Mormon Country* brought the American West's waning rural culture to a national audience the same year. Fawn Brodie's biography of Joseph Smith in 1945, *No Man Knows My History,* was the bombshell. Belief cultures which accept faith-promoting stories uncritically are generally uncomfortable with external examination and complicating histories. The church was beginning to lose control to the discussion of its past. With new evidence and interpretations, appeals to authority became less effective. At this point the church's response to the attention of scholars and their books became studiously immobile.

Initially the church lashed out at Brodie's work in a stinging editorial critique written by apostle Albert E. Bowen but printed anonymously. A lawyer rather than a historian, his critique deflated when key documents Bowen asserted as invalid turned up after additional research. Thereafter Brodie's book and its author were simply studiously and noticeably ignored. In 1957, Thomas F. O'Dea would publish another sociological study titled simply *The Mormons,* which would stand for a generation as the objective external summation and explication of Mormon culture. By that time the church had learned a lesson about attacking scholarship reactively—doing so no longer worked.

As he corresponded on issues and evidence relating to the Mormon book, Morgan's most cogent critic among the Latter Day Saints was RLDS librarian Samuel A. Burgess, whose scholarly training in mathematics, logic, and law made him quite capable of debunking the old facts and arguments about polygamy and hearsay evidence. He was a convert to the Reorganization, baptized as an adult in 1890. Burgess practiced law in St. Louis, served briefly as president of Graceland College in the 1910s, and pursued a PhD in psychology under G. Stanley Hall at Clark University in Worchester, Massachusetts. Prevented from attending his oral defense by an emergency, the degree was never awarded.

By the time he began exchanging letters with Dale Morgan in the 1940s, Burgess had been the church's librarian and unofficial historian for two decades. The church presidency of the time typically turned to Burgess for any question involving historical research. He was as poor a typist as Morgan was an exceptional one, but shared one common trait with the younger man: he was also completely deaf.[55] Burgess's calm and forthright remonstrance that "faith is not a blind credulity" provided an argument Morgan could not effectively counter. "Every scientist, everyone who works, must exercise the right kind of faith [for their field]," Burgess noted to Morgan in 1948. He pointed to the younger man's contradictory hyperbole defending Brodie's *No Man Knows My History,* noting that "if her work were really definitive there would be no place for your work."

A genuine believer untroubled by factors in his church's history that defied simple explanations, Burgess also calmly bypassed Morgan's historicism and picked apart his unassailable social-origin arguments about Joseph Smith and Mormonism. "[A]fter examining all the offered evidence," the old lawyer noted, "we hold he was a good man. He was a prophet when, and as he himself said only when, he was acting under the inspiration of God." Even Smith's polygamy did not ruffle him. "You should understand by now our real position; whether he was or was not [a polygamist] is incidental. The great point at issue is that God is and that He will speak to man."[56] Burgess, however, was talking past Morgan, who could neither grasp nor allow the argument. Morgan's inductive method of history possessed its own natural limits. "With my point of view on God, I am incapable of accepting the claims of Joseph Smith and the

Mormons," he had once written Juanita Brooks, aware of the fatal flaw in his own logic. "If God does not exist, how can Joseph Smith's story have any possible validity? I will look everywhere for explanations except to the ONE[*sic*] explanation that is the position of the church."[57]

Dale's correspondence in the late 1940s indicates that at this point he recognized but did not quite comprehend in believers like Samuel Burgess, Juanita Brooks, and Wilford Poulson their tenacious nonempirical faith in their branch of the church and to the latter-day Restoration of the gospel itself. Unlike many in the church who tried to address both spheres from one point of view, Juanita Brooks adopted an outside perspective on Restoration history, which allowed her to study church history and its actors without imposing moral judgments, but maintained an internalized faith in divinity and the mission of the church. In more modern terms, she compartmentalized her world somewhat, but doing so allowed her to look at church history and historical figures critically and historically. The institutional Mormons of the day strove ardently to adopt a unified view of their own existence. The problem was that the two spheres of reality only intersected, they did not precisely overlap.

Fawn Brodie and Dale Morgan, among the first generation of historicists, in their own way mirrored the myopia they decried in the church. While they looked down on Latter-day Saint leadership for trying to measure objective human history using the subjectivity of faith, they were attempting to do precisely the same thing in reverse—expecting to measure the subjectivity inherent in faith with the objective rod of factual human history. John A. Widtsoe advanced a theological rationale for LDS history, Dale L. Morgan a sociological one. In the context of the 1940s, neither side was comfortable allowing the other room enough to coexist culturally. In succeeding generations, LDS believers began to admit that God might not direct *everything* that happened and that choices and decisions happened in Mormonism under the exercise of mortal agency (sometimes ill-considered mortal agency). Likewise LDS scholars eventually acknowledged that belief and faith lay beyond the scope of straightforward natural force, objective accounts, or documentation. With those shifts, later generations would create a body of scholarship that neither attacked the Restoration churches nor ignored historical complexities. In the 1940s Brodie's biography and Morgan's history represented Latter Day Saint *ethical* or *utilitarian* or *presentist history* being scrubbed vigorously with the stiff bristles of modern historicism. Once the questions were asked, they could be deflected (as Joseph Anderson did in denying

Morgan access to the CHO material) but not pushed back. Defenders of LDS cultural tradition could only react, they had lost the initiative in the opening salvos of the modern culture wars.

* * * * *

By now even more worried that he would be shut out of Church Historian's Office at publication of the first Mormon book, just as he would launch into research for his second volume, Morgan made a fateful decision. Rather than work on the Mormon history, for which he had a publishing contract, he would concentrate first on extending and completing the preliminary bibliographic survey of Latter Day Saint publications. By the end of February 1949 the checklist was reasonably complete and Dale was ready to begin drafting historical notes for each of the bibliographic entries. Marguerite (Sinclair) Reusser suggested that the *Utah Historical Quarterly* publish the bibliography in several parts, but Dale insisted on conditions of length and the number of separately produced offprints he would later bind into volumes, terms that the USHS could not meet contractually, as a state agency. The latter was not merely selfishness; he wanted the bibliography to be described in library catalogs on its own as a monographic item, rather than see it buried and undescribed within the topically diverse issues of a serial publication. It was never completed nor published. The carbons of the checklist continued circulating, however.

Dale turned now to the University of Utah. Despite the fact that the draft of the first Mormon history book was due to Farrar & Rinehart in September, Morgan's drive to locate and manage all possible facts was quickly outweighing his ability to accomplish any work on the book at all. He drafted a 21-page sample of preliminary bibliographic notes for Harold "Hal" Bentley of the Humanities Research Foundation at the University of Utah. In May, he carried the sheets from his basement apartment on Tenth East up the hill to the university, and in one of his laborious face-to-face conversations—partly spoken, partly gestured, partly written—explained his ideas and handed the bibliography manuscript to William "Bill" Mulder. Morgan had estimated to Hal Bentley that the Mormon bibliography would run between six and eight hundred entries, but he told William H. Cadman of the Church of Jesus Christ that he planned "to publish, over a period of time, a bibliography of all the publications of the various churches which have grown out of the church founded by Joseph Smith in 1830."[58] This project was far different than what he anticipated with the

1830–1849 bibliography. Due to conflicts with other projects and despite Morgan's intention to prioritize it, the 1830–1849 historical bibliography manuscript itself never progressed much past sample pages and was marooned in checklist form. By the time he had a positive answer from the University of Utah, Dale was already committed to other projects.[59]

At the same time, Dale was conducting an intense round-robin correspondence about overland trail routes with Rod Korns and Charlie Kelly. Morgan's letters presented careful, systematic conversations in written form, summarizing geographic knowledge gleaned from a wide variety of sources, correcting and arguing with the other men. Korns had stumbled across the published diary of a German emigrant who had crossed Utah on Hastings Cutoff across the Great Salt Lake Desert in 1846. A careful following of leads eventually led him to the owner of the original diary. Morgan was thrilled. "Although I do not myself read German, I'm damned if I wouldn't buy a German dictionary and undertake to translate this part of his narrative, if necessary, to settle some of the questions I have wondered about," Dale wrote the owner in what turned out to be prophetic pronouncement.[60]

By late spring, Marguerite Reusser was with her husband and stepdaughter, managing the Utah State Historical Society from her new home in Oakland, California. Morgan's contact at the capitol offices was now Elizabeth Lauchnor. With Auerbach gone, change was at last afoot in the Utah State Historical Society. Juanita Brooks was appointed to the Board of Control early in 1949. Board member Arthur Crawford immediately suggested that Dale Morgan was the person to take over the organization. Juanita liked the idea. Early in May she wondered to Dale in a letter whether he would be interested in taking the helm, building a public research collection for the state, and expanding its publications program. Morgan demurred. He wanted a job—needed a job—but would not accept a job that promised to come with strings that could compromise his independent assessment on the Mormons. Morgan concluded that any institution in the state, even the Utah State Historical Society, was "too young, and too exposed to political reprisal" and employment there would hamper his ability to write objectively.[61]

* * * * *

By the middle of May 1949, Dale Morgan had lived and worked for a year in Salt Lake City without permanent employment. Given the type of writing he preferred to do, he was beginning to look eastward again. Through the rest of May and into June, Dale puttered ineffectively between obligations. One matter on which he attempted to take action was correcting inaccuracies on the newly erected Pioneer Monument above Salt Lake City, memorializing the Mormons' entrance into the Salt Lake Valley. It was, he felt, long on inspiration but short on fact. "To me it seems a reflection upon the intelligence and knowledge of the people of Utah that they should be content to have their history told in any way that shows them careless or ignorant."[62] But the monument remained uncorrected, as he suspected it would.

Morgan had other frustrations as well. The Mormon bibliography continued to lag, and he had not yet written a word on the Mormon book, so none of these could produce him any more income than his advance. With these pressures, during the late spring Dale turned his hand back to fiction with the hope of selling a few short stories, but his submissions again only yielded rejections from a shrinking market of popular fiction magazines and "slicks." While he looked for work and hoped for a break, Morgan also labored furiously on half a dozen small projects: editing a diary documenting the 1847 Mormon ferry on the last Platte River crossing, helping Rod Korns with his trail notes, and fielding newly arrived photostats, the precursors of photocopies, transcriptions, and notes from all over. He also launched into indexing the double volume of Powell journals, for which the Society paid him a badly needed $50 premium, though the alphabetizing and typing the 100-plus page manuscript was handled by Historical Society staff.

Rod Korns returned to the hospital with heart trouble at almost the same time Dale delivered the *UHQ* index manuscript, and Dale despaired over his condition. Morgan wrote Charles Kelly that he had proposed to Reusser that an entire issue of the *Utah Historical Quarterly* be devoted to publishing Korns's work on pre-Mormon travel across the state. He even volunteered to generate the footnotes for publication under Korns's name. A few days later John Selby inquired about progress on the Mormon book manuscript. In a return letter Morgan admitted that he had managed to avoid stewing and eating the wolf at the door, but that the work was not half complete. In fact, though he did not admit it to his editor, the manuscript was not really even started. He instead said he planned to complete the manuscript in August (implying that there *was* a manuscript) and would then revise it while completing research on the second volume.[63] He also made apologies for Madeline McQuown's biography of Brigham

Young, even though it was not formally under contract with the press. Selby observed that she had changed due dates half a dozen times without submitting anything at all; in return Morgan plead the perpetually precarious state of her health.

A few days after that correspondence on July 2, Rod Korns looked through the text for the Donner party journal from his hospital bed. Around 10 a.m., he set aside the pages, saying that he was uncomfortable. Sara noticed that his responses were slowing. Something was obviously wrong. About 3 p.m., J. Roderic Korns slipped quietly away. His younger son Bill telephoned Emily, asking her to relay the news to Dale.[64] Wrapped in the grief of losing a close friend who had never even begun the marvelous study that captivated them both, Dale impetuously but solemnly promised Sara Korns at the funeral that he would see her husband's work through publication over his name. "Rod's whole literary immortality depended upon me after he died," Dale later told Juanita Brooks.[65]

Late in the month, Utah State Historical Society politics took another turn. With the deceased Auerbach no longer a factor, the dominant figure on the Board of Control became Joel Ricks, a history professor at Utah State Agricultural College in Logan. Ricks desperately wanted the USHS to seize the honor of publishing a major study of the Domínguez-Escalante expedition by Herbert E. Bolton. Bolton was the towering figure of the period in the subject of Spanish borderlands, having supervised over two hundred graduate students at the University of California, Berkeley, and with many published studies to his credit. Marguerite Reusser confided to Dale that the Society could never secure the money to fund a separate publication of Bolton's work, so Ricks was pressing hard for something by Bolton to be published monographically in the *Quarterly*, as Morgan's *State of Deseret* and the Powell journals had been. He wanted it desperately enough to verbally assent to Bolton's demand for an astronomical $2,500 fee—a figure approaching the Society's monthly staff budget and equivalent to nearly $30,000 today. Morgan realized he was headed into a political wrestle between the Bolton manuscript and the memorial publication for Rod Korns on overland trails. Ahead of the upcoming Board meeting Dale quickly wrote a three-page proposal for a collection of edited primary sources on emigrant trails across the state.[66]

A week later Juanita Brooks reported to Dale that discussion of Morgan's proposal at the Board meeting received less than three minutes consideration. Board chair Joel Ricks and the three-member Executive Committee had decided to commission Bolton and called in the three other Board members "simply [to] vote yea and nay on what had already been decided by 'your president and Executive Committee.'"[67] Her ire up, Brooks insisted the chair bring Morgan's proposal before the Board for discussion on its merits. Ricks reluctantly summarized Morgan's plan.

Inconveniently for Ricks, the Board liked the idea. UHS secretary Elizabeth Lauchnor was charged to meet with Morgan and settle arrangements. Part of Ricks's problem with a Korns memorial volume, frankly, had been Korns's negative view of the Mormons and his challenging relationship with the Church Historian's Office staff. On the other hand, a final publication commitment on Ricks' proposal for Bolton's manuscript was postponed until its October meeting, but the board agreed that publication would be committed if arrangements for funding and submission date could be secured.[68]

Ricks' actions propelled yet another turning point in Morgan's career. By this point, Dale felt that he accurately read the political situation existing between church and state and decided no room remained in Utah for anyone in the objective middle. He could not find work in Salt Lake City and could not seem to make writing pay. During July, he decided to return to Washington, DC, but the Mormon book still hung over everything. Dale committed himself to try to get at least a rough draft completed before a tentative departure in November. In late summer he began recalling books loaned to friends, preparing at last to get serious about his Mormon book, even as he made plans to return east.

While the Utah Historical Society dispatched University of Utah history professor Leland Creer to talk over matters with Bolton in California, they queried Dale about how soon the Korns material would be available.[69] Dale hedged a bit on his reply. His friend's notes were in disarray, and not a word of the footnotes had actually been set to paper. He really needed to start on his own Mormon book.

* * * * *

As Dale Morgan finally launched himself into writing his biography of Mormonism, his approach to the documents and experience of the early church was shaped both by prior experience and by disposition. In the early 1940s he felt he had grasped the essential elements of good history. He also had proven himself a capable and engaging writer and a careful editor. His nonfiction writing was accurate, well-documented, readable, and could be entertaining. It drew praise that his collegiate short fiction never achieved. Second, keenly aware of the way assumptions and allegiance shaped a story, he was committed to basing any narrative on documentary records, without preconceptions, to in-depth familiarity with source material, and not to impose present sensibilities backward onto the record. Factual research looked like the irresistible force which would overturn interpretation and cut bias asunder.

Morgan's writing process for the Mormon book differed greatly from writing *The Humboldt* and *The Great Salt Lake,* and indeed, it differed from any of his later works. Most of the time he set down a text sequentially from beginning to end, editing and supplementing as he went. The chapters of the Mormon book proceeded in fits and starts, perhaps not only a function of his fragmented time, but also because while confident in his conclusions, he was still uncertain of exactly how to present them and what to emphasize. The process began piecemeal, by occasionally typing out "conceptual drafts," five-to-twelve-page narratives of a thought, or approach to a topic, whenever he had time and opportunity to write. These segments were neither sequential nor complete. The ideas simply spilled out, and the draft ended when the fire of the moment flickered out. They stacked up, giving him a dozen or more different introductions to the Smith family circumstances in Palmyra, New York, half a dozen treatments of the First Vision, as many about money-digging and Palmyra treasure-seeking. Eventually he would add fits and starts of an examination of the Book of Mormon. Nearly a year after signing the contract, the Mormon book had progressed to a loose collection of conceptual drafts but not a manuscript, and yet the due date crept ever closer.

Morgan summarized his now-proceeding venture to Kansas Historical Society librarian Louise Barry. The "Mormon book" was to break into three volumes by periods defined by the life spans of two major characters, Joseph Smith Jr. and Brigham Young. The first volume, Dale said, would include the contemporary cultural background of Mormonism, address the Book of Mormon and organization of the church and growth in Ohio, Missouri, and Illinois (inevitably including the origin of the church's practice of polygamy), concluding at its natural break with the death of Joseph Smith. Elements of two shorter preliminary manuscripts, his 1944 study of the Danites in Missouri and the 1940 work on the origins of the Kingdom of God would almost certainly have been integrated into the first volume.[70] The second volume would pick up in Nauvoo, Illinois, and therefore address the succession crisis, the Mormon Diaspora (generally regarded as the period between about 1840 and 1870) through the early years of the Reorganization, westward movement and settlement of Utah, and conclude with the death of Brigham Young. [71] A third volume, barely contemplated, would then necessarily carry the story from the federal anti-polygamy crusade, through the political accommodations of the 1880s to 1910s, the cultural centennial in 1930 and the rise of the polygamy sects in the same decade, up to the then-present day.

This last volume would carry a social criticism of contemporary Mormonism, in which Morgan fully intended to sit in judgment. Two years earlier, as the book's plan still rattled in a loose conceptual stage, Morgan responded to the *Utah Humanities Review*'s rejection of Austin Fife's article on LDS folklore because of a back-channel intervention from First Presidency member J. Reuben Clark: "When my big Mormon history reaches contemporary times, I am going to discuss all this question thoroughly, you may be sure. There is something damnably sick about a society and system of social beliefs antipathetic to proper functioning of scholarship."[72] Despite being denied access to the Church Historian's Office collections, enough source material was seeping into the emerging research libraries from trunks, closets, and attics, that Morgan felt justified that he could write substantively. The work would be grounded solidly in contemporary source material, though in his drafts, Morgan looked to DeVoto's *Mark Twain's America* as model, learning from the older ex-Utahn how to "stretch a fact" to cover a lot of descriptive ground with very little source material.

* * * * *

"I have had enough of working all day and trying to write all night," Dale told Fawn Brodie in 1948, "after all, I have been calling myself a writer; now is the time to demonstrate that I can make my writing support me. I feel it is mostly in the nature of a challenge."[73] Morgan saw the West stretching sky-wide all around him and could not help but imagine the interest such drama should attract. He was betting on declining odds. Having learned his craft in Writers' Project work, Morgan desperately wanted the western regionalism he knew to produce massive national sales, but he was trying to do so within a completely re-formed publication market. In the late 1940s supporting a career as a historian on book sales alone, as he planned a decade earlier, had become exponentially more challenging. "The kind of books I want to write cannot be expected to provide a living in themselves," he finally admitted to himself and to Juanita

Brooks in May 1949. "I will have to marry these books to other sources of income which will also permit me to live a normal social life."[74] It proved one of the truest professional observations he ever made.

Since Salt Lake City was now struck from his list of locations for the career he wanted, Morgan had to leave Utah a second time. His possible destinations were limited. Dale wanted work that allowed him to write, yes, but he also wanted to be in a place with a research library having substantive sources about Mormonism and western Americana. About the only options were Connecticut, Boston, New York City, a couple locations in California, and Washington, DC. In the second week of August, Dale wrote his sister Ruth that he planned to return to the Washington, DC, area and asked if he could stay temporarily with their family.[75]

Dale also began writing other friends and contacts with the news that he was moving back east. Most were sympathetic, some were irked. "It's a reflection upon the state," wrote Juanita Brooks, "that it has not enough to hold a man like you."[76] Dale waved her off: "The economic thing boils down to this, that I can either make a living freelancing or can write my histories, but not both. If I want to write the latter, a job will have to provide the wherewithal."[77] Charlie Kelly was blunt: "I'm sorry to hear you are leaving Utah, but actually I'm surprised you ever came back." "I hope some day you can write the things you have planned, and I know you will do a better job than has been done before. But I can't possibly see how you can make a living at it."[78]

Before leaving the state a second time, Dale made one more fishing trip with Jerry Bleak, a coincident opportunity to look over the stretch of Escalante route by Duchesne, Utah, and on the way back fishing the Strawberry Reservoir. Jerry came home with a string of trout; Dale was skunked. Though he could not know it then, this fishing expedition proved to be Morgan's last.

Dale's days through August and September 1949 were a patchwork of effort on the Korns notes and local research on emigrant trails across Utah, occasional work on his bibliographies, and beginning what would be a long, painful, and frustrating round of registration within the federal Civil Service Commission. Before leaving the west, Morgan really wanted to take some personal time to do a bit of exploring in its mountains, the National Parks, and California beaches. "But as it is," he wrote to Juanita Brooks, "I sit here trying to write a book, probing the Washington job situation at long range, and wondering just when I will be able to get away."[79] None of the pieces moved precisely into place, and he had to act without the certainty he desired. Dale finally terminated his lease on the 1000 East apartment with a September 30 date and got busy packing.

Short of funds on which to make the move, Dale resorted to an expedient he had hoped could wait five years or more. Addressing letters to the Utah State Historical Society, to Yale University librarian James Babb, and to the New York Public Library, Dale offered to sell carbons of his transcripts of articles from U.S. newspapers between 1800 and 1860. Though microfilm was becoming common in libraries and historical societies, many of these newspaper files were unique and unavailable to researchers in any format beyond the original printed papers. Under the title "The Mormons and the Far West," the transcripts (each filling a good-sized packing box) included contemporary documentation on the Latter Day Saints and Latter-day Saints, but also the fur trade, exploration, the California gold rush, transcontinental emigration, and trade with Mexico. It was a peerless collection and inherently limited resource. Morgan retained one set for his own use. Philanthropist William Robertston Coe bought a set for Yale University and eventually the Huntington Library got another, each for $300 or twice the monthly salary Morgan had made a few years earlier at the UWP. The Utah State Historical Society got its set at a discount rate, $150.[80]

As news of Morgan's pending move circulated, former USHS typist/clerk Lorraine Stout, now working in New York, paid Morgan perhaps the greatest compliment when she asked rhetorically how the society could possibly get along without him: "Just about every new project that we've embarked upon for the past year or so has been the result of a suggestion of yours—and more often than not the actual work involved has fallen upon your shoulders!"[81]

Dale's October 1 departure date didn't hold. Dale spent days ferrying material from 1000 East to his mother's basement on Hollywood Ave. The Hudson could not carry the swollen files and crates with him back to DC, nor could he afford to ship them, so those that were not absolutely essential to the Mormon book and Utah history were organized as best he could arrange along the walls in the low-ceilinged space. With a bit of planning Emily could retrieve and mail files individually to him as needed.

By the second week of October, Darel McConkey wrote back reporting his activity on Dale's behalf with the Civil Service Commission. In filling out the Information Specialist examination application, McConkey inadvertently put the wrong papers with the correct card, so Morgan was not registered and would have to correct matters when he arrived and re-indicate his interest in federal Information positions. A week later he wrote Morgan again that the Civil Service Information Specialist qualifying exam slated for October 28 could not be given on his expected October 31 arrival date. The best he could recommend was to stop in Columbus, Ohio, and take the exam there. [82]

Dale's plans to make the eastward drive into another research trip evaporated with McConkey's news. He hastily loaded the Hudson and left Salt Lake City on October 24 in a mad dash across the continent. At St. Louis, Dale turned north along US-61, racing for Quincy, Illinois. There he hoped against hope to take the Information Specialist exam at a subregional Civil Service Commission center, but the staff there merely referred him to the Chicago office. From Quincy, Dale dashed toward the state capital at Springfield, where a General Delivery letter from McConkey reported the unwelcome news that the exam could only be taken at a Civil Service Regional Center and only on October 28. It was already the 28th and there was no time to get to either Chicago or Columbus, Ohio. Morgan gave it up, resigned to take the exam on its next cycle in Washington, DC. Along the way the temperamental Hudson began dying at stoplights. Dale pulled into a garage in Zanesville, Ohio, to replace distributor points. Outside of Frederick, Maryland, the fan belt snapped. Morgan installed the spare himself and finally glided into a parking space in front of Ruth and Doug Barton's home in Alexandria, Virginia. Not an auspicious beginning.

PART II

An Uncomfortable Interlude

CHAPTER 9

Digression

Books and History in the Postwar Context

History is a hussy much disinclined to support herself.[1]
—Dale Morgan

MORGAN RETURNED to the national capital in 1950 for two reasons. Not only did he need access to the source material the capital offered, but he was beginning to realize that to establish himself as a writer of "the kind of books I want to write" might be more difficult than he assumed. He also needed a salaried job to subsidize his time devoted to research and writing. In fact, his ideal was rooted in assumptions about writing, publishing, and history he had developed in a prewar world. He was likely unaware of the broader changes affecting the American market for books and writing. Morgan seems to have planned his foray into the postwar world by hauling along his expectations formulated in the 1930s. Setting Dale Morgan's study of Mormonism into the context of both scholarship and the publishing industry of the time helps understand how rocky his prospective career path was likely to be.

The American book market on which Dale Morgan set his sights had endured two decades—a professional lifespan—that were anything but stable or orderly. A fundamental shift in the economics of publishing and reading, set in motion immediately *before* the Depression, changed the landscape. By the end of the Second World War, still reeling from realignment, the American publishing industry entered its second shift in a generation.

* * * * *

American publishing welcomed the twentieth century as a genteel club of family and founder-run businesses. Since the end of the Civil War, reading had been Americans' chief form of private entertainment. Prior to 1920, reading may not have been the United States' only form of personal recreation, but it was generally the most commonly shared recreation, particularly in non-rural communities. Reading crossed classes and geographies but was served from very different marketplaces. Inexpensive fiction magazines of several hundred pages printed on soft, cheap paper—known popularly as "the pulps"—exploded in the 1910s, catering thematically to those preferring romance, adventure, fortune, or the supernatural. Newspapers and magazines in the country regularly carried story serializations. Book and magazine publishers, second-generation firms based chiefly in Boston and New York with newer upstarts sprinkled liberally across the rest of the country, pushed out novels and descriptive adventure tours of everywhere on earth. The nation's sectarian interest newspapers and magazines were concentrated in Chicago and Nashville, Tennessee. Individual reading, whether highbrow novels or lowbrow police gazettes, was joined by the emerging phenomenon of middle-brow Book-of-the-Month clubs, curated reading lists lending culture to aspiring readers.

Reading was everywhere, but geographically the U.S. market for books and magazines was uneven. For instance, in 1930 an economic survey conducted by the book industry found that the entire state of Virginia, the twentieth most populous state, consumed *less* than two percent of the nation's books. The rest of the eleven Southern states together could collectively muster less than 13 percent, while New York and Illinois together counted 17.26 percent of the nation's book-buying. Those two states held over a quarter of the nation's urban population, but five states accounted for 62 percent of the books sold in the country, and of that figure, more than 30 percent of the nation's books were bought in New York, with California (even before it became a megalopolis), Illinois, Massachusetts, and Pennsylvania rounding out the figure. Demographically, in terms of the urban-rural market share, and given the sea of other printed material, the economics of book consumption was regionalized.[2]

At precisely the same time yet another problem facing the publishing industry was the wildfire success of the historical novel, fueled by Margaret Mitchell's 1936 book *Gone with the Wind*. Between June and December of 1936 alone, *Gone with the Wind* sold a million copies. By 1937 every US publisher was looking for historical novels that would turn over copies even fractionally as well as Mitchell's spectacular bestseller. Within four years of its initial publication, at least seven editions of Mitchell's book were available with prices ranging from an illustrated photoplay or movie tie-in edition at an unheard-of price of $7.50 down to a 69-cent paperback. Four of the five bestselling books of fiction in the country in 1940 were historical novels. Dozens of new titles began appearing in a new genre being called *Americana*.[3] Publishers were actively looking for what Michael Korda described as "ambitious novels with a big theme, a big scope, larger-than-life-size characters, whether written at the 'popular' level ... or at the literary level." Publishers were constantly hunting for potential bigness: "big in length, big in concept, with a big, central moral conflict, trying hard to be solid, serious, challenging, as well as entertaining."[4]

The Mormons were not ignored. Vardis Fisher's 1939 historical novel *Children of God,* dismissed by some Latter-day Saints as not suitably praising their pioneers, nevertheless drew outside attention to the church's history. Churchman Marvin O. Ashton returned from a tour of Latter-day Saint congregations in the Midwest reporting that at Carthage, Illinois, he had encountered "students of an entire school"—*not* Latter-day Saints—whose interest in the site had been attracted by Fisher's novel. In places where the Mormons had been, rather than where they were, people were awakening to the idea that Latter Day Saint history could be good business—but that didn't mean that *every* book on the subject was good business.[5] Brodie's biography of Joseph Smith proved to be good business because it interpreted a key figure for readers at large, much to the chagrin of believers. Morgan's book probably would have done the same, but Dale Morgan staked his would-be writing career on a thin, ground-level slice of regional Americana at a time that readers and publishers were looking for grandeur and sweeping scope.

The search for bigness was trumped only by the perennial quest for "the great American novel," of which *Gone with the Wind* was the most recent and *Moby Dick* probably the first. In his history of American popular reading, literary historian James D. Hart reminds us that historical fiction of the national past was in demand during this period partly "because many of its most widely read examples dealt with an earlier America, [perceived as] more serene or more triumphant, appealing to the nostalgic urge of people living through a period of distress." Distress in the 1930s came not merely in the form of the obvious economic depression but also in the challenge of mechanistic, fast-paced, impersonal Modernism.

Literary Americana tended to portray characters and settings of bygone times remembered or known, but not personally experienced by readers, something that was out of the reader's ordinary. A work could be nostalgic across any range of senses, from teary-eyed patriotic affirmation to bitterly negative social indictment, like Steinbeck's *Grapes of Wrath*. Americana was "concerned with the exploration of salient national characteristics," qualities that could be lauded even as they oversimplified the messy complexity of real people living in real times. Literary Americana was partly a response to the Depression itself, and rose out of "a people frustrated by the present and hoping to find comfort in the [perceived] happier, younger days of their land."[6] Strongly fueled by that nostalgia, modern classics like Stephen Vincent Benét's *John Brown's Body* (1928), Marjorie Kinnan Rawlings's *The Yearling* (1938), and Thomas Wolfe's *Of Time and the River* (1935) became important books. Even an urban slum became a bitter but nostalgic setting in Betty Smith's *A Tree Grows in Brooklyn* (1943). Each of these works evoked time and place, and quality and simplicity as well, in ways that had little previous parallel in American literature—or in earlier realities, for that matter. At the same time, *Americana* was a word which was also applied to a genre of old, historical imprints: rare-book works reporting the continent's exploration, the nation's history, and the activities of its people's progenitors. Both uses of the word looked back fondly on America's allegedly kinder, gentler, more adventuresome, and heroic past. Morgan's study of the Mormons promised to be anything but nostalgic.

Then the world descended again into war, replacing the Great Depression with a new and different type of disruption and dislocation. Men left for military service, women went to factories, and everyone looked east and west into two-front maelstroms. Yet, for all the horror and suffering it imposed on humanity, the Second World War represented an exceptional opportunity for American publishers. Following the dramatic downturn experienced during the late 1920s and early 1930s, the U.S. book industry had to cope with a nearly exponential demand for reading material during the war, including coordinating with the War Department to produce more than 122 million copies of pocket-sized Armed Services Editions—1,322 different genre and literary novels, as well as some nonfiction works—for soldiers and sailors. Reading once again became popular on the home front as well with other pastimes such as cinema and radio curtailed due to travel restrictions and blacked-out electricity.

The upswing in reading created something of a vacuum in the book market, one that sucked in publishable work not quite indiscriminately, but its gigantic draft created a bubble of opportunity. Material demonstrating lesser technical skill, marginal themes, outdated topics, and hack ideas and plots suddenly had a much greater chance at publication. The yearn for Americana nostalgia shifted from a reaction to economic conditions to a deep yearning for calmer times without war—which, after the war, had already receded safely into the past. Americana fiction continued to be popular, but its forces were paralleled in a focus on human experience in nonfiction drawing partly upon the pride of place expressed in the WPA projects' American regionalism.

* * * * *

The end of the Second World War in 1945 left publishers, executives, bookstore owners, and librarians unsure whether they were at the leading edge of a growth curve or near the precipice of a postwar bust. "Apparently," observed the introduction to one industry study, "no one in the book business had any authentic information as to what was actually happening, particularly in relation to 'People and Books.'" Eventually wartime price controls would be lifted, ensuring that production costs were certain to rise, whether from additional investment in plant capacity or postwar inflation. Publishers, like all other US businesses, adopted the view that "profitable future operation becomes increasingly dependent upon the accuracy with which market trends can be gauged."[7]

As book sales slowed from the wartime boom, publishers realized that they could not sustain the practices they had followed from the 1860s to the mid-1940s, the "gamble" George Bernard Shaw explained.[8] That process consisted of picking up manuscripts and pushing them through the expensive publication process based on a general feeling about what the public would *likely* buy and hoping for decent sales—precisely the way *The Humboldt* had been acquired. Because of rising costs for paper and especially printing and binding machinery, margins became much slimmer even as the volume of printed material increased.

In response, publishers were learning the value of targeting specific buyers. Since book production involved months of investment in editing, production, and manufacturing *before* a title was on shelves for sale, studying readership seemed like a good idea. "The ever-recurring phrase is that we will increase our business by ten-percent over what it was before the war," wrote one recently demobilized New York bookman, A. van Duym. "Sure the soldiers have acquired a taste for reading books, but does that necessarily mean that they will want to own them too?"[9] That question was entirely open, and no one had a good answer. What van Duym did realize presciently was that competition for book sales would not be between publishers, but between the book trade and the entire rest of the manufacturing economy. Both were chasing shares of the postwar market not only for entertainment, but also for appliances, automobiles, furniture, audio equipment, and even housing.

Learning well from federal war-planning efforts, the American publishing industry abandoned its traditional basis of making decisions based on literary instinct, replacing hunch with modern sales-forecast business models. In 1945, publishers commissioned a major study of reading habits in the United States. The fundamental question the industry wanted to know was this: "was the buying of books in recent years a war-time luxury which will abate now that the war has ended?" Some of what the industry learned from Henry C. Link and Harry Arthur Hopf's commissioned study, published in 1946 and titled simply *People and Books,* was not surprising—that level of education was a better predictor of readership than income or economic status, and reading of all sorts declined among older Americans. In the 1940s, America's older generation was generally not well educated and tended not to be readers, so the demographic decline in reading could be more related to amount of schooling and culture than to age. As public education reforms of the 1920s now produced its second generation of citizens, and as the general level of education increased within the population, reading should have increased as well—but didn't. The study missed a key factor.

Van Duym nailed the key difference in the postwar economy: radio and movies had inextricably joined books on the front line of competition for American leisure time. To publishers, the figures for recreational reading were sobering. Half of one statistical study's subjects had read a book or magazine within the preceding month. They were classed as active readers. Inactive readers, those who had read something only sometime within the past year, represented 21 percent (the same percentage which had read something only the day before). The remaining 29 percent had not read recreationally in a year and were considered nonreaders. Of the latter figure, nearly half could not recall having read something within the previous five years. Thus, 70 percent of the books sold in the U.S. in 1945 could be attributed to the activity of merely 21 percent of the population, and 94 percent of reading material of any type was handled by merely half of the country's potential readership. Even the popular historical novel genre did not rank high on readers' priority lists, landing only 6 percent of respondents' first preferences in the book survey.[10]

This study clanged alarm bells for the publishing industry because its results suggested that half the American population, more literate in 1945 than ever before, now read effectively nothing at all. Despite the boom in book sales and the increase in reading during the war, of the people who had read a book the previous day (21 percent of all respondents), the average time spent reading was merely thirteen minutes, less than the average time devoted to movie-going the previous day. By far the most significant recreational activity reported by respondents was listening to the radio, which now occupied eight times the number of minutes devoted to reading. More Americans were reading, but that reading still occupied only 40 percent of daily time available for recreation and improvement.

Overall, publishing generally seemed to be on good ground and was probably poised to grow after the war. As Americans became dramatically more mobile, publishers now needed to sell well *nationally* rather than appealing to niche regional markets, but in 1945, the relative importance of fiction to the book market was declining over the halcyon days of two decades earlier. One reason was that books were not nearly as significant in daily life as were radio, film, newspapers, and magazines.[11] What remaining reader interest existed for colorful story settings was being drawn away from fiction toward nonfiction. To be sure, hundreds of novels were still being released, but the Depression and the Second World War swelled readers' interest in nonfiction as American fiction markets began slumping. Fiction's importance as a fractional part of the whole trade-book market was lessening rapidly. Though the proportional balance between fiction and nonfiction book publications changed by only a few percentage points, it represented a sea change in American book sales and readership, showing how deeply war affected the country's reading habits. One writer, Harry Harrison Kroll, whose work had flourished during the war, recognized at least that aspect himself. "Novels don't seem to do as well as these 'I-was-the-last-man off Something-or-other' books," he complained as early as 1943.[12] And after one of his many postwar scouting trips, New York publisher Alfred A. Knopf's scout Herbert Weinstock reported back that "Among the booksellers I saw ... there was a unanimous depression about fiction, but also a general feeling that the book business is a healthy and going concern."[13]

This news should have been a flash of opportunity for a writer like Dale Morgan, but Morgan was not interested in nonfiction generally, just history specifically. For those who cared to look, the nonfiction bestseller lists revealed the dramatically changed nature of postwar America: *Betty*

Crocker's Picture Cook Book; The Baby; Look Younger, Live Longer; How I Raised Myself from Failure to Success in Selling; and *Your Dream Home* were among the top-selling nonfiction books for 1950. "The war had restored American productivity," observed Michael Korda, "brought a final end to the Great Depression, and made Americans yearn for a quiet life at home in the new suburbs that were already redefining the American Way of Life. Succeeding at your job, buying your dream house, looking younger and living longer, and cooking food that looked pretty was what Americans wanted after the deprivations of the Depression and the excitement of war, though even as people settled into 'the good life,' the first tremors of [social] changes were taking place around them."[14] Niche publishing markets began proliferating, but competition within them skyrocketed as publishers looked for bestsellers rather than simply interesting, insightful, or compelling works.

Regional history's thinning sliver of the postwar American book market was where Dale Morgan tried to stake his writing career. American readers seemed interested less in reading for personal diversion than in reading for personal improvement—how-to and self-help. History itself, a diversion, was not a necessary part of "success." As Morgan experienced with the success of both *Humboldt* and *Great Salt Lake,* a popular market for solid, readable history emerged during the 1940s. The problem Morgan faced was that the bulk of the nonfiction book market was not dominated by the kind of history Dale Morgan wanted to write. In short, to succeed as a historical writer in the postwar world, rather than write the kind of books he wanted to write, Morgan would have to write the kind of books people want to buy. After the Second World War, sustaining a writing career independently by sales alone would be much, *much* more difficult than it had been in the 1920s or 1930s.

* * * * *

American publishing also was being both riven and braided by a new financial force at almost exactly the same time—Wall Street money. The country's distinguished publishing firms, long individually or family owned, were about to be hijacked by corporations. "The Wall Street wolf was already at the door," wrote one prominent executive who came to work in publishing at this time, "impressed by the growth of [postwar] textbook and educational publishing and eager for a new industry to take public, while book publishers themselves were already trying to figure out how much they would be worth if they opened that door."[15] By the early 1960s American publishing houses were on the cusp of a four-decade corporate feeding frenzy of mergers, acquisitions, and consolidations. Publishers also established textbook divisions as a means of offsetting the general decline in fiction buying and to capitalize on first the influx of veterans into higher education and later the Baby Boom as that generation reached school age during the 1950s and 1960s.[16]

One of the first shocks of the earthquake would be Alfred A. Knopf's 1959 private sale of his imprint and its prestige to Bennett Cerf of Random House. Two years later, the "perennial optimist" himself took Random House public in a stock offering that attracted Wall Street interest to book publishing as only potential profits can. Old publishing families began selling off companies in a wave of acquisitions that culminated in the media and publishing conglomerates of the 1990s. The firms of hands-on owner/publishers—individuals who had or who wanted to publish Morgan, like Knopf, D. L. Chambers of Bobbs-Merrill, John Farrar, and Stanley Rinehart—quickly began disappearing into corporate maws as privately owned imprints and businesses became corporate fodder. Through the 1950s, American publishing, which for a century had been a men's club of old money, staffed on the strength of personal relationships, was taken over by accountants and thereafter ruled by the iron hand of balance sheets, market estimates, and contract terms. Over a decade and a half, by the time of Morgan's passing in the early 1970s, the American tradition and culture of trade publishing passed almost completely from private into corporate hands.[17]

* * * * *

At the same time, changes in the publishing market sparked an opportunity for new developments. Two of them affected Morgan directly. First was a mid-century proliferation of academic publishers. In 1901, the entire list of colleges and universities in the United States fielded merely four academic presses. By 1920 there were a dozen, and by 1927 more than two dozen. Between 1949 and 1969 the Association of American University Publishers membership more than doubled. The emergence of the university press was so dramatically sudden that one contemporary comment from the private sector voiced the existential questions "what is it that distinguishes a university press from any responsible commercial book publisher?" and "are university presses a permanent part of the academic landscape?"[18]

The postwar rise of academic publishing created a new opportunity for university-affiliated writers, including historians. In the 1930s and 1940s the bulk of history written by academics was published for informed non-specialists and released through mainstream trade-book publishers for the "middle brow" reading consumer eager for sophistication and knowledge. With the exception of dedicated textbooks, only incidentally did books of history appear in classrooms. That flow changed after World War II with the proliferation of university presses and the rising number of young PhDs moving into tenurable employment. Suddenly the production of not merely a book but of *scholarship* became increasingly important. Where trade publishers had been fairly cavalier about what *might* sell as long as it was "good," university presses were willing to invest in publishing works too specialized or detailed for the taste of balance-sheet driven mass-marketing. Often these were revised doctoral dissertations, such as the one Morgan himself copyedited in 1943. Operating with the security of institutional backing (the public sector analog of corporate ownership of trade publishers), academic presses operated on slim cost-recovery margins, content to sell a few hundred copies of a book chiefly to the rapidly expanding collections of burgeoning college and university libraries, rather than thousands or tens of thousands of copies to general readers.[19]

Just as importantly, these new academic publishers discovered a newly important factor of the age: the value of paperback books. Where hardcover books were attractive to libraries, paperbacks sold at lower prices to individuals. Paperbacks had been publishing's disreputable child of the 1930s. The products were notoriously cheap—inexpensive paper, printing which ranged between adequate and terrible, all kept together in marginal adhesive bindings sized for pockets. For two decades paperback houses were looked on as scavengers by mainstream publishers. By the 1950s, rather than sell off a book's reprint rights to a paperback house, trade publishers began establishing their own paperback imprints while university presses generally continued producing hardback books. Cornell University Press and the University of Chicago Press, however, began publishing successful paperback series in the mid-1950s, adapted to meet academic and library market expectations. Their paperback titles were produced in larger formats and on better quality paper, so that unsold copies could be returned for redistribution and sale elsewhere without disintegrating in the process.

As the Baby Boom began to hit colleges in 1960, the stock-in-trade of university presses generally became paperbacks. Cheaper to produce and thus cheaper to sell, paperbacks put large numbers of back-list and new scholarly titles directly into the hands of college and graduate students cost-effectively—not for casual reading, but as textbooks to involve those students with the conversations of scholarship.[20]

Dale Morgan's career transected these trends in academic publishing. He published one book through the University of California Press, his edition of William Perkins' *Three Years in California* (1964), which paid him almost nothing, but the paperback edition of *Jedediah Smith and the Opening of the West* (1964) from the University of Nebraska Press secured him consistent readership by college students and preserved his scholarly reputation across generations. The former book he did not want to do, while the latter he did not want done. Neither represented the writing he wanted to do. The tension between Morgan's expectations, systemic changes in publishing, and the opportunities which remained for publishing the ground-level work he was known for, pushed his writing career toward another publishing development of the period.

* * * * *

A second shift in America's publishing market after the Second World War was the rise of a much smaller class of publisher, one that already produced Morgan's work: the limited-edition press. During the nineteenth and into the twentieth century, reminiscences and personal narratives were often published privately by a local printer. These typically scarce publications eventually provided fuel for Americana book collectors and emerging rare-book collections. Private publication was partly overtaken in the first half of the twentieth century by the emergence of a new strain of limited-edition niche publishers. A commercial publisher took a risk on producing 3,000 to 20,000 copies of a work hoping that the mass market would (eventually) provide a return on the investment, which usually involved a high expense for marketing and a low price point. On the other hand, fine-press printers/limited-edition publishers like the Grabhorn Press in San Francisco, Champoeg Press in Oregon, the Old West Publishing Company operated by Fred Rosenstock, the California Historical Society, or Talisman Press could advertise directly to an interested mailing list and quickly sell all or most of three or five hundred copies of a fine-press work at a fairly high price point to select libraries and committed buyers. Morgan's own *Jedediah Smith and His Maps of the American West* (California Historical Society, 1954) was an early success story of this type.

The net effect of limited-edition-press publishing in the west provided an opportunity for important works of regional and antiquarian history to be published outside of the trade-publishing mainstream, carving out a whole series of new regional and state niche markets.[21]

Nearly fifteen years earlier, slightly flush with the success of *The Humboldt,* Morgan confessed to Jerry Bleak that "I'll never get rich writing the books I want to write," but he expected that he could make "a basic income" from his writing.[22] The "books I want to write" as he tried to launch a writing career in the 1940s were by the 1960s subjects too specialized for the mass-market, trade book publishers Morgan hoped to interest. By the mid-1960s the publishing world where Morgan expected to flourish had been largely replaced by corporate cost-benefit management, scholarship high on prestige but of low returns, and niche editions. Morgan's masterworks, his two great studies published as a preeminent researcher and historian of Western Americana, were products of this niche market for limited editions, fine-press printing, and subscription publishing. The market for works of extraordinary detail and focused narrative remained strong, but the branch of specialized history which attracted Dale Morgan and many like him never flourished in the new garden of corporate-dominated trade publishing.

While Morgan was a scholar committed to his subject, he also saw publishing partly as a revenue stream. As his career at UC Berkeley unfolded, Morgan ended up chasing small-press publication projects because that was the last venue for the kind of history he wrote. Writing commissions and royalties from small presses paid immediately, even if not very well. Ironically, the success of these small works distracted him from the one trade-book project which might have promised a substantive return: editing the William B. Lorton diary for Knopf.

Morgan published three trade books to critical success in the 1940s and early 1950s, though through the rest of his career his publishing sank ever more deeply into genres which receded further and further from the core of American trade-book publishing in which he wanted to succeed. In fact, never again in his career could Morgan successfully return to trade publishing. Why? Getting a book into trade publishing was becoming harder and harder, for one reason. Publishers increasingly adopted the convention of private literary agents as gatekeepers to begin separating good writing from the rest.

Also, as the number of academic historians climbing into higher education and the tenure pipeline increased, academics in the country tended to look askance at the antiquarianism of limited-edition publishing, at the same time that their own emerging academic writing style did not much interest trade publishers. "Serious" history was gravitating toward university presses, which themselves tended to specialize by region or discipline. Ian Tyrell points out that, in the 1950s, academic historians began disengaging with public readership, turning their arguments and writing inward, writing for each other rather than for the wide American population. The 1930s through the 1950s represented a high point in historians' published involvement with America's reading public. From virtually every angle, the American publishing culture that Morgan faced in 1950, and certainly at the peak of his career in the 1960s, was no longer the one he had been introduced to in the 1930s.[23]

Beyond the evolving style of academic history and proliferation of university presses, the growth of academic history after the Second World War strengthened other related developments. One was rising numbers of field-specific academic organizations and their conferences. The society which concerned Morgan most directly was the Western History Association (WHA), which enters his story somewhat later. A second development, specifically because of the rise of professional organizations, was the explosion in the number of scholarly journals. As organizations proliferated, so did the number of new topical journals catering to historical specialists. Even history's flagship journals expanded in scope if not issue length: the *Mississippi Valley Historical Review* became the *Journal of American History* in 1964.[24] Over the years its content shifted, presenting readers almost as many pages of book reviews—the kind of works Morgan could do but didn't interest him financially—as it did of articles.

* * * * *

The postwar expansion of higher education and shake-ups in publishing paralleled changes in the American economy and society itself. Increases in personal automobile ownership pushed railroad passenger lines into steep decline but fueled an explosion in automobile-related infrastructure, including services within national parks. While park "visitation" became a hiss and byword to preservationists, cities and towns perceived opportunity. Local historical features, historic sites, and battlefields were graded for roads and trails and reconstructed as attractions. There was a tradeoff, of course. In the emerging heritage industry of living-history museums and local history publishing, historical interpretation became a vehicle for tourism rather than a quest for understanding. The national past was mined for theme-park opportunities, such as Disneyland's Frontierland.[25] New industries in motels, corporate fast-food chains, and highway construction catered to the movement and interests of a post-war generation of automobile-mobile families. Tourist dollars were far more valuable than the promise of opportunities for engaged understanding that scholarly books or microfilmed archival collections promised institutions. Perhaps it was ironic that the study of history was being publicly underfunded at the same time that public interest (and tourist dollars) continued growing.

CHAPTER 10

"I Am in for a Long Pull"[1]

Job Seeker in Washington, DC, and Salt Lake City, 1950–1952

> *This financial crisis in my life is something that has to be fairly faced now;*
> *nothing is to be gained by turning my back on it for a year or two or five.*
> *I can't work out a satisfactory life for myself until I put a new financial*
> *floor under it.*[2]

—Dale Morgan

THE PACE OF CHANGE and growth in the postwar capital had accelerated even beyond the tense bustle experienced during World War II. After the war, industry was specializing and scaling upward rapidly. Finance, transportation, and communication were creating national networks and markets. Economically, the nation was becoming national, rather than merely a collection of regions. Frankly, modern governance required a modern government. The character of federal hiring fundamentally changed to manage this ballooning growth.

Though Herbert Hoover warned against it, the federal bureaucracy began expanding rapidly under Hoover during the 1920s as it organized to feed American business with data and expertise. Relief jobs created during the next decade, the recovery measures of the 1930s, whether in CCC camps or the federal offices that administered relief programs, were short-term opportunities never intended to be permanent. They disappeared as the country mobilized through 1940 and 1941. Within the federal government, the sheer size and complexity of organizing a nation for foreign war forced the federal mechanism, especially at its lower levels, to turn to utterly impersonal hiring factors to sift the hordes of applicants. Hiring processes were completely objectified by erecting a series of standardized and publicly accessible gates: announcements, qualification lists, applications, and review processes. Even at the state level and with wartime hiring frenzy, Utah WPA Administrator Darrell Greenwell issued a circular about jobs in which he reminded staff that "there are such opportunities, but the vacant jobs must be filled by trained persons."[3]

By the time the country sat back on its heels at the end of the war, if one wanted a government job in Cold War Washington, then one had to pass through the trial by fire that was the Civil Service Commission qualifying examinations and application process. Government service was no longer a gentlemen's club of country lawyers and second sons. Personal connections to power were still profoundly important, but by 1949 government service had outgrown the scope of relationships between one's father and the local Congressman. The need to differentiate between the skyrocketing numbers of applicants, gave credentialing—applicants' technical qualifications and formal credentials—a newly important place in postwar America, within industry as well as government.

Beyond its long-standardized application system, Civil Service began relying heavily on credentials as objective benchmarks, the means of containing, shaping, and directing the explosion of applicants to the federal workforce. However, confusion over "objective" submission, distribution, filing, and recall of Civil Service Commission forms was symptomatic of postwar bureaucracy. Morgan completed the government's standard employment application form and career information in color-coded quadruplicate well before leaving Salt Lake City, which effectively meant that his documentation was submerged in a sea of similar applications.

Of course, knowing someone still counted for much (at least, informally). Morgan began working his network of friends and professional acquaintances before leaving Salt Lake City. Once he arrived in late October, Darel McConkey and a mutual friend working at Civil Service helped Dale immediately set his job hunt in motion. One of Morgan's first informal personal calls was to former federal Historical Records Survey (HRS) director, Dr. Luther H. Evans, now the Librarian of Congress. Evans had praised Morgan's HRS writings and still remembered the author. Morgan asked Evans about employment prospects at the Library, or whether the Library was in the position to fund his work completing at least the Mormon bibliography.[4] Dale felt the bibliography gave him a potentially golden key to open a position at the Library of Congress, where the production of checklists and bibliographies were traditional foundations of professional service in the huge library.

Before computer-based digital automation shifted library routines in the 1980s, a principal way librarians improved the intellectual grasp of the massive book collection was to compile long topical lists of works within specific subjects. Verner W. Clapp, a former reading room assistant at the Library of Congress, reminisced about such work: "Each of us had his private bibliographic project. These not only served to occupy spare time and to motivate browsing that might otherwise have been aimless but also gave prestige. Of course, many collections of useless [card files] were generated, but some achieved lasting value."[5] The Library of Congress had a public-service staff of nearly sixty, nine of whom did nothing *but* bibliography, yet Morgan's deafness still chronically overbalanced the scale against him in hiring decisions. There was another catch. "Job descriptions for these positions indicate that the assistants in charge need at a minimum a college degree and graduation from an accredited library school or equivalent training and experience. Also desirable was experience (three years or more) in reference and bibliography in a large research library."[6]

Dale put enormous trust in the phrase "or equivalent training and experience." Given his practical HRS research experience and the Mormon bibliography well underway, Dale felt he had demonstrated that he was capable of detailed bibliographic work. What he did not understand was that the shift towards credential requirements affected an institution even as staid and seemingly monolithic as the Library of Congress. While the Library was chronically short-staffed and could have used his services, preemployment technical training had become a standard expectation of job applicants across many fields, carried from the war industries even to the library. Whether in government service, skilled labor, or corporate employment, requiring formal training and credentials became a way to reduce the sheer numbers of difficult to classify *–or equivalent training and experience* applicants. Morgan regarded highly his "practical training" as an HRS and Federal Writers' Project historian. "I worked four years for WPA," he wrote in an unpublished essay about his experience, "and those four years seem to me equivalent to about sixteen years in any other kind of work."[7] Unfortunately, he was the only one who thought that.

Yet, by the late 1940s on-the-job training and practical experience were no longer regarded as equivalent to graduation from an accredited degree program. Morgan survived college without accommodation for his deafness and maintained a credible B average, but impatient to be away in his writing career, he had seen no need to set aside his writing projects long enough to scratch his way through an advanced or specialized degree. Dale Morgan was capable, but tried to open a door into a profession that was now firmly locked to outsiders by its credentialing requirements.

Regardless of his complicating deafness, his informal work-experience credentials simply did not qualify him.

Nor did his specific work experience set him apart from the teeming crowd. Dale wrote his mother that the small handful of higher-paid positions for which he had applied through Civil Service attracted 4,000 applicants in two weeks. Even lower-paid press positions attracted over a thousand.[8] Civil Service hiring registers and iron-clad examination schedules also made the federal hiring process interminably slow. In the last months of 1949, the government hiring cycle was in ebb anyway; he would have to wait for the next cycle of hiring in the spring.

*　*　*　*　*

Three days after arriving in the capital, the mail delivered a Civil Service envelope, forwarded from Emily Morgan's address in Salt Lake City. Dale slit it open to discover a formal notice that his application for a rating as "Historian-Social Science Analyst" had been ruled ineligible since his rating failed to meet minimal requirements. A day or two later, two more envelopes arrived holding similar notices. One ruled him ineligible as "unable to hear the conversational voice," the other, as he put it, "just plain ineligible."

Dale immediately asked Darel McConkey to arrange a meeting with the Civil Service. Two days later the pair learned that barely two hundred of 4,000 applicants had secured the highest of the three ratings for which Morgan had applied. Gentle probing revealed that the reviewer had ignored Morgan's publication record, references, previous Civil Service rating, federal employment experience, and Guggenheim Memorial Foundation fellowship to disqualify him on the grounds of his service with the WPA, assuming that he had been employed on the Utah Writers' Project as an unskilled relief worker.

The reviewer's assumption—within the federal government's hiring agency, no less—illustrated a cold political reality: those gatekeeping federal employment disregarded the very activity Morgan valued as his primary training in historical method. Dale Morgan may have been proud of what he and the UWP had accomplished, but that was part of the problem. Despite proving his deafness a mere inconvenience rather than an actual handicap, he never seemed to grasp that, in terms of postwar Washington DC, his adult work experience in two of the most politically despised prewar federal agencies was as much a liability as it was a credential. Even Dale finally admitted to himself and a correspondent that "to many employers WPA experience was more damaging on an employment record than total unemployment."[9] In simple terms, the practical "graduate training" in writing of which he had been so proud, actually did not count for much.

On top of that, the Servicemen's Readjustment Act or "G.I. Bill" routed over two million veterans, who once would have considered blue-collar work as a career, into higher education and other training. By 1950, the number of educationally qualified applicants for positions everywhere had increased dramatically, lending added value to formal credentials as hiring standards.[10] Despite his wartime federal service, Morgan could not rely on hiring preference under the G.I. Bill. By the time of his second stint in Washington, DC, Morgan's 1939 strategic decision to base a career as a historian on native talent and hard work looked increasingly like a risky gamble. To add injury to insult, Civil Service clerks could not locate Morgan's application documents to double-check his prior employment status as a technical specialist.[11]

Finally in the first week of March, Morgan went personally to the Civil Service Commission building and spent a good part of the day circulating between offices trying to identify which ratings applied to which applications, which of his ratings were not yet filed, and why his previous CAF-9 rating with the Office of Price Administration was considered irrelevant.[12]

He also worked distractedly on the Mormon book, sending the draft for a fourth chapter to the Utah Historical Society on March 11. "This is depressingly slow progress in view of the deadline I have been trying to meet," he wrote his mother.[13] "Every page, paragraph, and sentence has to be tested for its soundness," Morgan asserted to his editor John Selby. "Already I have rewritten some parts of it eight or nine times, and none of it less than three."[14]

Coincidentally, however, Dale filed a revised federal employment application for an appointment as "Historian" in September 1950. His supplementary statement began with a confident but telling choice of words: "My stature as a historian is based only in part on my formal employment record." In the absence of academic credentials, he emphasized instead his practical research experience and publication record. Again, his document sank like a stone into the sea of applications. By the end of the month Morgan still had not heard about either his employment status or rankings revision. McConkey finally nudged a friend of his at

Civil Service in late May to see what had become of Morgan's appeal. The friend responded that not only had the original application, but also now Dale's appeal and supplementary documentation gone missing without a trace. After nine months, Morgan's job search had not even gotten to Civil Service square one.[15]

In desperation, Morgan finally called in a favor. Senator Elbert D. Thomas, the ranking member of the Utah congressional delegation, was a fan of Morgan's work and the two men were on a first-name basis. What Morgan's polite pleas to Civil Service could not shake loose, the formal inquiry of a sitting US Senator could, and did. Morgan's appeal surfaced inexplicably among the files of the Civil Service medical section. Senator Thomas and Morgan received a letter stating that based on the applicant's added data that "it has been found possible to assign him eligibility for Historian," the most specialized of the ratings for which Dale had applied.[16]

Dale wrote Thomas with genuine thanks: "faith, it is said, has power to move mountains, but it seems to require a more active principle to move the Civil Service Commission at times."[17] Morgan, at last, had in hand a valid hunting license for a suitable job. He immediately sent inquiries to half a dozen federal agencies.

* * * * *

Ironically, while Dale Morgan was energetically trying to find a writing job in the federal bureaucracy, the study of the national past was being infused with new energy and support. During the 1930s the documentary approach had careened into the nineteenth-century style of expository and often heroic narrative, emphasizing the experience of common citizens over individual political figures. Evidence—citations to primary and secondary works—became as important to historical writing as explanatory narrative had been during prior decades.

During and immediately after the war, both liberal historians such as Richard Hofstadter and Louis Hartz and conservative historians like Daniel J. Boorstin (who became Librarian of Congress in late life) drifted closer together. In the face of national unity to prosecute a foreign war, these writers began reemphasizing the general unity of national history, an interpretive viewpoint which took on the name *consensus school*. Every generation writes history anew to answer its concerns and serve its own purposes. By the 1950s, with Depression a memory, consensus historians felt the nation needed a "return to the true Americanism rooted in liberal capitalism and the pursuit of individual opportunity," in other words, back to the nation's bootstrap-success myths.[18] Generally, the consensus approach asserted "that America owed more—and particularly more of its successes—to a tradition of consensus about fundamental principles than to a tradition of internal conflict" over complications like labor or race.[19] Its theme was the basic continuity of American values, producing affirming narratives that emphasized the nation as a unified (and though unstated, white) society of common goals, minimizing the conflicts of slavery, western settlement, labor, and the "authentic color" but complex realities of ethnicity, gender, regionalism, and local priorities.[20]

The burgeoning growth of higher education both reflected and fueled a rise in an expansive new approach to documentary histories and publishing source material. In 1950 President Harry Truman commissioned the National Historical Publications Commission (NHPC) to generate a report on "what can be done—and should be done—to make available to our people the public and private writings of men whose contributions to our history are now inadequately represented by published works." Following the consensus approach to history, most newly commissioned documentary projects were for publishing the papers of the nation's Founders.

Within a year the administrator of the newly founded General Services Administration (GSA) noted that a report to President Truman by the NHPC provided "plans for cooperation between the Commission and appropriate state and local agencies in publishing hitherto unpublished letters, diaries, and other documents that are important to acknowledge of the history of the United States."[21] Most projects, however, were based at individual universities and not in federal service. Ironically, since most editing projects operated outside Washington, DC, Dale Morgan, perfectly suited to the editorial tasks of a dozen different NHPC projects, was less interested in documentary projects for their own sake.

* * * * *

As Morgan struggled for recognition in Washington DC, two completely unrelated events in Utah the same year set the stage for another development in Latter Day Saint historiography. The most visible was a journalistic kerfuffle. In honor of the University of Utah's centennial, the student literary magazine, *The Pen,* compiled an anthology of collegiate works by notable alumni. Dale Morgan's 1935 essay "Perspective on Platitude" led the anthology, behind only a work by Ray B. West, Jr., and which included scholastic work by alumni Bernard DeVoto, Wallace Stegner, Richard Scowcroft, and a dozen others. Most importantly, the issue included Will Jarvis' mostly positive review of Fawn Brodie's *No Man Knows My History* and a similar review of Vardis Fisher's *Children of God*. Because of these two comments, a front-page *Deseret News* editorial savaged the entire collection as a "flagrant, gratuitous, and scurrilous insult to the people who laid the foundation of Utah's greatness."[22]

For a moment it looked like the thunderous newspaper editorial scored a direct hit, but the culturally righteous salvo backfired. In the climate of the early Cold War, national publications mocked the newspaper's comment, the cultural high-handedness it implied, and made a direct comparison with similar Soviet tactics.[23] The "*Pen* controversy" became virtually the last of the Church of Jesus Christ of Latter-day Saints' blunt-object offensives in public cultural enforcement. The Historian's Office staff and the church's leadership thereafter contented themselves with oblique salvos in General Conference addresses, employed private counsel, or sat out historical storms with scant notice and stony silence. Morgan's essay in *The Pen Centennial* had nothing at all to do with the Latter-day Saints, but he was tarred by association. "Let this be a warning to you, Dale," Fawn wrote about the church editorial. "If, after five years, the Church can still get so wrought up about me, think how long you are likely to be public enemy No. 1[*sic*], with your not one but three volumes to raise their hackles."[24] Brodie's warning sunk deeply into Dale's thinking.

The second, the more broadly important development of the time began with a pair of informal meetings at the Logan Institute of Religion, adjacent to the campus of what was then the Utah State Agricultural College (now Utah State University), and at the University of Utah. At the latter, LDS faculty members with professional interests that included their local culture—Sterling M. McMurrin, Waldemer P. Read, Obert C. Tanner, and others—began meeting informally to discuss Latter-day Saint culture through the lenses of their scholarly disciplines. A similar meeting in Logan collected several Institute instructors and half a dozen USU professors to talk through challenges facing LDS education, specifically. The participants included a young economics professor still working on his dissertation, Leonard J. Arrington.[25] Within three months the separate monthly events were each regularly drawing thirty to forty individuals, most of them professors, Seminary and Institute instructors, and a handful of graduate students and nonacademics.

The two groups connected in Ogden and agreed to meet jointly. At that meeting the idea of beginning a scholarly journal on Mormon history, culture, and ideas was raised. The journal did not get off the ground, but by midyear the self-styled "Mormon Seminar" was meeting regularly to explore each other's work and thoughts relating to the Latter Day Saints and Latter-day Saints.[26]

The Mormon Seminar meetings drew interested LDS faculty from not only the Salt Lake Valley and Logan, but also from Brigham Young University in Provo. Nominally coordinated by University of Utah English Department faculty member Bill Mulder, presenters were drawn from anyone whose research employed scholarly approaches to the Mormons and was known to one or more group members. The subjects were wide open. Stan Ivins related findings from his long personal research into the history and sociology of polygamy. University of Utah anthropologist Charles Dibble discussed the Book of Mormon in terms of ancient Americas archaeology. Adam S. Bennion spoke about the challenges of academic freedom in terms of Latter-day Saint university faculty. Samuel Woolley Taylor talked about Mormons in fiction.

Over the years it was held, Mormon Seminar members and organizers repeatedly invited Dale Morgan to participate, but Morgan consistently held the group at arm's length. Despite his stated interest in the subject, recognized expertise, and repeated invitations, Morgan's demurrer was probably less because he was uncomfortable among the credentials or any vestiges of religious sentiment than because it was largely an oral forum. Jim Morgan recalled his older brother saying that "to talk with people very intimately or at very great length" involved real effort.[27] Dale could generally track an impromptu speaker he knew well personally, but the give-and-take discussion of the seminar setting among people whose speech patterns he did not recognize would have been at best extremely challenging for Dale to follow.[28]

The Mormon Seminar never organized formally nor attracted attendees much beyond university faculty, but over the succeeding half decade it was the first semiformal forum for intellectual curiosity involving study of the Latter-day Saints, as well as the first venue connecting Latter-day Saint academics who were extending their professional interests into their local culture. Despite his open advocacy of documentation and an intellectual approach, and undoubtedly because he did not participate, Morgan was never considered a part of this emerging circle of academics. For that matter, neither were the other members of Morgan's circle: Fawn

Brodie (by this time living in Los Angeles), Wally Stegner and Dick Scow-croft (both teaching creative writing at Stanford), Bernard DeVoto in the East (and who died in 1955), and Nels Anderson, now working in Europe. Juanita Brooks was the only one who remained in the state and within its mainstream culture, but despite her scholarly courage and junior college teaching career, she was never an academic.

In a cultural sense, meetings of the Mormon Seminar undoubtedly set the sails propelling an objectified, scholarly tone and drawing an indefinite but real line between scholarship and Utah's ethical or faith-promoting master narrative. Interpersonally the Seminar also reduced the distances between "liberal" thinkers within an increasingly conservative society. Leaving Utah in late 1949 took Dale Morgan out of range of the Mor-mon Seminar's early meetings, but the group effectively enacted what Morgan had argued needed to happen—that study and history had to get beyond right and wrong, angels and plates, to talk dispassionately about people, evidence, and ideas.[29] For its time the Mormon Seminar was engagingly useful.

* * * * *

Toward the end of the summer of 1950 and after nearly a year rooming with Ruth and Doug Barton, Dale finally located and signed a lease for an affordable single-bedroom space on the second floor of a new two-story apartment block on Condon Terrace, the extreme southern point of the District of Columbia.[30] Moving from Ruth's to his own place proved a bit problematic. The apartment was not actually finished, so Dale took mate-rial being cataloged on commission from New York booksellers Edward Eberstadt & Sons to the McConkeys for the space needed to complete the descriptions, and labored on the various sections of the Korns trails volume as he could make time. He again pressed Elizabeth Lauchnor to publish the trails collection as the *UHQ*'s 1950 volume ahead of Bolton's contribution, which that author continued to postpone. She, in turn, again pushed Board chair Joel Ricks, but Ricks would not budge.[31]

By the end of August, the Korns manuscript awaited only American University professor Ernst Correll's check of the Lienhard journal trans-lation, and Dale produced a corrected typescript of his bibliography of James J. Strang's following. Dale shoehorned himself and his research material into the Condon Terrace apartment. It was too small, but would be adequate quarters until he could find better. Once the move was made,

Morgan struggled to complete Eberstadt cataloging commissions because they were the only one of his activities that generated any money at all, and plunged back into the search for employment.

By mid-month Dale was completing job applications and queries all over the federal government: the U.S. Army Signal Corps, Army Historical Division, Bureau of Reclamation, Department of Commerce. Nothing took. Many agencies did not even have vacancies. From the latter, he at least received a personalized response: "The normal information services of peace-time life are slowing down. I do not foresee any hiring in the near future in any of our agencies."[32] Even with a vastly expanded federal workforce, by 1950 the government bureaucracy had reached employment saturation. By the end of the month Dale was forced to write John Selby again, pleading that the need to provide for himself had prevented him from working on the Mormon book manuscript since May.[33]

A ray of fiscal hope arrived with a query of Charles Badgerow of the Fideler Company, a Michigan-based textbook publisher. The company offered Morgan three cents per word for twenty 450-word chapters of a junior high school geography textbook on the American West, plus a $50 bonus for on-time delivery of the manuscript. The commission amounted to about $270, plus the bonus.[34] The firm would supply an outline and handle all photograph research and permissions; all they needed was a text. Dale wrote that he was very busy with his book, but that he would consider the offer. Under the circumstances he could hardly afford to say no; in fact, he offered to do a similar volume on the Great Plains as well.

Though he did not drive the Hudson often, the police finally noticed that its registration plates were outdated. Dale took the car in for its mandatory safety inspection prior to relicensing, where the garage discovered that the entire front axle was loose, a $60 repair job he could not afford. Morgan put the car up for sale, but in the postwar boom of American consumer spending, fueled by savings accounts fat with wartime wages, used cars were no longer desirable. Dale faced a buyer's market. He advertised the 1940 Hudson at $425, dropped the price to $375 before he got a single query, and still could not unload it at $350. The vehicle was his last financial reserve and his only marketable asset, but he was unable to sell the car and the attempt cost him fifteen badly needed dollars in newspaper advertisements.[35] Rather than risk a citation in the city, in early December Dale drove the balky, rattling car to the McConkeys' house in Burke, Virginia, and left it parked there until he was in better financial straits.

While Dale Morgan struggled in Washington, the Utah State Historical Society's Board of Control secured the services of precisely the sort of person Morgan had recommended two years earlier: a young PhD who was unknown in Utah and therefore not a threat to the church. A. Russell Mortensen was a recent widower who moved with his children from California partly to escape their family tragedy. He was also historically qualified and, fortunately, politically astute, an energetic and eminently practical man with enough vision to give the society and its *Quarterly* the guidance it needed to flourish. One of Mortensen's graduate students later pinned him as "a hustler—but a good one."[36] Elizabeth Lauchnor suggested that Dale write him immediately about the Korns manuscript.[37] By this time, Dale was devoting his days to a hunched-over study of manuscript journal photostats, trying to pull meaning out of the pages, and occasionally sending historical article queries to magazines, looking for a writing commission.

With all the other pressures on him, progress on the Mormon book manuscript came far too slowly. Then, of course, there were the inevitable distracting tangents. Dale wrote Wally Stegner asking for advice about a Jedediah Smith biography. Dale expected to write one between his first two Mormon books, but if Stegner thought the biography might be more marketable, well, a higher priority was worth more thought.[38] The only real break Dale got was his mother's offer to loan him as much as $750—if he needed it.[39]

* * * * *

In late April, Dale received news that the Department of the Navy had inquired about his availability. The Navy looked to fill a position for "Publications Writer," basically, the co-editor of an internal publication for the Bureau of Ships. As a trial, Morgan was handed instructions and a deadline and asked to produce a typewriter-based layout complete with text, suitable for reproduction by varitype machine, an early duplicator. He sought Darel McConkey's interpretations of the instructions to be certain he understood what was expected and fell to work on it immediately, though it hardly filled his days. Dale finally submitted the requested material to the Navy and replied that they had not supplied enough details for him to make a proposal for the publication, basically writing off the chance of getting the job. Five days later, a telegram arrived inviting him for an interview.[40]

Morgan arrived at the Main Navy Building early on the morning of May 10. He visited at length with the Publications section head and extensively with the other office staff. He was asked how he felt about working with a black clerk (which did not trouble him at all), and participated in a staff meeting. His earlier frustration in practicing speech reading consistently showed up in his mind as a glaring problem. The supervisor noticed and asked Morgan to outline how he would compensate in the office for his hearing loss. The man also wrote that he expected to fill the job before departing for Europe in June, and Dale left the meeting in the afternoon confident he would shortly receive a report-to-service directive from Civil Service. Writing internal Navy technical publications was not a job he particularly wanted, but employment of any sort would relieve his greatest problem and ensure that he would have the financial stability needed to complete the first Mormon book.[41]

May passed, and Dale did not receive word on the Navy appointment from Civil Service. The first week of June passed without any communication as well, and Dale wrote Madeline McQuown gloomily that he figured the job search would have to begin again.[42] She represented another problem. Madeline complained that her biography of Brigham Young was getting nowhere and blamed Dale for problems over source material. He would have none of it. "Better that I should send you whole files of documents for you to find yourself one note," he wrote, challenging her on the assertion and pointing out that in more than ten years she had still not shown him a single page of manuscript, "than that you should . . . show me what your problem was. . . . And all this to vindicate yourself before me."[43]

Frankly, the work on his own opus was progressing no faster. He did not tell Selby that he had taken on another yet cataloging project for the Eberstadts. He had to have an income somehow, however small. At this low point, the Naval Air Station inquired about Morgan. This second Navy opportunity fell through immediately; they wanted someone to interview engineers and reduce the technical data to a nontechnical level, which would require not only hearing to facilitate discussions but also an engineering background.

With no job offers and only one interview in two years, Emily Morgan worried about her oldest son and could finally not hold back her suggestion: "I have been thinking over very seriously your situation there and have come to the conclusion you are no better off there than here[,] as far as work possibilities are concerned."[44] He could not disagree, and complications continued to mount. The Department of Agriculture transferred

Darel McConkey to Mexico on a cooperative project. With the McConkeys headed out of the country, Dale had to get the Hudson into running order and back in front of the apartment. That cost him another badly needed sum, making it even more urgent for him to find another way to make money. Morgan had been unable to complete the Mormon book and suspected that Farrar & Rinehart would be loath to advance the last $250 of the contract against royalties—and he didn't want to lose future income either.

Dale pivoted. In August, he wrote the Utah State Historical Society's Board of Control. Studying the Mormons required him to make his own tools for the job. He had, he pointed out, a massive card file listing published works from various library collections. Luther Evans explained once that early bibliographers "started with no bibliographical preconceptions, made no investigations of purpose or method, but did something that was useful to himself and which ought to be useful generally."[45] Morgan wrote to the USHS board: "My idea has been all along that this labor should some day come to comprise a sort of Union Catalog of works relating to Mormonism and the Mormons, that this catalog should be placed in a Utah depository, and thus enable scholars to have at their fingertips all the bibliographical resources of our country." Morgan further explained that he once hoped to find time to check his card file against the National Union Catalog at the Library of Congress. Morgan proposed that the USHS pay him to make the comparison of his work against the NUC, and then Morgan would ship the Society the bibliographic cards. Today we take aggregated data for granted; in Morgan's day and time, it was unusual. Even the Library of Congress had completed its catalog only in 1927, and a project to assemble a "National Union Catalog" (NUC), adding the records of other libraries, had only been compiled in 1939—a paper database of several million cards, filed alphabetically, which existed in only one location and required manual searching.

When typed and organized, the project would create the first catalog of works relating to Mormonism ever compiled. "You will understand that I do not propose to sell the fruits of my past labors," he asserted, estimating the project would require four to six weeks of effort. "[T]housands of dollars would not reimburse me for the time I have expended in this work. What I am now proposing is simply a financial arrangement by which the results of all these years of work can be placed in such shape that the historical society can reap the benefit." He asked for a fairly rapid answer, because it was possible that writing a biography of fur trader Jedediah Smith would require his return west.[46]

* * * * *

If this chapter focuses rather excessively on finances, the reason is because efforts to sustain himself during his second Washington residence defined Dale Morgan's existence. Simply making these proposals shows how desperate Morgan's financial condition had become by August 1951. His options were exhausted. Freelance article/story queries and submissions to magazines had been fruitless. The federal bureaucracy had proven impervious. He had a contract for the first Mormon book, one he had reluctantly accepted in 1949 as the best option available at the time, and on which he had drawn three-quarters of the advance due him. Two years later, the obligation for the manuscript was still outstanding. He had no income on which to support himself to write the contracted work and fulfill the obligation. The Mormon bibliography was, perhaps, his last marketable professional asset. Two days after his letters to the Humanities Research Foundation (HRF) at the University of Utah on the Strang bibliography and the USHS Board of Control on the card file, Dale wrote his mother that he was facing the inevitable. He would either work out matters financially (how, he didn't say) or once again return west, at least for a while.[47]

Through the rest of August, Dale corrected galley proofs for the Fideler textbook. Knowing Dale's pinched situation, Charles Eberstadt sent along the firm's copy of the newly published Peter Skene Ogden and William Kittson journals of 1824–1825. Despite the pressure on him, Dale was immediately drawn into the work he had wanted to see so badly for so long. Browsing and reading the volume consumed Morgan for two full days. The journals were revelatory, providing a firsthand context for the fateful confrontation between the Hudson's Bay Company fur brigade and American free trappers in Ogden's Hole, an encounter which stemmed the British advance from the Pacific Coast into the North American interior. Having digested the Ogden/Kittson journals, in September Dale wrote to George Hammond of the Bancroft Library that he was beginning a Jedediah Smith biography, which would involve "a general rewriting of the history of the American fur trade for the period 1820–1830."[48]

Later in the month, Dale filed job queries directly with two agencies, bypassing Civil Service entirely, the Board on Geographic Names

(BGN) and the Bureau of American Ethnology (BAE), a branch of the Smithsonian Institution. After a few weeks the BGN director replied that upper-level positions were filled only from internal candidates, but Paul Oehser, chief of the BAE's Editorial Division, replied to Morgan's query immediately; he did not have a position open, but was expecting a vacancy to open the following March and wanted to talk with Morgan personally. Dale brushed his suit, shined his shoes, and visited Oehser a few days later. The discussion went well and though no promises were made, the prospect looked promising. BAE was essentially a cultural anthropology organization, which meant it dealt with subjects in which Morgan was comfortable and building an expertise: the history and culture of western Native Americans and their interaction with European Americans. The job prospect meshed so ideally with his interests that Dale effectively quit looking for work elsewhere.[49]

Meanwhile, Juanita Brooks championed Morgan's bibliographic research proposal on the USHS Board of Control and engineered its approval. Dale acknowledged to Mortensen his relief on August 25: "I thank you and the Board for making it possible for me in the end to do what I have been trying to do for the Society free for nothing." Mortensen observed earlier in the month that the legislature had finally formalized the USHS's designation as the state's public archive and that they would need a full-time archivist. He asked—preliminarily, to be sure—whether Dale would be interested in returning to Utah as the first state archivist. Morgan replied that he felt "split," drawn by the character and setting of the American West, yet also by the opportunities and resources of the East, specifically Washington, DC. He remained concerned about fall-out that was sure to come in the wake of his Mormon book, but told Mortensen that this time he would seriously consider accepting the job if an offer was made.[50]

Dale sent the corrected and checked card file to Salt Lake City in several batches as he completed his march through the file drawers. On November 17, he shipped the R–Z section and posted two letters to Mortensen, an official one and a personal one, describing the project and cards. Since it took another month for the Utah State Controller to forward the $300 payment, Dale (again) drew reluctantly on Emily's bank account to cover current expenses. Completing the project in November left him relatively uncommitted time to work on his book manuscript, but no income. Cataloging a few manuscripts for the Eberstadts brought in something. He also caught up on the never-ending flow of correspondence. "If I myself live to be 900 years old," he wrote friend and Americana collector Thomas W. Streeter in New Jersey, "I already have a good idea as to things that will be making pressing demands upon my time for the next five years after that."[51]

"Sundry Kinds of Hackwork"[1]

Writing in Washington, DC, 1950–1952

I hope some day to achieve a literary independence, to live on my wits and my typewriter.[2]
—Dale Morgan

JOB HUNTING WAS NOT MORGAN'S sole occupation in postwar Washington. He never did secure employment. In its place, writing provided Morgan his sole source of income, though it was a thin, irregular stream, and much of the writing that consumed him paid nothing at all. In mid-November 1949, Dale wrote John Selby, his editor at Farrar & Rinehart, with an update on the Mormon book. No, the manuscript was still unfinished. "I am established finally in some study space at [the Library of Congress] and am working like hell on my book," he reported.[3] But he wasn't, really; Morgan dabbled at it when he could free up the time. During his fruitless job search during his second residence in Washington, DC, Morgan filled his days with writing, but mostly writing that did not pay. By doing so, he set himself a standard to which he returned several times in his career—writing on behalf of others displaced his own personal writing commitments, even when it challenged his ability to make a living for himself. He also came to understand that writing commissions paid more immediately than book contracts.

In fact, though by this time he had pulled together perhaps a dozen or more conceptual drafts for the Mormon book's early chapters, he had begun a new draft upon arriving in Washington. What he also did not tell Selby was that he was busy with the mutually beneficial process of cataloging the papers of Oliver Olney, an early LDS dissenter, for the Eberstadts while transcribing them for himself. Neither did he mention having received word that the Utah State Historical Society's Board of

Control finally approved—and more remarkably, the Utah state legislature had agreed to fund—the astounding $2,500 payment to Herbert E.
Bolton for his not-yet-written study of the Domínguez-Escalante exploration, which the Society committed to publish sight-unseen in 1950. In the
same meeting, almost as an afterthought and at Juanita Brooks' vigorous
insistence, the Board finally formally committed to publication of the
proposed Korns memorial volume in 1951, allocating a $25 payment to
cover publication rights of the Heinrich Lienhard journal extract, and yet
nothing at all for the individual producing that manuscript.[4]

Beyond Morgan's promise to Sara Korns, the Board's action gave
Morgan a green light to go to work but obligated him to the USHS and
to a timeline. Thankfully the desk at the Library of Congress provided
private space for drafting and revising the Mormon book's initial chapters as he waited for the Civil Service Commission to grind out his "status"—its ability rating for Morgan's competence based on his examination
scores and prior experience. Status would peg him to the federal hiring
registers, and placement there would allow him to apply for graded vacancies in various agencies.

Meanwhile, Dale worked rather less doggedly on the Mormon book.
Elizabeth Lauchnor proposed that USHS staff act as his typing service in
exchange for continued advice.[5] Having competent typists readily at hand
took a load off of Dale's mind and his wallet. On December 6, two weeks
before his thirty-first birthday, Morgan finally dispatched the initial batch
of edited first-rough manuscript to the USHS for retyping, including a
draft appendix. The clean manuscript of the Mormon book appendix and
first chapter came back from the typist after the 1950 New Year, along with
Charles Kelly's file of Korns's notes. In late January, Dale reported to Sara
Korns that he had spent the previous six weeks on her husband's work
"night and day, so that my own affairs are beginning to suffer badly," which
was mostly true, though he had devoted a week at the Library of Congress
studying the chronology of Palmyra revivals documented in denomina-
tional newspapers.[6] As January turned to February, Morgan confided to
Kelly that he hoped to complete Korns's "manuscript" on emigrant trails
by the end of March, since Elizabeth Lauchnor reported that Bolton had
submitted nothing at all.

Morgan focused on resolving this setback when John Selby wrote
again, inquiring about progress on the Mormon book's manuscript. Dale
had nothing to report other than he had been at work on the book—
and he was. In mid-February he dispatched another chapter draft to the

USHS for typing, and on February 25 two more, but the work was progressing slowly—too slowly. Selby sympathized and told Morgan that he would schedule the book for the autumn list, which gave the author about another month to complete the manuscript.[7] Selby also denied that anyone at Rinehart had suggested Madeline McQuown's biography of Brigham Young and Morgan's study of the Mormons needed to be published simultaneously. She complained to Dale that her health was being compromised by stress to meet such an unrealistic demand. His reply to her was a long letter that said much about their curious relationship. "After five years, I have not read two words of your book, not even one, to be exact," Dale wrote Madeline.

> All along, you have tied yourself, and thus me, into such knots over your book.... You have been so damned touchy about your book throughout that I have found it the part of wisdom to keep my mouth shut and let you do as you liked. When I have volunteered information and advice, I have had my ears smacked down for trying to tell you how to write your own book and acting as though I knew more about it than you; and when I have kept quiet, I have been accused of taking no interest in it, having no confidence in you, and so on and so forth.[8]

While the organizers of the Mormon Seminar were taking their first collective steps, Dale Morgan was struggling to get his own work on the Mormons back on track. Working heavily on cataloging manuscripts for the Eberstadts while waiting for the clean typescripts to arrive from USHS typists, Dale wrote Selby that the editor could expect the draft of the Mormon book in June. Also, since Bolton had not been forthcoming with his Domínguez-Escalante manuscript, Dale suggested to Elizabeth Lauchnor that he would have Korns's trail volume in her hands by August if she would consider trading publishing commitments on the two volumes.[9] What he did not tell his contracted publisher was how little he had actually produced, leaving both Selby and Rinehart to infer he was talking about a complete book manuscript rather than a few early draft chapters. He also did not mention how hard it was for him to find time to work on his own writing at all.

Dale was chafing for personal space after nearly eight months as the Bartons' houseguest and made another effort at freelance writing. He set aside mornings for this effort and worked on his Mormon book drafts in the afternoons.[10] Another round of queries to the major "slick" general circulation magazines—*Saturday Evening Post, Atlantic,* and *Collier's*—bore no fruit. Unable to break into the major slicks, Dale began directing inquiries about freelance articles to travel magazines. Ruth Plassey of *Holiday* magazine was one of the few who responded, saying that her magazine editors were willing to look at an article on trails if Morgan wanted to write it on speculation. "It is only fair to warn you," another editor replied, "that the chances for acceptance of unsolicited material of this kind are very slim indeed."[11] That reply and others like it were not enough encouragement to spend the time on freelance article drafts.

The only opportunity—and one he didn't want—seemed to be back in Utah. Elizabeth Lauchnor wrote to tell Dale she was expecting a baby and resigning from the USHS. She asked if he would consider returning to Utah to run the society himself. As committed as Morgan was to a public research institution in the state, he did not even entertain the thought. Insulating the society from his work on the Mormons had been the key reason he resigned his informal status as editor of the *Utah Historical Quarterly* the previous year. "[S]ince the Society is still young and struggling," he wrote Lauchnor, "I do not want to see it [be] attacked as a way of getting at me hereafter, something that is entirely within the bounds of possibility."[12] The recent *Pen* controversy only reinforced his decision.

* * * * *

While he huffed and waited on the Civil Service, Dale worked evenings on the second of his Latter Day Saint bibliographies, this one on the Strang branch of Mormonism. With a stroke of good fortune, New York bookman Charles Eberstadt commissioned Morgan to catalog the collection of James Strang material which the firm had just purchased from Milo Quaife.[13] Desperate for money, Dale agreed to drop everything else to do the job.[14] The task proved invaluable to his Strang bibliography, and the notes would likewise be invaluable to the second volume of his Mormon trilogy. While the wrestle with Civil Service slowly unfolded, Dale cataloged the Strang papers in his sister Ruth's apartment working sixteen hours a day, seven days a week through three weeks of June.[15] After the intense, exhausting effort concluded, he was just glad to ship the two cartons back to New York with the catalog notes and entries.

While he tapped away at Mormon bibliography and occasionally on the history drafts, he also pursued his interest in the fur trade and overland travel, corresponding with many noted researchers and writers. To Harvey Tobie, Dale wrote in early July that he had conceived writing a biography of Jedediah Smith "in the grand manner," but was waiting for the Hudson's Bay Record Society to publish the Peter Skene Ogden and William Kittson journals documenting the 1824–1825 fur brigades.[16] The volume's publication was forecast for summer 1951.

Dale confessed to Chicago book collector Everett Graff that "I haven't been able to escape the necessity of working at [the Mormon book] instead of on more remunerative things, but at the same time I have not been able to give it the kind of relaxed attention it has required."[17] He wrote Selby again, citing the demands of the summer and apologizing that the manuscript certainly would not be complete until September. Selby acknowledged, thankful that it would not be later than that, since a September submission would still allow Farrar & Rinehart a spring 1951 publication date.[18] Dale also wrote Sara Korns, feeling an obligation to explain why her husband's work had not yet appeared. It, like everything else, had been shoved around by circumstances, particularly by Bolton's cavalier unwillingness to deliver his manuscript on time.[19]

In late July Morgan finally dove into the transcripts for the Korns memorial publication between hacking out entries for the Strang bibliography. Notes could be added later and as he found it convenient. With a week's worth of effort Morgan successfully sent off introduction manuscripts for the journals making up the *UHQ* volume. The sticking point was the journal of Swiss emigrant Heinrich Lienhard, a remarkable record of 1846 travel over the Hastings Cutoff and across the Salt Desert just a few days before the ill-fated Donner-Reed party, but published in German. Two years earlier Morgan had turned over his copy of the Lienhard memoir to Will Lund at the Church Historian's Office for a German-to-English translation. Even though he did not read German, Dale could tell that the translation came back with many of the key trail geography and date details missing. Rod Korns then had produced a translation, which Dale had checked for accuracy by American University professor Ernst Correll, but it also didn't pass. A better rendition was essential.

In the first week of September, photostats of the Lienhard diary manuscript itself arrived from the Bancroft Library. Even with a cursory comparison and no facility with German, Dale could tell that the journal was far more detailed than was this published reminiscence.[20] None of his contacts could turn up a German speaker willing to take on a transcription. Dale, however, was flatly unwilling to let Korns's work on emigrant trails go to publication carrying the translation of an inferior abridgment, not when he had the original document in hand. He wrote Kelly explaining a plan to juggle the available time to "carry forward the work on this [Mormon] book during the daylight hours; and during the evenings to complete Rod's manuscript and also a job that is in the offing for [Fideler]" while still looking for government-office work.[21] After having the Library of Congress make a positive print of the Lienhard negative photostat, Dale sat down to see what he could decipher of the text, and only nominally to work on his Mormon book.

Someone once asked me to gauge how Morgan's effort in transcription and editing compared to similar work done by other historians. Other than using contract typists to produce clean drafts from pencil or ink-corrected earlier versions (common to almost any project before computers), a question of scale or quantity may not be answerable, but it is certainly useful to compare support platforms. A benchmark project from a few years later, Donald Jackson's three-volume collection of John C. Frémont letters, had institutional backing in the form of a steady salary, defined time to pursue scholarship as part of an academic appointment, and the benefit of a dedicated staff. Most documentary editions did. Conversely, Morgan had none of those, not until he began working at the Bancroft Library in 1954, and then the single asset afforded him by the university was a salary. With the exception of the USHS staff's occasional typing assistance, Morgan worked alone in all of his historical transcription and editing. He absorbed time and most costs personally (though he got into a habit of using work time for scholarly projects), with the sole exception of cooperating with Eleanor Towles Harris on the William Marshall Anderson memoir. For "editing" her husband's work, Sara Korns supplied occasional subventions for paper or typists or photostat copies, but the real expense Morgan incurred was time. While he was unemployed, Morgan's time was his own, surely, but labor on the Korns volume meant he robbed his personal well-being to complete this and most subsequent projects.

* * * * *

On the morning of his thirty-sixth birthday, December 18, 1950, Dale opened his apartment door to find the calling card of RLDS president Israel A. Smith atop his newspaper. He had not heard Smith's knock. The visit portended neither birthday wishes nor exactly a social call. Dale might have been surprised to read a scrawled note on the card that Smith would return that afternoon. What Morgan did not know then was that the call was an informal acknowledgement of how influential Morgan's historicism-infused personal knowledge of Mormonism was perceived to be. Morgan's planned study on Mormon origins seemed threatening to believers who held firmly that history—especially Latter Day Saint history—was an ethical and moral enterprise whose purpose was to reinforce faith. Smith's visit was a signal that the collision between ethicism/presentism and historicism among the Latter Day Saints was more than merely a wrestle over a few facts.

Within Latter-day Saint culture at least, the nature of history itself was in flux. Swiss-born scientist Louis Agassiz once commented that "facts are stupid things until brought into connection with some general law"—that is, until they are given meaning with interpretation. But when conflicting facts collided, which facts had precedence? If facts make history and if history intends to tell a story, what story should be told? Instead of accepting the personal witness of church leaders' memory, and not particularly welcome in the Church Historian's Office, Morgan and a new generation of scholars were began looking into contemporary documentation existing outside of the culture's accepted stories and memory. What they found was a different set of facts that did not entirely support the traditions that had become the inspirational legends of the faith. Borne of his far-flung queries, news of Morgan's fellowship and rumors of his progress on "the Mormon book" filtered through the small community of writers and individuals interested in Latter Day Saint history. Everyone in Mormondom was still on edge from publication of Fawn Brodie's biography of Joseph Smith, *No Man Knows My History* which was, for believers, finding unfortunate success among American readers at large and had gone through three printings in less than six months. It was common knowledge among those who cared that Brodie and Morgan shared naturalistic views of LDS history. To believers, the possibility of a carefully documented skeptical study on the broad history of Mormonism was disquieting, and the story of Smith's visit involves one of the private counsels mentioned earlier to which LDS leaders resorted after the *Pen Centennial*.

On August 17, 1949, shortly before Dale left for the east and a year before Israel Smith arrived in Washington, Salt Lake City educator Francis W. Kirkham visited Morgan at home. In 1942 Kirkham had compiled a documentary collection on Mormon origins, privately publishing the work. Like Morgan, Kirkham and his study enjoyed the encouragement of professional chemist, apostle, and former University of Utah President Dr. John A. Widtsoe. Like Morgan, Kirkham was convinced that the historical record would ultimately bear out the origin story of the Book of Mormon, though in the opposite direction. Kirkham was well aware of the subject of Morgan's Guggenheim fellowship and highly interested in what the younger man had found, especially in light of the publication of new documentary sources in Brodie's *No Man Knows My History*. During his visit Kirkham studiously avoided directly discussing Morgan's book or his documentary research. Instead, he inquired about the Mormon bibliography. However, after the discussion, Kirkham met with Widtsoe, who brought him to First Presidency member J. Reuben Clark. The trio agreed to press first the Guggenheim Foundation and then Morgan himself for an advanced view of what they were certain was a nearly complete book manuscript.

Shortly after Morgan arrived back in Washington, Clark, a former U.S. State Department lawyer and U.S. Ambassador to Mexico, telephoned and then addressed David D. Moffatt of the Utah Copper Company. Clark wanted Moffatt to raise the concern about Morgan and his work to contacts in New York. Clark framed his issues with lawyerly care, shaping the evidence to fit the argument. "What Mr. Dale Morgan thinks or says or writes about the Church is of no particular concern to me or the Church," Clark observed, "but I am just a bit concerned about the sponsorship by the Guggenheim Foundation of the writings of a man who, contrary to the fact, would make Joseph Smith an imposter and a fraud and a trifler with the most sacred feelings of men." He recommended Moffatt (who was LDS) warn the Guggenheim Foundation that one of its grantees might expose the Foundation to ridicule.[22] Essentially, Clark sowed concern without supplying a shred of supportive evidence to sustain his accusation.

Moffatt passed along Clark's letter to R. C. Klugescheid, general counsel for Kennecott Copper Corporation, who approached Guggenheim Foundation Secretary Henry Allen Moe with the Latter-day Saints' request. Moe was diplomatic, not only responding with a four-page missive about the Foundation and its aims but also firmly closing the back-alley door. Clark's complaint, Moe noted, was the only question ever received of Morgan's facts or objectivity. Clark's argument and Klugescheid's letter tacitly (though entirely intentionally) raised the question of whether the Foundation could or should control Fellows' work. No, the secretary concluded: "To do that would be to use the power of money to control expression, and that in our free America would be intolerable. We have a duty to our America to choose our Fellows with care for their character and ability—and ability, if they be historians, means that we must have due regard to their historical objectivity." The Foundation sustained open inquiry and would not compromise the freedom to do so. Klugescheid could not help but agree.[23] The back-channel door clicked shut. In April 1950, Israel A. Smith, president of the Reorganized Church of Jesus Christ of Latter Day Saints, took his turn, asking the Guggenheim Foundation outright that since the RLDS Church had sustained Morgan's research under the fellowship, "we believe it is only fair to us that we be given the privilege of inspecting what he has prepared for publication." Moe was courteous but similarly deflected that request.[24]

Given Clark's and Smith's failures working back channels, the following April with Clark and Widtsoe's stated blessings, Kirkham wrote to Israel A. Smith. He again expressed concerns about Morgan's forthcoming book and invited Smith to cooperate in a work of faith against skeptics (though without naming either Morgan or Brodie): "All believers in the divine mission of the Prophet Joseph Smith and the divine origin of the Book of Mormon may unite in this undertaking. Let us work together to present all of the facts in their proper historical setting."[25]

Smith agreed to accompany Kirkham eastward and confront Dale Morgan personally to see what together they could worm out of him about conclusions or statements in his forthcoming book. Weeks later and after leaving his card, later in the day Smith and Kirkham showed up again on Morgan's stoop in Washington. Morgan successfully put them off. Morgan had nothing but preliminary drafts to show them, after all, but he did not admit that. The three men's conversation was cordial but halting and stuttered, as conversations due to Morgan's deafness always were. Unaware that he was being pumped for information, "we discussed at length all the projects in Mormon history I am moving forward," Dale reported to his mother later that evening, "not only the three volumes in my Mormon history but the bibliography of the smaller Mormon churches I am serializing in the [*Western Humanities Review*] and the larger bibliography of Mormonism for the period of 1830–1849."[26]

The two churchmen left the apartment with a better idea of what Morgan was working at but without either a pledge to see the finished work or a timeline of when it would be completed. This uncertainty appeared to provide a window of opportunity for the believers. Kirkham worked feverishly through the rest of the year to supplement the third edition of his *A New Witness for Christ in America,* an attempt to publish the new historical sources about the church's early years which had been surfacing, and beat Morgan to the interpretive punch. Morgan was content to let him do so, in no position to accept the challenge for a literary race to completion. Of Kirkham, Morgan later observed that "I give Kirkham this credit; he has been *interested*. But of course his interest is entirely circumscribed by his emotional conditioning [as a believing church member]. It is impossible for him to do what Juanita [Brooks] has done in her book, that is, base her conclusions on the facts she has developed. His conclusions were fixed before he began organizing his facts."[27] Beginning from one's conclusions was the greatest historical sin Morgan could imagine committing.

On the day after the visit by Smith and Kirkham, a copy of Juanita Brooks' newly published *The Mountain Meadows Massacre* arrived in the mail. Dale was pleased. He had given Brooks about a third of the documentary material she used in the final book and convinced her the work had to be footnoted (the only one of her interpretive works that ever was). It was, Morgan told a former HRS friend, "the first book, written from within the church, which in the past generation has displayed any intellectual curiosity to speak of, and damned near the only book of its kind which bases its conclusions upon its facts rather than starting with the conclusions and using only such facts as serves that conclusion."[28]

* * * * *

Morgan was still laboring ceaselessly on the Lienhard transcription and translation in the closing month of 1950, the journal strewn across his available workspace in various renditions and stages of completion. The rest of the manuscript for Rod Korns's memorial volume was in Russ Mortensen's hands in Salt Lake City, and the journal editor was clamoring for this last piece. No good. Working with magnifying glass, dictionary, and copious patience, Dale generated thirty pages of handwritten transcription before he felt comfortable enough with the text and script to go back to using his typewriter. Working steadily through November he was able to bull his way through the available source material: a positive reverse print made from a negative print of the miniature diary, which had been recorded in a writing style out of use for two hundred years, in a foreign language that he did not speak and in which he had no formal training.

Working doggedly under these conditions, Dale managed to eke out two pages of identification, transcription, and translation a night. For a break he would return to his patchwork transcription of earlier diary pages to fill in blanks and begin the work of actual translation from German into English. By December 1950, Dale was able to report proudly to Sara Korns that he had "more or less put to shame the local German experts, and have been rather conspicuously successful in what we might call transliterating Lienhard's manuscript."[29]

Toward the middle of January 1951, Bill Mulder wrote Morgan for news of the Strang bibliography manuscript. Apart from the business at hand, he suggested Morgan approach a Salt Lake City businessman with a record of supporting publication in Latter-day Saint topics. From his apartment in Washington, DC, Morgan turned aside any thought of a private subvention: "What it boils down to is that the large bibliography will simply have to wait until I can afford the luxury of working on it,.... I would not solicit or accept financial help on this bibliography from anybody but a foundation or learned society or public institution of some kind."[30] With this in mind, Mulder again approached the University of Utah's research committee to support granting the alumnus a research fellowship. The request was turned down toward the end of 1951, not on the merits of the proposal, but because Morgan was not a registered student or faculty member. "Whether you are inside or outside the formal academic world makes a tremendous difference in tapping funds," Dale groused to Madeline.[31]

After the first of the year Dale took out a short bank loan using his car as collateral. His financial condition was approaching desperate. Still, in a ceaseless quest for relevant source material, Dale explored the cost of microfilming federal records relating to the early fur trade and Jedediah Smith, hoping that at his recommendation the Bancroft Library might be willing to foot the bill and that the USHS might buy a copy of the film later.[32]

He was still, however, buried in the Korns manuscript, working twelve to sixteen hours a day to get the text up to his standards. Progress on the manuscript created a serious financial drain. For months it required about half of his available work time and crowded out possibly paying assignments, though no article commissions had been received. It was a job he could ill afford, but Dale wanted it done, and done well, over Korns's name. Sometimes we do things we can't afford, he told his mother. "I suspect that in the end Rod's book will be received as a more truly original and valuable contribution to the history of the West than Bolton's," he wrote to Charlie Kelly, "and this is how we would have it, a memorial more enduring than any stone that can be placed on his grave."[33]

John Selby's latest query about the Mormon book came along as well. He was hoping for a mid-May manuscript submission date so that it could now appear on the fall 1951 book list. Dale responded once more that he would do his best. He wanted to apply for a Huntington Library fellowship to support research on Jedediah Smith but reassured Selby he would not do anything at all on the fur trade until the Mormon book was done.[34]

* * * * *

After two frustrating years in Washington, DC, it was becoming increasingly clear that with the federal bureaucracy able to choose between any number of qualified applicants, Morgan was constantly faced with the requirement not only to prove he was competent, but also that he was superior. He also was becoming resigned to the fact that complete hearing loss would always be a complicating problem for employment. "I have to be enough better at my job, at any job I tackle, to more than counterbalance the small inefficiencies which are consequent upon the ability to hear," he wrote one official.[35]

Yet, to write the books he wanted to write, not only a major library, but also a salaried office job was imperative. Though there was a wide readership for certain types of nonfiction in the postwar world, the books he wanted to write generally would not pay for themselves. "This will always be the case," he wrote Madeline, "and I will have to compensate for it by a special kind of authority and prestige. A [Jedediah] Smith book will serve to enlarge my professional reputation and perhaps widen the field of opportunity open to me."[36] Without employment Dale had time to pursue a wide variety of research and writing projects, but with one driving concern—to understand the field well enough to be ready to write when the opportunity came. Emily knew "or at least surmised" how much effort her son was pouring into both the Korns manuscript and to research, perhaps as a way to cope with his circumstances. "For a guy without regular employment you do more work than any one I ever knew," she told him.[37]

By March 1951, Mortensen had become anxious about the Korns material and Morgan's unwillingness to send the Lienhard section. Morgan explained that he was doing the translation and writing, not editing existing work, expecting that Bolton had delivered a manuscript long before now which the USHS had in press. In fact, the USHS had more of Morgan's Korns book than anything else. Bolton still had not submitted anything beyond promises, and yet the USHS had to pay for Korns's book during the current fiscal year or lose funding for it. Though he was already pressed, Dale set everything else aside to get the final details into his carbons of the other sections and complete the Lienhard translation. He also completed a Huntington Library fellowship application, without much hope of receiving it. "Fellowship or no," Dale wrote Juanita Brooks with what became prophetic irony, "you can be sure that I am going to write the Jedediah Smith book inside the next two years. It will be a welcome change of pace while I am engaged with my Mormon history."[38]

By mid-month Dale had sent all final changes to the Korns's work—except the Lienhard translation, and he was working tenaciously on the getting Lienhard's narrative through the Ruby Valley and around its mountains. After the rest of the manuscript went to press (except the Lienhard portion), the previously unknown James Mathers diary surfaced.[39] Mathers had travelled with the Harlan-Young party and provided detail on its activities unrecorded in any other source. Dale tore his proverbial hair, begging Mortensen to postpone the volume to include this diary as well for the sake of completeness. The editor, pressed by the reality of state funding policy, flatly refused, and Morgan had to be content to insert a notice of the discovery and a few landmark dates in a long note.

Meanwhile, Dale sent the Lienhard diary photostats and his translation to Dr. Ernst Correll of American University to check. "Considering that I didn't know 25 [sic] German words when I began this labor last fall," he wrote to his mother with both pride and exhaustion, "the translation of a 15,000 word German text from a handwritten manuscript German-reading people all threw up as too difficult is a feat which reflected credit on my obstinacy if not exactly my intelligence."[40] On April 1, Morgan sat down with Correll to review and clarify the transcription. Morgan's painstaking effort was vindicated when Correll pronounced the result not merely clean, but in fact one of the best he had seen. He offered to recommend Morgan to the Civil Service as a qualified German translator.[41] The next day Dale airmailed the Lienhard text to the USHS, where it finally joined the rest of the manuscript in production.

In late April, a day after receiving news that the Department of the Navy had inquired about his availability, a letter from Mortensen arrived reporting that Herbert Bolton had finally delivered a manuscript on the Domínguez-Escalante expedition. Despite Morgan's manuscript arriving first, due to the politics of the situation and the board president's adamant stance, Mortensen had to preempt issuance of the memorial volume and put out Bolton's first. Through the summer, the two books went through press at the same time, both racing the state's fiscal-year deadline.

On June 30, 1951, Mortensen wrote Dale that an advance copy of *West from Fort Bridger* was in the mail. The USHS managed to get both its commissioned volumes through press before the deadline, but Mortensen planned to hold distribution of the Korns's book for a month to allow Bolton's *Pageant in the Wilderness* to be advertised and sold widely. Ricks bet heavily on public interest in Bolton's exploration story, and against advice instructed Mortensen to print three thousand copies. Of Korns's work, 986 copies were delivered by the printer, most of them bound to match the *Quarterly* binding, and all for distribution to subscribers.[42] Dale suggested the society officially release the volume on Korns's July 24 birthday, but USHS politics held the work to a September 1 release. These two books completed the list of annual monographic publications with which Marguerite Reusser and Dale Morgan had successfully held the journal together across the low point in its career. Thereafter Mortensen held the *Utah Historical Quarterly* to account and resumed publication of the journal as a genuine quarterly in January 1952.

Across five months of ceaseless work, Morgan distilled Roderic Korns's rough notes and the interpretations of routes and company membership in their series of circular letters with Charles Kelly into a major work of history. Not a single word had actually been written by Korns. When Russ Mortensen asked about putting Dale's name on the title page, Morgan declined: "I have had other books, and will have still other books in time to come, to make my own reputation, so I don't require one at Rod's expense, no matter what my contribution has been. I want this thought of as his book, as it would have been had he lived."[43] Morgan also confessed to John Selby once again that the Mormon book was not done—and that he had not worked on it for months. He would begin again tomorrow.[44]

* * * * *

Completion of the Korns manuscript and the Navy's trial project left Morgan, for the first time since the previous October, time to edit and revise the chapter drafts for the Mormon book. It was hard going. "The materials are refractory, and I find it hard to make the book all I have so long wanted it to be," the author confessed to Chicago book collector Everett Graff.[45] Selby wrote with a bit of an edge in response to Morgan's earlier letter that "it goes without saying that we shall be glad to see the book next month."[46]

Darel McConkey critiqued the few draft chapters of the Mormon book and expressed some concerns about his friend's interpretations. Morgan wrote McConkey that "in light of the existence of the Book of Mormon, you have only two positions you can take. Either it is what he claimed it to be, a work produced by the gift and power of God. Or it is not." Morgan felt he had discovered and organized a new group of facts that the Latter Day Saint churches' master narrative could not explain. Of course, his straightforward objectivity would be received as anti-Mormon, he thought, and not just by the saints and their church in Utah. "The trouble about writing a history of the Saints is that by no stretch of the imagination can you please everybody," Dale predicted to correspondent Lloyd Flanders and also to Milo Quaife as early as 1948. "I will be considered anti-Mormon not only by the Strangites but by the Brighamites [Latter-day Saints], the Josephites [Reorganized Church], the half a dozen Temple Lot churches, and a dozen others—by everybody, in fact, except the anti-Mormons, who will complain of my pro-Mormonism. This must be the sad fate of anyone who tries to write objectively about the Mormons."[47] Looking at matters as an outsider, McConkey was not so certain that Morgan was as objective as he thought himself to be.[48]

The Hudson's Bay Record Society released its annual publication, the journals of Peter Skene Ogden and William Kittson, the same week. Morgan was eager, almost desperate to see the record of the British fur brigade's movements through Oregon, Idaho, and to the fateful encounter with American free trappers in the mountain valley above Ogden, Utah. It was a key piece of documentary evidence needed for any Jedediah Smith biography, one Maurice Sullivan lacked for his 1925 study. Morgan filed an order request with the Library of Congress as soon as the book was available. He also wrote an inquiry to a graduate student at UC Berkeley who had reportedly found the long-lost William Marshall Anderson journals. Jaquelin S. "Jim" Holliday was the scion of a steelmaking fortune, the son of Indiana magnate and noted book Americana collector William J. Holliday. The younger Holliday had no interest in the family business but a great interest in the American West sparked by his father. Morgan wanted to know if Holliday had found the actual Anderson journals, which had been alleged to have been discovered several times previously, and what they might relate about Jedediah Smith contemporary Étienne Provost. Holliday sent along a complete transcript, initiating a lifelong correspondence and professional friendship second only to what would later develop between Morgan and Carl Wheat or George Hammond.[49]

While Morgan waited anxiously on *West from Fort Bridger* and the Ogden-Kittson journals in the summer heat of Washington, DC, he occupied himself writing the text for the junior-high geography textbook. The rush on that job was not so much as to limit Dale's social activities. In late July Dale hosted Max and Louise North for dinner. The Norths, Louise in particular, were friends from his OPA days during the war, who had built a house about a dozen miles south of him in Accokeek, Maryland.[50]

In the meantime, Morgan turned his attention again to Jedediah Smith. If pressed to leave DC, he wanted to take as much primary source material with him as possible. Dale filled his empty workday hours with research in National Archives holdings. He hunted material in the Interior Department archives; looked for a William H. Ashley map among the records of Albert Gallatin, Secretary of the Treasury under President Thomas Jefferson; asked for photostats from book-collecting friends; and continued plaguing the Hudson's Bay Record Society for microfilmed material. Dale waited through September for the USHS to approve the expenditure on his catalog-checking proposal, which provided him $300 worth of breathing room, and for Fideler to pay him for the textbook, which it did not. He set to work with his file of bibliography slips and the ranks of National Union Catalog card drawers in the Library of Congress. Meanwhile the likelihood of federal employment receded further as the newspapers filled with reports of federal layoffs in the face of postwar Congressional economizing.

By mid-October, Morgan was spending ten or eleven hours a day checking his stacks of bibliography slips against cards in the Library of Congress, finding huge numbers of new works in the catalog and no longer thinking of returning west immediately. The bibliographic commission allowed him a thin living while he bided his time and the calendar crept along, hoping that the prospective Bureau of American Ethnology job would open. He was, however, also finding in federal records enough new material on William H. Ashley as well as Smith, that he began thinking about editing a documentary collection on Ashley himself. He filed away the idea mentally as he filed the various index slips and transcripts.[51]

The pressing reality continued to be the Mormon book, however, and in mid-October Dale finally wrote John Selby. The delay completing the Mormon book was money-driven, he explained, imposed by a need to make a living. "I hope to finish this [card project] before the end of the month, and then, damn it, if everybody will just pay their bills and enable me to pay mine, I shall be able to put in two solid months on my book."[52] Fideler finally did come through with the outstanding textbook payment just before Halloween, and Morgan used the money to clear his debts as quickly as the check cleared the bank. Fate took a turn, however. John Selby was not in when Morgan's letter arrived at the New York office; secretary Marguerite Reese handed it off directly to the Rinehart brothers, Stanley and Frederick, and editor John Lamont. Reese responded with sympathy, stating that Morgan should feel free "to send part of the manuscript to us at this time," but the letter put Morgan and his overdue commitments on the partners' radar.[53]

Around Thanksgiving, Dale collected the latest typed drafts for the first four chapters of the Mormon book and posted them to his publisher. They were nowhere near what he expected to submit as final manuscript, but the submission fulfilled an obligation and bought him some time. Ruth wrote her big brother with family news for his thirty-seventh birthday: Doug was being transferred to Tokyo, Japan, and the family was looking forward to the adventure.[54] A day earlier, John Selby wrote with delight that the draft chapters for *The Mormons* had arrived.[55] Dale spent Christmas with Max and Louise North at their new home down the Potomac.

* * * * *

By mid-January, the New Year revelers had sobered up and settled down to face 1952. Dale Morgan did as well. The USHS research contract that he had completed six weeks earlier provided a moment of fiscal stability, and he planned to fling himself back into the Mormon book while his time was subsidized. "I have been working hard on my book and feel better about it," he wrote Madeline McQuown, estimating that he now had sufficient fiscal basis to finish the manuscript by April.[56] On a cold January afternoon a few days later, Dale drew a Rinehart & Company stationery envelope from his apartment-block mail slot. Good—he was awaiting a response on the chapters sent to New York the previous month and as expected, this was from Stanley Rinehart himself. Tearing open the flap, he pulled out and unfolded the sheet. The letter was not what he anticipated.

The senior partner wrote that the draft chapters Morgan had sent in December were not what the publisher expected. "We have now received three [*sic*] chapters, so preliminary in nature that they give no indication of the projected book," Rinehart observed pointedly before being blunt: the publisher expected either a substantive draft manuscript or the advances against royalties returned. Now. Barring Morgan's immediate delivery of a publishable manuscript, Rinehart cancelled the five-year-old agreement on what he had been told was a nearly decade-old writing, not research, project.[57]

Ten years earlier, Rinehart had taken a risk on an unknown contributor to their popular and successful Rivers of America series, one who offered a study not of one of the country's great arteries of commerce and history, but of an almost-unknown brackish trickle of a stream across the Nevada desert. The firm was surprised and pleased with the reception *The Humboldt: Highroad of the West* had enjoyed in 1943. After that, it had not been difficult for the publisher to perceive the enormous potential in this young Westerner and his Mormon topic. Rinehart's recommendation was instrumental in securing for Morgan the Guggenheim Fellowship awarded in 1945. He knew *The Great Salt Lake* also had done well. The publisher jumped at the chance for the contract on the Mormon book when it was offered in 1948 and had patiently supplied periodic advances against royalties on the contract for the Mormon history that now seemed to have gotten nowhere, as books go.

Decades later, Michael Korda, editor in chief of Simon & Schuster, wrote of this precise situation in his memoir of midcentury American publishing: "Publishers had always shied away from asking for their money back, partly because gentlemen didn't do that sort of thing and partly because most publishing houses weren't efficient enough to do it on any reasonable scale—besides, the thinking went, the sums of money were usually relatively small."[58] John Farrar, who signed Morgan to the Mormon book contract, had been the firm's socialite, the cultivator, the risk-taker, and Farrar had taken the risk on Dale Morgan. Stanley Rinehart, however, was the hard-nosed businessman, and he wanted the money back.

As Dale stood with the envelope in hand, maybe on the stair landing or in his small kitchenette, he knew he had no publishable manuscript on hand and absolutely no prospect of producing one quickly. He had not been exactly free to work on it, as he had explained to John Selby repeatedly for three years. Morgan felt he had not misled Selby or Rinehart at all. The publisher's letter demonstrated how badly the editors misunderstood Morgan's circumstance and habits, or perhaps how well he knew them. "Celebrity authors always assume that the hard part of writing is the *thinking*," wrote Korda on the same page of his memoir, "whereas the truth, as every professional writer knows, is that the actual writing is what hurts—thinking comes easy, by comparison, and nothing exists until it has been put down on paper." The editors and publishers expected the latter, and that like many other writers, Morgan typed and methodically revised a succession of drafts. That perception did not reflect the intense storms of composition and revision that were the way Dale Morgan produced his work.

Rinehart's ultimatum left the writer without room for a satisfactory explanation or response. Instead, an aggrieved Dale Morgan wrote stiffly to the publisher reemphasizing the effort he had made despite setbacks and agreeing to return the advance money. Loss of the contract shook Dale to his emotional foundation. Rinehart's letter caromed into Morgan's plans for the year, his whole schedule of priorities, and ultimately his career choice. "It is a matter of regret to me that I should have underestimated the amount of work this book still required of me, and that I should not have been able to foresee the personal difficulties that would attend this work," Morgan wrote Rinehart with some heat a few weeks later. "For Rinehart this has been simply another book on your list. For me it is the book by which finally I hope to be remembered."[59]

* * * * *

Counterfactual history—speculating on the *maybe*s and *what-ifs* in the past—is an exercise in speculative fiction, not a fair subject for a historian or a biographer. It is, nevertheless, tempting to wonder how Latter Day Saint and Western American history might have unfolded differently if Dale Morgan had completed his Mormon book and not been forced to refocus himself on the subjects that became his career. It is a bit presumptuous to assume that the work of one writer would affect society very deeply. The case is improved somewhat when we consider how much was shifting within the world Mormonism inhabited during the late 1940s and 1950s. It is probably fair to state that Morgan's book may not have changed history, but it certainly would have shifted history at a time when the first generation of academic writers was about to bring Mormonism into the pale of academic scholarship, and as large institutions began actively collecting Mormon material seriously.

Dale spent some intense January days reviewing what immediate options remained open to him. The list was short and not encouraging. Most importantly, employment prospects in Washington, DC, remained bleak. His best option would not even become an option until March, at the earliest. To survive—quite literally, to survive—he had to nail down the financial stability of another research fellowship or book contract and fling himself into the manuscript immediately. Morgan leapt in both directions with the same proposal. He wrote a hurried proposal to the Guggenheim Foundation. His reference letters virtually glowed with praise, but the foundation turned down the request solely because the award committee chose to distribute funding to as many scholars as possible and eliminated its previous fellows from consideration.

The day after Rinehart's letter arrived, without a literary agent's services, and unwilling to risk an out-of-hand rejection from a major publisher with a cold call, Morgan moved in the direction promising the quickest return and least risk. He wrote his *Great Salt Lake* publisher, the Bobbs-Merrill Company, proposing a biography of American fur trapper, trader, and explorer Jedediah Smith. Upon receiving Morgan's proposal, the initial response of the firm's president and publisher, D. L. Chambers, was: "who?"[60]

Bobbs-Merrill has been called "the greatest [publisher] ever to come out of the Midwest," but in the national scope the Indiana-based firm was a solid second-rank house. Its reputation stood well behind publishers like Rinehart & Company, DeVoto's Little, Brown and Company, Stegner's Harcourt, and, of course, the apex of American literary publishing, Alfred A. Knopf, who would begin courting Morgan for its list in less than a decade.[61] Bobbs-Merrill had published American history for years and had a decent list of nonfiction to its credit, but most importantly, the editors already knew Dale Morgan. Its staff in Indianapolis had been as impressed with *The Great Salt Lake* as Rinehart had been with *The Humboldt*. The early nineteenth-century fur trade, however, was entirely new ground, and Chambers took some time to be persuaded that a book in the topic was marketable.

In negotiating the contract, Morgan requested a $750 advance on royalties. Once a Jedediah Smith contract was signed, and though it nearly bankrupted him, he reimbursed Rinehart & Company the $750 he owed them and immediately set to work. Thereafter Dale Morgan's career hove to and necessarily sailed on a different tack, following the fallback topic that had grown alongside his interest in the Mormons: the American fur trade of the early nineteenth century.

Even while Morgan began writing the Jedediah Smith biography, he kept pressure on the job quest, using any angle he could to pry at possible openings, and the historical bibliography of Mormonism was not ignored entirely. The actual bibliography manuscript had not and did not progress by a single page, entry, or note beyond the forty-five pages of hastily drafted sample text, which had been abandoned in April 1949, but on March 1, Dale could write friend Stan Ivins that forty-five titles recently had been added to his master checklist.[62] The bibliography became the centerpiece to the hurried second fellowship application that the Guggenheim Foundation declined. Dale described the work as "nearly ready for publication."[63] It was not quite a ruse; Morgan probably did have reasonably close at hand most of the material he felt was needed to compile the notes and complete the project. What he lacked was uncommitted time to work on it. His life as a researcher grew increasingly complicated, claims of imminence becoming useful devices for buying time on projects that could yet be put off just a little longer. The bibliography had been set aside nearly three years earlier, and despite his interest in it would never again receive the intention periodically lavished on his history of the Mormons. Still, nearly another year after Stanley Rinehart's cancellation of the book contract, Dale wrote a publication query for it to Yale University Press. He expected to expand the list from 1830–1849 to include 1850–1869.[64] However, the Church Historian's Office staff were not cooperating as effectively as promised toward confirming the new checklist against their holdings, and he could not actually complete the bibliography until that marked checklist carbon returned. Perhaps his letter to Yale was intended as a baited hook; Yale had the funds and Morgan could point to his descriptive work on elements of the Collection of Western Americana given by William Robertson Coe, often informally called the "Coe Collection," which was still being absorbed by the library a decade after being acquired. Editor Eugene Davidson, however, did not bite, and the line was left to drift.

In the shock of the moment, standing with Rinehart's letter in hand in early January 1952, Morgan could not possibly realize the larger sense of what it meant. Cancellation of *The Mormons* contract severed the moorings that had tied him to the study of Utah and the Latter Day Saints thus far in his career. It would never be recovered. Neither the "Mormon book" nor the bibliography of Mormonism ever again became serious writing projects. Rinehart's cancellation knocked Mormonism cleanly and completely from Morgan's writing priorities and effectively redirected his career. What little he did create in the subject existed as book reviews, as a minor theme in some western-trail topic, or as a personal confection (such as his 1969 essay on Mormon literature). With the exception of completing his third historical bibliography, Morgan never returned to substantive work on Mormonism.

Even so, he did not or found he could not confide to even his closest friends what had happened to *The Mormons*. To Juanita Brooks, Dale asserted that he had reoriented his life: "I have already taken steps to alter my publishing obligations. In place of the unlimited commitment of my Mormon book I am taking on the more limited commitment of my Jedediah Smith biography." To University of California paleontologist and Western Americana bibliographer Charles L. Camp, Dale could only say that the Smith biography "has been growing up around me with the greatest vigor; in fact, it has crowded aside my Mormon book itself."[65] Dale told Charles Kelly that Rinehart "was showing a disposition to press me on my Mormon book, and I was no longer in a mood to be pressed; the result is that I have shelved my Mormon book until next winter and have embarked upon the writing of my Jedediah Smith biography."[66] Darrell Greenwell and Dean Brimhall were told that Dale had "suspended work on my Mormon book until November."[67] Morgan glided artfully around the real circumstances even to his closest friends, confessing the truth only to Madeline McQuown.[68] Was it embarrassment? Probably. Dale Morgan put great value on fulfilling his pledges and he was not happy about the inability to do so in this case.

* * * * *

With cancellation of his book contract, Morgan's ability to remain in Washington hinged entirely on the prospective job at the Bureau of American Ethnology. A year after he first learned of it, the anticipated BAE vacancy had still not opened. Moreover, Morgan could never convince its editorial chief that he could offset his inability to hear with sheer competence. On January 28, 1952, Dale wrote both his mother Emily and sister Ruth that he planned to leave Washington and return to Salt Lake City.[69] The Bobbs-Merrill contract for the fur trader biography changed only his prospects, not his immediate circumstances. Dale was at the end of his fiscal rope. With resignation he also accepted Emily's offer to let him draw on her bank account for the money needed to wind up his affairs in the east and make the trip to Salt Lake City. There was really no decision to make. Within a few days Dale alerted his Condon Terrace landlord that he would be out by March 7 and once again began packing.

Then, Darel McConkey wrote excitedly from Mexico City that unofficially "I actually set eyes on a paper signed by J.S. Smith" in the Archivo General de la Nación and was laboring with the Mexican bureaucracy about permission to see the document officially.[70] Dale was highly interested but forced himself to focus intensely on moving preparations: packing, forwarding mail, getting the Hudson serviced, the thousand things that one never considers but must arrange. Once the books were packed, four wooden bookcases went to the Norths. They were still there twenty years later to receive a few of his books in 1971.

At about 10 p.m. on March 7, as planned, Dale pulled away from the curb on Condon Terrace and drove north to Silver Spring, Maryland, for an overnight stay with Naomi and Tobe Peres, his former OPA assistant and her husband. Over the next few days Dale passed through Uniontown, Pennsylvania, Indianapolis, and finally to St Louis for his first major stop at the Missouri Historical Society. For two days the portable typewriter perched on his knees as he hammered out notes and transcriptions of key fur trade documents. Then, on March 16, Dale drove across Missouri and seventy miles into Kansas to see the fur trade collections at the Kansas Historical Society. The next day he got as far west as Limon, Colorado, before being stopped by bad weather. Before daylight the weather had broken, and Morgan drove the remaining ninety miles to Denver.

The drive from Denver through Laramie, Wyoming, toward Salt Lake City became a litany of weather delays and mechanical cussedness. He did not even make it home. The Hudson's engine blew up as he was pulling into Fort Bridger, Wyoming. Dale wrestled the car into a gas station lot. "I found that a piece of the cylinder block as large as the palm of my hand had been blown or knocked out," he wrote Darel McConkey a few days later. "Coolant was pouring into the snow under the car, and the dip stick showed oil not merely full, but the whole length of the stick."[71] There was no hope of a repair. Unpacking his typewriter, gathering up clothes, leaving the rest of his possessions in the car and the car where it had come to a stop, he sat down at the station to wait for the Greyhound bus. Two young men stopped for fuel, heard about Morgan's plight, and offered him a ride into the city, which he accepted gratefully. A taxi got him and his luggage to Hollywood Avenue. A couple of weeks later, Dale's brother Jim retrieved the Hudson for him. Dale unloaded his files and luggage into Jim's basement in Ogden for the time being, carrying what he could with him on the interurban train back to Salt Lake City. He let Jim sell the Hudson at whatever price it would bring, without asking what it was and without an ounce of regret.

The Holmes sisters about 1913 (from left): Annie Holmes Bleak, Emily Holmes Morgan, Ada Holmes Ostler, and Clara Holmes Hardy. If this photograph was not taken at a family gathering, the occasion may have been Emily's normal degree graduation. DLM Papers, Bancroft Library, University of California, Berkeley.

Left to right: Emily, Dale, and Lowell Morgan, about April 1915. DLM Papers, Bancroft Library.

Dale L. Morgan as a toddler, ca. 1917. DLM Papers, Bancroft Library.

The extended Morgan family in the summer of 1920 (from left): Jim Morgan, Emily Morgan, Lowell's brother Alan Dale Morgan, Lowell's mother Pearl Pratt Morgan holding Bob Morgan, Lowell's sister Carolyn Morgan, Ruth Morgan, Dale Morgan. DLM Papers, Bancroft Library.

Dale Morgan as high school graduate, 1933. DLM Papers, Bancroft Library.

Jarvis and Madeline Reeder Thurston, ca. 1938. Courtesy of Jarvis Thurston.

Morgan recreates one of his locally famous chess victories, November 1938. Photo by Ray Kooyman from author's collection.

Utah Chess Federation meeting at Salt Lake City's Alta Club, 1938. Morgan stands third right, with Jarvis Thurston at his right shoulder. Author's collection.

Andrew Jenson, Joseph Fielding Smith, and A. William Lund, the three main figures of the Church Historian's Office during Morgan's WPA years, circa 1937. Courtesy of Church Historian's Office, Salt Lake City, Utah.

Maurice L. Howe, ca. 1940. Courtesy of Daniel Walker Howe.

Charles Kelly, ca. 1935. Courtesy of Utah State Historical Society, Salt Lake City.

Hugh F. O'Neil, director of the Utah Historical Records Survey, ca. 1939. Courtesy of Utah State Historical Society.

Darel and Anna McConkey, ca. 1948. Courtesy of Jim McConkey.

Pastel self-portrait of Morgan, ca. 1941. Courtesy of Special Collections, J. Willard Marriott Library, University of Utah.

Morgan, as director of the Utah Writers' Project, autographs the first copy of *Utah: A Guide to the State* for Governor Herbert B. Maw, March 29, 1941. Courtesy of Utah State Historical Society.

Morgan sketching at the Salt Lake Art Center, ca. 1941. DLM Papers, Bancroft Library.

Marguerite Sinclair Reusser, secretary/librarian for the Utah State Historical Society, was Morgan's ally in developing the entity as a public research institution. Courtesy of Utah State Historical Society.

Dale Morgan, Jim McConkey, and the infamous Hudson Eight at the McConkey home, May 30, 1947. Courtesy of Jim McConkey.

Louise North (center) with Concepción (Conchita) and Carlos Bosch García at the Norths' home in rural Maryland, September 1, 1947. DLM Papers, Bancroft Library.

Juanita Brooks writes for Dale on their trip into the Wasatch, May 16, 1948. Photograph by Vesta Crawford, Darel and Anna McConkey Papers, Manuscripts Division, Special Collections, J. Willard Marriott Library, University of Utah.

Samuel A. Burgess, archivist/librarian of the Reorganized Church of Jesus Christ of Latter Day Saints, 1948. Courtesy of Library and Archives, Community of Christ Temple, Independence, Missouri.

A. Russell Mortensen, first full-time director of the Utah State Historical Society, ca. 1960. Courtesy of Utah State Historical Society.

The Mormon menace

Lee, John Doyle, 1812-1877.
　　The Mormon menace; being the confession of
John Doyle Lee, Danite and official assassin
of the Mormon church under the late Brigham
Young; introduction by Alfred Henry Lewis ...
New York, Home Protection Pub. Co. ₍c1905₎
　　1 p.ℓ., xxii ₍23₎-368 p.　front.,3 plates,
port.　20 cm.

　　An abridged reprint of an earlier edition
(St. Louis, 1881) published under title:
Mormonism unveiled; including the remarkable
life and con-　　　　　　　fessions of John D.
Lee ...

One data cell in a manual database—a library catalog card. Image by the author.

A section of the Library of Congress card catalog in use, ca. 1952. Courtesy of Library of Congress, Washington, DC.

George P. Hammond, director of the Bancroft Library, ca. 1950. Courtesy of Utah State Historical Society.

The portrait shot for *Jedediah Smith and the Opening of the West* promotion, 1952. DLM Papers, Bancroft Library.

Madeline Reeder McQuown, ca. 1960. DLM Papers, Bancroft Library.

Joe Colgan, Navajo case research assistant, ca. 1970. Courtesy of Jim McConkey.

Carl I. Wheat, close friend and coauthor, ca. 1960. Courtesy of California State Library, Sacramento.

Norman M. Littell, Navajo tribal general counsel, 1959. Unattributed press publicity photo in author's collection.

Everett L. Cooley, ca. 1955. Courtesy of Utah State Historical Society.

Dale Morgan in the Navajo research project office, April 25, 1960. Author's collection.

Louise North, ca. 1969. DLM Papers, Bancroft Library, University of California Berkeley.

Morgan in his only personally delivered speech before the Jedediah Smith Society, University of the Pacific, March 18, 1967. Holt-Atherton Special Collections, University of the Pacific Library, Stockton, California.

Morgan mugging with the Bennion sword for Everett Cooley's camera, Utah State Historical Society, August 1968. Author's collection

"Half an Easterner and Three-Quarters a Westerner"[1]

Writing *Jedediah Smith* and Salt Lake City, 1952–1953

> *I am in the West for this spring and summer, and possible for the fall, in the interests of a new book on fur trade and exploration I have engaged to deliver by November. Although I have had to lay aside my labors in Mormon history until that time, there is no such thing as laying them aside absolutely.*[2]
>
> —Dale Morgan

THE FIRST FEW WEEKS through the early spring of 1952 following Morgan's arrival in Salt Lake City were filled with friends dropping by to welcome him back. Juanita Brooks was chaperoning the Dixie College debate team to the capital and arranged to meet Dale at the Utah State Historical Society (USHS), where she introduced him in person to Russ Mortensen. Wilford Poulson dropped by from Provo. Sterling McMurrin invited Dale once again to the "Mormon Seminar," the discussion circle of liberal academics at the University of Utah. Dale wrote letters, did research at the USHS, and reorganized his hastily packed research material, but he did not write on the Jedediah Smith book. Finally in April he settled down to the task, beginning with the story of trapper Hugh Glass—and now he went fiercely to work.

Morgan's spring and summer were filled with intense effort drafting, revising, and expanding the suite of known facts in the Jedediah Smith record and its context of the American fur trade of the 1820s. "For a guy who had as much information about Jedediah Smith to begin with as I did, I sure have had a lot of research to do on him as the book has progressed," he groused to Denver bookseller Fred Rosenstock.[3]

Morgan's undivided attention to the biography was diverted by unusually heavy spring rains flooding out of the canyons of the Wasatch Front. Between 900 South and 1700 South Street, ditches and watercourses were overflowing, and sandbag dikes were hastily erected to channel runoff water west along both 1300 South and 2100 South. In April, work on the book came to a screeching halt when the family discovered three inches of water in Emily's basement, where Dale's entire library and his crated papers sat stored on shelves and in file cabinets. The potential damage or loss of his research files was a staggering prospect, and he dropped everything to spend several days getting the crates and cabinets at least six inches off the floor—where they remained for the next eighteen years.[4]

By May, Dale was closing the loop on the shelved Mormon history, offering explanations for his change of direction to individuals and institutions that had helped or were interested in it. Yet despite the spring's general progress, the fur trade biography was nowhere near complete and he had to make a living somehow. He made a fast $50 writing a newspaper article about Miles Goodyear for former WPA administrator Darrell Greenwell, editor for the *Ogden Standard-Examiner*. Leonard Kirkpatrick, librarian at the University of Utah's Thomas Library, explored the possibility of hiring Morgan temporarily to survey the university's holdings on Utah and the Mormons with an eye toward expanding its holdings into a genuine research library on local and cultural history. The effort did not pan out, and the survey was never done.[5]

In the meantime, Morgan's dogged determination to chase leads and write inquiries was paying off. He interspersed his other tasks with correcting his draft material from answers to queries set afloat in his ceaseless ebb and flow of correspondence. New material on Jedediah Smith and the fur trade was surfacing across the country. Relevant letters were found in the hands of autograph collectors, postal collectors, in several state and local historical societies, and the papers of Peter Smith, a brother. There were frustrations as well. Harrison Dale's published transcription of the Harrison Rogers diary was unreliable, he discovered, and he ordered new microfilm of the manuscript to repeat the process himself. "I guess there is no substitute, ever, for going to the ultimate sources when you are doing a job in history," he told Missouri Historical Society librarian Barbara Kell.[6]

With *Jedediah Smith*, for the first and possibly only time in his life as a writer, Morgan followed the path a publisher expected, from rough draft through revision to final manuscript. Through the spring and summer Dale assembled a "line-of-battle manuscript," a rough rendition of detail and citations from notes, transcripts, and correspondence, and from which he was composing the actual first draft. Morgan finally wrote Bobbs-Merrill President D. L. Chambers that he planned to send the first section of the Jedediah Smith draft manuscript in the second week of September, 1952.[7] Adding that task to his stream of correspondence, most of Morgan's days were spent hunched over a typewriter in his Hollywood Avenue bedroom, as the late summer days tinted the high Wasatch scrub oaks and mountain mahogany to brilliant reds, and the patches of quaking aspen to a livid golden yellow.

The November manuscript deadline approached and as he mailed the draft manuscript to the publisher in batches, Dale also began looking beyond its completion toward the next step in whatever career direction he could make. To far-flung friends he noted that he was willing to accept about any reasonable offer involving history.[8] Charles Eberstadt asked if Morgan was ready to "turn pro." Edward Eberstadt & Sons had long used Morgan to catalog material for sale selectively, and Charles noted the firm might make room for Morgan, "even though it does not allow sufficient time to do the thorough-going work on historical material that crosses one's desk." Dale asked for time to consider the implications, but finally decided he wanted to remain a writer and to return to the Mormons as a topic.[9] Everett Graff talked to the Newberry Library in Chicago about securing a foundation grant for Morgan "to do a comprehensive job on the fur trade."[10] Likewise, that possibility went nowhere.

Meanwhile, Bobbs-Merrill was routing the draft manuscript of the Smith biography among internal readers. "Apparently the author is concerned only with the events that gave [Jedediah Smith] a claim to fame, and not with the portrayal of 'the whole man,'" complained one reader, perhaps not understanding just how little was known about Smith. Another was complimentary. "Mr. Morgan, in addition to being a good writer, is a historian of integrity. He will not include what he cannot confirm by written evidence. He will not read between the lines. It would not ever be worth proposing that he fill out the account with probabilities or conjectures." The manuscript supplied them was as much about Thomas Fitzpatrick, James Clyman, and Hugh Glass as it was about Jedediah Smith, and the firm waited anxiously to see which direction the author was going to take the text in revision.[11] The manuscript was still coming in small batches and at the rate at which Morgan was supplying it, would clearly not arrive in time for even a December 1 deadline, as the author had not even begun revisions or a final manuscript.

Harrison Platt at Bobbs-Merrill wrote Dale just before Thanksgiving with news that the publisher had given up on spring publication, and that the new manuscript deadline would be April 1, 1953.[12] Dale was reluctant to admit any delay but would not have been able to make the earlier December deadline. Still he was sending dozens of queries to resolve details he felt were inadequately clear or to locate sources that needed to be included. "My own book is still this side of completion," Dale wrote Charles Kelly, "I'd like to be done with it, but new stuff is still coming in, so I do not complain."[13] As if he did not have enough to do, during December alone Dale also proposed several entirely different publication commitments to historical journals.[14]

As the Jedediah Smith biography progressed, its scope grew far beyond the man and his circle of fur-trade actors. To Colton Storm in Chicago, Morgan wrote that the project "automatically interests me in everything pertaining to the exploration of the Missouri river and the farther West."[15] The scope of his research included the expansion of geographic knowledge, trade relations between Native peoples and Europeans and Americans, formal and informal exploration, and the entire sweep of published and unpublished documentary sources providing snippets of fact and fragments of clues. It circumscribed the maps of the Lewis and Clark expedition; every receipt, note, letter, account, reminiscence, or newspaper squib ever generated by or about an American fur brigade; and every journal article or book regarding a related figure of the time.

Even as he worked on the biography, Dale also floated a proposal to Missouri Historical Society president Charles van Ravenswaay for the eventual publication of a collection of "The Ashley Papers," to which van Ravenswaay agreed, provided the society did not have to publish the result.[16] William H. Ashley was another central figure in the American fur trade of the 1820s, and at different times Jedediah Smith's employer, supplier, and partner. The collection of Ashley papers would be one of the few projects Dale Morgan saw to fruition, but between obligations, assignments, and distractions the project would require more than a decade to complete. Morgan's research was reshaping knowledge of the scope and dynamics of the earliest American West.

* * * * *

In late January 1953, Mortensen asked Morgan a second time if he would entertain the idea of working as the first archivist for the state of Utah.

A new Republican Secretary of State was appalled at the condition of offices in the Capitol and wanted action to improve the state's public-records accessibility. Morgan was definitely interested, but the situation was complicated and ultimately killed by back-channel discussion of his positive review of Brodie's *No Man Knows My History* eight years earlier. The Board of Control would have to approve Morgan's appointment, and its chair Joel Ricks (with whom Morgan had tangled over the Bolton and Korns volumes) was a brother-in-law to LDS church president David O. McKay.[17]

At the same time, correspondence with Bernard DeVoto kept Morgan busy. The former Utahn was busily compiling a one-volume collection of the Lewis and Clark expedition journals and regularly plagued Morgan for source material and opinions. The older man appreciated the help and was a competent researcher himself, but, DeVoto wrote Morgan, "there are ways in which it's depressing to get a letter from you. You know so much and are careful and accurate by nature and you progress by intelligent sequences."[18]

Finally, with the "line of battle" fur trade manuscript complete, Morgan could launch into revision. He shortly knocked out a letter to his Bobbs-Merrill contact, Harry Platt. "I have completely rewritten the first half of the book," adding new information and cutting heavily the manuscript he had delivered last fall. "That was a rather lousy manuscript, you know," he admitted to Platt. "I have positively blushed in working it over."[19]

For all the progress made on three fronts at once—not only the Jedediah Smith biography but also a documentary series of articles on the Shoshoni tribe and a "Bibliography of the Churches of the Dispersion," a study of publications relating to the complications of Latter Day Saint tradition between 1840 and 1870, this frenetically fruitful period represented an emotional low point, one of his darkest personal struggles. He was, by many measures, successful and respected. Even so, he still found it difficult to look at himself at thirty-seven, unmarried, unemployed, and hardly embarked on a career. "It is acutely painful to me to see the apricot blossoms open up on the tree in the yard and know that I haven't yet achieved an equivalent flowering in my own living," Dale wrote Madeline despondently.[20]

And he still needed an income. Mortensen successfully found enough money and the USHS Board of Control approved an expenditure to commission Morgan to organize and describe the bulk of HRS and UWP files to which the USHS had fallen heir half a decade earlier.[21] After working at that task through the daylight hours, Dale raced home nightly to hammer furiously on the Smith biography revision and to pick up another hundred bucks writing *Encyclopedia Americana* entries at DeVoto's recommendation, prodding the publisher about others meriting updates.[22]

Bernard DeVoto had come closest to a nationally marketable American Western regionalism with his own book on the fur trade, *Across the Wide Missouri* (Houghton Mifflin, 1947), though the author himself was no longer confident that writing history was a paying proposition, particularly if it was American Western history. Six years after publication DeVoto told Morgan that sales of *Across the Wide Missouri* had finally cleared the five-figure sum advanced him, but "I must have spent at least as much money of my own, cash in hand, on the book itself—not to mention travel expense and the like. Count my time as worth nothing and forget that I have a family and a handful of other dependents to support— merely to fund the work on the book was a ghastly matter through six full years. I hope to God I'm bright enough not to tackle another job."[23]

* * * * *

Right at this busy time in April 1953, Dale Morgan's streak of poor employment luck finally broke. During the third week of the month, a letter arrived from George P. Hammond of the University of California, Berkeley. Hammond had long been one of Morgan's professional contacts and the pair met personally on Morgan's Guggenheim excursion. Raised by Danish parents in Minnesota and North Dakota, Hammond had taken an undergraduate degree at Berkeley under Bancroft Director Herbert E. Bolton in 1920, completed a Master's thesis in 1921, and earned a PhD in Bolton's field of Spanish borderlands history in 1924. A translator and scholar, Hammond taught at UCLA for eight years in the 1930s before accepting an appointment at the University of New Mexico. He also shared with Morgan a background in the Historical Records Survey, having directed New Mexico's office between 1936 and 1939. In 1944, when the University of California was looking for a successor to Bancroft Library Director Herbert I. Priestley, Bolton recommended his former student. Hammond returned to a split appointment at his *alma mater,* the Bancroft directorship, and a concurrent appointment in the history department.[24] He had now directed the Bancroft Library for almost a decade, but that wasn't entirely why Morgan interested him.

Early in 1953 Hammond was retained as an expert in early Southwest history by Norman M. Littell, legal counsel for the Navajo Tribe.[25]

Hammond offered Morgan a $15 per day commission as researcher for a historical project which, he explained, involved finding and transcribing from Utah institutions any written source documenting the geography occupied by Navajos around 1846, as well as contacts with Mormons after that time. The research files Morgan would help generate supported a lawsuit between the tribe and the federal government over land tenure. Morgan agreed, asking if the commission could be postponed until June to allow him time to finish cataloging the WPA papers for the USHS and to complete the Smith biography. "I am so damned rushed I hardly know whether I am coming or going," he grumbled when reporting the paying distraction to his publisher. Hammond agreed.[26] Over the next decade, the Navajo project interactions would dominate Morgan's time and attention.

A few days after accepting the offer, Morgan proposed employing Madeline McQuown as a research assistant. He had two reasons: first, because he trusted her as a researcher; second, that the Church Historian's Office staff had completely denied him access to manuscript diary and journal holdings five years earlier. "I cannot be absolutely sure until they are approached that the [Historian's Office] will grant access to anybody," Morgan told Hammond, "They are very capricious about such things even to their own members, for they regard their collections as for the use and benefit of the Church, and in no sense constituting a research library." He explained further: "Sometimes, they won't cooperate worth a cent on any project, no matter now meritorious, and sometimes they receive you with open arms."

Recommending McQuown as an assistant, however, nearly derailed Morgan's commission, since it implied an additional expense.[27] Always willing to make a personal sacrifice for Madeline's sake, Morgan sweetened the deal, offering to pay her out of his own wage. That tipped the balance in his favor. Littell, through Hammond, agreed. Hammond rode a train from San Francisco to Salt Lake City to get Dale and Madeline oriented within the project and to set the research team to work. They met at the USHS room in the capitol building on May 20. The next day, Hammond took McQuown a few blocks south of the capitol and introduced her to the Church Historian's Office staff. Hammond remained in town for a few days, looking generally at source material.[28]

As Dale negotiated with Hammond for the first reasonably stable income he had seen in six years, Harry Platt was pleading for the final manuscript of the Jedediah Smith biography, hoping to get it through editorial reviews and into production early enough in the year to hold a publication date in the fall of 1953. By the end of the month and after eleven weeks of day-and-night work, Morgan still hammered on Jedediah Smith. Dale began sending the revised chapters to Indianapolis in batches toward mid-April, and these were immediately distributed among the Bobbs-Merrill internal readers. They were very complimentary. The rough draft of the previous fall had been fitted into "an Allusive[*sic*], moving style with many touches of both art and artifice," Platt reported. "I'd say Morgan is really giving us [a] final manuscript of considerable power and freshness."[29]

Unfortunately, that manuscript was also much too long. By May the sheets were back in Dale's hands, and he was going through them cutting for length with "a red pencil and very hard heart."[30] The June 1 submission deadline was uncomfortably close, and May became a cyclone of corrections, proofs, map drafts, and approvals. Even trimmed of fat, the publisher's castoff calculated that the biography manuscript was still too long for the projected page count and price point. The lean narrative still required some regrettable structural cutting, but the book was finally really moving and missing only one thing: a title. Platt wanted "something to show that this is not only a biography of one man but a history of a significant era in the opening of the west." A few days later Dale sent a few options to Platt and told him to pick one. Platt did: *Jedediah Smith and the Opening of the West.*[31]

* * * * *

With Morgan and McQuown working quickly through the small manuscript holdings of Utah institutions, the Navajo research project was going stronger in Salt Lake City than it was in Washington, DC. By late summer 1953, Dale's letters suggest he had already been approached by Hammond about making a trip east to spur effort there. That assignment involved a story that had started the previous year, in the fall of 1952.

"I have puzzled for a long time," Dale had written Darel McConkey the preceding October, "over how I might turn to financial advantage my special range of knowledge and my professional interests." He considered establishing himself as a researcher for hire in the capital, which would provide both an income and proximity to the institutions he desired to haunt. "The obvious flaw has been that you can only make money from people who have money . . . and I couldn't see college professors, graduate students, and the like laying out enough money to provide a respectable financial base for such a business."[32] In the succeeding weeks and months Morgan recreated the series of clever query/proposal letters he had once written to magazines, this time directed toward institutions and well-placed collectors and friends. Two of those letters proved important.

One of those letters went to University of California paleontologist and avocational historian Charles L. Camp, a long-time correspondent, suggesting that the Bancroft Library would profit from a minutely descriptive listing or *calendar* of its manuscript holdings. Such a project "would serve the purpose both of making available to scholars a useable knowledge of what Bancroft now has, and establishing a basis for a reinvigorated collecting program covering each and all of the Western states which are Bancroft's legitimate concern. This would be a fascinating and useful job, and if Bancroft ever finds the money for doing it, I would be glad to have them discuss the project with me."[33] Coincidentally, Hammond was under pressure from the University of California librarian to do precisely that. The second important letter was dispatched the next month directly to Hammond, suggesting that the library would profit from selectively microfilming federal records for the library's growing research collection.[34] Camp talked to Hammond about the manuscript proposal, and together the ideas took hold in Hammond's mind. Dale Morgan was at the center of both.

In the decades before digital imaging was even imagined, microfilming—photographing documents on long rolls of transparent plastic film—provided a tangible and compact format that could be stored at a library and reviewed at researchers' convenience. In the technological context of the 1950s, microfilming was perhaps the most economical means of collecting and handling the vast amount of historical material supporting the Navajo lawsuit—certainly cheaper than sustaining a researcher to search through and transcribe from the mountains of federal records. Because microfilming the entire mountain would be too time-consuming, the project first required selecting historically relevant documents to be microfilmed. Morgan's casual suggestion and his own effectiveness in Salt Lake City research seem to have provided the seed which prompted Hammond to extend Morgan's commission to do just what he had proposed to Camp a year earlier.[35] On July 1 Hammond wrote Dale that the research team had acquired thirty reels of microfilmed records relating to the Utes and that he had talked to Littell about getting Morgan to National Archives "as soon as possible, to make a similar selection of records relating to the Navahos."[36]

With the *Jedediah Smith* draft manuscript in the publisher's hands (though he was still compiling the mass of notes), Dale used this research as an excuse to take a badly needed break and head to California for a few days to visit the McQuowns. It wasn't much of a vacation. He worked furiously cutting the *Jedediah Smith* manuscript at the McQuowns' apartment in San Jose, making a quick day-trip with Madeline to the Bancroft Library to confirm references and detouring to the Huntington Library to see if its collections held anything relevant on the Navajos. He did not finish with the manuscript until his Union Pacific train had crossed the Sierras and was well past Reno, Nevada, on the trip home. Dale arrived home on July 10 to post the remaining end matter manuscript to Indianapolis, but also to find Hammond's invitation to Washington, DC.

On July 14 Morgan mailed the final batch of corrected and cut *Jedediah Smith* manuscript, photos, and maps back to Bobbs-Merrill.[37] Three days later Platt sent a telegram with terrible news: the text was still about 36,000 words longer than the book's price point could sustain. Rather than compromise the already compressed narrative, the publisher proposed a three-way accommodation: a price concession from the printer, reduce the author's royalty slightly, and to enlarge the book's trim dimension and type area. All of this would allow Bobbs-Merrill to shoehorn the text into the available page count while holding the $4.50 retail price. "I'm sorry we have to ask the above concession of you," wrote Harry Platt, "but I'd wager you will prefer less money to very much less text."[38] Dale replied with his own telegram and a vigorous agreement. Two weeks later Hammond wrote that before heading to Washington, DC, Littell wanted Morgan to join the legal team at a conference planned for St. Michaels, Arizona, on August 1. Ignoring the demands of Morgan's book, Littell instructed Hammond to get Morgan there.

Morgan caught a bus for the two-day ride south from Salt Lake City to Window Rock, Arizona. He unfolded stiffly from the bus seat to settle into two days of meetings with the Navajos' legal team and its other research group, a collection of archaeologists similarly on retainer. At lunch on the second day, Hammond pulled Morgan aside and asked if he would be interested in a temporary half-time job at the Bancroft Library once the National Archives stay was completed in about October. Hammond wanted someone who understood the American West and historical sources to write short descriptions of manuscripts and collections for the use of researchers—cataloging. One of the library's staff had reduced their work schedule due to poor health, and the library had a lot of work to do describing its large and growing manuscripts collection. The position would last only to the end of the 1954 fiscal year but *might* extend into something longer. The work on Navajo research, based out of Hammond's project office in Dwinelle Hall, could occupy the other half of Morgan's day. Together the jobs offered Dale temporary but full-time employment. The clouds of bad luck over his employment prospects seemed to have finally broken.

As the session broke up, George and Carrie Hammond prepared to drive Dale to Albuquerque, where he would catch another bus to Denver and a visit with Lucie Howe and her boys. After an overnight visit with the Howes in Denver, Dale was back home in Salt Lake City by August 6. The next day *Jedediah Smith* galley proofs began arriving in the mail, long sheets of straight text printed from the newly set type. Two weeks later Dale boarded a train for Washington, DC, and the research assignment. Though he had begun reading and correcting the day the sheets arrived, he continued working galleys against the manuscript for the entire trip. A few days before leaving, a confirmation arrived from the University of California, Berkeley. The job offer was real.[39]

Morgan's trip east was interrupted by a stop in Chicago. Western Americana collector Everett D. Graff had issued a long-standing invitation for Dale both to come see his book collection and to introduce him to important figures in the city. The pair went to the University of Chicago, where Dale talked to one of the librarians about the library microfilming its Latter Day Saint newspaper collections and adding Morgan's own negative microfilm to complete the record of several publications. They visited the aging bibliographer Wright Howes, and Morgan was introduced at the Newberry Library, where Graff served on the board.[40] Dale arrived in Washington, DC, on August 21. The McConkeys offered to house him once again until he found a short-term rental of his own, and Darel picked up Dale at the train station.

* * * * *

Once Morgan arrived at National Archives, it became clear almost immediately that the research task of identifying among federal records primary sources documenting Navajo historical geography involved far more archival material than had been imagined by the tribe's lawyers. To both log and arrange material for National Archives' microfilming Dale needed two research assistants. Ideally, one or both would be competent to act as researchers as well. Within a week, Littell had approved the additional hires. One was Elek Horvath, a recent Hungarian refugee with a PhD in art history and, like Morgan, fairly desperate for paying work of any sort. For the other, McConkey introduced Dale to a personal and family friend, Joseph E. Colgan.

Colgan was a scrawny, divorced dyspeptic with a taste for alcohol and deep experience in art and design. He had worked as a museum-diorama modeler for one of the New England state WPA art projects. Outside of work he pursued a hobby as well, attempting to fix needy people, usually a woman. In Colgan, Morgan seemed to have found someone who shared kindred qualities. Utterly irreligious, a very organized researcher driven by work, Colgan was also a skilled raconteur who clearly shared Morgan's devotion to the personal letter. Their correspondence began in 1953 as a way of documenting the research and microfilming project in federal records. The letters eventually deepened to a much more personal level. Beginning with their shared experience of Navajo research, Colgan reported research and daily life in the sort of readable, descriptive letters that chronicled not only related business, but personal activities and insightful perceptions that Morgan loved to read for their human intimacy. To the end of Morgan's life, he and Colgan wrote no less than monthly, often weekly, and frequently more than weekly.

The trio of researchers went quickly to work. With a little effort and discussion, they settled on a division of labor and process for handling the mass of identified material, logging their finds ahead of microfilming. Morgan concentrated on skimming the contents of record files, identifying reports, drafts, and letters of historical bearing on the case and as potential exhibits. Since the lawsuit involved the historic tenure and use of the landscape, his target was material mentioning the loose cultural boundaries of Navajo domestic locations at United States' first contact, historic grazing and hunting areas, and subsistence sites. Colgan was set to hunting material in the War Department records, while Horvath handled file arrangement ahead of microfilming and returning material to the correct locations in the departmental files.

Before a month had passed the trio created a systematic process for logging targeted material and preparing it for microfilming without separating it from other material in its containers. Through the fall the three labored on file after file of federal records: territorial Office of Indian Affairs superintendency, State Department, War Department, General Accounting Office. The work was painstaking. Morgan reported to Hammond in mid-November that "I ha[ve] been trying to anticipate any and all questions [Norman Littell] might hereafter be called upon to answer in legal proceedings regarding the Navahos [*sic*], and that consequently I had been listing everything of real significance to the Navajos found in these papers."[41]

Since Hammond had pledged that the Bancroft Library would buy a positive microfilm of the material for its collections, Morgan instructed his assistants to be broadly inclusive rather than too topically focused with their selections. The result was a massive but concentrated selection of documents from federal records, a cornerstone of primary documentation on which could rest a Navajo cultural library, if the tribe eventually chose to establish one. Morgan's task also involved meticulous coordination with National Archives' microfilming staff. Most of the documents were still in their nineteenth-century file jackets; the sheets had to be unfolded and flattened ahead of being herded beneath the microfilm cameras. Document checklists required typing and replication. Littell was impressed, and Hammond was grateful. "You have covered every phase of it admirably," the latter wrote, "in fact, so well that I almost felt that I was working with you day by day."[42]

In early September, the page proofs of *Jedediah Smith* arrived from the printer, needing immediate attention if the book was to appear on schedule. "This whole year has been just one long scramble for me," Dale wrote Charles Eberstadt, "and the scramble is not over yet, either, for I am still a couple of weeks short of getting caught up on all the things that piled up on me during the spring."[43] No one on the legal team viewed the Navajo project as anything but temporary. By the end of the year Morgan planned to resume work on his Mormon history, expecting to complete at least the first volume in 1954.

Dale finally located a fully furnished sixth-floor walkup in the LaSalle Apartments on Connecticut Avenue, moving in during the second week of September. Having a place in town of his own provided not only an opportunity to get *Jedediah Smith* page proofs read and draft an index, but also a base from which he could do a bit of research on his own as time allowed. Until the book went to press, however, time did not permit. Just as he was ready to return the corrected pages, a long-delayed reply arrived from the Hudson's Bay Record Society with keenly relevant new material. Morgan was willing to absorb the high charges for alterations made by a publisher at page-proof stage, a charge designed specifically to discourage authors from changing a book's page breaks or carefully calculated (and budgeted) length. Morgan accepted the charges, preferring to present readers with the most accurate account possible.[44]

Once the book's page proofs and index manuscript were in the publisher's hands, the author's responsibility became merely a waiting game. Just before midmonth in November, Harrison Platt mailed the author ten copies of *Jedediah Smith and the Opening of the West*. It was a handsome volume in a jacket dominated by vivid yellows and tans. "I hope you like the looks of the book," Platt wrote the author on making the delivery. "Please don't find any typos."[45] Dale responded with an airy wave, "You can hold up a book forever, hoping for that last one percent that is lacking, and there is always something lacking, something more that can be and will be discovered, no matter how long you wait. Better to publish the book, organize everyone's ideas, and set the whole community of scholarship to working with you."[46] Even before its official November 19 publication Dale bought and mailed dozens of copies to friends, associates, and as formal acknowledgements to those who had contributed documents to his research. New material continued surfacing despite publisher deadlines and Morgan marked up his own copy so quickly and thoroughly as to make the newly published volume historically obsolete. The book was hardly in stores when Everett Graff wrote Dale excitedly that a California lawyer named Carl I. Wheat had visited him recently, bringing news about discovering a Frémont map which he said had Jedediah Smith's travel routes marked on it.[47]

The book publication was exciting, the Navajo research all-consuming, and the possibility of a volume of Ashley transcripts distracting in the ever-shortening time Dale had available at the end of 1953. His goal was to complete the selection work in federal records by mid-December, allowing him time for a cross-country trip to arrive in Berkeley to start his editorial position at the Bancroft Library by the first working day of the new year. As the list of documents selected for microfilming crept over a thousand, however, Dale pressed Hammond and the Bancroft's personnel manager to delay his start date.

Emily wrote her congratulations to Dale on his thirty-ninth birthday. Before entraining for California, he passed another Christmas holiday with Max and Louise North and their two young daughters, as well as New Year's with McConkeys, newly returned from Mexico. As 1953 closed and despite the busyness that plagued his last weeks in Washington, Dale Morgan could put the past few years behind him with relief. Yes, the Mormon book was on hold, but his long-desired Jedediah Smith biography was at last in print, even if he was already looking toward a heavily revised second edition. No, he did not have a full-time job, but he had a pair of half-time appointments that at least looked like reasonably stable incomes to support himself and his writing. For the first time in several years the coming year looked like it held promise. "This year has been a furiously busy year, all year, and the rest will probably be the same," Dale had written his mother in September as he headed to Washington, DC, "but it [is] something to be on my way again."[48]

PART III

Western American Historian

CHAPTER 13

"It Is Something to Be On My Way Again"[1]

Bancroft Library and the Navajo Project, Berkeley, California, 1954–1962

> *Whether I will wish, or be content, to spend the rest of my days here I don't know. We have to earn a living and make out the best we can as we go along. I am not less a divided soul. . . . All my life, I guess, I will feel the tug east and west, whether in the West or the East.*[2]
>
> —Dale Morgan

DALE MORGAN LANDED at the University of California, Berkeley, in the midst of one of the most energetic periods in American higher education. Reviewing some of the seething changes in academia helps to put Morgan's late career and choices into context. He brought to Berkeley a growing scholarly reputation, yes, but his understanding of "the university" was based solely on his time as a student at a regional college during the 1930s, disdain for its academic historians, and his dismissal of graduate education for himself—not quite an unbiased perspective. As Morgan's career at Berkeley unfolded, he found it both enormously rewarding and highly frustrating. Exactly which emotion he felt varied from year to year and sometimes from day to day.

As previously discussed, the United States emerged from the Second World War into a very different world than the one from which it had entered the conflict. American industry scaled up while local businesses remained basically the same, so perhaps the sector experiencing the greatest systemic change was higher education. Despite dips during the First World War and the onset of the Depression, college enrollments steadily increased through the first four decades of the twentieth century. High school enrollments remained flat or trended slightly downward during the Second World War, mostly a result of falling birth rates during the 1920s. The administrative groundwork and academic infrastructure of the "ivory tower" had been laid and built in the previous century, but well into the twentieth, a college education largely (but not exclusively) remained a perquisite of a socially, economically, or politically privileged class. Senior academic historians of Dale Morgan's generation—the likes of George Hammond, Ray Allen Billington, and John Caughey—came through graduate programs in the 1920s and 1930s when higher education was still a comparatively small and elite venue. Professorial appointments before the war tended to be few and far between. "Many fine young [PhDs] were fretting their lives away in minor posts," wrote one observer in 1944, "as they waited in vain for professional opportunities which never came."

Since most young American men did not attend college before the Second World War, no one was entirely certain what would happen to universities after the war, but generally, student body growth due to the GI Bill looked like it would open up employment opportunities. "If the present dammed-up flow of students turns out to be an unexpectedly heavy flood when it is finally unloosed," the writer continued, "the staffing of overflowing classrooms with competent teachers may prove to be a formidable problem."[3]

At the GI Bill's passage, many higher education leaders worried about more than numbers. One account by the U.S. Office of Education reported that a third of the eight million enlisted service men and women had not completed high school.[4] The report stated clearly that not all qualified to enter college would do so. Time proved that prediction correct—only about half of eligible veterans took advantage of the education benefit (and, in an accommodating nod to Congressional delegations from the segregated South, in exchange for their supportive votes, all 1.2 million black veterans were excluded from benefits extended under the GI Bill). Behind veteran ranks themselves, in the early 1960s would come an even larger army of their children—the Baby Boom. That population increase meant an urgent need to expand higher education dramatically.

Federal investment in higher education infrastructure and research for three decades after the war was partially responsible for the economic miracle enjoyed by that generation.[5] New public institutions were founded and existing ones grew dramatically. Faculties and facilities expanded, also providing better employment options for prewar PhDs and new opportunities for those who flew through graduate schools after the war. Whether in the sciences, social sciences, or humanities, federal funding provided the cornerstone on which modern public colleges and universities were built and expanded. The United States' structure for mass higher education has roots in the past but is essentially a creation of the first two postwar decades.[6]

*   *   *   *   *

Morgan arrived at UC Berkeley in time to participate in its local development of a broad current within modern higher education—creation of the research-library collection. The movement was sparked some thirty years earlier, but the postwar investment in libraries had long-reaching consequences. Texts alone were insufficient, argued Yale University English Literature Professor Chauncey Brewster Tinker, who asserted the existence of a fundamental relationship between faculty, students, and institution. "There are three distinguishing marks of a university," Tinker asserted:

> a group of students, a corps of instructors, and a collection of books; and of these the most important is the collection of books. By the interaction of these three factors the university manifests its twofold activity to the world. Its scholars, by means of the books provided for them, advance the cause of knowledge and the reign of truth, and so make of the university a seat of learning. In the second place, this corps of instructors mediates between the books and the students, and ... puts a new generation in touch with the stored-up thought of the world. Without books ... no university and, indeed, no civilization, is possible.[7]

Prior to the invention and creation of the Internet in the 1970s, Tinker's model was fundamentally true. From our hyperconnected and digitally omnivorous present, it is difficult to imagine how scholarship could have functioned without PDF files, HTML, and Google. Those living in the digital age often forget a time existed when a single college or university entity—the library—constituted the sole destination for all practical inquiry associated with almost all classroom education and much academic research. With limited possibilities for movement or study elsewhere, scholars expected to go first to the library. The term we typically use today, *access,* essentially meant *acquisition* in the 1950s. No library could hold everything, but in the pre-Internet age a library's usefulness was generally measured by the size and breadth of its holdings.

The expansion of academic libraries, as at Berkeley, often included Tinker's particular interest: rare book collections. Whether at Tinker's Yale or at Morgan's Berkeley, many rare-book collections, and perhaps most of them, grew through the agency of wealthy private donors and foundations. A second avenue of institutional growth was a new interest and push toward acquiring collections of unpublished material—manuscripts. A quest for primary sources—a competition, really—began for the unpublished works, letters, and old shopping lists of significant writers and political figures.[8] Within a very short time historically informative documents generated by anyone became valuable.

Seen with the benefit of hindsight, Dale Morgan's first year at the University of California, Berkeley's Bancroft Library redefined his career and public reputation as a researcher and writer of American history. However, those months also established fault lines that would provide trouble as frequently as the earthquakes that rumbled beneath the city. Employment at the Bancroft Library did not hold a visible clue to his gravitation toward rare-book collection development and manuscript acquisition, but focusing as he tended to do on opportunities of the moment, this progression was perhaps inevitable. At this point the biography changes focus slightly, stepping away from details to look at Morgan and his career more broadly, dipping only selectively into details of specific projects. This approach is, perhaps, less fulfilling, but hopefully it puts the historian and the disciplines changing around him into a clearer context.

* * * * *

On January 3, 1954, Morgan vacated the short-term lease on the Connecticut Avenue apartment in Washington, DC, and Darel McConkey drove him to the train station to begin his move to Berkeley, California.[9] The rail trip west involved a few intermediate stops: an overnight stay in St. Louis to exploit the newest acquisitions at the Missouri Historical Society collections, and a week's stay at his mother's home in Salt Lake City. Since the McQuowns now lived in San Jose, Dale arranged to room with them until he could locate an apartment of his own closer to campus. The accommodations with the McQuowns were convenient to arrange but required a long daily bus commute for months.

When Morgan arrived at the Bancroft Library on January 18 for his first day of work, the institution was well on its way to becoming one of the nation's great research libraries. It was founded with the University of California's 1918 purchase of the book, manuscript, and notes collection amassed by San Francisco publisher and writer Hubert Howe Bancroft. Much of the manuscript material—notes, transcriptions, and some original documentary material—had been bound for convenient use, a common practice of the time. The bound volumes were installed in a suite of rooms in the upper level of Doe Library. Its founding director was History Department Chair Herbert E. Bolton, and until former English Department Chair James D. Hart was appointed director in 1971, the Bancroft Library directorship was looked on by the university's history faculty essentially as a departmental sinecure.

Initially the directorial position was merely a convenient staffing arrangement. Trained librarians with experience in California and Spanish borderlands history were few in the early twentieth century. Bolton's magisterial domination of the library as its founding director strengthened under successor Herbert I. Priestley, another faculty member in history. George P. Hammond, who was offered the director's position after Priestly's death in 1944, similarly held a joint teaching appointment. As its director, Hammond was not content merely to curate the established collection. He embarked on a sustained campaign to expand and deepen the library collections dramatically. In the process, and like Chauncey Tinker before him, Hammond realized that the university budget allocated to the Bancroft would always be an insufficient basis for building a research collection. Hammond organized a Friends of The Bancroft Library to raise money for acquisitions from alumni and interested donors. Under Hammond, the library moved in 1950 from its original residence in the creaking upper reaches of Doe Library to the new east-wing Library Annex.

The task Hammond had in mind for Morgan involved identifying and describing publicly the mass of unindexed, undocumented material in the library's original collection, as well as among its growing manuscript holdings. Unless one took the time to leaf through each bound volume of the original Hubert Howe Bancroft collection and become familiar with its contents, there was no effective way to locate much of anything. Great libraries were producing printed catalogs describing their unique research collections. Yale University had published just such a catalog only a couple of years earlier.[10]

In 1948 the University of California's president and regents allocated money for a guide to the Bancroft Library manuscript collections, a volume that could be distributed to aid researchers in other libraries. The chief problem the project faced was not finance or will, but personnel.

The Library employed graduate student Doris Wright to do the work. She had completed one significant collection guide but was not proceeding quickly enough.[11] Quite simply, the director was in a bind. Hammond hoped that Morgan could bring a set of fresh eyes and values to the project.

Manuscripts librarian Julia Macleod conducted Dale on a three-hour, shelf-by-shelf tour of the Bancroft collection. Based on his work with the WPA papers in Salt Lake City, within a week Dale crafted a proposal to Hammond outlining a process for compiling and filing the descriptions.[12] Before the month was out, Dale made Hammond another offer, one that both defined and would plague him later in his career. Dale quickly realized that being associated with one of the emerging great libraries lent him a lever to pry at source material important to his own writing. In this matter, the interests of Dale Morgan, author, aligned precisely with the interests of the University of California, collector. "With your permission, I am going to assign myself to an additional 'spare-time' job here at the library," he told Hammond, "What I propose to do is to make myself responsible for chasing down every lead to a manuscript I hear about."[13] Hammond readily agreed, and Morgan became effectively a one-man acquisitions team for the Bancroft Library. Hammond began relying on Dale to assess western diaries, letters, and manuscripts offered to Hammond for his recommendation on whether they should be acquired for the library's collection.

During the second week of February 1954, Dale received his first paycheck from the University of California for $81.21, and from the Navajos' legal counsel a check for $200. Clearly his personal time had the greatest value. The Navajo research work, the other half of his position, he did mostly at the McQuowns' though it was officially conducted in a History Department office belonging to Hammond in Dwinelle Hall, just down the hill from the library. The work schedule between lawsuit research and Bancroft obligations was utterly unbalanced, dictated by expediency. For weeks at a time Dale might do nothing but work on Navajo documents, leaving him behind on the Bancroft catalog, and vice versa, seesawing between projects and feeling constantly behind on both. "Time, no kidding, is a real problem," he once again confessed to his mother, though he had worked at the library barely a month.[14] In fact, almost on the day he began work, Dale was busy enough that his own writing, specifically the Mormon history and the bibliography he hoped to produce, were set aside almost completely.

Finally, the McQuowns hauled Dale and his belongings from their house in San Jose to an apartment in Berkeley on Benvenue Avenue, just south of campus. The location put him within a fifteen-minute walk of both the Navajo project office and the Bancroft Library. Within two months, Dale was becoming George Hammond's factotum, his right hand in terms of the collection. He had already generated assessments of prospective acquisitions and his follow-through resulted in several valuable new gifts. "Thus far, as a matter of fact, I have done practically everything but work on the job Bancroft hired me to do," he observed wryly to Darel McConkey.[15] Though the term appointment expired at the end of the fiscal year on June 30, Hammond began an administrative campaign to have Morgan's contract extended substantially. Hammond, in fact, was eagerly hoping Morgan would settle in sufficiently that he would accept a permanent position if one could be arranged for him.

By the early summer of 1954 Dale Morgan was immersed in Bancroft activities, though he officially remained a half-time employee. Both the library and Navajo project kept Dale fully occupied. Rather than working two half-time jobs, each had become about a three-quarter-time job. For his part, Dale was optimistic. He expected the Navajo project to slow appreciably, which would allow him time to again pick up the Mormon history.[16] The spring of 1954 slid gently into California's endless summer and ever closer to the end of his contract date. On May 28, Hammond arrived at his desk with the good news that Morgan's position at Bancroft and his contract with the Navajo research project had both been funded until June 1955. That was a relief. Being regularly employed had allowed Dale to buy furniture for his apartment and to begin repaying his mother the money borrowed from her in the frustrating, barren months of 1950 and 1951.

While the Navajo case provided a tidy if irregular income, Dale Morgan's position as Bancroft Library editor provided him the mailing address and letterhead furthering his reputation. Upon receiving Hammond's word that his initial temporary appointment had been extended, with his stability assured for at least another year, Dale looked toward again buying a car. The problem in that step was that since he could not hear, he could not qualify for a California driver's license. For the moment, however, the lack of a license represented an irritation rather than an inconvenience. He was close enough to walk to work and do shopping. Bay Area public transportation handled most else. Morgan never owned or drove another automobile.

* * * * *

Morgan's half-time appointment launched him into direct conflict with
Doris Wright, the previously employed graduate student who realized
her own organizational preferences were compromised by his effort and
ideas. Wright preferred working alone, her work complicated by a streak
of rather inflexible perfectionism. Wright had been hired as the manuscripts cataloger but settled on a detailed process for description that
amounted to indexing the manuscripts rather than describing them. Over
Morgan's first year of service her attitude about controlling plans, structure, and preparation of the guide to manuscripts ossified. By April 1955
it had hardened into an open rebellion. Morgan was still wrestling the
Navajo project demands. "I could wish that the work was farther advanced
than it is," Dale complained by mail shortly after Hammond's departure
for Mexico on sabbatical leave pursuing Navajo research, "but in the first
place, the labor has been advancing only on the basis of my own theoretical half-time work on it; and in the second place, the half-time work is
purely theoretical."[17] Wright resented Morgan's proposals as challenging
her methods. Their relationship declined. Eventually Wright refused even
to talk to Morgan directly, instead leaving notes and memos on a desk that
was usually awash with paper anyway.

By the time the term started in September Morgan and Wright were
at an impasse. She refused to work with him except in terms of an "equal
partnership." Bancroft Deputy Director Robert E. Burke was certain
that the absolute equality effectively translated into doing things her way
or not at all.[18] By praising and supporting good ideas when they were
raised, seeking accommodations when necessary, and strategically asking
for Hammond's administrative decisions, Morgan steered the project for
another year until work relationships between the two strained again and
the project slowly ground down.

The closing months of the 1955 fiscal year saw Dale again wondering about his employment prospects. A second reprieve extending his
term employment for another fiscal year was approved in June 1955, but
extensions would not last forever. So long as the University of California
kept him on payroll, Morgan didn't want to chase grant funding independently. That strategy hadn't worked well for him. The Navajo commission amounted to a full-time job that paid much better than the Bancroft
appointment, but the latter was reasonably stable while the former could
be ended at any time and certainly would be within the year. Neither
contract provided the income stability he wanted to finance his interests
in research and writing, but he had neither time nor inclination to look

afield when both gave him enough (theoretically) to pursue the writing projects he had in hand.[19] He was not precisely sure what to do.

Then, Morgan's competitor, Doris Wright, resigned in November for health reasons, clearing the way for a full-time appointment if Hammond could get it approved. Hammond managed the administrative necessities and on February 1, 1956, at age 42, Dale L. Morgan began the first and only permanent full-time employment he ever held.

* * * * *

Morgan's position as a University of California employee presented only half of his workday complications. Managing the Navajo research project in Washington DC by mail required considerable effort for nearly a decade, even if Morgan's part in identifying file documents lessened after his move west. Once the selections had been made and microfilm delivered, he still busily worked on a checklist of the contents of more than fifty reels of microfilmed records. The Navajo research always seemed to have four or five tasks requiring immediate attention. "[N]o matter which you are working on," Dale commented to Hammond with a sense of tired exasperation, "you have the uneasy sense that it ought to be one of the others."[20] After working a full day on the Bancroft manuscript descriptions well into the summer of 1954, he switched between offices, walking down the hill to the microfilm reader in Dwinelle Hall. There he worked from 7 p.m. till nearly midnight daily confirming the list of Navajo documents selectively microfilmed from federal records, and then listing key items for typists to transcribe entirely as prospective legal exhibits.

The demands of Morgan's first year as a history consultant offered no openings for returning to the Mormon history. Littell "positively forbids me any intellectual diversions, saying I must treat even my [Bancroft] job as nothing but recreation," he reported to Russ Mortensen.[21] Four months after arriving in Berkeley, even the work on the Navajo documents microfilm had to be set aside to free up time for an entirely different assignment: an intense study of the historical limits of Navajo cultural area. Morgan accompanied Hammond to a legal-team meeting in New Mexico, returning after two weeks on the road. Six weeks of intense work after their return generated a 148-page manuscript which described about two-fifths of the tribe's cultural margins in terms of geography. The work schedule was crushing. "Another such vacation and I am a dead man," Dale wrote a friend in Utah.[22]

Within a year of Morgan's arrival in Berkeley, his assignment for the Navajo legal team evolved from straightforward document identification into a position as a key historical interpreter for the legal team. Norman Littell began occasionally handing off Navajo and Hopi legal briefs, petitions, and documentary arguments for Morgan's critical review and comment. As the Utah Historical Records Survey had discovered more than a decade earlier, Morgan had the sensibilities of a damn fine editor coupled to a mind and memory which could collate facts, further honed by years of assessing and linking disparate sources. Littell eventually drew his research historian into several other suits for which he served as legal counsel. Most of the advisory work on these was not paid. On one hand, the occasional demand for this advice ate even more deeply into his scarce free time (some of which may have been charged to the Navajo project). On the other hand and more than anything else, it made Morgan indispensable to the Navajo legal team and guaranteed his retention on it well beyond the slated closing of straightforward research activities in the summer of 1955.[23]

Busy to the point of distraction, Dale again gave up recreational sketching. Of course, letters from friends still eddied in and out of the mailbox, and he usually made time to respond. After all, correspondence was his only method of direct back-and-forth conversation with most people. He told Charlie Kelly that a college-aged Danny Howe was trading Denver for Harvard University. "There's a boy worthy of Maurice," Dale reported with pride.[24] Besides these eddies, unsolicited questions drifted in from all over, from academic scholars as well as American West aficionados and the idly curious. Book dealer Charles Eberstadt, even away in New York, wasn't surprised. "Having made yourself *the* great scholar, the one and only and final authority on matters of western history . . . I am afraid with it you have wished on yourself the inquiries and solicitations of so many of us lesser students."[25] Berkeley's academic historians might have chafed at that. Salt Lake City's certainly did.

Returned from Mexico, George Hammond showed up at Dale's desk in July 1955 asking that he drop everything to make a return trip to Washington, DC. Yes, he could stop first to visit his mother in Salt Lake City. When Morgan's plane lifted off on July 22, Dale might have been a bit relieved to let the cares and burdens of Berkeley, California, remain behind the jet's slipstream—but only for a moment. With Joe Colgan and Department of the Interior staff help at hand, for a month Dale sifted Office of Indian Affairs, Department of the Interior, and War Department records, unsure exactly why he had been brought East but making the most of the opportunity. At the end of the first week of August he wrote Littell that the remaining work was best left to Colgan's effort.[26]

Adding to the demands of the moment, he also needed to finish drafting the Navajo historical report, which had to be completed before Littell could write the case brief. A legal brief, a written summation of the arguments and evidence provided to the judicial panel hearing the case, had to be completed ahead of oral arguments and was usually a basis for testimony. The Navajos' brief as plaintiffs rested squarely on the foundation of Richard Van Valkenburgh's archaeological report and George Hammond's historical report. Hammond circumscribed Spanish and Mexican records for backstory, but the Navajo suit was a case in the United States. Morgan's historical analysis and supportive exhibits from US federal records provided the cornerstone to the Navajo pleading. At one conference with the legal team, Morgan argued persuasively that every document cited in a Hopi brief should be acquired for the Navajo historical team's growing collection.[27] Littell agreed, and the research team was given a new lease on life.

Part of Morgan's energy in the document argument had another motivation. Most of the Navajo pretrial interpretive work was done by 1957 when the research team was essentially disbanded. Well before the Navajo research program began showing signs of winding up, Morgan was also job-coaching Joe Colgan. Littell's approval extended the research and duplication phase of the Navajo case, but the pace of work was slowing and would eventually expire, leaving Colgan without an income or future plans—an unintended consequence imposed by the mental focus and drive that made him a superior researcher. Colgan shopped around an idea for establishing a Navajo cultural institution. The Navajo Tribal Council listened to Littell, so Morgan suggested that Colgan float the idea to him that the research program could be used as a basis for establishing a tribal historical museum.[28] For two years Dale energetically counseled and admonished Colgan in the museum proposal, laying out prospective arguments and identifying opportunities and tactics for approaching Littell and crafting a formal proposal. Eventually Morgan realized he could not inspire Colgan sufficiently to formally make the proposal, and though considered seriously as an informal idea, the institution never gained the financial support it needed from the Navajo tribe. Dale lectured Colgan for having squandered the downtime as an opportunity to line up new research work. Sadly, hoping for another sugarplum to drop his way as the Navajo project had, Morgan's co-researcher never held a professional position again, working a series of menial jobs and declining further into alcoholism.

Morgan's advice to Colgan was sound but missed the larger factors: experience alone was no longer enough to be competitive in a narrowing and increasingly competitive professional job market. Both men were at or just beyond the middle of their work careers. A new generation of young academics was emerging from colleges and universities with little experience, but bearing academic credentials. They flooded the job market. Securing a credential that would make Colgan competitive beyond the Navajo opportunity—a graduate degree, a certificate of additional professional training—was never raised in their correspondence.[29] Morgan remained confident that ability, experience, and energy alone made opportunity, and he was certain that reputation was its own currency. As early as 1957 Dale said archly to a sponsor that "My reputation is at stake in everything I publish; my name on a job of history by now has connotations of thoroughness, honesty, absolute command of the sources, and literary grace appropriate to the subject."[30] His view had not changed since dismissing the thought of graduate school in 1939 and 1940. Morgan counseled Colgan with the authoritative certainty of a man who has progressed from instability to stability, never acknowledging—perhaps never recognizing—that he was himself facing similar circumstances.

Hammond's administrative patronage anchored Dale Morgan at the University of California. Were it not for Hammond, Morgan would likely again have been in the same situation he faced in 1949: competent, talented, experienced, but without the credentials that opened doors. Men like Joe Colgan and Dale Morgan were the capable but uncredentialed casualties in the postwar professionalization of academic and public history. Now the lack of an academic credential was a factor limiting both men's marketability in the very different workplace that telling the American past had become.

* * * * *

For three years, between beginning at the Bancroft in 1954 and the end of the document phase of the Navajo research project at the close of 1957, Dale Morgan was so frenetically busy that he had invested little time in anything other than his California obligations, yet his reputation remained high in Utah (outside the state's academic institutions, that is).

Based on a long effort by Marguerite Sinclair Reusser, Russ Mortensen finally persuaded the legislature that the abysmally poor condition of the state's records merited direct attention. In early 1953, while Morgan was trying vainly to find enough stability to eventually push the Mormon history to completion, for a second time Mortensen gauged Morgan's interest in returning to Utah as the first State Archivist. Dale concluded then that his plans for a historically frank discussion of Mormon origins and its first prophet would likely complicate relations between the overwhelmingly LDS members of the legislature and the state's official keeper of its past. The next year Mortensen hired as the state's first archivist a newly minted University of California PhD, Everett L. Cooley. Since then, Mortensen secured legislative approval (but no funding) for the USHS to move from the Capitol to the former governor's mansion on South Temple Street. The Nicholas G. Morgan, Sr. Foundation financed a renovation to convert the building into a freestanding home for the society, which was nearly complete.

Now in 1957 Mortensen and Nick Morgan wanted to know if Dale would be willing to take on a different role in the expanding library organization that initially had been his brainchild. Dale laid the case before George Hammond, seeking his advice. The Utah State Historical Society was home to him, and yet Dale felt an obligation to help the Bancroft finish what had been started and so badly needed with its *Guide to Manuscripts*. Privately, Hammond had no interest in losing his prize. His diplomatic reply was that only Morgan could decide what to do about job offers in Utah but also noting coyly that "you will have to decide whether the opportunities there will be commensurate of those in the Bay Area." He padded the advice with a high compliment: "everyone on the staff recognizes the slot you have filled among us, [and] how much we rely on you (especially the director) in innumerable ways."[31]

After mulling over the invitation for a month, Dale finally wrote his mother that he was disposed to stay in Berkeley. The three-volume *Guide to Manuscripts* would be completed at some point, even if the first volume wasn't yet, leaving him a marvelous base from which to attack his own wish list of research and writing projects.[32] He chose to remain at the University of California. While Dale Morgan never considered himself a Californian, this decision marked the last time he seriously considered returning to his native state.

* * * * *

Morgan had recovered most of his sense of balance years earlier, but not entirely. These lingering effects of meningitis were sporadic things, a residual consequence of damage to his inner ear. He compensated by sheer concentration on visual cues and walking with a slight shuffle in his gait that allowed him to keep most of one foot on the ground. One day in the summer of 1957 Dale was returning from an errand to the Navajo project office in Dwinelle Hall, down the hill from the library. Leaving the north entrance he experienced a flash of vertigo in midstride. Dale endured periodic falls as an adult, most of them without notice; this time the world tipped on its side, and Dale fell hard, face down on the concrete. One arm was doubled under him, leaving a bruise on his chest sufficient that he had a doctor confirm that ribs were not broken. He'd experienced no fall this serious for a long time.[33]

He was less lucky a couple of years later. Dale's desk in the Bancroft was on the basement level of the Doe Library Annex, outside of the locked-cage secure book storage. To one side, a flight of open-framed stairs led up into the manuscripts reading room. Like most libraries of the time, the floor was concrete, finished in linoleum tile. The hard, durable tiles required periodic resurfacing. Late in the afternoon of August 24, 1959, just before closing, Dale headed from his desk upstairs on some errand. The floors had been freshly waxed and polished. As his steps neared the flight of stairs one shoe heel struck the floor at enough of an angle that his foot shot sideways on the slick surface. For a person with normal balance the sudden disequilibrium would have been risky; for Dale, with his perpetual inner-ear imbalance problems, it was catastrophic: he slammed hard into the metal column of the stair framing or perhaps into the framing of the metal cage around the secure area, and crashed to the floor. The impact cut a gash near the top his head. He picked himself up and staggered upstairs, streaming blood. In the resultant commotion the library service desk called campus police, who called an ambulance which took Morgan a few blocks down the street to Herrick Hospital. One of the impacts snapped cleanly the long bone in his upper arm below the shoulder and chipped the ball in its joint. At the hospital the arm was immobilized in a cast reaching from shoulder to wrist. The cut required six stitches.

Someone notified the McQuowns, and Madeline drove up immediately from San Jose. After a three-day hospital stay Dale was discharged into their care, but his arm remained immobilized in plaster for eight weeks. Sympathy and invitations poured in from friends, but he preferred to remain at home. Madeline cleaned and cooked. Dale slept as best he could, slumped to one side in an armchair, plagued by dreams of being buried to his chest in a rock pile. The uncomfortable sleeping posture pinched a nerve in his right hip or leg that bothered him for weeks longer than the arm did. Eventually he saw little point in remaining housebound in California when he could do the same at his mother's home in Salt Lake City. By the first of September he was ready for a break. His physician agreed. The McQuowns and their long-time boarder, Jerry Finnin, offered to drive him.

A recently retired Emily Morgan indulged her protective sensibilities for two weeks. During his stay, she took her oldest son (and his cumbersome cast) to Kaysville for a visit with Utah landscape artist LeConte Stewart and his wife Zip before flying with him back to Berkeley. By the time Dale returned to work, three weeks into his ordeal in the middle of September, he could only muster the energy to pick out letters one-handed on the typewriter, with the eccentricities and liabilities to error imposed by the circumstance. One letter went to Everett Graff in Chicago, catching him up on the arm's condition and the writing projects which had shuddered to a standstill: the Ashley book of course, a corrected edition of fur trader James Beckwourth's memoirs of which nothing had yet been committed to paper, an edited version of William McCollum's 1850 book of travel experiences to California via Panama, and an edition of William Marshall Anderson's 1834 fur trade diary, which Dale had agreed to edit for the Huntington Library only a few weeks before his fall. "I also have a book of 1846 diaries well advanced," he notified Graff, "which must now wait patiently for attention."[34]

With one arm propped in the cast, Dale occupied his library desk pecking slowly on the *Guide to Manuscripts* manuscript. He reported to Hammond the printer's castoff of an estimated 400 pages for the text, plus possibly another hundred for an index. The book was not yet complete but had already reached the practical limits of publication. The shoulder was x-rayed on September 30, the day Emily flew home, but the physicians found that the new bone growth was not yet solid enough to show up on the film. The cast remained in place through a second X-ray ten days later, then for another week and a half. His doctor removed the cast on October 20 but, after only a day of freedom, decided the bone was still too weak. A new cast was applied for an additional three weeks. Eventually the second cast came off to Dale's great relief on November 9. "It seems that I now have a bone," he wrote Colgan, "but I assure you, not an arm."[35] Unused and held rigidly immobile for so long by the cast, Dale found he could no longer rotate his left wrist sufficiently to type. Mobility returned with practice, but only after several additional weeks of discomfort as the muscles and tendons were stretched into shape and pressed into service. One of his first letters (though again carefully typed one-handed) was a recommendation to the Rhodes Scholarship committee on behalf of new Harvard University graduate Dan Howe.

Freed from his plaster confinement, friends eagerly invited Dale for Thanksgiving, but he had to decline each offer, having long before accepted the McQuowns' invitation. Shortly before the holiday, Madeline wrote him with terms for the traditional meal: either Dale could cook or they were going out to eat. With his arm barely returned to serviceable condition, the choice was obvious. The McQuowns and Finnin drove into Berkeley. They planned to attend a play and were approaching the theater when Madeline missed a step while leaving the restaurant and went down with a scream. She was rushed to Alta Bates Hospital where the emergency room physician discovered a badly broken ankle. It was set in a cast, and she was admitted. On the last day of the month she was released from the hospital, but the inseparable trio moved into Dale's apartment to allow her an opportunity to recover.[36] The extra houseguests were a strain which Dale absorbed a second time without complaint, despite yet being unable to raise his left arm. They remained for three weeks, departing Christmas Eve for their home in San Jose.

The job offer which Morgan had desperately wanted from Yale University ten years earlier finally arrived just as Dale returned home. Book dealer Charles Eberstadt asked on philanthropist Frederick W. Beinecke's behalf whether Morgan would be interested in a move to Yale specifically to catalog Beinecke's collection, which was pledged to the university. Dale considered the offer briefly but decided against it; too much had changed. His outlook was much different than it had been when he had been scraping for work a decade earlier. "Maybe I would have agreed, had this come up before I came to Bancroft," he wrote Eberstadt, "but I am involved in too many obligations out here to feel free to chase money eastward. Anyhow, my objective is to free myself ultimately to write my books, not get involved in jobs as such, no matter what they may pay."[37]

* * * * *

Shortly after Thanksgiving 1960, Littell arrived in Berkeley for the latest of the periodic conferences on the trial phase of the Navajo lawsuits. By that point George Hammond had headed the research team for about eight years. He was approaching retirement age and needed to concentrate on administratively cementing the emerging position of the Bancroft Library within the University of California's library system. The Bancroft Library was growing—quickly. With Littell's approval, Hammond began backing away from most of his responsibilities for Navajo research in December 1960. His withdrawal from the project left most of the remaining historical work squarely on the shoulders of Dale Morgan. Morgan remained on retainer (and on alert) until the case was settled in 1963.

At this stage in the lawsuits Morgan had little to do, but he played a key role in the Navajo legal efforts twice more before the cases were argued and decided. The first was in 1961 as Morgan worked toward meeting the latest deadline for extending the Navajo boundary report, gathering exhibits demonstrating occupancy at various periods and locations, and on topical reports as background information for the lawyers themselves. By then Morgan's historical research was supporting three different Navajo cases. All had progressed to the trial stage, involving three different judicial panels in Los Angeles, Arizona, and Washington DC. Ahead of an Arizona court date for *Healing v. Jones,* the interminable argument between the Hopis and the Navajos, the Proposed Finding of Fact arrived from the Hopis' lawyer. Since the document proposed the historical evidence each side agreed to regard as indisputable and could be used as case evidence, Dale dropped everything to provide an assessment for the Navajo legal team. Two days later the trial transcript itself arrived, and Morgan dropped the proposed finding of fact to read and assess the testimony and analyze the arguments. Within three days Dale generated fifty-four pages of a "destructive analysis" and sat in conference with Littell and assistant counsel Marvin Sonosky for hours. He added another dozen pages to his analysis before the end of the week, and before two weeks of twelve-hour days were out, he had mailed that document plus a manuscript of exceptions to the findings. Littell was impressed enough to recommend that Morgan sit for a bachelor of laws exam (the qualification for legal practice at the time).

"Cheer up," Dale wrote his mother after she lamented the pressure he seemed to be under, "they will run out of lawsuits soon and leave me to the more or less peaceable life of a Western historian, or writer of Western books."[38] His various projects were pushed as he could make time for each of them. Though his correspondence kept flowing, there was virtually no time for personal letters for several years. "These days," he wrote in a rare letter to Juanita Brooks in 1960, "I am so pressed for time in almost every waking hour, and never more since the further jam-up in my affairs occasioned by the broken arm of last August, that letters simply don't get written."[39]

At virtually the same time he was finishing pretrial documents for the Navajo team, Dale was able to supply Bancroft's director with a positive progress report on the *Guide to Manuscripts*. The second draft was being typed and would soon be ready for preparation of a printer manuscript.[40] Finally, a year later on March 4, 1962, a final typescript for the first volume of *A Guide to the Manuscript Collections of the Bancroft Library* was handed to the University of California Press. The project had consumed eight years of effort and would still require another full year before the bound books were issued, but for a while at least it was off Dale's hands.

The second instance of Morgan's non-research involvement with the Navajo lawsuits came in September 1962. The federal judicial panel hearing the Navajo-Hopi case (*Healing v. Jones*) finally handed down a decision in favor of the Hopis. After eight months without a single communication from the tribal counsel, Littell telephoned with instructions for Dale to once again "drop everything" and comb the 226-page decision for errors, compiling the factual basis on which the decision would be appealed and challenged. The appeal had to be filed within sixty days, which left Morgan far less time than that to do the review. After furious effort Morgan did so, but to no real result. The case was settled in 1963, though to no one's satisfaction.[41]

*   *   *   *   *

By 1962 the two initiatives which had drawn Dale to the Bancroft Library appeared to be reaching their conclusions. Both required additional work from him, of course, but the end was in sight and it was time to plan further ahead. He craved an opportunity to set aside at least some of the demands and retire the personal pledges he had made to half a dozen people. A productive, pre-retirement sabbatical for Hammond in Spain suggested one means for getting some of Dale's perennial projects cleared and he began thinking about applying for a sabbatical himself.[42] Toward the end of March he notified Jim Hart, Bancroft's Acting Director, that when the published *Guide* had been delivered he would apply for a sabbatical—if the university could be persuaded that his nonacademic position and activities were equivalent to an academic appointment.[43] The answer from Donald Coney, the university librarian, came back in mid-April: *no*. Policy provisions existed for granting sabbaticals only to University of California employees with a faculty appointment, a contract which required original research and scholarship as a condition of employment. A staff appointment, such as a library employee, however meritorious an incumbent's scholarly output might be, did not require the same expectation for the production of scholar works and was therefore ineligible for university support whether via grants or sabbatical. Dale could, however, take up to a year of leave without pay.[44] That option provided him only the more-valuable half to his problem—time. Of course, he still needed an income.

Coney's answer set the stage for Morgan's decision eventually to pursue a second Guggenheim Fellowship in 1969, though, in 1962, he did not yet see it as an option. Morgan played an important role in the Navajo land-claims and related cases, and it provided paychecks, but those demands ate deeply into some of his most potentially productive years as a historian. In the end Morgan traded off time for money, thinking he was getting the best end of the deal and that he had time to spare.

* * * * *

With the first *Guide* volume in print and the Navajo suits behind him, Dale Morgan was itching to move forward. "My major job now," he told Joe Colgan, "must be to get my books written and make them pay off." Unfortunately, neither the outstanding Anderson nor Ashley books were anywhere near complete. Dale had done little other than bemoan them for quite a while. "If I can just once get caught up with old obligations!" he wrote his mother, "That is what I have been trying to do ever since I arrived in these parts."[45]

The most significant and nominally successful period of Dale Morgan's professional career did not have an auspicious beginning, but rather one very typical of the ceaseless challenges he would face to complete his one masterwork and others for which he is best known. In terms of Morgan's scholarly output, the years 1962 to 1964 marked the apogee of his scholarly career, but the accomplishment very nearly required a human sacrifice to complete.

CHAPTER 14

"Too Many Things Have Been Going On at the Same Time"[1]

Writing, 1954–1963

My books, I think, are the largest contribution I can make to my world, more important than anything I can do in or out of an institution.[2]
—Dale Morgan

MORGAN'S MOVE into an academic research institution at the scale of the University of California, Berkeley set him near the center of developing one of the nation's great historical research libraries. The dual appointments provided him an income but also required from him the time he wanted to devote to his own research and writing. Between 1948 and 1953 he had time but no money. Beginning in 1954 he had money but no time. Despite the demands pressing on him from the Bancroft editorship, his role as Hammond's collection-development factotum, and as a researcher for the Navajo legal team, Dale Morgan launched himself into writing the "kind of books he wanted to write."

To make a living as a publishing historian required Morgan to either write books publishers wanted to sell and a large number of readers wanted to buy, or to simply ignore sales and accept writing projects on commission. Since the subjects on which he wanted to write did not fit into the trade markets (other than the Mormon book) and royalty income for "the kind of books I want to write" had not proven reliable, he was left with the alternative of writing on commission. Beyond his own historical interests, "If I could count on three or four big commissions a year for the indefinite future," Dale once grumbled to his mother, "I would be disposed to kiss regular jobs goodbye." Two of those large commissions involved a centennial atlas for Rand McNally & Company, in 1955, and

Kansas in Maps, a more intense ghost-writing project that paid spectacularly but consumed Morgan for a year, in 1960. The problem was that
these commissions were the only well-paying offers to come his direction,
and commissions proved a sandy foundation on which to build a career.[3]
He couldn't count on them.

Dale decided to invest the income windfall from his commissions
rather than spend it outright. After seeking advice from several friends,
the money went into a mutual fund—one step closer to an independent
income that would eventually allow him time and opportunity to write as
he pleased. He would tell Emily Morgan a year after depositing the check
from the Kansas maps project that "until the day arrives that I no longer
need work for a living, my books and other professional contributions will
have to be written in what for other people is 'leisure time.' And I have
a vast fund of information stored up in my mind now that I want to get
down on paper before my time on earth runs out."[4]

Still, partly because Morgan wanted writing to provide a working
income, he accepted virtually every writing commission or contract that
came his direction, large or small. Morgan's writing career between his
arrival in California in the mid-1950s and his passing less than two decades
later is a twisting tale of an unreal (and unrealistic) number of planned
research, writing, and editing projects, late nights, and tangents. It is,
sadly, also a chronological record littered with broken and unmet commitments. "Dale was a mass of exaggerated contradictions," a long-time friend
of his told me. "His dogged persistence and drive for perfection exalt
while his chronic overcommitments exasperate."[5] During Morgan's years
as a University of California system employee, he produced the works
for which he is best known, other than *The State of Deseret* and *Jedediah
Smith and the Opening of the West.* A critique, even a summation of Morgan's published works cannot be crowded meaningfully into a biography
(at least, not a readable one), but a list of his published work appears at
the end of this work in the Bibliography. A biography can only manage
a few triangulatory stories drawn from that list. This chapter focuses on
select examples of Morgan's writing to illustrate his evolving priorities,
decisions, and the challenges of his habits as a writer.

* * * * *

In January 1954, as Morgan began work in Berkeley, reviews of *Jedediah
Smith and the Opening of the West* began trickling in from newspapers

across the country; comments in scholarly journals would come later. Comments were uniformly positive, ranging between complimentary and rhapsodic. "It makes me laugh to have reviewers speak of [the book] as 'definitive,'" Morgan wrote Charles Camp three months after publication. "To my way of thinking, it is practically obsolete already."[6] New source material continued to surface. "Luckily, with this book of Ashley documents I have coming up," he told Bernard DeVoto, "I can lay the new information on the line almost at once."[7] Opinions in scholarly journals were similarly positive. Historian Abraham Nasatir identified Morgan's work as "one of the three foundation works for studies of the American fur trade," a work of the caliber of Hiram Chittenden's *Mountain Men and the Fur Trade* (1902) and Maurice S. Sullivan's *Travels of Jedediah Smith* (1934). This was true enough, Dale reported matter-of-factly to his mother, "but it was nice to have a qualified scholar say so in print."[8]

Still, unlike *Humboldt,* which benchmarked book sales and income in Morgan's mind, Bobbs-Merrill's Harry Platt could only describe *Jedediah Smith* sales as "not thrilling." The book sold only moderately well and never went into reprint. "You are roughly in the 3,000[*sic*] bracket," Platt told the author, which meant that the book had not yet sold quite three thousand copies in its all-important first quarter.[9] In fact, despite its critical reception, the publisher made comparatively little on its investment in the book. Morgan's *Humboldt* sold reasonably well across four printings for over twenty years; *Jedediah Smith* sold 3,300 copies between publication and April 30, 1954, but in the next full year sold fewer than a third of that figure and posted virtually no sales thereafter.[10] Despite positive reviews from both academic and trade reviewers, Morgan's most notable work gained its status as a classic only after being issued in paperback (and over his own vigorous protests) a decade later. History—especially regional history—did not sell in postwar America as well as might be hoped.

Despite its publication by a second-rank house and only adequate sales, *Jedediah Smith* was noticed by one astute reader: Alfred A. Knopf, Sr., one of the nation's most prestigious publishers. An urbane and influential connoisseur of literature, Knopf experienced a permanent personal conversion to the American West in the late 1940s. Constantly looking to attract new talent to his publishing list, with a longstanding interest in publishing good history, and trying to find suitable writers who addressed the American West specifically, Knopf assigned one of his internal editors to read and report on Morgan's new biography. Philip Vaudrin replied noncommittally that *Jedediah Smith* was "not exactly distinguished as to style, but on the whole a good job."[11] No matter. The review cemented Morgan in Knopf's personal awareness as a viable prospect. Knopf later confessed to one of his editors his personal opinion that "Morgan is a very, very dull writer. His scholarship is beyond reproach and in his field he is the great authority. I am sure we'd want to publish him if we had the chance, but I cannot read him with pleasure."[12]

Anyone who has read Morgan's fur-trade study would be left questioning the standards on which Knopf made his judgment. Knopf, however, acted immediately. On the day that Vaudrin routed his internal review, Knopf dictated to his secretary one of the breezy, personal letters with which he cultivated authors. Dropping the names of both Fawn Brodie and Bernard DeVoto, Knopf politely inquired about Morgan's history of Mormonism and asked whether either he or Madeline McQuown would be interested in writing a short biography of Brigham Young for the firm's Great Lives in Brief series.[13]

* * * * *

Even as *Jedediah Smith* was on sale and on the day Morgan began work at the Bancroft Library, the 1845 Frémont map located by Carl Wheat arrived on loan from the American Antiquarian Society in Boston. George Hammond immediately carried it across the bay to San Francisco, where it was carefully photographed to create a duplicate for Carl Wheat's files and eventually for reproduction. Dale got an individual look at the huge sheet when it came back a few days later. He was stunned. The map itself was commonplace. The sheet was mostly white space, showing only the line-of-sight geography charted during John C. Frémont's first and second expeditions (1842–1844) along the Oregon Trail, Pacific coast, and through the Southwest. Hugely influential, this map was one of the first to accurately (though incompletely) represent the geography of the "central route" through the American West to Oregon and California.

The Frémont map itself was not the find, but the penciled markings on this particular copy were what made it significant. It had been annotated by Oregonian George Gibbs sometime between 1849 and 1855. Jedediah Smith produced a map of his travels which had long been lost, but here was clear evidence that Gibbs had not only seen Smith's manuscript map, but translated its key content—Smith's travels—onto the best map available. With the possible exception of his illiterate contemporary, the legendary Jim Bridger, Smith probably carried around in his head the most comprehensive knowledge of the American West's varied rivers, valleys, mountains, and deserts. Had Smith's map, as well as an accompanying diary, gotten into the right hands at the time he drew it, Americans would have comprehended the geography of the continent's interior accurately a generation earlier than it was known.[14]

Carl Irving Wheat was a lawyer by trade, but his avocation as a serious student of maps and the cartography of the American West made his reputation nationally. Not much study was required to recognize the map's significance. On his way home to Palo Alto from Massachusetts in December 1953, Wheat stopped in Chicago to visit with book collector Everett Graff, who immediately wrote Morgan to report the discovery. *Jedediah Smith and the Opening of the West* had been in print less than three weeks. Wheat began planning a suitably scholarly, cartographic reveal of the new rediscovery. Aware that Morgan had just published the Jedediah Smith biography and had been attracted to Berkeley by Hammond, Wheat asked the latter if he thought Morgan would contribute a biographical introduction. Hammond suggested the two men simply collaborate, which the lawyer enthusiastically accepted.

Hammond made the introduction and the pair quickly became fast friends. The immediate result of the two men's cooperation as students of geography was the fine-press limited edition of *Jedediah Smith and His Maps of the American West* in 1954 for the California Historical Society. Comments on the Wheat-Morgan collaboration were even more laudatory than for the Jedediah Smith biography the previous year. "If you need any 'elevation' in the rank of American historians of the West, this puts you to the top rung," wrote Denver bookman Fred Rosenstock.

* * * * *

The year Morgan arrived in California he paid Pat Tull, a Utah State Historical Society typist, to produce a clean transcription of his collected Ashley documents as a basis for a future volume. Morgan always concentrated first on a text and left the task of compiling notes for later in the process. "The footnotes are in your head now," one publisher noted about another project, "[and] it's just getting them on paper."[15] Though he had yet expended no effort to produce notes, Russ Mortensen read the typist's copy of the revised Ashley pages. "I think it will be your magnum opus," he told Morgan. "Of course you are aware that it will not contribute to your advancement in the priesthood."[16]

Mortensen's cultural reference to Mormonism was also a reference to his employment in an academic-support position. Morgan held no tenurable faculty appointment; he would likely derive no institutional recognition from what was clearly destined to be a major accomplishment of scholarship. Dale probably didn't care—not at this point, anyway. The Ashley papers were a great work that needed doing, and he was in a position to do it. When Denver bookseller Fred Rosenstock learned of it, he was captivated. Having sold books for years, Rosenstock wanted to issue them as well. The Ashley project looked like a large work that could very likely revolutionize the understanding of the earliest American West. "I won't bother you about it—but I just want to emphasize my continued interest," Rosenstock wrote upon learning of the prospect.[17] He flew to visit Morgan in Berkeley the following April (1955) to discuss the prospective Ashely book, the first of many trips he would make on joint publication projects. Rosenstock departed their April meeting having settled commitments to the Ashley collection as a viable publication project in a three-way verbal agreement between himself, Morgan, and using San Francisco printer Lawton Kennedy: if Morgan completed the collection of William H. Ashley documents, Rosenstock would see it published with Kennedy handling production.[18]

The relationship between the historian and the bookseller was one of trust and confidence that stretched over years, but a curious one as well. Though each would undoubtedly deny it vigorously, reading two decades of letters between Fred Rosenstock and Dale Morgan, one can only conclude that their relationship seems to have existed on a basis of constructive and perhaps competitive one-upsmanship. Rosenstock's letters to Morgan contained litanies of family illness, the press of his book business, the demands of travel, and publishing deadlines, tempered with pleas for haste on whatever project the pair worked on. Morgan's letters held out to Rosenstock ceaseless rounds of spring, fall, or winter colds or summer sinus infections, the demands of the Bancroft guide project, the Navajo lawsuits, or pressure on other writing projects. For twenty years both men's invocations were not only plain-language exchanges between close friends, but also subtexts justifying the endless distractions, chronic delays, last-minute changes, and long hours each faced.

Dale may have craved writing commissions, but they were limited things. Almost all came to Morgan though the agency of friends and acquaintances; they did not materialize out of the air. Well, one did. An unanticipated opportunity reared up in the summer of 1956, one that offered the possibility of a genuine career change and real money. Television producer Irving Paley wrote Morgan, interested in *Jedediah Smith* as the possible basis for a television series on Smith himself or the fur trade generally. Working up a story from a nonfiction study seems a bit of an odd match until one recalls popular culture of the time. Since the end of the Second World War, postwar America turned inward toward its own cultures but still craved adventure. The mid-1950s was the high point of the Hollywood Western and "the frontier" was hot. Motion picture studios built on the runaway success of *Stagecoach* (1939) with Westerns like Gregory Peck's *The Gunfighter* (1950), Jimmy Stewart in *Winchester '73* (1950), *High Noon* (1952), *The Naked Spur* (1953), and virtually anything with John Wayne in it. *The Searchers* (1956) was playing everywhere. Walt Disney Productions' *Davy Crockett: King of the Wild Frontier,* released the previous year, sparked one of the company's earliest merchandizing successes and set off a popular culture frenzy in consumerism.

Network radio serials like *The Lone Ranger* thrilled young listeners of Dale's own generation. Westerns flooded the airwaves. Both radio and film *The Durango Kid* serials translated well to the small screen of television. By the mid-1950s Roy Rogers and Dale Evans lent polished wholesomeness to the small screen, counterbalancing the Lone Ranger's masculine adventurism. The well-remembered *The Adventures of Rin Tin Tin*—a low-budget television adventure series featuring a German Shepherd dog directed at young viewers, which ran for 164 episodes between 1954 and 1959—overshadows other series with similar structure that were similarly successful: *The Adventures of Jim Bowie* (which ran 76 episodes) and *The Adventures of Kit Carson* (103 episodes), and *The Adventures of Wild Bill Hickok* (113 episodes). The studios threw money eagerly at new ideas and content, so yes, there was certainly interest (and potentially substantial production and sponsorship money) in Jedediah Smith and the fur trade. Paley floated the idea of a thirteen-episode trial production. Morgan jumped in immediately offering to write the series himself. The producer noted a bit warily that Morgan had no experience with script writing but cautiously agreed that a single 39-page script would be a useful beginning point for discussion with the producers.

As capable a writer as Dale may have been, television dialogue was one medium for which he had absolutely no concept due to his inability to hear. Dale owned a television and watched TV regularly, but other than what he could snatch from its flickering shadows, Morgan had no idea how television narrative was structured or even what was said. He wanted the income that a television series would bring but knew he was out of his element. This setting was one he could not study or research his way into familiarity; even if he could, he had no time at all to do it himself. Dale therefore turned for help to the person in whose insight he had the deepest trust, who had time, and needed a diversion and income: Madeline. Dale invited his longtime friend to Berkeley in late July, and over lunch, offered to pay her to watch several television programs and summarize for him in a couple of pages how the characters interacted and dialogue worked. She set to the task eagerly but quickly bogged down. Initially she tried to capture the dialogue directly but found that it moved far too quickly to be set down accurately. Instead, she summarized what was unique or memorable about an individual program.

A week later Madeline wrote Dale in frustration. She sent along her entire output, saying that she would do no more until he reviewed and approved what had been done. It was, as nearly as can be told, the only writing of hers over their long acquaintance Morgan actually saw.[19] Summaries didn't help, however. He needed to capture the ebb and flow of television dialogue. Finally he gave it up. Unable to produce a script, the prospective television deal evaporated.

* * * * *

Morgan's agency became central to the arrival of new historical material to the Bancroft Library collections, whether by gift or by purchase. One of these was a typed transcript of a reminiscence by Jedediah Smith's former clerk, Robert Campbell. Though the Ashley volume had hardly been translated from an idea to the working-project stage, Dale wrote Joe Colgan that the Campbell reminiscence could provide a companion book to the Ashley collection, picking up the story of the American fur trade after Ashley's withdrawal from the business in the late 1820s. Two days later he formally proposed the idea to Rosenstock, who agreed readily—but first had a favor to ask.[20] The Denver dealer had bought the 1849 diary of James A. Pritchard from a descendant with a pledge to have the diary edited appropriately and published. Would Dale postpone the Ashley project to edit the Pritchard diary first? The fee the Denver bookseller could offer was limited by the high price paid for the diary, so in addition to shelving his own work Morgan would have to accept a cut rate for his efforts.[21] Dale had hoped to see the Ashley and Campbell volumes issued together but set them aside and agreed, mostly because he planned to edit the overland diary quickly and then still have at least the Ashley book completed and ready for the printer by the end of the year.

Work on the Pritchard diary reconnected Morgan with Jim Holliday, the young scholar with whom he had corresponded while writing *Jedediah Smith*. The elder Holliday's book collection had been auctioned in 1954 and included the 1834 William Marshall Anderson diary rediscovered by his son. As Morgan began working on Pritchard and the massive table of 1849 diaries, Morgan and Holliday resumed a correspondence that grew quickly into a close personal and professional association, first as individuals interested in the early American West, and later as colleagues when Holliday became the Bancroft's assistant director in 1958. As Dale had once mentored Juanita Brooks, Morgan's papers document a similar mentoring and friendship with Jim Holliday.[22]

By the time the Navajo project sent Morgan packing back to Washington, DC, for the three-month trip in July 1955, Carl Wheat was emerging slowly from his stroke-imposed ordeal. On the day before he left, Dale had received word that Wheat had been felled by a massive stroke. Its lingering effects sharply curtailed his native energy. The sudden condition left him with only partial use of his right hand and leg. He now walked slowly and very carefully. He was tired enough that drafting the first volume of his life's work, *Mapping the Transmississippi West*, was set aside until Morgan returned. "If it weren't for your backing I might bail," the lawyer confessed candidly.[23] From DC, Morgan dismissed any sense of obligation. He ordered Wheat to focus on the structural issues of the book; he, Dale, would handle the small matters—fact-checking, coordination, proofreading—when he returned. With typesetting for the first volume already underway, Wheat was as relieved as he was touched by Dale's generosity and thanked him sincerely, noting that Morgan was "the only person in the world who has the knowledge and on whom I can lean in this emergency."[24]

If a return to Berkeley in September promised to bury Morgan yet deeper in commitments than he already was, still the trip east provided tangential benefits. He enjoyed time with his sister Ruth and her family, still in Alexandria, and made opportunities for lunches with Darel McConkey, as well as an occasional dinner and at least one summer afternoon with Max and Louise North. Dale arrived back at work in the first week of the month, refreshed to some extent from the working vacation. After catching up on mail, Dale renegotiated his work schedule, working Monday through Wednesday for the library and Wednesday through Friday on Navajo obligations—and occasionally for himself.

This work "for himself" included assuming a large role in preparing Wheat's cartography manuscript to take the pressure off the still-recovering lawyer and to see the project progress toward publication.[25] Dale occasionally caught an express bus to Palo Alto to confer with Wheat at home. They talked through the complications Wheat faced, both personal and historical, as he tried to reduce to manageable size (and page count) the mass of detail and knowledge crammed into the first volume. "I was happy to know by your note that the mountain of detail confronting you was made to seem reduced somewhat by our talk," Dale wrote his friend after returning home after one visit. "But again I want to reiterate that you are to leave as much of that as you can to me."[26]

A duplicate set of galley proofs for Wheat's book began arriving at Dale's apartment at about the same time that he was eager to begin substantive editorial work on his own volume of Ashley documents. His mother and several family members, however, arrived for a California excursion ahead of Dale's own summer visit to Salt Lake City. From there, Dale, Emily, and Emily's friend and housemate Helen Sanders piled into Helen's car and set off on a road trip through western Wyoming in the interests of the Ashley book. In late August the trio drove north along US 89 and turned east to make a crooked loop following the Bear River to Bear Lake astride the Utah-Idaho border and the site of the 1827 and 1828 rendezvous. Crossing eastward into Wyoming their route took in the Popo Agie and broad expanse of the South Pass before turning back north and west at Lander, past the Wind River Range and across Togwotee Pass into Jackson's Hole and the Tetons. It was a glorious trip providing a broad, visual familiarity with the country Ashley frequented.

The next year he and his mother made another on-the-ground inspection. This time, Dale first accompanied his mother and two of her sisters to Yosemite before departing for a two-week trip to Salt Lake City, Idaho, and Montana benefitting a future Campbell book. He hoped to turn over the Ashley manuscript to Kennedy before leaving but carried to the San Francisco office only the first two parts, both of which were incomplete, to serve as a basis for Kennedy's cost estimate.[27] Dale remained confident and told Fawn Brodie in December 1956 that six weeks' work would settle the Ashley documents manuscript so that he could move on seamlessly to the companion volume on Robert Campbell. The Campbell volume would be done about six weeks after the Ashley, he estimated.[28]

As Morgan and Rosenstock were negotiating the latest developments on Dale's Ashley project through mid-July 1956, two days past Wheat's stroke anniversary, he suffered a second, massively debilitating attack. Its effects were probably magnified by a delay in treatment, since it struck while he was at the annual retreat of the private and exclusive Bohemian Club. Rushed back to San Francisco and out of immediate danger, this time he was hospitalized for rehabilitation. Manuscript for the first volume of *Mapping the Transmississippi West* had been put into the hands of San Francisco printer Lawton Kennedy merely days earlier. Carl's wife Helen wrote Dale that her husband was profoundly discouraged but counting on Morgan to help get the book through the endless routine of design, composition, proofreading, corrections, and indexing. Of course, he would, Dale responded: "You tell Carl not to trouble himself for a moment about the book. He has given me a thorough education on things cartographical, and of course I can lift practically the whole load from his shoulder on the mechanics of seeing this and his later books through the press."[29]

By the middle of September 1957, a year after his second stroke, Carl struggled on with physical limits imposed by it, unable to speak or use his right hand, but managing to complete a manuscript for the second volume largely on his own. Wheat was feeling his way along the cold edges of mortality and wanted Morgan to know about the fiscal arrangements that would see his life work through publication should worse things happen. Though no formal agreement was ever made, an unspoken understanding rose between the men that Dale would see to completion whatever volumes of *Mapping the Transmississippi West* the author was unable to complete himself. Everyone hoped it would not come to that, of course, but Helen Wheat confided in Dale a fear that her husband would be unable even to finish the second volume.[30]

Dale caught a bus to Palo Alto on the first Friday in February and worked till midnight on the manuscript for the second volume and took it back to Berkeley with him. Over the next several days he wrote Wheat several letters with queries. The increasing amount of work spent on Wheat's study quickly absorbed what little free time Dale had, but he was unwilling to let the project expire from Wheat's inability. "I know you're always too busy for your own good, but how are you otherwise?" his mother wrote. "Life has been an uninterrupted scramble," he responded.[31]

And it was. Virtually all of 1957 and 1958 was consumed by Wheat's proofs and the Pritchard project, which ballooned unnaturally. Rosenstock had not exaggerated: the James A. Pritchard diary was a remarkable documentary find, a lucid, detailed, and complete transcontinental record.

The Pritchard diary's high documentary quality and readability, and the fact that the Bancroft had already collected scores of diaries, sparked Dale's curiosity about how it fit into the general overland experience of 1849, the first great year of Gold Rush emigration. Within three weeks of beginning serious work on the notes, Dale decided to use the book as a vehicle to systematize what was known of 1849 diaries across the main trail via South Pass.[32] Initially he planned an appendix to tabulate movements of other diarists during the year. Dale mailed queries to libraries and researchers across the country, asking for microfilmed copies of 1849 diaries and letters in their holdings, and if duplication was unavailable, then for dates when the diarist recorded passing specific landmarks. Eventually he tabulated data for over a hundred trail documents, which provided a nightmare to represent in useful form. "No one else now living could produce such a wealth of material," Charlie Kelly opined in his typically blunt way when the book was published.[33]

* * * * *

A year earlier Morgan had tracked to a granddaughter in Westchester County, New York, the diary of William B. Lorton, a document that Dale latter identified as "the finest Forty-Niner diary I have ever laid eyes on."[34] At Dale's encouragement, the granddaughter, Valita Moran, had donated the manuscripts to the Bancroft Library for Morgan to transcribe and eventually edit for publication. Moran was greatly enamored with the inscribed copy of *The Overland Diary of James A. Pritchard* sent by Dale and, just as pointedly, looking forward to seeing the William B. Lorton diary handled at least as handsomely—and preferably distributed on a scale that would provide her an income. Acting on that commission, one letter he did write was to publisher Alfred A. Knopf, Sr., who had gently but tirelessly prodded Dale for a book on the American West for years. Morgan felt the Lorton diary was a book that would interest Knopf. "I think it merits something more than the usual limited edition format that is the customary destiny of Gold Rush diaries," he opined confidently, "that it has in fact real sales potential." Knopf bit hard immediately. "Dear Dale for heaven's sake don't let us be formal with each other after all this time." Of course, he was interested in the book. Send it on immediately.[35]

Knopf immediately assigned the proposal to one of his most trusted editors, Angus Cameron. On Cameron's rhapsodic report of the Morgan's initial transcription, the publishing house began planning for an elaborately illustrated, benchmark volume on the romantic but real history of the American West. Dale wrote to Mrs. Moran that Cameron had been "captured by your grandfather," but that publication would take more time for a book manuscript than for making a book proposal. And another prospective commission arrived from publisher Julian Messner Inc., this one offering a thousand dollars in advance for a single chapter in a large popular *The Book of the American West.* This one had not been solicited nor had a friend interceded; it looked like Morgan's reputation had finally reached a point that it began attracting lucrative commissions by its own mass.[36]

* * * * *

Dale wrote Everett Graff shortly after the turn of the season about his writing goals for 1961. As busy as he was, the research facet of the three Navajo lawsuits looked like it was about over (it wasn't). This work had eaten up his personal free time for eight years. Disconnecting himself from Navajo demands potentially left Morgan uncommitted time for his own work. Dale told Graff that he wanted to complete the long-stagnant Mormon bibliography for Antiquarian Press, requiring only sufficient time to write up the notes to fill out the list of bibliographic entries he felt was already basically complete. After seven years of occasional effort, the Ashley volume was slated for an October publication under Rosenstock's Old West Publishing imprint. Those were his two priorities.

In the midst of the Navajo project, Bancroft's *Guide to the Manuscript Collections,* editorial work and proofing for Wheat's *Mapping the Transmississppi West,* and Robert W. Baughman's *Kansas in Maps* centennial book, Morgan managed to complete some of the works for which he remains best known: the *Pritchard* diary with its massive tabulation of 1849 travel across the northern branch of the California trail; William McCollum's *California as I Saw It,* a similar study about gold-rush travel via Panama, for Talisman Press. Dale was confident time freed by the conclusion of his Navajo commitment would be sufficient for him to draft several more volumes as well: edit the William Marshall Anderson volume with Eleanor Towles for the Huntington Library, the James Beckwourth memoir already under contract to the University of Oklahoma Press, an edited collection of late fur trader David Adams' papers (documenting Fort Laramie in the 1840s) for the Missouri Historical Society, and that long-contemplated edited collection of 1846 diaries and letters he had mentioned the year before. Dale confided the same ambitions to other friends as well: 1961 was going to be his big step forward in terms of scholarship. The calendar was ambitious, but then Dale Morgan was perpetually optimistic about his ability to meet challenges and capitalize on opportunity.[37]

While Hammond explored the possibilities for the *Guide to Manuscripts* publication with University of California officials, tragic news came from Helen Wheat in Palo Alto: in early May, Carl suffered a another progressive stroke or perhaps a series of small strokes the effects of which came on only gradually. Wheat could no longer walk, could not swallow, could not speak, and was in utter despair that his fifth and final volume of *Mapping the Transmississippi West* would ever be completed. "We may need some help from you," she wrote Dale with an obvious plea tucked discretely behind the statement. "I hope that the last thing you will worry about is your book," Morgan wrote his friend in reply:

> You have set the framework so solidly in the past four volumes that it is crystal clear what the final volume should and must be; and your work on the actual maps for the last volume has set up even more of the basic structure for it. Anytime you would like me to lend a hand on the construction work, just sing out, Carl, and we will fix up the arrangements. I can take any amount of the manual labor off your hands so that you need only work over a rough text into a final form that suits you.[38]

To crowd matters further, the McQuowns moved into Dale's apartment yet again for a month between June and July for Madeline to have another round of medical attention, avoiding the stress of traveling from San Jose. They had hardly left when in early August, Helen Sanders arrived for a visit on one leg of a longer trip. Helen had herself retired, no longer lived with Emily Morgan, and had moved to Marysville, California. As ever, Dale enjoyed playing host, taking her to dinner at Jack's in San Francisco and to see *Fiorello* at the Geary Theater. Two days later Ruth and Doug Barton arrived with their family. The Bartons were only passing through, staying just for the day and Helen left soon after, leaving Dale finally ready to begin the fifth volume of Carl Wheat's book. Writing longhand, even hunt-and-peck typing, was now physically beyond Wheat's capacity, Dale told Joe Colgan, "hence it will be up to me to prepare the text."[39] The dedication to see Wheat's work completed came at the cost of completing his own Ashley opus, but like his commitment to Rod and Sara Korns a decade earlier, Dale could not bear to see a friend's life work left incomplete. Taking on the project personally and at his own expense was a cost Dale assumed willingly.

* * * * *

On August 16, Francis P. Farquhar, of the California Historical Society and a Friend of the Bancroft Library, wrote Morgan informally that the society's board had selected him for the Henry R. Wagner Memorial Award acknowledging unique contributions made to the understanding of California history. The award formally recognized the Pritchard and McCollum books. Each was a spectacularly edited journal, but Morgan's original supplementary material—the massive table of 1849 overland journal data and the ship lists at Chagres, Panama—were what made the individual documents into comprehensive studies for two of the three main thoroughfares to California in the earliest gold rush years. The award also indicated how deeply Morgan had become connected with the state's major organizations devoted to the past. Dale was publicly pleased with the award and gracious in accepting it, but privately held a different opinion. "Truth to tell, this business embarrasses me a bit," he confided to Joe Colgan, safely distant in Washington, DC. "I am not much in favor of such awards, even when they are given to me. What counts is the book itself, what you have put into it. And what people say about the book afterward matters not in the least."[40]

Juanita Brooks had no such reservations. She was thrilled Dale's work was finally being recognized, even if not by an academic institution. Yes, Morgan's star as a scholar of note had risen. Brooks compared the recent accolades acknowledging Hollywood women's swimwear designer Rose Marie Reid's recent gift to BYU and J. Willard Marriott's gift to the University of Utah to Morgan's scholarly contribution. Money was, she observed wryly, "a sure route to a gold tassel and a vari-colored hood, while genuine scholarship stands like Lazarus at the gate."[41]

Part of Brooks's ire was over something Morgan knew nothing about—that he had been denied an honorary doctorate. Unknown to Morgan, the University of Utah's Arthur L. Crawford moved that the institution acknowledge its alumnus with an honorary degree. Collating supportive recommendations was no problem, but the accolade wrecked on the opinion of one disgruntled faculty member. Since the prospective honoree fell within the history department's subject area, the university administration asked department chair Leland Creer's assessment of the prospective awardee. Creer never forgave Morgan's low opinion of his published writing. The department chair responded that Morgan was not a historian but merely a "dilettante to history." His opinion killed the proposal.[42]

Of course, laudatory recognition and the help Morgan provided to many others over the past few years brought neither the Ashley book nor his other publication projects much closer to completion.

* * * * *

Toward the end of the year Dale summarized for Fawn Brodie his success over the year and plans for 1962. He related the work on the Kansas book for Baughman, talked about the Wagner Memorial Award, and that he had been "virtually practicing law without a license for the Navajos." Yes, the Ashley book was nearly finished. He hoped to finish editing the Beckwourth memoir soon (though he had set not a word to paper) and, in May, to complete the collection of documents he planned to call *Overland in 1846* and had promised to Talisman Press. "There are a couple of other documentary projects on foot, probably about five altogether, but I anticipate that a winter's work largely devoted to cleaning up those things will enable me to tackle my long-deferred Mormon history, to be followed by a large general history of the fur trade after Lewis & Clark," conceived as a historical precursor to *Jedediah Smith and the Opening of the West.*[43] He did not mention Wheat's book, although Helen wrote that Carl now felt ready to work with Dale. He also did not mention that the Bancroft's *Guide to Manuscripts* was nearly at proof stage and would require his attention. Nor did he mention that a contract with Knopf for the Lorton diary had been signed by Valita Moran, committing him to a completed manuscript in a year.

Not that life was all work and no play. Morgan made opportunities to socialize. He went with friends Tasia and Michael Melvin to the Kirov Ballet performance of *Sleeping Beauty.* Helen Harding Bretnor, Dale's coworker at Bancroft, and her husband, science fiction writer Reg Bretnor, hosted him for dinner occasionally. However, he had not delivered his chapter for *The Book of the American West,* and the latter was being pushed by publisher Julian Messner, Inc. "Keep us at the top of your agenda and that is all I ask," editor Jay Monaghan wrote genially.[44]

Dale was doing so, sort of, but he was more interested in starting work on the huge compilation of 1846 travel narratives, which would draw together the records for an entire season of overland travel, including the Donner tragedy. In early November he raised the proposal with George Hammond and asked for the latter's recommendation. Knowing Dale's penchant for never saying no to a fascinating project, Hammond was diplomatic but blunt: "In view of the importance of completion of the Guide, and of its importance in your career, I feel it would be impracticable to commit yourself (and the Library) to such a big project as [Talisman Press publisher] Mr. Greenwood proposes. As I have mentioned to you on various occasions, the publication of the Guide ought to take precedence over everything now, for reasons that I do not need to review again."[45]

At the Thanksgiving holiday Dale quietly ignored Hammond's pointed advice and committed himself to Talisman Press for the 1846 book. He also wrote Carl Wheat that he planned to quickly produce a text for the fifth and final *Mapping the Transmississippi West* volume in January before moving forward on other work. He hosted the Macleods for his own forty-seventh birthday dinner on 18 December. A few days later, he roasted a Christmas goose for the McQuowns at their home in San Jose; Madeline had been discharged from a Salt Lake City hospital and arrived home only a few weeks earlier.

At the very end of December 1961, Dale received word that he had been named a Fellow of the California Historical Society. In the Wagner Memorial Award citation a month earlier, James D. Hart noted that "Dale Morgan has considerably enriched our understanding of various facets of the Western United States and of that entire frontier itself through his diverse ... research and publications[,] which include bibliographies scrupulously and intelligently compiled, carefully annotated editions of primary documents; knowing cartographic studies of important early maps; and his own firmly based historical studies marked both by breadth of treatment and depth of interpretation."[46]

A year earlier the Missouri Historical Society's bulletin called Morgan plainly "the foremost historian of the American West."[47] Dale Morgan arrived at Bancroft as a competent researcher and writer of history, but as a comparative newcomer to the field of academic history. Though he held no professional degree and did not teach professionally, by 1961 Morgan was a major figure in the study of the American West. Despite the recognitions, however, he had not made much progress on the writing projects of personal importance; for most of the past five years he had been trying with only marginal success to get them off of his priority list and into his typewriter.

* * * * *

Dale began devoting his weekends to the fifth *Transmississippi* volume, but further complications and new demands piled up. He quickly found Wheat's existing draft or outline basically unusable. Morgan decided to start over entirely. Before he could launch into the writing, with the *Guide to Manuscripts* ready to go to the printer, interim library director James Hart approached Morgan with a new publication project. To mark the acquisition of a major collection of material documenting Mexican history, the Bancroft wanted to mount a major exhibition with a substantial catalog. As the institutional publication arm, Morgan was handed responsibility for coordinating a text, illustrations, and handling the publication process. This task consumed him daily until March.

Expecting the author would hold the deadline he had himself proposed, by the end of January Monaghan had written again, noting that Morgan's chapter had not arrived. In fact, though Monaghan didn't know it, Dale had not yet set down a single word of the essay. He took a few days' break from work to have an ingrown toenail corrected surgically and told Monaghan he was working exclusively on the fur trade essay. However, "working on" in his language meant research, not writing. Consumed chiefly with restructuring Wheat's book and notes in his free time, Morgan would put off *The Book of the American West* editor repeatedly and not actually write anything until nearly April 1962.

Dale was invited to the Melvins' for Easter and enjoyed playing with his "adopted" niece and nephews. Later that week the latest of Alfred Knopf's polite queries on the status of the William B. Lorton diary also arrived. Though four years had passed since his first inquiry, Morgan had nothing to offer the publisher, explaining that he was busily at work on Wheat's volume.

In fact, the effort required to draft the text for the final volume of *Mapping the Transmississippi West* extended far beyond shaking together Carl Wheat's notes or arranging his maps and photostat prints, but at least they were not in the condition of the loose notes that made up *West from Fort Bridger*. Even crippled as he was by the three strokes, Wheat had drafted a few early chapters. Dale went through these carefully but employed his own knowledge of the field, frequently imposing major revisions on whatever Wheat had done. The mail carried a long succession of drafts, corrections, and eventually proofs back and forth between Berkeley and Palo Alto. Morgan was very careful to give his friend the last word on virtually everything in what was essentially Morgan's original work. The target deadline for Carl's manuscript stretched during 1962 from March, to May, then to August, finally to December.

Despite the "author's" wishes for haste and comparability with the other volumes, the fifth lengthened as well. By mid-June Helen Wheat had written Dale for her husband, begging him not to add any more new material or send additional maps. The work had to be held to the same size as the preceding volumes, however much interesting or relevant material might potentially be included. The printer had only enough paper on hand for a single volume, and the bound book had to be kept within the cost margins of the others in the series. Morgan, however, kept at work, consumed with the idea that Wheat's one masterwork was to stand unchallengeable in terms of definitive completion.

Without notice in early April, Dale received a Bobbs-Merrill check for $31.55, payment on the sale of British publication rights to *Jedediah Smith*. The author was not happy for at least two reasons. First, it was a cheap sale, and second, Dale desperately wanted to make a major revision to the book. Morgan feared that a new and unchanged version floating around discouraged possible publisher interest in a new edition. After a clarifying telephone call with the publisher, friend Lois Stewart returned a mollifying report that the payment was not a publication commitment. It was, rather, merely a one-year earnest-money option on the title for possible inclusion in the Eyre & Spottiswoode book series on the American West—Americana for Europe. Morgan insisted Bobbs-Merrill inform the English firm that he planned a revision. "I am averse to having a virtually obsolete book reprinted when it is possible to update the whole thing," he told Huntington Library's John Hawgood. Concern about Morgan's insisted-upon plan to update the work likely killed the British firm's interest; no market for a reprint would have existed if a revised edition was available.[48] The Eyre & Spottiswoode list later included Fawn Brodie's *No Man Knows My History* but never included *Jedediah Smith*.

In the midst of the press, typist Marguerite Reusser suffered a heart attack, which required finding a new typist for Wheat's printer manuscript.[49] The book Dale estimated in May would need three weeks of work, required four months of nearly constant effort daily from supper to midnight, and most of his weekends. During the summer of 1962 everything else was set aside; he attended no parties, made and received no social calls other than having Dan and Sandra Howe as houseguests for a week in late July while they looked for housing. By the third week of August, everything Dale had taken on was a pressing demand, again crowding his limited budget of time and energy, and galleys for the *Guide to Manuscripts* began arriving for review, adding yet more layers of demands and deadlines. Dale wrote his mother with uncharacteristic openness when he observed that "Time keeps slipping away on me, when what I need is for it to stand still a bit and give me a platform on which to get some necessary things done."[50] By this point Morgan had given up cooking for himself and was eating out for every meal. Money had become less valuable than time. It showed. Dale's lanky frame put on weight to the point that back in May his physician recommended he lose and keep off twenty pounds.

For a week before attending the presentation of the Wagner Memorial Award to longtime friend Thomas Streeter, Dale worked furiously on a "bibliocartography," the list of maps concluding what had grown to be a double volume of Wheat's final work. He dispatched batches of manuscript to Palo Alto daily as they were completed. Both demands were set aside on September 28 so Dale could spend the day with Tom Streeter. Though the pair were old friends, the visit was a formal one, and Streeter's time in California was filled with receptions, but Dale was on hand at the Chancellor's reception for Streeter. He hovered a bit anxiously as the collector met UC Berkeley librarian Donald Coney for the first time since Coney had made the donor-relations miscalculation of the century: in the 1940s Streeter had offered his large and growing collection of incredibly rare Americana to the University of California, Berkeley library; in an act beyond imagination today, Coney had turned it down.[51]

On November 20, Helen Wheat called George Hammond. Hammond brought the news downstairs personally to Dale's desk: Carl had suffered a fifth massive stroke and was in a coma. The fifth volume lacked an author's introduction, only part of the page proof had been reviewed and approved, and there was no one else but Dale Morgan to turn to. Would Dale please provide an introduction and correct the page proofs?[52] The introduction wasn't all that was involved; Helen Wheat's trust obligated Morgan to additional time dealing with map placement in the forthcoming volume, effectively making Morgan the project manager for the book as well. This work required months of conferences with typesetter Mackenzie & Harris, with printer Grabhorn Press on the book dummy, with the map lithographer to confirm reproduction quality, along with the necessary proofreading cycle and writing Wheat's volume introduction, for which no more than a collection of notes and thoughts existed. Wheat began a slow improvement. He came out of the coma after about two weeks. In another week he was coherent, if slow, and clearly in no condition to complete any of the remaining work on volume five. Dale agreed to do the work.

A few days after Thanksgiving typesetter Carroll Harris began delivering proofs for Wheat's volume. Dale took a bit of time out for another project—only a few pages for the outstanding and long-overdue commitment to *The Book of the American West*—and then settled into reading and correcting the *Transmississippi* proofs. Midway through December, Dale released all of the page proof of Wheat's fifth volume for printing. Carl was slowly regaining his speech capacity, but Dale found it painful to see his once vigorous, incisive mind trapped behind a muzzy web of damaged physical ability. Dale flew to Salt Lake City on December 22 for a family holiday. Before leaving he stopped at Mackenzie & Harris in San Francisco to pick up the page samples for the Ashley book designed by Lawton Kennedy. They were magnificent.

* * * * *

Perhaps no time in Dale Morgan's life represented both the success and the frustrations of writing history so effectively as did the years across the middle of his Bancroft career. Though he was perpetually behind with writing, these years were also the years in which his two largest and most important documentary works were published, and the point at which he had become a respected senior member among academics writing on Western American history. Coincidentally, as described earlier, those years reflected some of the greatest changes in the American publishing industry, the economic sector on which Morgan still wanted to pin a career. As rewarding as his work at the Bancroft Library may have been, Dale still looked longingly toward research and publishing as his real calling.

From his perspective, Morgan's desires existed in an uneasy balancing act. Scholarly books made a reputation, but popular nonfiction was what sold well enough to provide actual income. He was probably too close to his own output to recognize that his career reflected this modern conundrum. His scholarly reputation was made with the publication of Pritchard's diary and McCollum's *California as I Saw It* and similar works of painstaking scholarship but limited issue, yet it was *The Humboldt* and *The Great Salt*

Lake—dismissed as mere "stakes in my education"—which consistently supplied royalty checks. By the mid-1960s Morgan was looking less often for an exit from academia into full-time writing, but it was still a goal.

Ironically, at the time that individual institutions and the states legislatures initiated the humanities' long, slow decline in higher education, funding support for history began growing on the federal level. At about the same time, in the swirl of competing forces, public universities discovered the principle that Ivy League institutions had long understood—the value of private donors. Morgan's *alma mater*, the University of Utah, for instance, successfully solicited a million-dollar gift from Latter-day Saint hotel tycoon J. Willard Marriott. Half the sum provided the lead gift toward construction of a new central library, and half provided an acquisitions fund with which to fill it. Everett Cooley, who left the Utah State Historical Society to establish a rare-book department at the University of Utah's new Marriott Library, immediately set to work spending the allocation.

In terms of actual output, 1963–1969 stands as the high point of Dale Morgan's career. These years solidified his reputation as a scholar and would have laid the foundation for the works he would have generated later in life as an acknowledged authority in the field. In fact, in one of the last scholarly reviews of his work, the reviewer asserted that "Dale Morgan's name on a book is like a hallmark on sterling, a guarantee of quality without further testing."[53]

* * * * *

January 1, 1963 shone clear and cold in Salt Lake City. As Dale flew back to the Bay Area from a family holiday, relieved from the intense pressure that the Bancroft *Guide to Manuscripts,* Wheat's map book, and the fur trade chapter for Monaghan's *The Book of the American West* had extracted from him, he was certainly unaware that the dawning year would extract a still greater toll. The year 1963 would finally see simultaneous completion and release of two of Dale Morgan's greatest scholarly accomplishments and most complex works, making it the pinnacle of his career as a scholar, but the cost was enormous. From our privileged position looking back across Dale Morgan's lifespan, the intensity of 1961–1962 was little more than a warm-up act for the main event in 1963, a year which would nearly crush him physically and emotionally.

Dale returned home to Berkeley from Salt Lake City to find in his mailbox a letter from Bobbs-Merrill. The letter was the firm's formal notice that it was negotiating the outright sale of paperback rights to *Jedediah Smith* with the University of Nebraska Press. The sale, his publisher noted, "will assure the book's availability in some form during the period in which you are revising and up-dating[*sic*]. Considering all the irons you have in the fire, this revision may well take much longer than you anticipate at the moment." In essence, the letter called Morgan's bluff about the threatened new edition. Dale was furious. He fired back a bristling response, failing to understand that while authors were fired by the thought of new editions, publishers were chiefly interested in new printings. He had thought the idea of a reprint had been laid to rest the previous year with the British edition. Again, Morgan waved the threat of the new edition like a field-officer's sword, asserting vigorously that the new work would "destroy the market for the reprint."

This time the threat of a new edition had no effect. Bobbs-Merrill owned the rights to the book by contract and could do with it what they chose. The editor pointed out in return that a new edition would not necessarily find a publisher. Frankly, the firm was reorganizing and was not about to lose a cash-in-hand sale to vague plans for a new edition. The original edition had not sold well, anyway. To a student query about the book which chanced to arrive the same week, Dale asserted that an updated edition would be published simultaneously in Britain and the U.S.—perhaps an optimistic hope but certainly an intentional misdirection. The Bobbs-Merrill staff was right and had the contract to prove the point. Dale's threat ultimately proved hollow. The sale of paperback rights underscored that Bobbs-Merrill had no interest in an updated edition for its own sake and could prevent the author from publishing a second edition elsewhere.

Morgan was disappointed and upset, but he still cashed the check. The exchange effectively wrecked Morgan's hope of ever updating *Jedediah Smith and the Opening of the West*. Over the University of Nebraska Press imprint the original 1953 edition of the book has remained (and yet remains) in print, one of the classics of scholarly literature on the American West.[54] Despite the author's ire, it was specifically because the book went into paperback that Morgan's work remained accessible to succeeding generations of students (like me). Despite how badly he did not want the book to appear, the paperback scholarly edition remains the cornerstone of his literary legacy.

Carl Wheat came home to Palo Alto from the hospital at almost the same time that corrected page proofs were returned for Dale's two-part fifth volume of *Mapping the Transmississippi West*. Five strokes left Wheat in a wheelchair with slurred speech, which made discussion painfully difficult. He tired easily. Due to his condition Wheat had seen nothing at all of the fifth volume until now. On May 10, after several delays and complications, George Hammond and Morgan picked up the first copies of the conclusion to Wheat's life work and drove them south. Dale took great personal pleasure in laying the two-part volume in the author's lap, the printed culmination of a lifetime of interest and hard work.

Dale Morgan produced, by his own estimation, about half of the second volume, virtually all of the third, the chapter on Mormon maps in the fourth, and the entire two-part fifth volume—approximately half of the series, though he never claimed credit for doing so. The correspondence between the two men demonstrates clearly that Morgan also corrected and edited (sometimes amending to the point of rewriting) Wheat's text throughout the first and fourth volumes, and corrected proofs for all of them as well. Morgan was as generous in allowing Wheat alone to receive the praise for the volume as Wheat was insistent in trying to credit him for it. Dale did quietly include the fifth volume on the one list of his publications he generated himself.[55]

* * * * *

On January 30, 1963, Bob Greenwood of Talisman Press wrote Dale asking for an estimate of when the 1846 manuscript would be submitted. With Wheat's project gone to press Morgan replied that he had taken up the manuscript the previous week. Dale projected that both volumes would be ready in February—by March, at the latest. In March, with Wheat's work finally in press proofs, Dale leapt back into work on both the Ashley and the 1846 collections, revising his estimate. Now he expected to complete the Ashley manuscript by March 30 and the 1846 collection and notes by April 20.[56] He did neither. The Ashley text was in Kennedy's hands by April 11 (though including neither the extensive notes nor the lengthy introduction). A week earlier Morgan handed back to the University of California Press the last of the proofs for the Bancroft's *Guide to Manuscripts*.

Although projects were finally being cleared, the overlapping commitments exacted a high personal cost. By this point, Dale had largely given up personal diversions other than research or writing. He had not sketched or painted for several years. While he visited occasionally with friends in San Francisco and was social with a few Bancroft colleagues, those occasions seemed increasingly further apart. He almost never entertained at home any more, instead hosting friends at the university's Faculty Club. He barely had time for that.

Earlier in the spring Madeline had once again fled California to her doctor in Salt Lake City. The Brigham Young biography manuscript went with her to fill time while she was under more attentive medical care. Yet, when she returned home to San Jose after again running out of funds for medical attention, no notable progress had been made. Surely Dale could not preach to her. Writing to his mother in mid-April he again demonstrated a naively unrealistic optimism about calendars, obligations, and his ability to complete work. Looking ahead of Ashley, he fully expected to clear the Lorton diary and another unnamed Forty-niner project in May–June 1963, and then the Campbell volume before the end of the year. He had yet to set a single word to paper for any of these works, and he still had not completed either the Ashley book or the 1846 collection, which he now pledged for a late summer delivery.

By this point in his career one might expect Morgan to look at his own record and be more realistic about what could be accomplished at the level of sophistication and documentation he expected. Despite the projects completed in the past year, he could joke to Archie Hanna, curator of the Western Americana Collection at Yale, that "now I'm only about five years behind."[57] In retrospect, Morgan's sentiment looks uncomfortably like black humor. By the third week of May 1963, Dale plunged headlong into the Ashley papers and the compilation of 1846 material. Fred Rosenstock arrived on one of his trips to Berkeley and as usual stayed overnight with Morgan. The pair went to see Lawton Kennedy and finalize arrangements for design and typesetting on the Ashley book. Kennedy's typesetter went to work, and galleys began arriving in the middle of June. Meantime, with *Overland in 1846* already announced for the fall sales list, Greenwood wanted at least the first part of the manuscript to begin composition. The year was essentially half over, and he had nothing of the manuscript in hand.

Workdays still required full attention on the myriad of details relating to manuscript acquisition for the Bancroft Library collection, but it was the late nights that became incredibly wearing. By the end of July, while the Ashley galleys continued drifting in, Dale delivered the documentary text for the second volume of the 1846 compilation, though nothing yet of the first volume and none of his original contribution—the all-important introduction or the notes. On August 1, History Department faculty member Jim Scobie wrote that the University of California Press was ready for the William Perkins manuscript any time Dale could have it ready. Dale may not have even taken time to respond. By the tenth of the month, half a year after Morgan had promised the full manuscript of the 1846 book, Greenwood's letters were becoming visibly nervous. Volume 2 text galleys were ready, and Talisman needed manuscript of the first volume immediately. Printing the 1846 collection had to proceed from front to back and could not begin until the introduction was on hand. Greenwood and partner Newton Baird were beginning to discuss the uncomfortable reality that they were facing financial disaster if the book was not delivered to buyers in time for Christmas. The situation only worsened.

Despite obligations to three publishers, Dale had his own personal complications. His mother picked up Helen Sanders in Maryville, and they both drove down for a visit. Of course, Dale expected to play host. Both books went on hold, but taking the pair to lunch in San Francisco, Dale used the opportunity to drop the first part of the lengthy Ashley introduction at Lawton Kennedy's printshop, where Kennedy dropped a bombshell: the fur trade book was now running short and needed to be filled out to justify its advertised $35 price. That news allowed Morgan to resurrect nineteen pages of documents, but meant that he again had to renumber the manuscript pages. And fifty pages of notes and half the introduction still remained incomplete. That evening as Dale, Emily, and Helen went to dinner, Dale ordered a glass of beer with the meal. Emily said nothing, knowing her son no longer had a personal interest in his Latter-day Saint strictures.

By the third week of September Dale's guests had gone but their host had accomplished almost nothing during their visit. Bob Greenwood had passed anxiousness and was now desperate about the 1846 book. Dale still had not completed the introduction nor supplied Talisman with the notes. Proofs for the text had been pulled from the type, but Greenwood did not dare send them to the author lest Dale's penchant for corrections hamper delivery of the introduction. The publisher finally sent them anyway midmonth, needing something to move on the volume but with strict instructions to Morgan not to correct the proof until the complete introduction had been mailed.

As the year's daylight hours shortened toward winter, Morgan's workload on the two books lengthened. Whether he worked on either project did not matter; they were both scheduled for pre-Christmas publication and long overdue. Kennedy and Rosenstock were as anxious for corrected proofs as were Greenwood and Baird. Dale was now spending literally every waking moment on one set of proofs or the other—early mornings, coffee breaks, lunch times, and late, late evenings every day of the week and all weekends. He read the typeset galleys against his careful transcriptions, but it was painstaking work that his drive for precision always privileged when facing a deadline. Unfortunately, his attention to proofs crowded against the incomplete introduction, which was needed to plan the page count, paper order, and binding order.[58] The pressure from both Talisman and Kennedy increased.

By the end of September Dale considered staying home to work on the books rather than attending the annual Western History Association (WHA) meeting being held in Salt Lake City. He wrote Emily that "the best I hope for is that I can handle Ashley and 1846 so that both books don't have crises at the same moment."[59] It was rather late for that—both projects were *in* crisis. On October 7 Morgan finally sent forty-three pages of the introduction to Greenwood in Georgetown, California, barely a down payment on an introduction that would eventually run over a hundred printed pages. Dale enlisted the ever-broke Joe Colgan to draw a pair of maps for the Ashley book, and Morgan juggled a base map, drafting instructions, and data for that process. Greenwood needed Morgan's attention to a map reproduction for the end sheets. Kennedy needed photos to make printing plates of painter George Catlin's drawings to be used as illustrations. The Bancroft needed Morgan's involvement with its energetic campaign to the Friends of The Bancroft Library supporting the purchase of a major California art collection. When Alfred Knopf asked whether he would see Morgan at the WHA annual meeting, Dale begged off and cancelled the trip.

By October, Newton Baird was printing what he had of the introduction to the first volume of *Overland in 1846*. Greenwood instructed the author to mark proofs with only outright typographical errors. There was no time for anything else. Five days later, when Morgan did not turn around the corrections quickly enough, Greenwood wrote that it was too late; he would print an errata rather than make corrections to the type and reprint. Morgan still had not supplied the footnotes to the first volume. Dale sent a few pages to keep things moving. Greenwood was not happy; having a few pages merely ate up resources and time.

By November 1 Robert Greenwood was frantic. Morgan's delay compromised not only the publisher's investment but also the press's next publication. The publisher threatened to take the first volume to the binder to be made up without the notes.[60] Morgan had no notes manuscript to send him, committing instead to mailing daily what pages he could complete. By this point the printer had already been paid time-and-a-half to set type on a rush commission, and the publisher was worrying about possible bankruptcy. The stack of printed sheets for the first volume was sent on to the bindery for folding a day before Morgan supplied the final notes manuscript. It included far more material than what the publisher had estimated in the budget. Greenwood wrote bluntly that Morgan should now expect to pick up some of that bill.[61]

Even as Dale compiled notes doggedly for the 1846 volume and read the last page proofs for the Ashley book, he began planning for the marathon race that compiling indices for both books would require. On the advertised publication date of *The West of William H. Ashley*, Emily wrote to note the importance of the long-awaited day, an uncomfortable reminder of how far behind things actually were. Colgan still had not delivered maps for either book. Dale's personal diversion was now limited to the fifteen-minute walk back and forth between his apartment on Benvenue Avenue and work. He now made no pretense at cooking or housework; there was no time for pretense. He slogged back and forth through November and into December, staying up ever later to complete the remaining composition.

On November 22 the news of John F. Kennedy's assassination crashed into every citizen's psyche, but even Morgan's concern about the future of the country could not displace the burden that *Overland in 1846* had become. On the Monday before Thanksgiving Dale mailed about a third of the volume two notes to Greenwood, promising the remaining sixty-seven pages the next day. He enjoyed no holiday to speak of. Upon mailing the note manuscript the following Tuesday, he went to work without a breath compiling the *Ashley* index. Greenwood was livid upon receiving the notes. That manuscript was far longer than for volume one, ruining "finally and resolutely, as far as I am concerned, the schedule I had been trying to keep—and the cost picture," he fumed. "I doubt now if there can be any royalties."[62]

At Thanksgiving, Dale hardly looked at the Christmas cards that began arriving and made no attempt at all to send out his own greetings for the 1963 holiday season. Colgan had still not sent the map. It finally arrived in Berkeley on December 1. Dale gave it a hasty review before dispatching it to his publisher, while he struggled to complete the *Ashley* index. A few days later Colgan's three-part drawing for the *Ashley* map also arrived; Kennedy's engraver would join the parts into the large seamless image that would be photographically reduced and printed for the book. Greenwood did not have the same luxury; the map which was supposed to lead the second volume ended up tipped in at the end just to get it into the book at all.

A week later, Dale was trying to complete an index for each book at the same time. Both publishers sent telegrams saying the index manuscripts were needed immediately. In outright desperation, on December 9 Robert Greenwood wired Dale that he was driving to Berkeley to complete the index and carry it with him to press. When he arrived at Morgan's apartment, Dale was still at work on the notes for volume two and had not even begun indexing. Years later Greenwood related the experience: "We worked for two days and nights, breaking only for brief meals and a few hours' sleep. We typed through the night of the second day to finish the copy."

At one point, Dale glanced into the refrigerator and wrote Greenwood a note asking what he wanted to eat. The latter responded that he would order out. "He [Dale] looked puzzled. Dale had a telephone in his apartment, but he couldn't hear it ring. He seemed skeptical that prepared food would be delivered to his apartment door."[63] The food came, the index manuscript to *Overland in 1846* was finished, and with it Robert Greenwood raced to the typesetter on December 11, the presswork alone more than two months behind schedule.

* * * * *

With one book finally off his hands, Dale could finally concentrate properly on the *Ashley* index. He wrote his mother not to expect him either for Christmas or after. Nor should she plan to come to Berkeley; he was still buried with obligations and could not be an adequate host. "I feel as though I had been beaten with sticks," he told Jim Scobie. "Not that I ever lead a totally relaxed life, or can as long as I insist upon being a writer and have to be a writer on top of holding down a regular job."[64] Even with the *Guide to Manuscripts* at last in print, the "regular job" imposed its own demands. On the day before his forty-ninth birthday, Morgan was summoned to Hammond's office to talk with Bancroft Library donor Helen Kennedy about the library publishing a biography of her ancestor and Stockton, California founder Charles M. Weber. A prohibition on holiday visitors did not extend to the McQuowns, who came to stay for several nights while Madeline was enduring yet another surgical procedure at Alta Bates Hospital. Tom McQuown and Jerry Finnin cycled in and out of his apartment, while Dale worked doggedly on the *Ashley* index. Lawton Kennedy carried that manuscript from Berkeley to his San Francisco printshop on December 22. Typesetting for the index began at 1 a.m. on December 23.[65]

On Christmas morning, Dale set a goose to roast for his guests. Tom McQuown answered a knock at the door and returned with a box containing four copies of *Overland in 1846*. The binding had been completed only the previous morning, and the books had been shipped to the subscriber list on the afternoon of Christmas Eve, so the publisher did manage to deliver the books for Christmas even if they arrived no earlier than that morning. By the time the twin volumes were bound, the publisher's constant demand to deliver made Morgan so thoroughly sick of the book and its subject that he virtually abandoned the overland trail as a field of study for several years. Though he once wanted to compile a similar collection for 1841, the first year of transcontinental wagon travel, that project never again captured his attention. "I am never again going to permit a book to be published as that one was," he asserted archly, as if it was not his own choices that had forced the publisher's compromises.[66]

And yet, *The West of William H. Ashley* was everything the two-book overland set was not. Praise for the book echoed across the country from scholars and Western buffs. Morgan provided a ground-level documentary study of the economics of the American fur trade at its high point. Its notes captured a remarkable breadth of interactive detail, hinting at the narrative arc that might have been captured a few years later if Morgan had successfully finished his history of the North American fur trade. That story, however, was not yet a factor in his plans. Morgan was content to have *Ashley* as it was, with endnotes.

Privately, Dale grumbled to Joe Colgan that he did not much like *Overland in 1846*, compared with *The West of William H. Ashley*. Sure, he had to finish the *Ashley* index on his own, but "No corners were cut on this as Greenwood did (sometimes without my knowledge) on 1846, and [*Ashley*] continues a quality job from first to last."[67] However, Dale overlooked the point that the *Ashley* printer, binder, and publisher gave up the race at the end and simply postponed its publication to 1964.

For the first six weeks of 1964 Dale waited anxiously for the news that bound copies of the *Ashley* were available. On Valentines' Day he spent the day at the bindery in San Francisco, autographing sewn but unbound copies of the pages destined for the special leather-bound issue. When he returned with his pen three days later to sign the remaining books, Dale left a thick file of Campbell transcriptions from which Kennedy planned to work up a castoff and rough production estimate for the *Ashley* companion book. Assuming Dale's schedule held, the Robert Campbell book was to appear in print in about nine months, in time for the fall book season.

With the binding soon complete, on February 21, George Hammond drove Dale to Lawton Kennedy's shop, where the first special-edition copies of *The West of William H. Ashley* had been received. Kennedy pasted the folding map into the first bound book from the stack, and the trio left immediately for the hour-long drive to the home of Carl and Helen Wheat. Wheat had known for years that the fur-trade book would be dedicated to him, but as Dale placed the specially bound copy in his lap and turned to the dedication page, Wheat was visibly touched. Dale wrote words of thanks to his friend that, in Carl's weakened state, Morgan could no longer say clearly enough to be understood.

A few days later, Dale noticed that the copy of the book he had himself was missing an image—an irritating binding error that he hoped was unique, since presentation copies of the book had already been mailed to the University of Utah library and to his mother, and the bindery was working busily on the trade edition. The rest of his copies proved to be missing the same plate. A halt was called to distribution until all the books on hand could be checked for the missing image. Most of the specially bound presentation copies were missing the plate, and all were replaced at the bindery's expense, but a few flawed copies of the trade edition inadvertently got out to eager buyers.

*　*　*　*

I've focused attention on this year and these books because this desperate story illustrates so well the reasons why Dale Morgan's "practical training" in history allowed him to chronically wedge himself into long lists of unrealistic commitments. Beginning with his earliest days with the Historical Records Survey, Morgan got into a habit of writing only when he was pressed to do so by a deadline. He had thrilled to work hard and deliver good, almost polished written matter on a short schedule under pressure.

The process was something of a drug, and like a drug, he progressed rapidly from casual use to dependence.

Second, Dale Morgan consistently underestimated both time and effort needed for tasks. As a result, he consistently overcommitted to both interesting projects and to quick-buck projects. He turned down almost as many writing commissions as he ultimately accepted, but because he wrote only under deadline pressure, the tradeoff was that he was chronically in arrears.

A third factor is visible in Morgan's record of correspondence and individual letters. One can see in this specific circumstance with simultaneous books for Talisman Press and Old West Publishing Company, as in most others, that he was completing his research in a flurry of last-minute queries as the book was being written. The act of composing the text shaped the questions he needed resolved, and the new information from research shaped the text as he worked. He had always worked this way, but rarely with the stakes so high as in 1963. In fairness, the research for no book is ever really complete at the time of its writing, but Morgan's symbiosis between research query and composition and revision was very intertwined indeed.

Finally, Morgan did not have the convenience of a word processor and still tended to write from the beginning to the end of a work, starting with the text, then the notes, and finally the frontis matter with the all-important introduction. Unfortunately, if one does not supply a publisher with an entire manuscript when a project begins, then Morgan's preferences hamstrings the basic production sequences a publisher and printer must meet to issue a book on schedule. In the fall of 1963 Morgan dragged not one, but two publishers simultaneously into crisis and toward catastrophe.

Morgan expected to embark immediately on the *Ashley* companion volume on Robert Campbell. Like most of his work he had not yet set down a single page of draft text, but he was confident about what would be included. One definite piece was a few pages from an 1832 diary among the papers of a German sportsman, Maximilian zu Wied. The diary was essential to the Campbell book since the expedition members met and interacted with Campbell at Fort Union for several weeks. The prince's collection was owned by the Northern Natural Gas Company. Unfortunately, despite Morgan's site visit in 1964 to encourage permission, the document's corporate owners determinedly held to their inexplicable policy of buying, owning, and displaying artworks but not releasing accompanying historical documents for study.[68] The inability to include that single source, and the slight hope that it would become available in the future, kept Morgan from ever drafting the Robert Campbell volume.

* * * * *

Distilling eight incredibly busy years into fewer than a hundred pages simply does not do justice to the energy, the individual accomplishments, long nights, or the stress accumulated a drop at a time in thousands of letters, tens of thousands of pages of notes, drafts, proofs, and index sheets that flowed like a river past Dale Morgan's eyes. Nothing in Morgan's upbringing or training prepared him for an academic existence. That he accomplished so much and—in worldly terms—succeeded so arguably well is a testament to ... what? Surely native ability was a factor, as was a finely honed sense of commitment to a task.

Though he could not know it, Morgan's life was better than three-quarters over, even as he launched into real work on what might have been his greatest accomplishments as a historian. Had he known, would he have reordered his priorities? Possibly, but I don't think it would be by much.

CHAPTER 15

"Too Many Obligations Out Here"[1]

Turning Points and Departures

Behind the oft-repeated statement that each generation must write its own history lies a tragic situation. It implies that there can be no ultimate history, and that the historian is doomed to be forever writing in the sand. He can say little of permanent value. He must expect his work to be superseded again and again, and what he says today will, by the next generation, be considered nonsense.[2]

— Avery Craven

FOCUSING TOO CLOSELY on employment and writing obscures Morgan's social activity and the larger contexts swirling around him, far out of his control. Yet, Morgan's commitment to Carl Wheat and *Mapping the Transmississippi West* represented how effectively his social life and profession focus had shifted from the Salt Lake valley to the Bay Area. After 1957 it was never really drawn back toward Utah again.

For a short period Dale resumed participation in local life-drawing classes at the San Francisco Art Association as a free-time diversion. Occasionally he arranged private modeling sessions at his apartment with Tasia Melvin, one of the life models who posed regularly. Over time the pair struck up a personal friendship that soon drew Dale into association with her young family. Through the next decade Dale was a frequent guest at their San Francisco home, becoming good friends of Tasia and husband Michael. As their family grew, "uncle Dale," far from his own nieces and nephews, adopted the Melvins as family, becoming a fixture at the Melvin children's birthday parties and family holidays. Dale also settled into warm friendships with George and Carrie Hammond, Carl and Helen Wheat, Charles and Jessie Camp, Helen and Reg Bretnor, and Julia and Mac Macleod.

By 1958 Dale wrote Juanita Brooks only occasionally and his WPA and OPA friends not at all. About the only one of his Utah friends that Dale corresponded with more or less regularly was Charlie Kelly, though Russ Mortensen remained not only a friend but also provided important support to ongoing research. Morgan's connections to Utah were now mostly sentimental and through family. Yet, life kept moving for all of them.

Dale opened a letter from Anna McConkey in the first week of June 1959. It was her notice that Darel had suffered a second and much more severe heart attack. Since virtually no treatments were available at the time, the depleted oxygenation to Darel's brain affected the speech center of his cerebral cortex. He was recovering—slowly—but was now suffering from aphasia. Deprivation left thinking and reasoning functions unaffected, but perceptions and expressions were tangled in blind alleys of dead neural synapses that made it impossible for Darel McConkey to translate thought into coherent communication. He could comprehend what he heard and some of what he read but could not reply beyond yes and no. McConkey's mind was trapped inside his own brain. As he slowly regained strength, routine physical tasks around the house and yard were unaffected, Anna related, but he could not communicate meaningfully. As long as Darel did not sap his stamina, painting walls, woodworking, or light effort in the yard and garden were not a problem, but until (and unless) his brain could heal and reroute the synapses, he would not speak or write coherently again. His ability with arithmetic was largely gone. He also had trouble reading. The McConkey family endured weeks of their father's unintelligible sounds and scribbles, then occasional words, garbled short sentences, and finally halting, painfully difficult conversation. Eventually McConkey recovered his faculties sufficiently to begin typing later the same year. Even short letters were painful, slow, and filled with misplaced words and odd grammar. Darel McConkey's life as a man of words was clearly over.

Dale watched his friend at a distance through Anna's letters. He sent back encouraging letters, reporting his challenges with the library, the Navajo research, and his own writing, carefully avoiding laments or mentions of Darel doing again what he once had done eagerly for Dale—reviewing and editing book manuscripts as they came close to submission dates. When Anna mentioned that adult conversation was good for her husband's recovery, Dale immediately offered to buy and have a television installed. The family was delighted, and Anna was grateful. That elemental encouragement became even more important when in January

1960, Anna wrote that Darel had been referred to a rehabilitation and retraining program in the heart of the Shenandoah Valley, two hours by car southwest of their Lovettsville farm. He was assessed at the resident facility in March, then checked into it in early July.[3] Darel considered rehabilitation as merely a stopgap measure, for progress in manual training encouraged him to believe that he could eventually recover well enough to write and edit again. In rehabilitation he learned and refined manual skills which did not require the activity in the verbal centers of his damaged brain, finding renewed sense of purpose and direction in learning to build picture frames, upholster furniture. He positively fell in love with woodturning on a lathe.

Morgan's relationship with the McQuowns and their boarder Jerry Finnin was entirely different. By this time Tom and Madeline McQuown had hunted East Bay communities for a house they could afford for more than a decade. Madeline wanted a location closer to her doctors in Berkeley, but Jerry wanted a place of his own and Tom's salary from the Railway Mail Service alone was simply inadequate to buy without his contribution. Finally in March 1958 and after ten years of on-again, off-again efforts in the jungle of California real estate markets, the odd trio located a ranch-style house in Los Gatos, south of San Jose against the hills and directly east of Palo Alto.[4] Their move further south added a bit to Dale's occasional bus rides and to their drives north, but gave Madeline the backyard garden she craved at a price the three of them could afford.

After the move to Los Gatos, Dale and Madeline still exchanged letters frequently, sometimes twice weekly. Though she purged and destroyed most of Dale's letters to her, he saved her letters, filled with complaints of his lack of consideration for her feelings and circumstances, showing wide swings between an arch sense of independence and shuttered privacy, and expressing a fawning desire for his guidance and approval. Madeline alternately disliked Dale's directive suggestions about the way she handled serial installments of dire life-threatening health issues. Her responses suggest that his advice to her was as blunt as he provided to Joe Colgan and other close friends. She pled for understanding and openness even as she dismissed his efforts at both. As she never had a decade earlier, her letters now more often than not dismissed Morgan as callous and ignorant or insensitive, telling him what he was in ways she would never accept in reference to herself. "I had hoped that some of it could be done by mail," she wrote in the spring of 1960, "but you either feel great reluctance, or have no understanding of what I mean, or are so withdrawn in your struggles that you cannot talk to me." She mentioned a profound emotional development, noting that "This year has made a tremendous change in me—not in what I am, but in deepening what I am to almost intolerable depths."[5]

Madeline now began asserting that she existed at levels well beyond her closest friend's comprehension, dismissing or denigrating his attempts at understanding her and offering help. His responses may have been brusque (we don't know, for she destroyed most of his letters), but the few offers we know he made at least seem genuine. Conversely, letter after letter from her was filled with reasons that the Brigham Young biography remained incomplete though she dodged outright explaining why. With the benefit of hindsight, clearly the ties that had bound their relationship in the 1940s were slowly ravelling.

On a positive note, Madeline had introduced Morgan to the work of landscape painter LeConte Stewart, an artist from Kaysville, Utah. She had been one of Stewart's seventh-grade students during a brief period when the artist taught junior high school in Kaysville. While much of the fine art world of the 1950s was drinking the heady wine of Modernism, Stewart painted landscapes of the valleys and mountains of northern Utah. Morgan fell in love with Stewart's interpretive portrayals of Utah's seasons, rural reaches, and the hills of the Wasatch Range, a landscape of solid brick farmhouses, barns, fencerows, and open fields that was beginning to disappear under the urban sprawl of postwar America. Stewart was once quoted as saying that his art "cut a slice of contemporary life as it is in the highways and biways [sic] as I have found it."[6] His art presented not an idealized world and not an impression of it, but certainly a realistic, identifiable one. Stewart's style carried a visual nostalgia of the sort that appealed greatly to California-bound Dale Morgan. Stewart sold his own work through a small storefront in Kaysville, and Dale eventually bought dozens of oil paintings and pastels, giving many to family members yet keeping a score or more for himself. The Stewarts' oldest son, Maynard Dixon (Dick) Stewart, lived in California, where he painted and taught at San Jose State College. He and his family were close friends with Madeline, and Dale became a friend as well.

In the second week of January 1961, Darel McConkey pecked out a typewritten postholiday letter to Dale. It was about as much as aphasia would allow him to write now: "I appreciate how much you write about my letters. I hope they're some better, but one's brain can be very difficult to say things, or write, or read. My stomach hurts sometimes, to say things."[7] Dale was too busy with routine pressures to reply immediately, and without the benefit of foresight was unable to comprehend that he was holding his friend's last communication. Three weeks later Dale arrived home from work to find a telegram from Anna beneath his front door. Never, he wrote her the next day, had he opened a telegram with greater reluctance. He knew what news it must convey. The inevitable communication was short: "Darel died January 29 1961. Anna."

Pressing obligations of the moment evaporated as Dale stood in his doorway, the paper hanging limply in hand. He spent a sleepless night, grieving a second time in his life for the passing of his best friend. "Darel told us that he was not afraid to die," he wrote the new widow the next day, "he too prepared for what might happen, [but] the impact upon us is not any the less."[8] Anna wrote a few days later: "he loved you more than any man among his friends, and I'm more grateful than I can say that he had your friendship."[9] Dale had never been as close to Anna as he was to Darel, but his innate loyalty kept the pair in contact. They maintained a periodic correspondence through coming months and years, Dale offering counsel and encouragement as she sold the farm, moved back to the city with the younger children, and eventually took a clerical position with the United Planning Organization, one of the Great Society federal programs. For the rest of Dale's life he made a point to visit Anna McConkey on any trip to Washington, DC.[10]

* * * * *

Although Dale was now in employment squarely situated within academia, because of his appointment and his deafness Morgan operated only at the edges of broader changes happening in his field of American, and specifically, Western American history.

In *The Structure of Scientific Revolutions,* published at almost the same time as Morgan's Wagner Award was presented, Thomas Kuhn explained that the advance of knowledge within a scholarly field is neither sequential nor orderly. Instead, developments unfold in fits and starts, irregular and often competitive.[11] Today we might say the same thing using a term borrowed from business—*disruption.*

American history has had its encounters with disruption. Prior to Frederick Jackson Turner's "frontier thesis," scholars asserted the similarities of American and European institutions, emphasizing the evolutionary continuity from Europe to North America. Citing what later was described as *germ theory,* writers of the late nineteenth century concluded that American civilization was the mature end of a linear progression, the full flower sprung from seed sown in the medieval forests of Germany and Britain (where most of that generation earned their doctoral degrees, as well).

Turner's compelling 1893 essay, "The Significance of the Frontier in American History," claimed that the social necessity to shape and reshape institutions to fit the receding line between civilization and the continental wilderness to the west—the frontier—was the determining factor creating an entirely new and unique American civilization. Far from seeing continuity, Turner's *environmentalism* asserted that ever since settlement, the land west beyond city limits and county lines served as an outlet for the expansive social and economic pressures of American civilization. In other words, the presence of a continuously receding frontier had *defined* American civilization. The West *was* the national story.

Turner pointed out that as of the 1890 census, settlement density across the entire continental U.S. at two persons per square mile had finally exceeded the official definition of "unsettled"; in other words, for the first time in national history there was no longer an unpopulated "frontier." With the American West subdivided into geopolitical order and drawn fully into the Union, and with no areas of the continental U.S. statistically "unpopulated"—that is, without a frontier—Turner asked, what direction would national history take? What force would develop and maintain national character?[12]

Turner's conception of frontier became one of the first American perspectives of American national history, taking the country out of the arc of European influences and ideas. The U.S. was no longer simply an inheritor of European culture, but rather an original cultural entity shaped by its very environment. Turner's thesis was adopted widely and became the explanation of America for a generation, the "received wisdom" for those who were interested in the transmississippi reaches of American regionalism. The West was a place of flux. Most importantly, however, it was a factor that was now gone irretrievably. Turner's idea was a powerful one, shaping after 1900 a generation of scholars trained by Turner, particularly Herbert E. Bolton. As noted in an earlier chapter, interest in the history of the American West as a region distinct from the Eastern seaboard and Midwest, exploded in the late nineteenth and early twentieth centuries in a flurry of state and local historical societies and history publications. The first scholarly conference on the history of the American West was held in Boulder, Colorado, in 1929, attracting a young new generation of academics. Bolton delivered the keynote address.

By the early 1930s, however, the historiographic page was beginning to turn again. With the onset of the Depression, scholars began wondering whether the American West had ever been a land of golden opportunity. There were too many losers in it. Turner's "frontier thesis" was challenged and largely dismissed by this new generation. They were more interested in the robber barons of extractive industry, while other scholars tinged with Depression-fueled Marxism mocked Turner's heady ideas about culture as vacant, missing entirely the ground-level experience of those working in rail yards, farms, and cattle ranges. In 1945, Carlton J. H. Hayes delivered a presidential address to the American Historical Association titled "The American Frontier—Frontier of What?" Hayes was among the first to openly question Turner's frontier model.[13]

A few years after Hayes' address, in his introduction to Stegner's *Beyond the Hundredth Meridian*, Bernard DeVoto asserted that Turner's thesis was outright myth. It was myth in the sense of a founding story, yes, but also myth in the sense of being fundamentally false, one that artificially but very effectively set the American West *apart* from the national story. DeVoto saw the West's history as a national failure to reshape its cultural expectations to match geographic realities, rather than its institutions being shaped by its geography. There had been, he said, little success integrating the arid American West into the rest of the nation.[14]

On the heels of Stegner's book, University of Oregon historian Earl Pomeroy published a provocative article in the prestigious *Mississippi Valley Historical Review*, one of the chief journals of American history, arguing that the American West was treated too provincially by its chroniclers.[15] Perhaps Pomeroy's views came partly as a reaction to the release of Walt Disney's *Davy Crockett: King of the Wild Frontier* to theaters the same year of 1955, on top of the public fascination with the stylized cowboy culture of Gene Autry, Roy Rogers, and the Lone Ranger. That American West was (despite being utterly unrealistic) romantic and intensely individualistic, a place of personal risk and daring, cultural counterweights to the Soviet model of Cold War socialism.

* * * * *

Morgan didn't care much for the philosophical arguments fueling academic historians. He wanted to tell the story from the sources and get it right, whether the fur trade, or—sometime, hopefully sooner than later—where he started, with the Mormons. During the late 1950s the Latter-day Saints were finally welcomed from a position on the cultural periphery into the mainstream. They assimilated seamlessly with the descendants of other European forebears, like Irish and Italian and Polish in Eastern cities, into a white American middle class. Within a decade the church would begin an outward turn toward internationalism, but for the moment Mormons were content to be among the most American of Americans. The polemics of earlier generations were left conveniently behind as new LDS publishers like Bookcraft and the Nicholas G. Morgan Sr. Foundation catered works of inspirational storytelling by writers like Preston Nibley and E. Cecil McGavin.[16]

Morgan's long-held perspective, that Latter Day Saint history was more whitewash than it was pedestal, was shared rather more quietly by many contemporaries. Prominent rancher and later philanthropist Charles Redd observed to a correspondent that "altogether too much of our Mormon writing has been on the side of sheer extravagance. We'll never have a good history of the Mormon people . . . until someone can do it in a detached, down-to-earth fashion. But," Redd qualified, "I want that historian to have the same feeling and affection for the people and their effort as you and I have." Against this backdrop, Bill Mulder presented one of the first public scholarly presentations on Latter-day Saints history in the University of Utah's annual faculty lecture.[17]

A bit later, the turn toward scholarly detachment happening outside the culture was exemplified in a 1959 observation made by Marvin Hill, a professor of American history at Brigham Young University. Hill's comment was the first scholarly treatment of Latter Day Saint historiography, published two years after Redd's private admonition. Hill concluded that Mormonism's historiography "has been plagued by too much emotion, too much description and too little interpretation," and that "most of it has been written from too narrow a base [of evidence]."[18] Hill stated formally and academically what Dale Morgan asserted privately with little success more than a decade earlier, a viewpoint that also fueled Charles Redd. The generation who would fulfill Redd's wish were either rising or already beginning their work.

From Washington, DC, in June 1952, Morgan responded to a query by a young LDS scholar in the University of North Carolina's economics doctoral program who was then teaching at Utah State Agricultural College. He sent for comment a manuscript on the law of consecration and history of early Latter Day Saint tithing practice. "Reluctant though you may be to face up to it," Dale wrote Leonard J. Arrington in response, "you had better reconcile yourself to the fact that you are a historian." He praised Arrington for "the quality that for me has been so painfully lacking in scholars who have concerned themselves with the Mormon scene, intellectual curiosity combined with enough energy to take that curiosity where it sees the need to go." Arrington wrote back in thanks: "I wish I knew you well enough to call you Dale." The response offered Morgan an opening which the latter left swinging like an unlatched door, still wary of Mormondom's church-affiliated writers in general. A month later, after Arrington displayed a degree of historical objectivity in correcting a few interpretive errors on the strength of better research, Morgan warmed up to the budding scholar, who later in life would define the revision of history among the Latter-day Saints.[19]

Arrington was one of the Latter-day Saint veterans of the Second World War who used their GI Bill benefits toward graduate study. These veterans encountered other students working on a thesis, dissertation, or article in the Church Historian's Office, creating a network of acquaintances. Familiarity generated invitations to the Mormon Seminar and became the basis for more formal activity a decade in the future. During Morgan's time in the Historian's Office, he was allowed almost no access to manuscript sources. This new generation had somewhat better success in seeing documents.

The familiarity among Arrington and his Mormon academic contemporaries underscores how alone Morgan was as he planned and struggled toward completing his "Mormon book." He had effectively left Latter Day Saint studies just as the field was beginning to emerge. He never pursued graduate study. He never participated in the Mormon Seminar, despite repeated invitations. The Seminar ceased meeting regularly in 1955, effectively disbanding as an informal professional conference, but a few participating couples continued meeting informally in what they dubbed the "Monday Nighters." Nevertheless, the Seminar's rise and demise both raised awareness and provided perceptional space for the eventual organization of a more formal, academically reputable, and hopefully more stable organization.

A year after the Mormon Seminar ceased its meetings, Utah State University history professor S. George Ellsworth circulated a questionnaire to LDS scholars—not merely in Utah but across the country—assessing interest in formally organizing some sort of meeting for discussing

Latter-day Saint topics. On the heels of Ellsworth's survey, Arrington wrote to those he knew among academic historians and those with related interests in other fields. Among other recommendations, Arrington suggested to his colleagues that Latter-day Saint studies really needed a formal department or think-tank on Latter-day Saint history at BYU, as well as to organize some form of a professional organization as a vehicle for annual meetings in the subject.[20] A nod toward formalizing Latter-day Saint studies got a boost as early as 1960, when BYU President Ernest L. Wilkinson's assistant, John Bernhard, wrote Arrington with a proposal that the economics professor come to "the Y" to initiate an "Institute of Mormon Studies."[21] Arrington was disinterested in leaving Utah State University but advised Wilkinson on the possible structure and personnel needed. The "Institute" was never established, but Latter Day Saint history was changing anyway, just like the rest of academic scholarship.

* * * * *

Another development within academic history was reflected in an explosion of scholarly journals and academic-field associations. "The boom in post-war funding for research," according to scholars Aileen Fyfe and Anna Gielas, "enabled the development of the commercially successful, internationally oriented journal-publishing industry that would come to dominate late 20th-century science (and academia)."[22] The Latter-day Saints were included as scholarly attention broadened. Though Morgan, Brooks, and others had blazed a new trail into scholarship two decades earlier, the earliest commonly read academic studies were released within a decade after the end of the war. Among the churches, however, studied non-comment was the tack taken at publication of one of the first intentionally scholarly treatments of the saints, Thomas F. O'Dea's *The Mormons* (University of Chicago Press, 1957).[23]

Scholarship in the humanities itself also was transforming. Prior to the Second World War the scholarly hallmark of peer review was commonly limited to scientific publications. After the war, though the movement was slow, the social sciences and humanities adopted peer review as a basis for publishability within their own expanding list of journals. As the number of historical publications increased and their nature evolved, readers changed as well. Over the coming decades academic writers generally gravitated toward peer-reviewed scholarly journals and away from the state historical publications and magazines that previously had been an important base for scholarship.

Paralleling the growth of academic journals was the expansive growth of scholarly organizations and their conferences, and in this Dale Morgan participated.[24] Dale agreed to present a paper on the importance of overland journals at the Conference on the History of Western America in Santa Fe, New Mexico, in mid-October 1961. Dale had never been to a conference and planned to read the paper himself. Bob Burke, Dale's coworker at the Bancroft, persuaded Dale to make a sound check in the empty banquet room the next evening. Dale's vocal delivery in a flat, high monotone and his slurred pronunciations did not come through the microphone or speakers adequately, so Burke agreed to read the piece for him. In Santa Fe, Dale certainly met for the first time many people with whom he had corresponded, but unable to hear the spoken presentations, the scrum of dinner-table conversations and receptions must have been wearying and difficult to follow. Conversation in groups of more than two or three other people always frustrated him.[25] "Once, for a frolic," he later wrote his mother about conference attendance, "but that's enough of these conferences for me."[26]

The 1961 "Santa Fe conference" in which Morgan participated represents a watershed in western American historiography. The overwhelming response—organizers planned optimistically for ninety participants and got three hundred—confirmed that the American West was a viable subject for academic scholars as well as avocational buffs. It also marked an intellectual resurgence in Turner's historical model.

In the introduction to the published conference proceedings, Ray Billington summarized the broad scholarly trends in Western historiography, beginning with the "germ theory" and ending with the present day. Since the 1929 conference, Billington pointed out, two streams of thought were informing Western historiography. One was the contextual, interpretive approach of academia, where once again Turner's frontier model was being picked up and dusted off, his grand ideas both supplemented and challenged by the rising generation of trained and credentialed historians. Billington pointed to Oscar O. Winther's bibliography of American Western writing and scholarship as evidence. The first edition, published in 1942, cited 3,500 periodical articles about the American West published between 1811 and 1938; a second edition, extending the inclusive date to 1957 and published the same year as the Santa Fe conference, cataloged more than 9,000. Clearly the Transmississippi West was becoming an academic field on its own.[27]

And yet, the conference marked the turn of another historiographic page. Billington also damned with faint praise the second strain of Western Americana study, the "legion of antiquarians, popular writers, and dedicated probers of the past's minutiae" who burdened publishers with ever more detailed studies of what academics had begun to view as the hopelessly romantic and popular "antique West" of cowboys and cattlemen, gold miners, fur trappers, and westering pioneers. In arguing the existence of separate approaches, and whether intentionally or unwittingly, Billington drew a line across his field separating the popular and the academic. Along this line the literature, the writers, the credentials, and eventually the scholarly discipline would divide.

CHAPTER 16

"Struggling to Get My Disordered Life Back Under Control"[1]

Bancroft Library, Berkeley, 1964–1965

There is no more miserable way of life than publishing books, especially when they stack up on you.[2]

—Dale Morgan

THROUGHOUT 1963 DALE MORGAN'S attention was distracted from virtually everything other than the 1820s fur trade, 1846 overland travel, and Bancroft manuscript descriptions. Shortly after the new year, while Dale began planning his activities for 1964, other minds were mulling over his future. One afternoon, George Hammond summoned Dale out of the library to his faculty office in Dwinelle Hall, relaying confidentially that he planned to retire the following year. Hammond had brought Morgan to the Bancroft and worked hard to keep him there, but his retirement raised questions about Morgan's functions and employment status. Prior to announcing his retirement, Hammond and Bancroft Associate Director Robert Becker privately discussed rewriting Dale's job description to make his position into more than just an informal assistant. If Morgan was to have real job security after Hammond's departure, it would take time to get the request drafted and approvals secured through the University of California bureaucracy.[3]

In the first week of February, Paul Cracroft of the University of Utah wrote Dale with an invitation to his alma mater's 1964 Founders' Day celebrations; Morgan had been selected as the year's Distinguished Alumnus. Dale was publicly bemused but privately quite pleased. This was not quite one of the awards in which he typically put little confidence, though he replied that he would be unable to get away from business to receive the honor in person. He also had a practical motive for declining to attend: his declining speaking ability. With few exceptions he had given up addressing historical conferences in person, as his own monotone, complicated by microphone pickup and speaker amplification in a large space, made understanding his speaking voice virtually impossible. The less he used his voice in public the more he lost control over its quality, volume, timbre, and diction. He was finding it harder and harder to be understood clearly by strangers. Dale asked his mother to attend the University of Utah event in his stead and sent her the text of a speech for the occasion.

Although by this time the Utah State Historical Society had given up attempting to lure Dale Morgan home to Utah, the Wasatch Front's one last attempt came later that spring. The size of the University of Utah had tripled since Dale Morgan first attended as a student three decades earlier. Little more than a regional college back then, despite its name, the institution now swelled with postwar investment. The administration was intentionally positioning resources to develop the school into a research institution. In 1960, a major gift from hotel magnate J. Willard Marriott became a lead gift toward construction of both a new library and a suitable collection to fill it. The new library director, Ralph D. Thomson, wrote one of the university's notable alumni mentioning that plans were being laid to establish a Western Americana research collection. He was looking for advice. Thomson dangled the lure in front of Morgan, noting that the institution would love to have "someone like you come to the Library," but by 1964 Morgan was no longer tempted by an opportunity to return to the Wasatch Front.[4] He was no longer really a Utahn, and while he still refused to consider himself a Californian, his career was now largely defined by that state and by the larger West.

Other matters in his life and relationships were straining. After a trip to Albuquerque on a late-breaking Navajo legal matter in April, Dale caught a flight to Salt Lake City specifically to visit Madeline McQuown, who had left San Jose to become a Holy Cross Hospital (now Salt Lake Regional Medical Center) patient yet again. She lay in bed weakly, pleading that she was too ill to carry on much of a conversation during his visit, expressing the latest installment of ennui, loneliness, and boredom. Her insightful criticism and intellectual rigor—forces that attracted him and had formed the basis of their friendship twenty-five years earlier—were wilting. Their relationship was straining. Dale could not understand her need to be constantly cared for nor her seeming unwillingness or inability to take any positive step to remedy matters; she accused him of utterly misunderstanding what was actually going on around him. "One trouble about communicating with me is that you never *ask* me a question; you tell me the *answers*," she complained, which was very likely true.[5]

Madeline's observation seems to have been more than just a complaint about Dale's inability to draw conclusions and understanding in routine verbal discussion, which was unquestionably part of the problem. Consigned by deafness to observe and analyze in order to make sense of the world streaming around him, Morgan's flaw as a friend may have grown out of his own coping mechanism: his straightforward analyses of circumstances created in him a tendency to dictate resolutions to others' perceived problems. Madeline snapped at him once that "it never occurs to you that forbearance is needed in a relationship with you, just as with everyone else."[6] His diagnoses tended to be rational, self-contained, and brusque, leaving little room for others to make choices: *Here is the problem you face. Here is a solution. Do it.* Dale never could figure out why Joe Colgan kept trying to fix needy women, or why Madeline could not just work systematically to complete her Brigham Young biography.

As critical of Madeline's serial illnesses and perpetual neediness as he might have been, her letters conversely were becoming ever more strident and critical of his concern and effort to help. It may be reading in too much, but she seems to have resented Morgan's growing professional success and stability even while she praised it. Dale still defended her stridently, even to his mother Emily, and his relationship with Madeline remained a point of unusual contention between them. Emily deferred to her oldest son when it came to Madeline, but "To me she will always be the same selfish, rude person I have always met and tried to be nice to . . . [and I] don't feel I am as narrow minded as you suggest."[7]

The turn of December 1964 brought the usual flurry of holiday cards and birthday greetings from friends. Juanita Brooks, whose reputation was rising quickly enough in Utah to eclipse her mentor, complained of "a barren, wasted year" for herself but praised Dale's recent books. "Alone and single-handed you do more than all the other historians of the state combined," she wrote.[8] Life had drawn him far from the friends of Salt Lake City and Latter-day Saint history. Fawn Brodie acknowledged the distance that had crept into their friendship. "Do write," she noted with some wistfulness, "We never get a letter from you anymore."[9] She was right. Consumed with the Bancroft's publication program and collection development, and in chronic arrears from his personal writing projects, Dale rarely corresponded with his oldest friends. He remained in contact

with Marguerite Reusser only because he paid her as a typist and tran-
scriptionist. Other than an annual lunch with grade school chum Ab
Heiner, now working for Kaiser Steel, Dale saw Utah friends almost not
at all. Correspondence continued unabated but now focused more on
Bancroft contacts and California friendships, such as rare free weekends
spent with the Melvin family. Otherwise, Morgan's free time consisted of
a steady diet of writing or research to inform writing. His time and attention "belonged to everybody but myself." This reality was, he confided
separately to George Hammond at about the same time, "one reason I
have done absolutely nothing about either my large Mormon history or
my large narrative history of the fur trade."[10]

On December 18, 1964, Dale passed his fiftieth birthday, musing to
George Hammond that the event brought him to an age twice that of his
father at his death. The occasion awakened a spirit of self-reflection on
the generational changes that had broadened and fragmented the small,
safe world of his youth among a tight-knit family. "What takes the place
of our rare summer visits to Saltair and Lagoon," he asked his mother and
sister rhetorically, "or the family picnics in Liberty Park, or the jaunts to
Wasatch? Or the intermixing of cousins that always went on at Christmas
and other holiday seasons."[11] Dale was feeling for the first time twinges of
personal nostalgia. The swell of reverie that colored his letters to his family
was reflected in comments to Edgar Carter in Los Angeles, once again putting off an untouched biography of his father William H. Carter, another
of the many projects to which Dale had committed himself, in this case,
as long ago as 1954. "I have the sense always of living on borrowed time—
and in this I must contrive to live a little too, beyond existing as a writing
machine. I have not done enough of that in the past."[12]

* * * * *

One relief to his workload seemed to be coming sooner rather than later—
conclusion of the retainer for his research assistance with the Navajos'
legal cases. In its place he needed another paying project that would be
just as stable, whether or not it was quite as remunerative. In early January the opportunity was handed to him. Everett Graff came for a visit on
behalf of Chicago-based R. R. Donnelley & Sons, one of the largest book-
printing companies in the country. Through its private Lakeside Press
imprint the firm produced an edited Lakeside Classics volume of Americana as a Christmas gift for its employees and business associates. Graff

knew Donnelley's executives well. Just after Dale had started at Bancroft in 1954, Graff offered to introduce him, and Graff and Wright Howes periodically encouraged the firm's interest in Morgan.[13] In 1957 the series' longtime editor (and Morgan's series editor for *Great Salt Lake*), Milo Quaife, retired from the series shortly before his death. Quaife planned and delivered Lakeside Classics content years in advance. Despite his retirement Quaife's foresight left the firm breathing room to find just the right new editor. Graff stepped up his lobbying for Morgan. At Graff's prompting and with his support, Dale wrote to Donnelley Advertising Manager Harry J. Owens, who was very interested in the practical credentials Dale offered.

Despite the tidal changes in American publishing isolated pockets of tradition remained that produced an income from writing history. In terms of actual work the position would be a dream job for Dale, limited to identifying and recommending books for the Lakeside Classics series, and then editing, composing a decent introduction, and historical notes. Donnelley would pay all expenses, as well as a commission for the work on delivery of a finished text, a sum that represented better than a month's salary at Morgan's pay scale. The opportunity was, quite simply, the kind of sinecure Morgan craved, a stable income that could go a long way toward subsidizing a full-time career as a nonfiction writer.[14]

Early in 1963 Harry J. Owens, the corporate officer in charge of the Lakeside Press, began directly courting Morgan. Late that same year, taking time away from Ashley and his 1846 books, Morgan informally proposed, and the company accepted a title for Christmas 1965, Harriet E. Bishop McConkey's *Dakota War Whoop,* a memoir of the 1862–1863 "Sioux War" in Minnesota.

With Quaife as a model, Donnelley evidently felt no rush to get Morgan involved or start him on the first book needing his attention. Owens wrote confidently that "Our search work [for the Lakeside volume] has been extended farther and farther into the future. This makes it easier on the editor, and easier on our production people." The executive could afford expansive generosity with time—he had not yet wrested a manuscript from Dale Morgan.[15] Ignoring the Donnelley commissions in 1963 to complete *Ashley* and *Overland in 1846* consumed the time cushion afforded by the final volumes Milo Quaife had left completed. Still Dale's choice to delay work on his first commissioned Lakeside Classic for other projects pushed the research and editing process uncomfortably close to the publication year—normal for him but concerning for yet another publisher, who late in 1963 asked Morgan about the books for 1966 and 1967.[16]

The West of William H. Ashley and *Overland in 1846* were resigned to the shelf early in 1964, and Morgan wrote Owens confirming that he was beginning editorial work on the McConkey volume, but he felt that he needed to see the Minnesota ground himself to do an adequate job as editor. In the second week of January, Donnelley formally accepted Morgan's 1965 book proposal and informally his editorship, probably assuming he had completed his part of the work. Owens also confirmed the title for 1966 would be Laura Fish Judd's *Honolulu* unless a suitable title from Alaska's history was discovered. Dale wrote Everett Graff in Chicago with news that he would likely be coming to town, adding: "I am slowly clearing away the backlog, and I may be able to direct my attention to my Mormon bibliography before long. But there are still a half dozen books in different stages of completion."[17]

Morgan slated a circuitous itinerary for his research trip from mid-April through mid-May: Salt Lake City, to surprise his mother on her seventieth birthday; Denver, to see Lucie Howe and Fred Rosenstock; Chicago, for conferences with Donnelley staff; Minneapolis, to visit locations of the Sioux war; New York City to meet with Knopf and his staff about the Lorton diary (before whom he also dangled the idea for a one-volume fur trade history), to see the Eberstadts, and to escort Emily, who flew out for this part of the trip, through the World's Fair; Omaha, Nebraska, to visit the Joslyn Art Museum to see the Alfred Jacob Miller watercolors of the fur trade and art by Karl Bodmer commissioned by Prince Maximilian zu Wied-Neuwied for his Missouri River expedition. The trip also involved an inevitable stop in Washington, DC. There, besides lunch with Anna McConkey and dinner with former assistant Naomi Peres and husband Tobe, Dale made a side trip to the east shore of Chesapeake Bay to visit friends from OPA days, Max and Louise North. Max North's inability to travel was the motivation for Dale's side trip. Six months earlier physicians had discovered Max's cancer. Dale spent a pleasant weekend with his old friends and their two daughters.

Dale arrived back in Berkeley from his month-long eastward excursion on June 1, 1964. "My apartment is a mess, so is my desk at Bancroft," he confessed to an acquaintance, "and so is my mind."[18] Dale returned to work in time for the university's announcement of A. Hunter Dupree as George Hammond's replacement in the Bancroft Library directorship, effective at Hammond's retirement in June 1965. Dupree was another

History Department member, though a historian of science—not a field of study associated with the Bancroft Library's topical strengths, Dale observed quietly to a distant friend. By then, the administrative proposal of Hammond and Burke bore fruit. A memo arrived on Dale's desk noting his promotion from Editor III, a staff appointment, to Associate Specialist II, which was technically an academic (but not faculty) appointment.[19]

Despite the promotion, Morgan's new appointment was only a partial victory. It involved a pay raise but no formal resolution about his professional standing in terms of leave policy. Unwilling to push too much more after the promotion, Dale wrote his mother some time later that "I shall have to wait for some dust to settle to find out exactly what this means and what my academic (as distinguished from nonacademic) prerogatives may be."[20] The university bureaucracy immediately regretted approving his change in standing and eventually went to the librarians' advisory council seeking to reverse the action on a policy basis. With one of their number finally ascending to at least partial faculty status, the librarians flatly rejected the proposed reversal.[21] Unfortunately for Morgan, the change in status was never adequately defined, the opportunity was lost, and the failure to do so opened the first crack in Morgan's allegiance to his employer.

* * * * *

Despite having lost an editorial year to other commitments, in March 1965, Tek Osborn, Morgan's production contact for the Lakeside Classics, began asking for the manuscript to commence typesetting for the volume so as to be ready in time for its pre-Christmas release. Dale forwarded a photocopy of Harriet McConkey's original 1865 edition marked with his strikeouts so that typesetting could begin. Dale had worked hard and long enough, and Osborne had pled and cajoled often enough, that a manuscript had been delivered—in batches, of course—and could go to press. Even at the end of March, however, nine months ahead of its release date, *Dakota War Whoop* was late. Unlike Talisman or Rosenstock, the Lakeside Classics had a much less sympathetic or accommodating publisher. The exchange between Morgan and Osborn proved to be but the first time, not the only time, in Morgan's short editorial tenure that Donnelley staff pressured him to hold to the annual production schedule.

Barely a month later, arriving home from a trip to Salt Lake City in April 1965, Dale found a reminder notice about the 1966 volume on Hawaii, which required him to travel for site research within the current year in order to deliver a manuscript on schedule. Dale did not get away to Hawaii for research until late the following February 1966, the year in which the book was due to be published. Donnelley's management had made connections for him across the island. He met with descendants of the Judd family, spent time in several local libraries, and toured the islands. Once again he returned to California ready to begin just as Tek Osborn began chafing him about a final delivery date for the manuscript.[22]

It was a good thing that the Donnelly production editor got in line early, for on the same day and after a decade of effort with Eleanor Harris, Dale signed a publication contract for the William Marshall Anderson diaries. Angus Cameron, however, was handed yet another IOU for the Lorton book. "I must say," the New York editor wrote Morgan with a bit of pique, "that I'm in a little bit of an embarrassment with one postponement after another to explain to my colleagues." Cameron could have noted that Alfred A. Knopf had already waited through two contracts and a seemingly endless litany of delays and postponements.[23]

The back-to-back rushes on the McConkey and Judd books finally persuaded Morgan that he needed to allow the comparatively short volumes more of his time. For the third Lakeside book, this one on the Yukon gold rush, Morgan planned a late-summer 1966 research trip, well ahead of a self-imposed manuscript due date in December.[24] As it was, the two-and-a-half-week Yukon trip was an ordeal. In July, Morgan flew to Juneau via Seattle, took a ferry to the historic Klondike departure point at Skagway and crossed the White Pass to Whitehorse on the Yukon Railway. From there, the site trip to Dawson City required a 360-mile bus ride out and another one back. Unlike his palatial experience in Hawaii the previous spring, the subarctic was still isolated and Spartan, its roads unpaved and its accommodations comparatively meager.[25]

Scheduling his site research a full year and a half ahead of publication meant that Dale, at least for the time being, was finally following something like a customary production schedule. Unfortunately, he missed the self-imposed December deadline for the Klondike manuscript, and in late January 1967 he wrote apologetically to Tek Osborn in Chicago that it was coming soon. After three more months of delays he pledged to personally deliver the notes on a trip to Chicago and did so on April 4, asking about plans for the following year. This time Osborn wrote coolly that Morgan need not bother, adding that no decision about a Lakeside title had yet been made for 1968 season "and until this is done we cannot make a definite commitment on editorship."[26] Dale missed Osborn's unstated implication, dribbling in various corrections on the introduction for another month. At the end of April and though he was officially retired, Harry J. Owens informed Dale that Donnelley planned to take its annual Lakeside Classics series in a different direction and had appointed Paul Angle of the Newberry Library as the series editor.[27] As late as August Donnelley staff had to remind Dale pointedly that he had yet submitted neither the introduction nor index to the Lynch book.[28]

Had Dale read between the lines he would have noticed he had been fired as editor for the Lakeside Classics. Without directly saying so, the company officers—who ran their international printing concern as a tight, methodical business—had communicated that Morgan's repeated inability to meet clear deadlines had compromised his reputation with them. The loss of the Chicago editorship cut off part of the income stream he had planned to depend upon in financing an early retirement. He took the loss philosophically. "If I have to go on working beyond that time, well, nothing is lost," he wrote Emily Morgan with a literary shrug.[29]

Perhaps Morgan's writing habits were suited more to windfall opportunities than to systemic ones. No matter how much he coveted external writing commissions, they required individual investments of time and effort, but Dale Morgan's approach to research and writing did not change much. His writing habits suited Bob Baughman's intense *Kansas in Maps* project; they served him much less well when dealing with the hard schedule required to produce the Lakeside Classics.

* * * * *

In March 1965, while working after-hours on the Lakeside books and in his day job as the publication arm of the Bancroft Library, Dale was completing the first draft of descriptive material that would become the calendar to the recently acquired Charles M. Weber papers. He was also discretely collecting and editing the essays that would be George Hammond's retirement *Festschrift* when a staff member appeared at his desk to relay an urgent, mid-day telephone call from Dale's youngest brother, Bob. Emily Morgan was in the hospital following what appeared to be a stroke. Dale dashed off a note to his aunt Ida Holmes, who lived in nearby Walnut Creek, as he bolted for Salt Lake City. Over succeeding days Emily Morgan's condition deteriorated, causing paralysis on her right side and descent into a coma.[30] Worse, the stroke complicated treatment of her diabetes. Dale remained with his family for a bit longer than a week, sitting with his mother through the afternoons and evenings, working on book galleys from his brother's kitchen table as he found time in the morning. Emily reemerged and recovered slowly. The previously handwritten letters to her eldest son after her stroke were thereafter painstakingly written out in block letters. By August she was confident enough to begin handwriting again, but the result was laborious, like the papers of the grade-school children she had taught for years.

His mother's emergency was not the only personal blow that spring. During the last week of May, Dale received an unexpected letter from Louise North. She let him know that Max had succumbed to cancer a few short weeks after Dale's visit the previous year. Once Morgan recovered from the immediate shock of losing another close friend, Louise's news set their long-term friendship on a different footing, freeing Morgan to begin giving her openly the affection that he seems to have harbored privately since they met in the early 1940s.[31] Morgan was confident enough in their relationship to suggest to Louise within a few months of her news that she break cleanly with her past and move herself and the girls to California, where he could care for them more directly, effectively proposing marriage to his longtime friend. Like most of his personal correspondence, the letter does not survive to confirm how directly he put it.

Louise responded that she liked the idea, but even after a year she was not yet prepared to embark on another marriage, though she invited him to visit her and the family. Dale was as close to ecstatic as he ever became. "If things continue as hopefully as they have begun at long range I might be able to go after the three of them at the end of August," he confided to the Wheats with characteristically unrealistic optimism, "Maybe Louise will not be able to make the adjustment at all, but I must find out."[32]

As he juggled commitments, Dale managed to free time in April for the Kaiser Permanente clinic to run the battery of tests required by his health insurance coverage. The results, he reported to his recovering mother, were "all normal."[33] In June, however, Dale's personal physician decided otherwise, noting a potential health concern that had come up in a more careful review the laboratory work: "one of your laboratory tests indicated the possibility of diabetes."[34] The doctor recommended Morgan schedule a day for a glucose-tolerance test to confirm or dismiss the possibility. In late August, Dale finally set aside his usual crush of writing and received medical confirmation that he was a Type II diabetic, but the doctor assured him that his condition was rather mild and could be controlled largely by diet. Because of this early diagnosis, Morgan was recruited to participate in a long-term clinical study of early-stage diabetes being conducted by the Kaiser Foundation Research Institute's diabetic research program.[35]

Susceptibility to diabetes has since been linked strongly to family genetics, but in 1965 modern biomedical research was still a comparatively young field. The genetic factor was not yet understood, nor was diabetes then recognized as a biological mask to liver dysfunction, a potentially more serious condition. In fact, cancer research conducted decades later correlates an increased risk of colorectal cancer in individuals with Type II diabetes, such as Morgan had developed. A month later he could report to a friend of his medical ordeal that "except for some bowel griping, I seem reasonably back to normal."[36]

* * * * *

Dale busied himself through the summer of 1965 with Hammond's retirement preliminaries, page proofs for his first Lakeside Classics volume, plans for a long-delayed trip to see Hudson's Bay Company archival records in Ottawa, and furious work to complete the Weber collection inventory. For reasons internal to the university, the book had to be completed prior to Hammond's retirement. Dale also planned a detour to Washington, DC, on the Ottawa trip, to see Louise's family and assess his standing with her. "The thing is balanced on a knife edge," he confided to Carl and Helen Wheat, "watching Max die left deep scars, and their home in Accokeek is not just a home but a way of life."[37]

Dale flew out of San Francisco on the first leg of his midsummer trip on June 18. Louise and her two daughters met him at the airport. After dinner in the city the quartet drove along the Potomac River to the North home directly across the river from Mount Vernon. Dale stayed for a week. While Louise worked and the girls were at school, Dale remained at the house correcting the Lakeside proofs and puttering around doing odd jobs for his hostess. He proposed formally to Louise before continuing on to New York City. She said only that she would think about it, but Dale left with hope and a dinner appointment scheduled for his return trip from Ottawa.

Morgan continued first to New York to meet with Knopf's Angus Cameron about rescheduling the Lorton contract (yes, he was confident a manuscript could be done and delivered by November). Then in Ottawa, he spent two weeks with his head buried in microfilm readers at the Public

Archives of Canada, combing Hudson's Bay Company records for half a dozen pending and future writing projects. The trip was a tremendously fruitful one, marred (quite literally) only by a gash on his forehead sustained in a vertigo-induced fall on the Archives' staircase.[38]

Dale returned to Washington in the second week of July, expectantly meeting Louise for dinner—and to receive her demurrer on his proposal. Still aching from Max's agonized passing, she was not ready for such change. Disappointed, Dale proceeded to Chicago, which provided the opportunity to report to Donnelley, to confirm proofs on the McConkey book, and to resolve questions from frantic letters that chased him across the eastern U.S. and Canada. Morgan was home on Benvenue Avenue on July 18, tired, but mostly disappointed and yet fanning a small spark of inextinguishable hope. He confided to Helen Kennedy and the Wheats that he had been as successful as could be reasonably hoped for: "the most Louise would agree to was a sort of engaged-to-be-engaged arrangement, saying she would make no promises."[39] Part of that complication was imposed by mere distance. "It would be far simpler if she were in the same town, or even in the same state, with me, and if a life with me didn't involve turning her past life inside out," he told his mother candidly.[40]

* * * * *

George Hammond's retirement and A. Hunter Dupree's succession as Bancroft Library director was affected in the early summer of 1965 while Morgan was in the East. Dale returned to work to find that the new director's freshly employed secretaries did not know who he was. He also returned to find Dr. Markell's letters about his possible diabetes and tracked through the notices to discover that he had missed his rescheduled appointment through a clerical error. Another glucose tolerance test confirmed the diabetes diagnosis and Morgan's diet changed immediately, causing him to fret irritably about the inadequacies of Sucaryl over sugar as a sweetener, "which makes my coffee taste like powdered bone."[41]

Madeline wrote begging a favor in late August. She and Tom were struggling financially after a heart attack forced his retirement from the Postal Service. To qualify for unemployment herself, she needed to demonstrate her work record. Since Madeline had not drawn a paycheck of any sort since her brief stint at the WPA in 1941, she pleaded with Morgan that he confirm a "white lie" that she had been working privately for him. Dale improved on the opportunity, responding with a formal job offer that would turn his periodic gifts into a genuine income stream, a plan he felt was perfectly adapted to her ceaseless health concerns. For an open-ended amount of time he would employ her formally as a research assistant, paying $300 a month for her to check material against details in his checklist of printed works on Mormonism. He would handle all the tax arrangements and applied for a federal employer tax number to ensure her taxes were paid properly. "I'd like you to have a degree of financial independence, and this is one aspect of it," he wrote his oldest friend. Dale encouraged her to bring along the Brigham Young biography manuscript as they worked.[42]

Dale's offer finally cornered Madeline. Despite complaints and protests, and except for the few months she had worked for the Utah Writers' Project in 1941, she had never held or sought regular employment, but this time she did not have a sound reason to decline her friend's generosity. Over the next month she deflected the offer as effectively and from as many directions as she could by asserting the burdens it would impose and attacking his presumptions: she was too ill to work regularly; Dale always failed to appreciate her delicate condition; he was cruel to play psychological games about her obvious disability; the offer required too much travel. Despite at least one face-to-face conversation, negotiation and compromise could not resolve her protests. In fact, the offer strained relations between them. "I think I may be rather longer on guts than you are, if it comes to that," she snapped at Dale in mid-October, "for you are more concerned with your own security than with anything else in the world."[43] Their friendship had always been stormy, bordering on codependent, but the exchange seemed to have opened the final crack that would rupture permanently two years later.

For years Madeline had asserted that she wanted discussion rather than instruction from Dale Morgan, but as her needs changed she waffled over needing direction rather than simply support. For his part, Morgan trusted that his detached observations allowed him an objective view of her problems. He never seemed to have understood that his self-directed study and detachment as an amateur psychologist often came across as arrogant, indulgent, or disinterestedly analytical. He wanted her to have an opportunity to stand firmly on her own reputation and brilliance; she wanted to be coddled without accountability. To Morgan, Madeline faced paths she merely needed to see clearly in order to act; to her, his generosity was alternately smothering, domineering, and neglectful. It did not help that she vacillated between wanting emotional companionship and an alternate decision-maker who would absolve her of responsibility for shortfalls. She was above all, a survivor, willing to do or be nearly anything necessary to sustain her comforts and indulge her neuroses. Having others make decisions allowed her to claim credit for her heroic efforts when things worked out, and to deflect criticism when she changed her mind or failed to complete obligations. The cables of mutual respect that had bound them together for so long were now worn and fraying.

Tensions between himself and one of his oldest friends were not the only strong undercurrents against which Dale swam. Though as late as October 1965 Morgan observed confidentially that the new Bancroft director's presence in the library had "scarcely registered."[44] At the announcement of Hunter's appointment, Dale told Eleanor Harris confidentially that the new director's lack of expertise in fields for which the Bancroft was noted "may heighten my own value to the Bancroft, for with GPH's departure, I will be the only person around the place with national stature."[45]

Morgan's observation was perfectly true but the hope it expressed did not last long. By January 1966, although Dupree had been at the helm for six months, Dale reported quietly to George Hammond (teaching on a Fulbright fellowship in Spain) that he had interacted with the new director on library business just that week for only the third time. No new acquisitions or funding could be documented. Tensions were rising between Dupree and key members of the staff. Dupree imposed rules and regulations but was reluctant to commit directives to writing. He also ignored the recommendations of his assistants in hiring decisions. Morgan had functioned as Hammond's factotum outside of the library's official structure, his "man Friday" to whom the director turned for assessments of prospective acquisitions for the collection, who drafted speeches and letters, who acted as liaison with the Friends of The Bancroft Library, and who handled the publications program. Other than confidentially confirming facts and rumors simmering among the staff, Morgan held himself aloof from an escalating conflict and increasingly personal confrontations. Whispered rumors eddied between American Historical Association attendees that Dupree would step down to return to full-time teaching—a common cover for the academic equivalent of a dismissal.

By mid-January 1967 interactions between the director and library staff entered freefall. Reprimands for routine leave requests or personal use of telephones exploded into shouting matches. Suspicions grew on both sides. The director finally insisted on reading and approving every letter or memo written by the staff to an entity outside the library, resulting in long approval delays. Morgan told his mother that by the end of January "I am almost the only member of the senior staff on speaking terms with him, and that only because I don't have much to do with him."[46] After another week of desperate intrigue, Dupree resigned his appointment, citing an obligation to a National Science Foundation grant and an inability to adequately balance an administrative appointment with research obligations. The embattled director agreed to remain in place, an isolated lame duck, until a successor was named.[47]

The university began casting about for Dupree's replacement, seeking input from many directions, hoping to avoid a repeat of the wreck that had attended the straightforward appointment made by the chancellor. James D. Hart was mentioned, a UC professor of English and former interim director. Even considering Hart upset the History Department faculty, which still tended to look upon the Bancroft Library as their private sinecure. A month after Dupree's resignation, Chancellor Edward W. Strong asked UC Librarian Donald Coney to act as the nominal head of the Bancroft, with assistant director Bob Becker to have functional management of the library.[48]

The unpopular former library director might no longer have had effective charge of the Bancroft Library, but in returning to a faculty office in Dwinelle Hall, any comment made there about the library went unchallenged. As the Bancroft's *de facto* administrator, Becker was saddled with damage control. Upon Dale's return from the East, Becker wrote him confidentially that the library staff faced a genuine challenge to show that grumbling about its staff and programs was without merit. In terms that involved the library editor, Becker explained that "I am in the delicate position of having to explain to the University Librarian, the BL faculty committee, and to the Chancellor's office the reason why the [multi-volume manuscripts] Guide languishes while DLM continues to produce other works."[49] Political pressure put on Bob Becker to complete the remaining two volumes of the *Guide to Manuscripts in the Bancroft Library* prompted the assistant director to assign a typist to Dale Morgan. Dale set his half-time assistant to typing clean copies of the descriptions that would go into the second volume on the library's Latin American holdings. By September 1, Dale had three typists busy. "Other works" mentioned by Becker certainly included the Weber book, which was bound and nearly ready for distribution to Friends of The Bancroft Library buyers. It did not include the William H. Carter biography and never would. In early April, Edgar Carter asked Morgan to return the manuscript he had begun on his father and entrusted to Morgan in 1954.[50] Twelve years of waiting had worn out Carter's gratitude for Dale's offer to complete the biography.

* * * * *

As Dale Morgan stewed in his obligations and opportunities, larger developments far beyond his ken were moving apace. By 1965, Fawn Brodie's *No Man Knows My History* was approaching the end of its second decade in print. It had proven a steady seller to the ire of both the Latter-day Saints and Reorganized Church. The following year Knopf put the book into its eighth printing—ninth, if its separate British edition counted. Other than the scriptures and James E. Talmage's *Jesus the Christ,* Brodie's book had sold more copies than any other work on Mormonism and certainly seen a wider distribution. The book's naturalistic assessments and gritty documentation still reverberated within the LDS community. Though the author directed her attention toward other subjects, the Latter Day Saints and Latter-day Saints were attracting the interest of a new generation of scholars. While BYU's Ernest Wilkinson had been unsuccessful creating an "Institute for Mormon Studies," related measures were enacted at BYU and beyond. Publication of the first issues of *BYU Studies Quarterly* in 1959 provided a dedicated venue for scholars writing on Mormonism to disseminate their research. This journal was the first serial publication to take Latter-day Saint perspective seriously. It was followed in 1966 by the commencement of an independent journal, *Dialogue: A Journal of Mormon Thought.* New outlets for thinking about the Restoration attracted a new type of writing about the Mormons.

Though Morgan clearly had not produced anything on the Latter Day Saints or Latter-day Saints since the visit of Israel A. Smith, RLDS president, and Francis Kirkham in Washington, DC, fifteen years earlier, Morgan's work represented enough of a potential threat that the Latter Day Saints kept the lines open. Kirkham arrived in Berkeley to see Morgan again in 1955. Smith flew to meet Morgan a second time the next year, specifically to secure an update on the still-unpublished Mormon study. "The whole record of Mormon history is incredibly involved," Morgan explained in a follow-up letter to their visit. "There is no doubt that it is badly in need of a reordering; there has been too much appeal to *ipse dixit* [an assertion without proof], and not enough looking at the facts in times past. Even studies of the Mormons, or various phases of Mormon history, which attempt to be objective are not really so, for they come down to merely verbal objectivity . . . without actually attempting to establish what are the facts in the matter, thus abdicating the responsibility of judgment."[51]

Perhaps the clearest public statement of how poorly Mormon history was regarded outside of the church appeared in Wallace Stegner's introduction to his history of the church's overland experience, *The Gathering of Zion*. Stegner noted that the westward movement of the church was *myth* (i.e., origin story) of first order, "fully, even monotonously, documented," but in perceiving higher meaning and divine intent, and uncomfortable with complications, Latter-day Saint officialdom and popular writers still frequently invoked faith-promoting legend over hard facts, ignoring evidence in favor of inspirational narrative. The result was so often incredible that Stegner cited Bernard DeVoto's stubborn empiricism, trusting no Mormon account as evidential unless he could see an original document, and because he was not of the faith he was unable to see most.[52]

Though the first threads of archival modernization were beginning to stir within the church's historical institution, for their part, the guardians of the past at the Church Historian's Office and Daughters of Utah Pioneers were quite content to expect readers to take their versions of the master narrative as gospel. To those who looked for evidence and wrote on corroboration, parts of the official Mormon story simply could not be documented. Yet, the landscape of history also had changed much in the U.S. since Morgan and Stegner came to the field prior to the Second World War—even within Latter Day Saint cultures. They had been part of that generational and perspectival challenge to utilitarian narrative and helped initiate the shift to documentation over testimony.

Around them the landscape was poised to change again, but in the hands of a younger generation. Neither Stegner nor Morgan were directly involved this time. Morgan remained a notable character, as did Juanita Brooks, but the turn toward documentary objectivity that they and their circle had pioneered in the 1940s had been replicated more formally by young Latter-day Saints pursuing professional academic training in the postwar years. By the middle years of the 1960s these academics, who had been junior faculty across a wide variety of fields in the previous decade, were becoming tenured professors in college and university departments. They were scattered among academic institutions, mostly in Utah and California.[53]

Responses to S. George Ellsworth's survey of scholars, circulated in 1956 at the demise of the Mormon Seminar, suggested that enough Latter-day Saints with academic training existed that a formal organization might draw them together. In the mid-1950s the time still had not been right. Now, not quite a decade later, interest was gelling. The group of Latter-day Saint academic students who once introduced themselves to other graduate students at tables in the Church Historian's Office now gravitated toward each other at meetings of the Organization of American Historians (OAH), American Historical Association (AHA), and the still-new Western History Association (WHA). People began discussing shared interests by mail.

At Leonard Arrington's suggestion, interested parties agreed to an independent meeting of a Mormon History Association (MHA) in San Francisco at the 1965 AHA conference. Eventually a dozen or so academic scholars met informally to organize the Mormon History Association.[54] After its initial meeting in 1965, the group collected in sponsored sessions during the Pacific Coast Branch meetings of the OAH between 1966 and 1969 before beginning an independent MHA meeting in 1970.

On one level, MHA was merely one more scholarly association founded during the rapid growth of academic organizations across higher education. On another level, its organization reflected a deep desire for a reflective, evidence-based, objectified middle ground for study of the Latter Day Saint past that was not utilitarian—neither anti-Mormon diatribe nor faith-promoting pageant. Addressing fellow academics at the WHA meeting in 1965, Arrington focused attention on the "secularization of Mormon history and culture." Convinced that scholars segregating history from theology was a new departure for the field, Arrington turned away from his nonacademic predecessors, who had made the same break a generation earlier. Arrington's ignored Morgan's generation and focused on academic scholars alone in an article "Scholarly Studies of Mormonism in the Twentieth Century," which appeared in the initial issue of *Dialogue: A Journal of Mormon Thought* the next year.[55] Defining "scholarship" as the output of credentialled academics alone pushed aside the pioneers of the field.

Morgan recognized not only that the field was in the midst of a tidal change but also that he was no longer one of its driving forces—though the numbers of LDS scholars who sought advice or input from him suggested that they considered him a force to be reckoned with. In 1966 Morgan commented on the draft of a conference paper by Rodman W.

Paul about the Latter Day Saints as a theme in American West historical writing. Morgan pointed to Robert Bruce Flanders' recent book *Nauvoo: Kingdom on the Mississippi* as evidence of the cultural and intellectual maturation of the field. Flanders had been raised in the Reorganized Church of Jesus Christ of Latter Day Saints but used material from the LDS branch of the culture in Utah. Morgan wrote to Paul that Flanders' work on Nauvoo "represents a coming together, a growing together, in the field of responsible scholarship such as we have not been accustomed to see." He added: "we are now reaching the point where the young scholars emerging out of either church are prepared to deal with what I might call 'the whole data.'"[56] Paul responded with encouragement for Morgan to return to work on his own now-legendary Mormon history: "we need it very badly."[57]

Dale fielded news of another major development in Mormon studies the same year. Beginning in 1949, a succession of Utah State Historical Society typists had converted Morgan's handwritten slips to a card catalog, separate files of duplicate cards organized alphabetically or numerically by title, author, and publication year. In fifteen years that collection had become an indispensable research tool. Like all library card catalogs, its content was inaccessible beyond the file drawers the cards occupied. In January 1966, however, the new University of Utah Press returned a positive response to a catalog publication pitch, sparking a collaboration between Utah colleges and universities. The state's academic librarians convened a Checklist of Mormon Literature Committee. Cooley reported to Morgan that with financial support through the USHS, which was (despite growth in the universities) still the largest history-research library available in the state, the committee of librarians had organized to push for the publication of the catalog resulting from Morgan's checklist.[58] Librarian Chad Flake of Brigham Young University took up the commission to edit the card catalog into a single published list.

In the few hours a week Morgan was not at work, the previous year's news of the effort toward a formalized Mormon bibliography prodded Morgan to scramble through his papers for the draft of his bibliography of Mormonism, which he had not touched since 1949. Morgan's notes on individual publications were too large and expansive for the catalog envisioned by the publishing committee. Instead, Morgan resurrected his idea for a study of Mormonism's first two decades through its books, a historical bibliography that certainly would have been similar to his own "Bibliography of the Churches of the Dispersion" or Thomas Streeter's massive *Bibliography of Texas, 1795–1845.*[59] A few months later, in a letter to Yale University's Archie Hanna, Dale wrote that he was considering a trip to New Haven to pick up that project again, since "being only about [eight] books behind now, I consider I am making progress."[60]

* * * * *

Perhaps as important as the development of a cadre of academic historians within Mormonism, or perhaps a natural outgrowth of that fact, was the increase in books and articles on the Latter Day Saints. The earliest scholarly study was probably Richard T. Ely's *Harper's Monthly* article "Economic Aspects of Mormonism" published in 1903.[61] Philosopher E. E. Ericksen and rural sociologist Lowry Nelson were among the earliest academics to study and publish on the Mormons, though not in history. Within a decade of Morgan's arrival at Berkeley important scholarly works focusing on the Mormons had begun appearing. A list might include Nelson's collected studies of Utah's rural social and geographical organization, *The Mormon Village* (1952). It was followed quickly by Thomas O'Dea's broader and more sociological study titled *The Mormons* (1957), which was followed immediately by Bill Mulder's *Homeward to Zion* (1957) on Scandinavian migration, and Leonard Arrington's broad, seminal exploration of regional economics in *Great Basin Kingdom* (1958). Sociology opened the way to occasional similar studies through the 1930s and 1940s until Marvin Hill could generate the first published historiographic treatment of Latter Day Saints in 1959.[62]

Articles on Mormon history came nearly as thickly as other new explorations of the Mormons, soon appearing regularly in major scholarly journals. By the mid-1960s Dale Morgan watched this activity from the sideline of the movement, though the mail continued to bring queries and requests from most of the scholars and students of the day. He responded liberally to each and liked some of them very much, but he remained wary of both academic history and of LDS academics generally. Twenty years earlier Dale seems to have expected that Latter Day Saint culture could not produce the kind of analysis he felt the churches and their people merited. It did, it seems, and within just six years the field he left a decade and a half earlier matured far faster than he could possibly expect.

* * * * *

Carl Wheat suffered yet another stroke on June 1, 1966, which left him unable to speak, barely able to swallow, and with an impaired ability to understand or respond to others. Dale wrote encouragingly on June 11, avoiding mention of the demon seizing Wheat, presenting chatty personal news and that William H. Goetzmann's magisterial new book *Explorations and Empire: The Explorer and the Scientist in the Winning of the American West*, published by no less than Alfred A. Knopf, drew heavily from Wheat's *Mapping the Transmississippi West*. The letter did not reach the intended recipient. On June 8, Wheat suffered another "episode," and most of his remaining time was spent asleep as his body slowly shut down. On June 24, someone on the Bancroft staff brought Dale a message. Helen Wheat had telephoned to tell him that Carl had slipped away the previous day.

By this time and after nearly ten years of sporadic effort, Dale and Eleanor Harris were busily reading galleys and then page proofs on the long-awaited publication on the William Marshall Anderson diaries for the Huntington Library and giving "concentrated attention" to the Lorton diary, he reported to his mother.[63] The attention was not actually editing or writing, but rather that he was completing the revisions to the basal text of Lorton's remarkable narrative. Rather than a straight transcription, Morgan inserted punctuation, corrected spelling, smoothed out the rough or incomplete language, broke the running text into paragraphs to facilitate reading, and divided the five volumes into chapters. Angus Cameron was ecstatic with the result, but when Morgan mentioned discovery of the diary of fellow overland company member Vincent A. Hoover, Cameron became a bit wary with his compliments. Worried over Morgan's tendency for distraction and mission creep, he inquired precisely when Knopf could expect the introduction and notes to Lorton.[64]

A few days later, Dale was pleased to see Donald Jackson of the University of Illinois arrive for research in the Bancroft. He took Jackson to lunch for an opportunity to talk about progress on Jackson's editing of the John C. Frémont papers, on whose editorial board Morgan served. Jackson's visit introduced Morgan to the work of a young school teacher, Todd I. Berens. They had exchanged letters the year before, but Jackson's praise of Berens's master's thesis on the 1848 Frémont map and its value to the 1849 emigration along the Southern Route, thus relating directly to Lorton, caught Morgan's attention. Berens harbored a fascination for the impact of landscape on human experience, a new manifestation of antiquarianism but giving him a perspective within "environmental determinism" which Morgan shared. Berens was also committed to providing his junior high school students with a look at history from the ground. Berens guided his student "Explorers' Club" members on excursions along the trails, expecting the students to read, think, propose, and solve questions, and to report carefully. Dale was impressed. At Jackson's urging, he wrote Berens about the latter's research into the Forty-niner southern route, which Lorton and Hoover had taken with nearly disastrous outcome.[65] Jackson's introduction opened a mutually profitable relationship between Berens and Morgan.

Dale also continued his series of apologetic delays on the Lorton diaries to Valita Moran. Richard Thurman, director of the new University of Utah Press, asked about Morgan's increasingly legendary history of the Mormons. Dale did not rise to the bait. He had not forgotten it, but the Mormons had to take their place among the ceaseless swirl of changing priorities. "I'll clean up my Mormon bibliography before I tackle my Mormon history again," Dale told the press director confidently, "but neither will occur inside the next few weeks."[66] There was good reason, besides chronic busy-ness. By late summer 1966, Madeline's letters began commenting upon how tired and drawn Dale looked on her occasional visits to Berkeley. Donald Jackson said the same thing.[67] Dale shook it off to complete another glucose-tolerance test and to return page proof corrections for his second Lakeside Classic book before departing for Alaska on site research for the third.

* * * * *

Having worked for the University of California for more than a decade by this point, Dale had long chafed over what he felt were inequities in its sabbatical policy. The *defacto* decision not to request a clear statement about the privileges of his unique academic-but-not-faculty standing at his 1964 promotion now haunted him. Hammond was no longer available as Morgan's administrative champion. In the fall of 1966 a proposal to revise the university leave policy on research was submitted to the faculty senate. This revision specifically excluded staff. The genie was out of the bottle. Morgan wrote the university librarian, pointing out that the proposal created a tiered class system. "A scholarly project undertaken by a member of the faculty is regarded as meritorious in the highest degree, reflecting credit upon the University, and deserving of financial support from the university. Exactly the same project undertaken by citizens of the second class is regarded as something of an inconvenience."[68] He was correct, but in making his critique, Morgan failed to note just how unusual his position was. Dale Morgan's scholarly career was an exception to the rule, and the university had to have a rule.

Morgan's argument nonetheless struck a chord with University Librarian Donald Coney, none of whose other staff held academic or faculty appointments despite many with doctoral credentials. Coney asked Morgan to list the projects in which he was engaged that would qualify for research leave. Dale grabbed at the opening, mentioning the large fur trade history that had long been a goal, but emphasizing a library-related project which had already garnered support abroad: his historical bibliography of Mormonism. Nevertheless, Morgan was disingenuously optimistic. "If this project were just now beginning, three or six months of leave would not nearly suffice for all the work to be done," he asserted to Coney. Still, he felt able to assert honestly, "but it is near the capstone stage after many years of labor."[69] In fact, besides recently jotting a few scribbled notes on the typed pages, he had not touched the manuscript since 1949 and had expended no measurable effort besides that.

Secure in his employment and reputation, again Morgan probably did not recognize that the discipline of history itself was changing. He came to history in the late 1930s, a time at which more than half of US faculty members worked in private institutions. Many faculty held only master's degrees or no advanced degrees at all. Morgan earned his practical experience in the school of applied history, what today might be considered "public history." As a whole, by the late 1960s, the history read by most Americans tended to be written by journalists, by talented paraprofessionals like himself, and by local people proud of their communities. Shortly after beginning at the Bancroft Library in early 1954 he wrote an admirer of *Jedediah Smith and the Opening of the West* that "I have found that the so-called amateurs have more interest and enthusiasm, and more often than not more actual knowledge, than the so-called professionals who merely make a livelihood out of history, and I would be reluctant to give up whatever might remain of my own amateur standing."[70] The problem was, that at Berkeley he worked for one of the nation's top research universities, with an entirely different set of criteria for measuring professional credentials.

* * * * *

By the time Dale vainly applied for sabbatical in 1966, statistics alone signaled how much the discipline of history in the United States had changed. The number of U.S. teaching academics doubled between 1940 and 1960, and nearly doubled again between 1960 and 1970.[71] The number of new professorial positions created between 1965 and 1970 (as the Baby Boom generation began entering college) outstripped the entire population of the U.S. professorate as it stood in 1940.[72] The number of professorships in humanities fields grew, but even the swelling growth in the humanities masked a more profound change: over the same period the ratio of humanities positions declined in proportion to the overall number of academic faculty. In short, the sciences grew at a much faster rate. Higher education's encouragement of its traditional, *humanitas* curriculum was fading to lip service, swapped out in favor of business acumen, career training, and both hard and applied sciences.

Morgan's own output also reflected the realities of the postwar world of publishing: regional studies held only regional appeal. Unlike the *Humboldt, Great Salt Lake,* and *Jedediah Smith and the Opening of the West,* which had been intentionally general-reader, mass-market works, the rest of Morgan's completed output appealed only to small, exclusive audiences. The publishers catering to those niches in California and the American West tended to produce collectible limited-editions which appealed to those of an antiquarian mind, in turn relying on the last of the commercial fine-letterpress printers. Morgan's own output also reflected those realities of limited-edition historical publishing.

Despite Leland Creer's disparaging assertion that Dale Morgan was "a dilettante to history," a broad, deep vein of antiquarianism certainly colors his published work. Perhaps this is natural, given the WPA's "school of hard knocks" and the documentary style in which Morgan was introduced to history and learned his craft. Focusing on externally objective precisions of geography, chronology, and demography, an antiquarian's interest bypasses questions of meaning and larger significances. Rich with detail and even with color, Morgan's emphasis on the source documents renders experience with precision. To him, inferring motivations and meaning was unsuitably speculative. An antiquarian approach to the past elementally strives to correct and confirm. Perhaps the paragon antiquarian study of the period in Morgan's field is Carl P. Russell's *Firearms, Traps, and Tools of the Mountain Man* (Knopf, 1967).

The modern discipline of "public history" and the remaining involvement in regional history is the bloodline inheritor of the antiquarianism of bygone days. Supplemented by archaeology and informed by material-culture studies, the nation's history museums, historic preservation programs, state and national parks, and school programs are the richer for this perspective. Antiquarianism documents what was *actual* rather than restating what was traditional or assumed, presenting to harried tourists and wide-eyed children what *would have been*. Academic historians of Morgan's time were beginning to ask very different questions and present very different accounts of the past. Taking Morgan's preferred fields as examples, topics might include how white trappers perpetuated Native gender roles, or how the loss of a keystone species might have affected Native social systems; why Mormon converts were attracted to the appeals of the new faith if it was not all that different from mainline Protestantism, and why claimants to Joseph Smith's legacy insisted on publishing and distributing their own revelations; what forces pushed emigrants who made the westward trip, and what can be inferred about national pressure of slavery for new land? All of these are the kinds of questions that academic scholars were being trained to ask by the 1970s.

Merely pointing out that elemental division in American historiography during the twentieth century is not to say one interpretive perspective is more valuable. Morgan was an outstanding scholar in his field, but at Berkeley he was out of his class as well as outranked by individuals with doctoral degrees and faculty standing—and academic history had long diverged from the fact-correcting antiquarian structure, the approach in which he had staked out his professional aspirations three decades earlier.

CHAPTER 17

"I Seem to Work All the Time"[1]

Shifting Priorities, Berkeley, 1966–1968

I was 10 years behind five years ago, and maybe I am just five years behind, so maybe we can regard that as progress.[2]
—Dale Morgan

PASSING HIS FIFTY-SECOND BIRTHDAY in December 1966, Dale saw the likelihood of an official leave from the University of California receding ever more distantly from possibility, while his personal attention was drawn toward Louise North in Maryland. For the first time Dale considered the possibility and complications of retirement. He now had not only his investments, but by 1972 would be old enough at 55 and have adequate term-in-service to qualify for a modest retirement income. Since coming to Berkeley in 1954, the need for dependable income had been the tradeoff against which writing time had been balanced. Morgan's professional reputation flourished while at the University of California, but if he had reached a point that a moderate income could at last be secured, then it made sense to begin considering retirement as an intentional career move.

Though Morgan continued working on the third Lakeside Classic book to the point that he was getting tired of "one continued round of Klondikery,"[3] it was still in his hands in the first week of February when Madeline McQuown arrived unannounced. Dale let her in, of course. Through the evening, various disappointments metastasized into disagreements which exploded into perhaps the most serious confrontation of their thirty-year friendship. Madeline's side of the matter is unknown, but after she stormed back to San Jose, Dale sat down to his typewriter on February 9 to clarify what was at stake in their "debacle"—and for the first time in years, he made and retained a carbon of his follow-up letter to her.

"What you want is a justification for not doing what you basically don't want to do," he wrote, "and the only justification that is worthwhile[*sic*] for you is one that involves casting the blame on me." Morgan stripped away her pretenses for the Brigham Young biography's incompletion: preferential conveniences, arguments justifying progress and lack of progress, personal travel, stuck in a marriage she admitted she did not want but would not leave, and mired in an adult lifetime of fruitless medical attention. There was scant evidence, he told her bluntly, that she existed any longer as "anything but a bundle of compulsions." Though he had accommodated to her illnesses and demands for years, his letter finally openly shredded the arguments she had used to cover her inability to finish the Brigham Young biography. "[T]he only way you will now work on the book is in the self-destructive pattern I have observed for years, but stripped now of all pretense," he wrote with a bite to his own words. "What you want is to demonstrate that it is not possible for you to finish the book; and that this is not your fault. 'Dale, I worked night and day to finish this book. The doctors warned me against it, but you forced me into this position; in an effort to satisfy you, I worked far beyond my strength. Now you see me, shattered and ill in a hospital bed, forced there by your cruelty and lack of understanding.'" He recognized that completing the book "would have left you without excuse for continuing with a marriage you professed to have done with."

Morgan's letter was a sharp, incisive, and completely pitiless assessment. It broke down her fundamental codependence that held together their relationship, acknowledged the wreck of her second marriage (and tacitly, the first as well), and laid in the open the excuses about the book that had been her mainstay.[4] Upon reflection, Morgan evidently decided not to mail Madeline his letter, for the signed sheet is among his papers. The pair eventually patched up their differences, as friends do, but the tone of his few surviving letters thereafter reveal that the hold Madeline McQuown once held over Dale Morgan's priorities and allegiance had finally broken.

Dale's act of finally setting down to paper his doubts about her motivations seems to have finally affected a cathartic change in his perception of their friendship. While an emotional need for Madeline dominated him in 1937, Louise North held his affections in 1967. He no longer needed Madeline. Dale continued writing her frequently but his letters became chatty activity reports which she considered shallow gossip. "Let me hear something besides the kind of thing you have been writing," she complained.[5]

Madeline could sense his withdrawal. Dale no longer wanted the most from their relationship, which had long given her the dominant power in it. Their roles reversed. Her reaction was one of complaint, trying to recapture the control she had lost. "I have wanted to avoid trouble, tried to make things easy for everyone but myself," she wrote him. "No one has ever appreciated my efforts which have been truly heroic when they are properly understood."[6]

Madeline, of course, reserved sole discretion to determine when or if another person "properly understood" her or her efforts. Jerry Finnin, the friend who lived with McQuowns for two decades and saw Madeline far more than did Dale Morgan, considered her more of a hypochondriac than an invalid.[7] As time passed and she could no longer bully, plead, or wheedle to retain Dale's attention to her chronic illnesses and setbacks, her letters became increasingly bitter. She craved advice and direction even as she resented him for supplying it. With Louise North's place growing in his affection, Morgan's letters to Madeline do not survive, but based on her replies, which he retained, they evidently grew less intense and certainly less interested in her well-being. Madeline chastised him for a growing emotional distance, as he had once mourned to her twenty-five years earlier.

The relationship between Dale Morgan and Madeline McQuown remains difficult to understand, mostly because we have only one side of their correspondence, but neither person can fairly be understood without the other. In his examination of the story behind the Brigham Young biography, Craig L. Foster concluded that toward the end of their relationship McQuown was "at best, indifferent."[8] I think she was hardly that. My view is that Madeline developed a codependence on Morgan and his support. If he was pushing her, she needed not push herself. She seemed to use his encouragement as not only a support but also something to collapse against, allowing her to position herself as a martyr for her art, her justification for making no progress on the biography. Foster's reading of her indifference is probably correct for their relationship in the 1940s, but by the 1960s she relied heavily on Morgan's letters and their periodic personal interactions to never meet her inner needs, allowing her to feel neglected despite his attentions. By the middle of 1968 she slipped a barb or cutting remark into every surviving letter she wrote him. Dale continued to send her money occasionally. By August that year, however, Dale withdrew and Madeline demanded ever more. If they continued to write beyond that point, neither retained the letters.

A few months after their February 1967 confrontation, Dale forwarded to Madeline a letter from Fawn Brodie. Having published to acclaim her biography of Richard Francis Burton, *The Devil Drives,* Brodie was looking with renewed interest toward Brigham Young as a biographical subject. The thought of Brodie and her national reputation rang an alarm for McQuown. "I am disturbed at Fawn's desire to write a book about Brigham Young just as you may have been," Madeline wrote Dale leadingly. She also fired off a letter to Brodie, emphasizing how exhaustive her research had been and how close her manuscript was to completion. Commenting breezily that she had two other works partially complete from the same material, McQuown cavalierly stated that she did not discourage Brodie from writing on Young herself. She had seen Brodie's recent Burton biography at Dale's apartment, as well, "but understandably I have not had a moment to do any reading outside the Mormon field"—which was an outright fiction.[9] In none of her letters to Morgan for nearly a decade had she reported reading or consulting even a reasonably relevant book title. Yet, McQuown's artful boasts nudged Young from Brodie's focus, to be replaced with an interest in Thomas Jefferson, which would eventually result in her most successful yet controversial book.[10]

Over the years, Dale Morgan helped McQuown fend off would-be writers on Young so successfully that no biographies of the "American Moses" were published between M. R. Werner's *Brigham Young* (Harcourt, Brace & Company, 1925) and Stanley P. Hirshson's *The Lion of the Lord* (Knopf, 1969), and not another until Arrington's *Brigham Young: American Moses* (Knopf, 1985).[11] Brodie had begun teaching at UCLA at the beginning of the 1966 fall term. She was reticent about the appointment. "I cannot do serious research ... and teach full time," she wrote Dale, torn between the conflicting priorities of a "double regimen." Having tried to master a "double regimen" himself—though without Brodie's immediate family obligations—he could certainly sympathize. Both of them were caught in a quandary: research and writing required time and wouldn't pay well, and a steady paycheck required time and attention taken from research and writing. It seemed very much like an either/or proposition, or a requirement to scale back the research and writing to the available time. Dale could hardly imagine doing the latter when so much untouched opportunity in the field lay before him.

* * * * *

Toward the end of February 1967, Dale accepted an invitation to speak—
actually *speak*—before the Jedediah Smith Society at the University of the
Pacific in Stockton, California.[12] At nearly the same time, Alfred Knopf
got word that Morgan had discussed and planned to edit with Jim Holliday a book featuring the previously published journal of H. M. T. Powell,
entitled *The Santa Fe Trail to California*. Holliday had made virtually the
same progress with the diary of Forty-niner William Swain over the preceding decade as Morgan had with the Lorton—that is, none—and before
Knopf was willing to issue a contract for the Powell book, he wanted to
hear about the state of the Lorton contract. Dale dodged making a direct
response to Knopf's pointed query by admitting only that the books
would appeal to the same market, but that no content would overlap
between them.[13] After mulling over the opportunities, and having for two
decades unsuccessfully hunted for books on the American West having
the literary standards he expected, Knopf wrote to author Oscar Lewis
that he was interested in pursuing the Powell volume, but "we should
begin, I think, by including Dale Morgan out. For years he has owed us
his edition of the Lorton Journals, but there is still no sign at all of his
being able . . . to deliver them."[14]

Later that year Angus Cameron quietly approached Holliday about
doing the Powell volume without Morgan, unaware that Holliday would
complete far less scholarship during his much longer career than Morgan. Unfortunately for the publisher, Holliday refused to consider the
project without Morgan's direct involvement. Knopf was piqued. "I am
Missouri [i.e., the "Show-Me State"] as far as Dale is concerned," he said
with a grumble, adding that he would "believe in [Morgan's] capacity
to carry out in good faith jobs he undertakes when I see him make the
finish line in time with one of them."[15] The root of the problem was,
of course, that Morgan never considered the completion of any project
to be unmanageable.

Morgan addressed the Jedediah Smith Society meeting in person, the
first time in his adult life that Dale stood at a podium and spoke to an
audience with his own voice. From his own account in a letter to Emily,
he stumbled slightly in the high, nasal monotone that friends accepted.
Without an audible check on their shape or tone, the effort slightly mud-
dling consonants from a tongue and lips long out of sync with the mind
that shaped them, the speech provided perhaps the only opportunity to
record Morgan's own voice, but no one thought of doing that.[16] Returning
up the Bay to Berkeley, Dale immediately begin drafting an address to the

Missouri Historical Society, as well as both to finish and to begin reducing the length of his notes for the still-incomplete Klondike Lakeside Classics book. He only finished editing and retyping his notes while he was in Missouri at the conference. He also finished his second speech, "a love-letter [*sic*]" to the Society, only the night before it was delivered on his behalf.[17]

Returning west, Dale arrived at the Kaiser clinic for his first biennial comprehensive physical exam, hoping the physicians "don't add anything to their last discovery, the mild diabetes. Enough is enough!"[18] Nothing new resulted, though a day later Dale was handed a note by another staffer: colleague Helen Harding Bretnor's cancer had progressed to the point that even her native optimism could no longer deny its reality or the toll it imposed on her physical abilities. Dale had known, corresponded, and worked with Helen since he first began serious historical research in the 1940s, over twenty years earlier. "Helen simply could not believe that anything very drastic could happen to *her*," he wrote George Hammond somewhat prophetically. "This is one thing I learned long ago, to accept the fact that anything that could happen to anybody else could also happen to me."[19]

* * * * *

By 1967 Dale Morgan had lived in the apartment on Benvenue for nearly fourteen years. Its single bedroom and living/kitchen area was crowded with so much material that even the occupant referred to domestic space wryly as "something like a cross between the Library of Congress, the National Archives, and a warehouse."[20] That summer the residents of his apartment block were told that the building had been sold and that the new owner planned to increase monthly rent substantially.[21] Dale began looking for new accommodations which, since he did not have a car, would still have to be within walking distance of the library at the center of campus. On her way to work one morning in July, Bancroft colleague Lois Stone noticed a unit for rent in a two-level duplex on La Loma Avenue, a block below her house on the opposite side of campus. The owner lived in the ground-level section. Morgan signed a lease and prepared to move in September 1, but before then, he had to correct and clear proofs for the *Klondike* text and complete notes for a new commission editing a long gold rush reminiscence by Howard Gardiner. By early August he had essentially completed the latter task, adding 140 pages of notes to the 531-page transcript of the memoir.[22] However, he still had to organize and clear the apartment on Benvenue, which he admitted would require positively heroic effort.

Dale sorted and consolidated dunes of paper during his early mornings before work and again evenings often past midnight.[23] Packing the teetering cliffs of books into ninety boxes required successive nights working till 2 a.m. Even so, a moving company had Dale packed, trucked, and installed into his new residence on schedule. The duplex sat on the north side of campus but still about the same distance from the library as the place on Benvenue. In addition to being near to Stone, it was also a block from Lawton and Renée Kennedy. Morgan's new L-shaped accommodation occupied the top floor, up a short flight of exterior stairs from the walk beside the garage. This one had two bedrooms. The largest, at the front of the house above the garage, was eventually rimmed with shelves for the library, but could be pressed into service as an ersatz guestroom. On the other end, a brick fireplace ornamented one wall of the generous living room, which opened to a narrow deck and another set of stairs descending to the steep hillside yard. In the angle to one side of the living room was a kitchen-dining area. Large windows in both spaces framed a clear, unobstructed view west across Berkeley and the bay to San Francisco, where the Golden Gate Bridge glowed orange in morning light. To the south, the Campanile stood tall against the skyline with Oakland as a backdrop, its new downtown construction just beginning to reach skyward.

The new location still provided Dale a fifteen-minute walk to work: down La Loma's hilly twists, across Hearst Avenue, and following the Campanile like a compass needle across the Esplanade directly to the front doors of the Doe Library Annex, which housed the Bancroft Library. Several days were required to settle the books, papers, and personal effects. Still a bit unsteady on her feet, Emily arrived on September 8 for a visit, accompanied by Jim and Mary Beth and their daughter, Linda, joined shortly by Linda's sister, Susan. The next day the group picked up Jim McConkey, who was visiting California with a friend, for a day trip through San Francisco. Dale hosted them all for lunch on Fisherman's Wharf, introducing them to cracked Dungeness crab. They drove past Golden Gate Park to Ocean Beach. On the eleventh, Jim and Mary Beth Morgan continued on to Carmel, and Jim McConkey and friend flew south to Los Angeles. Dale finally not only hung his collection of LeConte Stewart paintings but also completed correcting the William Marshall Anderson index proofs.

Buoyed by the success of his spring talk before the Jedediah Smith Society, Dale planned to deliver an invited address to the annual Utah State Historical Society gathering in Salt Lake City in person as well. Charles Kelly advised him against it, saying that while he and Everett Cooley understood Morgan's speech, most attendees would not.[24] Dale reluctantly took his advice, but he attended the Utah event. Juanita Brooks drove up from St. George, their first personal meeting in years. Fawn Brodie also attended, specifically for her installation as a Fellow of the Society, a far cry from the hue and cry in Utah which had followed her biography of Joseph Smith two decades earlier. It was the only time all three friends occupied the same space. Acknowledging the cultural climate change in Utah, Dale later observed to Fawn that her Fellowship "gave me far more pleasure than any award that has ever been made to me."[25] Morgan's visit to the Wasatch was never complete without a field excursion, and a few days after the Historical Society meeting, Everett Cooley drove him and two others along the stretch of Oregon Trail northwest from Fort Bridger to the Bear River and back through Woodruff and Ogden. Dale grabbed handfuls of sagebrush to bring the gray-green, windswept tang of the Wasatch Mountains back to his urban-California bedroom.

* * * * *

Late in 1967 Dale Morgan was perhaps involved with more book-length writing and prospective writing projects than he had ever been before, and still he looked further afield. Too many fascinating discoveries had been made, and too many possibilities lay in front of him. The American West and its history remained a compelling subject. Recalling the financial success of the Rivers of America and American Lake series, Morgan floated the idea for a book series on California history to Lloyd Lyman at the University of California Press. As one who produced and marketed the output of the new generation of eager academics, Lyman looked more critically at trends, not merely titles. The editor responded that he felt the time for book series was passing. He was looking for works that synthesized what had been learned.[26]

Lyman's reply was perhaps the first intimation Morgan received that the field of Western American history itself had changed around him, and not merely Latter Day Saint history. By the mid and late 1960s the adoption of new interpretive tools, like quantitative methods, and a shift toward filling omissions in the national story provided a basis for a challenge to the consensus approach—social history. The postwar generation of historians, young people in graduate schools in the mid- and late 1960s, were turning to study the experiences of overlooked and marginalized populations. History was no longer solely grounded in ideas, politics, economics, or in documents found chiefly among the papers of notable individuals. New tools were creating new approaches to telling the story of the past. Statistical studies of population and changes gave rise to *cliometrics*.[27] Studies of race, class, and gender began asking questions about society outside the previous mainstream. Informed by developments in the sciences and archaeology, environmental history provided another new approach to the past. Scholars were straying from the mainstream to study the fringes and boundaries of American society. In Hunter Dupree's graduate student colloquium, one presenter and fellow history department faculty member, Gunther Barth, was described as "literally cascading ideas, to demonstrate how in the field of social history scores of topics awaited investigation."[28]

Concurrently the rise of individual field specialties effectively narrowed the scope of the histories being written. Some areas of study fell out of fashion and all but disappeared. As noted previously, academic history left behind the fact-correcting drive of antiquarianism. Journal articles and books began to serve a new function as statements within a formalized conversation (or argument) between informed specialists proposing interpretive ideas. In terms of historical writing, an increasing percentage of contemporary history books were being written, published, and read with an entirely different set of eyes and with different expectations than they had a generation earlier. For good or ill, an author's formal credentials took on an elevated importance in determining a work's reception and standing within the readership and its appeal to other scholars. Unless one wrote for trade publishers and a general readership, "serious" history was quickly disappearing as the province of well-informed amateurs like Dale Morgan and was becoming the preserve of formally credentialed professionals.[29]

Yet, despite these trends, Dale Morgan's scholarly reputation stood at its apex. A graduate student wrote Morgan that "your critical editorial ability is today unsurpassed by anyone in the field of Western American history."[30] The questioner wanted to catalog Morgan's publication record, too. Dale wrote back, not entirely tongue-in-cheek, that the grad student might be decent enough to wait until Morgan was good and dead before embarking on something with the air of such scholarly finality as a bibliography. "I have scarcely made a good beginning yet on my lifework in

history," he responded, "and even an interim bibliography seems prema-
ture."[31] His pending-project list trailed out a dozen specific works which
he expected (or had once expected) to complete, and he had "not in the
least abandoned my intention of tackling large general works" including
a history of the Mormons and a broad history on the North American
fur trade." Disbelieving in prophecy himself, Morgan's confident response
and list of forthcoming projects confirmed that he did not recognize that,
as of 1967, his professional bibliography *was* essentially complete.

* * * * *

By 1967, Dale had been out of contact with Louise North for nearly two
years. As he worked ever more closely and smoothly with Eleanor Harris, his attention seemed to be drifting her direction. In November, Dale
described Eleanor as "one of the most intelligent women I have encountered."[32] If he was beginning to feel a romantic attraction, she seems to
have sensed the direction of the drift and gently settled a barrier to it.
"I do not want to be found lacking in my share of our commitment,"
she wrote, but explained that her emotions were still bound up by the
hurt experienced in a recent divorce. "To engage in a sincere relationship
frightens me, as do outward demonstrations of love."[33] As he had with
Madeline years earlier, Dale tried to make haste to ease her into a bond,
inviting the younger woman into a mutual emotional intimacy "let come
of that what may. Even a deeper friendship, if those are the ultimate limits,
is sufficient justification." He recalled her gentle gesture of once taking
his arm walking through an airport, noting that neither of them spoke
lightly about the emotion of love, but that "I look forward to the evolution
of a more intimate relationship with you, an intimacy that begins in the
mind and sometimes does not evolve beyond that point."[34] Though they
continued to work together happily, Eleanor Harris did not respond to
his proposed affections, and he pressed no further.

Meanwhile Mormon scholarship was complicated by new developments. Aziz Atiya identified several fragments of the papyri rolls once
owned by Joseph Smith, which Smith had cited as manuscript for the
historically problematic Book of Abraham. Separately, Brigham Young
University publicly announced a commitment to developing the scholarly study of the Church of Jesus Christ of Latter-day Saints. Personally,
Dale's reconnection with Fawn Brodie encouraged her to push *No Man
Knows My History* into a revised edition. The queries and news that cycled

through his mailbox at the end of 1967 drew Mormonism back into Morgan's active interests. Wesley Walters contacted Dale, eager to share his research into the religious revivals in the Palmyra, New York, region and asking about Morgan's old drafts on the Mormon history. Chad Flake finally produced a draft manuscript that became *A Mormon Bibliography, 1830–1930* a decade later. Cooley forwarded a massive photocopy to Dale as a prompt for an introduction; "after all," he had written Dale when the project was picking up steam several years earlier, "it is Dale L. Morgan's Mormon Bibliography, and none of us have forgotten it."[35]

At the beginning of December, Cooley invited Morgan to Salt Lake City for a conference with Flake about the bibliography and publication challenges it might face. He arranged for the University of Utah Press to fund Morgan's travel, which allowed Dale a trip home over the Christmas-to-New Year's holiday.[36] Before leaving, in the spirit of the season Morgan hosted grade-school friends Ab Heiner and John Silver at lunch. He also hosted a series of evening dinners with the Macleods and now-widowed Reg Bretnor, as well as the Michael and Tasia Melvin family, and, of course, he invited the McQuowns. "You must be out of your mind," Madeline snapped in response, "with my blood pressure ... I am not going anywhere but the hospital."[37] Dale nearly didn't make the trip to Salt Lake City himself. Just before leaving he experienced another vertigo which pitched him down the stairs outside the library's east door. His legs tangled and were so bruised that he took a few days of sick leave to nurse his injuries at home before departing.[38]

Once Dale arrived in Salt Lake City, Emily Morgan held her first full family party in several years two days after Christmas, paving the small living room on Hollywood Drive with a layer of Holmes extended-family nieces and nephews and a new generation of their small children. It was Dale's favorite occasion. A few days later Morgan met Cooley and Flake at the new Utah State Historical Society (USHS) quarters on South Temple Street for a daylong session to discuss standardizing entries and eventually typesetting *A Mormon Bibliography, 1830–1930*. Dale compiled and sent ahead a long letter, his review of the manuscript as it stood. His review laid out five large issues for discussion and made eighteen specific suggestions ranging from capitalization style and census symbols to the practice of using later editions of a work as catalog entries, as well as identifying fictional works.[39]

Dale headed eastward again in February 1969 with a roundabout circuit to Missouri and a stop for a conference in Illinois. A short flight to

Chicago put Morgan at dinner with the R. R. Donnelley staff, quietly but vainly hoping that he could mend fences and return to the position as Lakeside Classics' editor. He spent several days in the Newberry Library collections before flying on to Washington, DC, partly to visit niece Anne Stebbins, who delivered a daughter just before Dale landed at the airport, but chiefly to attempt to pick up again with Louise North.

Dale remained perhaps uncertain of how to reconnect with Louise, or if he could. His official excuse for the Washington visit was to court Carl Wheat's son Frank and National Archives map librarian Herman Friis toward establishing a national cartography award in Wheat's name. That mission, however, provided an excuse or opportunity to explore whether Louise's views had changed. Dale wrote her in February before leaving and was pleased, perhaps relieved, to receive an invitation in reply. They met for supper in the city on March 3. One dinner engagement led to another, "a sort of advance celebration of Louis's birthday."[40] The door apparently was not entirely closed.

The stay allowed a series of reunions as well. He lunched with Anna McConkey and Lucie Howe, visited Naomi Peres, and lunched repeatedly with his sister Ruth Barton's family. The highlight of the week for him, however, was the return engagement with Louise and daughter Lisa at Hall's, one of the dining spots Dale frequented while working in the city two decades earlier. Dale gave Louise an early birthday present of a double-strand necklace of serpentine stone and a bit of cash to pay for one or more trees or bushes to be planted at her home on the east shore of the Potomac River. Dale remained as Louise's guest, and Lisa made pancakes for breakfast the next morning. After Dale found a take-up reel that fit Louise's movie projector, the three spent the day watching and reminiscing over home movies.[41]

That evening, after Lisa went to bed, Dale and Louise had a long discussion. "It was perfectly evident that each of us has still had the warm and deep regard for each other we had finally been able to express before I left Washington in July, 1965," Morgan wrote his mother. "Louise talked about the confusion and doubt she had felt at that time ... and her long conviction that when she was uncertain, the best thing was to do nothing." They agreed that matters might have worked out differently had Dale lived in the area and they could have worked out a new relationship together that did not involve a move across the country. Dale must have quietly filed away that idea for future reference. The barrier of uncertainty and change that existed between their worlds thinned slightly, and its shape and texture began to look less daunting. "I don't have any answers yet," he confessed, "and am disposed to let Louise go her own pace in the light of our discussion, and see where we come out after a while."[42]

The North daughters, Lynn and Lisa, sent Dale a tie for Easter, confirming that he was following cautiously along the right track. He had known both for their whole lives, first as their "Uncle Oscar" and then simply Dale for as long as either could remember. Their affections he had never needed to win over; the challenge was their mother. After the tie arrived, he wrote Emily Morgan that he hoped he was reading Louise's reticence and emotional fears correctly, "that there is a kind of pattern to her, that rejection is a stage on the way to acceptance, giving her a kind of floor to stand on and adjust to circumstances." He was willing to wait as she became comfortable with the idea of remarriage and of Dale himself, for he felt that "if she can resolve her doubts and inclination against change, she will marry me completely holding back nothing of herself."[43]

Dale invited Louise and the girls to California over summer vacation, but Louise's time was committed elsewhere, and Dale began laying plans for another trip eastward himself. "If I can keep her in motion, even walking backward," he wrote to his mother, "one of these days she will laugh and turn around and recognize where we are."[44] Dale confided his budding romance to George Hammond and Helen Kennedy, and eventually months later to Jim Holliday, but to no one else besides his mother. To Kennedy, he unfolded a new plan to retire at the University of California's minimum retirement age of 55 to devote himself fully to writing while he still kept his faculties and his reputation was strong. That target was now only a year and a half away. He had long mused and complained, seriously and in jest, about being chronically five to ten books behind. Retirement would provide him both an income and unencumbered time to work, as well as an opportunity to pursue his choice among the scores of projects that had captured his attention briefly, only to be set aside because of more pressing commitments.

Toward the middle of June at his physician's insistence, Morgan sat down for a long and serious conversation with the Kaiser dietician. They pointed out that his diabetes, though officially mild, was still a medical reality that could not be neglected. Morgan agreed to pay greater attention to his culinary choices.[45] Given his age, Dale's annual physical exams through the Kaiser clinic now included a colorectal exam, though his diabetes always took forefront in any comment he made about his health or medical treatments. As unpleasant as the exams might be, if he was looking for a flash of empathy from Madeline McQuown, one of the few people he told about them, the news was wasted. She had recently endured a kidney removal and wanted both books to stave off boredom and money to stave off creditors. "Are you suggesting you are my friend?" she snapped at him, "One wonders. The last thing I remember of you was your gloating over my blood pressure."[46] He sent both.

A month later Madeline wanted him to intercede with the Social Security Administration to increase payments so she had more support to finance her writing rather than paying her caretaker—not that she actually wanted to write. "If I had the faintest idea that you really cared I'd try harder to write," she wrote caustically, "but it's scarcely worth it. I've had too much experience with you."[47] He sent more money.

Several weeks later Madeline mourned to her longtime friend that the Brigham Young biography was "almost finished" and that its incompletion, perhaps like so much of Morgan's work, inspired in her nothing but hopelessness.[48] One last drop to their long stream of exchanges, a final envelope and its mournful, biting contents came from her a month later. Beyond that their letters did not continue. Their thirty-year friendship and correspondence was effectively over. In 1943 Dale had named Madeline as his sole literary beneficiary, leaving her his books, papers, and manuscripts. In 1954 he reserved for her a portion of his retirement and any insurance payout. In 1969, Morgan edited both his retirement and investment accounts, naming Louise his primary beneficiary and her daughters equally as his secondaries.[49] Once his closest friend and chief confidante, Madeline McQuown was no longer listed at all.

Dale caught a flight to Utah in late August. This late in his career Dale Morgan visited the USHS irregularly, but the staff there began making his infrequent visits into colloquia for those seriously writing on Western American history. Everett Cooley remembered two decades later:

> we had two staff members who, while they were working there, got their degrees in history at the University [of Utah], but they said the greatest learning experience they had were these seminars we had with Dale Morgan, sitting around the coffee table—Stan Ivins, Wally Stegner, uh, Bill Mulder—Leonard [Arrington] was there frequently, Tom Alexander, and these were great sessions—Sam and Ray Taylor. And they'd go on for some time, we'd take more than a fifteen minute coffee break but: we felt justified in it because it was enlightening us. These were great times.[50]

By October, the beginning of the autumn book season, Angus Cameron wrote Morgan with only veiled sarcasm that yet another production season had passed without not only Lorton, but now also without measurable progress on the H. M. T. Powell diary.[51] Of course, neither Morgan nor Holliday had anything to return but apologies. In fact, neither book would ever be completed by either man. No matter, Dale returned East in the middle of the month to carry on his long-distance courtship at closer range, though he expected nothing as dramatic as the emotional breakthrough of the past March.

Louise and Lisa picked up Dale at the airport and returned to Accokeek. This time, however, he roomed down the road at Marian Crane's house; word had gotten back to Louise that the neighbors disapproved of her having a man in the house back in March. Dale was fine with the arrangement and settled into a domestic routine. While Louise ebbed and flowed between home and her work as a public information officer for the Department of Housing and Urban Development, Dale puttered contentedly, painting the house's trim, feeding the family animals including Lisa's horse and Tom, the donkey. The pace was bucolic, slower and more intentional than he had experienced in years.

Dale devoted a few days to research in the National Archives or the Library of Congress, using one trip into the city as an opportunity for dinner with an increasingly desperate Joe Colgan. On another evening he hosted Anna McConkey and Lucie Howe. Louise and Lisa drove in to attend a play with him, followed by a late supper. Before leaving, Louise took Dale around to meet her brother. Dale and Louise were clearly growing into a couple. "When I ask Louise who she is she says 'I am your girl,'" he told his mother contentedly. "I think something finally will become possible, how and when I don't undertake to say yet."[52]

As pleasant as the visit was and as comfortable as he felt with the Norths, a hurt was still to come. Louise drove Dale to National Airport for his return flight to California but exploded an emotional bombshell in the car, telling him that she did not love him "as a wife should love a husband." She was, now, convinced she neither would nor could remarry.[53] Louise's words stung a heart certain they were moving in rhythm toward a bright end. Dale climbed aboard his flight emotionally empty. Several weeks passed before he could confide to his mother what had happened.

Louise's parting seems to have inspired in Morgan a resolution to clear up loose ends and rearrange his priorities, perhaps his first preparation for an eventual move east. Highest on his list of obligations was to get the second volume of the *Guide to Manuscripts* completed, but most of his time was devoted to sorting fourteen years' worth of accumulated correspondence layering his desk in the Bancroft Library lower level, a daunting and inane but essential bit of drudgery. He got the mass preliminarily separated into alphabetical order by correspondent but had no time for further organization. By November the letdown from Louise's parting words, an overcrowded list of commitments, and constant pressure at work and in his own writing were taking a toll. Morgan finally realized that he could not meet his present commitments in his present circumstances or with the time available. Since he was unwilling to give up the commitments, circumstances had to give.

On November 12, Dale sent a memo upstairs to Bob Becker. The memo suggested changes on several fronts. He pointed out that the Bancroft and its staff had essentially drifted for over three years since Hammond's departure. A new director for Bancroft, when or if appointed, should not have to step into a vacuum. The new university librarian, James E. Skipper, seemed open to new ideas, and ideas often in turn generated the means required to enact them. Dale had ideas; the circumstances could change from the inside, if there was a will to move forward. "I am calling for a longer-range point of view on the Library and the direction of its growth," he admitted quietly to George Hammond.[54] The memo concentrated on administrative concerns, but tucked unobtrusively in the middle was an administrative suggestion masking an intensely personal dimension. Dale observed that his two weeks in the East not only had been a "refreshment," but also that they underscored how deeply he and others in the library needed a break, or leave of absence.

The issue of sabbatical leave he left quietly alone, having fought and lost on that point two years earlier. Morgan instead pointed out that the University of California's library system had no policy provision for unpaid leave. He pointed out that a leave without pay would be personally prohibitive for an employee, hinting that the purpose of having a leave-without-pay policy would be pointless. The scramble for both a renewal and sustenance would leave the University without a refreshed and reenergized staff member. Dale expressed his commitment to the library, though intimating that his need for a substantive break was great enough that he was leaning toward making such a request.[55]

The personal dimension lurking behind the memo had been broached on his recent visit. Dale and Louise mutually agreed that a courtship between 1965 and 1968 *could have* flowered in a different outcome had

Dale been closer at hand. Morgan's memo looks very much like an explor-atory step toward resolving the transcontinental distance hampering their relationship, an attempt to create time and space for him to work first and foremost on his "Maryland project"—changing Louise's mind about marriage. If he got some writing done in the process, so much the better.

Dale updated his editor at Knopf on December 11, just before depart-ing for American Historical Association annual conference in New York City. Since writing last in early November, he reported "an unrelieved diet of Lorton, far into every night." The effort there was paying off—not in progress on the manuscript itself, but in new material that could be added to the volume. Dale now planned to add parts of Lorton's letters to the *New York Sun,* the text of another letter by fellow traveler Henry Gregory, and the overland company's official journal by Adonijah Welch to the text, plus the Cephas Arms journal as an appendix. None of the documents had been seen by another scholar, and "it all hangs together beautifully," he wrote Angus Cameron. "No doubt about it, this is going to be an extraordinary book, any way you look at it,"[56] he crowed—but it would not be ready in December. January 1969 at the very latest.

At home, Morgan began focusing on disentangling the precise geog-raphy of Lorton's route south through Utah. In doing so, he returned to his old research habit: pouring over source material, consulting maps, collating sources mentally. Once again his letters, now to Todd Berens, became the long, winding, but carefully argued explanations of his reason-ing and conclusions, teasing out geographic detail from inference-based clues sketched in the documents, the kind of letters he had written thirty years earlier to Rod Korns, Charles Kelly, and Juanita Brooks. In Berens, he found a mind who similarly understood the importance of landscape to overland travel and who similarly harbored a penchant for geographic precision. Drawing Lorton back to the fire put Hoover on the back burner to stew.[57]

Dale flew to Salt Lake City a few days before Christmas, meeting Ber-ens and several of his students at the USHS and spending the day with his mother and extended family. He contracted the flu at Emily's home and spent the holiday in bed, so sick he missed news reporting the Apollo 8 moon orbit and almost deciding not to go on to New York City on December 27 to attend the American Historical Association annual con-ference. He did, ultimately. From there, after the conference concluded, Dale took a commuter flight from New York to Washington, where lunch with Louise topped his priority list, a welcome midday interruption to time spent in National Archives. All three of the Norths drove in later to meet him for dinner, and he returned with them to Accokeek, taking time to paint window trim he had missed in October. Since it was an indoor job, Dale refused to let Louise pass in or out of the kitchen him until she kissed him on the cheek. "I felt better on leaving than I had in October," he reported to Emily, "a trifle more hopeful about the future."[58]

Dale was also hopeful about the Lorton project. So much new material had cropped up in the past six months that Dale promised Cameron that he would have the finished Lorton manuscript by May 1, 1970.[59] Nevertheless, though not a word of notes or introduction had yet been set to paper, in his far-flung research queries he insisted on noting that the work was "about to go to press," the most liberal use of the wording imaginable.[60]

Unbeknownst to Morgan, at the beginning of the year Everett Cooley, now an employee and faculty member at the University of Utah, began a second campaign for Morgan's *alma mater* to award Dale an honorary doctorate. Cooley involved Juanita Brooks, who had become the doyen of regional history within the state, and Brigham D. Madsen, a credentialed academic historian, the university's administrative vice president, and one of the few state residents with both academic credentials and a solid political reputation. Yet Leland Creer was still the history department chair at the University of Utah. This time Creer argued Morgan and his growing body of highly regarded work were not notable enough to merit the recognition, which again killed the honor.[61]

While Cooley's effort percolated beyond his awareness, Dale and the rest of the Morgan family were dealing with Emily Morgan's physical decline. News that his mother had been taken to the hospital two days after Christmas and right after he left her, dizzy and weakening noticeably, did not reach Dale while traveling through December. Testing later suggested a series of small strokes. She was hospitalized in January as Dale returned to California, and on her physician's warning that she was no longer sufficiently stable to live alone, she became a guest of Jim and Mary Beth. Fiercely independent since her widowing four decades earlier, Emily found inability and dependence hard to accept, but her physician told the family that medically nothing more treatment-wise could be done to reverse the effects of the strokes. Emily slept for long periods and became emotional easily. By the middle of the month the family was exploring options for long-term care.[62]

While Dale followed his mother's decline from afar, he acted on a matter discussed with Louise on his last visit. At the beginning of February he wrote inviting Lynn North to Salt Lake City for a road trip through the west and on to California. Lynn, at school in Michigan, was thrilled. Dale first scheduled his own colonoscopy. It returned no concerns. Flying to Salt Lake City for his mother's seventy-fifth birthday and niece Linda Morgan's wedding reception two weeks later, Dale delightedly introduced Lynn, her cousin Georgiann, and a friend, to his gathered family. After celebrating Emily's May 1 birthday, Dale rented a car. With the trio of young women splitting the driving, the quartet made a circuitous trip through Ogden and Evanston, Wyoming, before turning back through Provo and ending up in Fillmore. Dale was following the 1849 southern-route trail of William Lorton, Vincent Hoover, Adonjiah Welch, and Cephas Arms along the rim of the Great Basin into southern Utah. For the benefit of the young women, the car wandered along the highways, stopping at Bryce Canyon and Zion National Parks, Las Vegas, and a side trip in and out of Death Valley before turning north to Reno and Lake Tahoe, and descending west across the Central Valley of California into Berkeley. Dale put up his entourage in his apartment, letting them have La Loma Avenue as a base for a run of the Bay Area and weekend excursions to Yosemite National Park and Carmel. After two weeks, a thrilled Lynn North flew back to Washington and her mother, while the other pair of girls returned to Michigan.

Lynn's excited report of the trip Dale had given her upset Louise's previously firm decision against a future marriage. She was deeply grateful that Dale would take her oldest daughter on the kind of excursion across the west that she had longed for. Though Morgan was simply being characteristically generous, that generosity was a gentle tonic for Louise's still-aching and independent soul. She wrote Morgan on the day before Lynn left for home that he would be losing a "daughter" while she regained one. "It was not a matter of politeness, how the girls were received in Utah," Dale wrote to Bob Morgan and his wife Audry, "but simply extending the family to include them." After Louise's own letter of thanks, Dale could speculate to George Hammond that "I would say the odds [for him with Louise] have shifted from 50–50 to 70–30, anyhow."[63]

On Memorial Day, shortly before the trio of Dale's houseguests departed, Emily Morgan suffered another stroke. This one left her memory clouded. Once the girls had been safely dispatched, Dale flew to Salt Lake City. Dale arrived at the hospital and was admitted to her room without being recognized. He patted her shoulder, and when Emily suddenly turned her head to see who it was, her awareness began to return.

On the drive to the Salt Lake City airport for his return flight, Dale told Bob that he was sure he had seen their mother alive for the last time.[64]

Dale had flown first to Denver to see Rosenstock before planning to return to Berkeley, and he was still there two days later when Bob's telephone call informed him that Emily Holmes Morgan had passed away. Dale returned to Salt Lake City immediately, and Bob retraced the route from the airport the brothers had taken so recently. Ruth arrived from Florida the next day, and Emily's funeral was held at the Ivins Ward church on June 21. After a couple of days devoted to beginning estate matters and settling responsibilities, Dale and his sister travelled by air together to Chicago. Dale flew on to Washington, DC, arriving on June 24. The distance between him and Louise had lessened appreciably, and Dale determined to reduce it further. He pulled Louise and daughter Lynn into the kitchen, slid an arm around both and launched into a straight-faced interrogation:

> Lynn, you are designated as the official chaperone on this visit, so I have some official questions to put to you officially. Question No. 1, am I allowed to kiss your mother? (Louise began to laugh, and Lynn nods her head yes.) Am I allowed to take liberties with her, such as patting her on the behind? (Lynn shakes her head, no.) This needs further work, obviously. But Question No. 3, am I allowed to kiss the official chaperone?" (Lynn nods her head, yes.) And am I allowed to take liberties with the official chaperone, such as patting her on the behind? (Lynn shakes her head, no; and by now we are all laughing.) So I pat them simultaneously on the behind and say, "We shall see, we shall see, this matter needs more investigation."[65]

The unscripted melodrama perhaps helped Louise feel a little less self-conscious in front of her oldest daughter about her growing affection for Dale, which he certainly intended all along.

Dale settled in for a lengthy visit. He extended the trip by a week to stay with Lynn so that Louise could travel to Florida on a family matter. She was back on July 9 in time for Dale to leave on July 13. Before he left, Dale insisted that it was the Norths' turn to visit and invited them to spend Christmas with him in California. A few days after his departure Louise wrote Dale poignantly, "We miss you! ... but most of all I miss you. I miss the way your eyes light up when you look at me and the way your voice croons to me when you tell me about your love. But more than that, I miss sitting on the porch with you in the evening, shopping at the Giant with you and seeing you come in all hot and tired from working in the garden. We did have such a lovely three weeks together." The scale was tipping in his favor—slowly, but tipping nonetheless.[66]

* * * * *

By the middle of 1969, Dale's life was both very much the same, and yet he had crossed a summit. On one hand, he was still committed to research projects and writing commitments far beyond realistic capacity, a backlist that could only be cleared through time and careful attention to priorities and by avoiding distractions down enticing tangents. Dale remained remarkably busy at the Bancroft, embroiled with collection development and all sorts of related relationships. That much was still stable.

On the other hand, much had changed or would change in the near future. Emily was now gone, and with his mother gone he lost his surest anchor to Utah, his youth, and his extended family. In the next month, the Bancroft Library would finally have a new director, who would take the institution in an entirely new direction. Most importantly, there was Louise. Morgan wrote Rosenstock optimistically that despite Louise's continued reticence, "everything is different now, and I feel that we have crossed a great divide. There are all sorts of problems that will have to be worked out, and I don't have a solution for them at the moment, monetary or otherwise. But those are mere details as compared with the fundamental matter of emotional commitment."[67]

There was a way forward. Life was good.

CHAPTER 18

"There Are All Sorts of Problems That Will Have to Be Worked Out"[1]

New Directions, Berkeley, 1969–1970

My objective is to free myself ultimately to write my books.[2]
—Dale Morgan

A DECADE-LONG GROWTH in the number of credible scholarly works about the Latter Day Saints impressed ethnic historian Moses Rischin. Writing in a 1969 essay from within the flowering climate of academic historicism, Rischin proposed Thomas O'Dea's sociological study, *The Mormons* (1957), as the beginning point. He mentioned by title and author most of the books cited in the previous chapter. By the time the San Francisco State College scholar set down his observations, he could also cite more recent works by Mario De Pillis, Klaus Hansen, and even a British scholar, Philip A. M. Taylor's treatment of English convert emigration in *Expectations Westward* (1965). The books were accented by a score or more articles in respectable scholarly journals. Citing the founding of both *BYU Studies* and *Dialogue: A Journal of Mormon Thought* as more evidence of a maturing new discipline, Rischin christened this scholarly, objectified approach "the new Mormon history."

"This seems to be only a beginning," Rischin observed, "a giant step from church history to religious and intellectual history seems in the offing." The scholarly interest of inquiring academics lay behind the shift, he asserted. The scholarly approach to the Latter Day Saints and Latter-day Saints was less polemic than the work produced by previous generations—in fact, *not* polemic at all, neither against or for the church. Professional training in scholarship, Rischin claimed, lent even scholars who elected to remain practicing Latter Day Saints the interpretive equipment and the personal discipline to step beyond tradition. "They believe," he wrote, "that the details of Mormon history and culture can be studied in human or naturalistic terms—indeed, must be so studied—and without thus rejecting the divinity of the Church's origin and work."[3]

Rischin's single-page essay provided a turning point in Latter Day Saint historiography. Coining a name and identifying a foundational work fixed scholarly attention on academic historians as the focus and the drivers of the New Mormon History. By implication, Rischin claimed the detached historicism earned in graduate training was what made credentialed academics, who, in turn, created the meaningful break with the Latter-day Saints' and Latter Day Saints utilitarian storytelling.

It sounds good, but Richin's evidence misses some important points.

If academic training and credentials sparked this transformation, then academically trained students like John A. Widtsoe, Leland Creer, Milton R. Hunter, and Levi Edgar Young should have succeeded in objectifying Latter-day Saint history in an earlier generation. This group of scholars tried to create a scholarly underpinning to a study of the Latter-day Saint and Latter Day Saint past, but their training and credentials gave their historical writing merely the academic trappings of scholarship. They failed to challenge or recognize utilitarian functions of Latter-day Saint history of their day, or to dive meaningfully into source material. To do so required a different generation with different values. Beginning in the 1940s graduate training made a few LDS students intensely aware that they were pushing against something older and more entrenched. Academic training perhaps contributed to an intense self-awareness that was new within Latter Day Saint studies. Reflected perhaps best in the title of Leonard Arrington's 1965 presentation before the Western History Association (WHA): "The Secularization of Mormon History and Culture,"[4] the scholastically driven "New Mormon history" was as much an intentional departure from the cultural insularity of an earlier history as an application of new techniques and motivation. And yet, between these generations stood the circle of "Lost Generation" non-academics who spaded the ground of documentation and from it harvested the first fruits of non-polemic studies regarding the Latter-day Saints.

If the philosophical approach of historicism was what fueled the New Mormon History, then Rischin's setting of inclusive boundaries effectively excluded and ignored the Lost Generation and nonacademic scholars generally, those without credentials, who developed and publicly practiced an objectified historicism independently, well before academic writers did so openly. Rather than the academics of Leonard J. Arrington's generation, I see the fundamental groundwork that cleared much of the utilitarian ground in LDS history as having been done by the writers and works of the generation preceding Rischin's 1957 origin date. Specifically, Morgan's circle, who generally lacked academic credentials, brought to Latter-day Saint and Latter Day Saint history the earliest commitment to historicism, and they made the stylistic break with utilitarian polemics and inspirational patriotism. They plunged far more deeply into archival documents, emphasizing documentary source material and less intentional reliance on testimonial memory.

Rischin's essay, written to fellow inhabitants of the ivory tower, rather seems an example of academic historians' mid-century inward turn—a cultural bias focusing on its own. He drew a line around the New Mormon History that defined away its nonacademic Lost Generation pioneers: Nels Anderson, Juanita Brooks, Bernard DeVoto, Fawn Brodie, Francis W. Kirkham; novelists like Claire Noall, Virginia Sorensen, Vesta Crawford. This circle of informal, sometimes disagreeable relationships was perhaps initially catalyzed by Maurice Howe, but its membership was extended and linked individually by Dale Morgan. They spaded the hard ground, pointed out the primacy of source material, and left the academic historians of the 1950s and later room to work. The academic scholars of the New Mormon History extended the value of historicism without having to fight utilitarianism for cultural legitimacy—not until later, anyway.

Partly because he lauded the virtues of scholarship to those who were already credentialed scholars, Rischin's observation was adopted as an article of faith. But what of those who came to historicism without the benefit of modern academic training? For all his implied praise of scholarly detachment, Rischin's assertion about the New Mormon History is a bit utilitarian itself, focusing on the emergence of perspectives its then-current practitioners valued. True, the first generation of academically trained scholars were trained in the 1940s, independent of Mormondom's Lost-Generation writers, but LDS scholars also were not the first to look at the Latter Day Saint past through the interpretive lens of historicism. That credit (or blame) belongs with the loose circle of nonacademic Lost-Generation writers.

A year after Rischin's comment appeared in print, the Mormon History Association held its first independent annual meeting (since 1966 its gatherings had been held as thematic sessions within the Organization of American Historians conference). None of the generation whose work predated the academic "New Mormon History" attended. DeVoto was dead. Fawn Brodie had left Mormon studies entirely. Despite her growing reputation, Juanita Brooks remained somewhat intimidated by credentialled scholars and therefore aloof from those with formal training. Plus, she was already past a traditional retirement age herself. Anderson, working in government, was simply ignored. Stegner, a professor of English composition, didn't seem interested in pursuing history with that much detail. For his part, Dale Morgan remained active in the WHA, fielding and responding to queries from academic writers of the New Mormon History but seemingly never tempted toward participation in the Mormon History Association. Morgan and his circle's absence ceded that pursuit to the Mormon academics.

* * * * *

On July 17, 1969, Berkeley Chancellor Roger W. Heyns and University Librarian James E. Skipper announced the appointment of James D. Hart, former university vice chancellor and English Department chair, as director of the Bancroft Library effective January 1, 1970. By the date of its announcement, the appointment was an open secret among the library's senior staff. Hart had been the Bancroft's acting director in 1961 when Hammond was on sabbatical in Spain, and Hammond had urged Hart's appointment at his retirement in 1965. Appointment of a new director provided the opportunity to realign the history-only focus of the library and raise its stature to that of a truly great research library. At the same time, the UC Berkeley Main Library's rare books department and the Mark Twain Collection (later the Mark Twain Papers) were added to the Bancroft's portfolio, which already included University Archives and the Regional Oral History Office. The new organization closely followed the outline proposed by an external advisory committee several years earlier.[5]

Dale wrote Louise in mid-July, proposing that they marry in New Orleans that fall. At the end of July, Louise wrote Dale again, retreating back down the path they had walked together on his recent visit. Yes, she admitted openly, she had grown to love him in ways she had not thought possible a few months earlier, yet she did not feel prepared for remarriage. "For the past week I've been turning over in my mind just how I feel and what I want out of the remainder of my life," she wrote candidly. "I've always postponed such thoughts in the past and turned my attention to more pressing current problems." Dale's proposal of a wedding in New Orleans forced her to confront both feelings and fears, something she didn't really want to do. "The answer that keeps recurring is that I don't want any drastic change," she responded candidly. "I am content to let well enough alone and just drift. It's so much easier than making a big decision."[6]

"Well," Dale confided to Nancy Holliday shortly after receiving the letter, "I haven't brought Louise this far through so many adversities to let things rest here."[7] True to form, Dale created an analysis of her response in the way he had analyzed Madeline McQuown's motivations—indeed, in the analytical way he understood most intimate human relationships. Whether or not he polished and sent Louise his analysis, he drafted it longhand. "The tragedy," he wrote, "is that with so much intelligence sensitivity to mood and thought and insight into people you are able to apply none of this to your own living or even understand yourself very well." He continued:

> You have been in flight from responsibility more than you know. It has been at the heart of your confusion with respect to me[.] You have neither been willing to enter wholeheartedly into my world nor to stand apart from it. The passivity that has paralyzed all your relations with me has saved to rob you of a great many of the things you have felt to be lacking in your world. You have wanted the sense of security[,] of excitement that comes from having a world made in what you may dwell. But you have fought against any suggestion that you might have some responsibility for shaping that world that it should be required of you to give love as well as receive it, create happiness as well as receive it as your responsibility.[8]

Citing a family record of poor remarriages, Louise later wrote him: "You are right, I think, when you observe that it is not so much that I reject you as a husband as that there is some conflict within me that makes me resist marriage now with everything I am."[9] Louise's near-rejection underscored the truth of what Dale had written Bob Becker a year earlier—he needed a break. While it might be granted with professional writing in mind, he needed time to draw Louise closer to himself, and he felt he had to do that in person, not by mail. Berkeley, California was not close enough to Accokeek, Maryland to accomplish that feat.

On the heels of Louise North's plea for emotional distance, a more ominous memorandum arrived from Bob Becker. "Our old ways we may not keep; nothing that we have done can be justified simply because we have always been doing it," he asserted discretely. Becker pointed out

Morgan had made no appreciable progress toward completing the library's most recent promotional brochure, the map book for Mrs. Kennedy, nor the second volume of the *Guide to Manuscripts* since Morgan listed them as ranked priorities the preceding April. "It is impossible to remain ignorant of the fact that you do not work on your assigned responsibilities, nor have you done so for many, many months," Becker stated, adding: "you are not what a member of the History Department once termed you to me: A Scholar-in-Residence. You are a member of the staff." Just as Dale was finally making progress on the magnificent new material reinforcing the edition of the Lorton diary, Becker insisted that Morgan confine his activity during work hours to Library-assigned tasks.[10] The rebuke was tactful, diplomatic, but stinging, yet also clearly Becker's attempt to give Morgan time to show a record of accomplishment before Hart took over in six months.

Thus, a push from Bob Becker and a pull from Louise North coincided. Both underscored that Morgan's position at the Bancroft Library was no longer viable to accomplish either purpose he valued—neither professional writing nor personal relationship. Two days later Dale wrote George Hammond confidentially looking for advice. "Is it not singular that the staff should have ethical obligations to Bancroft which Bancroft does not have toward the staff?" He had been a Bancroft Library employee for better than fifteen years, was ineligible for sabbatical leave, and in his staff position an unpaid leave was unlikely to be approved, yet he was more widely known than anyone else who worked there. "Anything I can do along this line must be strictly on the self-help basis, I think; and the way the world is set up, this would involve, at present, a grant from some foundation or learned society."

The leave without pay that a fellowship represented was a terrific gamble, for during an absence his responsibilities could be reallocated and he might be left with effectively no position at a grant or fellowship's conclusion. Still, Dale decided the risk was worth the prospective return. "I feel that I have less and less time to do some of the big work in history that I expect of myself, something that should be given its proper weight." In his estimation, the application would have to be filed in the coming autumn if a grant were to be available in the spring of 1971.[11] What most concerned Morgan was not his job at Bancroft but rather "what I want to do with history, in the uncertain amount of time that may still remain to me." Plus, "if I want Louise, it may ultimately come down to ... pulling up my base here and putting down new roots in the East."[12] Applying for an individual research fellowship was a first step taken toward disconnecting himself from California. Wary of change and craving stability, Louise would bring an emotional sacrifice to the altar to make the marriage, but Dale would bring a professional one. Dale Morgan had been willing but not yet ready to stand on his own reputation in 1948, but by 1969 he thought that he probably could.

While Dale worked steadily to reduce the pile of correspondence that had sifted onto his desk over his three-week absence in Maryland, Hammond came to see Dale personally to answer the question about a fellowship. Certainly, he recommended, try for a second Guggenheim Foundation grant. Other foundations, however, seemed to be decreasing their direct support of scholarship. Hammond recommended "a strong offense" suggesting "for mid-1971, a major study on the Mormons (or whatever you feel should come first[)]."[13] Morgan planned to say nothing to Becker about a fellowship application, instead waiting for Hart to come on board, but he wrote the Guggenheim Foundation for an application form and instructions on August 5.[14]

Despite their recently renewed courtship, Louise again began pulling further away from Dale and the emotional commitment that remarriage would require. She wrote him that a relationship was "what I have retreated from in all directions, because it places an additional responsibility on me—the responsibility for your happiness as well as for the happiness of Lynn and Lisa."[15] Finally the pattern that characterized their relationship seemed to becoming clear to him: when they were in close proximity, he was able to keep her fears at bay, but when they were apart, doubts and fear crowded out her affection. A fellowship—if he could get one—promised both an opportunity to close the gap and a convenient opportunity to take Louise along.

On August 21, Dale wrote Fred Rosenstock than he planned to seek a Guggenheim Fellowship. He felt the likelihood of being awarded the fellowship was small, but was going to apply anyway.[16] Through the next month he told more close friends: Donald Jackson at the University of Virginia, Ray Allen Billington at the Huntington Library, and Wallace Stegner at Stanford University, each of whom he asked to serve as references. He also told his coauthor, Eleanor Harris. The motivation for telling her, besides the trust and confidence he had in her discretion, was that he enlisted her to postpone work on the Hoover book for several months. Despite the progress made recently, he even set aside Lorton once again to concentrate on the fellowship application.

Though Hammond assumed Dale would return to the Mormons, the theme of his first Guggenheim Fellowship, Dale decided to hang the proposal on the fur trade. He had contemplated the idea of a three-volume study at least as early as 1954, when he considered that *Jedediah Smith and the Opening of the West* would be the middle volume.[17] In intervening years, however, he was not the only writer in the field, and scholarship had continued. Richard Oglesby completed a book on Manuel Lisa (Morgan's own choice as a central character for his study), which lessened the need for a comprehensive study of the trade's early years. With the collection of Robert Campbell material stalled over permissions, Dale's contemplated third volume looked like it would not move soon. He began mulling over the challenges and opportunities that a single-volume work would offer.

After a few days of careful thought, he finally settled on the scope for his new Guggenheim Foundation application: a study of the *entire* North American fur trade between the expulsion of the French from Canada in 1763 and the 1870 Deed of Cession by the Hudson's Bay Company, the document which cleared the latter's charter claims to the west and made possible the founding of the Dominion of Canada.[18] The proposal was a return to the grand narrative Morgan craved, the kind of historical synthesis of his earliest works "and not the documentary works that have principally preoccupied me since coming to Bancroft."[19] A work of this size and scope would be a magisterial undertaking which probably no other scholar before or since had a sufficient grasp of resources to produce. In the early days of October 1969, Morgan complied his proposal and posted the application to the John Simon Guggenheim Memorial Foundation in New York City. His narrative laid out the scope he intended to address:

> I shall devote equal attention to the Canadian and American West during this significant century, which was also the great age of the exploration of the interior West, make clear the intimate interaction of the Canadian and American fur trades, ... and analyze the economic base with particular attention to the marketing of furs, the entrepreneurs who entered the trade, their resources, limitations, and mode of conducting their business, the ever-recurring problem of manpower (sources, competition for it, its character, manpower as a perpetual limiting factor in all plans and action), and the continental wealth in furs—an unevenly distributed wealth.[20]

While the Bancroft awaited its new director and the grant proposal winged eastward, as Dale planned and hoped, Jim and Bob Morgan unitedly struggled with Emily Morgan's estate. Dale, however, was none too patient with what he saw dimly from afar as delay and inexcusable laziness. He dabbled with the idea of buying the Hollywood Avenue house himself, partly out of sentiment and partly with the thought of using it as a rental property. That thought was more of a dream than a plan. Ultimately the family decided the aging structure required too much investment and determined to sell the family home. Family treasures, none of which were valuable in their own right beyond the pale of family, were divided. Dale suggested Bob hang onto an old frying pan: "the interest may be sentimental rather than rational, but I would hate to see it just thrown away, going back as it does to the last Sunday before Dad was taken ill."[21] That single sentence was the only time of record among his hundreds of letters to family that he ever referred to their father, Lowell Morgan, with the informality that families typically share.

During the month Dale also made quiet queries to Berkeley's personnel office about what benefits would be due him as an early retiree. He discovered later he would net a meager $200 monthly if he retired in 1970, which was less than Louise would lose in widow's benefits from her Civil Service annuity and Max's US Navy pension, should she remarry. Waiting to retire until the beginning of 1971 would net him only about another $30 monthly. This information imposed an inconvenient complication to his scheme, and he confided to Anna McConkey that "I am making it a serious objective to set up a more favorably[sic] retirement picture" in 1972.[22] Dale also declined to attend the WHA meeting in Omaha, too busy to make the trip and planning to make another visit to Maryland, anyway. As he struggled with the fellowship application and retirement planning, the La Loma property's owner was transferred to Indiana and put up the duplex for sale for the second time in two years. With the fellowship as his highest priority and potential ticket out of California, there was now no question of Morgan's interest in buying it.

* * * * *

Dale spent the fall of 1969 dashing off two marvelous pieces of writing, his last works on the Mormons and very nearly his last published works of any sort. One was an essay for *Dialogue* about literature and literary value in Mormonism, a reprise of the assessment he had written in 1942. His writing sparkled with personal insight and character even as he discussed the merits of nonfiction, hymns, and personal narrative as "literature of a high order." The other piece was a personal narrative, an explanation of his experience with Latter Day Saint bibliography, requested by Everett Cooley as a prospective introduction to the catalog Chad Flake would publish (eventually) as *A Mormon Bibliography, 1830–1930*. As the father of that work, Morgan's lengthy explanation summarized his long history with bibliography and what it meant to the growing body of scholarship on Mormonism. Though the catalog was not published for nearly a decade after Morgan dispatched his sheets to Salt Lake City, the essay appeared in the front of the volume with a commemorative note from the publication committee. The catalog was, as Cooley had said earlier, Dale Morgan's work, after all.[23]

Dale delayed his October visit east by a week to deal with some dental work and to rush the index to the Howard Gardiner book, but was in Maryland again by the middle of the month because, as he told Helen Wheat, "letters just don't do the work with my girl, the thing needs the personal touch."[24] He stayed part of the time in the city, working more on the Gardiner index and at the Library of Congress from his preferred accommodation at the Mayflower Hotel, interrupted by visits south to Accokeek. There he fell into routine chores, gathering and sawing wood and sacking dry leaves as winter bedding for the animals.[25] The stay was shorter than usual, for Morgan had arranged a stop in St. Louis, where he was the guest of Missouri Historical Society manuscripts librarian Frances Hurd Stadler and her husband.

Dale was back in Berkeley on November 17 in time to arrange a trail ride with Todd Berens over the Thanksgiving weekend. With their mother gone, his siblings gathered their own families for holidays, so Dale stayed in Berkeley to spend Thanksgiving with Mac and Julia Macleod. The next day he caught a flight to Los Angeles where Todd Berens picked him up. This time they followed Jedediah Smith's 1827 trail, beginning around Needles and tracing the geography westward, turning south around Soda Lake and through Afton Canyon, then back onto the interstate and into the Los Angeles plains across Cajon Pass. He flew back to the Bay Area on December 1.[26] Once at home his attention turned eastward again. Dale cajoled Louise to either bring her daughters or follow them to California for the Christmas holiday, but as often in relationships, with the most at stake, he had the least control. She declined. The girls wanted to spend Christmas at home, and Louise was out of leave.[27]

Though the fall of 1969 Dale corresponded widely, confident that 1970 would see several book projects completed. Gardiner was merely the first.[28] He wrote Fawn Brodie that his plan was to use the year to clear "five or six" books and then to concentrate on the fur trade study and then return to the history of the Mormons. The goal was ambitious but possible, certainly, if the list included only his own projects (which, according to his own correspondence, included William B. Lorton and Vincent A. Hoover diaries, the Robert Campbell compilation, letters by English botanist Joseph Burke, and several works of lesser priority, none of which had proceeded as far as a rough draft; only Lorton and Hoover existed as complete transcripts at that point). Still, the plan was naïvely optimistic at best, given his track record over the previous five years. Dale spent Christmas with the Hollidays at their home in Lafayette, east of Berkeley. On December 28, Lynn North and a friend arrived at Dale's doorstep after a cross-country road trip. He was delighted; Louise was relieved that her oldest daughter opted for Dale in Berkeley over who-knows-what in Haight-Ashbury across the bay. The young women enjoyed a three-day reprise of Lynn's trip with Dale earlier in the year before pulling out on New Year's Eve.

* * * * *

James D. Hart assumed his responsibilities at Bancroft at the turn of 1970, and the staff and their new director began the inevitable period of accommodation to new ideas and personalities. Hart and Morgan had known and worked around each other for years. In the second week of the new year, Dale sent the scholar of American literature the tear sheets of his recent article on Mormon literature, noting innocently later in the memo that he had applied for a Guggenheim Foundation fellowship and would complete the book on Stockton maps for Helen Kennedy and the second *Guide to Manuscripts* volume before departing.[29] He hoped the University of California system would grant him leave in acknowledgement of the fellowship if it was awarded, but was not hopeful on that point, he told a sister-in-law: "I am quite prepared to break out of my present pattern, and either show that I can make as much money writing books and articles on my own time as a regular job produces, or look for a new job in the Washington area."[30]

Hart responded later in the month, clearly skeptical about Dale's plans for the fellowship—and also about taking on an announced plan to provide an introduction and notes to Helen Bretnor's translation of the diary of a French gold seeker. "All of these things, wonderful as they are," he wrote in response, "are not central to your daily obligations at the Bancroft Library."[31]

Shortly after Hart's wary note, Eleanor Harris sent Dale a revised, corrected, and retyped transcript for the Vincent Hoover diary. Never able to say no to an opportunity, Dale suddenly elevated that project to the center of his attention. In his optimistic budget of calendar time, Dale told Todd Berens that he would deliver the notes for both Lorton *and* Hoover by March 1, which he might have realized from past experience was an utterly unrealistic assumption.[32] Morgan devoted himself completely to the various southern-route projects, working at his desk at the library every night till 10 p.m. and all day on weekends. He was not actually writing, however, just working out the chronology, geography, and relationship of the documents to the other source material.[33] In other words, he was placing notes and structuring the source material.

The cost of the lack of actual progress on existing commitments was increasing. Valita Moran's patience had worn thin, and after nearly fifteen years, she now stated openly that she regretted allowing the Lorton material to pass out of her hands. Friends wagged their heads, she complained, saying that she had been taken as a fool. Dale responded that her friends plainly did not understand what was involved in making a historical document into a work of history. Crafting history involved "a living entity, growing and changing character like any living thing."[34] Sending her a prospective title and a table of contents mollified her concerns and he kept working—nominally. Even so, he would assure Angus Cameron in May that the Lorton book was "on the absolute verge of completion," even though he had not written much more than a few pages of outline for an introduction.[35] By late February Dale was no longer even thinking of the Lorton and Hoover as two books, and he suggested to Eleanor Harris that they join the diaries into a larger and more substantial book on 1849 travel along the southern route, one to make LeRoy R. and Ann W. Hafens' 1954 collection *Journals of Forty-Niners* obsolete.

The Lorton diary was becoming for the southern route what his Pritchard and McCollum books had become for the northern trail and the Panama crossing respectively, and what *The West of William H. Ashley* had become for the high years of the American fur trade: Morgan's attempt at a comprehensive grand narrative.[36] Dale told Jim Holliday, who had been offered and assumed leadership of the California Historical Society, that delivery of what now he conceived of a vastly expanded project involving the Hoover diary, would have to be delayed.[37] In fact, the volume's scope was nearly exploding.

Meeting his obligations at work involved almost as much pressure. At the end of the first week of February, Morgan forwarded a status report to Hart, noting that shaping the text of the Stockton maps book being financed by Helen Kennedy through the Friends of The Bancroft Library was more complicated than imagined, and he warned that the project might not be completed for a year. Morgan also noted that he had not been directly involved with the second *Guide to Manuscripts* volume on Mexican and colonial resources, which was not precisely accurate; he had not written the text but certainly had been charged with coordinating staff work toward completing the volume. Separately, toward the end of February Dale received a request for a prospective itinerary and budget from the Guggenheim Memorial Foundation, a strong indication that his fellowship request was likely to be funded. No matter what pressure faced him on publication projects or at work, Dale set them aside to make a spring trip to see Louise early in 1970. It was not an option or an indulgence, he wrote Joe Colgan, for "there is just so much I can accomplish by mail in bringing her to the point of marriage, and I don't expect to reach that exact point next month either."[38]

* * * * *

Morgan's transcontinental flight from California landed in time for Dale to meet Louise for dinner the same evening. Earlier the same day, Gordon N. Ray, president of the John Simon Guggenheim Memorial Foundation, posted a letter to Morgan's Berkeley address, formal notice that the foundation had awarded Dale L. Morgan a second Guggenheim Fellowship.[39] On March 25, Lois Stone, who had been picking up his mail, telephoned the news to Dale's hotel in Washington, DC. Dale's luck in finding a path out of Bancroft professionally and personally had finally opened. Not only was his second award quite unusual, it was also achieved despite a much more competitive field. Where in 1945 the Foundation awarded ninety-six fellowships, 218 awards were made in 1970. Morgan's project for a history of the continental fur trade ranked competitively with projects proposed by fellow awardees Utah folklorist Jan Harold Brunvand, Princeton historian Robert Darnton, and computer scientist Len Kleinrock, whose work on the mathematical theory of data networks helped provide the conceptual backbone for developing the Internet (and later, he personally invented the concept of email).[40]

Dale waited until returning to California to accept the Guggenheim award formally, confirming in his acceptance letter that the required physical exam would be filed. He notified Hart of the award as well, stating that he had requested the beginning date for April 1971 to provide more time to clear his Bancroft obligations.[41] The fellowship imposed on him and his priorities a hard deadline.

The litany of Dale Morgan's obligations in the spring of 1970 was staggering, and for perhaps the first time he began to realize how badly he had overpromised himself. The best he could do was characterize the situation to his brother Bob as "a hellish amount of advance preparation," in addition to planning for the travel and research itself.[42] Beyond the verbal or contractual commitments that stood at the last holiday, he had also pledged to complete a major revision of the diaries of trapper/cartographer Warren Angus Ferris for Rosenstock by June 1, as well as an introduction and notes to Helen Bretnor's translation of the French diary for the University of California Press. He also was currently reading and correcting galleys for both the first volume of John C. Frémont's exploration diaries edited by Donald Jackson, and Charles Camp's revisions for a fourth edition of *The Plains and the Rockies* bibliography. On top of that, he now needed to identify and buy books on the Canadian fur trade, and he still hoped to capture Louise's matrimonial agreement before the end of the year, which portended additional travel. As he ramped up communication coordinating his eventual departure, Morgan seems to have taken entirely for granted the idea that the University of California would grant him an extended leave without pay; that inconvenient detail had yet to be negotiated and approved as well. Despite the stated writing priorities he intended to clear before leaving, toward the end of April 1970, however, he confessed to Eleanor Harris that he had made no meaningful progress on either the Lorton nor Hoover books, nor in fact on any current writing commitment.[43]

News of the Guggenheim award was communicated to friends and acquaintances in the routine blizzard of correspondence. Others learned of it through the announcement made either by the University of California or the foundation's own published list. Congratulations, wrote a UC Berkeley library administrator, "one is always relieved, if rarely so, to be told libraries can be distinguished for something besides collecting."[44] Fawn Brodie saw the notice and wrote her congratulations. Dale was as irked as he had been in 1946 that she found out before he had been able to tell her personally, but he responded optimistically that "now for the first time it is really possible for me to do the uprooting."[45]

Dale also quietly composed an inquiry to the Library of Congress, asking about potential vacancies on staff, asserting that he needed to decide whether to apply for a sabbatical. Morgan's letter reads as if he was trying not to appear too eager and was willing to negotiate. It did not say that Morgan had resigned himself that he would never qualify for a sabbatical and was making career plans beyond the fellowship. As he had in the 1940s, in 1970 Dale still badly misunderstood the hiring dynamics of the nation's largest library. Unlike George Hammond, who had budgetary control and a reasonably free hand with hiring, federal hiring authority was not vested in Library of Congress staff, and they could not simply hold an open vacancy, however talented or notable the applicant.[46]

* * * * *

If Louise North provided a pull, emerging discontentment at work served to push Morgan beyond the academic library career he had once gratefully accepted. In 1946 George Hammond had been charged with building the Bancroft Library into a research institution. By 1970 that task had been effectively accomplished, and the Bancroft stood as one of the nation's great historical-research libraries. In part, the transition from one status to another meant the library formalized activities or arrangements which had been informal, as well as securing what had once been open and accessible. Where Hammond could afford to be intentionally indulgent of the historical work Morgan did and his growing reputation as a scholar, Hart came to the helm of an institution that grew only in size and not generally in its sophistication.

A noisy, excited herd of Morgan nieces and nephews arrived for a stay with Uncle Oscar in the first week of June at about the same time that Dale posted his second progress report to Hart. Other than receipt of the fellowship award, no real progress had been made on the Stockton map book or the second volume of the *Guide to Manuscripts*. This time Morgan's report rang an alarm bell for the new director. Hart's response came as a formal memorandum, a dated catalog of estimates, goals, pledges, delays, and nonperformance. It looked very much like the administrative foundation for a pending personnel action.[47] The barefaced formality of the question about his work performance must have stung, but Dale responded with measured reason about his unorthodox position, neither librarian nor university faculty and yet the "library's consulting scholar" for public queries. His professional reputation extended well beyond mere employment service to the university, a point that some staff resented. Dale observed that he kept personal accomplishments out of the library's formal reports, partly to keep from antagonizing egos already bruised by his reputation. As a result, most of his notable work was not pursued on university time. The university had not supported his scholarly work, he noted, and Morgan pursued the second Guggenheim application to address that lack of compensation. "I am not dependent on the Library for either a job or professional status," he noted with more than a tinge of boastfulness. "So what I do for the Library ... I do out of my own sense of commitment not less than the Library's welfare." Dale also pointed out somewhat disingenuously that he could have walked away from the library to embark on the fellowship immediately and had postponed the award out of a sense of loyalty to complete the *Guide to California Manuscripts* (the third volume of the catalog).[48]

Privately, Dale wrote to Dan Howe, reporting a tentative fellowship plan and expressing that he was thinking seriously about retiring from the University of California rather than merely taking a leave of absence. He expected to embark on the fellowship in April 1971, spend time in institutional collections around the Pacific Northwest and three months in England, as well as to devote several more months to northeastern libraries and archives before settling permanently in or around Washington, DC. "Time is rapidly passing without my ever seeming to get as much done as needs to be done," he stated, adding that the fellowship timeline might have to be pushed back to accommodate his employment and other writing obligations.[49]

Hart remained concerned about progress on the library's publishing program but accepted Dale's explanation and general plans. Some of his coworkers held distinctly different opinions of their colleague and his work. Years earlier Madeline McQuown had warned her friend that "the chief thing at Bancroft is that the people there feel you write book after book on Bancroft time[,] becoming rich and famous on the salary they have and drudge for—rightfully or wrongfully."[50] Longtime public services librarian [John] Barr Tompkins, by disposition a stickler for rules and regulations and a former member of the University of California's School of Librarianship, was one of the coworkers Madeline had warned Dale about. Relations between the two had always been fairly stiff but finally snapped in an exchange of letters in the summer of 1970. The breaking point was a procedural change for staff paging books from the collection for internal use.

Dale had long enjoyed the informal privilege of pulling and returning books from the collection at his convenience on Tier 3, the basement storage area where his desk was located. As library processes standardized and staff became more careful about documenting the movement of its valuable collection material, Tompkins, as head of the Bancroft Library's reading room, required library paging procedures and records be filed and followed precisely. He was clearly irked that Morgan wanted to bypass rules that now applied to everyone else. Finally, Tompkins snapped at Morgan in a memo, which is worth quoting, for it shows how the tenor of the place had changed for Morgan since Hammond's retirement:

> For too long now you, as a paid member of the staff . . . have been the notable, or notorious, exception in that you have done so little for The Bancroft Library. Some of us have repeatedly been put in the position of making some sort of apology for the failure of the *Guide* to appear; I have very often found it necessary to report that you were not on hand when patrons asked for you. We, if not you, have a deep concern for the public image of the Library we serve. Your long-term failure to get on with your work is a matter of growing unrest among your working colleagues who see you serve yourself at the Library's and our expense. It is that simple, actually, and if it's painful, I cannot apologize, because it's true. You talk of being helpful, in the face of your last several years of procrastination, during which you have used the Library and its staff for your own ends, is meaningless. . . . To all this there is a very simple solution: Do your job. You'll find the atmosphere will improve in contrast to the deterioration which will surely develop if you persist in disregarding the procedures set up for the general operation of the library.[51]

To be sure, Dale was well-liked and socially active with friends among the staff, but those relationships were only part of his experience. Many factors were at play. Deafness imposed its own form of isolation. Madeline was correct about the resentment of his reputation beyond the library functions. Hammond was no longer on hand to insulate and deflect discontent for Morgan's freedoms. The library and its administrative, public access, and internal security structures were institutionally maturing. In sum, the Bancroft Library in which Dale Morgan worked in 1970 was a very different place than the one to which he had been invited in 1954.

Demands on his time were not simplified when on June 15 a North American Van Lines truck pulled into La Loma Avenue with Morgan's two overstuffed, four-drawer steel file cabinets and a dozen or more crates of books and papers emerging from nearly twenty years in Emily Morgan's basement. These items arrived together with some of her furniture, Dale's portion of his mother's estate. This delivery put all of Morgan's papers at hand in the same location for the first time in his career, though little room for them was available in the quickly filling library at the front of the house. Later in the day a Pacific Intermountain Express van delivered a few more boxes, his mother's personal correspondence, photographs, and collected family papers.[52] Dale had almost no time to organize the jumble of boxes, furniture, papers, and a room of shelves already overflowing with books.[53]

In this midst of the work storm, Dale made another trip to Washington in early July. Officially the purpose was Bancroft collection development, but it provided a subsidized opportunity for a bit of contact with friends—and Louise, of course. Earlier in the year she had turned down a proposal for a June wedding because they would have to live apart. In July, Dale returned with the hope a wedding could take place in October. "Louise and I attain a closer relationship on each succeeding visit, and she was especially a joy on this last one, full of perky and impish humor which showed how totally relaxed she is with me now," Dale told his sister Ruth confidently. "We got past the point where she agreed that she is going to marry me, 'sometime or other,' as I put it; that we are 'engaged to be engaged.'"[54]

This year portended another change in Maryland. Lisa planned to follow Lynn to college in Michigan at the end of the summer, leaving Louise genuinely alone in her home for the first time. Before leaving, Dale personally delivered the now-traditional invitation to the North family to meet him in California for the Christmas holidays. He returned in hopeful spirits, but on July 15, he arrived at work to find that during his absence his desk (and its deep strata of unfiled correspondence and papers) had been cleared and moved elsewhere in the building as part of a space reallocation—one more nudge reinforcing his plan to leave. Given their exchange the preceding month, Hart accorded Morgan some personal and emotional space to play catch-up, noting that "You look to be so assiduously at work every time I am in your area that I don't want to disturb you."[55]

At the end of August, Morgan was surprised and delighted to receive a $250 check from Retendex Internation for his portion of the option to television and film rights to *Jedediah Smith and the Opening of the West*.[56] The book, which had finally been issued in paperback, was on its way to status as a classic of Western Americana, but neither option was ever exercised. Receipt of this windfall may have been the motivation to invite Louise to meet him in early October and at the height of fall color along the Wasatch Mountains that rimmed Salt Lake City. She initially agreed but then could not come. Meanwhile, Dale was working frantically on virtually everything but the tasks that most needed to be done, confessing in one letter that "I am as far as ever from catching up with the work piling up on every hand." He was, at least, hard at work and making slow but measurable progress on the Friends of The Bancroft Library book on Stockton maps, which hung most closely over his head.[57]

* * * * *

On October 3, Dale returned to Salt Lake City for the first time since his mother's death, making a weekend trip to attend the inaugural advisory board meeting of the American West Center at the University of Utah. During the meetings and social gatherings he was bothered by an indefinite sense of a tightening or drawing on the right side of his abdomen. He thought that his now-constant exhaustion was due to the weight of overwork finally catching up with its perpetrator.

Probably this visit to Salt Lake City was when Dale revealed to Everett Cooley he intended to pick up the history of the Mormons again on his fellowship, rather than work solely on the fur trade history. Cooley told me in 1997 that he remembered challenging Dale on the point, saying that he thought the fellowship had been solely to support the fur trade book. Morgan waved off the librarian. "He said 'Cooley, you don't understand how these things work.' He says 'you can get a grant, and as long as you make progress on whatever you're doing you can spend your time [doing what you want].'"[58] Cooley wasn't so certain on that point.

The highlight of the trip for Morgan, however, was attending a presentation by Fawn Brodie at a standing-room-only event in the Hotel Utah titled "Can We Manipulate the Past?" The apostate had come publicly home again, and to a platform literally next door to the Church

Administration Building. Fawn handed Dale a copy of her speech so that he could follow along as she read her presentation. Afterwards, Dale scrawled her a note of how proud he was of one of his oldest friends.[59]

When the board meeting concluded, Morgan accepted an invitation to a weekend football game and an invitation from Bob and Audry for a road trip south though Utah Valley and around Nephi to look northward at Mount Nebo, the last Wasatch Front landmark visible as one headed toward Los Angeles along the southern route to California. Dale felt a tinge of regret, however, upon receiving a special-delivery letter from Louise about his pending visit later in the month: no wedding bells, please.[60] He flew back to Berkeley the next day.

Upon his return, Dale consulted with his physician about the results of his latest glucose-tolerance lab work. His blood-sugar level was up again.[61]

CHAPTER 19

"As Liable to Happen to Me as to Anyone Else"[1]

Lafayette, California, and Accokeek, Maryland, 1970–1971

I shall fight this out to the end, and hopefully the end may be a good deal longer than the usual.[2]

—Dale Morgan

SHORTLY AFTER RETURNING to Berkeley in August 1970, Morgan was jerked awake with a sharp pang of what he thought was a pinched nerve in his right side, just below his rib cage. The sensation was uncomfortable, but he shrugged it off and went to work. Within a few days he felt himself tiring noticeably through a typical day. Before two weeks were out, after walking home from work he was resting on the couch for longer and longer periods before diving into an evening of research. Dale began waking in the morning wringing in sweat. He shrugged it off as age or something and, on October 16, caught a flight to Washington, DC, for a visit with Louise and her daughters. Despite plans for research and other activities, Morgan spent much of the time resting on the bed in his favorite accommodation at the Mayflower Hotel, completely wrung out from comparatively little exertion. Dale wrote Jim Holliday mentioning the odd pain in his side. Holliday fired back a letter that he was to have the doctor look into it as soon as Morgan returned, fearing either a kidney stone or prostate trouble.[3] Dale returned to Berkeley on November 2.

On the next day, Dale went to a hastily arranged appointment at the Kaiser clinic. The attending physician immediately identified an enlarged liver and ordered a battery of blood tests and an isotope-enhanced X-ray of Dale's abdomen. Morgan left with strict instructions for a vegetarian diet and orders to retain six days of stool samples for analysis. On the day after his medical appointment, November 4, Dale went home from work at lunchtime and spent the next two days in bed absolutely wrung out. He recovered well enough to return to work on November 7, but something was obviously wrong.[4] Dale kept a follow-up appointment at the clinic on November 9. A telephone call later that same afternoon set up another appointment with his physician the following day.

Learning that one has cancer is not a gentle experience—especially not when cancer is at an advanced stage, and certainly not in a major organ. "It was obvious from his manner that he didn't like the news he had for me," Morgan later recalled for his family, "and I put the question to him at once, there was a possibility I had cancer? 'Perhaps,' he said. Assuming the worst, what was the prognosis for cancer of the liver, I asked. He shook his head, and I said 'It is invariably fatal.' He nodded."[5]

Morgan's physician explained that far into his large intestine, just past the opening from the small intestine, a small patch of cells had reproduced wildly, their corrupted status taking over the cells next to them. This growth seems to have happened at a bend where one of the liver's lobes lays against the colon wall. A cancerous tumor can affect the cells of another organ lying against it. This site, where the two organs nestle against each other, is probably where Morgan's colorectal cancer found its entry to his liver's hepatocyte tissue. There is a reason that in English the organ is called "the *liver*." In medieval medicine, the heart and brain were secondary organs—the liver was the seat of life itself. The liver's centrality to body function, however, also makes it somewhat vulnerable to damage or systemic interruption. As Dale was about to leave the consultation, the doctor said directly "Maybe we are all wrong" and put an arm about Morgan's shoulders. To the patient, this uncharacteristic action by a physician was a meaningful communication in itself.[6]

Leaving the clinic, the implications of his short interview crashed into Dale's psyche, a black flood of confusion and emotion. He did not return to the library after the appointment. Instead, he climbed on a transit bus for San Francisco. His cancer diagnosis, terminal or not, convinced him to make a symbolic but material step toward Louise and marriage. Even if she rejected his proposal, he needed to give her a token to remind her that it had been made. A diamond did not fit his sentiment or carry appropriate meaning; he went looking for something suitably informal and distinctly western. The ride through Oakland, across the water, and into San Francisco could not have been pleasant. The trip provided an uninterrupted stretch of thoughts, fears, and uncertainty chasing him like the tatters of scudding clouds over the Bay Bridge: all the possible complications that cancer and its treatment flung at him, knocking over his carefully built house of cards—the book contracts, the job search, his plans for the fellowship, travel to Europe with Louise. Marriage. Louise.

Morgan's destination was Marion Davidson's storefront on Union Street, a small shop specializing in Native American handiworks and arts. Dale requested Davidson dial Jim Holliday at the California Historical Society a few blocks away. Dale relied on others to serve as his vocal and aural intermediary, the only practice Morgan had ever known as an adult. Davidson placed the call, handed over the telephone receiver, and Dale asked Holliday to come to the shop. Dale's use of the telephone himself was "an astounding situation—my God, it was frightening," Holliday recalled years later. "I knew something dreadful had happened or he wouldn't be calling me."[7]

While Dale waited for his friend, he looked distractedly for a suitable ring in silver and turquoise, finally settling on and buying a shell necklace instead. Alarmed by the sudden and cryptic request delivered from an unlikely setting in the middle of the day, Holliday double-parked on the narrow Russian Hill pavement of Union Street to come in and retrieve Dale. Returning to Holliday's car, the pair sat stock still in San Francisco's city traffic as Dale choked out his news. Within a few minutes, a police officer insisted Holliday move out of the street. Jim pulled around the corner and parked long enough to get from Dale the rest of the sketchy information about his medical condition.

Colon cancer is insidious and often has no symptoms. It begins with a genetic mutation in one of the stem cells that constantly divide and redivide in the healthy tissue lining the large intestine. When left untreated, the longer-lived, mutated cells pile up, forming masses of polyp tissue. According to the National Institute of Diabetes and Digestive and Kidney Diseases, between 15 percent and 40 percent of the U.S. population, both men and women, develop polyps.[8] These are usually easy to identify in a colonoscopy. Not all polyps turn cancerous, but even in 1970 regular colonoscopies provided opportunities to remove polyps before they became cancerous and formed distinct tumors.

All this medical detail came out later. For the moment, all Jim Holliday needed to hear was the essentials: Dale had cancer, and it was serious. Holliday drove immediately back to the California Historical Society office on Mission Street, called his wife Nancy, and with her approval told Dale pointedly that he would be staying at their home. Despite working as

the society's director for less than two weeks, Holliday cleared his schedule with his secretary and drove Dale back across San Francisco Bay and
east to his family home in Lafayette. They stopped in Berkeley to retrieve
clothes from Dale's apartment, giving Jim an opportunity to telephone
the clinic and clarify medical details Dale did not have. Holliday needed
to know as much as possible before placing the inevitable phone call to
Louise North later that evening.

Jim dialed the long-distance call to the Accokeek, Maryland, exchange
with operator assistance. Louise picked up the telephone. Holliday had
often talked to her, and a call from Dale through Jim was no surprise. This
time, however, rather than acting as Dale's voice and ears, he told Louise
that she needed to hear from Dale directly and handed over the receiver,
allowing Dale himself to stumble out the news in his own way to the
woman he loved, knowing he would not hear her reaction. Having buried a husband from cancer, and only slowly and somewhat shyly coming
around to the possibility of another marriage, Louise was terribly upset
to have the promise of new happiness yanked from her as well. When
Holliday reclaimed the telephone to mediate the rest of the conversation,
Louise wanted him to book Dale on a flight to Washington the next day.
Holliday patiently explained the medical reasons why Dale needed to stay
in California for now, and Louise relented, but insisted Dale come east
for Thanksgiving.

Through the next week, Jim and Nancy ferried Dale to and from Alta
Bates Hospital. On November 12 Dale was admitted for a needle biopsy
of his liver and a twenty-four-hour medical observation spent flat and
unmoving on his back. The experience was more than uncomfortable,
"the general effect was that of having been kicked in the belly by a horse,"
he later mused.[9] The next day Nancy returned to retrieve him and sat with
Dale through a follow-up visit with Dr. Feldman. Having absorbed the
shock, this visit was less tenuous and more openly frank about medical
matters. They discussed the cancer's likely sequence, and Feldman outlined a recommended treatment regimen in detail. His problems were not
limited to his liver, Dale learned. His pain in that location had just tipped
off the physician. Much more testing would have to be endured before
any real answers could be given and treatment plans made. Dale decided
to wait before alarming his own family members. He was back the next
week for a barium enema and battery of colon X-rays.[10]

The treatment ordeal was scheduled. Before beginning, Morgan traveled to Maryland for a Thanksgiving holiday gathering with the Norths.

Lynn and Lisa were home from Michigan; Louise made dinner. This time there was little horseplay. A stark reality was too close for comfort. The best solace either Dale or Louise could receive was each other's company. Neither left a record about the shell necklace, but the stay wasn't long. Dale was back in Berkeley a few days later to receive the test results: Feldman found generally "that I was in great shape, barring a little cancer here and there," Dale later joked. As nearly as anyone could tell, the tumor had formed in the upper reach of his large intestine in or just below the right colic or hepatic flexure. The X-rays revealed no blockage to the colon from a tumor, nor had he experienced pain other than the "bowel griping" of a few years earlier, which made the condition nearly asymptomatic and suggested an origin in a sessile polyp, hard to see or remove, being merely masses that form flat in the wall lining the large intestine. The polyp might have originated as much as a decade earlier, right at or just beyond the edge of what a routine colonoscopy could effectively inspect. He had endured one just the year before. The diabetes that worried his physician in 1965 could have been an early symptom of the cancerous tumor spreading to the liver and beginning to affect its function, or conversely, his diabetes could have provided a biotic opportunity for cancer to develop. In either case, Dale had no anemia, often a telltale symptom of colon cancer, but because the tumor had become metastatic to the liver, his case was beyond surgery as a treatment option. The one treatment available was grounded on aggressive chemotherapy, given by a regular injection.

Hart had undoubtedly been told by Holliday that his staff member faced a serious medical diagnosis, probably before Morgan left for Thanksgiving. Dale, however, formally informed the Bancroft Library staff of his cancer in a general letter on December 5, pledging that he would work at least part-time while undergoing treatment, which was beginning immediately. Despite his best intentions, he was in no condition to keep such a promise. Two days later he rolled a stack of paper and carbons into the typewriter on the Hollidays' dining room table. Now the diagnosis and prognosis were confirmed, and he knew it was time to tell his brothers and sister. "Dear Ruth and Doug, Jim and Mary Beth, Bob and Audry, and Helen," he typed in the greeting, "This is not an easy letter for me to write, and it will be no easier for you to read. But I have always understood that anything that could happen to anybody else could happen to me, and in this sense I am well prepared for what I have to tell you." Dale explained matter-of-factly that he had metastatic cancer, "and it is not to be supposed that I have a very long life expectancy, from here on out." The letter went on for four pages, describing his symptoms, diagnosis, and the anticipated treatment regimen.[11]

* * * * *

If one wanted to identify the formal end of Dale L. Morgan's career, that date would be during the second week of November 1970. As far as his letter files or others' reminiscences can confirm, work on any project was dropped after his first medical appointment informing him of the cancer diagnosis. Every project was abandoned where it lay. All his attention turned to sustaining himself through the exhaustion imposed by impaired liver function and the side effects of the chemical poison counteracting the cancer's invidious spread. One side effect of the chemotherapy was lassitude that acted like a dam impounding his river of correspondence, which dried immediately to an occasional drip.

Jim Holliday became Dale's contact with the rest of the world. Other than the Bancroft staff, Dale informed few immediate friends of his prognosis; there is no evidence that Madeline McQuown was among them. Information about Dale's condition filtered out only in piecemeal fashion through the network of his hundreds of correspondents, too many to notify individually. None of his Utah contacts or friends, other than his family, had the news from him directly. One of the few who did get an individual notice was historian Donald Jackson, one of Dale's references for his Guggenheim application. The personal letter to Jackson, written on December 11, was one of the last Morgan wrote.[12] The Melvins, across the bay in San Francisco, found that Uncle Dale was no longer responding but had no idea why. He finally broke his news to Tasia in a handwritten letter in early January, literally the last drip of his once-flowing correspondence.

Most of Morgan's oldest friends found out about his cancer through their network of professional relationships. Wally Stegner, Fawn Brodie, Juanita Brooks, Charles Kelly, Ev Cooley—all wrote their sympathies, but none had received the news from Dale directly. "I simply refuse to face the fact that your life is in danger," wrote Fawn Brodie from Los Angeles, who would succumb to her own cancer in another decade. "Meanwhile I shall pray for you, with every confidence that my prayers, under the circumstances, will be heeded with even more respect that those of the brethren in Salt Lake City. This is a time when, damn it all, a seeker after truth like you should have a little miracle."[13] Juanita Brooks was effusive. "We are all so indebted to you, Dale! Your work out-weighs that of all the others combined. Historians and Sham Historians all put together cannot match your contribution. I myself owe so much to your guidance, though I can hardly claim to be an historian."[14] When Dale failed to reply to *anyone's* written wishes—completely unlike him—the network began its own investigations and discussions amongst themselves. Charles S. Peterson, director of the Utah State Historical Society, began preparing the obituary for the *Utah Historical Quarterly* that would inevitably be needed. He approached Charles Kelly for a personal comment. Kelly, now totally blind and only a year or so away from his own death at age 98, deferred and asked Everett Cooley to write the piece.

By a stroke of good fortune, on a visit to Berkeley in August 1969, Fred Rosenstock had helped Morgan create a fair-market estimate of his massive library for an insurance policy.[15] A year later, when the bookman tried to arrange one of his flying consultations with Lawton Kennedy, printer for the Old West Publishing Company, he found the usual accommodations at Dale's apartment were no longer available. It took some doing to even find Dale. Rosenstock made a point of visiting Dale at the Hollidays' in Lafayette, and with the library appraisal in mind his initial estate plan—to allow select institutions to choose from among his books—was scrapped. Dale proposed to sell Rosenstock nearly the entire book collection outright and asked Rosenstock to broker a sale *en bloc* to the University of Utah to serve as the core of a Western Americana collection Ev Cooley was beginning to build. An outright sale would help finance his hoped-for post-cancer research trip and reduce the bulk and expense of moving east, which Louise insisted upon.[16]

Jim Hart telephoned Gordon Ray at the Guggenheim Foundation, whom he knew as a professional acquaintance, and suggested that under the circumstances Morgan might be allowed to take up the fellowship without delay. On December 16, Hart received a telephone call with the Foundation's decision to activate the Fellowship immediately, a concession to allow Dale to take advantage of its support and begin the work.[17] The Bancroft staff rallied around him as well. Morgan received detailed instructions about leave policy. Hart made a personal appeal to both UC Berkeley's chancellor and president to allow Morgan to draw full pay while on the fellowship, which was granted in an exceedingly generous and unusual concession.[18]

Lynn and Lisa North arrived in Berkeley from Michigan in mid-December, a day before Dale's fifty-sixth birthday, his last and merely a week after his letter to Donald Jackson. Otherwise the event didn't leave so much as a trace within his correspondence. Louise could not get the leave time off from work before the holiday but arrived herself by air on Christmas Eve. Dale at last had gotten "his girls" to California. Though he and Louise were not married and would never marry, they were at least informally a couple, and he gently claimed the girls as well. Dale Morgan enjoyed the Christmas of 1970 as his one and only immediate-family holiday gathering. The North trio remained with him until January 3, then returned east to get their home in Accokeek ready for his arrival.

Two days later, Dale's younger brother Jim and his wife Mary Beth Morgan drove to Berkeley to help Dale pack his apartment for the impending move to Maryland. For a week they sorted the volumes he would take to support the ambitious fur trade volume, setting aside the hundreds being sold to Fred Rosenstock. Several Bancroft staff members joined them to box the deep piles of manuscript material drifted across every surface of the La Loma apartment: stacks of unsorted correspondence, boxes and drawers of transcriptions, sheaves of notes, piles of old proof material from earlier publications. The chemotherapy regimen made Dale lethargic nearly to the point of immobility. Jim, Mary Beth, and the Bancroft staff were content to do the work. The most Dale could do was doze lightly on the living room couch, rousing himself when a decision needed to be made.[19]

One evening during their weeklong stay, Jim and Mary Beth Morgan drove Dale to dinner with Gordon Holmes, aunt Ida's boy and their youngest Holmes cousin. Dale was worn from his chemotherapy treatments but upbeat, determined on recovery and to carry though the terms of the fellowship. The promised research trip to Europe with Louise was a lodestone of hope. Holmes was a physician. During the evening Gordon pulled Jim aside and told him quietly, based only on what he knew of Dale's treatment and the dinner-table rendition of the story, not to hold out hope for recovery.

On another evening the trio accepted a dinner invitation from Gordon's sister, June, and brother Sam Holmes. Sam, a lawyer, handled a revision to Dale's will. That evening, with the practical business done and before the group was called to dinner, as a practicing Latter-day Saint, Jim asked his older brother if he would accept a priesthood blessing. "He was a little bit noncommittal, but he kinda shook his head, he would," Jim remembered years later. A few minutes later, Jim and Sam pulled out a chair for Dale to sit on, preparing to lay their hands on his head in the accepted form for a blessing. Now Dale waved them off. Jim asked why, when he had agreed a few minutes earlier. Jim recalled that Dale explained "'when I lost my hearing, when I was ill,' he said, 'I was administered to for a fare-thee-well'—[those] were the words he put it—'and nothing ever happened. So, through with that.'"[20] It is impossible to say whether in a moment of mortal weakness Dale entertained a momentary flicker of his old faith, but his closely held naturalism eventually pushed the thought back into whatever mental corner it may have come from.

When the packing was complete and with the crated books due Rosenstock dispatched by truck to Denver, Jim and Mary Beth returned home to Utah. Dale moved back to Lafayette with the Hollidays. The apartment on La Loma Avenue had been cleared, the lease terminated. With plans in place for Dale's departure east to join Louise, Jim and Nancy Holliday hosted a reception for Dale at their home. It was more of a wake than a retirement or send-off event. Everyone invited knew that this was their final opportunity to say goodbye.[21]

Outside California among the long list of Dale Morgan's contacts and obligations, those not connected to his personal circle were simply left without any indication of the changed circumstances. By this point Angus Cameron could make no more excuses for Morgan about the Lorton diary. "You have seemed so close on finishing it for so long that I just can't imagine what finally held you up," he had written in December, and like everyone else received no answer.[22] Midway through January, Alfred Knopf himself dictated one of the iron-hand letters about the William B. Lorton project which had hung on promises and preliminaries since 1959, the kind of letter counterbalancing the cultivated, velvet-glove correspondence for which he was famous. "Well, Dale, there is not much I can do about this, except tell you that I think your behavior toward me and Angus over the years has been absolutely outrageous and I am ashamed of it, as well as very, very resentful." Unlike Stanley Rinehart, Knopf had no advance against royalties to recover, but he wrote warmly and with more prophetic insight than he was aware that "life is too short to endure patiently any more of this kind of thing, and I can only regret what I had hoped would be an enduring, pleasant, and creditable association has come to nothing."[23]

Spurred by Knopf's letter, Dale roused himself enough to endure a car ride from Lafayette into the university on January 18, 1971. Morgan returned to his desk at Bancroft to gather up what he could find of his collected source material on Lorton, hoping to begin settling the text into at least a draft form. The desk had likewise been cleared of the dunes of paper that had drifted and eddied across its disordered surface for years. While there, Dale addressed a letter to Knopf, explaining his cancer and, in its face, invoking a deflective claim reminiscent of the rash pledge made to John Selby about his Mormon opus in 1948: "the [Lorton] book is so nearly finished that I cannot endure its incompletion, and it has priority over all other books I have in progress."[24] Given his agreed-upon writing plans, his rapid decline, and its inevitable conclusion, one may wonder whether books had any priority at all for him. In truth, however, other than a few sheets of conceptual draft, Dale Morgan had not set to paper one page of introductory text or a single explanatory note on the William B. Lorton diary; the book was "nearly finished" only as a neural net of remembered references and quotations in his remarkably comprehensive mind. The book *may have been* more or less complete; it remained merely to be written and documented. Its final form would emerge from the inevitable queries that would fly out and back as questions arose in composition, just as had every one of his publications.[25] A few days later Dale again rallied enough energy to generate a typed description of his research files and collected material for the Bancroft staff, an outline of his crated papers.[26] It was virtually his last act of record as an historian or correspondent.

*   *   *   *   *

During the week of January 24, 1971, Louise flew back to the Bay Area. With the Hollidays' help she got Dale to the Oakland Airport and aboard a flight to Washington, DC. The drive across the District of Columbia from Dulles Airport to the east bank of the Potomac River threaded the arterial rush of Beltway traffic that now flowed ceaselessly in all directions. She pulled into the tree-lined drive of her twelve acres and helped Dale into the house he had visited so often and of which he was now finally a resident. Despite his optimistic insistence in shipping to her home the crated fur-trade books and his collection of LeConte Stewart paintings of Utah, Louise knew what she was facing. She had endured it barely six years earlier with Max. Letters, forwarded from California, came to Dale occasionally, but he no longer made any effort to respond. The once-chattery typewriter sat silent.

Dale Morgan's last nine weeks of mortal existence are known only to the members of the household in Accokeek, Maryland. Louise arranged hospice care for Dale while she was at work. Anne Stebbins, Ruth's oldest daughter, and her husband John were living in nearby Silver Spring, Maryland. As word filtered through the family and plans solidified, Anne dropped nearly everything to come regularly to Louise's home and help care for her favorite uncle. Jim McConkey made a day trip to visit; his mother, Anna, must have come at least once. As the cancer crept quietly through his organs and Dale Morgan's body failed, Louise cared for him with the emotional tenderness the deaf, brilliant, self-sufficient man had craved through his whole adult life.

On the next to last day of March 1971, Dale L. Morgan "went on the long hunt," joining the generation of mountain men, fur traders, and overland emigrants that so fascinated him.

"If History Is Going to Stay Viable"[1]

A Historian's Life and Contexts

> *My research is likely to stand as monumental when my book is finished . . .*
> *but I will always have an apologetic feeling about it, for no one can know*
> *as well as I do all the deficiencies in this research, the unexplored areas, the*
> *unsettled questions which more time and energy and money might dispose*
> *of once and for all. But life is real, life is earnest, etc., and also life is short.*
> *Too damned short.*[2]
>
> —Dale Morgan

TO EVERY MORTAL PASSING, there is an aftermath, the necessary uncoupling of an individual's immortal identity from the banalities of their material existence. Much of that process happened ahead of Morgan's move from California to Maryland. Dale closed up his apartment on La Loma Avenue, deeding his papers and a collection of several hundred scarce Mormon books and pamphlets to the Bancroft Library before his departure. Everett Cooley, understanding Dale Morgan's scholarly significance, began soliciting donations of his letters from friends and family immediately after Morgan's death.[3] His efforts made possible the personal connections necessary for the University of Utah to eventually acquire the papers of Morgan associates Fawn Brodie, Dean Brimhall, Charles Kelly (though Kelly's were divided between the University of Utah and Utah State Historical Society), Wallace Stegner, and Bill Mulder.

Although Morgan promised the pick of his library to Bancroft and the Utah State Historical Society (USHS) long before his cancer was diagnosed, the bulk of Western Americana books boxed by Jim and Mary Beth Morgan went to Denver; they were joined not too long after by the fur trade material he had taken to Maryland. As planned, Fred Rosenstock offered Dale's library to the University of Utah library. By that time, unfortunately, the

J. Willard Marriott acquisition fund had been exhausted. Everett Cooley set about raising money to meet the $12,500 purchase price. The price seems laughable in the context of today's book market, but in the dollars of the time represented about a year's salary at Morgan's pay grade. The university did not get the collection Cooley wanted and Morgan himself wanted it to have. The librarian later made two conflicting statements about why the sale fell through, though both could be true. Cooley wrote Marguerite Reusser that the money could not be raised, but years later he told me that the collection development librarian protested that Morgan's books would likely duplicate holdings the library already owned, and wouldn't approve the purchase.[4]

Rosenstock then offered Morgan's book collection to Brigham Young University, where the fiscal situation may have been similar, but collections librarian A. Dean Larsen jumped at the offer. In reviewing the collection, Cooley noted that "so many of his books have marginal entries [the library is] almost manuscript in nature."[5] Unfortunately, BYU failed to see Morgan's heavily annotated collection as a reflection of a significant historian; it was simply an opportunity to acquire a topically specific group of thematic materials, an academic collection-building process common in the 1960s and 1970s as libraries grew rapidly. No list of the acquired titles was ever made. Select volumes were added to the Harold B. Lee Library's Special Collections and the rest dispersed into the library's general collection. The remainder were sold to Salt Lake City bookseller Sam Weller's Zion Bookstore. "There were sufficient duplicates that BYU was able to sell them and reimburse themselves for the expense of the entire library," Cooley later grumbled.[6]

Settling Dale Morgan's estate imposed individual pain as well. Madeline McQuown, always at ends for money and perhaps looking forward to the pleasure that a disbursement from Dale's long-time life insurance policy would afford her, learned that Dale had replaced her with Louise North as the policy beneficiary. Madeline was furious with disappointment. That sense of being wronged might have been still simmering when Everett Cooley approached her in 1973 or 1974 about donating her own papers to the University of Utah. She agreed, but in McQuown's intense native sense of personal privacy and perhaps harboring a sense of betrayal, she purged her papers of Dale's letters. Though her papers include two dozen letters to her from Dale, there are also folders full of strips torn from his typed sheets—the inoffensive but also unintelligible and mostly useless remains of the purge. She destroyed hundreds of others she felt were too intimate or that reflected poorly on her.[7]

* * * * *

I began this book with the bold claims that Dale L. Morgan is probably the key figure in the pre-academic period of Latter Day Saint history, and was among the last of the great amateur historians of the American West. "No scholar knew more about the Far West," Ray Allen Billington claimed of Morgan after his passing, "and none did more to retell its history accurately than did Dale Morgan."[8] A few months after his passing, Alfred L. Bush, the Philip Ashton Rollins Curator of Western Americana at Princeton University, posed perhaps the inevitable question to Fawn Brodie, who was then elbow-deep in her own biography of Thomas Jefferson. "I alas to think," observed the librarian, "what might have been produced if a Dale Morgan had the vast sums of money [Thomas Jefferson papers editor Julian] Boyd has had at his disposal for thirty years, and the staff..., and the time ... and a full 68 years."[9] Such speculation falls within the realm of counterfactual history, but given Morgan's long string of choices and bad luck, it is a tempting question to pose, nonetheless. Neither statement suggests that Dale Morgan was a main figure in the midcentury pursuit of the American West's history. In fact, with no graduate students to carry on his interpretive legacy, acknowledgement of Morgan's scholarly legacy began evaporating soon after this death.

As the chapters of this biography have unfolded, I have tried to weave in some of the developments within the disciplines that happened around him and largely outside his ken. Of course, scholarship on neither the Mormons nor the American West ended with Dale Morgan's passing. In fact, the disciplinary perspective of both histories was undergoing massive redirections that would come to the surface within a few years later. Postwar expansion of higher education would be reflected in both Western American history and religious history involving the Latter Day Saint traditions. A biography of a "last great" someone cannot end without at least introducing the changes that followed his career.

WESTERN AMERICAN HISTORY

Dale L. Morgan died almost precisely at a point in which Western American historiography began actively segregating readerships, disconnecting along fault lines that had been forming for two decades. Shortly after Morgan began his work, the historical discipline began fracturing into two veins. Along with the strictly narrative perspective of history itself, the tradition of the untrained chronicler and interpreter was being relegated to decidedly popular works and antiquarian editing. "Serious" history of the American West was becoming an academic discipline reinforced with comparative perspective, rounded out by ideological synthesis. The movement towards professionalizing study of the American West had begun with the trained (if self-promoting) Frederick Jackson Turner in the 1890s and shifted increasingly toward professionalization and the academically credentialed in Turner's students' generation, the likes of Southwest historian Herbert E. Bolton and Great Plains historian Walter Prescott Webb. Morgan was thus among the last great amateurs not only for the abilities and interest he cultivated, but because his career dovetailed so neatly with a time in the field when it was still possible to compile and publish landmark studies that individually shaped the discipline.

In the decades following Morgan, the field has changed so dramatically that individuals find it difficult to shape an entire discipline themselves. Western American history has become somewhat schizophrenic, divided into subspecialties of cultural regions and wary camps of institutional professionals: of institutional academic and public historians, who frequent the Western History Association (WHA) conferences, and the enthusiastic amateurs who populate affinity organizations such as the Oregon-California Trails Association and Jedediah Smith Society, as well as heritage groups like the Daughters of Utah Pioneers and Mormon Battalion. Morgan represents one of the last figures who was at home among the denizens of both camps. Like the scarps and faults that divide the American West, the geologic strata of Western American history has shifted, perhaps permanently (at least "permanently" as measured by careers and lifetimes). It will take time to weather and erode the divides. Both these twentieth-century shifts merit careful historiographic studies of their own, but Morgan is my vehicle for introducing and commenting briefly on both. Other scholars will have to tease out the crosscurrents and branching streams.

On one side were the scholarly historians, those whose careers profited from the postwar investment made in higher education and from the population explosion of the Baby Boom. The process began much earlier, but it was effectively accomplished in the early 1970s. The split was certainly visible to people on the ground. Dale Schoenberger commented in one of the early issues of the *Western Historical Quarterly* that the academic side of the divide sought to "upgrade the field of Western history from the former trend of mere narration and reporting, but it pooh-poohs a biography of a gunfighter or a mountain man as an adolescent [pursuit] and beneath the standards of their profession."[10] Required to function within the realm of peer review, scholarship, and tenure requirements, this redirection was perhaps natural. "The trend is one which lives in fear of glamorizing the West," Schoenberger observed, with its focus toward narrow specializations and a captive audience of peers and classrooms. Academics pursued seriousness above all.

The academic pursuit of the American West stalked away from the other side of the divide, exactly the uncredentialled amateurs who read in the field and attended the early scholarly conferences precisely *for* the glamor in the subject which academics generally dismissed. These were fact-correcting zealous avocational storytellers, who came to the field out of personal fascination, most of them self-instructed in their pet interests—lawyers and librarians and public officials and dentists and who knows what else. The results of their zeal, like those who write about railroading, could bury a reader in antiquarian precision or in uncritically rendered myth. Some of the written results of pet interests were abysmally poor, but others, such as the work of Charles Camp or Carl Wheat or Carl P. Russell, are remarkable.

The watershed division in Western American historiography unfolding during Morgan's lifetime is illustrated by trends in Western History Association meeting programs. Jim Holliday's program committee for the fifth annual conference in 1967 were charged to put together a program that was "90% buffs and 10 per cent[*sic*] academics."[11] Merely five years later the proportion of presenters had essentially reversed. Thereafter WHA existed, and has been conducted since, as a formal academic conference. At that 1972 meeting, Yale historian Howard R. Lamar's presidential address threw a raking light across the widening divide, delivering a provocative comment on the status and direction of history of the American West and calling not for a rapprochement, but for the pace of the division to accelerate.

The following year Lamar's presidential successor, John Caughey, echoed his predecessor's sentiments, urging fellow historians to break out of their self-imposed imprisonment in Frederick Jackson Turner's early, antique, and glamorous "frontier" American West to broaden the parameters of the field. "We [Turner's] disciples are the ones who made the quantum jump of equating frontier and West and assuming therefore an end to western history in 1890 and, indeed, the disappearance of the West,"[12] Caughey stated. He supported emphatically that statistical population density had little to do with actual frontiers and argued that the American West had not gone and that there was much more to it than fur traders, explorers, covered wagons, and cowboys. A generation later, UCLA historian Stephen Aron noted that "because Turner's formulation equated frontier and West, the closing of the former meant the end of the latter's historical significance."[13] The academics of Morgan's generation had successfully uncoupled the two.

The addresses by Lamar and Caughey provided an all-clear signal to the discipline that the twentieth century was an acceptable study period for the American West, that modern concerns like the environment, business, gender, and water were fair game, and that historians were really writing as part of a conversation among themselves. The social history juggernaut was having its effect, and academic history forged ahead to blaze its own trail through the cultural memory of the past.[14] A new generation of scholars took up the charge.

The problem was that Lamar, Caughey, and others such as University of Oregon historian Earl Pomeroy were also within the vanguard of American historians' inward turn, the more or less intentional abandonment of the nonacademic reading public. The WHA was not the only collection of academics to strike out independently for themselves. Academic historians generally abandoned the uncredentialled "buffs" in most fields with or without outright disdain. Not all academics agreed. Cooley was horrified at the academic snobbery exhibited by University of Utah department chair Leland Creer's sniffy dismissal of Morgan as a "dilettante to history" chiefly because Morgan lacked credentials beyond the work itself.

In his study, titled *Historians in Public: The Practice of American History, 1890–1970,* Ian Tyrrell noted that the entire discipline of academic history made "a crucial error" in the early 1970s. The discipline tragically narrowed its audience to students and other academics. History's "large public audience" was left behind as "the profession retreated into 'narcissism.'"[15] Tyrell documents how academics quit writing for an interested public readership and began writing for each other. Some of that change can be seen in just the list of buyers of for the work of fine-press printer/publisher Talisman Press. Talisman's buyers were not academic historians,[16] though its books seem to have been acquired energetically by library collections. Focused on the opinions of peers and scholarly rigor and arguments, by the 1970s academics seemingly dismissed the large number of individuals in America who bought and read history for personal enjoyment.

In developing a post-Turnerian historical approach to Western American history, "real" historians—meaning the academic practitioners of history—left behind the culturally important function of history: the narrative of storytelling. They abandoned antiquarianism, Dale Morgan's trappers and trails, to pursue new topics, to wield new interpretive tools like cliometrics, to explore connections and dependencies, and to take comparative approaches. In the place of Morgan's microhistorical narratives, chronological corrections, and geographic clarification, a deeper interest grew in the twentieth century American West, together with new emphases on Hispanic and Native peoples, economics, relationships with the East, women's experience, and the environment. Within a decade, topics such as water, urbanization, gender roles, and environmental change had supplanted scholarly interest in trails, pioneers, settlement, and the cattle industry. Personified by Pomeroy, Western American history also began to drink deeply from the interpretive abstractions of historical theory as well. Studying the past trended toward comparison and synthesis, heavily analytical rather than documentary or descriptive narratives.[17]

Dale Morgan's career was as a paragon of primary source material. As large and important as they are, his two major works of trail history, *The Overland Diary of James Avery Pritchard* and *Overland in 1846,* stand as mere slivers of their subjects, more antiquarian than scholarly. This point heralded that the last chance for the American West's last great amateur historian was passing, even within his chosen specialties. In 1979, a key work in the new approach blended Morgan's grasp of the factual with the new interpretive, theoretical turn to history and at a stroke consigned Morgan's great works on the trail to antiquarian near oblivion: John D. Unruh's *The Plains Across: The Overland Emigrants and the Trans-Mississippi West, 1840–60.*[18] Where Morgan concentrated on the microhistory of specific experiences, Unruh's study looked at the broad sweep, the grand narrative of the overland experience, exploring patterns and making inferences about the experience and meaning of the trip.

By this point, it should be clear that in his quest for source material and to understand the environment of historical happening, Morgan drank deeply of not only of historicism but also of philosophical empiricism. In Morgan's eyes, truth could be had only by gaining a grasp of the documenting sources. Therefore a historian who lacked *any* fact, however minor, lacked truth. The historian's mission became to command any and all documentary sources, and to hew to them alone. Inductive reasoning was an appropriate tool, but deductive reasoning was unsuitably speculative. As Morgan demonstrated with dozens of other projects, he was willing to wait until the last possible source either became available or was shown to be inapplicable. He would scrap projects entirely if the source material he wished for could not be had. The criticism Dale Morgan most feared was not being wrong; it was far worse to have his research proven incomplete, even fractionally.

Early in his writing career Morgan responded to a public librarian's request for an autobiographical statement. His comments communicated a personal philosophy of history:

> I think that a historian is required to be continuously skeptical, to accept nothing on faith, and prepared at a moment's notice to set up a yell for the facts. I think that nothing can take the place of persistent intellectual curiosity, or the willingness to look at even the oldest of settled ideas with a fresh and lively interest. I feel one must be prepared to follow his intelligence wherever it leads him, and damn the consequences. [I]n this readiness there is a healthy recognition that there are always many ways of looking at any situation, and no man, one's self included, will ever have a monopoly on truth. In the writing of history I think one has to be prepared to face the anger and resentment of those who do not want their settled ideas unsettled but at the same time and while seeing this in proper perspective. In short, above all else a historian must be responsible to himself. He can only please everybody for a very short time if at all, within the narrow limits of an insular society. The final constancy must be to one's self.[19]

Since Dale Morgan's time, his unshakable trust of historical fact and its reflection of John Adams' 1772 observation that "facts are stubborn things" have been overtaken, superseded, outdated. To be fair, Morgan's view of the facts of history was also evolving. He realized that historical sources were not inherently objective. Late in Morgan's life, Todd Berens asked the older man about his philosophy of history. Dale responded with a comment on the need to have a sense for the weight and value of fact:

> They say that the poets are entitled to whatever readers can get out of their poems, and I suppose the same applies to historians. But I have never been much concerned with a philosophy of history as such. I have been more interested in practical questions, straightening out the enormous distortions of the record that I have found on every hand; and beyond that, being continuously interested

in the causes that produce certain effects, and the effects that are produced by certain causes. Historians seem to have trouble enough with all these elementals, to say nothing of wrestling with large abstractions. In any case, to me "history" is not limited to human experience as such. Why scrub oaks grow in one place and not in another, or how and why they spread from one place to another, or what becomes of the Pleistocene fauna, or for that matter, how the universe itself is put together, is all "history" to me, while the cause-and-effect relationship can be profitably studied. Such things may relate back to the human experience, in that so far as we know, only human minds concern themselves with these matters, but I am also prepared to accept the possibility of non-human intelligence being found in the universe somewhere, sometime, which would do away with the human referent entirely, and establish history as such independent of the human minds that are now cognizant of it. So, you see, this does not have a great deal to do with history conceived as "the missing link that binds the individual to that chain of human experience which transcends time and space to give man his identity."[20]

Morgan's comment to Berens brings him much closer to sociologist Johan Goudsblom's point of reference, made when discussing human religious history, that nothing is ever self-evident and there is always room for inquiring how things have become what they now are.[21] It also edges him towards American historian Hayden White's assertion that "the facts do not speak for themselves, but that the historian speaks for them, speaks on their behalf, and fashions the fragments of the past into a whole whose integrity is . . . a purely discursive one."[22] White's reminder is, in essence, what Leopold von Ranke envisioned a century and a half earlier as the founder of Germanic historicism. But in humanities fields like history, relying too heavily upon empiricism threatens to condemn disciplines to the realm of the technical and historically superficial: who had done what, when, and where? In short, it threatens to replicate the antiquarianism decried by modern scholarship. Cataloging facts, even a breathtaking catalog of facts, threatens to miss the essence of history by failing to address *why*.

The *whys* of history exist as interpretations, therefore beyond the factual record, and interpretation is shaped by the student's perspective, not the actors of history. Dale Morgan was singularly skilled, but his approach makes Morgan an environmental historian, rather than social historian. Historian Charles S. Peterson identifies Morgan as an American Western regionalist.[23]

* * * * *

Present-day academics bemoan the "death of the humanities" and lament that "no one reads history any more" with blinkers on. It is more accurate to say that no one outside academic specialties reads narrowly specific academic history. That outcome is partly the natural result of choices made during Morgan's lifetime. Reflecting on that changed circumstance a generation later, a pair of recent scholars noted that "[academic] disciplines now enjoy a monopoly over what counts as scholarly."[24] Early writers on the American West—the likes of Francis Parkman or William Prescott—"regarded romantic conventions not as meaningless stereotypes, but as effective ways of communicating a message that all their literate contemporaries would understand." History has become a discipline of describers and explainers. If anything, in the process Western American history—and American historical writing generally—has lost its engaging storytellers. Historians' place as keepers of the national story has been supplanted by talented, book-writing journalists and "edutainment" media outlets such as the History Channel.[25]

One cannot be too harsh on academic history, which since the rift of the 1970s has extended a welcome to practitioners of public history and has become somewhat less unwelcoming to talented aficionados. It may be more correct to observe that Western American history involves a large complement of participants from the world of "public history" approaches in museums and historical interpretation. In that sense, the post-Morgan discipline has institutionalized rather than turned to pure academic history. The divide is yet unbridged, however, between scholars and the members and organizations with preservationist tendencies that still find fire in the glamorous antique American West, like the Oregon-California Trails Association, Old Spanish Trail Association, the Westerners International, or the Jedediah Smith Society, and of fine artists living and dead.

Historiography is always in flux. That ebb and flow is the very nature of human inquiry, but toward the end of the 1960s and through the early 1970s, the academic historiography of the American West intentionally pushed itself free of the dragging weight of history buffs and amateurs.

The point is that the *practice* of history itself was changing. It is partly because this rift occurred that I feel confident characterizing Dale Morgan as arguably the last great amateur historian of the American West. Morgan's career was one of the last focusing on the antiquarian interest in source documents and narrative history before the avocation of Western American history had become nearly fully a credentialed profession.[26]

Today scholars of the American West consider Morgan either as a fellow professional or dismiss him, as did Leland Creer, as merely a talented, detail-driven amateur. With the exception of *Jedediah Smith and the Opening of the West,* which thrived (and still thrives) in the paperback edition the author resented, by the 2010s Morgan and his work all but disappeared from the ranks of the profession. John R. Wunder's book *Historians of the American Frontier* included pioneering nonacademic writers Hubert Howe Bancroft, Hiram Chittenden, Bernard DeVoto, and Theodore Roosevelt, as well as popular writer Walter Stanley Campbell (who under the pen name of Stanley Vestal became the stylistic predecessor of David McCullough), but listed only PhD-holding writers of Wunder's directly preceding generation. Dale L. Morgan did not qualify.[27]

Morgan recognized the early signs of the shift and occasionally expressed concern himself about the academic ossification of history. Irene Paden held his respect. He once praised Kansas Historical Society librarian Louise Barry as a chronicler. "What is especially gratifying is to find someone not a professional historian lured into such scholarly pursuits. If history is going to stay viable, that has to keep happening, the more often the better."[28] Western American history is now a respected academic field, but its place in academia has come at the cost of alienating many of the nation's interested but avocational readers outside of the ivory tower, leaving the affinity and heritage associations, and state history journals to collect the work of well-informed graduate students and enthusiastic amateurs.

After the 1967 WHA meeting, Eleanor Harris wrote her coauthor to relate the constant stream of people who, after realizing her working relationship with Dale Morgan, poured into her ears their experiences of his generosity with sources, advice, or criticism: "another interesting demonstration to me of how modest you are of your contributions to Western historians—[W. H. Hutchinson] being only one of the many who spoke to me at the conference of your eminence in this field."[29] In the late 1960s Dale Morgan had been generally accepted as one of the grand old men of Western American history. That high estimation was part of the challenge he struggled to meet. The trouble, Everett Cooley recalled George Hammond saying of Dale Morgan, "is [that] he had such wide interests, and he takes on more than he can ever accomplish even though he works fourteen, fifteen hours a day lots of times."[30] What Morgan did accomplish in his short career, which is listed in the bibliography, is impressive. The individual works of few other writers of his time have proven so durable, populating citation lists and recommended readings for two generations. Yet, despite the great volume of his published work, his never-published, never-begun material—most of it driven by his own intense curiosity about first causes and relationships—was undoubtedly far greater. Morgan's remarkable memory was a blessing, allowing him to work with tremendous grasp of material, but it also means we have among his massive papers nowhere near what he simply carried around in his head.

To be perfectly fair, Morgan himself yearned to transcend the historically small scale, intensely detailed documentary work for which he was known. He yearned to recapture the challenge of tying together threads and narratives into large-scale, genuinely historical works such as what he had accomplished in *Jedediah Smith and the Opening of the West,* and though it was of a more popular slant, with *The Great Salt Lake.* Stegner's *Beyond the Hundredth Meridian* would certainly have been a parallel. Morgan's massive history of the North American fur trade, had he been able to complete it, might have been such a study. Robbed of a late career in which to unfold his wings, he is remembered chiefly for being a documentary historian, an editor, and a writer of antiquarian narrative. A pity, that.

LEGACY IN MORMON STUDIES

Moses Rischin's term "New Mormon History" integrated quickly.[31] It has become an article of faith that the movement grew around O'Dea, Arrington, and others named in the pioneering essay. Academics have since pushed back Rischin's date to 1950, specifically to claim Juanita Brooks' *Mountain Meadows Massacre* as one of their own.[32] In 1988 Davis Bitton, a founding member and president of the Mormon History Association and former Assistant Church Historian (1972–1982), asserted that the New Mormon History approach referred "not to the fact of being produced recently but to distinctive approaches and questions asked."

I agree with Rischin, Bitton, and other interpreters to a point, yet lauding the academic flowering in this way masks the real collision that stirred the soil from which that flower grew: the avocational writers engaged *before* Arrington's generation of scholars began their scholarly training. Something inquisitive was stirring energetically years earlier, and Dale Morgan, Fawn Brodie, and Juanita Brooks—though nonacademics—had been in the thick of the conflict it generated. To be sure, the generation of the 1930s and 1940s also had precursors and antecedents. If this book makes a contribution beyond biography, it is to suggest that this earlier period of historiologic conflict during the WPA years and after World War II blazed the trail and smoothed the way for the rise of academic interest in Mormonism in the 1950s, as well as in new scholarship on Mormonism in the 1960s and 1970s.

Dale Morgan and his circle were seminal figures in the first generation of Latter Day Saint historicism, looking at it from a position other than affirmation or polemic. Nels Anderson, Dale Morgan, Bernard DeVoto— to them belongs the real beginning of the New Mormon History. Morgan was among the first to cultivate hard evidence for religious development, particularly the largely unplowed ground of contemporary sources. Each of those in Morgan's immediate circle, other than Wallace Stegner and Nels Anderson, were academically untrained but competent amateurs (Anderson worked in federal service, returning to academia only in the 1970s). Each developed a strong reliance on pinning down source material in ways that earlier writers, interested chiefly in communicating an overarching message, had not.

James D. Tabor reflected the approach Morgan assumed by observing that historians of religion "can evaluate what people claimed, what they believed, what they reported, and that all becomes part of the data, but to then say, 'A miracle happened,' ... goes beyond our accessible methods."[33] The writer of history must rely on sources, but must also avoid on their personally held viewpoints about Truth—yes, with a capital "T"—which are part of that story. D. Michael Quinn's "functional objectivity" is what the distinguished Arnold Toynbee encouraged when insisting that historians "lay their cards on the table."[34] Morgan functioned within a different time and trusted in an objectivity that has never been possible.[35] Morgan felt that an absolute objectivity could be achieved, but only by rejecting the faith he was trying to contextualize. Discussing by letter Brodie's *No Man Knows My History* with Bernard DeVoto, the pair accused each other of bias, Morgan tagging the Harvard writing professor as a

frustrated psychologist, and the professor pointing to the western neo-
phyte as a frustrated sociologist. In truth, both men's dismissal of faith
disqualified either from effectively understanding the Mormons (or any
other denomination). Historian Perry Miller wrote insightfully about the
Puritans, not because he shared their faith or because he rejected it, but
because he accepted their faith as meaningful to them, a defining factor
in their worldview and choices. Dale Morgan might have matured into a
similar perspective, but his extant writing on the Latter Day Saints suggests doing so would have required a major shift in personal perspective
and a softening of his self-proclaimed "objectivity."

In identifying the New Mormon History, Rischin focused his attention on the writing and interactions among academic historians and their
dispassionate focus on the Latter-day Saints and early Latter Day Saint
culture. Later scholars accepted Rischin's timeline, proposing that the
change in Mormon historiography identified by Rischin occurred because
of the emergence of professionally trained historians from within Mormon culture, really the rise of a topical specialty within academically practicing and teaching historians. Thus the New Mormon History becomes
merely one facet of the larger institutionalization of history during the
mid-twentieth century.

The new generation of academically trained Mormon scholars did
abandon the insular expectation that the church's truth claim could be
proven or disproven historically, a point that fueled the Lost Generation's
earlier work. The academic historians tended to follow the outline that
Morgan encouraged two decades earlier, to see the saints as historical
actors and not merely divine puppets (or intentional scoundrels), but they
stopped short of making judgments. Their failure to do so rankled one of
the pioneers of Latter Day Saint historicism. In the fall of 1964, Morgan
took Arrington to task for what Morgan considered the younger scholar's
conveniently opportunistic historicism, an attitude content to document
and describe rather than explain and make a final judgment of "what is."
He wrote the Utah State University economics professor:

I for one cannot agree that the "true historian" should exhibit
"suspended judgment." On the contrary, I think it is the ultimate
responsibility of the historian, after he has dug as deeply into the
facts as possible, and when he is supposed to know more about his
subject than the average reader can hope to know, that he should
stand up and render judgement. It may keep a historian out of

trouble to abstain from judgment, but it is not the primary business of a historian to keep himself out of trouble. He should be sufficiently humble, recognizing that the whole record is rarely recoverable about anything. But his attitude finally should be: "Insofar as the facts are known to me, this is what I make of them."[36]

Morgan's desire to pass judgments on motivation and meaning based on empirical evidence was where Morgan's lack of formal training in humanities fields hampered him. By the early 1960s Morgan began realizing that the emerging subfield of Mormon studies had grown well beyond his own contributions of ploughing up new material. He remained a figure respected privately, but his published work was increasingly overshadowed by an entire generation of new approaches and scholarship. "We were well-meaning, and all right in our day," Morgan wrote Fawn Brodie somewhat nostalgically in 1967, "but of course the new generation of Church-oriented [academic] historians are more solidly grounded and have a greater maturity."[37] Credentials alone—lacked by the likes of Morgan, Brodie, and DeVoto—suggested the inquiry into Mormonism by those new young scholars could be taken seriously, at least by other academics. As the New Mormon History began to flower, Morgan became tangential. His reputation held weight—almost all of the early academic scholars of Mormonism wrote him asking advice or seeking review of their work—but his inability to complete the "Mormon book" ultimately limited his scholarly relevance within Mormon studies.

YouTube and Internet sites are rife with modern detractors, critics, and those who have left the churches charging that Latter Day Saint culture has falsified its history. Making those assertions is part of claimants' own ethical approach to the history they perceive, providing a departure point justifying their own "enlightenment" and assertion of historical objectivity. It is probably fairer to note that the Latter Day Saints' understanding has evolved, mirroring the adoption but eventually abandoning the ethical history which emerged in the early Republic of the late eighteenth and early nineteenth century at the hands of writers like Mason Weems, though in nationalist rather than religious terms.

Paraphrasing a comment made about utilitarian or patriotic history in an earlier chapter, the Latter Day Saints would never have an reliable view of their own past until they had writers more committed to historical evidence than to inspiring readers.[38] Wallace Stegner complained to Morgan as late as 1948 that "it seems to me utterly impossible to write anything about the church except from within the hierarchy and [to] avoid upsetting the first presidency."[39]

Dale Morgan, however, was a key figure in this transition away from Mormonism's insular ethical history and anticipating the development of the heavily academic New Mormon History. As Lamar and Caughey said of Western American history generally in 1971 and 1972, Marvin Hill said of Mormonism in 1959: that it was time to address what had happened after 1900.[40] Rischin's comment touched a chord among historians of the Latter-day Saints. In the 1970s Richard Bushman called the New Mormon History: "a quest for identity rather than a quest for authority." A figure no less significant than University of Chicago religion scholar Martin E. Marty acknowledged the inevitable clash that the Mormons' *primitive naiveté* would experience about their mythic past. "Someday the crisis had to come," he reasoned.[41]

Arrington codified four foundational principles of historicism from which to craft history: to relate the past on its own terms, rather than projecting present sensibilities onto it; to explore contemporary sources deeply and exhaustively before rendering historical judgment; to allow for human nature and foibles in existence; and to understand that circumstances and therefore policies and standards, change.[42] Morgan would have wholeheartedly agreed, even as his own comment to Arrington (quoted in chapter 8) suggests that Morgan would have struggled with the first point. As evidence of Morgan's struggle, I offer his book reviews, generated ten years apart, for Fawn Brodie's *No Man Knows My History* and Leonard Arrington's *Great Basin Kingdom*. Arrington's study he damns with faint praise, while Brodie's he praises with faint damns. The chief difference between the two reviews is that Morgan agreed warmly with Brodie's naturalistic criticisms and mistrusted Arrington's refusal to be openly critical of the church as subjective ethicism.

Within a year of Morgan's death, Milton V. Backman would publish a volume comparing historical accounts of Joseph Smith's "first vision," and he would do so by discussing at least one firsthand account from Smith himself that pushed the story to 1832—and was in Smith's own hand. While still compelling, Dale Morgan's assertions were becoming as dated as the traditional evidence he had challenged. Now newer historical evidence was available. Within two years of Morgan's passing the first collection of scholarly essays on the faith appeared. Significantly, it drew in the work of academic scholars from both Utah's Latter-day Saint and Missouri's Reorganized Latter Day Saint traditions.[43]

Even more significant, in 1972 the Church of Jesus Christ of Latter-day Saints responded to an administrative consultant's recommendation on its non-ecclesiastical structures. In many offices through the early part of the decade, apostles surrendered daily management responsibilities in favor of hiring professional staff. The Church Historian's Office was no exception. The shift was not only administrative, but also generational. A. William Lund, custodian (and guardian) at the Church Historian's Office, died two months before Dale. Joseph Fielding Smith, the longtime Church Historian who had become president of the church at David O. McKay's passing in 1970, himself passed from the scene less than two years later. The church's historical arm and official institutional memory was professionalized with the appointment of a trio of professional historians to the new Church History Department, led by Leonard J. Arrington.[44] In a conversation with outgoing Church Historian and apostle Howard W. Hunter, Arrington noted Hunter's opinion that in 1972 "the church is mature enough that its history should be honest." Hunter further asserted: "the best way to answer anti-Mormonism is to print the truth."[45] One might say, *is to print the complicated truth of mortals.* Within the former bastion of LDS utilitarianism, historicism was poised to have its day.

Therefore, it is perhaps no surprise that Morgan is among the least remembered of his circle. Although, in 1940, he generated arguably the first work of scholarship on the Mormons that met modern standards (*The State of Deseret*), he never completed the masterwork of Latter Day Saint history on which he was widely known to be laboring, and the seminal bibliography he began was completed only by another's hands. Yet Morgan is arguably the link that associated the historical writers Gary Topping addressed.[46] Juanita Brooks and Fawn M. Brodie are better remembered because they produced foundational controversial books, and yet both works were profoundly reshaped by Morgan. Brodie's *No Man Knows My History* was rescued from being one more polemic on Joseph Smith to become probably the most significant book on Mormonism of the twentieth century. Morgan helped Brooks craft *Mountain Meadows Massacre* from a story into a genuine scholarly study, her sole publication sustained and not merely contextualized with notes and citations. Stegner and DeVoto also earned their reputations by the general excellence of their work and both acknowledged their debt to the younger man.

The generation of scholars who were graduate students in the late 1960s reshaped the telling of cultural and administrative history, revolutionized the church's record-keeping, and opened new relations to the rest of Latter Day Saint community. Its participants, steeped in historicism, affected the cultural narrative for the second half of the twentieth and through the first quarter of the twenty-first century. On this firm foundation, a revitalized commitment to inquiry and documentary integrity was reflected, partly to defuse critics proliferating in the creation of the Internet. With the establishment of the Joseph Smith Papers project (2001) and later the Church History Library (2009), the Latter-day Saints' approach to its past now generally reflects a comment by Harold B. Lee to Leonard Arrington that "the best defense of the church is the true and impartial account of our history," or as Spencer W. Kimball told Arrington later: "Our history is history, and we don't need to tamper with it or be ashamed of it."[47]

No matter what was happening to the field at large, not all among the church's central officers shared the viewpoint of Lee, Kimball, or Hunter, nor did they see the shift toward professionalism as positive. Less than a decade after its flowering, the creation of this historical "Camelot" under Arrington was challenged in the 1990s by a reenergized, culturally conservative ethicism—Arrington's "Holy Ghosters"—which tried to recapture or deflect the liberalizing historicism offered by the New Mormon History.[48] Morgan would have expected and denounced this attempt to again retreat inwards. Only with the inevitable shift in church leadership, and with the encouragement of President Gordon B. Hinckley (1995–2008), the denomination readopted openness and the broad inquiry that re-embraced historicism and encouraged scholarship. And the past does not stay still nor our perspective of it remain fixed in place. Jan Shipps's review of Richard Lyman Bushman's *Joseph Smith: Rough Stone Rolling* perceives another recent turn in the wheel of Latter Day Saint history, suggesting that the externally informed but inward-facing New Mormon History may be giving way in turn to something still newer.[49]

Although the field outgrew him well before his passing, a shadow of Morgan's influence lingers over the field of Latter Day Saint studies. To its first generation of scholarly writers, he was both benchmark and bugaboo, the one to consult for fear that one had missed something relevant. Being one of the first to plow the fields of untouched sources created for him a reputation as one who might be dismissed but could not be ignored. The field has grown dramatically since then, but in its early years even Leonard Arrington did not loom so large. Content to have made a transition into a related subject, Morgan's comments to Cooley in fall 1970, just before his

cancer diagnosis, about how he planned to use the Guggenheim fellowship, suggest he always nourished a desire to return topically to the Mormons. Perhaps his most notable legacy in the field was completed in 1978
with publication of Chad J. Flake's *A Mormon Bibliography, 1830—1930*.
Today a second edition remains the standard catalog of works by and
about the Latter Day Saints.

* * * * *

Traditionally a biographer provides the last word on his subject. After a
lot of thought I've decided to let my subject have the last word, a couple
of admonitory epigrams that both warn and tantalizingly invite.

Romanticism aside, it is a truism that those who came to the American
West, whether trapper, explorer, argonaut, rancher, or settler, did hard
things. Some succeeded spectacularly. Most did not. What it *meant* to
dare greatly is no less than what a deaf man from Depression-era Salt Lake
City would have said his life meant: he did the best he could with what
circumstance dealt him. Some of the results were notable, others were just
projects that needed doing. I think Morgan would agree that daring to
come west at all was by itself a human accomplishment, as was his wrestle
with being a deaf writer in a hearing world.

The first quote from Morgan stands as something of a warning about
the very methodology to which he held so rigorously. "The 'truth,'" he
observed, probably in the 1940s as he was at work on his unfinished Mormon book, "is never simple, and history can never have the exactitude
of mathematics, say, or chemistry. There are too many variables, too many
missing elements, for very many final judgments, and any history, when
all is said and done, is an oversimplification of a total situation."[50]

The second comment, frankly, could have been said by anyone who
wished to make a living at writing, but it was invoked as advice to the
coming generations of writers and readers—both professional and avocational—in the ever-unfolding tally of stories told from within: "He whose
final objective is the relaxed life has no business taking up with history."[51]

But what an adventure it is, anyway.

A Dale L. Morgan Bibliography[1]

I. WORKS BY DALE L. MORGAN (IN CHRONOLOGICAL ORDER)

BOOKS

[With Ray Kooyman]. *1938: The Book, The Utah Tournament*. Salt Lake City: Utah Chess Federation, 1938.

A History of Ogden. Ogden, UT: Ogden City Commission, October 1940.

The State of Deseret. Ogden: Utah Historical Records Survey Project, in *Utah Historical Quarterly* 8, no. 2–4 (April–October 1940): 65–251. [Written as an intended "Introduction to the Inventory of State Archives of Utah"]

The Humboldt: Highroad to the West. Rivers of America Series. New York: Farrar & Rinehart, 1943.

The Great Salt Lake. American Lakes Series. Indianapolis: Bobbs-Merrill, 1947.

West from Fort Bridger, edited by J. Roderic Korns, *Utah Historical Quarterly* 19 (1951). [Despite credit to Korns, Morgan transcribed, edited, and wrote the entire work.]

Life in America: The West. Grand Rapids, MI: Fideler Company, 1952. Reprinted 1955, 1958, 1960, 1962.

Jedediah Smith and the Opening of the West. Indianapolis: Bobbs-Merrill, 1953. Paperback. Lincoln: University of Nebraska Press, 1964.

A Bibliography of the Churches of the Dispersion (Western Humanities Review, 1953).

With Carl I. Wheat. *Jedediah Smith and His Maps of the American West*. California Historical Society Special Publication no. 26. San Francisco: California Historical Society, 1954.

Rand McNally's Pioneer Atlas of the American West Containing Facsimile Reproduction of Maps and Indexes from the 1876 First Edition of Rand, McNally & Co.'s Business Atlas of the Great Mississippi Valley and Pacific Slope, Together with Contemporary Railroad Maps and Travel Literature. Chicago: Rand McNally, 1956. Reissued, 1969.

Robert W. Baughman, *Kansas In Maps*. Topeka: Kansas State Historical Society, 1961. [Despite credit to Baughman, Morgan ghost-wrote the entire work and coordinated publication]

With Charles Kelly. *Old Greenwood: The Story of Caleb Greenwood, Trapper, Pathfinder, and Early Pioneer*. Revised ed. Georgetown, CA: Talisman Press, 1965. [Morgan wrote virtually the entire work.]

Captain Charles M. Weber: Pioneer of the San Joaquin and Founder of Stockton, California. Friends of The Bancroft Library General Publication no. 1. Berkeley, CA: Friends of The Bancroft Library, 1966.

EDITED VOLUMES

Utah: A Guide to the State. New York: Hastings House, 1942. Reprinted 1945, 1954, 1959, 1972.

Tales of Utah 1941–1942: Collection of News Stories. Salt Lake City: Utah Writers' Project, 1942.

Santa Fe and the Far West. Los Angeles: Glen Dawson, 1949.

Wheat, Carl I. *Mapping the Transmississippi West, 1540–1861*. 5 vols. in 6 books. San Francisco: Institute for Historical Cartography, 1957–1963. [Morgan advised on and edited the entire series, and wrote entirely the two-part volume 5]

The Overland Diary of James A. Pritchard from Kentucky to California in 1849. Denver: Old West Publishing Co., 1959.

McCollum, William S. *California As I Saw It: Pencillings by the Way of Its Gold and Gold Diggers! and Incidents of Travel by Land and Water*. Los Gatos, CA: Talisman Press, 1960.

Mexico Ancient and Modern: As Represented by a Selection of Works in the Bancroft Library. Keepsake no. 10. Berkeley, CA: Friends of The Bancroft Library, 1962.

A Guide to the Manuscript Collections of the Bancroft Library. Vol. 1. Edited with George P. Hammond. Berkeley, CA: University of California Press, 1963.

Overland in 1846: Diaries and Letters of the California-Oregon Trail. 2 vols. Georgetown, CA: Talisman Press, 1963.

Platt, P. L., and B. Slater. *Travelers' Guide across the Plains upon the Overland Route to California*. San Francisco: John Howell, 1963. [Morgan also wrote the introduction (v–xi).]

Frémont, John C. *Geographical Memoir upon Upper California*. Edited with Allan Nevins. Sacramento: Book Club of California, 1964. [Morgan contributed "The Map of Oregon and Upper California" (xxi–xxxi) and essentially rewrote Nevins' contribution.]

Perkins, William. *Three Years in California: William Perkins' Journal of Life at Sonora, 1849–1852*. Edited with James R. Scobie. Berkeley: University of California Press, 1964.

The West of William H. Ashley: The International Struggle for the Fur Trade of the Missouri, the Rocky Mountains, and the Columbia, with Explorations beyond the Continental Divide, Recorded in the Diaries and Letters of William H. Ashley and His Contemporaries. Denver: Old West Publishing Co., 1964.

McConkey, Harriet E. B. *Dakota War Whoop: Indian Massacres and War in Minnesota.* Lakeside Classics, no. 63. Chicago: Lakeside Press, R. R. Donnelley & Sons Co., 1965.

Judd, Laura Fish. *Honolulu: Sketches of Life in the Hawaiian Islands from 1828 to 1861.* Lakeside Classics, no. 64. Chicago: Lakeside Press, R. R. Donnelley & Sons Co., 1966.

Anderson, William Marshall. *The Rocky Mountain Journals of William Marshall Anderson.* Edited with Eleanor T. Harris. San Marino, CA: Huntington Library, 1967.

Lynch, Jeremiah. *Three Years in the Klondike.* Lakeside Classics, no. 65. Chicago: Lakeside Press, R. R. Donnelley & Sons Co., 1967.

Gardiner, Howard Calhoun. *In Pursuit of the Golden Dream: Reminiscences of San Francisco and the Northern and Southern Mines, 1849–1857.* Stoughton, MA: Western Hemisphere, 1970.

ARTICLES, ESSAYS, AND CONTRIBUTIONS TO LARGER WORKS

"Historical Sketch of Tooele County." *Inventory of the County Archives of Utah: No. 23 Tooele County (Tooele City).* Ogden: Utah Historical Records Survey Project, June 1939.

"Historical Sketch of Daggett County." *Inventory of the County Archives of Utah: No. 5 Daggett County (Manila).* Ogden: Utah Historical Records Survey Project, August 1939.

"Historical Sketch of Weber County." *Inventory of the County Archives of Utah: No. 29 Weber County (Ogden).* Ogden: Utah Historical Records Survey Project, January 1940.

Origins of Utah Place Names, 3/e. Salt Lake City: Utah State Dept of Public Instruction, March 1940.

Thornley, John D., ed. *History and Bibliography of Religion,* vol.1. In *Inventory of Church Archives of Utah.* Salt Lake City: Utah Historical Records Survey, June 1940.

"Historical Sketch of Carbon County." *Inventory of the County Archives of Utah: No. 4 Carbon County (Price).* Ogden: Utah Historical Records Survey Project, July 1940.

"Historical Sketch of Utah County." *Inventory of the County Archives of Utah: No. 25 Utah County (Provo).* Ogden: Utah Historical Records Survey Project, September 1940.

"Historical Sketch of Uintah County." *Inventory of the County Archives of Utah: No. 24 Uintah County (Vernal).* Ogden: Utah Historical Records Survey Project, November 1940.

"Historical Sketch of Emery County." *Inventory of the County Archives of Utah: No. 8 Emery County (Castle Dale).* Ogden: Utah Historical Records Survey Project, March 1941.

"Places You Should Know: High Uintah Primitive Area." *Travel West,* 16 June 1941.

"Utah's Years before the Beginning." *Salt Lake Tribune*, 6 July 1941.

"Utah: A Viewpoint." *Rocky Mountain Review* 5, no.2 (Winter 1941): 1–2.

"Mormon Story Tellers." *Rocky Mountain Review* 7, no. 1 (Fall 1942): 1–7.

[Grace Winkleman]. *Provo: Pioneer Mormon City*. Portland, OR: Binfords & Mort, 1942, chapter 2 [uncredited].

"Historian Insists Carson Carved Island Cross." *Ogden Standard Examiner* (Ogden, UT), 8 October 1943.

"Cities of the Rockies 1: Salt Lake City." *Rocky Mountain Review* 9, no. 1 (Fall 1944): 39–44.

Chester Bowles. "Black Market." "Office of Price Administration." In *1944 Britannica Book of the Year: A Record of the March of Events of 1943*. Encyclopedia Britannica, 1945. [as ghost-writer]

"Rain (An Excerpt)." "Mormon Storytellers." In *The Rocky Mountain Reader*, edited by Ray B. West, Jr. (New York: E. P. Dutton & Co., 1946), 283–97.

"The Great Salt Lake," *Think Magazine* 12 (May 1946): 18–21, 40.

Introduction to *The Exploration of the Colorado River in 1869*, edited by William C. Darrah [and Dale L. Morgan]. *Utah Historical Quarterly* 15 (1947): 1–8.

Introduction to *The Exploration of the Colorado River and the High Plateaus of Utah in 1871–72*, edited by William C. Darrah [and Dale L. Morgan]. *Utah Historical Quarterly* 16/17 (1948–1949): 1–9.

"The Administration of Indian Affairs in Utah, 1851–58." *Pacific Historical Review* 17, no. 4 (November 1948): 383–409.

"The Mountain States." In *American Guide: A Source Book and Complete Guide for the United States*, edited by Henry G. Alsberg, 1072–1090. American Guide Series. New York: Hastings House, 1949.

"Salt Lake City: City of the Saints." In *Rocky Mountain Cities*, edited by Ray B. West, Jr., 179–207. New York: W. W. Norton, 1949.

"Letters by Forty-niners." Edited by Dale L. Morgan. *Western Humanities Review* 3, no. 2 (April 1949): 98–116.

"The Mormon Ferry on the North Platte: The Journal of William A. Empey." Edited by Dale L. Morgan. *Annals of Wyoming* 21, no. 2–3 (July, October 1949): 111–67.

"Pioneer Barrier," *Deseret News Magazine*, 9, no. 9 (September 1949).

"A Bibliography of the Church of Jesus Christ, Organized at Green Oak, Pennsylvania, July 1862." *Western Humanities Review* 4, no. 1 (Winter 1949–1950): 44–70.

"A Bibliography of the Church of Jesus Christ of Latter Day Saints (Strangites)." *Western Humanities Review* 5, no. 1 (Winter 1950–1951): 42–114.

Introduction to *Gazetteer of Utah Localities and Altitudes*, vii. Salt Lake City: University of Utah Division of Biology, 1952.

"The Miles Goodyear Story." *Standard Examiner* (Ogden, UT), 18–26. July 1952. [serial article]

"Book of Mormon." "Mormons." "Reorganized Church of Jesus Christ of Latter Day Saints." "Smith, Joseph Fielding." In *Encyclopedia Americana*. New York: Grolier, 1953.

"Miles Goodyear and the Founding of Ogden." *Utah Historical Quarterly* 21, no. 3–4 (July, October 1953): 195–218, 307–29.

"Washakie and the Shoshoni: A Selection of Documents from the Records of the Utah Superintendency of Indian Affairs." 10-part series. *Annals of Wyoming* 24–29 (July 1953–April 1958).

"Introduction." "A Bibliography of the Churches of the Dispersion." *Western Humanities Review* 7, no.3 (Summer 1953): 255–66. [The bibliography itself was issued to subscribers only as a separate imprint]

"The Diary of William H. Ashley, March 25 to June 27, 1825." Edited by Dale L. Morgan. *Bulletin of the Missouri Historical Society* 11, no. 1–3 (October 1954, January, April 1955): 9–40, 158–86, 279–302.

"The Reminiscences of James Holt: A Narrative of the Emmett Company." Edited by Dale L. Morgan. *Utah Historical Quarterly* 23, no. 1–2 (January, April 1955): 1–33; 151–79.

"Board of Trustees: Juanita Brooks." "Utah State Historical Society: Sixty Years of Organized History." *Utah Historical Quarterly* 25, no. 3 (July 1957):193–95.

"The Contemporary Scene." In *Among the Mormons,* edited by William Mulder and A. Russell Mortensen, 467–74. New York: Alfred A. Knopf, 1958.

"The Changing Face of Salt Lake City." In *The Valley of the Great Salt Lake,* edited by A. Russell Mortensen. *Utah Historical Quarterly* 27, no. 3 (Summer 1959): 209–32. The entire number was issued separately the same year.

"The Ferries of the Forty-niners." 3-part series. *Annals of Wyoming* 31–32, no. 1–2, 1 (April, October 1959, April 1960): 5–31; 145–89; 51–69.

"The Significance and Value of the Overland Journal." In *Probing the American West: Papers from the Santa Fe Conference*, edited by K. Ross Toole, John Alexander Carroll, Robert M. Utley, and A. R. Mortensen, 29–36. Santa Fe: Museum of New Mexico Press, 1961.

Foreword to *Trappers and Mountain Men,* by Evan Jones, 8. American Heritage Junior Library. New York: American Heritage; distributed by Golden Press, 1961.

"The Significance and Value of the Overland Journal." *El Palacio* 69, no. 2 (Summer 1962): 69–76.

Introduction to *California Manuscripts: Being a Collection of Important, Unpublished and Unknown Original Historical Sources*, Catalog no. 159, 3–6. New York: Edward Eberstadt & Sons, 1962.

"Contemporary Biography: George P. Hammond." *Pacific Historian* 7, no. 3 (August 1963):142–48.

"Opening the West: Explorers and Mountain Men." In *Book of the American West,* edited by Jay Monaghan, 9–82. New York: Julian Messner; Copp Clark Publishing Co., 1963.

"Early Maps." *Nevada Highways and Parks.* Centennial issue (1964): [13]–17.

"A Western Diary: A Review Essay." *American West* 2, no. 2 (Spring 1965): 46–47, 93.

"GPH." In *GPH: An Informal Record of George P. Hammond and His Era in the Bancroft Library,* 1–12. Keepsake no. 13. Berkeley, CA: Friends of The Bancroft Library, 1965.

Foreword to *Letters of George Catlin and His Family: A Chronicle of the American West,* edited by Marjorie Catlin Roehm, xv–xviii. Berkeley, CA: University of California Press, 1966.

"The Wheat Legacy." *Bancroftiana* no. 39 (November 1966): 2–3.

"The Fur Trade and Its Historians." *Minnesota History* 40, no. 4 (Winter 1966):151–56, and *American West* 3, no. 2 (Spring 1966): 28–35, 92–93.

"A New Ashley Document." *Westerners' New York Posse Brand Book* 12, no. 4 (1966): 73–77, 87–88.

"The Fur Trade and Its Historians." In *Aspects of the Fur Trade: Selected Papers of the 1965 North American Fur Trade Conference,* edited by Russell W. Fridley, 151–56. St. Paul: Minnesota Historical Society, 1967.

"Brigham Young." *Encyclopedia Britannica,* 13th ed., 1967.

"Jedediah Smith Today." *Pacific Historian* 11, no. 2 (Spring 1967): 35–46.

"Susanna Bryant Dakin." *Bancroftiana* no. 40 (May 1967): 1.

"Literary Conception, Gestation, Publication." "Helen Harding Bretnor." *Bancroftiana* no. 41 (December 1967): 2–3, 6.

"The Mormon Way Bill." "The Wheat Collection." *Bancroftiana* no. 42 (May 1968): 3.

"An Informative Dialogue-by-Letter about Kit Carson's Early, Uncertain Chronology." *Montana: The Magazine of Western History* 18, no. 3 (Summer 1968): 86–90.

"New Light on Ashley and Jedediah Smith." *Pacific Historian* 12, no. 1 (Winter 1968): 14–22.

"Utah before the Mormons." *Utah Historical Quarterly* 36, no. 1 (Winter 1968): 3–23.

"The Archivist, the Librarian, and the Historian." *Library Journal* 93, no. 22 (15 December 1968): 4621–23.

"Edmund Green." *Bancroftiana* no. 44 (April 1969): 8.

"Mistaken Identity." *Bancroftiana* no. 45 (July 1969): 8.

"Mutual Respect but Another Round about Kit Carson's Lost Year." *Montana: The Magazine of Western History* 19, no. 3 (Summer 1969): 79.

"Literature in the History of the Church: The Importance of Involvement." *Dialogue: A Journal of Mormon Thought* 4, no. 3 (Autumn 1969): 26–32.

"Ashley, William Henry." "Great Salt Lake." Logan (Utah)." "Ogden, Peter S." "Ogden (Utah)." "Provo (Utah)." "Salt Lake City." "Smith, Jedediah Strong." "Utah." *Encyclopedia Britannica,* 14th ed., 1969.

"Erwin Gustav Gudde, 1889–1969." *California Historical Society Quarterly* 49, no. 2 (June 1970): 183–84.

"Western Travels and Travelers in the Bancroft Library." In *Travelers on the Western Frontier,* edited by John F. McDermott, 100–111. Urbana: University of Illinois Press, 1970).

CONFERENCE PRESENTATIONS
"The Significance and Value of the Overland Journal." Conference on the History of Western America, Santa Fe, NM, 12–14 October 1961.

"Some Problems of Fur Trade History." North American Fur Trade Conference, St. Paul, MN, 1–2 November 1965.

"Jedediah Smith Today." California Historical Foundation-Jedediah Smith Society meeting, University of the Pacific, Stockton, CA, 18 March 1966.

"Utah Before the Mormons." Utah State Historical Society annual meeting, Salt Lake City, 23 September 1967.

"Travels in the Bancroft Library." Travelers on the Western Frontier Conference, Southern Illinois University, Edwardsville, 21 February 1968.

MAPS
Utah Historical Trails Map: The Routes of Explorers, Early Wayfarers, and Immigrant Trails Depicted in Relation to the Modern Highway System of the State. Salt Lake City: Utah State Department of Publicity and Industrial Development, 1948. Two printings.

Historical Trails Map of Utah. Salt Lake City: Utah Tourist and Publicity Council, 1965.

BOOK REVIEWS
"Sound Views on Pressing Issue of Present Day." Review of *Social Security,* by Maxwell S. Stewart. *Salt Lake Tribune,* 11 July 1937.

"Political Social Forces Shaped the Man Napoleon." Review of *Bonaparte,* by Eugene Tarlé. *Salt Lake Tribune,* 1 August 1937.

"Nationalism an Evil World Must Accept." Review of *Foreigners Aren't Fools,* by Christopher Hollis. *Salt Lake Tribune,* 8 August 1937.

"Chemistry's Value to Man Reiterated." Review of *Man in a Chemical World,* by A. Cressy Morrison. *Salt Lake Tribune,* 22 August 1937.

"Chronicle of New Mexico Too Forcedly Directive, Yet Valuable Americana." Review of *New Mexico's Own Chronicle,* edited by Maurice Garland Fulton and Paul Horgan. *Salt Lake Tribune,* 22 August 1937.

"Asch Reports Findings as to American Contrasts." Review of *The Road: In Search of America,* by Nathan Asch. *Salt Lake Tribune,* 29 August 1937.

"Strike Novel Handles Theme Superficially." Review of *The Strikers,* by Goetze Jeter. *Salt Lake Tribune,* 12 September 1937.

[Under heading "Books on Miscellaneous Subjects."] Review of *Planning for College,* by Charles Maxwell McConn. *Salt Lake Tribune,* 12 September 1937.

"Editor's Work Recalls Era 1913–1933." Review of *Twenty Eventful Years,* by Lawrence Kaye Hodges. *Salt Lake Tribune,* 26 September 1937.

"Ruthless Financial Giant a City-Builder of Vision." Review of *Ralston's Ring,* by George D. Lyman. *Salt Lake Tribune,* 10 October 1937.

"Ogalala Tribe Finds Honest Historian." Review of *Red Cloud's Folk,* by George E. Hyde. *Salt Lake Tribune,* 24 October 1937.

"Nippon Nation Wears Tougher Aspect to US." Review of *Japan in American Public Opinion,* by Eleanor Tupper and George E. McReynolds. *Salt Lake Tribune,* 12 December 1937.

"Viereck Book Not Unbiased Criticism, but Significant in Some Aspects." Review of *The Kaiser on Trial,* by George Sylvester Viereck. *Salt Lake Tribune,* 19 December 1937.

"Sane Analysis Given Vital Contemporaries." Review of *Modern Fiction: A Study of Values,* by Herbert J. Muller. *Salt Lake Tribune,* 2 January 1938.

"Man's Conception of World, of Society and Himself." Review of *Architects of Ideas,* by Ernest R. Trattner. *Salt Lake Tribune,* 26 June 1938.

"Panoramic View of Town's Growth in Novel Form." Review of *American Years,* by Harold Sinclair. *Salt Lake Tribune,* 3 July 1938.

"New Respect for Cherokee Tribe Follows Account of Its Worthy History." Review of *A Political History of the Cherokee Nation,* by Morris L. Wardell. *Salt Lake Tribune,* 17 July 1938.

"Penetrating Discussion of Labor's Problem." Review of *What Are We to Do?,* by John Strachey. *Salt Lake Tribune,* 14 August 1938.

"Farrell Offers Brutally Realistic Picture of One Phase of American Life." Review of *No Star is Lost,* by James T. Farrell. *Salt Lake Tribune,* 9 October 1938.

"Story-Teller Hemingway Takes Playwright's Role." Review of *The Fifth Column and the First Forty-Nine Stories,* by Ernest Hemingway. *Salt Lake Tribune,* 20 November 1938.

"'American Dream' Can Be Realized Analyst Argues." Review of *Roads to a New America,* by David Cushman Coyle. *Salt Lake Tribune,* 27 November 1938.

"Ancient Civilizations In Relation to Today's." Review of *The Romance of Human Progress,* by Arthur Stanley Riggs. *Salt Lake Tribune,* 18 December 1938.

"Nazi Ideology Explained." Review of *Germany Speaks,* a symposium. *Salt Lake Tribune,* 8 January 1939.

"Exposition of Philosophy Penetrating and Readable." Review of *Guide to the Philosophy of Morals and Politics,* by C. E. M. Joad. *Salt Lake Tribune,* 22 January 1939.

"U.S. 'Isolation' Policy Examined and Condemned." Review of *The United States and World Organization, 1920–1933,* by Denna Frank Fleming. *Salt Lake Tribune,* 19 February 1939.

"Aztec Downfall as Seen by One of Cortez' Men." Review of *The True History of the Conquest of Mexico,* by Captain Bernal Díaz del Castillo. *Salt Lake Tribune,* 26 February 1939.

"Reporter Bitterly Scores Late Mid-Europe Events." Review of *Betrayal in Central Europe,* by G. E. R. Gedye. *Salt Lake Tribune,* 19 March 1939.

"Einstein Personality Yet to Be Revealed; Present Study Able, but Limited." Review of *Albert Einstein: Maker of Universes,* by H. Gordon Garbedian. *Salt Lake Tribune,* 2 April 1939.

"Out of Prison Comes Strong Human Story." Review of *Spanish Prisoner,* by Peter Elstob. *Salt Lake Tribune,* 23 April 1939.

"Naziism a New Religion, Hitler Its Prophet!" Review of *Mein Kampf,* by Adolph Hitler. *Salt Lake Tribune,* 30 April 1939.

"Admirable, Able Paper on Democracy's Nature by an Advocate." Review of *Democracy Works,* by Arthur Garfield Hays. *Salt Lake Tribune,* 14 May 1939.

"Evaluation of America's Immediate Past a Book Of Profound Importance." Review of *American in Midpassage,* by Charles A. Beard and Mary R. Beard. *Salt Lake Tribune,* 4 June 1939.

"America's Connection with One Famous Corsican." Review of *The Bonapartes in America,* by C. E. Macartney and Gordon Dorrance. *Salt Lake Tribune,* 2 July 1939.

"Man's Pilgrimage Theme of Thomas Wolfe's Last Literary Production." Review of *The Web and the Rock,* by Thomas Wolfe. *Salt Lake Tribune,* 9 July 1939.

"Whole Story of Northwest's Pioneer Mission in Detail." Review of *The Whitman Mission,* by Marvin M. Richardson. *Salt Lake Tribune,* 19 June 1940.

"They Happened to Be Mormons." Review of *Children of the Covenant,* by Richard Scowcroft. *Saturday Review of Literature* 28, no. 33 (18 August 1945): 16.

"Two Western Books." Reviews of *Pardner of the Wind,* by N. Howard (Jack) Thorp; and *The Wild Horse of the West,* by Walker D. Wyman. *Rocky Mountain Review* 10, no. 1 (Autumn 1945): 58–60.

"Scenic Backdrop with People." Review of *This is the Place: Utah,* by Maurine Whipple. *Saturday Review of Literature* 28, no. 45 (10 November 1945): 17.

"A Prophet and His Legend." Review of *No Man Knows My History,* by Fawn M. Brodie. *Saturday Review of Literature* 28, no. 47 (24 November 1945): 7.

Review of *The Midnight Cry,* by Francis D. Nichol. *Rocky Mountain Review* 10, no. 3 (Spring 1946): 172–74.

"Craftsman vs. Artist." Review of *On This Star,* by Virginia Sorensen. *Saturday Review of Literature* 29, no. 21 (25 May 1946): 14–15.

"Strange and Savage." Review of *The Colorado,* by Frank Waters. *Saturday Review of Literature* 29, no. 39 (28 September 1946): 28.

"Jim Bridger, In Part." Review of *Jim Bridger, Mountain Man,* by Stanley Vestal. *Saturday Review of Literature,* 29, no. 43 (26 October 1946): 37.

"Atoms to Dog Fights." Review of *I Hate Thursday,* by Thomas Hornsby Ferril. *Saturday Review of Literature* 29, no. 49 (7 December 1946): 62.

"Symbiosis of Mine and Men." Review of *Vermilion,* by Idwal Jones. *Saturday Review of Literature,* 30, no. 20 (17 May 1947): 19.

"Western Panegyrics." Reviews of *Along Sierra Trails: Kings Canyon National Park,* by Joyce and Josef Muench; *Exploring Our National Parks and Monuments,* by Devereux Butcher; and *One Hundred Years in Yosemite: The Story of a Great Park and Its Friends,* by Carl Parcher Russell. *Saturday Review of Literature,* 30, no. 38 (20 September 1947): 29–30.

"The Wild and Furry West." Review of *Across the Wide Missouri,* by Bernard DeVoto. *Saturday Review of Literature,* 30, no. 45 (8 November 1947): 14–15.

"Pacific Highroad." Review of *The Overland Trail,* by Jay Monaghan. *Saturday Review of Literature* 31, no. 2 (10 January 1948): 10–11.

"Captains of the Great Exploration." Review of *Lewis and Clark: Partners in Discovery,* by John Bakeless. *Saturday Review of Literature,* 31, no. 3 (17 January 1948): 8–9.

"Horses, Good Whiskey, and Art." Review of *Frederick Remington: Artist of the Old West,* by Harold McCracken. *Saturday Review of Literature,* 31, no. 4 (24 January 1948): 26–27.

"What's Going On in the Rockies." Review of *The Big Divide,* by David Lavender. *Saturday Review of Literature,* 32, no. 3 (15 January 1949): 29–30.

"Wild West Bad Man." Review of *Wicked Water,* by MacKinlay Kantor. *Saturday Review of Literature,* 32, no. 7 (12 February 1949): 17.

"Honey and Gold." Review of *Sierra Nevada Lakes,* by George and Bliss Hinkle. *Saturday Review of Literature* 32, no. 16 (16 April 1949): 21.

"Fruits of Rebellion." Review of *The Evening and the Morning,* by Virginia Sorensen. *Saturday Review of Literature* 32, no. 17 (23 April 1949): 13–14.

Review of *The Journal of Madison Berryman Moorman 1850–51,* by Irene D. Paden. *Western Humanities Review* 3, no. 2 (April 1949): 161–64.

"Fusing Red and White Cultures." Review of *Beulah Land,* by H. L. Davis. *Saturday Review of Literature* 32, no. 24 (11 June 1949): 15, 29.

"American Folk Outlaw-Hero." *Review of Jesse James Was My Neighbor,* by Homer Croy. *Saturday Review of Literature* 32, no. 26 (25 June 1949): 18–19.

"Call of the Wild West." Review of *The Bubbling Spring,* by Ross Santee. *Saturday Review of Literature* 32, no. 36 (3 September 1949): 14.

"Shipwrecked and How." Review of *Silverlock,* by John Myers Myers. *Saturday Review of Literature* 32, no. 36 (3 September 1949): 28.

"The Meteoric Pike." Review of *The Lost Pathfinder: Zebulon Montgomery Pike,* by W. Eugene Hollon. *Saturday Review of Literature* 32, no. 38 (17 September 1949): 17–18.

"Two Cutoffs from South Pass." Review of *Prairie Schooner Detours,* by Irene D. Paden. *Saturday Review of Literature* 32, no. 48 (26 November 1949): 16.

"Life According to the Prophet Smith." Review of *The Peaceable Kingdom,* by Ardyth Kennelly. *Saturday Review of Literature* 32, no. 53 (31 December 1949): 15.

"Of Men and Taxes." Review of *American Heartwood,* by Donald Culross Peattie. *Saturday Review of Literature* 32, no. 53 (31 December 1949): 17–18.

"Colorado Montagnes." Review of *Rocky Mountain Country,* by Albert N. Williams. *Saturday Review of Literature* 33, no. 14 (8 April 1950): 11.

"The West's Wildest." Review of *The Last Chance: Tombstone's Early Years,* by John Myers Myers. *Saturday Review of Literature* 33, no. 19 (13 May 1950): 50.

"The West Tomorrow." Review of *America's New Frontier: The Mountain West,* by Morris E. Garnsey. *Saturday Review of Literature* 33, no. 23 (10 June 1950): 12.

"Deseret News That Is Fit to Print." Review of *The Voice in the West,* by Wendell J. Ashton. *Saturday Review of Literature* 33, no. 28 (15 July 1950): 27.

"Personal History Notes." Review of *Them Was the Days,* by Martha Ferguson McKeown. *Saturday Review of Literature* 33, no. 30 (29 July 1950): 19.

"Minister's Niece Astray and Descendants." Review of *Diamond Wedding,* by Wilbur Daniel Steele. *Saturday Review of Literature,* 33, no. 31 (5 August 1950): 15.

"Gallant Lady." Review of *Family Kingdom,* by Samuel W. Taylor. *Saturday Review of Literature* 34, no. 19 (12 May 1951): 17–18.

"The Need for Roots." Review of *The Proper Gods,* by Virginia Sorensen. *Saturday Review of Literature* 34, no. 29 (21 July 1951): 17.

"Western Territories and States." Review of *Peter Skene Ogden's Snake Country Journals, 1824–25 and 1825–26,* edited by E. E. Rich and A. M. Johnson. *American Historical Review* 57, no. 3 (April 1952): 773.

Review of *The Larkin Papers,* Vol. 1, edited by George P. Hammond. *Utah Historical Quarterly* 20, no. 4 (October 1952): 385–86.

Review of *The Road to Santa Fe,* edited by Kate L. Gregg. *Utah Historical Quarterly* 21, no. 1 (January 1953): 82–84.

Reviews of *Before Lewis and Clark,* edited by A. P. Nasatir; *The Course of Empire,* by Bernard DeVoto; *David Thompson's Journals Relating to Montana and Adjacent Regions, 1808–12,* edited by M. Catherine White. *Utah Historical Quarterly* 21, no. 3 (July 1953): 271–75.

Review of *The Larkin Papers,* Vol. 4, edited by George P. Hammond. *Utah Historical Quarterly* 22, no. 3 (July 1954): 277–79.

"Polygamy in Practice." Review of *Isn't One Wife Enough?,* by Kimball Young. *Saturday Review* 37, no. 34 (21 August 1954): 14–16.

"Adobe Emporium." Review of *Bent's Fort,* by David Lavender. *Saturday Review* 38, no. 5 (29 January 1955): 12, 28.

Review of *The Fur Hunters of the Far West,* by Alexander Ross. *Montana: The Magazine of Western History* 6, no. 3 (Summer 1956): 56–58.

Review of *Rufus B. Sage: His Letters and Papers, 1836–1847,* edited by LeRoy R. and Ann W. Hafen. *Pacific Historical Review* 25, no. 4 (November 1956): 404–5.

Review of *Joseph Reddeford Walker and the Arizona Adventure,* by Daniel Ellis Conner. *Utah Historical Quarterly* 25, no. 3 (July 1957): 265–66.

"Mr. Meeker and the Red Men." Review of *Massacre: The Tragedy at White River,* by Marshall Sprague. *Saturday Review* 40, no. 30 (27 July 1957): 25–[*inc.*].[2]

"The Mormon Story." Review of *Kingdom of the Saints,* by Ray B. West, Jr. *Saturday Review* 40, no. 30 (27 July 1957): 26.

Review of *Journal of Captain John R. Bell,* edited by Harlin M. Fuller and LeRoy R. Hafen. *Pacific Historical Review* 26, no. 3 (August 1957): 293–95.

"Of Indians, Cowboys, and Ladies." Review of *This is the West,* by Robert West Howard. *Saturday Review* 40, no. 34 (24 August 1957): 28–29.

"The 'Peculiar People.'" Review of *The Mormons,* by Thomas F. O'Dea. *Saturday Review* 40, no. 52 (28 December 1957): 9.

Review of *Among the Mormons: Historic Accounts of Contemporary Observers,* edited by William Mulder and A. Russell Mortensen. *Pacific Historical Review* 27, no. 3 (August 1958): 303–4.

Review of *Great Basin Kingdom,* by Leonard Arrington. *Utah Historical Quarterly* 27, no. 2 (April 1959): 191–93.

Review of *Army Exploration in the American West, 1803–1863,* by William H. Goetzmann. *California Historical Society Quarterly* 39, no. 1 (March 1960): 83–85.

Review of *Robert Newell's Memoranda: Traveles in the Territory of Missourie...,* edited by Dorothy O. Johansen. *Oregon Historical Quarterly* 61, no. 1 (March 1960): 70–74.

Review of *Bill Sublette, Mountain Man,* by John E. Sunder. *Pacific Northwest Quarterly* 51, no. 2 (April 1960): 86–87.

"With the Help of a Beaver Hat, a Continent Was Settled," *The Fur Trade,* by Paul Chrisler Phillips. *New York Times Book Review,* 13 August 1961, 7–8.

Review of *The Gila Trail,* by Benjamin Butler Harris, edited by Richard H. Dillon. *Arizona and the West* 3, no. 3 (Autumn 1961): 294–95.

Review of *The Diary of James J. Strang,* edited by Mark A. Strang. *Michigan History* 45, no. 3 (September 1961): 277–78.

Review of *Peter Skene Ogden's Snake Country Journal, 1826–27,* edited by K. G. Davies. *Pacific Northwest Quarterly* 54, no. 3 (July 1963): 126.

Review of *John Doyle Lee,* by Juanita Brooks. *Southern California Quarterly* 45, no. 4 (December 1963): 364–66.

Review of *Josiah Belden, 1841 California Overland Pioneer,* edited by Doyce B. Nunis, Jr. *California Historical Society Quarterly* 42, no. 4 (December 1963): 335–36.

"Clark Papers," *The Field Notes of Captain William Clark, 1803–1805,* edited by Ernest Staples Osgood. *Minnesota History* 34, no. 4 (Winter 1964): 164–65.

"When the Saints Came Marching In." Review of *The Gathering of Zion,* by Wallace Stegner. *Saturday Review* 48, no. 3 (16 January 1965): 31.

"A Western Diary." Review of *On the Mormon Frontier: The Diary of Hosea Stout,* edited by Juanita Brooks. *American West* 2, no. 2 (Spring 1965): 46–47, 93.

Review of *The Beaver Men: Spearheads of Empire,* by Mari Sandoz. *The American West* 2, no. 1 (Winter 1965): 68.

Review of *Mountain Men and the Fur Trade of the Far West,* Vol. 1 and 2, edited by LeRoy R. Hafen. *Utah Historical Quarterly* 34, no. 2 (Spring 1966): 183–84.

Review of *The Mountain Men and the Fur Trade of the Far West,* Vol. 3, edited by LeRoy R. Hafen. *Utah Historical Quarterly* 35, no. 3 (Summer 1967): 270–71.

Review of *Quest for Empire,* by Klaus J. Hansen. *Utah Historical Quarterly* 35, no. 4 (Fall 1967): 352–53.

Review of *America's Western Frontiers,* by John A. Hawgood. *Minnesota History* 41, no. 1 (Spring 1968): 46–47.

Review of *Australians and the Gold Rush,* by Jay Monaghan. *Arizona and the West* 10, no. 1 (Spring 1968): 72–73.

Review of *Wilderness Kingdom,* by Joseph P. Donnelly, trans. *Oregon Historical Quarterly* 69, no. 1 (March 1968): 63–65.

Review of *The California Gold Discovery,* by Rodman W. Paul. *Pacific Historical Review* 37, no. 2 (May 1968): 235–36.

Review of *Exploration and Empire: The Explorer and the Scientist in the Winning of the American West,* by William H. Goetzmann. *Journal of American History* 55, no. 1 (June 1968): 141–53.

Review of *Father Kino in Arizona,* by Fay Jackson Smith, John L. Kessell, and Francis J. Fox. *Journal of American History* 55, no. 1 (June 1968): 115.

Review of *The Recollections of Philander Prescott,* by Donald Dean Parker. *Journal of the Illinois State Historical Society* 61, no. 2 (Summer 1968): 211–12.

Review of *George C. Yount and His Chronicles of the West,* edited by Charles L. Camp, *California Historical Society Quarterly* 48, no. 1 (March 1969): 88–89.

"Where We're At," *The Records of a Nation,* by H. G. Jones. *Library Journal* 94, no. 7 (1 April 1969): 1423.

Review of *Joshua Pilcher: Fur Trader and Indian Agent,* by John E. Sunder, *Pacific Historical Review* 38, no. 4 (November 1969): 484–85.

Review of *An Artist on the Overland Trail,* by James F. Wilkins. *Western Historical Quarterly* 1, no. 1 (January 1970): 77–79.

Review of *The Overland Journey of Joseph Francl, the First Bohemian to Cross the Plains to the California Gold Fields,* edited by Richard Brautigan and Patricia Oberhaus, *California Historical Society Quarterly* 49, no. 1 (March 1970): 72–73.

Review of *The California Gold Rush Diary of a German Sailor,* by W. Turrentine Jackson. *Pacific Historical Review* 39, no. 1 (February 1970): 118–19.

Review of *The Lion of the Lord,* by Stanley P. Hirshson. *Utah Historical Quarterly* 38, no. 4 (Fall 1970): 361–62.

Review of *The Lost Trappers,* by David H. Coyner. *American West* 8, no. 2 (March 1971): 54.

JUVENILIA

BYLINED ARTICLES AND COLUMNS

"The Spirit of Christmas." *West Red & Black* 15 (18 December 1931).

The Lone Survivor [pseudonym]. "Love Arrives at U; Quarry Narrates Story of Stark Horror." *Utah Chronicle*, 30 April 1935.

"Freshmen Get Lowdown on Life as Lived at Utah University." *Utah Chronicle*, 26 September 1935.

"Burleque of Italo-Ethiopia." *Utah Chronicle*, 3 October 1935.

"Man Is Low, Says Writer as Skies Appear Dark and Gloomy." *Utah Chronicle*, 10 October 1935.

"Denver Falls Before Redskin Pass Attack." "Many Factors Seen as Causes For Utah Student Apathy." *Utah Chronicle*, 31 October 1935.

"None of These Sad Pecks, Says Columnist of Kissing Scene." *Utah Chronicle*, 7 November 1935.

"Belly-Laughs Still Aroused by Political Tub Thumpers." *Utah Chronicle*, 14 November 1935.

"Goates-Type Turkey Day Dope Gives Writer a Sour Stomach." *Utah Chronicle*, 27 November 1935.

"All-American Fable Must Have Been Dreamed, Columnist Opines." *Utah Chronicle*, 21 November 1935.

"Utah's Oscar Voices Fear for Large Mouths." *Utah Chronicle*, 27 November 1935.

"Exams Held Inadequate Test of Student's Subject Mastery." *Utah Chronicle*, 5 December 1935.

"Peace or Chaos Seen as Alternatives Facing Nations." "'Technical Knowledge Unnecessary to Appreciate Art,' Explains Professor." *Utah Chronicle*, 12 December 1935.

"Dismal Sounds of Orchestra Is Lure to Native Curiosity." *Utah Chronicle*, 16 January 1936.

"This Column 'For Men Only' Says Writer as He Tells All." *Utah Chronicle*, 23 January 1936.

"Admission Wrenches Soul, but Pen Has Vanished." *Utah Chronicle*, 30 January 1936.

"Death Rattle of Elephant and Donkey Wafts Up from Gutter." *Utah Chronicle*, 6 February 1936.

"Surging of Public Opinion Obscured View of Strange Case." *Utah Chronicle*, 23 April 1936.

"Propaganda in Films Useful but Conflagration Lurks in Offing." *Utah Chronicle*, 30 April 1936.

"Bogey Man Tactics Displace Merit in New Advertising." *Utah Chronicle*, 14 May 1936.

"2 Piddling Fish, Red Hot Sunburn Reward One Utah Fluff-Head." *Utah Chronicle*, 21 May 1936.

"'Lead Kiiindlyy Liight,' Warbles Eastman, While Ab Weeps Faster." *Utah Chronicle*, 28 May 1936.

"Writer Thinks Peace Plan Will Be Marked by Generalities." *Utah Chronicle*, 9 January 1936.

"Murky Depths of Union Lounge Harbor Grim, Ill-Boding Grunt." *Utah Chronicle*, 13 February 1936.

"War Cannot Be Bound by Set of Laws, Opines Columnist." *Utah Chronicle*, 20 February 1936.

"Kicking of Supreme Court's Pants Irks Utah Columnist." *Utah Chronicle*, 28 February 1936.

"Freshmen Go in Here, but Few Come Out Here, Moans Columnist." *Utah Chronicle*, 5 March 1936.

"Indigestion—or Is Man About to Follow The Dinosaurs." *Utah Chronicle*, 12 March 1936.

"Writing on Life That Is Known to Authors Produces Better Pen." *Utah Chronicle*, 12 March 1936.

"Radical Parties Revolt Students Even Though They Be Liberal." *Utah Chronicle*, 26 March 1936.

"Flowers That Bloom in Election Sprout from the April Grass." *Utah Chronicle*, 16 April 1936.

"Selassie Finale Given as Italians Terminate Ethiopian Strife." *Utah Chronicle*, 7 May 1936.

"Frosh Warned to Hold Noses in Presence of Sopht Species." *Utah Chronicle*, 24 September 1936.

"Free Snatchers Swoom[sic] with Joy over Fat Purses." *Utah Chronicle*, 29 September 1936.

"Tragic Picture of Modern War Is Painted by New Writer." *Utah Chronicle*, 10 October 1936.

"Zest Added by Rubbernecks," *Utah Chronicle*, 13 October 1936.

"As the Fancy Strikes Us." *Utah Chronicle*, 19 November 1936.

"3rd Annual Art Exhibit Deemed Impressive." *Utah Chronicle*, 3 December 1936.

"As the Fancy Strikes Us," *Utah Chronicle*. 10 December 1936.

FICTION AND ESSAYS

"A Student Speaks." *University Pen*, Autumn 1934, 2.

"Insight into Confusion." *University Pen*, Winter 1935, 12–13

"Perspective on Platitude." *University Pen*, Spring 1935, 6–9. Reissued in *Pen Centennial* (1950).

"Atheist." *Salt Lake Tribune*, 12 May 1935.

"Cold." *University Pen*, Autumn 1935, 12–13, 24–27.

"For the Sun Will Be Always Bright." *University Pen*, Spring 1936, 3–5, 19–21–28.

"A Small Dog." *Salt Lake Tribune*, 14 June 1936.

"Eve." *University Pen*, Autumn 1936, 9–10, 22–25.

"On Realism in Literature." *University Pen*, Winter 1937, 8–9, 22–25.

"Business Man." *University Pen*, Spring 1937, 5–7, 18–21.

"Twenty-nine Dollars." *Salt Lake Tribune*, 31 October 1937.

POETRY
"The Gold-digger." *West Red & Black,* magazine issue no. 3 (1932).
"Blank Verse." *West Red & Black,* magazine issue no. 4 (1933).

POSTHUMOUS PUBLICATIONS
Review of *The Mountain Men and the Fur Trade of the Far West,* Vol. 4, edited by
    LeRoy R. Hafen. *Utah Historical Quarterly* 39, no. 4 (Fall 1971): 380–81.
Foreword to *The Beginning of the West: Annals of the Kansas Gateway to the
    American West, 1540–1854,* by Louise Barry, vii–viii. Topeka: Kansas State
    Historical Society, 1972.
Introduction to *A Mormon Bibliography, 1830–1930,* by Chad J. Flake, xv–xxvi.
    Salt Lake City: University of Utah Press, 1978.

NEW EDITIONS AND ANTHOLOGIES
The Humboldt: Highroad to the West. Santa Clarita, CA: Books for Libraries
    Press, 1970; Paperback. Lincoln: University of Nebraska Press, 1985.
The Great Salt Lake. American Lakes Series. Introduction by Ray Allen Billing-
    ton. Albuquerque: University of New Mexico Press, 1973.
Dale L. Morgan's Utah. Woodcuts by Royden Card. Salt Lake City: Red Butte
    Press, 1987.
Overland in 1846: Diaries and Letters of the California-Oregon Trail. Edited by
    Dale L. Morgan. 2 vols. Lincoln: University of Nebraska Press, 1993.
West from Fort Bridger, by J. Roderic Korns, edited by Will Bagley and Harold
    Schindler. Logan: Utah State University Press, 1994.
Carl I. Wheat. *Mapping the Transmississippi West, 1540–1861.* 5 vols. in 6. Storrs-
    Mansfield, CT: Mauritzio Martino; Parsippany, NJ: About Books, 1995.
"Salt Lake City: City of the Saints." In *Great and Peculiar Beauty: A Utah
    Reader,* edited by Thomas Lyon and Terry Tempest Williams, 244–60. Salt
    Lake City: Gibbs Smith, 1995.
*Shoshonean Peoples and the Overland Trail: The Frontiers of the Utah Superinten-
    dency of Indian Affairs.* Edited by Richard L. Saunders. Logan: Utah State
    University Press, 2007.
Dale Morgan and the Mormons. 2 vols. Edited by Richard L. Saunders. Norman,
    OK: Arthur H. Clark Co., 2012–2013.

II. REVIEWS OF MORGAN'S WORK

SCHOLARLY REVIEWS
CALIFORNIA AS I SAW IT, 1960
Nunis, Doyce B. *California Historical Society Quarterly* 40, no. 1 (March 1961):
    74–76.
Baur, John E. *Pacific Historical Review* 30, no. 1 (February 1961): 86–87.
Caughey, John W. *Arizona and the West* 3, no. 2 (Summer 1961): 178–79.

CAPTAIN CHARLES M. WEBER, 1966
Robinson, W. W. *Southern California Quarterly* 49, no. 3 (1967): 348–49.
Nunis, Doyce B. *Arizona and the West* 9, no. 2 (Summer 1967): 174–75.
McGowan, Joseph A. *California Historical Society Quarterly* 47, no. 1 (March 1968): 81–82.
Knuth, Priscilla. *Oregon Historical Quarterly* 68, no. 4 (December 1967): 339–40.
Hardeman, Nicholas P. *Pacific Northwest Quarterly* 58, no. 1 (January 1967): 44.
Davis, W. N., Jr. *Montana: The Magazine of Western History* 18, no. 2 (Spring 1968): 84.

DAKOTA WAR WHOOP, 1965
– none –

GEOGRAPHICAL MEMOIR UPON UPPER CALIFORNIA, 1964
– none –

GREAT SALT LAKE, 1947
Stegner, Wallace. *Pacific Historical Review* 16, no. 3 (August 1947): 330–31.
Tobie, Harvey Elmer. *Oregon Historical Quarterly* 48, no. 4 (December 1947): 336.
Thomas, Elbert D., Senator. *American Historical Review* 53, no. 1 (October 1947): 127–28.

A GUIDE TO THE MANUSCRIPT COLLECTIONS OF THE BANCROFT LIBRARY, VOL. 1, 1963
Arizoniana 4, no. 3 (Fall 1963): 19.
Spence, Clark C. *Agricultural History* 38, no. 1 (January 1964): 62.
Storm, Colton. *Southern California Quarterly* 46, no. 1 (March 1964): 89–90.
Hager, Anna Marie. *California Historical Society Quarterly* 43, no. 1 (March 1964): 61–62.
Lapp, Rudolph. *Pacific Northwest Quarterly* 55, no. 2 (April 1964): 54.
Winther, Oscar Osburn. *Indiana Magazine of History* 60, no. 2 (June 1964): 215–16.
Davis, W. N., Jr. *American Archivist* 27, no. 3 (June 1964): 414–16.
Morgan, George T., Jr., and Brownell, Jean B. *Oregon Historical Quarterly* 65, no. 2 (June 1964): 198–99.
Caughey, John W. *American Historical Review* 69, no. 4 (July 1964): 1164–65.
Cutter, Donald C. *Hispanic American Historical Review* 44, no. 3 (August 1964): 398–99.
Tyler, S. Lyman. *Utah Historical Quarterly* 32, no. 1 (Winter 1964): 83–84.
Howell, Warren R. *Book Collector* 14, no. 2 (Summer 1965): 253–54.

HONOLULU, 1966
– none –

THE HUMBOLDT, 1943

Stephens, Eleanor S. *Oregon Historical Quarterly* 44, no. 3 (September 1943): 328–29.

Knoles, George Harmon. *Pacific Northwest Quarterly* 34, no. 4 (October 1943): 410–11.

Hutcheson, Austin E. *Pacific Historical Review* 12, no. 4 (December 1943): 410–11.

Lockey, J. B. *Mississippi Valley Historical Review* 30, no. 3 (December 1943): 432–33.

Wier, Jeanne Elizabeth. *California Folklore Quarterly* 3, no. 1 (January 1944): 74–76.

Davidson, Levette J. *Journal of American Folklore* 57, no. 223 (January/March 1944): 86–87.

IN PURSUIT OF THE GOLDEN DREAM, 1970

Cleaver, John D. *Oregon Historical Quarterly* 71, no. 4 (December 1970): 359–60.

Nunis, Doyce B. *Western Historical Quarterly* 2, no. 1 (January 1971): 84–86.

Smith, William. *New York History* 52, no. 1 (January 1971): 102–4.

Jensen, Billie Barnes. *Montana: The Magazine of Western History* 21, no. 1 (Winter 1971): 73.

Spence, Clark C. *Journal of American History* 57, no. 4 (March 1971): 918–19.

Leary, David T. *California Historical Quarterly* 50, no. 1 (March 1971): 84.

Andrews, Thomas F. *Southern California Quarterly* 53, no. 2 (June 1971): 162–63.

Elliott, Russell R. *Arizona and the West* 13, no. 2 (Summer 1971): 185–86.

Caughey, John W. *Pacific Historical Review* 40, no. 4 (November 1971): 545–46.

Gilbert, Benjamin F. *Pacific Northwest Quarterly* 62, no. 4 (October 1971): 155–56.

JEDEDIAH SMITH AND THE OPENING OF THE WEST, 1953

Keene, Martin S. *Montana: The Magazine of History* 4, no. 4 (Autumn 1954): 60.

Nasatir, A. P. *American Historical Review* 59, no. 4 (July 1954): 943–44.

Breck, Allen D. *Western Folklore* 13, no. 2/3 (1954): 217–18.

Wiley, Francis A. *Pacific Historical Review* 23, no. 3 (August 1954): 286–87.

JEDEDIAH SMITH AND THE OPENING OF THE WEST, 1964
(PAPERBACK)

Wood, R. Coke. *California Historical Society Quarterly* 44, no. 2 (June 1965): 167–68.

JEDEDIAH SMITH AND HIS MAPS OF THE AMERICAN WEST, 1954
Cleland, Robert G. *Pacific Historical Review* 24, no. 2 (May 1955): 179–81.

MAPPING THE TRANSMISSISSIPPI WEST, 1957–1963
Hanna, Archibald, Jr. *American Historical Review* 63, no. 4 (July 1958): 1000–1001.
Pritchett, V. S. *Scientific American* 201, no. 1 (July 1959): 166–67.
Kemble, John Haskell. *Pacific Historical Review* 28, no. 3 (August 1959): 296–97.
Kemble, John Haskell. *Historical Society of Southern California Quarterly* 41, no. 3 (September 1959): 273–75.
Riegel, Robert E. *American Historical Review* 65, no. 1 (October 1959): 139–40.
Reith, John W. *Historical Society of Southern California Quarterly* 43, no. 2 (June 1961): 230–31.
Wyman, Walker D. *American Historical Review* 67, no. 1 (October 1961): 153–54.
Kemble, John Haskell. *Pacific Historical Review* 30, no. 4 (November 1961): 407–09.
Wake, William H. *Historical Society of Southern California Quarterly* 43, no. 4 (1961): 471–72.
Kish, George. *Imago Mundi* 18 (1964): 98.

MEXICO ANCIENT AND MODERN, 1962
Flaccus, Elmer Wm. *Hispanic American Historical Review* 44, no. 1 (February 1964): 96–97.

OLD GREENWOOD, 1965
Sunder, John E. *Southern California Quarterly* 48, no. 2 (June 1966): 213–14.
Hawgood, John A. *California Historical Society Quarterly* 46, no. 3 (September 1967): 260–61.
Jacobs, Wilbur R. *Arizona and the West* 9, no. 1 (Spring 1967): 69–70.

THE OVERLAND DIARY OF JAMES A. PRITCHARD, 1959
Nunis, Doyce B. *Arizona and the West* 1, no. 4 (Winter 1959): 385–86.
C. C. W. *Journal of the Illinois State Historical Society (1908–1984)* 52, no. 4 (Winter 1959): 559–61.
Wheat, Carl I. *California Historical Society Quarterly* 38, no. 3 (September 1959): 275–76.
Rolle, Andrew F. *Historical Society of Southern California Quarterly* 41, no. 4 (December 1959): 394–95.
McKee, Irving. *Mississippi Valley Historical Review* 46, no. 4 (March 1960): 714–15.
Johansen, Dorothy O. *Pacific Northwest Quarterly* 51, no. 2 (April 1960): 91–92.
Paul, Rodman Wilson. *Pacific Historical Review* 29, no. 2 (May 1960): 188–89.

Mattes, Merrill J. *Montana: The Magazine of Western History* 10, no. 2 (Spring 1960): 56–57.

Knuth, Priscilla. *Oregon Historical Quarterly* 61, no. 2 (June 1960): 224–25.

Solberg, Winton U. *Wisconsin Magazine of History* 43, no. 4 (Summer 1960): 297–98.

OVERLAND IN 1846, 1963

Carter, Harvey L. *Journal of American History* 51, no. 2 (September 1964): 307–9.

Caughey, John W. *Arizona and the West* 6, no. 4 (Winter 1964): 322–23.

Holliday, J. S. *California Historical Society Quarterly* 44, no. 1 (March 1965): 64–65.

Cline, Gloria Griffen. *Pacific Historical Review* 33, no. 4 (November 1964): 472–73.

Johansen, Dorothy O. *Oregon Historical Quarterly* 65, no. 4 (December 1964): 405–6.

Billington, Ray Allen. *Southern California Quarterly* 47, no. 3 (September 1965): 333–34.

Ellsworth, S. George. *Utah Historical Quarterly* 32, no. 4 (Fall 1964): 393–94.

RAND MCNALLY'S PIONEER ATLAS OF THE AMERICAN WEST, 1956

Meinig, Donald W. *Geographical Review* 48, no. 2 (April 1958): 298–300.

THE ROCKY MOUNTAIN JOURNALS OF WILLIAM MARSHALL ANDERSON, 1967

Carter, Harvey L. *Montana: The Magazine of Western History* 18, no. 2 (Spring 1968): 89–90.

Athearn, Robert G. *American Historical Review* 73, no. 5 (June 1968): 1640–41.

Sunder, John E. *Southern California Quarterly* 50, no. 2 (June 1968): 209–10.

Bartlett, Richard A. *Journal of American History* 55, no. 2 (September 1968): 393.

Saum, Lewis O. *Pacific Northwest Quarterly* 59, no. 4 (October 1968): 223.

Loos, John L. *Arizona and the West* 11, no. 1 (Spring 1969): 66–67.

THREE YEARS IN CALIFORNIA, 1964

Rolle, Andrew. *The Americas* 21, no. 4 (April 1965): 422–23.

Jackson, W. Turrentine. *Southern California Quarterly* 47, no. 2 (June 1965): 219–20.

Franklin, William E. *The Historian* 27, no. 4 (August 1965): 595–96.

Davis, W. N., Jr. *Montana: The Magazine of Western History* 15, no. 3 (Summer 1965): 80.

Hinckley, Ted C. *Journal of American History* 52, no. 2 (September 1965): 370–71.

Dumke, Glenn S. *Pacific Historical Review* 34, no. 4 (November 1965): 471–72.

Hammond, George P. *Arizona and the West* 8, no. 2 (Summer 1966): 176–78.

Paul, Rodman W. *American Historical Review* 70, no. 3 (April 1965): 901.

[Unsigned]. *Journal of the West* 4, no. 1 (January 1965): 113–14.

[Notice only]. *American West* 2, no. 2 (Spring 1965): 88–89.

THREE YEARS IN THE KLONDIKE, 1967

– none –

TRAVELERS' GUIDE ACROSS THE PLAINS UPON THE OVERLAND ROUTE TO CALIFORNIA, 1963

Nunis, Doyce B. *Southern California Quarterly* 45, no. 3 (September 1963): 275–76.

Hager, Everett Gordon. *California Historical Society Quarterly* 43, no. 3 (September 1964): 251–52.

THE WEST OF WILLIAM H. ASHLEY, 1964

Camp, Charles L. *Journal of the West* 3, no. 3 (July 1964): 418–19.

Danker, Donald F. *Plains Anthropologist* 9, no. 25 (August 1964): 206–8.

Clokey, Richard M. *Wisconsin Magazine of History* 47, no. 4 (Summer 1964): 353–54.

Athern, Robert. *Montana: The Magazine of Western History* 14, no. 4 (Autumn 1964): 75.

Lavender, David. *Southern California Quarterly* 46, no. 3 (September 1964): 280–81.

Carter, Harvey L. *Journal Of American History* 51, no. 2 (September 1964): 337–38.

Nasatir, A. P. *American Historical Review* 70, no. 1 (October 1964): 267.

Smith, G. Hubert. *Nebraska History* 45, no. 4 (December 1964): 379–83.

Sunder, John E. *Pacific Historical Review* 34, no. 1 (February 1965): 84–86.

Russell, Carl P. *Oregon Historical Quarterly* 66, no. 1 (March 1965): 63–65.

Nasatir, A. P. *Pacific Northwest Quarterly* 56, no. 2 (April 1965): 91.

Carstensen, Vernon. *Arizona and the West* 8, no. 1 (Spring 1966): 91–92.

Nunis, Doyce B. *California Historical Society Quarterly* 45, no. 3 (September 1966): 275–77.

[Unsigned]. *American West* 1, no. 3 (Summer 1964): 66–67.

WEST FROM FORT BRIDGER, 1952

Greever, William S. *Pacific Northwest Quarterly* 43, no. 1 (January 1952): 73–74.

Carstensen, Vernon. *Mississippi Valley Historical Review* 38, no. 4 (March 1952): 711–12.

Paden, Irene D. *Pacific Historical Review* 21, no. 2 (May 1952): 182–83.

Goodykoontz, Colin B. *The American Historical Review* 57, no. 4 (July 1952): 989–91.

UTAH: A GUIDE TO THE STATE, 1942

Creer, L. H. *Pacific Northwest Quarterly* 32, no. 3 (1941): 330–31.

Hunter, Milton R. *Pacific Historical Review* 10, no. 3 (1941): 367–68.

III. WORKS WRITTEN ABOUT OR INVOLVING DALE L. MORGAN

Hart, James D. "Dale Lowell Morgan." *California Historical Society Quarterly* 40, no. 4 (December 1961): 367–70.

Wood, R. Coke. "The Members of the Jedediah Smith Society..." *Pacific Historian* 15, no. 4 (Winter 1971): 82.

Cooley, Everett L. "Dale L. Morgan (1914–1971)." *Dialogue: A Journal of Mormon Thought*, Vol. 6, No. 1 (Spring 1971): 101.

Billington, Ray Allen. Introduction to *The Great Salt Lake*, by Dale L. Morgan, vii–xxviii. Albuquerque: University of New Mexico Press, 1973.

Cooley, Everett L. "A Dedication to the Memory of Dale L. Morgan, 1914–1971." *Arizona and the West* 19, no. 2 (Summer 1977): 103–6.

Morgan, Dale L. *Dale Morgan on the Mormons: Correspondence and a New History,* edited by John Phillip Walker. Salt Lake City: Signature Books, 1986.

Peterson, Charles S. Introduction to *The State of Deseret*, by Dale L. Morgan, vii–xiv. Logan: Utah State University Press, 1987.

Saunders, Richard L. *Eloquence from a Silent World: A Descriptive Bibliography of the Published Writings of Dale L. Morgan*. Salt Lake City: Caramon Press, 1990.

Peterson, Charles S. "Dale Morgan, Writer's Project, and Mormon History as a Regional Study." *Dialogue: A Journal of Mormon Thought* 24, no. 2 (Summer 1991): 47–63.

Saunders, Richard L. "'The Strange Mixture of Emotion and Intellect:' A Social History of Dale L. Morgan 1933–1942." *Dialogue: A Journal of Mormon Thought* 28, no. 4 (Winter 1995): 39–58.

Novak, Gary F. "'The Most Convenient Form of Error': Dale Morgan on Joseph Smith and the Book of Mormon." *FARMS Review of Books* no. 1 (1996): 122–67.

Foster, Craig L. "Madeline McQuown, Dale Morgan, and the Great Unfinished Brigham Young Biography." *Dialogue: A Journal of Mormon Thought* 31, no. 2 (Summer 1998):111–23.

Saunders, Richard L. "The Utah Writers' Project and Writing of *Utah: A Guide to the State.*" *Utah Historical Quarterly* 70, no. 1 (Winter 2002): 21–38.

Topping, Gary. "Dale L. Morgan." In *Utah Historians and the Reconstruction of Western History*, by Gary Topping, 113–73. Norman: University of Oklahoma Press, 2003.

Morgan, Dale L. *Shoshonean Peoples and the Overland Trails: Frontiers of the Utah Superintendency of Indian Affairs, 1849–1869*. Edited by Richard L. Saunders. Logan: Utah State University Press, 2007.

Morgan, Dale L. *Dale Morgan and the Mormons.* 2 vols. Edited by Richard L. Saunders. Norman, OK: Arthur H. Clark Co., 2012–2013.

Saunders, Richard L. "Lost in Time: Dale L. Morgan and the Forty-niner Journal of William B. Lorton." *Southern California Quarterly* 98, no. 4 (2016): 457–86.

Saunders, Richard L. "Postscript: Dale Morgan and the Elements of Utah History," *Utah Historical Quarterly* 85, no. 4 (2017): 308–9.

Saunders, Richard L. "Placing Juanita Brooks among the Heroes (or Villains) of Mormon and Utah History," *Utah Historical Quarterly* 87, no. 3 (2019): 218–37.

Saunders, Richard L. *Dale L. Morgan: Mormon and Western Histories in Transition.* Salt Lake City: University of Utah Press, 2023.

Notes

FOREWORD

1. Charles Kelly and Maurice L. Howe, *Miles Goodyear* (Salt Lake City: Western Printing Company, 1935).
2. Dale L. Morgan (hereafter DLM), "The Significance and Value of the Overland Journal," in *Probing the American West: Papers from the Santa Fe Conference,* eds. K Ross Toole, John Alexander Carroll, Robert M. Utley, and A. R. Mortensen (Santa Fe: Museum of New Mexico Press, 1962), 28.

INTRODUCTION

1. DLM to Jerry Bleak, 13 August 1938, Ms 579 1:10, Manuscripts Division, Special Collections, J. Willard Marriott Library, University of Utah, Salt Lake City (hereafter UU-Ms).
2. DLM to Obert C. Tanner, 7 May 7 1943, reel 8: frame 1655, DLM Papers, Bancroft Library, University of California, Berkeley (hereafter CU-Banc), BANC MSS 71/161 c, microfilm (80 reels) at UU-Ms. Hereafter Morgan's correspondence is cited by date as [*reel*]:[*frame*].
3. DLM to Juanita Brooks (hereafter JB), 31 July 1943, Mss B103 1:6, Utah Division of State History library, Salt Lake City (hereafter UHi); DLM to Barbara Kell, 4 September 1952, DLM Papers, 4:948.
4. John Berger, *A Seventh Man: The Story of a Migrant Worker in Europe* (Cambridge: Granta Books, 1989), 93–94.
5. Gary F. Novak, "'The Most Convenient Form of Error': Dale Morgan on Joseph Smith and the Book of Mormon," *FARMS Review of Books* 8, no.1 (1996): 122.
6. DLM to D. L. Chambers, 16 October 1952, DLM Papers, 2:638.
7. Avery O. Craven, "An Historical Adventure," *Journal of American History* 51, no. 1 (June 1964): 5; H. J. Jackson, *Those Who Write for Immortality: Romantic Reputations and the Dream of Lasting Fame* (New Haven, CT: Yale University Press, 2015), 60.
8. John Toland, *Captured by History: One Man's Vision of Our Tumultuous Century* (New York: St Martin's Press, 1997), xi.
9. Carl E. Rollyson, *A Higher Form of Cannibalism: Adventures in the Art and Politics of Biography* (New York: Ivan R. Dee, 2005).
10. George M. Marsden, *Jonathan Edwards: A Life* (New Haven, CT: Yale University Press, 2003), 170.
11. David Herbert Donald, *Lincoln* (New York: Simon and Schuster, 1995), 13.
12. DLM to JB, 29 November 1952, Ms 486 1:6[c]; 2:27, UU-Ms.

13. DLM, *Dale Morgan on Early Mormonism: Correspondence and a New History,* ed. John Phillip Walker (Salt Lake City: Signature Books, 1986); Gary F. Novak, "The Most Convenient Form," 122–67.

14. DLM to Donald L. Parman, 23 July 1964, DLM Papers, 8:1183.

CHAPTER 1

1. Dale L. Morgan (herafter DLM), untitled autobiographical novel (hereafter UAN), page 37, DLM Papers, 54:1122.

2. DLM to A.R. Mortensen, 1 February 1951, Mss B40 1:7, UHi; 5:1045.

3. Jacquelin S. (Jim) Holliday, interview by author, 17 October 1994, transcript in the author's possession; Lynn North, interview by author, 30 March 2020, transcript in the author's possession; "Dale Morgan, UC Scholar, Dies at 56," *San Francisco Chronicle* (San Francisco), 31 March 1971; A. Russell Mortensen, "Dale L. Morgan: A Personal Appraisal," Ms 201 50:2, UU-Ms.

4. Parley P. Pratt, *The Autobiography of Parley Parker Pratt, One of the Twelve Apostles of the Church of Jesus Christ of Latter-day Saints, Embracing His Life, Ministry, and Travels* (Chicago: Law, King & Law, 1888), 30–44.

5. Orson Pratt, *New and Easy Method of Solution of the Cubic and Biquadratic Equations, Embracing Several New Formulas, Greatly Simplifying This Department of Mathematical Science* (Liverpool, England: Longmans, Green, Reader, & Dyer, 1866).

6. Twenty years later, Pratt's logical gifts once put Orson on a parity against the formidable likes of Dr. John P. Cardinal Newman, U.S. Senate Chaplain, in a debate over the strength of the scriptural case for the Mormons' peculiar marriage practices. The debate lasted three days, and Newman was unable to negate Pratt's scriptural and logical case. *The Bible and Polygamy: Does the Bible Sanction Polygamy? A Discussion between Professor Orson Pratt . . . and the Rev. Doctor J. P. Newman* (Salt Lake City: Deseret News Printing and Publishing, 1879).

7. Robert H. (Bob) Morgan, interview by author, 19 March 1994, transcript in the author's possession; James S. (Jim) Morgan, interview by author, 9 May 1998, notes in the author's possession.

8. "Crushed to Death," *Deseret Evening News* (Salt Lake City), 19 January 1877.

9. Emily Holmes transcript, Registrar's Office, University of Utah, Salt Lake City, 1913.

10. "Transcript of Ward Record 1914, Form E," p. 251, Twenty-second Ward (Salt Lake City), Record of Members Collection 1836–1970, Church History Library, Church of Jesus Christ of Latter-day Saints, Salt Lake City (hereafter USlC).

11. Morgan was born at home. One version of the birth certificate (DLM Papers, 25:1776) lists the address as 455 North 300 West.

12. Salt Lake County birth certificate for DLM, 25:1775; DLM to Maurice Howe, 23 December 1940, DLM Papers, 26:388.
13. "Transcript of Ward Record 1915, Form E p.604–5, Twenty-second Ward (Salt Lake City), Record of Members Collection 1836–1970, USlC.
14. Works Division, *A Report of the Works Division* (Salt Lake City: Utah Emergency Relief Administration, 1935), 14.
15. Tim Sullivan, *No Communication with the Sea: Searching for an Urban Future in the Great Basin* (Tucson: University of Arizona Press, 2010), 104. South Salt Lake incorporated in 1936.
16. "Hundreds of Babies are Entered in Show," *Salt Lake Telegram* (Salt Lake City), 14 September 1916; "Baby Crop Overflows Cradle," *Salt Lake Herald* (Salt Lake City), 14 September 1916; "Automobile Parade Attracts Thousands," *Salt Lake Tribune* (Salt Lake City), 14 September 1916.
17. Samuel Holmes, interview by author, 6 March 1994, transcript in the author's possession. Entries in Personal Ancestral File (a discontinued free genealogy software provided by FamilySearch, a website operated by the Church of Jesus Christ of Latter-day Saints) date Mary Holmes' death as January 4, 1917. Family tradition holds that her death was incident to Spanish Flu, but that outbreak did not strike the US until the following year.
18. Hal Morgan to DLM, 29 March 1956, DLM Papers, 23:1696.
19. DLM to Emily Holmes Morgan (hereafter EHM), 23 April 1956, DLM Papers, 21:990.
20. 1920 United States Census, Salt Lake City, Salt Lake County, Utah, digital image, s.v. J. Lowell Morgan, Emily Morgan, FamilySearch.org.
21. Hal Morgan to DLM, 29 March 1956, DLM Papers, 23:1696.
22. "Traveling Salesman Will be Buried Sunday," *Deseret News* (Salt Lake City), 13 March 1920.
23. UAN draft 1, DLM Papers, 25:1763–65.
24. Ward record #323, Church Census, CR 4 311 #139, USlC; Robert Morgan, interview, 19 March 1994; Robert Morgan, though a baby at the time, recalled that his mother first moved to a rented house on 400 North (Robert Morgan, interview, 30 May 2002, notes in the author's possession).
25. DLM to Eleanor Towles Harris (hereafter ETH), 14–15 December 1967, DLM Papers, 4:389; Marie Fox Felt to DLM, 11 July 1954, DLM Papers, 19:26.
26. Diary entry for 27 March 1920 is cited in Kenneth R. Hardy, *Samuel Holmes Family History* (West Valley City, UT: Family History Publishers, 2008), 221–22.
27. Hardy, *Samuel Holmes Family History,* 226; DLM to ETH, 14–15 December 1967, DLM Papers, 4:389.
28. DLM to ETH, 14–15 December 1967, DLM Papers, 4:389.
29. James S. (Jim) Morgan, interview by author, 9 May 1998, notes in the author's possession.

30. Utah Light and Traction Co., *Salt Lake City: Where to Go and How to Get There* (Salt Lake City: Utah Light and Traction Co., 1940); map 379, UHi.

31. James S. (Jim) and Mary Beth Morgan, interview by author, 25 April 1991, transcript in the author's possession.

32. James S. (Jim) and Mary Beth Morgan, interview, 25 April 1991.

33. Robert D. (Bob) Morgan, interview by author, 25 April 1994, transcript in the author's possession.

34. The baptism was recorded as 27 January 1923 and the confirmation as 4 February 1923, "Transcript of Ward Record, 1923," p.482, Wells Ward, Record of Members Collection 1836–1970, USlC.

35. This ideal is most clearly described in UAN, p.42–46, DLM Papers, 54:1127–33.

36. "Transcript of Ward Record 1927," p.670, Record of Members Collection 1836–1970, USlC.

37. "Record of Officers 1928," Wells Ward, Record of Members Collection 1836–1970, USlC.

38. Bob Morgan to DLM, 15 December 1958, DLM Papers, 23:1072.

39. UAN, DLM Papers. The specific direct-mail firm was never recorded by the family, but the description hints that Morgan may have worked for Harry B. Walker, who worked out of an office on Cleveland Avenue, about five blocks north of the Morgan home. The only other option would have been Reynolds Distributing Service. Both Jim and Bob Morgan recalled that the Morgan boys also delivered direct-ad flyers for Dunn's Grocery, the corner-grocery down the block (James S. [Jim] and Mary Beth Morgan, interview with author, 25 April 1991).

40. "Utah, Salt Lake County Death Records, 1908–1949," s.v. Ernest Eldredge Holmes, FamilySearch.org. Younger brother Richard provided an account of Eldredge for the family newsletter published privately by Kenneth Holmes, "The Fourth Brother: Memories of Edge," *Holmes Family Heritage* 1, no. 2 (Fall 1985).

41. This section is drawn from the UAN. Dale's near-death experience is confirmed in the Robert H. [Bob] Morgan interview, 19 March 1994.

42. DLM used this experience as the opening material of the initial UAN first-person drafts (DLM Papers, 25:1709–10), which was then transferred to and rewritten slightly in later drafts and eventually the edited revised draft (54:1087–90).

CHAPTER 2

1. DLM to EHM, 2 September 1938, DLM Papers, 21:12.

2. Undated conversation [1936–1937], DLM Papers, 54:768.

3. Ross E. Mitchell, "How Many Deaf People are in the United States?: Estimates from the Survey of Income and Program Participation," *Journal of Deaf Studies and Deaf Education* 11, no. 1 (2006): 112–19. Mitchell sets up the

problem, noting that until 1940 the decennial census of population counted
those who were deaf. Reporting on this census characteristic proved to be
chronically unreliable, and the category was dropped after the 1930 census,
as demonstrated by the first census in which Morgan would have been
counted. United States Census Bureau, *The Blind and Deaf-mutes in the
United States, 1930* (Washington, DC: Government Printing Office, 1931),
1–3, 21. If the population ratios have not changed much, then Gallaudet
University calculates that 0.22 percent of the population, or two persons per
1,000 across all age groups, do not use hearing for communication (Charles
Reilly and Sen Qi, "Snapshot of Deaf and Hard of Hearing People, Postsecondary Attendance and Unemployment" [Washington, DC: Gallaudet
Research Institute, 2011], https://www.gallaudet.edu/office-of-international
-affairs/demographics/deaf-employment-reports). The figure is widely used
and probably applies equally well to 1930. Western Interstate Commission
for Higher Education, Mental Health Program, *Information Gaps on the
Deaf and Hard of Hearing Population: A Background Paper* (Boulder, CO:
Western Interstate Commission for Higher Education, 2006), https://www
.nasmhpd.org/sites/default/files/InformationGapsResearchPaper.pdf.

4. DLM to Darel McConkey, 9 September 1940, Accn 3206, UU-Ms.
5. UAN edited revised draft, 52, DLM Papers, 54:1135.
6. Edna Sullivan to DLM, 24 September 1929, DLM Papers, 20:495.
7. UAN, second revised draft, 92, DLM Papers, 54:1177.
8. Robert H. (Bob) Morgan, interview, 19 March 1994.
9. UAN edited revised draft, 64–65, DLM Papers, 54:1149–50.
10. "Transcript of Ward Record 1930," Wells Ward, 142, Record of Members Collection 1836–1970, USlC.
11. Edwin Ross Thurston, "Teaching the Deaf," *Improvement Era* 49, no. 1 (Jan 1946): 24, 56.
12. UAN second revised draft, 90, DLM Papers, 54:1175.
13. UAN, DLM Papers, 54:768.
14. DLM to Madeline Reeder (Thurston) McQuown (hereafter MRM), 10 June 1951; Morgan, Dale L., *Dale Morgan on Early Mormonism: Correspondence and a New History* (hereafter *DMEM*), ed. John Phillip Walker (Salt Lake City: Signature Books, 1986), 189.
15. UAN, second revision, 77, DLM Papers, 54:1162.
16. DLM to Marguerite Sinclair Reusser (hereafter MSR), 22 May 1951, DLM Papers, 6:409.
17. Gerald T. (Jerry) Bleak, oral history interview, 17 March 1994, notes in author's possession.
18. UAN, second revised draft, 92, DLM Papers, 54:1177.
19. DLM, "To Those With Ears" (April–May 1937), DLM Papers, 54:674–96.
20. Robert H. (Bob) Morgan, interview by author, 25 April 1994, transcript in author's possession. Dozens of interaction fragments illustrating how

he navigated are scattered in the margins and on the backs of Morgan's research transcriptions (DLM Papers, cartons 15–25), most dating to his two stints in Washington, DC, from 1943–1947 and 1950–1952. He selectively retained "conversations," mostly from his Bancroft Library years, in the first box of his papers.

21. UAN edited revised draft, 78–79, DLM Papers, 54:1163–64. June confirmed her part in this story to me personally in 1994, notes in author's possession.
22. UAN edited revised draft, 80, DLM Papers.
23. Phyllis M. Tookey Kerridge, "Aids for the Deaf," *British Medical Journal* 1, no. 3886 (29 June 1935): 1314–17.
24. Johnson's observation is cited in Douglas C. Baynton, "Deafness," in *Keywords for Disability Studies,* eds. Rachel Adams, Benjamin Reiss, and David Serlin (New York: New York University Press, 2015), 48; Michel David and Sandra E. Trehub, "Perspectives on Deafened Adults," *American Annals of the Deaf* 134, no. 3 (July 1989): 200–204; Elizabeth Charlson, Michael Strong, and Ruby Gold, "How Successful Deaf Teenagers Experience and Cope with Isolation," *American Annals of the Deaf* 137, no. 3 (July 1992): 261–70.
25. Ethel B. Warfield, "Problems of Deafness," *American Annals of the Deaf* 83, no. 4 (September 1938): 300–305.
26. George Morris McClure, "On Being a Teacher of the Deaf," *American Annals of the Deaf* 92, no. 2 (March 1947): 133–41. cf. Ian M. Sutherland, "Everybody Wins: Teaching Deaf and Hearing Students Together," in *Worlds Apart?: Disability and Foreign Language Learning,* eds. Tammy Berberi, Elizabeth C. Hamilton, and Ian M. Sutherland (New Haven, CT: Yale University Press, 2008), 42–69.
27. Jody Becker Kinner, "Utah Deaf History and Culture," accessed March 14, 2023, http://utahdeafhistory.com.
28. Jack R. Gannon, *Deaf Heritage: A Narrative History of Deaf America* (Washington, DC: Gallaudet University, 2012), 211–12.
29. UAN edited revised draft, 82–84, DLM Papers, 54:1167–69. Morgan could have attended East High School, which was closer, but he and his cousins were in the West district.
30. T. Gerald (Jerry) Bleak to DLM, 4 September 1938, DLM Papers, 9:1283.
31. UAN edited revised draft, 93–94, DLM Papers, 54:1178–79; Robert H. (Bob) Morgan, interview, 19 March 1994, 28.
32. DLM, "To Those with Ears," DLM Papers, 54:674–96.
33. James S. (Jim) and Mary Beth Morgan, interview, 25 April 1991, quoting DLM to Ida Holmes, n.d.
34. Robert K. Greenwood (hereafter RKG), personal communication with the author, April 1990, notes in author's possession.
35. West High School graduation program, DLM Papers, 25:1782.

CHAPTER 3

1. Conversation notes, ca. 1937, DLM Papers, 55:11ff.
2. DLM to EHM, 2 September 1938, DLM Papers, 21:14.
3. Alma Vernon Rasmussen, "The Government Work Relief Program in Utah, 1932–1940" (master's thesis, University of Utah, 1942), 8.
4. J. W. Gilliman, "Address by Mr. J. W. Gilliman, Director of the State Department of Public Welfare before the State Conference of Social Work," 13 November 1937, DLM Papers, 26:1887–98. The figures cited in the text are on page 4.
5. Michael Barone, *Our Country* (New York: Free Press, 1990), 95–96.
6. Robert Gottlieb and Peter Wiley, *America's Saints: The Rise of Mormon Power* (G.P. Putnam's Sons, 1984), 69–70; D. Michael Quinn, *The Mormon Hierarchy: Extensions of Power* (Salt Lake City, Utah: Signature Books, 1997), 358.
7. This unusual situation was a response to the high unemployment of the Depression. It reduced the number of idle, unemployed young people by keeping them in school. Bleak, notes from personal communication to author, undated (ca. 1995).
8. Bleak, oral history interview notes, 17 March 1994. Jerry's memory for the camp numbers was faulty, as documented by Kenneth W. Baldridge, *The Civilian Conservation Corps in Utah: Remembering Nine Years of Achievement, 1933–1942* (Salt Lake City: University of Utah Press, 2019), 374.
9. DLM to Bleak, 25 July, 1 August, 10 August 1933, Dale L. Morgan Collection, MS 579 1:6, UU-Ms.
10. DLM to Bleak, 25 July 1933, MS 579 1:6, UU-Ms.
11. Glen C. Dawson, interview by author, 24 May 1995, transcript in possession of author.
12. Jim Morgan, personal communication, 25 April 1992.
13. DLM to Bleak, 25 July 1933, MS 579 1:6, UU-Ms.
14. DLM to EHM, 2 September 1938, DLM Papers, 21:14.
15. Peter H. Lindert and Jeffrey G. Williamson, *Unequal Gains: American Growth and Inequality since 1700* (Princeton, NJ:Princeton University Press, 2016), 194–218.
16. DLM to Bleak, 6 October 1937, MS 579 1:8, UU-Ms.
17. DLM, "To Those With Ears," DLM Papers, 54:674–96.
18. Some of these are among DLM Papers in C15:39–41.
19. Undated diary entry, DLM Papers, 25:1687.
20. cf. Richards Durham to DLM, 30 November 1940, DLM papers, 12:155; Richard L. Saunders, "'The Strange Mixture of Emotion and Intellect:' A Social History of Dale L. Morgan 1933–1942," *Dialogue: A Journal of Mormon Thought* 28, no. 4 (Winter 1995): 39–58.
21. DLM to EHM, 2 September 1938, DLM Papers, 21:14.

22. Stegner completed his degree from the University of Iowa in 1935, the year *before* the founding of Wilbur Schramm's influential Iowa Writers' Workshop. He was not a graduate of that prestigious program.

23. "The Utah Chronicle," *Utah Chronicle,* 5 December 1935, 4.

24. DLM, "Atheist," *Salt Lake Tribune* (magazine section), 12 May 1935.

25. DLM Papers, 55:18–19; "Pen Associate Appointed," *Utah Chronicle,* 31 October 1935, 3.

26. See DLM Bibliography in this volume; DLM to EHM, 2 September 1938, DLM Papers, 21:12ff.

27. A few of these are scattered in his papers. See DLM Papers, reels 54 and 55.

28. For a list of Morgan's published fiction, see DLM Bibliography in this volume; his papers contain incomplete drafts for dozens more in carton 15.

29. UAN draft part 3, page 6, DLM Papers, 54:1324.

30. Undated note [1936–1937], DLM Papers, 54:768.

31. Conversation, DLM to unidentified person, ca.1936–1937, DLM Papers, 55:24.

32. DLM, "Perspective on Platitude," *University Pen* (Spring, 1935), 6–7, and reprinted in *Pen Centennial* (Salt Lake City: University of Utah Press, 1950), 87–90; manuscripts of both essays about deafness are in carton 15 of the DLM Papers, folders 25 and 29 respectively (i.e., 54:566–77, 54:674–96).

33. Undated conversation, DLM Papers, 54:770.

34. DLM to Durham, 4 December 1940, DLM Papers, 2:1543.

35. John Taylor, "The Organization of the Church," *Millennial Star,* 15 Nov 1851, 339. Italics added to quote by author.

36. "Sigma Upsilon Announces Initiates," *Utah Chronicle,* 26 April 1934; Jarvis Thurston, interview by author, 16 June 1994, pages 2–4, transcript in author's possession. Madeline's uncle was William Reeder, a judge who the HRS staff engaged as a reader and critic for local history.

37. DLM to Jerry Bleak, 16 July 1937, MS 579 1:7, UU-Ms.

38. DLM to Jerry Bleak, 5 October 1938, MS 579 1:9, UU-Ms.

39. "23,892 Jobless in Utah, Faddis Says," *Ogden Standard-Examiner,* 19 April 1937. Comparatively, the state's working-age population (20–65) reported in the 1930 census was less than 250,000; if one considers men only, the state's working-age figure falls to 131,000. About 18 percent of the working-adult population was unemployed at that date (Table 3, "Population—Utah," United States Census Bureau, *Fifteenth Census of the United States: 1930, Population,* vol. 3, pt. 2 (Washington, DC: Government Printing Office, 1932), 1088.

40. DLM to Bleak 23 May, 21 June, 16 July 1937, MS 579 1:7, UU-Ms. A list of the 33 reviews appears in the bibliography.

41. DLM to Bleak 6 October 1937, MS 579 1:8, UU-Ms.

42. DLM to Bleak, 30 November 1937, MS 579 1:8, UU-Ms.

43. DLM to Bleak, 28 January, 25 February 1938, MS 579 1:9, UU-Ms. Some of the plots written at this period survived in DLM Papers. See 55:233f.

44. Jarvis Thurston, interview by author, 21 April 2001, notes in author's possession.

45. [Arnold Gingrich] to DLM, undated [1936–1939], DLM Papers, 19:207–10.

46. Jarvis Thurston, interview, 14 June 1994; DLM to Bleak, 13 August 1938, MS 579 1:10, UU-Ms. Maurice Howe had tried first to get Thurston into one of the projects "but the quota was down, he had a job already, was not certified and etc and etc." Howe to DLM, 11 June 1939, DLM Papers, 26:533.

CHAPTER 4

1. Darrell Greenwell to DLM, September 19, 1942, DLM Papers, 12:1098.

2. This chapter is a much condensed compilation of two earlier works: my introductory matter to *Dale Morgan on the Mormons,* vol. 2 (Norman, OK: Arthur H. Clark Co., 2012–2013), 21–54, and "Dear Dale, Dear Juanita: Two Friends and the Contest for Truth, Fact, and Perspective in Mormon History" (36th Juanita Brooks Lecture, Dixie State University, St. George, UT, 28 March 2019), which appeared as a shortened version in "Placing Juanita Brooks among the Heroes (or Villains) of Mormon and Utah History," *Utah Historical Quarterly* 87, no. 3 (Summer 2019): 218–37.

3. Definition from Sandra M. Gustafson, "Histories of Democracy and Empire," *American Quarterly* 59, no. 1 (March 2007): 110. A marvelous case study in Western antiquarianism is Amanda Laugesen, "George Himes, F. G. Young, and the Early Years of the Oregon Historical Society," *Oregon Historical Quarterly* 101, no. 1 (Spring 2000): 18–39.

4. Frank Winn, "The Book Rack," *Deseret News,* 30 December 1938.

5. See DLM, *Shoshonean Peoples and the Overland Trails: Frontiers of the Utah Superintendency of Indian Affairs, 1849–1869,* ed. Richard L. Saunders (Logan: Utah State University Press, 2007); Paul W. Reeve, *Religion of a Different Color: Race and the Mormon Struggle for Whiteness* (Oxford, UK: Oxford University Press, 2015); Max Perry Mueller, *Race and the Making of the Mormon People* (Chapel Hill: University of North Carolina Press, 2017).

6. William A. Wilson, introduction to *The Roll-away Saloon: Cowboy Tales of the Arizona Strip,* ed. Deirdre Murray Paulsen (Logan: Utah State University Press, 1985), x, and quoted in William G. Hartley, "The Nauvoo Exodus and Crossing the Ice Myths," *Journal of Mormon History* 43, no. 1 (January 2017): 57–58.

7. Louis Reinwand, "Andrew Jenson: Latter-day Saint Historian," *BYU Studies* 14, no.1 (Autumn 1973): 29–46; Davis Bitton, "B. H. Roberts as Historian," *Dialogue* 3, no. 4 (Winter 1968): 25–44; Reid L. Neilson and

Scott D. Marianno, "True and Faithful: Joseph Fielding Smith as Mormon Historian and Theologian," *BYU Studies* 57, no. 1 (2018): 7–64; M. R. Werner, *Brigham Young* (New York: Harcourt, Brace & Co., 1925); Jessica E. Black, Molly Oberstein-Allen, and Jennifer L. Barnes, "Tell Me A Story: Religion, Imagination, and Narrative Involvement," *Journal for the Cognitive Science of Religion* 5, no. 1 (2017/2019): 37–62; untitled, undated bibliography that may have been generated for an early *State of Deseret* draft, DLM Papers, 26:93–103; Joseph Fielding Smith, *The Origin of the Reorganized Church: The Question of Succession* (Salt Lake City: Skelton Publishing, 1907); Joseph Fielding Smith, *Essentials in Church History* (Deseret News Press, 1922); B. H. Roberts, "History of the 'Mormon' Church," *Americana* 4–10 (1909 July–1915 July); B. H. Roberts, *Comprehensive History of the Church of Jesus Christ of Latter-day Saints,* 6 vols. (Salt Lake City: Deseret News Press, 1930).

8. Ingolf U. Dalferth, *Creatures of Possibility: The Theological Basis of Human Freedom,* trans. Jo Bennett (Grand Rapids, MI: Baker Academic, 2016), 197, cited by Deidre Nicole Green, *Jacob: A Brief Theological Introduction* (Provo, UT: Neal A. Maxwell Institute, 2021), 46.

9. Paul Ricoeur *The Symbolism of Evil* (New York: Harper & Row, 1967), 351–53, cited in Martin E. Marty, "Two Integrities: An Address to the Crisis in Mormon Historiography," *Journal of Mormon History* 10 (1983): 3–19. Marty summarized this perspective as "they receive and accept more or less without question a world, a world view, and views from . . . teachers" (6). It is also suitably described as *presentism* (and undoubtedly pejoratively as *utilitarianism*).

10. The mission statement of the National Society of the Sons of Utah Pioneers is openly ethical: "Come to know our fathers, and turn our hearts to them. Preserve the memory and heritage of the early pioneers of the Utah Territory and the western US. Honor present-day pioneers worldwide who exemplify these same qualities of character. Teach these same qualities to the youth who will be tomorrow's pioneers." National Society of the Sons of Utah Pioneers, "Mission and Activities," accessed April 8, 2023, https://www.sup1847.com.

11. Roberts, *Comprehensive History*, vol. 1, vii–ix.

12. JB to DLM, March 6, 1947, DLM Papers, 10:687. Brooks twice explicitly and publicly rejected Kate Carter's bowdlerizing approach: first, in "The First One Hundred Years of Southern Utah History," *Proceedings of the Utah Academy of Sciences, Arts and Letters* 24 (1946–1947):71–79; and second, in "Let's Preserve Our Records," *Utah Humanities Review* 2 (July 1948): 259–63.

13. DLM to EHM, 3 February 1943, DLM Papers, 21:104.

14. T. B. H. Stenhouse, *Rocky Mountain Saints: A Full and Complete History of the Mormons . . .* (New York: D. Appleton & Co., 1873); Fanny Stenhouse,

Exposé of Polygamy in Utah: A Lady's Life among the Mormons (New York: American News Co., 1872) and *"Tell It All": The Story of a Life's Experience in Mormonism, an Autobiography* (Hartford, CT: A. D. Worthington, 1874); J. H. Beadle, *Polygamy; or, The Mysteries and Crimes of Mormonism . . .* (Philadelphia: National Publishing Co., 1882); William A. Linn, *The Story of the Mormons: From the Date of Their Origin to the Year 1901* (New York: Macmillan, 1902); Ruth Kauffman and Reginald Kauffman, *The Latter Day Saints: A Study of the Mormons in Light of Economic Conditions* (London: Williams & Norgate, 1912).

15. Eric A. Eliason, "Curious Gentiles and Representational Authority in the City of the Saints," *Religion and American Culture* 11, no. 2 (Summer 2001): 155–90.

16. Peter Novick, *That Noble Dream: The "Objectivity Question" and the American Historical Profession* (Cambridge, England: Cambridge University Press, 1998), 33–37; Laurence R. Veysey, *The Emergence of the American University* (Chicago: University of Chicago Press, 1965), 121–73; Robert B. Townsend, *History's Babel: Scholarship, Professionalization, and the Historical Enterprise in the United States, 1880–1940* (Chicago: University of Chicago Press, 2013), 155–79.

17. Thomas W. Simpson, *American Universities and the Birth of Modern Mormonism, 1867–1940* (Chapel Hill: University of North Carolina Press, 2016), 90–113.

18. Simpson, *American Universities*, 90–113. Morgan privately claimed Levi Edgar Young discontinued his doctoral dissertation on polygamy and did not complete his graduate degree in history because he "could not accept" the personal and historical realities encountered in his research (DLM to JB, 23 June 1951, Mss B103 2:13, UHi).

19. DLM to Nels Anderson, 14 November 1941, DLM Papers, 1:849; DLM to JB, 20 April 1948, DLM Papers, 1:1699. Andrew L. Neff, *The History of Utah, 1847–1869*, ed. Leland Creer (Salt Lake City: Deseret News Press, 1940). Morgan thought even less of Creer's dissertation, published as *Utah and the Nation* (Seattle: University of Washington Press, 1929).

20. DLM to JB, 23 June 1951, DLM Papers, 1:1982. Milton R. Hunter, *Brigham Young, The Colonizer* (Salt Lake City: Deseret News Press, 1940), *The Mormons and the American Frontier* (Salt Lake City: LDS Department of Education, 1940); Levi Edgar Young, *Chief Episodes in the History of Utah* (Chicago: Lakeside Press, 1912), *The Story of Utah* (Danville, NY: Hall & McCreary, 1913), "The Great West in American History," *Bulletin of the University of Utah (new series)* 11, no. 9 (1920): 3–9, and *The Founding of Utah* (New York: Scribner, 1924).

21. DLM to JB, 15 November 1949, DLM Papers, 1:1951.

22. David Whittaker, ed., *Mormon Americana: A Guide to Sources and Collections in the United States* (Provo, UT: BYU Studies, 1994). In 1938 the

Utah State Historical Society was barely functional and is treated later. A snapshot of LDS-related library holdings is visible in a handlist generated by a BYU psychology professor and early twentieth-century book scout and collector: M. Wilford Poulson Papers, MSS 823 5:5, UPB. The only published catalog of the time is: New York Public Library, "List of Works in the New York Public Library Relating to the Mormons," *Bulletin of the New York Public Library* 13, no. 3 (March 1909): 183–39.

23. Maurice Howe to DLM, May 19, 1942, DLM Papers, 26:987.

24. There does not seem to be a record or explanation of what this tiff concerned, but it did not likely concern anything Morgan had written.

25. DLM to Maurice Howe, 23 July 1939, DLM Papers, 26:205; William Warner Bishop, "Rare Book Rooms in Libraries," *Library Quarterly* 12, no.3 (July 1942): 375–85. The now-common practice of general patron access does not seem to have emerged for another decade (cf. Henry J. Browne, "A Plan of Organization for a University Archives," *American Archivist* 12, no. 4 (October 1949): 355–58).

26. Peter N. Carroll, *Keeping Time: Memory, Nostalgia and the Art of History* (Athens: University of Georgia Press, 1990).

27. Jerrold Hirsch, *Portrait of America: A Cultural History of the Federal Writers' Project* (Chapel Hill: University of North Carolina Press, 2003), 3. "Documentary is the presentation or representation of actual fact in a way that makes it credible and vivid to people at the time. Since all emphasis is on the fact, its validity must be unquestionable as possible ('Truth,' Roy Stryker [head of the Farm Security Administration photo office] said, 'is the objective of the documentary attitude'). Since just the fact matters, it can be transmitted in any plausible medium" (William Stott, *Documentary Expression and Thirties America* [New York: Oxford University Press, 1973], 14). Also: "The heart of documentary is not form or style or medium, but always content." And "social documentary … shows man at grips with conditions neither permanent nor necessary, conditions of a certain time and place" (Stott, *Documentary Expression*, 20). Peter Novick points out that evidence-based scientific method was a major influence on the field as academic history professionalized in the US (Peter Novick. *That Noble Dream*, 25–28, 31–40). On the other hand, by focusing solely on academic historians, Novick similarly misses the importance of the federal projects' challenge to American antiquarian and presentist tendencies, just as the New Mormon History would also do a generation later.

28. DLM to JB, 5 November 1941, quoted in Charles S. Peterson, introduction to Juanita Brooks, *Quicksand and Cactus: A Memoir of the Southern Mormon Frontier* (Logan: Utah State University Press, 1992), xxviii.

29. "This does not mean, however, that all are of equal importance in every context, nor certainly that all should be put before the audience" (Stott, *Documentary Expression,* 117).

30. Maurice Howe to Darel McConkey, 27 February 1940, Accn 3206, UU-Ms; DLM to Howe, 7 February 1939, DLM Papers, 26:163.

31. Leonard J. Arrington, *Confessions of a Mormon Historian: The Diaries of Leonard J. Arrington, 1971–1997,* ed. Gary James Bergera, vol. 1 (Salt Lake City, Utah: Signature Books, 2018), 164. For a similar comment, see JB to Ettie Lee, 15 March 1967, in *The Selected Letters of Juanita Brooks,* ed. Craig S. Smith (Salt Lake City: University of Utah Press, 2019), 322.

32. DLM to Samuel A. Burgess, 13 August 1948, P79-2f3, Reorganized Church of Jesus Christ of Latter Day Saints Library and Archives (now Community of Christ Library and Archives; hereafter MoInRC), Independence, MO; MS 360 7:11, UU-Ms; 2:123; *DMEM,* 163.

33. This was the gist of an exchange of letters with apostle John A. Widtsoe existing in Morgan's papers and is the perspective which limits the scope of existing drafts for *The Mormons* solely to factual documentation. On the other hand, as nearly as I can conclude from his private letters, Dale Morgan did not dismiss the divine claims of Mormonism as untrue merely because they were inadequately documented. Though he was not a believer, he refused to denigrate others' beliefs, but he would not accept tradition (i.e., unsupported assertion) as historical fact. Chess partner Richards Durham, while on an LDS proselyting mission, critiqued Morgan's naturalism in what is probably the finest assessment of his personal perspective on religion and history. See Durham to DLM, 20, 28 March 1941, DLM Papers, 12:166.

34. DLM to Bernard DeVoto, March 2, 1942, DLM Papers, 2:2147.

35. Stott, *Documentary Expression,* 104–17; Jerre Mangione, *The Dream and the Deal: The Federal Writers' Project, 1935–1943,* 2nd ed. (Philadelphia: University of Pennsylvania Press, 1983), passim.

36. Gary S. Topping, "Personality and Motivation in Utah Historiography," *Dialogue* 27, no. 1 (Spring 1994): 73–89.

CHAPTER 5

1. "My mind consists in large part of a typewriter keyboard." DLM to John Farrar, 30 June 1942, DLM Papers, 3:330.

2. DLM to Bleak, 2 December 1938, Ms 579 1:10, UU-Ms.

3. *Utah Historical Quarterly* 6 (1933), title page verso. The next issue would not appear until 1939.

4. Dee Bramwell, "Report of Interview with Miss Wilcox...," undated, DLM Papers, 27:75; Larry H. Malmgren, "A History of the WPA in Utah" (Master's thesis, Utah State University, 1965).

5. Luther H. Evans, "The Historical Records Survey," *American Political Science Review* 30, no. 1 (February, 1936): 133–35. Utah expressed this mission within the state in its own publication: Utah Historical Records Survey, *WPA Historical Records Survey Project* (Ogden: WPA, 1940); a copy exists

in the University of California, Berkeley Library collection. Cedric Larson, "The Cultural Programs of the WPA," *Public Opinion Quarterly* 3, no. 3 (July 1939): 491–96; Julian P. Boyd speech, 29 December 1936 to Society of American Archivists meeting, Providence, RI, extracted in HRS "Circular Letter No. 8 to State Directors," 17 February 1937, US Works Progress Administration Collection, 1:3, Library of Congress. How well the Survey managed its charge nationally is considered in Edward F. Barrese, "The Historical Records Survey: A Nation Acts to Save its Memory" (PhD dissertation, George Washington University, 1980). The National Archive Survey Commission isn't a known office; the federal entity is taken from Bramwell, "Report of Interview," 27:75, but may be an error; the more likely entity was the Public Archives Commission. The national developmental context leading up to this period is addressed in Townsend, *History's Babel*, 155–73; William F. Birdsall, "The Two Sides of the Desk: The Archivist and the Historian, 1909–1935," *American Archivist* 38, no. 2 (April 1975): 158–73.

6. Dean Brimhall to DLM, 8 October 1945, Ms 114 18:11, UU-Ms; DLM Papers, 10:18.

7. "Larger Staff In Historical Records Work," *Ogden Standard Examiner* (Ogden, UT), 17 July 1938. The project's story is addressed in Monty Noam Penkower, *The Federal Writers' Project: A Study in Government Patronage of the Arts* (Urbana: University of Illinois Press, 1977); Mangione, *The Dream and the Deal*, 1983; Hirsch, *Portrait of America*, 2003.

8. Hallie Flanagan, *Arena: The History of the Federal Theatre* (New York: Benjamin Blom, 1940).

9. Robert D. Leighninger, "Cultural Infrastructure: The Legacy of New Deal Public Space," *Journal of Architectural Education* 49, no. 4 (May 1996): 228.

10. DLM to Jerry Bleak, 13 August 1938, Ms 579 1:10, UU-Ms.

11. Barratt Chadwick, "On the Home Front," 7 June 1942, DLM Papers, 25:1794.

12. "Notes for the attention of Mr. Slover," 1938, DLM Papers, 27:703; Hugh O'Neil to DLM, undated [August–November 1938], 27:720.

13. DLM to EHM, 2 September 1938, DLM Papers, 21:12.

14. Samuel Holmes, interview, 6 March 1994.

15. DLM to Durham, 4 December 1940, DLM Papers, 2:1543.

16. DLM to Durham, 4 December 1940.

17. DLM to Durham, 4 December 1940; DLM to JB, 12 April 1942, JB Papers, UHi, cited in Levi S. Peterson, *Juanita Brooks: Mormon Woman Historian* (Salt Lake City: University of Utah Press, 1988), 125; DLM to MSR, 21 December 1940, Ms 143 2:23, UU-Ms; DLM Papers, 2:95.

18. "WPA Survey Editor Names Salt Laker [E. Geoffrey Circuit] as Assistant," *Salt Lake Tribune,* 27 August 1938, DLM Papers, 80:1207. Morgan was hired a few weeks before Circuit, but the matter of seniority and assignment isn't clear from what little documentation exists.

19. DLM to Maurice Howe, 21 January 1939, DLM Papers, 26:156. He had been on the job for five months.

20. "Inventory of Mormon diaries, journals and life sketches, in the Library of Congress," undated, C2:6, and "Report for Project for Collection of Social and Historical Data in Washington County, Juanita Brooks, Supervisor," DLM Papers, C6:29 [37:1785–91].

21. DLM to Bleak, 5 October 1938, Ms 579 1:10, UU-Ms. The one personal introduction to historiography (Maurice Howe to DLM, 18 May 1939, DLM Papers, 26:518) did not come for another six months. cf. Charles S. Peterson, "Dale Morgan, Writers' Project, and Mormon History as a Regional Study," *Dialogue* 24, no.2 (Summer 1994): 47–63.

22. Bernard DeVoto, "The Centennial of Mormonism," *American Mercury* 19, n. 73 (January 1930): 1–13. A year before beginning with the HRS, Morgan confirmed that he accepted DeVoto's perspective (DLM to Jerry Bleak, 30 November 1937, Ms 579 1:8, UU-Ms). Linn, *Story of the Mormons*, 1902.

23. The shift in then-recent American history is explored in William C. Binkley, "Two World Wars and American Historical Scholarship," *Mississippi Valley Historical Review* 33, no. 1 (June, 1946): 3–26.

24. DLM to EHM, 20 October 1938, DLM Papers, 21:28; DLM to Jerry Bleak, 2 December 1938, Ms 579 1:10, UU-Ms; "Title Contender Will Play Mass Contest," *Ogden Standard-Examiner,* 1 December 1938.

25. Morgan wrote Charles Kelly for the first time late in 1938 asking for information about the early settlement in Tooele County, directly west of Salt Lake City. DLM to Charles Kelly (hereafter CK), 2 November 1938, Mss B114 1:2, UHi.

26. Several of Brooks' letters to Morgan are included in JB, *The Selected Letters of Juanita Brooks,* ed. Craig S. Smith (Salt Lake City: University of Utah Press, 2019).

27. Willa Dean Derrick, personal communication with the author, 28 March 2019.

28. Levi S. Peterson, *Juanita Brooks*, 120.

29. JB, *Quicksand and Cactus: A Memoir of the Southern Mormon Frontier* (Logan: Utah State University Press, 1992), 336.

30. Most of this essay material is scattered widely through cartons of the WPA papers, Mss B57, UHi. Not all of Morgan's histories were published, cf. Weber County historical sketch "For Preliminary Edition," Mss B57 165:2, UHi.

31. "Memorandum for Dale Morgan," 15 October 1938, DLM Papers, 26:2050.

32. DLM to Dee Bramwell, 23 March 1940, DLM Papers, 7:1075.

33. DLM to Fawn M. Brodie (hereafter FMB), 16 April 1946, MS 360 7:7, UU-Ms; DLM Papers, 1:1643.

34. DLM to EHM, 7 March 1939, DLM Papers, 21:26; Jarvis Thurston, interview, 16 June 1994.

35. Robert H. (Bob) Morgan, interview, 19 March 1994.

36. MRM to DLM, 11 May 1940, DLM Papers, 15:12.

37. Undated diary entry [likely 22–23 March 1940], DLM Papers, 25:1687.

38. Undated diary entry [likely 22–23 March 1940], DLM Papers, 25:1687.

39. DLM to Maurice Howe, 9 May 1939, DLM Papers, 26:178.

40. Maurice Howe to DLM, 15 May 1939, DLM Papers, 26:514.

41. DLM to Maurice Howe, 22 May 1939, DLM Papers, 26:182.

42. Maurice Howe to Darel McConkey, 18 May 1939, DLM Papers, 19:340.

43. G. B. Hotchkiss to DLM, 19 October 1939, DLM Papers, 19:638.

44. DLM to Maurice Howe, 12 June 1939, DLM Papers, 26:192.

45. Novick, *That Noble Dream,* 361–411.

46. DLM to DeVoto, 6 February 1953, M0001 117:352, Stanford University Special Collections Ms 579 1:3, UU-Ms; DLM Papers, 2:1473.

47. MRM to DLM, 2 June 1951, DLM Papers, 15:1219.

48. Doyce Nunis to DLM, 23 June 1966, DLM Papers, 16:1166.

49. Robert H. (Bob) Morgan, interview, 19 March 1994.

50. Walter Prescott Webb, "History as High Adventure," *American Historical Review* 64, no. 2 (January 1959), 272.

51. DLM to [*unstated*], 13 June 19[39], DLM Papers, 27:1054; DLM to Bleak, 12 August 1939, Ms 579 1:11, UU-Ms.

52. DLM to Shawl, Nyeland & Seavey, 23 June 1939, DLM Papers, 8:1494.

53. Alan [Morgan] to DLM, 25 April 1939, DLM Papers, 20:1049.

54. DLM to Bleak, 12 August 1939, Ms 579 1:11, UU-Ms; DLM to Norman D'Evelyn, 24 October 1939, DLM Papers, 8:108. DLM to Anderson Jewelry Company, 7:892; DLM to Boyle's Furniture Company, 7:1073, DLM to Hotel Ben Lomond, 8:561; DLM to Minnoch Glass & Paint Company, 8:1012, all 25, 28 May 1939.

55. "Garner Demands Ban on WPA Politics Now," *Washington Daily News,* 1 June 1939.

56. DLM to Maurice Howe, 5 June 1939, DLM Papers, 26:190.

57. Maurice Howe to DLM, 9 June 1939, DLM Papers, 26:530.

58. Muriel Taylor to DLM, 8 May 1939, DLM Papers, 20:537; diary entry dated 22 March [1940], 25:1687.

59. DLM to Maurice Howe, 30 June 1939, DLM Papers, 26:201; Howe to DLM, 8 November 1941, 26:928; DLM to Howe, 18 November 1942, 26:454. Howe died in 1945, and the book was never begun.

60. DLM to Durham, 15 July 1939, DLM Papers, 2:1539, 20:1280.

61. DLM to Maurice Howe, 23 July 1939, DLM Papers, 26:205; J. M. Scammell to DLM, 30 July 1939, 20:191.

62. DLM to D'Evelyn, 24 October 1939, DLM Papers, 8:108.

63. DLM to MRM, 30 July 19[39], DLM Papers, 5:802. Train fare from Salt Lake City to Ogden was 75 cents.

64. DLM to Maurice Howe, 5 August 1939, DLM Papers, 26:226.

65. DLM to Bleak, 22 May 1938, Ms 579 1:9, UU-Ms.

66. DLM to Bleak, 13 August 1938, Ms 579 1:10, UU-Ms.

67. DLM to Bleak, 12 August 1939, Ms 579 1:11, UU-Ms.

68. DLM to Bleak, 6 October, 7, 30 November 1937, Ms 579 1:8, UU-Ms.

69. Thurston, interview, 16 June 1994.

70. Edward A. Geary, "Mormondom's Lost Generation: Novelists of the 1940s," *Brigham Young University Studies* 18, no. 1 (Fall 1977): 89–98.

71. The manuscript, unidentified in the DLM Papers, is divided between C15:36–38 (54:1087–62), with another, perhaps earlier draft interfiled (54:1264–96); part 2 begins in C15:37 (54:1298–18), part 3 (54:1319–30).

72. DLM to Maurice Howe, 14, 17 August 1939, DLM Papers, 26:231, 26:233.

73. DLM to Farrar & Rinehart, 1 October 1939, DLM Papers, 3:310. The literary-agent system that characterizes trade publishing today had been borrowed from film and Broadway but not yet been implemented much beyond the most notable writers. It helped tremendously that Morgan's proposal was specifically made for a title in a thematic series rather than a general manuscript query.

74. Quoted in James L. W. West III, "The Divergent Paths of British and American Publishing," *Sewanee Review* 120, no.4 (Fall 2012): 503–13.

75. DLM to Farrar & Rinehart, 18 November 1939, DLM Papers, 3:313; DLM to Stanley M. Rinehart Jr., 13 March 1943, 6:473.

76. Nels Anderson to DLM, 27 December 1939, DLM Papers, 27:285; Bramwell to Maurice Howe, 18 June 1939, 27:72; Bramwell to Luther Evans, 28 July 1939, 27:124.

77. DLM to Maurice Howe, 6 and 20 February 1940, DLM Papers, 26:301, 26:304.

78. For a description of both, see the Morgan bibliography in this volume, pp. 433–55. *The State of Deseret* was reprinted by Utah State University Press (Logan) in 1987, edited with an introduction by Charles S. Peterson.

79. DLM to Farrar, 26 February 1940, DLM Papers, 3:314; undated diary entry, 25:1687.

80. Maurice Howe to DLM, 16 January 1939, DLM Papers, 26:611.

81. DLM to Maurice Howe, 21 January 1939, 26:156.

82. DLM to Charles K. Madsen, 17 January 1940, DLM Papers, 8:915; DLM to Maurice Howe, 17 January 1940, 27:303.

83. DLM to Maurice Howe, 6 February 1940, DLM Papers, 26:301.

84. Maurice Howe to DLM, 18 February 1940, DLM Papers, 26:646.

85. Undated conversation [10–15 February 1940], DLM Papers, 27:738.

86. "Morgan," DLM Papers, 27:330.

87. DLM to Darel McConkey, undated [March–April 1940], Accn 3206, UU-Ms.

88. DLM to Darel McConkey, undated [15–22 April 1940], Accn 3206, UU-Ms. Morgan later said that the writing "comes too close to the truth in

the lives of a number of people I know and have known" (DLM to Darel McConkey, undated [25–26 April 1940], Accn 3206, UU-Ms).

89. Darel McConkey to DLM, 24 April 1940, DLM Papers, 14:1316.

90. DLM Papers, carton 3:90; review carbon of 3:89. The date in DLM's hand reads "Tues. April 30–40."

91. DLM to Darel McConkey, 22 June 1940, DLM Papers, 5:554.

92. Darel McConkey to DLM, 2 June 1940, DLM Papers, 14:1319.

93. DLM to EHM, 29 June 1940, DLM Papers, 21:30.

CHAPTER 6

1. DLM to Darel McConkey, 15 July 1940, Accn 3206, UU-Ms.

2. DLM to Robert Allen, 12 April 1942, DLM Papers, 1:796.

3. Henri C. Flesher to DLM, undated [July 1940], DLM Papers, 27:1230.

4. DLM to Darel McConkey, 15 July 1940, Accn 3206, UU-Ms.

5. DLM to Darel McConkey, 8 July 1940, Accn 3206, UU-Ms. Some of the staff's letters can be found on DLM Papers, 27:678, 681, 755, 765, 1100–1110, 1230.

6. Maurice Howe to DLM, 4 December 1940, DLM Papers, 26:770; Richard L. Saunders, "The Utah Writers' Project and Writing of *Utah: A Guide to the State*," *Utah Historical Quarterly* 70, no.1 (Winter 2002): 21–38.

7. DLM to Henry F. Pringle, [6–8] August 19[40], DLM Papers, 8:1270. The letter is misdated 1942, the year the book was published. Morgan's project-sponsorship correspondence was collected into Mss B40, UHi.

8. DLM to Farrar & Rinehart, 10 August 1940, DLM Papers, 3:320; DLM to Maurice Howe, 17 August 1940, 26:349; DLM to DeVoto, 2 February 1941, M0001 117:351, CSt-Sc; Ms 579 1:1, UU-Ms; DLM Papers, 2:1416.

9. Charles S. Elzinga to DLM, 7 December 1940, DLM Papers, 27:429.

10. "Article Discusses State of Deseret," *Salt Lake Tribune*, 19 July 1940; "Utah Historical Issue Is Sent," *Deseret News* (Salt Lake City), 20 July 1940.

11. CK to DLM, 3 August 1940, DLM Papers, 13:1801.

12. Jarvis Thurston, interview, 16 June 1994; Jarvis Thurston to Richard Saunders, personal correspondence, 19 July 1994, in author's possession; DLM to MRM, 14 March 1940, Ms 143 2:1, UU-Ms; Diary entries 22, 23 March [1940], 251687; Marriage certificate 105603, 29 January 1941, Clark County, Nevada, vol. 20, 206. That Thurston and Morgan never saw each other again is a bit hyperbolic on Jarvis's part; Thurston worked for the UWP for a few months prior to the massive staff cut in 1941, though probably from Ogden and not with Morgan directly.

13. Robert H. (Bob) Morgan interview, 19 March 1994. The first part of the story was told after the interview concluded and is related from my memory.

14. DLM to Farrar, 12 September 1940, DLM Papers, 3:321.

15. "Maw Receives First Copy of WPA Guide to Utah State," *Salt Lake Tribune*, 29 March 1940.

16. Press Release W-18, 27 February 1942, Mss B57 207:2, UHi; Saunders, "Utah Writers' Project," 4–38.

17. DLM to JB, 3 February 1943, Mss B103 1:6, UHi. A decade later Wallace Stegner would also ask Morgan to read and correct the manuscript for his *Beyond the Hundredth Meridian: John Wesley Powell and the Second Opening of the West* (1954; reis., New York: Penguin Books, 1992).

18. "Resume of Meeting in Chicago by Mr. Greenwell," undated [July 1941], DLM Papers, 27:742; DLM to Maurice Howe, 10 July 1941, 26:435; "Workers on W. P. 5025", Mss B57 207:2, UHi.

19. DLM to Darel McConkey, 14 August 1941, Accn 3206, UU-Ms.

20. DLM to Farrar, 24 September 1941, DLM Papers, 3:323; Farrar to DLM, 29 September 1942, 12:608.

21. DLM to JB, 7 September 1941, Mss B103 1:5, UHi.

22. DLM to DeVoto, 26 October 1941, DLM Papers, 2:1427.

23. DLM, "Utah: A Viewpoint," *Rocky Mountain Review* 5, no.2 (Winter 1941): 1, 4; DLM, "Mormon Story Tellers," *Rocky Mountain Review* 7, no. 1 (Fall 1942): 1, 3–4, 7.

24. DLM to MSR, 18 September 1941, DLM Papers, 6:329.

25. DLM to Maurice Howe, 12 August 1941, DLM Papers, 26:440.

26. J. Cecil Alter to DLM, 5 August 1941, DLM Papers, 9:430. Cf. DLM to Darel McConkey, 14 August 1941, Accn 3206, UU-Ms.

27. JB to DLM, 11 August 1941, DLM Papers, 10:405; DLM to JB, 12 August 1941, Mss B103 1:5, UHi; DLM to Maurice Howe, 12 August 1941, DLM Papers, 26:439.

28. DSS Form 57 [draft registration card], DLM Papers, 25:1791.

29. "Morgan Keeps Chess Title," *Salt Lake Telegram*, 2 September 1941.

30. "Separations and Transfers on WP 5025," [1 July–30 September 1941], Mss B57 206:9, UHi; HRS state supervisor report for 1 July–31 December 1942, Mss B57 206:7, UHi.

31. DLM to MRM, 10 July 1942, DLM Papers, 5:744. See also 27:563.

32. Diary, 8 December 1941, DLM Papers, 25:1684.

33. Maurice Howe to DLM, 11 December 1941, DLM Papers, 26:942.

34. MRM to DLM, 26 December 1941, DLM Papers, 15:31.

35. DLM to Maurice Howe, 1 May 1941, DLM Papers, 26:418.

36. MRM to DLM, 8 January 1942, 15:39; undated diary entries, DLM Papers, 25:1687.

37. DLM to Farrar, 22 February 1942, DLM Papers, 3:326.

38. Unsigned, undated note [DLM to "Stew" Powell, 10–21 March 1942], DLM Papers, 27:1114.

39. DLM to JB, 21 May 1942, Mss B103 1:6, UHi; *DMEM*, 29–33.

40. DLM to Stella Drumm, 2 April 1942, DLM Papers, 8:150; DLM to JB, Mss B103 1:6, UHi; Ms 486 1:1[c], UU-Ms; *DMEM*, 25–29.

41. DLM to JB, 12 April 1942, Mss B103 1:6, UHi; Ms 486 1:1[c], UU-Ms; *DMEM*, 25–29.

42. Ian Tyrell, *Historians in Public: The Practice of American History, 1890–1970* (Chicago: University of Chicago Press, 2005), 155.

43. DLM to MRM, 10 July 1942, DLM Papers, 5:744.

44. DLM to EHM, 2 September 1938, DLM Papers, 21:12.

45. DLM to Maurice Howe, 17 January 1940, DLM Papers, 26:292.

46. DLM to [Ruby] Garrett, 30 May 1942, DLM Papers, 8:299.

47. Form 107(NR), number 5-827-501 [War Manpower Commission certification of DLM on the list of "National Register of Scientific and Specialized Personnel"], DLM Papers, 25:1793.

48. DLM to Wallace Stegner, 13 July 1942, DLM Papers, 6:1126; DLM to Farrar, 27 September 1942, 3:332. Stegner's editor sent the *Mormon County* galleys with a telling comment on Morgan's growing authority: "I like the way [Stegner] explains to me, 'This [i.e., having DLM correct proofs] is the best way I know of insuring against bonehead mistakes'" (Charles A. Pearce to DLM, DLM Papers, 19:1554).

49. DLM to EHM, 5 October 1942, DLM Papers, 21:36.

CHAPTER 7

1. DLM to CK, 11 March 1943, CK Papers, Mss B114 1:2, UHi.

2. DLM to Alvin Smith, 11 May 1943, DLM Papers, 8:1523.

3. Civil Service Commission, *Tips to Newcomers to Washington, DC* (Washington, DC: Civil Service Commission, 1942).

4. Nels Anderson to DLM, 21 January 1942, DLM Papers, 9:519.

5. DLM to EHM, 8, 13 October 1942, DLM Papers, 21:42, 44.

6. DLM to EHM, 13, 15, 23, 29 October 1942, DLM Papers, 21:44, 49, 54, 60.

7. DLM to EHM, 8 October 1942, DLM Papers, 21:42.

8. DLM to EHM, Bob and Audry Morgan, 29 October, 4 November 1942, DLM Papers, 21:60; DLM to MSR, 22 October 1942, Mss B40 1:1, UHi.

9. Clark [Tyler] to DLM, 17 December 1941, DLM Papers, 20:1136.

10. DLM to EHM, 5 December 1942, DLM Papers, 21:79.

11. Luther Gulick, "V. War Organization of the Federal Government" in "The American Road from War to Peace," *American Political Science Review* 38, no. 6 (December 1944): 1166–79.

12. Wilson D. Wallis, *Messiahs: Their Role in Civilization* (Washington, DC: American Council on Public Affairs, 1943).

13. DLM to Farrar, 30 November 1942, DLM Papers, 3:339.

14. DLM to EHM, 4 November 1942, DLM Papers, 21:65.

15. DLM to Farrar, 16 November 1942, DLM Papers, 3:337.

16. Farrar to DLM, 1 December 1942, DLM Papers, 12:624; DLM to Farrar, 21 December 1942, 3:340.

17. DLM to Farrar, 27 December 1942, DLM Papers, 3:341.

18. DLM to EHM, 9 January 1943, DLM Papers, 21:93.

19. DLM to EHM, 14 January 1943, DLM Papers, 21:95.

20. DLM to CK, 11 March 1943, CK Papers, UHi. The Office of Price Administration (OPA) was created by Executive Order 8875 on August 28, 1941, and was abolished by the General Liquidation Order, May 19, 1947. Best contemporary data is found in Office of Price Administration, *OPA Is Our Battle Line: Employee Handbook*. Region 7 ed. (Washington, DC: Government Printing Office, 1943); cf. Andrew H. Bartels, "The Office of Price Administration and the Legacy of the New Deal, 1939–1946," *Public Historian* 5, no. 3 (Summer 1983): 5–29.

21. Conversation notes with Jim Holliday, 7 November 1967, DLM Papers, 1:98.

22. W. J. Ghent to Maurice Howe, 16 February 1942, DLM Papers, 26:963, 27:59.

23. FMB to DLM, 15 June 1943, DLM Papers, 10:35.

24. Newell Bringhurst, "Juanita Brooks and Fawn Brodie: Sisters in Mormon Dissent," *Dialogue* 27, no. 2 (Summer 1994): 105–27; Gary S. Topping, *Utah Historians and the Reconstruction of Western History* (Norman: University of Oklahoma Press, 2003); Geary, "Mormondom's Lost Generation," 89–98.

25. DLM to [Glory Harris, 9–10 August 1943], DLM Papers, 1:94; DLM to EHM 12, 17, 19, 21 November 1943, 21:203; 206, 207, 209.

26. MRM to DLM, 15 January 1944, DLM Papers, 15:218. Jarvis Thurston married Iowa native Mona Van Duyn as the pair were finishing master's degrees at the University of Iowa's prestigious writing program. The couple founded *Perspective* in 1947, which became one of the country's most important poetry journals of their generation, and taught at Washington University in St Louis, MO, for most of their careers. As a writer, her poetry was awarded a Bollingen Prize and the National Book Award in 1971, a Guggenheim fellowship in 1972, and a Pulitzer Prize in 1991. She was admitted to the Academy of American Poets in 1981 and became a life-appointed Chancellor four years later, was elected a Fellow of the National Institute of Arts and Letters (1986), and capped her professional career as United States Poet Laureate in 1992. The couple welcomed me at their St. Louis home on several occasions between 2001 and her death in 2004. Madeline's bitter characterizations do not match my experience with either individual.

27. Elliot [Marple] to DLM, 20 October [1943], DLM Papers, 25:2283.

28. Barton J. Bernstein, "The Removal of War Production Board Controls on Business, 1944–1946," *Business History Review* 39, no. 2 (Summer 1965): 243–60.

29. Marple to DLM, undated [spring 1944], DLM Papers, 25:2288; Harriet W. Jones to DLM, 2 March 1944, 25:2221; Jones to DLM, 8 March 1944, 25:2222.

30. Marple to DLM, 12 June [1944], DLM Papers, 25:2281.

31. Milo Quaife to DLM, 9 November 1944, DLM Papers, 15:1829; DLM to Quaife, 13 November 1944, 6:243. Morgan had been recommended by a B-M

salesman and confirmed by DeVoto; unsigned note dated 5 April [1944], and "Pro-file—The Great Salt Lake," undated, Bobbs-Merrill mss., 123:"Morgan, Dale Lowell. Great Salt Lake. R.R. & Promotional Material," InU-Li.

32. Processors of the DLM Papers did not attempt to order the undated OPA memos and correspondence. The order of events is my own reconstruction based on contextual clues. DLM to [Del Beman], undated [15–17 January 1945], 25:2296; [Marple] to DLM, undated, 25:2278–80; Beman to DLM, 17 January 1945, 25:2264.

33. DLM to Durham, 24 February 1946, DLM Papers, 2:1548; *Federal Chess Club Newsletter,* January 1946, 25:2029.

34. H. M., "Joe Smith, the Mormon Prophet," *New York Tribune,* 20 July 1844.

35. Ronald O. Barney, *Joseph Smith: History, Methods, and Memory* (Salt Lake City: University of Utah Press, 2020), 10.

36. Fellowship application dated 22 January 1945, "Morgan, Dale L.," John Simon Guggenheim Memorial Foundation archives, New York.

37. DLM to FMB, 28 January 1946, Ms 360 7:7, UU-Ms.

38. DLM to J. Roderic Korns/CK, 28 February 1945, Mss B114 1:4, UHi; 5:191.

39. Henry A. Moe to DLM, 5 April 1945; "Morgan, Dale L.," 1945 application, John Simon Guggenheim Memorial Foundation archives, New York; DLM Papers, 17:1042

40. DLM to EHM, 9 April 1945, DLM Papers, 21:365.

41. DLM to JB, 23 April 1945, Ms 143 2:22, UU-Ms. The "no friendly critic" was a reference to Charles Kelly, who also claimed to be at work on a history of the Mountain Meadows Massacre that was never published. DLM to JB, 30 May 1945, Mss B103 1:9, UHi; *DMEM,* 75–78.

42. DLM to UHi Board of Control, to MSR, 27 May 1945, DLM Papers, 9:70, 6:351. The administrative history of the organization is related summarily in Cory Nimer and J. Gordon Daines III, "The Development and Professionalization of the Utah State Archives, 1897–1968," *Journal of Western Archives* 3, no. 1 (2012): 1–30, which misses both the 1934 federal grant and Morgan's early involvement with the development of the Archives.

43. DLM to JB, 15 June 1945, Mss B103 1:9, UHi. Jim Morgan served a tour of duty in the Allied occupation of Japan, and Bob was a radio operator through the entire war in the US and Canada.

44. DLM to EHM, 15 August 1945, DLM Papers, 21:406; DLM to JB, 20 August 1945, Mss B103 1:9, UHi.

45. Bernstein, "Removal of War Production Board Controls," 252–54.

46. DLM to FMB, 25 August 1945, Ms 360 7:6, UU-Ms.

47. Darel McConkey to DLM, 28 August 1945, DLM Papers, 14:1392.

48. DLM to FMB, 28 October 1945, Ms 360 7:6, UU-Ms; DLM Papers, 1:1626; *DMEM,* 79–83.

49. See Ernst Troeltsch's comments on church history cited in Martin E. Marty, "Two Integrities," 7.

50. M. Wilford Poulson to FMB, 18 October 1943, DLM Papers, 20:1644.

51. Stanley S. Ivins to Herbert O. Brayer, 2 May 1946[c], J. Reuben Clark papers MS 303 234:9, Brigham Young University (hereafter UPB), Provo, UT.

52. JB to DLM, 9 December 1945, DLM Papers, 10:629.

53. Greenwell to DLM, 6 December 1945, DLM Papers, 12:1087; EHM to DLM, 8 January 1946, 22:724.

54. John Henry Evans, *Joseph Smith: An American Prophet* (New York: Macmillan, 1933). Admittedly, the volume had been reprinted several times before 1946.

55. Stanley S. Ivins to DLM, 10 August 1946, DLM Papers, 13:1131.

56. Wallis, *Messiahs,* 4.

57. John Mecklin, *The Story of American Dissent* (New York: Harcourt, Brace, and Company, 1934).

58. EHM to DLM, 30 October 1945, DLM Papers, 22:696.

59. DLM to Bleak, 13 December 1945, Ms 579 1:12, UU-Ms.

60. DLM to Hudson's Bay Company Governor and Committee, 9 August 1945, DLM Papers, 8:582; DLM to CK, 28 November 1945, Mss B114 1:3, UHi; 4:1008.

61. DLM to EHM, 16 February 1946, DLM Papers, 21:454.

62. DLM to Edmund F. Hackett, 23 February 1946, DLM Papers, 8:390.

63. Marriner Eccles, *Hearings before the Committee on Banking and Currency . . . on S. 2028, a Bill to Amend the Emergency Price Control Act of 1942, as Amended, and the Stabilization Act of 1942, as Amended, and for Other Purposes,* 79th Congress, 2nd session (Washington, DC: Government Printing Office, 1946), 2: 1614–16. Eccles testified before the Senate committee; the House version was the Price Control Renewal Act. An "Analysis of the Price Control Bill passed by the House" appears in DLM Papers 2: 1749–53. Barton J. Bernstein, "Removal of War Production Board Controls on Business, 1944–1946," *Business History Review* 39, no. 2 (Summer 1965): 243–60.

64. MRM to DLM, 16, 18 July 1946, DLM Papers, 15:636, 638.

65. Ray Allen Billington, Introduction to Dale L. Morgan, *The Great Salt Lake* (Albuquerque: University of New Mexico Press, 1973), xix.

66. Robert Kaye to DLM, 21 October 1946, DLM Papers, 19:886; DLM to MSR, 19 November 1946, 6:371.

67. Everett M. Reimer to DLM, 30 November 1946, DLM Papers, 25:3026; Ethel B. Gilbert to DLM, 30 November 1946, 25:3022; Advice of Personnel Action, 30 November 1946, 25:3032.

68. DLM to JB, 16 December 1946, Mss B103 1:12, UHi; 1:1885.

69. DLM to Guernsey Van Riper, Jr., 9 December 1946, DLM Papers, 6:1474.

70. DLM to Axel J. Andreson, 19 February 1947, DLM Papers, 7:906; Arthur J. Babcock to Chambers, 1 March 1947, 11:128. John A. Widtsoe, "On the Bookrack," *Improvement Era* 50, no. 4 (April 1947): 218.

71. Van Riper to DLM, 22 January 1947, DLM Papers, 17:1736.
72. DLM, "Salt Lake City, City of the Saints," *Rocky Mountain Cities,* ed. Ray B. West Jr. (New York: W. W. Norton, 1949).
73. DLM to Moe, 24 February 1947, "Morgan, Dale L.," 1945 Application, John Simon Guggenheim Memorial Foundation archives, New York; DLM Papers, 6:971.
74. MRM to DLM, 1 March 1947, DLM Papers, 15:753.
75. Arthur L. Crawford to DLM, 9 April 1947, DLM Papers, 11:1537.
76. DLM to Harrison C. Dale, 28 July 1947, DLM Papers, 8:24.
77. MRM to DLM, 12 April 1947, DLM Papers, 15:781.
78. DLM to MRM, 14 April 1947, Ms 143 2:3, UU-Ms.
79. MRM to DLM, undated [August 1947], DLM Papers, 15:799.
80. DLM to FMB, 2 August 1947, Ms 360 7:10, UU-Ms; Ms 143 2:21, UU-Ms.

CHAPTER 8

1. DLM to EHM, 11 January 1948, DLM Papers, 21:593.
2. DLM to JB, 8 September 1942, Mss B103 1:6, UHi.
3. DLM to Bleak, 26 February 1939, Ms 579 1:11, UU-Ms.
4. DLM to EHM, 3 October 1947, DLM Papers, 21:560; EHM to DLM, 14 October 1947, 22:1150.
5. DLM to Stanley M. Rinehart Jr., 16 October 1947, DLM Papers, 6:481.
6. DLM to Israel A. Smith, 20 December 1947, DLM Papers, 6:928.
7. DLM to FMB, 12 July 1950, Ms 360 7:12, UU-Ms; 1:1721.
8. DLM to FMB, 25 January 1948, Ms 360 7:11, UU-Ms; 1:1694; *DMEM,* 150–54.
9. DLM to EHM, 11 January 1948, DLM Papers, 21:593.
10. DLM to Moe, 3 January 1948, "Morgan, Dale L.," John Simon Guggenheim Memorial Foundation archives, New York; DLM Papers, 6:976
11. DLM to Harvey E. Tobie, 12 February 1948, DLM Papers, 6:1384.
12. MRM to DLM, 10 March 1948, DLM Papers, 15:884.
13. DLM to Tobie, 30 March 1948, DLM Papers, 6:1385.
14. DLM to Burgess, 13 August 1948, P79-2f3, MoInRC; Ms 360 7:11, UU-Ms; 2:123; *DMEM,* 160–65.
15. DLM to FMB, 12 July 1950, Ms 360 7:12, UU-Ms; DLM Papers, 1:1721.
16. Nels Anderson to JB, 29 May 1942, Mss B103 1:6, UHi.
17. John A. Widtsoe to DLM, 25 March 1946, DLM Papers, 20:879. Widtsoe encouraged inquiry at many levels and disciplines; cf. Michael Austin and Ardis E. Parshall, "The Novelist and the Apostle: Paul Bailey, John A. Widtsoe, and the Quest for Faithful Fiction in the 1940s," *Journal of Mormon History* 42, no. 3 (July 2016): 183–210.
18. DLM to George Albert Smith, 29 March 1948, DLM Papers, 8:1536.
19. Leonard J. Arrington, "Coming to Terms with Mormon History: An Interview With Leonard Arrington," *Dialogue* 22, no. 4 (Winter 1989): 38–54.

20. Daryl Chase, *Joseph the Prophet: As He Lives in the Hearts of His People* (Salt Lake City: Deseret Book, 1944), 8.

21. Richard L. Evans, *At This Same Hour* (New York: Harper, 1945–1949), 96.

22. Joseph Anderson to DLM, 14 April 1948, DLM Papers, 18:828. President Smith was evidently not consulted at all; cf. George Albert Smith to DLM, 19 April 1948, DLM Papers, 20:343.

23. DLM to JB, 19 February 1949, Ms 486 1:4[c], UU-Ms; DLM Papers, 1:1915.

24. DLM to Joseph Anderson, 20 April 1948, Ms 360 7:11, UU-Ms; 7:896; *DMEM*, 157–58.

25. Within a year of Morgan's passing, new library leadership, with academic training and archival expertise, promoted a professionalization of the Church History Department during the 1970s and 1980s. A reasserted cultural conservatism dampened "Camelot" for a few years after that, until under Gordon B. Hinckley's leadership, the church realized the merits of a general open-door research policy. The Church History Library and its research policy now provides a level of access to its material which Dale Morgan, Daryl Chase, and others encouraged a professional lifetime earlier. Leonard J. Arrington, *Adventures of a Church Historian* (Urbana: University of Illinois Press, 1998); Gregory Prince, *Leonard Arrington and the Writing of Mormon History* (Salt Lake City: University of Utah Press, 2016), 79–88, 152–91, 201–23, 276–305, 338–44. See also Cory Nimer, "The Old Guard and Rearguard Actions: Professionalization and the Church Historian's Office," *Journal of Mormon History* 45, no. 1 (January 2019): 110–38.

26. DLM to FMB, 15 June 1948, Ms 360 7:11, UU-Ms; 1:1703.

27. DLM to Austin Fife, 14 June 1948, DLM Papers, 3:372.

28. Moe to DLM, 24 March 1948, "Morgan, Dale L.", 1948 Application, John Simon Guggenheim Memorial Foundation archives, New York; DLM Papers, 17:1054.

29. DLM to JB, 16 April 1948, DLM Papers, 1:1892. Morgan said essentially the same thing to Fawn Brodie a week earlier; cf. DLM to FMB, 11 April 1948, Ms 360 7:11, UU-Ms; DLM Papers, 1:1698.

30. DLM to Darel McConkey, 11 April 1948, Accn 3206, UU-Ms.

31. DLM to John W. Caughey, 5 May 1948, DLM Papers, 2:548.

32. DLM to CK, 11 May 1948, DLM Papers, 4:1061.

33. Virginia Sorensen to DLM, 20 April 1948, DLM Papers, 17:1088.

34. Milton R. Hunter, *Utah: The Story of Her People, 1540–1947* (Salt Lake City: Deseret News Press, 1946); Leland H. Creer, *Founding of an Empire: The Exploration and Colonization of Utah, 1776–1856* (Salt Lake City: Bookcraft, 1947); DLM to FMB, 20 April 1948, Ms 360 7:11, UU-Ms; DLM Papers, 1:1699.

35. DLM to FMB, 22 May 1948, Ms 360 7:11, UU-Ms; DLM Papers, 1:1701.

36. [Unsigned] to DLM, undated [July 1948], DLM Papers, 20:1196.

37. DLM to Utah Industrial Commission, 4 August 1948, DLM Papers, 9:74.

38. DLM to Arthur L. Crawford, 2 June 1948, DLM Papers, 2:1312.

39. Sherril W. Taylor, "Young Utahn Becomes Recognized As Authority on Western History," *Deseret News* (Salt Lake City), 13 June 1948.

40. Rulon S. Howells to DLM, 19 June 1948, DLM Papers, 19:653.

41. DLM to EHM, 7 August 1948, DLM Papers, 21:612.

42. John Selby to DLM, 22 July 1948, DLM Papers, 17:778; DLM to Selby, 26 July 1948, Ms 143 2:28, UU-Ms; *DMEM,* 158–60.

43. DLM to Fredrick R. Rinehart, 31 August 1948, DLM Papers, 8:1340.

44. DLM to Stegner, Ms 676 18:53, UU-Ms.

45. MRM to DLM, 5 September 1948, DLM Papers, 15:913.

46. Henry G. Alsberg to DLM, 8 October 1948, DLM Papers, 9:418.

47. MSR to William Culp Darrah, 21 October 1948, Mss B361 2:9, UHi.

48. DLM to Alsberg, 25 November 1948, DLM Papers, 1:808.

49. DLM to Rulon S. Wells III, 14 December 1948, DLM Papers, 7:69.

50. Widtsoe to DLM, 7 January 1949, DLM Papers, 20:881.

51. DLM to Widtsoe, 24 January 1949, DLM Papers, 9:237.

52. DeVoto to DLM, 28 December 1945, in Bernard DeVoto, *Letters of Bernard DeVoto,* ed. Wallace Stegner (New York: Doubleday, 1975), 174–282; DLM Papers, 12:40.

53. Topping, "Personality and Motivation in Utah Historiography," 73–89.

54. Carroll, *Keeping Time,* 90. Carroll (205–7) lays out four alternatives to history *qua* historicism: ignorance, irrelevance, nostalgia (or antiquarianism), authoritative deceptions (invention; which we might call "faithful history").

55. Burgess lost his hearing around 1920 in a botched surgical attempt to halt progressive hearing loss. David M. Brugge, "The Career of Samuel Burgess," *Saints' Herald* 98, no. 2 (8 January 1951): 9, 22.

56. [Burgess] to DLM, undated [February 1948], P79-2f3, MoInRC; DLM Papers, 10:1084.

57. DLM to JB, 15 December 1945, Mss B103, 1:10, UHi; DLM Papers, 1:1850; *DMEM,* 84–91.

58. DLM to William H. Cadman, 12 March 1949, DLM Papers, 2:150.

59. They were eventually published in DLM, *Dale Morgan on the Mormons,* vol. 1, 315–75.

60. DLM to Marguerite Eyer Wilbur, 24 February 1949, DLM Papers, 9:242; DLM to Mrs. E. J. Magnuson, 15 April 1949, DLM Papers, 5:808.

61. DLM to Brimhall, 6 September 1949, Ms 114 18:12, UU-Ms; DLM Papers, 2:132; DLM to Greenwell, Ms 114 18:12, UU-Ms; DLM Papers, 3:663.

62. DLM to George Albert Smith, 26 May 1949, DLM Papers, 8:1539.

63. DLM to Selby, 17 June 1949, DLM Papers, 6:861.

64. DLM to JB, 3 July 1949, Ms 486 1:4, UU-Ms; DLM to Mrs. E. J. Magnuson, 5 July 1949, DLM Papers, 5:814.

65. DLM to JB, 18 November 1951, DLM Papers, 1:1991.

66. DLM to Joel E. Ricks, 20 July 1949, DLM Papers, 8:1332; DLM to JB, 21 July 1949, 1:1939; UHi budget sheet, Joel E. Ricks Papers, Mss 114 3:5, Utah State University Special Collections and Archives, Logan (hereafter ULA).

67. DLM to MSR, 30 July 1949, DLM Papers, 6:396.

68. JB to DLM, 29 July 19[49], DLM Papers, 10:1044; DLM to CK, 29 July 1949, 4:1087.

69. DLM to Harold Bentley, 1 August 1949, MS 44 11:2, UU-Ms; EL to DLM, 2 August 1949, DLM Papers, 14:1019.

70. Both manuscripts appear in *Dale Morgan on the Mormons,* vol. 1, 217–44, 103–47. Neither was ever completed. On Morgan's plans for the histories, cf. DLM to W. R. Coe, 21 October 1949, DLM Papers, 7:1263.

71. DLM to Fife, 24 January 1948, DLM Papers, 3:371; DLM to Beatrice D. Johnson, 24 January 1948, 4:893; DLM to Louise Barry, 13 August 1949, 1:997.

72. DLM to JB, 30 April 1947, Mss B103 2:1, UHi; DLM Papers, 1:1888; DLM to Fife, 4 May 1947, 3:366. By this point, Morgan had probably given up his earlier plan (and the contract, which had been signed in 1943) for a fourth, preliminary book with his publisher tentatively titled *This Was America,* which was to set the stage of American social and religious ideas during the first half of the nineteenth century (DLM to MSR, 15 April 1943, Mss B40 1:2, UHi). Morgan's preparation for this volume seems to have been limited to extensive reading of *Niles* and contemporary newspapers. With no training in intellectual history, it is fascinating to speculate whether he could have carried off in a single volume a subject which has provided entire careers for other historians.

73. DLM to FMB, 11 April 1948, Ms 360 7:11, UU-Ms; DLM Papers, 1:1698.

74. DLM to JB, 3 May 1949, DLM Papers, 1:1932

75. Ruth Barton to DLM, 22 August 1949, DLM Papers, 23:1374.

76. JB to DLM, 17 August 1949, DLM Papers, 10:783.

77. DLM to CK, 11 October 1949, Mss B114 1:5, UHi; DLM Papers, 4:1094.

78. CK to DLM, 17 October 1949, DLM Papers, 14:129.

79. DLM to JB, 6 September 1949, DLM Papers, 1:1950; DLM to FMB, MS 360 7:12, UU-Ms; 1:1717; *DMEM,* 174–76.

80. DLM to Elizabeth Lauchnor, 24 September 1949, DLM Papers, 5:352; DLM to James T. Babb, 26 September 1949, 2:133; DLM to Leslie Bliss, 23 November 1949, HIA 31.1.1 32:6, Huntington Library, San Marino, CA; 1:1526; Bliss to DLM, 25 November 1949, HIA 31.1.1 32:6, Huntington Library; 9:1350. Morgan first offered the set to New York Public Library, which turned down the offer. DLM to New York Public Library, 26 September 1949, DLM Papers, 5:1344.

81. Lorraine Stout to DLM, 9 November 1949, DLM Papers, 16:1392.

82. Darel McConkey to DLM, 12, 19 October 1949, DLM Papers, 14:1428, 1426.

CHAPTER 9

1. DLM to Selby, 18 November 1949, DLM Papers, 6:866; "It is a sad fact that history is a jade who will not support herself" (DLM to Paul W. Gates, 26 July 1948, 8:308).

2. O. H. Cheney, *Economic Survey of the Book Industry, 1930–1931* (New York: R. R. Bowker, 1949), 50–51.

3. Alice Payne Hackett, *Seventy Years of Best Sellers, 1895–1965* (New York: R. R. Bowker, 1967), 153–55. Carl F. Kaestle and Janice A. Radway, eds., *Print in Motion: The Expansion of Publishing and Reading in the United States, 1880–1940* (Chapel Hill: University of North Carolina Press, 2009). James L. W. West, III, *American Authors and the Literary Market Place since 1900* (Philadelphia: University of Pennsylvania Press, 1988).

4. Michael Korda, *Making the List: A Cultural History of the American Bestseller, 1900–1999* (New York: Barnes & Noble, 2001), 81.

5. "Fisher's Book Fans LDS History Study," unidentified clipping dated in manuscript, 22 May 1940, DLM Papers, 80:250.

6. James D. Hart, *The Popular Book: A History of America's Literary Taste* (New York: Oxford University Press, 1950), 265.

7. Henry C. Link and Harry Arthur Hopf, *People and Books: A Study of Reading Habits and Book-buying Habits* (New York: Book Industry Committee, Book Manufactures Institute, 1946), 22.

8. Quoted in James L. W. West III, "The Divergent Paths of British and American Publishing," 503.

9. A. A. van Duym, "Where Is the Book Business Heading?" in "Strictly Personal," *Saturday Review of Literature,* 24 November 1945; cf. John Tebbel, *A History of Book Publishing in the United States,* Volume 4: *The Great Change, 1940–1980* (New York: R. R. Bowker, 1978), 98–102.

10. Link and Hopf, *People and Books,* 9, 22, 122, 138–66.

11. Link and Hopf, *People and Books,* 56, 113, 122; Dorothy V. Knibb, "Reading Trends Stir Book Trade," *Domestic Commerce* 33, no. 11 (Nov. 1945). Within a decade television would dominate that list.

12. Harry Harrison Kroll to Jesse Stuart, [18 May 1943], Jesse Stuart Papers, University of Louisville, KY. Cheney, *Economic Survey,* 21ff, provides an excellent summary of the geographic distribution of book-buying in the country during the 1930s, trends which become only more concentrated after the war. For comparison, Leigh Ann Duck, *The Nation's Region: Southern Modernism, Segregation, and US Nationalism* (Athens: University of Georgia Press, 2006) usefully illustrates some of the broad literary changes across time in regionally defined themes.

13. Herbert Weinstock, "Report on Trip to Louisville, St. Louis, Dallas, Austin, San Antonio, Houston," Feb. 1951, Alfred A. Knopf records, 537:7, Harry Ransom Center, University of Texas, Austin (hereafter TxU-Hu).

14. Korda, *Making the List*, 100, 104; William Darby, *Necessary American Fictions: Popular Literature of the 1950s* (Bowling Green, Ohio: Popular, 1987); Joan Shelly Rubin, *The Making of Middle-Brow Culture* (Chapel Hill: University of North Carolina Press, 1992).

15. Michael Korda, *Another Life: A Memoir of Other People* (New York: Random House, 1999), 45. Korda spent his career at Simon & Schuster, heading the firm's editorial division for three decades. On general prospects, see American Book Publishers Council, *The Situation and Outlook for the Book Trade* (New York: American Book Publishers Council, 1951).

16. Jennifer Kavins Hannifin, "Changing Sales and Markets of American University Presses, 1960–1990, *Publishing Research Quarterly* 7, no. 2 (Summer 1991): 11–35.

17. Korda, *Another Life*, 199–201, 385–91.

18. Carroll G. Bowen, "When Universities Become Publishers," *Science,* new series 140, no. 3567 (10 May 1963): 599–05; Albert N. Greco, *The Growth of the Scholarly Publishing Industry in the US: A Business History of a Changing Marketplace* (Cham, Switzerland: Palgrave Pivot, 2019); Hannifin, "Changing Sales and Markets," 11–35.

19. Gene R. Hawes, *To Advance Knowledge: A Handbook on American University Press Publishing* (New York: American Association of University Presses, 1967). A pointed criticism of the postwar economies of scale in university publishing is found in Roger W. Shugg, "The Professors and their Publishers," *Daedalus* 92, no. 1 (Winter 1963): 68–77.

20. Frank L. Schick, *The Paperbound Book in America: The History of Paperbacks and Their European Background* (New York: R. R. Bowker, 1958); Thomas L. Bonn, *Heavy Traffic & High Culture: New American Library as Literary Gatekeeper in the Paperback Revolution* (Carbondale: Southern Illinois University Press, 1989); Tebbel, "*History of Book Publishing*," Vol. 4, 347–65; August Frugé, *A Skeptic Among Scholars: Recollections of a University Publisher* (Berkeley: University of California Press, 1993), 85; David McKitterick, *A History of Cambridge University Press: New Worlds for Learning, 1873–1972* (Cambridge, UK: Cambridge University Press, 2004), 327–28. My version of paperback history is a necessarily large generalization and drastic oversimplification, though the American Book Publishers' Council's *Annual Trends Survey of the General Book Publishing Industry* (New York: American Book Publishers' Council, 1962) reported that fifty-seven academic presses sold 6.5 million books for an income of $15 million in 1961.

21. Frank Stevens, "Is the Limited Edition the Solution to the Dollar Book Problem?" *Publishers Weekly,* 19 July 1930, 250–51; Robert D. Harlan and Bruce L. Johnson, "Trends in Modern American Book Publishing," *Library Trends* 27, no. 3 (Winter 1979): 389–407; Carol Porter Grossman,

The History of the Limited Editions Club (New Castle, DE: Oak Knoll Press, 2017); Megan Benton, "Measured Markets: Limited Edition Publishing and the Grabhorn Press, 1920–1930," *Publishing Research Quarterly* 11, no. 2 (Summer 1995): 90–102; Donald E. Bower and S. Lyman Tyler, *Fred Rosenstock: A Legend in Books & Art* (Flagstaff, AZ: Northland Press, 1976).

22. DLM to Jerry [Bleak], 8 December 1944, Ms 579 1:12, UU-Ms.
23. Tyrell, *Historians in Public*, 155.
24. The last issue under the name *Mississippi Valley Historical Review* contained one of the first expressions of identity crises that the study of the American West expressed nearly annually over the coming half-century. W. N. Davis, Jr., "Will the West Survive a Field in American History: A Survey," *Mississippi Valley Historical Review* 50, no. 4 (March 1964): 672–85.
25. Richard Francaviglia, "Walt Disney's Frontierland as an Allegorical Map of the American West," *Western Historical Quarterly* 30, no. 2 (Summer 1999): 155–82; David Lowenthal, *Possessed by the Past: The Heritage Crusade and the Spoils of History* (New York: Free Press, 1996), chapters 4–7.

CHAPTER 10
1. DLM to EHM, 5 November 1949, DLM Papers, 21:638.
2. DLM to EHM, 29 April 1950, DLM Papers, 21:669.
3. Greenwell to WPA Administrator, 17 July 1941, DLM Papers, 27:1640. Morgan landed in DC as the Classification Act of 1949 took effect and everyone scrambled to understand new rules.
4. DLM to Luther H. Evans, 2 September 1949, DLM Papers, 3:295; DLM to Civil Service Commission, 3 September 1949, 9:22.
5. Josephus Nelson and Judith Farley, *Full Circle: Ninety Years of Service in the Main Reading Room* (Washington, DC: Library of Congress, 1991), 23
6. Vernor W. Clapp, "Three Ages of Reference Work," *Special Libraries* 57 (Jul/Aug 1966): 379–84; Robert Gooch, "Report of Reference Chief Robert Gooch," *Report of the Librarian of Congress* (1947), 4.
7. DLM, "WPA Was People," DLM Papers, 32:0136–50.
8. DLM to EHM, 5 November 1949, DLM Papers, 21:638.
9. DLM to Harold W. Landin, 9 August 1943, DLM Papers, 8:797. In 1967 journalist Henry Lee Moon recalled the attitude of "stay on the Project as long as you had to, and get off as quickly as you could"; interview, quoted in Penkower, *The Federal Writers' Project*, 161.
10. Wilbur J. Cohen, "The Federal Government's Program for Ex-servicemen," *Annals of the American Academy of Political and Social Science* 238 (1945): 63–70; Robert C. Serow, "Policy as Symbol: Title II of the 1944 GI Bill," *Review of Higher Education* 27, no. 4 (2004): 481–99; Suzanne Mettler, "The Creation of the GI Bill of Rights of 1944: Melding Social and Participatory Citizenship Ideals," *Journal of Policy History* 17, no. 4 (2005): 345–74;

Patricia Strach, "Making Higher Education Affordable: Policy Design in Postwar America," *Journal of Policy History* 21, no. 1 (2008): 61–88.

11. DLM to EHM, 5 February 1950, DLM Papers, 21:657; DLM to MRM, 6, 15 February 1950, Ms 143 2:6, UU-Ms; DLM to Gilbert A. Schulkind, 7 February 1950, DLM Papers, 8:1461.

12. DLM to Civil Service Commission, 4 March 1950, DLM Papers, 9:25, 28.

13. DLM to EHM, 13 March 1950, DLM Papers, 21:662.

14. DLM to Selby, 5 April 1950, DLM Papers, 6:869.

15. DLM to EHM, 20 May 1950, DLM Papers, 21:672.

16. William C. Hull to Elbert D. Thomas, 27 June 1950, DLM Papers, 17:1490; W. A. McCoy to DLM, 27 June 1950, 19:1136.

17. DLM to Thomas, 3 July 1950, DLM Papers, 6:1332.

18. Jack Pole, "Richard Hofstadter" in *Clio's Favorites: Leading Historians of the United States, 1945–2000*, ed. Robert Allen Rutland, (Columbia: University of Missouri Press, 2000), 68–83.

19. J. R. Pole, "Daniel J. Boorstin," in *Pastmasters: Some Essays on American Historians,* eds. Marcus Cunliffe and Robin W. Winks (New York: Harper and Row, 1969), 211.

20. In the hands of writers like Hofstadter, Hartz, Boorstin, Henry Comager Steele, and Allan Nevins, the mainstream Consensus version of US national history did not account adequately for the rural or the poor and included virtually nothing about the experiences of Black, Hispanic, or Native American citizens. The Consensus perspective ignored the social immunities color afforded mostly to urban Euro-Americans, a group that accommodated white ethnic minorities into a single and "colorblind" form of economic, social, and racial nationalism. It thus rested on unstated but inherent racial assumptions simply taken for granted at a time when America was still starkly segregated. The powerful image of America as a cultural "melting pot" had grown out of the Progressive era nearly half a century earlier, but the Consensus approach reflected a strain of largely white, inspirational, and nationalist ethicism. Its inspirational enterprise was expressed by illustrator Norman Rockwell's *Four Freedoms* paintings and the Office of War Information's highly effective propaganda campaign. The latter successfully challenged prewar isolationism by linking World War II with the American Revolution, thus converting military service from involvement in foreign affairs into a crusade for "liberty" and "freedom." In sum, Consensus work tended to minimize the nation's cultural and racial diversity to concentrate on "shared" heritage, the "melting pot" myth of cultural integration and broad national stories. Cf. Peter Novick, *That Noble Dream*, chapter 11; Peter Charles Hoffer, "The Rise of Consensus History," in *Past Imperfect: Facts, Fictions, Fraud* (New York: Public Affairs, 2004); Mario DePillis, review of *History's Memory*, by Ellen Fitzpatrick, *Journal of Social History* 37 (Summer 2004): 1116–18.

21. National Historical Publications Commission, *A National Program for the Publication of the Papers of American Leaders: A Preliminary Report to the President* (Washington, DC: General Services Administration, 1951), iii. State historical societies had been collecting and publishing extracts of diaries and reminiscences since the 1870s, even in the American West, but the volume of material was inconsistently presented in print, and sometimes bowdlerized in fits of local sentiment.

22. *Deseret News* (Salt Lake City), 5 March 1950.

23. "Voice in Deseret," *Time*, 20 March 1950, 42.

24. FMB to DLM, 14 March 1950, DLM Papers, 10:233.

25. Arrington diary entries dated 1 September 1950 (a summary of the discussion follows the diary entry), 21 February 1951, 29 March 1951, 1 November 1951, 13 May 1954, 23 June 1954, Leonard J. Arrington Historical Archive, ULA (hereafter LJAHA); the initial Logan meeting is documented in "A Symposium of Opinions: Certain Aspects of LDS Education with Suggestions for Making It Less Theological and More Functional in Individual and Community Life," September 1950, ULA.

26. Arrington diary, 29 March 1951, LJAHA; Stan Ivins to DLM, 1 March 1951, Mss B31 13:5, UHi; DLM Papers, 13:1177.

27. James S. and Mary Beth Morgan, interview, 25 April 1991.

28. Bill Mulder to DLM, 12 January 1952, 16:731; 7 July 1952, DLM Papers, 16:724.

29. Thomas A. Blakely, "The Swearing Elders: The First Generation of Modern Mormon Intellectuals," *Sunstone* 10, no. 9 (1985): 8–13; Richard D. Poll, "The Swearing Elders: Some Reflections, a Response to Thomas Blakely," *Sunstone* 10, no. 9 (1985): 14–17.

30. DLM to Michael Sessor, 18 September 1950, DLM Papers, 8:1484.

31. Lauchnor to Joel E. Ricks, 10 August 1950, MS 201 6:11, UU-Ms.

32. Donald R. Burgess to DLM, 20 September 1950, DLM Papers, 18:1187.

33. DLM to Selby, 29 September 1950, DLM Papers, 6:871.

34. Charles R. Badgerow to DLM, 2 September 1950, DLM Papers, 9:604; Badgerow to DLM, 24 October 1950, 9:601.

35. DLM to EHM, 20 November 1950, DLM Papers, 21:694; DLM to EHM, 28 November 1950, 21:696.

36. E. Leo Lyman, personal communication, 17 February 2022.

37. DLM to A. R. Mortensen, 29 November 1950, DLM Papers, 5:1036.

38. DLM to Stegner, 28 November 1950, Ms 676 18:53, UU-Ms; 6:1145.

39. DLM to MRM, 4 December 1950, Ms 143 2:12, UU-Ms; EHM to DLM, 2 December 1950, DLM Papers, 22:1400.

40. Buships[*sic*] to DLM, 9 May 1951, DLM Papers, 20:1099.

41. DLM to EHM, 10 May 1951, DLM Papers, 21:736; DLM to Darel McConkey, Accn 3206, UU-Ms; [unsigned] to DLM, 10 May 1951, 20:1100.

42. DLM to MRM, 8 June 1951, MS 143 2:7, UU-Ms; DLM to Darel McConkey, 9 June 1951, Accn 3206, UU-Ms.

43. DLM to MRM, 10 June 1951, Ms 143 2:7, UU-Ms; *DMEM,* 188–92.
44. EHM to DLM, 4 August 1951, DLM Papers, 22:1546.
45. Luther H. Evans, "Bibliography by Cooperation," *Bulletin of the Medical Library Association* 37, no. 3 (July 1949): 198.
46. DLM to Mortensen, 9 August 1951, DLM Papers, 5:1106.
47. DLM to EHM, 11 August 1951, DLM Papers, 21:756.
48. DLM to GPH, 8 September 1951, DLM Papers, 3:936.
49. DLM to Dean [Brimhall], 7 May 1953, DLM Papers, 1:1600.
50. DLM to Mortensen, 25 August 1951, DLM Papers, 5:1108.
51. DLM to Thomas Streeter, 9 December 1951, DLM Papers, 6:1240.

CHAPTER 11
1. DLM to Selby, 26 July 1948, Ms 143 2:28, UU-Ms; *DMEM,* 159.
2. DLM to Bleak, 26 February 1939, Ms 579 1:11, UU-Ms.
3. DLM to Selby, 18 November 1949, DLM Papers, 6:866; 15 November 1949, 6:866.
4. DLM to MSR, 14 November 1949, 6:402.
5. Lauchnor to DLM, 4 November 1949, DLM Papers, 14:1025.
6. DLM to EHM, 19 January 1950, DLM Papers, 21:655; DLM to Sara Korns, 27 January 1950, 5:313.
7. Selby to DLM, 23 February 1950, DLM Papers, 17:797.
8. DLM to MRM, 27 February 1950, Ms 143 2:6, UU-Ms. This is the point at which Morgan forwarded to Madeline the four drafts which John Philip Walker published in DLM, *Dale Morgan on Early Mormonism: Correspondence and a New History,* ed. John Philip Walker (Midvale, UT: Signature Books, 1986).
9. DLM to John Selby, 5 April 1950, DLM Papers, 6:869; DLM to Lauchnor, 6 April 1950, 5:370.
10. DLM to EHM, 29 April 1950, DLM Papers, 21:669.
11. Ruth Plassey to DLM, 27 November 1950, DLM Papers, 19:1249.
12. DLM to Lauchnor, 3 May 1950, DLM Papers, 5:373.
13. DLM to Charles Eberstadt, 27 May 1950, DLM Papers, 3:46. This material was the same he had seen in Detroit three years earlier.
14. Charles Eberstadt to DLM, 1 June 1950, DLM Papers, 12:286. He also agreed to produce a separate assessment of the Strang "appointment letter." Morgan's study of the letter and its historicity (reproduced in *Dale Morgan on the Mormons,* vol. 1, 487–93) was the major source of information for Charles Eberstadt, "The Letter that Founded a Kingdom," *Autograph Collectors' Journal* 3, no. 1 (October 1950): 2–5, 32.
15. DLM to Gilbert A. Schulkind [Civil Service Commission], 7 Feb 1950, DLM Papers, 8:1461.
16. DLM to Tobie, 6 July 1950, DLM Papers, 6:1390.
17. DLM to Everett D. Graff, 15 July 1950, Trustee Personal Papers, ser. 3 7:28, Newberry Library, Chicago; 3:590.

18. DLM to Selby, 11 July 1950, DLM Papers, 6:870; Selby to DLM, 18 July 1950, 17:800.

19. DLM to Sara Korns, 16 July 1950, DLM Papers, 5:287.

20. DLM to Sara Korns, 6 September 1950, DLM Papers, 5:296; DLM to Lauchnor, 7 September 1950, 5:392; DLM to GPH, 8 September 1950, 3:935; DLM to Mrs. E. J. Magnuson, 8 September 1950, 5:819.

21. DLM to CK, 5 November 1950, DLM Papers, 4:1105; DLM to Sara Korns, 20 November 1950, 5:303.

22. J. Reuben Clark to David D. Moffatt, 21 November 1949, "1949 Mormon Church Correspondence," in "Morgan, Dale L.," file, John Simon Guggenheim Memorial Foundation archives, New York. A carbon of the letter is in M-correspondence, J. Reuben Clark papers, MS 303 380:4, UPB. Moffatt was a director of the Utah Copper Company and the son-in-law of First Council of Seventy president Rulon S. Wells, which, ironically, also made him the uncle of Morgan's good friend Rulon S. Wells III. "Family Dinner Marks Rulon S. Wells Birthday," *Deseret News* (Salt Lake City), 8 July 1940.

23. R. C. Klugescheid to Moe, 29 November 1949; Moe to Klugescheid, 29 November 1949, "1949 Mormon Church Correspondence," in "Morgan, Dale L." file, John Simon Guggenheim Memorial Foundation archives, New York.

24. Israel A. Smith to John Simon Guggenheim Memorial Foundation, 12 April 1950, Moe to Smith, 24 April 1950, "1949 Mormon Church Correspondence," in "Morgan, Dale L." file, John Simon Guggenheim Memorial Foundation archives, New York.

25. Francis W. Kirkham to Israel A. Smith, 6 September 1949, P13 f1802, MoInRC.

26. DLM to EHM, 18 December 1950, DLM Papers, 21:701. cf. DLM to MRM, 18 December 1950, Ms 143 2:6, UU-Ms; *DMEM,* 179–81.

27. See various letters in collection P13, Community of Christ archives, Independence, MO, including f1819, f1821, f1825, f1834, f1836, f1842; "Morgan, Dale L.," John Simon Guggenheim Memorial Foundation archives, New York; DLM to MRM, 18 December 1950, *DMEM,* 179–81; DLM to MRM, 26 December 1950, Ms 143 2:6, UU-Ms. Francis W. Kirkham, *A New Witness for Christ in America: The Book of Mormon,* 2 vols. (Independence, MO: Zion's Printing and Publishing Co., 1951). Widtsoe's query to Morgan was likely part of his own research for *Joseph Smith: Seeker after Truth, Prophet of God* (Salt Lake City: Deseret News Press, 1952).

28. DLM to John D. Thornley, 19 December 1950, DLM Papers, 6:1358.

29. DLM to Sara Korns, 1950 Dec 1, DLM Papers, 5:304.

30. DLM to Mulder, 14 January 1951, DLM Papers, 5:1281.

31. DLM to MRM, 24 January 1952, MRM Papers.

32. DLM to Mortensen, 4 January 1951, DLM Papers, 5:1042.

33. DLM to EHM, 27 January 1951, DLM Papers, 21:712; DLM to CK, 8 January 1951, 4:1112.

34. DLM to Selby, 28 January 1951, DLM Papers, 6:872.

35. DLM to Paul Oehser, 1 January 1952, DLM Papers, 8:1120; Paul Oehser to DLM, 4 September 1952, 19:1457.

36. DLM to MRM, 28 January 1951, Ms 143 2:7, UU-Ms.

37. EHM to DLM, 31 January 1951, DLM Papers, 22:1437.

38. DLM to JB, 18 March 1951, Mss B103 2:13, UHi.

39. Clyde Arbuckle to DLM, 22 March 1951, DLM Papers, 9:551.

40. DLM to Ernst Correll, 25 March 1951, DLM Papers, 7:1300; DLM to EHM, 25 March 1951, 21:727.

41. DLM to Sara Korns, 3 April 1951, DLM Papers, 5:324.

42. Mortensen to DLM, 14 July 1951, DLM Papers, 16:569 [300 in paper *UHQ* cover, 700 in fabrikoid *UHQ* bindings, 2,000 in red cloth as monographs]; "Cost of [UHQ] Volume 19," J. Roderic Korns letters, A2597, UHi. Only 800 copies of the Bolton press run sold in the critical first month. The USHS stocked unsold Bolton books for decades, unloading what they could very slowly at steep discounts (Mortensen to DLM, 17 August 1951, DLM Papers, 16:574).

43. DLM to Mortensen, 3 April 1951, DLM Papers, 5:1065.

44. DLM to Selby, 12 April 1951, DLM Papers, 6:875.

45. DLM to Graff, 4 May 1951, DLM Papers, 3:591.

46. Conversation: [Darel McConkey] to DLM, DLM Papers, 1:422–27; Selby to DLM, 3 May 1951, 17:805.

47. DLM to Lloyd A. Flanders, 11 January 1948, DLM Papers, 3:429.

48. Darel McConkey to DLM, 19 May 1951, DLM Papers, 14:1456.

49. DLM to Jim Holliday, 20 October 1951, DLM Papers, 4:482. Holliday worked with Morgan as assistant director at the Bancroft Library after taking his PhD in history at UC Berkeley in 1958, resigning in 1961 to teach full-time at San Francisco State University. Morgan tried for years to help Holliday get the William Swain letters and diary edited for publication. It finally appeared as *The World Rushed In: The California Gold Rush Experience* (New York: Simon & Schuster, 1981), one of the fundamental scholarly studies of the Gold Rush and which accomplished for its author what Morgan never could achieve—a financially successful book of history.

50. At the time the Norths and their Accokeek neighbors were the subject of an FBI investigation as communist subversives. David H. Price, *Threatening Anthropology: McCarthyism and the FBI's Surveillance of Activist Anthropologists* (Durham, NC: Duke University Press, 2004), 180–84.

51. DLM to Mortensen, 13 October 1951, DLM Papers, 5:1123.

52. DLM to Selby, 16 October 1951, DLM Papers, 6:878.

53. Marguerite J. Reese to DLM, 29 October 1951, DLM Papers, 19:1735.

54. Ruth Barton to DLM, 14 December 19[51], DLM Papers, 23:1511.

55. Selby to DLM, 17 December 1951, DLM Papers, 17:809.

56. DLM to MRM, [1–5 January 1952], fragment, Ms 143 2:15, UU-Ms.

57. Stanley Rinehart, Jr. to DLM, 5 January 1952, DLM Papers, 17:266.

58. Michael Korda, *Another Life*, 197.

59. DLM to Stanley Rinehart, Jr., 4 February 1952, DLM Papers, 6:481.

60. Letters were from Harrison Dale, Bernard DeVoto, and LeRoy Hafen (application file, John Simon Guggenheim Memorial Foundation archives, New York); D.L. Chambers to Patty, Bobbs-Merrill mss. 123: "Morgan, Dale Lowell. Jedediah Smith. R. R. & Promotional Material," Bobbs-Merrill Company records, Lilly Library, Indiana University, Bloomington.

61. Richard J. Schrader, "Introduction," *The Hoosier House: Bobbs-Merrill and Its Predecessors, 1850–1985: A Documentary Volume, Dictionary of Literary Biography*, vol. 291, ed. Richard J. Schrader (Farmington Hills, MI: Thomson Gale, 2004), xvii; also John Tebbel, *A History of Book Publishing in the United States, Volume 3: The Golden Age between the Wars* (New York: R. R. Bowker, 1978), 559–60.

62. DLM to Ivins, 1 March 1952, Mss B31 13:5, UHi; DLM Papers, 13:1188.

63. DLM to James Mathis, 30 January 1952, "Morgan, Dale L.," John Simon Guggenheim Memorial Foundation archives, New York.

64. DLM to Eugene Davidson (Yale University Press), 10 December 1952, DLM Papers, 2:1349.

65. DLM to JB, 26 January 1952, Ms 486 1:6[c], UU-Ms; DLM Papers, 2:12; DLM to Charles L. Camp, 3 February 1952, DLM Papers, 2:246.

66. DLM to CK, 16 February 1952, DLM Papers, 4:1173.

67. DLM to Greenwell, 12 May 1952, DLM Papers, 3:644; DLM to Brimhall, 7 May 1952, DLM Papers, 1:1600. cf. DLM to Israel A. Smith, 12 May 1952, 6:942.

68. DLM to MRM, 26 January 1952, Ms 143 2:9, UU-Ms.

69. EHM to DLM, 28 January 1952, DLM Papers, 22:1668; Ruth Barton to DLM, 28 January 1952, 23:1523.

70. Darel McConkey to DLM, 24 February 1952, DLM Papers, 14:1498.

71. DLM to Darel McConkey, 31 March 1952, DLM Papers, 5:585.

CHAPTER 12

1. DLM to Darel McConkey, 2 September 1952, Accn 3206, UU-Ms; DLM Papers, 5:594.

2. DLM to Israel A. Smith, 12 May 1952, DLM Papers, 6:942.

3. DLM to Fred Rosenstock, 7 November 1952, Ms 487 1:5, UU-Ms; DLM Papers, 6:575.

4. DLM to Darel McConkey, 4 May 1952, DLM Papers, 5:587.

5. DLM to CK, 27 May 1952, DLM Papers, 4:1178; DLM to JB, 28 May 1952, Ms 486 1:6[c], UU-Ms; 2:20; Leonard H. Kirkpatrick to DLM, 5 June 1952, 19:961; Kirkpatrick to Carl Christensen, 12 September 1952, 20:1535.

6. DLM to Kell, 4 September 1952, DLM Papers, 4:948.

7. DLM to Chambers, 7 September 1952, DLM Papers, 2:636.

8. DLM to Darel and Anna McConkey, 2 September 1952, DLM Papers, 5:594; DLM to Graff, 12 September 1952, Trustee Personal Papers, ser.3 7:28, Newberry Library, Chicago; DLM Papers, 3:598.

9. Charles Eberstadt to DLM, 17 September 1952, DLM Papers, 12:404; DLM to Eberstadt, 19 September 1952, 3:148; DLM to Eberstadt, 26 September 1952, 3:151; Eberstadt to DLM, 3 October 1952, 12:408.

10. Graff to DLM, 24 September 1952, Trustee Personal Papers, ser. 3 7:28, Newberry Library, Chicago; DLM Papers, 12:975.

11. Reader reports, Bobbs-Merrill mss. 123: "Morgan, Dale Lowell. Jedediah Smith. R. R. & Promotional Material," Bobbs-Merrill Company records, Lilly Library, Indiana University, Bloomington.

12. Harrison Platt to DLM, 20 November 1952, DLM Papers, 16:1648.

13. DLM to CK, 12 December 1952, DLM Papers, 4:1184.

14. These included an edited documentary series on the Eastern Shoshoni to the *Annals of Wyoming* (DLM to Lola Homsher, 8 December 1952, 4:621; publication of this series is considered in DLM, *Shoshonean Peoples and the Overland Trail: Frontiers of the Utah Superintendency of Indian Affairs, 1849–1869,* ed. Richard L. Saunders [Logan: Utah State University Press, 2007]); Morgan asked Bill Mulder if the *Western Humanities Review* was ready for the Dispersion bibliography (DLM to Mulder, 16 December 1952, Ms 44 11:3, UU-Ms; DLM Papers, 5:1292); and Morgan promised the *Utah Historical Quarterly* he would edit the James Holt reminiscence (DLM to Charles Eberstadt, 17 December 1952, DLM Papers, 3:165).

15. DLM to Colton Storm, 5 January 1953, DLM Papers, 6:1213.

16. DLM to Charles van Ravenswaay, 23 January 1953, DLM Papers, 9:86; DLM to Rosenstock, 6 February 1953, Ms 487 1:5, UU-Ms.

17. DLM to Camp, 3 February 1953, DLM Papers, 2:309; DLM to McConkey, 11 February 1953, 5:615. We have only Morgan's word on this point; state records from the officials involved were never transferred to archival custody.

18. DeVoto to DLM, 12 February 1953, DLM Papers, 12:49. In 1944 Stegner had written Morgan that "Benny DeVoto and I are determined, sooner or later, to pool our resources and send you at least one page of errata on one of your books." (Wally [Stegner] to DLM, 24 July 1944, Ms 143 2:41, UU-Ms; cf. DLM to MRM, 1944jul10, Ms 143 2:11, UU-Ms).

19. DLM to Platt, 24 March 1953, DLM Papers, 6:131.

20. DLM to MRM, 20 March 1953, Ms 143 2:9, UU-Ms.

21. DLM to JB, 15 March 1953, Ms 486 1:6[c], UU-Ms; DLM Papers, 2:36. The project provided Morgan about six weeks of income and finally gave the massive files a useable finding aid.

22. DLM to Darel McConkey, 2 April 1953, UU-Ms; DLM to Drake de Kay, 6 April 1953, DLM Papers, 8:77.

23. DeVoto to DLM, 12 February 1953, DLM Papers, 12:49.

24. DLM, "GPH," in *GPH: An Informal Record of George P. Hammond and His Era in the Bancroft Library* (Berkeley: The Friends of The Bancroft Library, 1965), 1–20.

25. The Navajo Tribe officially changed its name to "Navajo Nation" in 1969.

26. DLM to Platt, 19 April 1953, DLM Papers, 6:132.

27. DLM to George P. Hammond (hereafter GPH), 22, 28 April 1953, BANC MSS 70/89 14:1, CU-Banc; cf. GPH to Norman M. Littell, 1 May 1953, BANC MSS 70/89 14:1, CU-Banc.

28. GPH notes, 20 May 1953, BANC MSS 70/89 14:1, CU-Banc.

29. Harry [Platt] to Chambers, internal memo dated 28 Apr 19[53], Bobbs-Merrill mss. 123: "Morgan, Dale Lowell. Correspondence," Bobbs-Merrill Company records, Lilly Library, Indiana University, Bloomington.

30. DLM to Platt, 2 May 1953, DLM Papers, 6:135.

31. DLM to Darel McConkey, 11 May 1953, Accn 3206, UU-Ms; DLM to Harrison Platt, 19 May 1953, DLM Papers, 6:140.

32. DLM to Darel McConkey, 29 October 1952, Accn 3206, UU-Ms; DLM Papers, 5:598.

33. DLM to Camp, 20 October 1952, DLM Papers, 2:287. Morgan's comment may have been a response to a summary description by GPH published in GPH, "Manuscripts Collections in the Bancroft Library," *American Archivist* 13, no. 1 (January 1950): 15–26.

34. DLM to GPH, 19 November 1952, DLM Papers, 3:940.

35. GPH to DLM, 13 April 1953, BANC MSS 70/89 14:1, CU-Banc; DLM to Darel McConkey, 12 April 1953, Accn 3206, UU-Ms; 5:617; DLM to JB, 12 April 1953, Ms 486 1:6[c], UU-Ms. William Jerome Wilson, "Manuscripts in Microfilm: Problems of Librarian and Custodian," *Library Quarterly* 13, no. 3 (July 1943): 212–26.

36. GPH to DLM, 1 July 1953, BANC MSS 70/89 14:1, CU-Banc.

37. DLM to Platt, 14 July 1953, DLM Papers, 6:152.

38. Platt to DLM, 17 July 1953, DLM Papers, 16:1696.

39. DLM to Charles L. Camp, 3 September 1953, DLM Papers, 2:317.

40. DLM to EHM, 29 August 1953, DLM Papers, 21:809; DLM to GPH, 22 August 1953, BANC MSS 70/89 14:1, CU-Banc; DLM to Pat Tull, 19 September 1953, 6:1439.

41. DLM to GPH, 14 November 1953, BANC MSS 70/89 24:17, CU-Banc.

42. GPH to DLM, 5 December 1952, BANC MSS 70/89 24:17, CU-Banc.

43. DLM to Charles Eberstadt, 5 September 1953, DLM Papers, 3:172.

44. DLM to Charles Eberstadt, 19 September 1953, DLM Papers, 3:174.

45. Platt to DLM, 5 November 1953, DLM Papers, 16:1722.

46. DLM to Platt, 17 December 1953, DLM Papers, 6:172.

47. DLM to Graff, 26 October 1953, Trustee Personal Papers, ser.3 7:28, Newberry Library, Chicago; DLM Papers, 3:607; DLM to GPH, 15 December 1952, BANC MSS 70/89 14:1, CU-Banc. Morgan's annotated copy of the

book either never arrived at Brigham Young University in 1971 or was discarded afterward; in any case, it has since disappeared.

48. DLM to EHM, 13 September 1953, DLM Papers, 21:813.

CHAPTER 13

1. DLM to EHM, 13 September 1953, DLM Papers, 21:813.
2. DLM to Darel and Anna McConkey, 23 December 1954, Accn 3206, UU-Ms.
3. Benjamin W. Frazier, "Postwar Faculty Recruitment," *Journal of Higher Education* 15, no. 9 (December 1944): 476–81.
4. Ernest V. Hollis and Ralph S. M. Flynt, "Some Factors Influencing Postwar College Enrollments," *Bulletin of the American Association of College Professors* 30, no. 4 (Winter 1944): 525–34; R. H. Eckelberry, "The Approval of Institutions under the GI Bill," *Journal of Higher Education* 16, no. 3 (March 1945): 121–26.
5. Charles B. Nam, "Impact of the 'GI Bills' on the Educational Level of the Male Population," *Social Forces* 43, no.1 (October 1964): 26–32; Carl L. Bankston III, "The Mass Production of Credentials: Subsidies and the Rise of Higher Education Industry," *Independent Review* 15, no. 3 (Winter 2011): 325–49.
6. Roger L. Geiger, *The History of American Higher Education: Learning and Culture from the Founding to World War II* (Princeton, NJ: Princeton University Press, 2015), 423–78, 548–51.
7. Quoted in William L. Joyce, "The Evolution of the Concept of Special Collections in American Research Libraries," *Rare Books & Manuscripts Librarianship* 3, no.1 (Spring 1988): 19; Bishop, "Rare Book Rooms in Libraries," 375–85.
8. Amy Hildreth Chen, *Placing Papers: The American Literary Archives Market* (Amherst: University of Massachusetts Press, 2020).
9. DLM to FMB, 11 April 1954, DLM Papers, 1:1734.
10. Mary Withington, *A Catalogue of Manuscripts in the Collection of Western Americana Founded by William Robertson Coe, Yale University Library* (New Haven, CT: Yale University Press, 1952).
11. Doris Marian Wright, *A Guide to the Mariano Guadalupe Vallejo Documentos para la Historia de California, 1780–1875,* Guides to the Manuscript Collections no. 1 (Berkeley: University of California Press, 1953).
12. DLM to GPH, 27 January 1954, DLM Papers, 3:950.
13. DLM to GPH, 31 January 1954, DLM Papers, 3:954.
14. DLM to EHM, 16 February 1954, DLM Papers, 21:843.
15. DLM to Darel McConkey, 13 March 1954, Accn 3206, UU-Ms.
16. DLM to EHM, 7 April 1954, DLM Papers, 21:856; DLM to FMB, 11 April 1954, 1:1734.
17. DLM to GPH, 12 February 1955, BANC MSS 70/89 24:19, CU-Banc; DLM Papers, 3:1001.

18. Doris Wright to DLM, 1 September 1954, DLM Papers, 20:973; DLM to GPH 1 September 1954, 3:956; DLM to Wright, 1 September 1954, 9:286, 288.

19. DLM to EHM, 3 November 1955, DLM Papers, 21:965.

20. DLM to GPH, 21 November 1954, BANC MSS 70/89 24:18, CU-Banc.

21. DLM to Mortensen, 19 September 1954, DLM Papers, 5:1191.

22. DLM to Mortensen, 14 July 1955, DLM Papers, 5:1218.

23. DLM to Joseph E. Colgan, 18 May 1955, DLM Papers, 2:769.

24. DLM to CK, 20 October 1955, DLM Papers, 4:1204.

25. Charles Eberstadt to DLM, 1 February 1956, DLM Papers, 12:453.

26. DLM to Norman M. Littell, 7 August 1955, BANC MSS 70/89 14:2, CU-Banc.

27. DLM to GPH, 2 December 1955, BANC MSS 70/89 14:6, CU-Banc. Anthropologists argued strenuously about the ethics of this case. Cf. Wilcomb E. Washburn, "Anthropological Advocacy in the Hopi-Navajo Land Dispute," *American Anthropologist* 91, no. 3 (1989): 738–43; Richard O. Clemmer, David F. Aberle, Joseph G. Jorgensen, and Thayer Scudder, "Anthropology, Anthropologists, and the Navajo-Hopi Land Dispute: Reply to Washburn," *American Anthropologist* 91, no. 3 (1989): 743–53; Peter M. Whiteley and David F. Aberle, "Can Anthropologists Be Neutral in Land Disputes? The Hopi-Navajo Case," *Man* 24, no. 2 (1989): 340–44.

28. DLM to Colgan, 25 September, 31 October 1957, DLM Papers, 2:906, 2:915.

29. DLM to Colgan, 5 September 1957, DLM Papers, 2:901.

30. DLM to Edgar Carter, 8 March 1957, BANC MSS 70/89 14:3, CU-Banc; DLM Papers, 2:340.

31. Mortensen's first exploratory offer of the Utah State Archivist position was in 1951 (Mortensen to DLM, 22 August 1951, DLM Papers, 16:576; DLM to Mortensen, 13 October 1951, 5:1123). The second offer, conditional on funding which never came, was in early 1953 (DLM to Camp, 3 February 1953, 2:309; DLM to Darel and Anna McConkey, 11 February 1953, Accn 2306, UU-Ms). Another flutter came in 1954 (Mortensen to DLM, 26 April 1954, 16:628) before Cooley was hired in July (Mortensen to DLM, 15 July 1954, 16:633). DLM to GPH and GPH to DLM, 9 January 1957, BANC MSS 70/89 14:2, CU-Banc.

32. DLM to EHM, 6 February 1957, DLM Papers, 21:1021; DLM to JB, 28 May 1957, 2:60.

33. DLM to Rosenstock, 21 August 1957, Ms 487 1:6, UU-Ms.

34. DLM to Graff, 21 September 1959, Trustee Personal Papers, ser.3 Graff 7:28, Newberry Library, Chicago; 2:1153.

35. DLM to Colgan, 9 November 1959, DLM Papers, 2:988.

36. MRM to DLM, 19 November 1959, DLM Papers, 15:1695; DLM to EHM, 14 December 1959, 21:1145.

37. DLM to Carl I. Wheat, 29 December 1959, DLM Papers, 7:456.

38. DLM to EHM, 24 March 1961, DLM Papers, 21:1208.
39. DLM to JB, 10 March 1960, DLM Papers, 2:69.
40. DLM to GPH, 1 April 1960, DLM Papers, 3:1134.
41. James M. Goodman and Gary L. Thompson. "The Hopi-Navaho Land Dispute." *American Indian Law Review* 3, no. 2 (1975): 397–17; David M. Brugge, *The Navajo-Hopi Land Dispute*; cf. Richard O. Clemmer, "Crying for the Children of Sacred Ground: A Review Article on the Hopi-Navajo Land Dispute," *American Indian Quarterly* 15, no.2 (Spring 1991): 25–30.
42. DLM to GPH, 6 May 1961, DLM Papers, 3:1163; DLM to Graff, 10 February 1962, Trustee Personal Papers, ser.3 Graff 7:28, Newberry Library, Chicago; 2:1168; DLM to Colgan, 26 March 1962, 2:1066.
43. DLM to James D. Hart, 27 March 1962, DLM Papers, 4:408.
44. Donald Coney to Hart, 19 April 1962, DLM Papers, 20:1358.
45. DLM to EHM, 7 January 1962, DLM Papers, 21:1248.

CHAPTER 14
1. DLM to Carl Wheat, 29 December 1959, DLM Papers, 7:456.
2. DLM to Darel McConkey, 8 April 1959, DLM Papers, 5:646.
3. DLM to EHM, 11 March 1956, DLM Papers, 21:984; DLM to Mortensen, 3 April 1956, 5:1227; DLM to FMB, 2 April 1956, 1:1786.
4. DLM to EHM, 22 July 1961, DLM Papers, 21:1225.
5. Jim McConkey to author, 27 November 2021, letter in author's possession.
6. DLM to Camp, 2 February 1954, DLM Papers, 2:322.
7. DLM to DeVoto, 23 February 1954, M0001 117:352, CSt-SC; Ms 579 1:3, UU-Ms; DLM Papers, 2:1482.
8. DLM to EHM, 11 August 1954, DLM Papers, 21:894.
9. Platt to DLM, 15 April 1954, DLM Papers, 16:1734.
10. Royalty statements for *The Humboldt: Highroad to the West*, DLM Papers, 25:3204–26; for *Jedediah Smith and the Opening of the West*, 25:2190–597.
11. [Philip Vaudrin], "Morgan: Jedediah Smith," Alfred A. Knopf records, 157:7, TxU-Hu.
12. Alfred A. Knopf, Sr., to Clifford Crist, 17 November 1949, Knopf records, 252:12, TxU-Hu.
13. Knopf to DLM, 12 January 1954, Knopf records, 157:7, TxU-Hu; DLM Papers, 14:408.
14. Robert Utley, *A Life Wild and Perilous* (New York: Holt, 1997), later published as *After Lewis and Clark: Mountain Men and the Paths to the Pacific* (Lincoln: University of Nebraska Press, 2004). DLM to Carl Wheat, 4 March 1954, DLM Papers, 7:114. Despite his own careful search of federal records, Morgan failed to discover an 1855 letter of George Gibbs to John Lambert among US Department of the Interior records, in which Gibbs reported that a "joint commission of army and navy officers" bought Jedediah Smith's original map (drawn for Smith by Charles DeWard, not

by Smith himself) in 1850 while in Oregon (George Gibbs to John Lambert, 25 April 1855, Entry 725, Record Group 48, National Archives, Washington, DC, published in "Archives Corner," *Castor Canadensis* [Spring 2020]: 11).

15. Conversation: RKG to DLM, 12 January 1962, DLM Papers, 1:599.
16. Mortensen to DLM, 1 November 1955, DLM Papers, 16:671.
17. Rosenstock to DLM, 17 January 1955, DLM Papers, 17:464; 13 March 1955, 17:469
18. DLM to Carl Wheat, 20 April 1955, DLM Papers, 7:186.
19. MRM to DLM, 24, 31 July 1956, DLM Papers, 15:1498, 1502.
20. DLM to Colgan, 4 July 1956, DLM Papers, 2:824; DLM to Rosenstock, 6 July 1956, Ms 487 1:6, UU-Ms; DLM Papers, 6:593.
21. Rosenstock to DLM, 15 July 1956, Ms 487 1:6, UU-Ms.
22. Parke-Bernet Galleries, *Western Americana, Many of Great Rarity, Formed by W. J. Holliday* (New York: Parke-Bernet Galleries, 1954); Jim Holliday, interview, 1994. Morgan coached and prodded Holliday politically through an abbreviated career as a municipal museum director, but particularly for fifteen years in his editing of the William Swain diary, which finally made it to print a decade after Morgan's death as *The World Rushed In: The California Gold Rush Experience* (New York: Simon & Schuster, 1981).
23. Carl Wheat to DLM, 26 August, 1 September 1955, DLM Papers, 18:147, 18:148.
24. Carl Wheat by Helen Wheat to DLM, 25 July 1956, DLM Papers, 18:171.
25. DLM to EHM, 24 September 1955, DLM Papers, 21:959.
26. DLM to Carl Wheat, 28 September 1955, DLM Papers, 7:204.
27. Rosenstock to DLM, 15 August 1957, DLM Papers, 17:499.
28. DLM to FMB, 21 December 1956, MS 360 7:13, UU-Ms.
29. Helen Wheat to DLM, 22 July 1956, DLM Papers, 18:169; DLM to Helen Wheat, 24 July 1956, 7:242.
30. DLM to EHM, 10 September 1957, DLM Papers, 21:1042.
31. EHM to DLM, 4 February 1958, DLM Papers, 22:2186; DLM to EHM, 14 February 1958, 21:1061.
32. DLM to Carl Wheat, 12 April 1958, Accn 1106 1:1, UU-Ms.
33. CK to DLM, 5 September 1959, DLM Papers, 14:224.
34. DLM to GPH, 14 November 1960, DLM Papers, 3:1148.
35. DLM to Knopf, 14 March 1961, Knopf records, 464:5, TxU-Hu (DLM Papers, 4:1365); Knopf to DLM, 17 March 1961, Knopf records 464:5, TxU-Hu (DLM Papers, 14:430).
36. Jay Monaghan to DLM, 25 March 1961, DLM Papers, 16:417.
37. DLM to Graff, 4 January 1961, Trustee Personal Papers, ser.3 Graff 7:28, ICN; DLM Papers, 2:1159; DLM to Archie Hanna, 25 January 1961, 3:1400.

38. Helen Wheat to DLM, 11 May 1961, DLM Papers, 18:308; DLM to Carl and Helen Wheat, 15 May 1961, 7:531.

39. DLM to Colgan, 9 August 1961, DLM Papers, 2:1054.

40. DLM to Colgan, 12 September 1961, DLM Papers, 2:1056.

41. JB to DLM, 11 September 1961, Mss B103 4:8, UHi; Ms 579 2:14, UU-Ms.

42. Arthur Crawford to JB, 22 December 1958, Mss B103 4:2, UHi. Cf. JB to DLM, 11 September 1961, Mss B103 4:8, UHi; Everett Cooley to JB, 28 January 1969, Mss B103, 7:1, UHi; Cooley to Ray A. Billington, 26 December 1973, Ms 579 2:14, UU-Ms.

43. DLM to FMB, 22 October 1961, DLM Papers, 1:1751.

44. Monaghan to DLM, 16 November 1961, DLM Papers, 16:426.

45. GPH to DLM, 18 November 1961, DLM Papers, 12:1652.

46. James D. West, "Dale Lowell Morgan," DLM Papers, 25:2506.

47. DLM to EHM, 3 May 1960, DLM Papers, 21:1161; "Among Our New Acquisitions," *Bulletin of the Missouri Historical Society* 16, no. 3 (April 1960): 282.

48. Check stub, DLM Papers, 25:2198; DLM to Bobbs-Merrill, 1 May 1962, 7:1039; Lois Stewart [Bobbs-Merrill] to DLM, 14 May 1962, 20:448; John A. Hawgood to DLM, 31 October 1962, 19:513; DLM to Lois Stewart, 5 November 1962, 8:1591; DLM to Hawgood, 15 November 1952, 8:462; John Bright-Holmes [Eyre & Spottiswoode] to DLM, 29 November 1962, 18:1120.

49. DLM to Carl Wheat, 16 August 1962, DLM Papers, 7:616

50. DLM to EHM, 8 August 1962, DLM Papers, 21:1264.

51. DLM to GPH, 18 August 1955, BANC MSS 70/89 14:2, CU-Banc. Howell J. Heaney, "Thomas W. Streeter, Collector, 1883–1965," *Papers of the Bibliographical Society of America* 65, no. 3 (1971): 243–56. Streeter's collection of Texas imprints and manuscripts had been sold to Yale University in 1957. The high points of the remaining collection were auctioned in the legendary seven-part, twenty-three-session "Streeter Sale" between 1966 and 1969, arguably the greatest bibliographic event of US history. Parke-Bernet Galleries, *The Celebrated Collection of Americana Formed by the Late Thomas Winthrop Streeter,* 8 vols. (New York: Parke-Bernet Galleries, 1966–1970).

52. Helen Wheat to DLM, 19 November 1962, DLM Papers, 18:345.

53. Richard Dillon, review of *In Pursuit of the Golden Dream,* by Howard C. Gardiner, *Colorado Magazine* 47, no. 4 (1970): 339.

54. Lois Stewart to DLM, 28 December 1962, DLM Papers, 20:449; DLM to Stewart, 3 January 1963, 8:1592; Stewart to DLM, 11 January 1963, 20:450. In 1969, Bobbs-Merrill alerted Morgan that Eyre & Spottiswoode, a British reprint house, wanted to issue *Jedediah Smith and the Opening of the West* in a European edition if Morgan was no longer planning to revise the work. Dale fired back a letter that he certainly did plan to revise the work—heavily. He pointed to new discoveries with the confident projection that

a major revision would be published perhaps in 1970. Though the firm produced a British edition of Fawn Brodie's *No Man Knows My History* in 1963, it never got Morgan's book—but then the *Jedediah Smith* revision was never completed either (Robert H. Andersen [Bobbs-Merrill] to DLM, 9 December 1968, 18:824; DLM to Robert M. Amussen [*sic*], 12 December 1968, 7:888; Andersen to DLM, 31 December 1968, 18:825.).

55. DLM to FMB, 11 September 1962, MS 360 7:13, UU-Ms; 1:1755.
56. DLM to Frances H. Stadler, 28 March 1963, DLM Papers, 6:1064.
57. DLM to Hanna, 16 April 1963, DLM Papers, 3:1417.
58. DLM to RKG, 18 September 1963, Talisman Press records, 2143:2, California State Library, Sacramento; DLM Papers, 3:759; RKG to DLM, 18 September 1963, 12:1237.
59. DLM to EHM, 29 September 1963, DLM Papers, 21:1306.
60. RKG to DLM, 1 November 1963, DLM Papers, 12:1258.
61. DLM to RKG, 14 November 1963, Talisman Press records, 2143:2, California State Library, Sacramento; DLM Papers, 3:784.
62. RKG to DLM, 26 November 1963, DLM Papers, 12:1282.
63. RKG, "Foreword" in Richard L. Saunders, *Eloquence from a Silent World* (Salt Lake City, Caramon Press, 1990), vii.
64. DLM to James R. Scobie, 16 December 1963, DLM Papers, 6:851.
65. The best single account of the dual editorial debacle is DLM to Barry, 17 January 1964, DLM Papers, 1:1071.
66. DLM to Barry, 17 January 1964, DLM Papers, 1:1071.
67. DLM to Colgan, 27 December 1963, DLM Papers, 2:1103.
68. Mildred Goosman to DLM, 30 June 1964, DLM Papers, 12:912. The volume was finally published as Prince Alexander Philipp Maximilian, *The North American Journals of Prince Maximilian of Wied,* eds., Stephen S. Witte and Marsha V. Gallagher, trans. by William J. Orr, Paul Schach, and Dieter Karch (Norman: University of Oklahoma Press, 2017).

CHAPTER 15

1. DLM to Carl Wheat, 29 December 1959, DLM Papers, 7:456.
2. Avery O. Craven, "An Historical Adventure," *Journal of American History* 51, no. 1 (June 1964): 5.
3. Darel and Anna McConkey to DLM, 10 April 1960, DLM Papers, 14:1763.
4. MRM to DLM, [undated], 15:2259; MRM to DLM, 4 March 1958, DLM Papers, 15:1609.
5. MRM to DLM, undated [19 May 1960], DLM Papers, 15:1724.
6. "Former University of Utah Art Department Chair Reflected Contemporary [*sic*] Life on His Canvas," *The Eagle* (Utah State University Eastern, Price), 4 December 2003.
7. Darel McConkey to DLM, 8 January 1961, DLM Papers, 14:1812.

8. Anna McConkey to DLM, 31 January 1961, DLM Papers, 14:1819; DLM to Anna McConkey, 1 February 1961, Accn 3206, UU-Ms; DLM Papers, 5:698.

9. Anna McConkey to DLM, 3 February 1961, DLM Papers, 14:1821.

10. Anna McConkey discovered she had breast cancer in 1968 at age 60 but was unable to afford treatment until qualifying for Medicare at 65. By then it was too late. She died of the cancer in May 1978 (interview with Jim McConkey, 2018, transcript in author's possession).

11. Thomas S. Kuhn, *The Structure of Scientific Revolutions,* 4th ed, University of Chicago Press, 2012), passim.

12. Frederick Jackson Turner, "The Significance of the Frontier in American History," in *The Frontier in American History*, ed. Ray Allen Billington (New York: Holt, Rinehart and Winston, 1962), 1–38. Turner continued (and modified) his thematic explorations in *Rise of the New West, 1818–1829* (Harper & Bros., 1906) and *The United States, 1830–1850: The Nations and Its Sections* (1935; reis., New York: Peter Smith, 1950). Being a pioneer in the field, Turner's work has engendered dozens of responses and comments which are too many to be cited here.

13. Carlton J. H. Hayes, "The American Frontier—Frontier of What?" *American Historical Review* 51, no. 2 (January 1946): 199–216.

14. Bernard DeVoto, introduction to *Beyond the Hundredth Meridian: John Wesley Powell and the Second Opening of the West*, by Wallace Stegner (1954; reis., New York: Penguin Books, 1992), xv–xxiii.

15. Earl Pomeroy, "Toward a Reorientation of Western History: Continuity and Environment," *Mississippi Valley Historical Review* 41, no. 4 (March 1955):579–600. cf. William H. Lyon, "The Third Generation and the Frontier Hypothesis," *Arizona and the West* 4, no. 1 (Spring 1962):45–50.

16. c.f. Preston Nibley, *LDS Adventure Stories* (Salt Lake City: Bookcraft, 1953), *Stalwarts of Mormonism* (Salt Lake City: Bookcraft, 1954); Bryant S. Hinckley, *The Faith of Our Pioneer Fathers* (Salt Lake City: Bookcraft, 1956); E. Cecil McGavin, *The Mormon Pioneers* (Salt Lake City: Stevens & Wallis, 1947).

17. Charles Redd to Leonard Arrington, 25 July 1957, LJAHA series X, 79:2, ULA; William Mulder. "The Mormons in American History." Twenty-first Frederick Williams Reynolds Lecture, 14 January 1957 (1959, reis.; Salt Lake City: University of Utah Press, 1981), 59–77.

18. Marvin S. Hill, "The Historiography of Mormonism," *Church History* 28, no. 4 (December 1959): 418–26. The theme was continued in Rodman Paul, "The Mormons as a Theme in Western Historical Writing," *Journal of American History* 54, no. 3 (December 1967): 511–23.

19. DLM to Leonard J. Arrington, 24 June 1952, LJAHA ser. X 26:3, ULA; DLM Papers, 1:885; Arrington to DLM, 28 July 1952, 9:562.

20. Arrington to S. George Ellsworth, 23 October 1956, LJAHA ser. X 26:5, ULA.

21. John T. Bernhard to LJA, 5 December 1960, Arrington to Bernhard, 8 December 1960, LJAHA ser. X 27:5, ULA. Given Wilkinson's insistence on loyalty and control, it is doubtful such an entity could have succeeded.
22. Aileen Fyfe and Anna Gielas, "Introduction: Editorship and the Editing of Scientific Journals, 1750–1950," *Centaurus* 62, no. 1 (February 2020): 5–20.
23. Howard M. Bahr, "Simple, Common-sense Explanation": Thomas F. O'Dea and the Book of Mormon," *Journal of Mormon History* 32 no. 3 (Fall 2006): 104–40.
24. Patricia J. Gumport and Stuart K. Syndman, "The Formal Organization of Knowledge: An Analysis of Academic Structure," *Journal of Higher Education* 73, no. 3 (May/June 2002): 375–408;
25. DLM to FMB, 2 April 1956, DLM Papers, 1:1786.
26. DLM to EHM, 21 October 1961, DLM Papers, 21:1235.
27. This section is summarized from the able historiographic overview presented at the conference by Ray A. Billington, "The Santa Fe Conference and the Writing of Western History," in *Probing the American West: Papers from the Santa Fe Conference*, eds. K. Ross Toole, John Alexander Carroll, A. R. Mortensen, and Robert M. Utley (Santa Fe: Museum of New Mexico Press, 1962), 1–16; Oscar Osburn Winther, *A Classified Bibliography of the Periodical Literature of the Trans-Mississippi West, 1811–1957*, 2nd ed. (Bloomington: Indiana University Press, 1961).

CHAPTER 16
1. DLM to EHM, 1 June 1964, DLM Papers, 22:32.
2. DLM to Allan Nevins, 15 February 1964, DLM Papers, 5:1326.
3. DLM to EHM, 18 January 1964, DLM Papers, 22:14; Robert H. Becker to DLM, undated [15–28 Mar 1964], 9:1031. Morgan's similarly undated draft job outline is found in DLM to Becker, 1:1365.
4. Ralph D. Thomson to DLM, 18, 27 March 1964, DLM Papers, 20:561, 20:563.
5. MRM to DLM, undated [10–14 September 1961], DLM Papers, 15:1795.
6. MRM to DLM, undated [10–14 September 1961], DLM Papers, 15:1795.
7. EHM to DLM, 7 November 1961, DLM Papers, 23:272.
8. JB to DLM, 9 December 1964, DLM Papers, 10:968.
9. FMB to DLM, [December 1964?], DLM Papers, 10:311.
10. DLM to GPH, 4 December 1964, DLM Papers, 3:1246.
11. DLM to EHM and Ruth Barton, 30 December 1964, DLM Papers, 22:49.
12. DLM to Edgar Carter, 23 December 1964, DLM Papers, 2:520.
13. Graff to DLM, 11 January 1954, Trustee Personal Papers, ser.3 7:28, Newberry Library, Chicago; 12:989; DLM to Graff, 14 January 1960, DLM Papers, 2:1157; DLM to Darel and Anna McConkey, 31 March 1960, Accn 3206, UU-Ms; DLM Papers, 5:677
14. Graff to DLM, 11 January 1954, 29 December 1959, Trustee Personal Papers, ser.3 7:28, Newberry Library, Chicago.

15. Harry J. Owens to DLM, 10 September 1963, DLM Papers, 16:1274. Morgan himself suggested the first book he edited for Lakeside Press. Owens to DLM, 9 January 1964, 16:1280.

16. Owens to DLM, 3 January 1963, DLM Papers, 16:1273; Owens to DLM, 10, 19 September 1963, 16:1274, 1276.

17. DLM to Graff, 23 March 1964, DLM Papers, 3:630: "They grow up around me, and now and then I harvest one."

18. DLM to Floyd Risvold, 2 June 1964, DLM Papers, 6:518.

19. GPH to DLM, 7 August 1964, DLM Papers, 12:1675.

20. DLM to EHM, 9 October 1964, DLM Papers, 22:39.

21. GPH to DLM, 7 August 1964, DLM Papers, 12:1675; DLM to GPH, 4 December 1964, 3:1246.

22. DLM to Tek Osborn, 21 March 1966, DLM Papers, 5:1461.

23. DLM to Angus Cameron, 21 March 1966, Knopf records 464:5, TxU-HU; DLM Papers, 2:197; Cameron to DLM, 24 March 1966, Alfred A. Knopf records 464:5, TxU-Hu; DLM Papers, 10:1279.

24. DLM to R. C. Swanson, 31 August 1966, DLM Papers, 6:1312.

25. DLM to Risvold, 4 October 1966, DLM Papers, 6:537.

26. Osborn to DLM, 29 March 1967, DLM Papers, 16:1232.

27. Owens to DLM, 27 April 1967, DLM Papers, 16:1316; Harold W. Tribolet to DLM, 1 May 1967, 17:1661.

28. Swanson to DLM, 7 August 1967, DLM Papers, 17:1467.

29. DLM to EHM, 30 April 1967, DLM Papers, 22:192.

30. Bob Morgan to DLM, 31 March 1965, DLM Papers, 23:1086; DLM to Ida Holmes, 2 April 1965, 22:421.

31. DLM to EHM, 6 June 1965, DLM Papers, 22:74.

32. DLM to Carl and Helen Wheat, 15 June 1965, DLM Papers, 7:712; DLM to EHM, 6 June 1965, 22:74; Jim Holliday to DLM, 28 October 1965, 13:664. Morgan's side of the correspondence was not retained.

33. DLM to EHM, 30 April 1965, DLM Papers, 22:62.

34. Edward K. Markell to DLM, 15 June 1965, DLM Papers, 19:1223.

35. Conversation notes, [23 August 1965], DLM Papers, 1:701–2; DLM to EHM, 23 August 1965, 22:93; Robert Feldman and Dwight Fitterer to DLM, 24 August 1965, 20:1009; DLM to EHM, 26 August 1965, 22:94; Mary Larsen [Kaiser Foundation Research Institute Diabetic Research Program] to DLM, 16 February 1966, 19:1019.

36. Paul J. H. L. Peeters, Marloes T. Bazelier, Hubert G. M. Leufkens, Frank de Vries, and Marie L. DeBruin, "The Risk of Colorectal Cancer in Patients with Type 2 Diabetes: Associations with Treatment Stage and Obesity," *Diabetes Care* 38, no. 3 (March 2015): 495–502; MRM to DLM, 26 August 1965, 17:142; DLM to MRM, 20 September 1965, 5:797.

37. DLM to Carl and Helen Wheat, 15 June 1965, DLM Papers, 7:712.

38. DLM to ETH, 31 July 1965, DLM Papers, 4:193.

39. DLM to Helen Kennedy, 19 July 1965, DLM Papers, 4:1271; DLM to Carl and Helen Wheat, 19 July 1965, 7:715

40. DLM to EHM, 26 July 1965, DLM Papers, 22:87.

41. DLM to EHM, 16 September 1965, DLM Papers, 22:97.

42. MRM to DLM, 26 August 1965, DLM Papers, 17:142; DLM to MRM, 20 September 1965, 5:797.

43. MRM to DLM, 11 October 1965, DLM Papers, 16:2076; 14 October 1965, 15:2074.

44. DLM to GPH, 20 October 1965, DLM Papers, 3:1269.

45. DLM to Anna McConkey, 4 June 1964, Accn 3206, UU-Ms.

46. DLM to GPH, 10 January 1965, BANC MSS 70/89 14:4, CU-Banc; DLM Papers, 3:1285.

47. DLM to GPH, 18 January 1966, BANC MSS 70/89 14:4, CU-Banc; 3:1293; Hunter Dupree to DLM, 18 January 1966, DLM Papers, 12:104.

48. DLM to GPH, 16 February 1966, BANC MSS 70/89 14:4, CU-Banc; DLM Papers, 3:1305.

49. Becker to DLM, undated [21–28 March 1966], DLM Papers, 9:1033; Becker to DLM, undated [30 March–15 April 1966], 9:1034.

50. Edgar Carter to DLM, 10 April 1966, DLM Papers, 10:1625.

51. DLM to Israel A. Smith, 9 July 1956, DLM Papers, 6:944.

52. Wallace Stegner, *The Gathering of Zion: The Story of the Mormon Trail* (New York: McGraw Hill, 1965), 1–13.

53. Leonard J. Arrington and Davis Bitton, *Mormons and Their Historians* (Salt Lake City: University of Utah Press, 1988), 126–46.

54. Leonard J. Arrington, "Reflections on the Founding and Purpose of the Mormon History Association, 1965–1983," *Journal of Mormon History* 10 (1983): 91–103. cf. Ted Warner to Arrington, 5 September 1965; Arrington to M. R. Merrill, 31 August 1965, LJAHA ser. 1 12:59, ULA.

55. Leonard J. Arrington, "The Secularization of Mormon History and Culture" (presentation at 5th Annual Western History Association Conference, Helena, Montana, October 14–16, 1965); Arrington, "Scholarly Studies of Mormonism in the Twentieth Century," *Dialogue* 1, no. 1 (1966): 15–32.

56. DLM to Rodman W. Paul, 4 August 1966, DLM Papers, 6:86. Paul's presentation was eventually published as "The Mormons as a Theme in Western Historical Writing," *Journal of American History* 54, no. 3 (December 1967): 511–23.

57. Paul to DLM, 11 August 1966, DLM Papers, 16:1363.

58. UHi Publications Committee report, Ms 114 15:1, UU-Ms.

59. Thomas W. Streeter, *Bibliography of Texas, 1795–1845,* 5 vols. (Cambridge, MA: Harvard University Press, 1955–1960). Peter Crawley's *Descriptive Bibliography of the Mormon Church,* 3 vols. (Provo, UT: Brigham Young University Religious Studies Center, 1997–2012), published years later, is the closest approximation to what Morgan wanted to produce.

60. DLM to Cooley, 19 September 1966, DLM Papers, 2:1190; DLM to Hanna, 16 September 1965, 3:1426. Where Crawley included only works produced by the Mormons, Morgan's bibliography would have included anything at all relative to the church, positive or negative.
61. Richard T. Ely, "Economic Aspects of Mormonism," *Harper's Monthly Magazine* 106 (1903): 677–78.
62. Marvin S. Hill, "The Historiography of Mormonism," *Church History* 28 no. 4 (December 1959): 418–26.
63. DLM to EHM, 9 July 1966, DLM Papers, 22:149.
64. DLM to Cameron, 11 July 1966, Knopf records 464:5, TxU-Hu; 2:198; Cameron to DLM, 23 July 1966, DLM Papers, 10:1281.
65. DLM to Todd I. Berens, 20 July 1966, DLM Papers, 1:1412.
66. DLM to Richard Y. Thurman, 3 August 1966, DLM Papers, 8:1698, 20:571.
67. MRM to DLM, 21 September 1966, DLM Papers, 15:2124; 14 November 1966, 15:2137; Conversation with [Donald Jackson], undated [July 1966], 1:184.
68. DLM to Coney, 28 October 1966, DLM Papers, 7:1280.
69. DLM to Coney, 21 November 1966, DLM Papers, 7:1283. The work, which was hastily rough-drafted only through 1836 (not 1849), is reprinted in DLM, *Dale Morgan on the Mormons,* vol. 2, 348–75. Morgan was not the only library employee upset. Donald Coney addressed the matter in his annual "Report of the University Librarian, 1966–67," *CU News* 22, no. 26 (29 June 1967): 7–8. Research was a stated expectation for a faculty appointment, and, as such, the system supported effort toward meeting the requirement; staff appointments—even if the individual had a terminal degree—had no such expectation and therefore no cause.
70. DLM to Joel E. Ferris, 30 March 1954, DLM Papers, 8:220.
71. National Center for Education Statistics, *The Condition of Education 1980, Statistical Report* (Washington, DC: Government Printing Office, 1980).
72. Seymour Lipset and Everett C. Ladd, Jr, "The Changing Social Origins of American Academics," *Qualitative and Quantitative Social Research: Papers in Honor of Paul F. Lazarsfeld,* eds. Robert Merton, James S. Coleman, and Peter H. Rossi (New York: Free Press, 1979), 319–38.

CHAPTER 17
1. DLM to Tobie, 26 August 1966, DLM Papers, 6:1410.
2. DLM to Tobie, 26 August 1966, DLM Papers, 6:1410.
3. DLM to ETH, 7 February 1967, DLM Papers, 4:227.
4. DLM to MRM, 7 February 1967, DLM Papers, 5:799.
5. MRM to DLM, 5 October 1967, DLM Papers, 15:2185.
6. MRM to DLM, 22 August 1967, DLM Papers, 15:2169.
7. Gerald "Jerry" Finnin, interview with Everett Cooley and Della Dye, transcript, 1976, Ms 143 1:2, UU-Ms.

8. Craig L. Foster, "Madeline McQuown, Dale Morgan, and the Great Unfinished Brigham Young Biography," *Dialogue: A Journal of Mormon Thought* 31 (Summer 1998): 111–23.

9. MRM to FMB, undated [22 August 1967], DLM Papers, 15:2171.

10. Fawn M. Brodie, *Thomas Jefferson: An Intimate History* (New York: W. W. Norton, 1974).

11. Foster, "Madeline McQuown," 122. Craig Foster is certainly correct that Dale Morgan "carried the weight of [McQuown's] deceit by encouraging and promoting a book that would never appear, thus risking his reputation as a scholar and mentor," but Morgan was as deceived about the work as effectively by McQuown as was everyone else. Newell Bringhurst, "Fawn Brodie's Thomas Jefferson: The Making of Popular and Controversial Biography," *Pacific Historical Review* 62, no. 4 (November 1993): 433–54.

12. DLM to Leland D. Case, 21 February 1967, DLM Papers, 2:541.

13. DLM to Knopf, 22 February 1967, Knopf records 525:8, TxU-Hu; DLM Papers, 4:1375.

14. Knopf to Oscar Lewis, 22 August 1967, Knopf records addenda 17:8, TxU-Hu. Neither Morgan nor Holliday began the project, and Powell's diary was finally published as a limited-edition book as H. M. T. Powell, *Santa Fe Trail to California, 1849–1852,* ed. Douglas S. Watson (New York: Sol Lewis, 1981).

15. Cameron to Jim Holliday, 29 August 1967, Knopf to Cameron, 4 October 1967, Knopf records addenda 17:8, TxU-Hu.

16. DLM to EHM, 24 March 1966, DLM Papers, 22:189.

17. DLM to Cooley, 9 April 1967, DLM Papers, 2:1204.

18. DLM to GPH, 2 May 1967, DLM Papers, 3:1358.

19. [Unsigned] to DLM, 4 May 1967, DLM Papers, 20:1123; DLM to GPH, 16 May 1967, 3:1359.

20. DLM to FMB, 1 June 1963, DLM Papers, 1:1756.

21. DLM to EHM, 24 June 1967, DLM Papers, 22:195.

22. DLM to ETH, 4 August 1967, DLM Papers, 4:266; DLM to Eugene L. Schwaab, 7 August 1967, 6:838.

23. DLM to Risvold, 30 August 1967, DLM Papers, 6:540.

24. CK to DLM, 18 July 1967, DLM Papers, 14:261.

25. DLM to FMB, 27 October 1967, MS 360 7:14, UU-Ms; DLM Papers, 1:1763.

26. Lloyd G. Lyman to DLM, 4 October 1967, DLM Papers, 14:1304.

27. Novick, *That Noble Dream,* 332–39; Jerome M. Clubb and Howard Allen, "Computers and Historical Studies," *Journal of American History* 54, no. 3 (December 1967): 599–07.

28. DLM to GPH, 2 December 1965, DLM Papers, 3:1279.

29. Jack W. Schuster and Martin J. Finklestein, *The American Faculty: The Restructuring of Academic Work and Careers* (Baltimore, MD: Johns

Hopkins University Press, 2006); William G. Bowen and Eugene M. Tobin, *Locus of Authority: The Evolution of Faculty Roles in the Governance of Higher Education* (Princeton, NJ: Princeton University Press, 2015).

30. Robert C. Post to DLM, 18 November 1967, DLM Papers, 19:1643.
31. DLM to Post, 21 November 1967, DLM Papers, 8:1253.
32. DLM to Dawson, 6 November 1967, DLM Papers, 2:1413.
33. ETH to DLM, 27 November 1967, DLM Papers, 13:427.
34. DLM to ETH, 29 November 1967, DLM Papers, 4:306.
35. Cooley to DLM, 8 April 1965, DLM Papers, 11:1098.
36. Cooley to DLM, 1 December 1967, DLM Papers, 11:1128.
37. MRM to DLM, 3 December [1967], 5:2190.
38. DLM to Helen Kennedy, 21 December 1967, BANC MSS 70/89, 12:42, CU-Banc.
39. DLM to Chad Flake, 5 December 1967, MS 3330, USlC; 3:381.
40. DLM to Jim Holliday, 6 March 1968, DLM Papers, 4:551.
41. DLM to EHM, 11 March 1968, DLM Papers, 22:234; 21 May 1968, 22:246.
42. DLM to EHM, 14 March 1968, DLM Papers, 22:235.
43. DLM to EHM, 16 April 1968, DLM Papers, 22:242.
44. DLM to EHM, 21 May 1968, DLM Papers, 22:246.
45. DLM to ETH, 15 June 1968, DLM Papers, 4:343.
46. MRM to DLM, 22 May 1968, DLM Papers, 16:2192.
47. MRM to DLM, 18 June 19[68], DLM Papers, 15:2198.
48. MRM to DLM, undated [17 July 1968], DLM Papers, 15:2201.
49. Manuscript is dated 28 September 1943, 25:1796; University of California Retirement System, Designation of Beneficiary, 18 July 1969, 18 July 1969, 25:2341; Cooley to FMB, 5 June 1979, Ms 360 4:6, UU-Ms.
50. Cooley, interview, 27 June 1997, transcript in author's possession. cf. Charles S. Peterson and John A. Peterson, "Charles S. Peterson," in *Conversations with Mormon Historians* (Provo: Brigham Young University Religious Studies Center, 2015), 449–92.
51. Cameron to DLM, 1 October 1968, DLM Papers, 10:1311.
52. DLM to EHM, 19 October 1968, DLM Papers, 22:274.
53. DLM to EHM, 5 November [1968], DLM Papers, 22:283.
54. DLM to GPH, 18 November 1968, DLM Papers, 3:1370.
55. DLM to Becker, 12 November 1968, DLM Papers, 1:1338.
56. DLM to Cameron, 11 December 1968, Knopf records addenda 17:8, TxU-Hu; DLM Papers, 2:204; DLM to Todd Berens (transcript), 21 January 1969, Ms 491 1:1, UU-Ms; DLM to Berens, 30 January 1969, Ms 491 1:1, UU-Ms; DLM Papers, 1:1425
57. George L. Harding to DLM, 2 February 1969, DLM Papers, 13:225.
58. DLM to EHM, 7 January 1969, DLM Papers, 22:295.
59. DLM to Cameron, 13 Jan 1969, Knopf records addenda 17:8, TxU-Hu; DLM Papers, 2:207.

60. DLM to Wisconsin Historical Society, 15 January 1969, DLM Papers, 6:1118
61. Cooley to JB, 28 January 1969, Mss B103, 7:1, UHi; Cooley to FMB, 2 December 1970, Accn 0073 16:15, UU-Ms.
62. Ruth Barton to DLM, 4 February 1969, DLM Papers, 23:1479; Mary Beth Morgan to DLM, 6 February 1969, 23:963.
63. Louise North (hereafter LN) to DLM, 28 May 1969, DLM Papers, 16:897; DLM to Bob and Audry Morgan, 4 Jun 1969, Ms 579 2:20, UU-Ms; DLM to GPH, undated [June 1969], BANC MSS 70/89 14:2, CU-Banc; DLM to Jim and Nancy Holliday, 15 July 1969, DLM Papers, 4:561.
64. DLM to Helen Wheat, 23 July 1969, DLM Papers, 7:738; DLM to Ruth Barton, 20 June 1970, 22:407.
65. DLM to Ruth and Doug Barton, Jim and Mary Beth Morgan, Bob and Audry Morgan, 9 July 1969, Ms 579 2:20, UU-Ms.
66. LN to DLM, 16 July 1969, DLM Papers, 16:908.
67. DLM to Rosenstock, 22 July 1969, Ms 487 1:13, UU-Ms.

CHAPTER 18

1. DLM to Rosenstock, 22 July 1969, Ms 487 1:13, UU-Ms.
2. DLM to Helen Kennedy, 22 May 1968, DLM Papers, 4:1302.
3. Moses Rischin, "The New Mormon History," *American West* 6, no. 2 (March 1969): 49. cf. Matthew Bowman, "The Birth and Life of the New Mormon History," *Nova Religio* 24, no. 1 (August 2020): 77–87.
4. Leonard J. Arrington, "The Secularization of Mormon History and Culture," LJAHA ser. 12 154:6, ULA.
5. "A New Decade, A New Director," *Bancroftiana*, no. 45 (July 1969), 1–2.
6. LN to DLM, 27 July 1969, DLM Papers, 16:916.
7. DLM to Nancy Holliday, 31 July 1969, DLM Papers, 4:564.
8. Undated draft [28 July–5 August 1969], DLM Papers, 5:1367.
9. LN to DLM, 10 August 1969, DLM Papers, 16:925.
10. Becker to DLM, 28 July 1969, DLM Papers, 9:1029.
11. DLM to GPH, 31 July 1969, DLM Papers, 3:1374.
12. DLM to GPH, 7 August 1969, DLM Papers, 3:1375.
13. GPH to DLM, 6 August 1969, DLM Papers, 13:161.
14. DLM to John Simon Guggenheim Memorial Foundation, 5 August 1969, "Morgan, Dale L.," 1970 Application, John Simon Guggenheim Memorial Foundation archives, New York.
15. LN to DLM, 12 August 1969, DLM Papers, 16:930.
16. DLM to Rosenstock, 21 August 1969, Ms 487 1:13, UU-Ms; DLM Papers 6:802.
17. First statement about a three-volume history of fur trade was made to CK, 8 October 1954, DLM Papers, 4:1194; DLM to Carl H. Mapes, 4 April 1955, 5:838.

18. DLM to Post, 21 November 1967, DLM Papers, 8:1253; DLM to Billington, 27 September 1969, Ms 579 2:14 [c], UU-Ms; 1:1503. His application narrative, besides the John Simon Guggenheim Memorial Foundation files, may be seen in the GPH Papers, BANC MSS 70/89 14:3, CU-Banc.

19. DLM to Stegner, 2 October 1969, Ms 676 18:53, UU-Ms.

20. BANC MSS 70/89 14:3, CU-Banc.

21. DLM to Bob Morgan, 25 September 1969, Ms 579 2:20, UU-Ms; 22:357.

22. DLM to Anna McConkey, 18 October 1969, Accn 3206, UU-Ms.

23. DLM, "Literature in the History of the Church: The Importance of Involvement," *Dialogue: A Journal of Mormon Thought* 4, no. 3 (Autumn 1969): 26–32; DLM, introduction to *A Mormon Bibliography, 1830–1930*, ed. Chad J. Flake (Salt Lake City: University of Utah Press, 1978); both works are reprinted in *Dale Morgan on the Mormons*, vol. 2, 424–48.

24. DLM to Helen Wheat, 8 October 1969, DLM Papers, 7:741.

25. DLM to Helen Wheat, 19 November 1969, DLM Papers, 7:743.

26. DLM to ETH, 4 December 1969, DLM Papers, 4:370.

27. LN to DLM, 9 December 1969, DLM Papers, 16:976.

28. DLM to Camp, 8 December 1969, DLM Papers, 2:386.

29. DLM to Hart, 12 January 1970, DLM Papers, 4:426.

30. DLM to Mary Beth Morgan, 16 January 1970, DLM Papers, 22:342.

31. Hart to DLM, 26 January 1970, DLM Papers, 13:514.

32. DLM to Berens, 2 February 1970, Ms 491 1:1, UU-Ms; DLM Papers 1:1461.

33. Cf. DLM to Berens, 9, 10, 16 February 1970, Ms 491 1:1, UU-Ms; DLM Papers, 1:1464, 1470, 1474.

34. DLM to Valita Moran, 12 February 1970, DLM Papers, 5:1021.

35. DLM to Cameron, 5 May 1970, Knopf records addenda 17:8, TxU-Hu; DLM Papers, 2:217. The files Morgan did complete are in C16:17, with notes and research material in folders 18–31.

36. DLM to ETH, 26 February 1970, DLM Papers, 4:379.

37. DLM to ETH, 6 March 1970, DLM Papers, 4:382.

38. DLM to Colgan, 17 February 1970, DLM Papers, 2:1134.

39. Gordon N. Ray to DLM, "Morgan, Dale L.," 1970 Application, John Simon Guggenheim Memorial Foundation archives, New York; DLM Papers, 17:1073.

40. *John Simon Guggenheim Memorial Foundation Fellows*, pamphlet (New York: John Simon Guggenheim Memorial Foundation, 1970).

41. DLM to Hart, 31 March 1970, DLM Papers, 4:435; DLM to Ray, 31 March 1970, "Morgan, Dale L.," 1970 Application, John Simon Guggenheim Memorial Foundation archives, New York; DLM Papers, 6:994.

42. DLM to Bob Morgan, 2 April 1970, DLM Papers, 22:379.

43. DLM to ETH, 23 April 1970, DLM Papers, 4:386.

44. Julian Michel to DLM, 16 April 1970, DLM Papers, 19:1281.

45. DLM to FMB, 13 May 1970, MS 360 7:15, UU-Ms; DLM Papers, 1:1776; *DMEM*, 211–16.

46. DLM to Roy P. Basler, 19 May 1970, DLM Papers, 7:968; Basler to DLM, 25 May 1970, 18:954.

47. Hart to DLM, 18 May, 9 June 1970, DLM Papers, 13:517, 519.

48. DLM to Hart, 31 May, 10 June 1970, DLM Papers, 4:440, 445.

49. DLM to Dan Howe, 11 June 1970, DLM Papers, 4:690; DLM to Ernst and Frances H. Stadler, 12 June 1970, 6:1103.

50. MRM to DLM, 27 March 1964, DLM Papers, 15:1976. A year earlier, Tompkins had reprimanded Morgan for making marginal notes and corrections in books from the collection, a longstanding practice in his own books but another unpardonable library sin (John Barr Tompkins to DLM, 11 September 1969, DLM Papers, 17:1657).

51. Tompkins to DLM, 24 June 1970, DLM Papers, 17:1659. Morgan told another staff member that "I have long been aware that Barr regarded me as an excrescence on the staff, in violation of all his ideas of order" (DLM to Estelle Rebec, 25 June 1970, DLM Papers, 8:1294).

52. DLM to Bob and Audry Morgan, 22 June 1970, DLM Papers, 22:386; DLM to Ruth Barton, 20 June 1970, 22:407.

53. DLM to Bob and Audry Morgan, 22 June 1970, DLM Papers, 22:386.

54. DLM to Ruth Barton, 20 July 1970, DLM Papers, 22:410.

55. Hart to DLM, 4 August 1970, DLM Papers, 13:524.

56. DLM to Bobbs-Merrill, 27 August 1970, DLM Papers, 7:1040.

57. DLM to Michael Ginsberg, 4 September 1970, DLM Papers, 3:544; DLM to Hart, 4 September 1970, 4:456.

58. Cooley, interview, 27 June 1997. Cooley reported the same thing to Alfred L. Bush at Princeton University Library in 1971 (Cooley to Bush, 29 April 1971, Accn 0073 19:5, UU-Ms).

59. Brodie held onto his note: MS 360 7:15, UU-Ms.

60. DLM to Jim Holliday, 7 October 1970, DLM Papers, 4:603.

61. DLM to Bob Morgan, 8 October 1970, Ms 579 2:20, UU-Ms; DLM Papers, 22:391.

CHAPTER 19

1. DLM to Ruth and Doug Barton, Jim and Mary Beth Morgan, Bob and Audry Morgan, and Helen [Sanders], 7 December 1970, Ms 579 2:20, UU-Ms.

2. DLM to Knopf, 18 January 1971, Knopf records 533:2, TxU-Hu; DLM Papers, 4:1378.

3. DLM to Hart and Bancroft Staff, 5 December 1970, DLM Papers, 4:460; Jim Holliday to DLM, 29 October 1970, 13:741.

4. DLM to Hart and Bancroft Staff, 5 December 1970.

5. DLM to Barton et al., 7 December 1970.

6. DLM to Barton et al., 7 December 1970.

7. Jim Holliday, interview, 17 October 1994.
8. National Institute of Diabetes and Digestive Diseases, "Definition and Facts for Colon Polyps," accessed April 7, 2023, https://www.niddk.nih.gov /health-information/digestive-diseases/colon-polyps/definition-facts#.
9. DLM to Barton et al., 7 December 1970.
10. DLM to Barton et al., 7 December 1970; DLM to Hart and Bancroft Staff, 5 December 1970, DLM Papers, 4:460.
11. DLM to Hart and Bancroft Staff, 5 December 1970.
12. DLM to Donald Jackson, 11 December 1970, DLM Papers, 4:820.
13. FMB to DLM, 30 January 1971, DLM Papers, 10:343.
14. JB to DLM, 10 February 1971, DLM Papers, 10:987.
15. DLM to Rosenstock, 14 August 1969, Ms 487 1:13, UU-Ms; DLM Papers, 6:801.
16. Conversation: [Rosenstock]/DLM, 2 pages, Ms 487 1:13, UU-Ms; Cooley to DLM, 11 December 1970, DLM Papers, 11:1178.
17. DLM to Jackson, 18 January 1971, 4:821; DLM to Gordon N. Ray, 31 December 1970, "Morgan, Dale L.," John Simon Guggenheim Memorial Foundation archives, New York.
18. Hart to DLM, 12 January 1971, DLM Papers, 13:527.
19. James S. and Mary Beth Morgan interview, 1994.
20. James S. and Mary Beth Morgan interview, 1994; Robert H. Morgan interview, 1994.
21. Tasia Melvin, interview, 13 February 2020, transcript in author's possession.
22. Cameron to DLM, 15 December 1970, Knopf records addenda 17:8, TxU-Hu; DLM Papers, 10:1335.
23. Knopf to DLM, Knopf records 533:2, TxU-Hu.
24. DLM to Knopf, 18 January 1971, Knopf records 533:2, TxU-Hu; DLM Papers, 4:1378.
25. Richard L. Saunders, "Lost in Time: Dale L. Morgan and the Forty-niner Journal of William B. Lorton," *Southern California Quarterly* 98, no. 4 (2016): 457–86.
26. DLM to Rebec, 21 January 1971, DLM Papers, 8:1296.

EPILOGUE
1. DLM to Barry, 2 March 1965, DLM Papers, 1:1101.
2. DLM to Sylvia Behart, 6 January 1948, DLM Papers, 1:1375.
3. Cooley to Jim Morgan and Bob Morgan, 6 April 1971, Accn 0073 19:5, UU-Ms.
4. Cooley to David Laird, 4 February 1971; Laird to Cooley, undated, Accn 0073 42:5, UU-Ms; Cooley to FMB, 18 February 1971, Ms 360 4:6, UU-Ms; Accn 0073 16:15, UU-Ms; Cooley to Hugh C. Garner, 7 May 1971, MS 579 2:19, UU-Ms; Cooley to MSR, 27 June 1975, Accn 0073 19:5, UU-Ms; Cooley, interview, 27 June 1997.

5. Cooley to FMB, 18 February 1971, Ms 360 4:6, UU-Ms; Accn 0073 16:15, UU-Ms.

6. Cooley to MSR, 27 June 1975, Accn 0073 19:5, UU-Ms.

7. Cooley to FMB, 5 June 1979, Ms 360 4:6, UU-Ms. DLM, Will, 1943, DLM Papers, 25:1796.

8. Ray Allen Billington, introduction to *The Great Salt Lake*, by DLM (Albuquerque: University of New Mexico Press, 1973), xxvii.

9. Bush to FMB, 7 July 1971, Ms 360 4:4, UU-Ms.

10. Dale T. Schoenberger, "Interpretation of Western History: Academics versus Buffs," *WHQ* 2, no. 2 (April 1971): 232–33.

11. DLM to ETH, 18 September 1967, DLM Papers, 4:276.

12. Howard R. Lamar, "Persistent Frontier: The West in the Twentieth Century," *Western Historical Quarterly* 4 (January 1973): 5–25; John Caughey, "The Insignificance of the Frontier in American History or 'Once Upon a Time There Was an American West,'" *Western Historical Quarterly* 5 (January 1974): 5–16. The admonitions of Pomeroy, Lamar, and Caughey to the discipline as agents of change were reviewed in Jack L. August, Jr., "The Future of Western History: The Third Wave," *Journal of Arizona History* 27, no. 2 (Summer 1986): 229–44.

13. Stephen Aron, "What's West, What's Next?" *OAH Magazine of History* 19, no. 6 (November 2005): 22.

14. Lamar's charge was significant enough that three decades later it remained the reckoning point in Western historiography. William Deverell, "Historiography, 1971 to Today," *Western Historical Quarterly* 42, no. 3 (Autumn 2011): 355–60.

15. Peter Stearns and Joel Tarr, "New, Public Uses for History," *New York Times,* 7 June 1980; Ian Tyrell, *Historians in Public*, 155. Tyrell's conclusions were presaged in a post-Vietnam volume by Jesse Lemisch, *On Active Service in War and Peace: Politics and Ideology in the American Historical Profession* (Toronto: New Hogtown Press, 1975).

16. Talisman Press archives, California State Library, Sacramento.

17. David Rich Lewis, "Forty-Seven Years: An Editor's Report and Inventory," *Western Historical Quarterly* 46, no. 4 (Winter 2015): 467–95.

18. John D. Unruh Jr., *The Plains Across: Overland Emigrants and the Trans-Mississippi West, 1840–60* (Urbana: University of Illinois Press, 1978).

19. DLM to Ora Lee Parthesius, 15 April 1951, DLM Papers, 8:1185.

20. DLM to Berens, 10 December 1965, Ms 491 1:1, UU-Ms. For another statement, DLM to Barry, 10 December 1965, DLM Papers, 1:1107.

21. This sentiment is lifted directly from a contextual statement by Johan Goudsblom, "Ecological Regimes and the Rise of Organized Religion," in Johan Goudsblom, Stephen Mennell, and E. L. Jones, *The Course of Human History: Economic Growth, Social Process, and Civilization* (Armonk, NY: M. E. Sharpe, 1996), 31.

22. Hayden White, "The Fictions of Factual Representation," in *Grasping the World: The Idea of the Museum*, edited by Donald Preziosi and Claire Farago (London: Routledge, 2004), 26.

23. Charles S. Peterson, "Dale Morgan, Writers' Project," 47–63.

24. Lorraine Daston and Sharon Marcus, "The Books that Wouldn't Die," *Chronicle of Higher Education* (Washington, DC), 22 March 2019, B16.

25. David Levin, *History as Romantic Art: Bancroft, Prescott, Motley, and Parkman* (Stanford, CA: Stanford University Press, 1959), ix.

26. Michael P. Malone, "Beyond the Last Frontier: Toward a New Approach to Western American History," in *Trails: Toward a New Western History*, eds. Patricia Nelson Limerick, Clyde A. Milner, and Charles E. Rankin (Lawrence: University Press of Kansas, 1991).

27. John R. Wunder, ed., *Historians of the American Frontier: A Bio-bibliographical Sourcebook* (Westport, CT: Greenwood Press, 1988).

28. DLM to Barry, 2 March 1965, DLM Papers, 1:1101.

29. ETH to DLM, 20 October 1967, DLM Papers, 13:424. William Henry "Hutch" Hutchinson taught at California State University, Chico.

30. Cooley, interview, 27 June 1997, relating a comment of GPH to Cooley.

31. Davis Bitton and Leonard J. Arrington, *Mormons and Their Historians* (Salt Lake City: University of Utah Press, 1988), 126–46; Robert Flanders, "Some Reflections on the New Mormon History," *Dialogue* 9 no. 1 (Spring 1974): 34–41; Grant Underwood, "Re-visioning Mormon History," *Pacific Historical Review* 55, no. 3 (August 1986): 403–26; James B. Allen, "Since 1950: Creators and Creations of Mormon History," *New Views of Mormon History: Essays in Honor of Leonard J. Arrington,* eds. Davis Bitton and Maureen Ursenbach Beecher (Salt Lake City: University of Utah Press, 1987), 407–38; Roger D. Launius, "From Old to New in Mormon History: Fawn Brodie and the Scholarly Analysis of Mormonism," in *Reconsidering No Man Knows My History: Fawn M. Brodie and Joseph Smith in Retrospect*, ed. Newell G. Bringhurst (Logan: Utah State University Press, 1996), 195–233; Davis R. Bitton, "Mormon Society and Culture," in *Excavating Mormon Pasts: The New Historiography of the Last Half Century*, eds. Newell G. Bringhurst and Lavina Fielding Anderson (Salt Lake City: Greg Kofford Books, 2004), 351.

32. Ronald W. Walker, David J. Whittaker, and James B. Allen, *Mormon History* (Urbana: University of Illinois Press, 2001), 60–112.

33. James D. Tabor, "Do Historians of Religion Exclude the Supernatural?," *HuffPost,* 5 September 2016, https://www.huffpost.com/entry/do-historians -of-religion-exclude-the-supernatural_b_57cda5cde4b06c750ddb3815

34. D. Michael Quinn, ed., *The New Mormon History: Revisionist Essays on the Past* (Salt Lake City, UT: Signature Books, 1992), viii–ix; Arnold J. Toynbee, *Toynbee on Toynbee: A Conversation between Arnold J. Toynbee and G. R. Urban* (New York: Oxford University Press, 1974), 12.

35. Novick, *That Noble Dream,* passim.

36. DLM to Arrington, 19 November 1965, LJAHA ser. V 21:10, ULA; DLM Papers, 1:892.

37. DLM to FMB, 21 August 1967, MS 360 7:14, UU-Ms; DLM Papers, 1:1759; *DMEM,* 205–10.

38. W. E. B. Dubois, *Black Reconstruction* (1935; reis. New York: Touchstone, 1992), 722. DuBois' original statement is that "we shall never have a science of history until we have in our colleges men who regard the truth as more important than the defense of the white race."

39. Stegner to DLM, 16 September 1948, DLM Papers, 17:1244.

40. Hill, "Historiography of Mormonism," 425.

41. Bushman's comment is reported in Robert Flanders, "Some Reflections on the New Mormon History," 34. Martin E. Marty, "Two Integrities," 8. In this case, *mythic* describes origin stories, not necessarily falsity.

42. Arrington, "Reflections," 91–103.

43. F. Mark MacKiernan, Alma R. Blair, and Paul M. Edwards, eds. *The Restoration Movement: Essays in Mormon History* (Lawrence, KS: Coronado Press, 1973). Milton V. Backman, *Joseph Smith's First Vision: The First Vision in Historical Context* (Salt Lake City: Bookcraft, 1971).

44. Leonard J. Arrington, "The Founding of the LDS Church Historical Department, 1972," *Journal of Mormon History* 18, no. 2 (Fall 1992):41–56; Arrington, *Confessions of a Mormon Historian,* 96–99, 106–9.

45. Arrington, *Confessions of a Mormon Historian,* 108 [26 January 1972].

46. Topping, *Utah Historians.*

47. Arrington, "Reflections," 101. cf. Arrington, *Adventures of a Church Historian*; Davis R. Bitton, "Ten Years in Camelot: A Personal Memoir," *Dialogue* 16, no. 3 (Autumn 1983): 9–20.

48. Topping, *D. Michael Quinn,* 93–123.

49. Jan Shipps, "Richard Lyman Bushman: The Story of Joseph Smith and Mormonism, and the New Mormon History," *Journal of American History* 94, no. 2 (2007), 498.

50. DLM, untitled comment on FMB, *No Man Knows My History,* DLM Papers, 9:361.

51. DLM to Parthesius, 15 April 1951, DLM Papers, 8:1185.

A DALE L. MORGAN BIBLIOGRAPHY

1. Updated from Richard L. Saunders, *Eloquence from a Silent World: A Descriptive Bibliography of the Published Writings of Dale L. Morgan* (Salt Lake City: Caramon Pres, 1990).

2. A printer's imposition error did not include the conclusion of the review in pages, leaving it incomplete.

Works Cited

MANUSCRIPTS AND ARCHIVAL MATERIAL

Dale L. Morgan (DLM) Papers, BANC MSS 71/161c, Bancroft Library, University of California, Berkeley.

Darel and Anna McConkey Papers, Accn 3206, UU- Ms.

Emily Holmes (Morgan) transcript, Registrar's Office, University of Utah, Salt Lake City.

Everett D. Graff Papers, Subgroup No. 15, Trustee Personal Papers, Newberry Library, Chicago.

Fawn M. Brodie (FMB) Papers, Ms 360, University of Utah Special Collections (UU- Ms), Salt Lake City.

Juanita Brooks (JB) Papers, Mss B 103, Utah Division of State History library (UHi), Salt Lake City.

Juanita Brooks (JB) Papers, Ms 486, UU- Ms.

Leonard J. Arrington Historical Archive (LJAHA), Utah State University Special Collections and Archives (ULA), Logan.

Madeline R. McQuown (MRM) Papers, Ms 143, UU- Ms.

"Morgan, Dale L.," "1949 Mormon Church Correspondence"; John Simon Guggenheim Memorial Foundation Archives, New York.

M. Wilford Poulson Papers, MSS 823 5:5, Brigham Young University (UPB), Provo, Utah.

Record of Members Collection 1836–1970, Church History Library (USlC), Salt Lake City.

Stanley S. Ivins Papers, Mss B 31, UHi.

Talisman Press records, boxes 2142–2182, California State Library, Sacramento. US Census. 1920, Salt Lake City.

"Utah, Salt Lake County Death Records, 1908–1949," index and images, FamilySearch .org.

Wallace Stegner Papers, Ms 676, UU- Ms.

Ward record #323, Church Census, CR 4 311 #139, USlC.

Works Progress Administration (WPA) Papers, Mss B 57, UHi.

INTERVIEWS AND ORAL HISTORIES

Bleak, T. Gerald ("Jerry"), oral history interview, 17 March 1994.

Cooley, Everett L., interview, 27 June 1997.

Dawson, Glen C., interview, 24 May 1995.

Finnin, Gerald ("Jerry"), interview transcript, 1976, Ms 143 1:2, UU-Ms.

Greenwood, Robert K., conversation notes, April 1990.

Holliday, Jacquelin S. (Jim) interview, 17 October 1994.

Holmes, Samuel, interview, 6 March 1994.

Melvin, Tasia, interview, 13 February 2020.

Morgan, James S., interview notes, 9 May 1998.

Morgan, James S., personal communication to the author, 25 April 1992.

Morgan, James S. and Mary Beth, interview, 25 April 1991.

Morgan, Robert H., interview, 19 March 1994.

Morgan, Robert H., interview, 25 April 1994.

Morgan, Robert H., interview notes, 30 May 2002.

North, Lynn, interview, 30 March 2020.

Thurston, Jarvis, interview, 14 June 1994.

Thurston, Jarvis, interview notes, 21 April 2001.

PUBLISHED WORKS

Allen, James B. "Since 1950: Creators and Creations of Mormon History." In *New Views of Mormon History: Essays in Honor of Leonard J. Arrington,* edited by Davis Bitton and Maureen Ursenbach Beecher, 407–38. Salt Lake City: University of Utah Press, 1987.

American Book Publishers' Council. *Annual Trends Survey of the General Book Publishing Industry, 1961.* New York: American Book Publishers' Council, 1962.

American Book Publishers' Council. *The Situation and Outlook for the Book Trade.* New York: American Book Publishers' Council, 1951.

"Among Our New Acquisitions." *Bulletin of the Missouri Historical Society* 16, no. 3 (April 1960): 282.

Aron, Stephen. "What's West, What's Next?" *OAH Magazine of History* 19, no. 6 (November 2005): 22–26.

Arrington, Leonard J. *Adventures of a Church Historian.* Urbana: University of Illinois Press, 1998.

Arrington, Leonard J. "Coming to Terms with Mormon History: An Interview with Leonard Arrington." *Dialogue* 22, no. 4 (Winter 1989): 38–54.

Arrington, Leonard J. *Confessions of a Mormon Historian: The Diaries of Leonard J. Arrington, 1971–1997.* Edited by Gary James Bergera. 3 vols. Salt Lake City: Signature Books, 2017.

Arrington, Leonard J. "The Founding of the LDS Church Historical Department, 1972." *Journal of Mormon History* 18, no. 2 (Fall 1992): 41–56.

Arrington, Leonard J. "Reflections on the Founding and Purpose of the Mormon History Association, 1965–1983." *Journal of Mormon History* 10 (1983): 91–103.

Arrington, Leonard J. "Scholarly Studies of Mormonism in the Twentieth Century," *Dialogue* 1, no. 1 (1966): 15–32.

Arrington, Leonard J. "The Secularization of Mormon History and Culture." Paper presented at 5th Annual Western History Association Conference, Helena, MT, October 14–16, 1965. LJAHA, Special Collections and Archives, Merrill-Cazier Library, Utah State University, Logan.

Arrington, Leonard J., and Davis R. Bitton. *Mormons and Their Historians.* Salt Lake City: University of Utah Press, 1988.

August, Jack L., Jr. "The Future of Western History: The Third Wave." *Journal of Arizona History* 27, no. 2 (Summer 1986): 229–44.

Austin, Michael, and Ardis E. Parshall. "The Novelist and the Apostle: Paul Bailey, John A. Widtsoe, and the Quest for Faithful Fiction in the 1940s." *Journal of Mormon History* 42, no. 3 (July 2016): 183–210.

Bahr, Howard M. "'Simple, Common-sense Explanation': Thomas F. O'Dea and the Book of Mormon." *Journal of Mormon History* 32 no. 3 (Fall 2006): 104–40.

Baldridge, Kenneth W. *The Civilian Conservation Corps in Utah: Remembering Nine Years of Achievement, 1933–1942.* Salt Lake City: University of Utah Press, 2019.

Bankston, Carl L., III. "The Mass Production of Credentials: Subsidies and the Rise of Higher Education Industry." *Independent Review* 15, no. 3 (Winter 2011): 325–49.

Barney, Ronald O. *Joseph Smith: History, Methods, and Memory.* Salt Lake City: University of Utah Press, 2020.

Barone, Michael. *Our Country.* New York: Free Press, 1990.

Barrese, Edward F. "The Historical Records Survey: A Nation Acts to Save its Memory." PhD dissertation, George Washington University, Washington, DC, 1980.

Bartels, Andrew H. "The Office of Price Administration and the Legacy of the New Deal, 1939–1946." *Public Historian* 5, no. 3 (Summer 1983): 5–29.

Baynton, Douglas C. "Deafness." In *Keywords for Disability Studies,* edited by Rachel Adams, Benjamin Reiss, and David Serlin, 48–51. New York: New York University Press, 2015.

Beadle, J. H. *Polygamy; or, The Mysteries and Crimes of Mormonism, Being a Full and Authentic History of This Strange Sect from Its Origin to the Present Time [...].* Philadelphia: National Publishing Co., 1882.

Becker Kinner, Jody. Utah Deaf History and Culture, accessed March 14, 2023, http://utahdeafhistory.com.

Benton, Megan. "Measured Markets: Limited Edition Publishing and the Grabhorn Press, 1920–1930." *Publishing Research Quarterly* 11, no. 2 (Summer 1995): 90–102.

Berger, John. *A Seventh Man: The Story of a Migrant Worker in Europe.* Cambridge: Granta Books, 1989.

Bernstein, Barton J. "The Removal of War Production Board Controls on Business, 1944–1946." *Business History Review* 39, no. 2 (Summer 1965): 243–60.

The Bible and Polygamy: Does the Bible Sanction Polygamy? A Discussion between Professor Orson Pratt . . . and the Rev. Doctor J. P. Newman. Salt Lake City: Deseret News Printing and Publishing, 1879.

Billington, Ray Allen. Introduction to *The Great Salt Lake*, by Dale L. Morgan, vii–xxviii. Albuquerque: University of New Mexico Press, 1973.

Billington, Ray Allen. "The Santa Fe Conference and the Writing of Western History." In *Probing the American West: Papers from the Santa Fe Conference*, edited by K. Ross Toole, John Alexander Carroll, A. R. Mortensen, and Robert M. Utley, 1–16. Santa Fe: Museum of New Mexico Press, 1962.

Binkley, William C. "Two World Wars and American Historical Scholarship." *Mississippi Valley Historical Review* 33, no. 1 (June 1946): 3–26.

Birdsall, William F. "The Two Sides of the Desk: The Archivist and the Historian, 1909–1935." *American Archivist* 38, no. 2 (April 1975): 158–73.

Bishop, William Warner. "Rare Book Rooms in Libraries." *Library Quarterly* 12, no. 3 (July 1942): 375–85.

Bitton, Davis R. "B. H. Roberts as Historian." *Dialogue* 3, no. 4 (Winter 1968): 25–44.

Bitton, Davis R. "Mormon Society and Culture." In *Excavating Mormon Pasts: The New Historiography of the Last Half Century*, edited by Newell G. Bringhurst and Lavina Fielding Anderson, 351–66. Salt Lake City: Greg Kofford Books, 2004.

Bitton, Davis R. "Ten Years in Camelot: A Personal Memoir." *Dialogue* 16, no. 3 (Autumn 1983): 9–20.

Bitton, Davis R., and Leonard J. Arrington. *Mormons and Their Historians.* Salt Lake City: University of Utah Press, 1988.

Black, Jessica E., Molly Oberstein-Allen, and Jennifer L. Barnes. "Tell Me A Story: Religion, Imagination, and Narrative Involvement." *Journal for the Cognitive Science of Religion* 5, no. 1 (2017/2019): 37–62.

Blakely, Thomas A. "The Swearing Elders: The First Generation of Modern Mormon Intellectuals." *Sunstone* 10, no. 9 (1985): 8–13.

Bonn, Thomas L. *Heavy Traffic & High Culture: New American Library as Literary Gatekeeper in the Paperback Revolution.* Carbondale: Southern Illinois University Press, 1989.

Bowen, Carroll G. "When Universities Become Publishers." *Science,* new series 140, no. 3567 (10 May 1963): 599–605.

Bowen, William G., and Eugene M. Tobin. *Locus of Authority: The Evolution of Faculty Roles in the Governance of Higher Education.* Princeton, NJ: Princeton University Press, 2015.

Bower, Donald E., and S. Lyman Tyler. *Fred Rosenstock: A Legend in Books & Art.* Flagstaff, AZ: Northland Press, 1976.

Bowman, Matthew. "The Birth and Life of the New Mormon History." *Nova Religio* 24, no. 1 (August 2020): 77–87.

Boyd, Julian P. Speech to Society of American Archivists meeting, Providence, RI, 29 December 1936. Extracted in HRS "Circular Letter No. 8 to State Directors," 17 February 1937, US Works Progress Administration Collection, box 1, fd. 3, Library of Congress, Washington, DC.

Bringhurst, Newell. "Fawn Brodie's Thomas Jefferson: The Making of Popular and Controversial Biography." *Pacific Historical Review* 62, no. 4 (November 1993): 433–54.

Bringhurst, Newell. "Juanita Brooks and Fawn Brodie: Sisters in Mormon Dissent." *Dialogue* 27, no. 2 (Summer 1994): 105–27.

Brodie, Fawn M. *Thomas Jefferson: An Intimate History.* New York: W. W. Norton, 1974.

Brooks, Juanita. "The First One Hundred Years of Southern Utah History." *Proceedings of the Utah Academy of Sciences, Arts and Letters* 24 (1946–1947): 71–79.

Brooks, Juanita. "Let Us Preserve Our Records." *Utah Humanities Review* 2 (July 1948): 259–63.

Brooks, Juanita. *Quicksand and Cactus: A Memoir of the Southern Mormon Frontier.* Logan: Utah State University Press, 1992.

Brooks, Juanita. The *Selected Letters of Juanita Brooks.* Edited by Craig S. Smith. Salt Lake City: University of Utah Press, 2019.

Browne, Henry J. "A Plan of Organization for a University Archives." *American Archivist* 12, no. 4 (October 1949): 355–58.

Brugge, David M. *The Navajo-Hopi Land Dispute: An American Tragedy.* Albuquerque: University of New Mexico Press, 1999.

"The Career of Samuel Burgess," *Saints' Herald* 98, no. 2 (8 January 1951): 9, 22.

Carroll, Peter N. *Keeping Time: Memory, Nostalgia and the Art of History.* Athens: University of Georgia Press, 1990.

Caughey, John. "The Insignificance of the Frontier in American History; or, 'Once Upon a Time There Was an American West.'" *Western Historical Quarterly* 5, no. 1 (January 1974): 5–16.

Charlson, Elizabeth, Michael Strong, and Ruby Gold. "How Successful Deaf Teenagers Experience and Cope with Isolation." *American Annals of the Deaf* 137, no. 3 (July 1992): 261–70.

Chase, Daryl. *Joseph the Prophet: As He Lives in the Hearts of His People.* Salt Lake City: Deseret Book, 1944.

Chen, Amy Hildreth. *Placing Papers: The American Literary Archives Market.* Amherst: University of Massachusetts Press, 2020.

Cheney, O. H. *Economic Survey of the Book Industry, 1930–1931.* New York: R. R. Bowker, 1949.

Civil Service Commission. *Tips to Newcomers to Washington, DC.* Washington, DC: Civil Service Commission, 1942.

Clapp, Verner W. "Three Ages of Reference Work." *Special Libraries* 57 (July/August 1966): 379–84.

Clemmer, Richard O. "Crying for the Children of Sacred Ground: A Review Article on the Hopi-Navajo Land Dispute." *American Indian Quarterly* 15, no. 2 (Spring 1991): 25–30.

Clemmer, Richard O., David F. Aberle, Joseph G. Jorgensen, and Thayer Scudder. "Anthropology, Anthropologists, and the Navajo-Hopi Land Dispute: Reply to Washburn." *American Anthropologist* 91, no. 3 (1989): 743–53.

Clubb, Jerome M., and Howard Allen. "Computers and Historical Studies." *Journal of American History* 54, no. 3 (December 1967): 599–607.

Cohen, Wilbur J. "The Federal Government's Program for Ex-servicemen," *Annals of the American Academy of Political and Social Science* 238 (1945): 63–70.

Coney, Donald. "Report of the University Librarian, 1966–67." *CU News* 22, no. 26 (29 June 1967): 7–8

Craven, Avery O. "An Historical Adventure." *Journal of American History* 51, no. 1 (June 1964): 5–20.

Crawley, Peter. *Descriptive Bibliography of the Mormon Church*. 3 vols. Provo, UT: Brigham Young University Religious Studies Center, 1997–2012.

Creer, Leland H. *Founding of an Empire: The Exploration and Colonization of Utah, 1776–1856*. Salt Lake City: Bookcraft, 1947.

Creer, Leland H. *Utah and the Nation*. Seattle: University of Washington Press, 1929.

Darby, William. *Necessary American Fictions: Popular Literature of the 1950s*. Bowling Green, Ohio: Popular, 1987.

Dalferth, Ingolf U. *Creatures of Possibility: The Theological Basis of Human Freedom*. Translated by Jo Bennett. Grand Rapids, MI: Baker Academic, 2016.

Daston, Lorraine, and Sharon Marcus. "The Books that Wouldn't Die." *Chronicle of Higher Education* (Washington, DC), 22 March 2019, B16.

David, Michel, and Sandra E. Trehub. "Perspectives on Deafened Adults." *American Annals of the Deaf* 134, no. 3 (July 1989): 200–204.

Davis, W. N., Jr. "Will the West Survive a Field in American History: A Survey." *Mississippi Valley Historical Review* 50, no. 4 (March 1964): 672–85.

DePillis, Mario. Review of *History's Memory*, by Ellen Fitzpatrick. *Journal of Social History* 37, no. 4 (Summer 2004): 1116–18.

Deverell, William. "Historiography, 1971 to Today." *Western Historical Quarterly* 42, no. 3 (Autumn 2011): 355–60.

DeVoto, Bernard. "The Centennial of Mormonism." *American Mercury* 19, no. 73 (January 1930): 1–13.

DeVoto, Bernard. Introduction to Wallace Stegner, *Beyond the Hundredth Meridian: John Wesley Powell and the Second Opening of the West*, xv–xxiii. New York: Penguin Books, 1992. First published 1954 by Houghton Mifflin Company.

DeVoto, Bernard. *Letters of Bernard DeVoto*. Edited by Wallace Stegner. New York: Doubleday, 1975.

Dillon, Richard. Review of *In Pursuit of the Golden Dream,* by Howard C. Gardiner, *Colorado Magazine* 47, no. 4 (1970): 339.

Donald, David Herbert. *Lincoln.* New York: Simon and Schuster, 1995.

Dubois, W. E. B. *Black Reconstruction.* New York: Touchstone, 1992. First published 1935 by Harcourt, Brace and Company.

Duck, Leigh Ann. *The Nation's Region: Southern Modernism, Segregation, and US Nationalism.* Athens: University of Georgia Press, 2006.

Eberstadt, Charles. "The Letter that Founded a Kingdom," *Autograph Collectors' Journal* 3, no. 1 (October 1950): 2–5, 32.

Eccles, Marriner. *Hearings Before the Committee on Banking and Currency . . . on S. 2028, a Bill to Amend the Emergency Price Control Act of 1942, as Amended, and the Stabilization Act of 1942, as Amended, and for Other Purposes.* 79th Congress, 2nd session. Washington, DC: Government Printing Office, 1946.

Eckelberry, R. H. "The Approval of Institutions under the GI Bill." *Journal of Higher Education* 16, no. 3 (March 1945): 121–26.

Eliason, Eric A. "Curious Gentiles and Representational Authority in the City of the Saints," *Religion and American Culture* 11, no. 2 (Summer 2001): 155–90.

Ely, Richard T. "Economic Aspects of Mormonism." *Harper's Monthly Magazine* 106 (1903): 677–78.

Evans, John Henry. *Joseph Smith: An American Prophet.* New York: Macmillan, 1933.

Evans, Luther H. "Bibliography by Cooperation." *Bulletin of the Medical Library Association* 37, no. 3 (July 1949): 198.

Evans, Luther H. "The Historical Records Survey," *American Political Science Review* 30, no. 1 (February, 1936): 133–35.

Evans, Richard L. *At This Same Hour.* New York: Harper, 1949.

Flanagan, Hallie. *Arena: The History of the Federal Theatre.* New York: Benjamin Blom, 1940.

Flanders, Robert. "Some Reflections on the New Mormon History." *Dialogue* 9, no. 1 (Spring 1974): 34–41.

Foster, Craig L. "Madeline McQuown, Dale Morgan, and the Great Unfinished Brigham Young Biography." *Dialogue: A Journal of Mormon Thought* 31 (Summer 1998): 111–23.

Francaviglia, Richard. "Walt Disney's Frontierland as an Allegorical Map of the American West." *Western Historical Quarterly* 30, no. 2 (Summer 1999): 155–82.

Frazier, Benjamin W. "Postwar Faculty Recruitment." *Journal of Higher Education* 15, no. 9 (December 1944): 476–81.

Frugé, August. *A Skeptic Among Scholars: Recollections of a University Publisher.* Berkeley: University of California Press, 1993.

Fyfe, Aileen, and Anna Gielas. "Introduction: Editorship and the Editing of Scientific Journals, 1750–1950." *Centaurus* 62, no. 1 (February 2020): 5–20.

Gannon, Jack R. *Deaf Heritage: A Narrative History of Deaf America*. Washington, DC: Gallaudet University, 2012.

Geary, Edward A. "Mormondom's Lost Generation: Novelists of the 1940s." *Brigham Young University Studies* 18, no. 1 (Fall 1977): 89–98.

Geiger, Roger L. *The History of American Higher Education: Learning and Culture from the Founding to World War II*. Princeton, NJ: Princeton University Press, 2015.

Gooch, Robert. "Report of Reference Chief Robert Gooch," *Annual Report of the Librarian of Congress for the Fiscal Year Ending June 30, 1946*. Washington, DC: Government Printing Office, 1947.

Goodman, James M., and Gary L. Thompson. "The Hopi-Navaho Land Dispute." *American Indian Law Review* 3, no. 2 (1975): 397–417.

Gottlieb, Robert, and Peter Wiley. *America's Saints: The Rise of Mormon Power*. New York: G. P. Putnam's Sons, 1984.

Goudsblom, Johan. "Ecological Regimes and the Rise of Organized Religion." In *The Course of Human History: Economic Growth, Social Process, and Civilization*, edited by Johan Goudsblom, Stephen Mennell, and E. L. Jones, 31–48. Armonk, NY: M. E. Sharpe, 1996.

Greco, Albert N. *The Growth of the Scholarly Publishing Industry in the US: A Business History of a Changing Marketplace*. Cham, Switzerland: Palgrave Pivot, 2019.

Green, Deidre Nicole. *Jacob: A Brief Theological Introduction*. Provo, UT: Neal A. Maxwell Institute, 2021.

Greenwood, Robert. Foreword to *Eloquence from a Silent World*, by Richard L. Saunders, vii–x. Salt Lake City: Caramon Press, 1990.

Grossman, Carol Porter. *The History of the Limited Editions Club*. New Castle, DE: Oak Knoll Press, 2017.

Gulick, Luther. "V. War Organization of the Federal Government." *American Political Science Review* 38, no. 6 (December 1944): 1166–79.

Gumport, Patricia J., and Stuart K. Syndman. "The Formal Organization of Knowledge: An Analysis of Academic Structure." *Journal of Higher Education* 73, no. 3 (May/June 2002): 375–408.

Gustafson, Sandra M. "Histories of Democracy and Empire." *American Quarterly* 59, no. 1 (March 2007): 107–33.

Hackett, Alice Payne. *Seventy Years of Best Sellers, 1895–1965*. New York: R. R. Bowker, 1967.

Hammond, George P. "Manuscripts Collections in the Bancroft Library." *American Archivist* 13, no. 1 (January 1950): 15–26.

Hannifin, Jennifer Kavins. "Changing Sales and Markets of American University Presses, 1960–1990." *Publishing Research Quarterly* 7, no. 2 (Summer 1991): 11–35.

Hardy, Kenneth R. *Samuel Holmes Family History*. West Valley City, UT: Family History Publishers, 2008.

Harlan, Robert D., and Bruce L. Johnson. "Trends in Modern American Book Publishing." *Library Trends* 27, no. 3 (Winter 1979): 389–407.

Hart, James D. *The Popular Book: A History of America's Literary Taste.* New York: Oxford University Press, 1950.

Hartley, William G. "The Nauvoo Exodus and Crossing the Ice Myths." *Journal of Mormon History* 43, no. 1 (January 2017): 57–58.

Hawes, Gene R. *To Advance Knowledge: A Handbook on American University Press Publishing.* New York: American Association of University Presses, 1967.

Hayes, Carlton J. H. "The American Frontier—Frontier of What?" *American Historical Review* 51, no. 2 (January 1946): 199–216.

Heaney, Howell J. "Thomas W. Streeter, Collector, 1883–1965." *Papers of the Bibliographical Society of America* 65, no. 3 (1971): 243–56.

Hill, Marvin S. "The Historiography of Mormonism." *Church History* 28 no. 4 (December 1959): 418–26.

Hinckley, Bryant S. *The Faith of Our Pioneer Fathers.* Salt Lake City: Bookcraft, 1956.

Hirsch, Jerrold. *Portrait of America: A Cultural History of the Federal Writers' Project.* Chapel Hill: University of North Carolina Press, 2003.

Hoffer, Peter Charles. "The Rise of Consensus History." In *Past Imperfect: Facts, Fictions, Fraud.* New York: Public Affairs, 2004.

Holliday, J. S. *The World Rushed In: The California Gold Rush Experience.* New York: Simon & Schuster, 1981.

Hollis, Ernest V., and Ralph S. M. Flynt. "Some Factors Influencing Postwar College Enrollments." *Bulletin of the American Association of College Professors* 30, no. 4 (Winter 1944): 525–34.

Holmes, Kenneth. "The Fourth Brother: Memories of Edge." *Holmes Family Heritage* 1, no. 2 (Fall 1985).

Hunter, Milton R. *Brigham Young, The Colonizer.* Salt Lake City: Deseret News, 1940.

Hunter, Milton R. *The Mormons and the American Frontier.* Salt Lake City: LDS Department of Education, 1940.

Hunter, Milton R. *Utah: The Story of Her People, 1540–1947.* Salt Lake City: Deseret News, 1946.

Jackson, H. J. *Those Who Write for Immortality: Romantic Reputations and the Dream of Lasting Fame.* New Haven, CT: Yale University Press, 2015.

Joyce, William L. "The Evolution of the Concept of Special Collections in American Research Libraries." *Rare Books & Manuscripts Librarianship* 3, no. 1 (Spring 1988): 19–29.

Kaestle, Carl F., and Janice A. Radway, eds. *Print in Motion: The Expansion of Publishing and Reading in the United States, 1880–1940.* Chapel Hill: University of North Carolina Press, 2009.

Kauffman, Ruth, and Reginald Kauffman. *The Latter Day Saints: A Study of the Mormons in Light of Economic Conditions.* London: Williams & Norgate, 1912.

Kelly, Charles, and Maurice L. Howe. *Miles Goodyear.* Salt Lake City: Western Printing Company, 1935.

Kerridge, Phyllis M. Tookey. "Aids for the Deaf." *British Medical Journal* 1, no. 3886 (29 June 1935): 1314–17.

Kirkham, Francis W. *A New Witness for Christ in America: The Book of Mormon.* 2 vols. Independence, MO: Zion's Printing and Publishing Co., 1951.

Knibb, Dorothy V. "Reading Trends Stir Book Trade." *Domestic Commerce* 33, no. 11 (Nov. 1945): 24–25.

Korda, Michael. *Another Life: A Memoir of Other People.* New York: Random House, 1999.

Korda, Michael. *Making the List: A Cultural History of the American Bestseller, 1900–1999.* New York: Barnes & Noble, 2001.

Kuhn, Thomas S. *The Structure of Scientific Revolutions.* 4th ed. Chicago: University of Chicago Press, 2012.

Lamar, Howard R. "Persistent Frontier: The West in the Twentieth Century." *Western Historical Quarterly* 4, no. 1 (January 1973): 5–25.

Larson, Cedric. "The Cultural Programs of the WPA." *Public Opinion Quarterly* 3, no. 3 (July 1939): 491–96.

Laugesen, Amanda. "George Himes, F. G. Young, and the Early Years of the Oregon Historical Society." *Oregon Historical Quarterly* 101, no. 1 (Spring 2000): 18–39.

Launius, Roger D. "From Old to New in Mormon History: Fawn Brodie and the Scholarly Analysis of Mormonism." In *Reconsidering "No Man Knows My History": Fawn M. Brodie and Joseph Smith in Retrospect,* edited by Newell G. Bringhurst, 195–233. Logan: Utah State University Press, 1996.

Leighninger, Robert D. "Cultural Infrastructure: The Legacy of New Deal Public Space." *Journal of Architectural Education* 49, no. 4 (May 1996): 226–36.

Lemisch, Jesse. *On Active Service in War and Peace: Politics and Ideology in the American Historical Profession.* Toronto: New Hogtown Press, 1975.

Levin, David. *History as Romantic Art: Bancroft, Prescott, Motley, and Parkman.* Stanford, CA: Stanford University Press, 1959.

Lewis, David Rich. "Forty-Seven Years: An Editor's Report and Inventory." *Western Historical Quarterly* 46, no. 4 (Winter 2015): 467–95.

Lindert, Peter H., and Jeffrey G. Williamson. *Unequal Gains: American Growth and Inequality since 1700.* Princeton, NJ: Princeton University Press, 2016.

Link, Henry C., and Harry Arthur Hopf. *People and Books: A Study of Reading Habits and Book-buying Habits.* New York: Book Industry Committee, Book Manufactures Institute, 1946.

Linn, William A. *The Story of the Mormons: From the Date of Their Origin to the Year 1901.* New York: Macmillan, 1902.

Lipset, Seymour, and Everett C. Ladd, Jr. "The Changing Social Origins of American Academics." In *Qualitative and Quantitative Social Research: Papers in Honor of Paul F. Lazarsfeld,* edited by Robert Merton, James S. Coleman, and Peter H. Rossi, 319–38. New York: Free Press, 1979.

Lowenthal, David. *Possessed by the Past: The Heritage Crusade and the Spoils of History*. New York: Free Press, 1996.

Lyon, William H. "The Third Generation and the Frontier Hypothesis." *Arizona and the West* 4, no. 1 (Spring 1962): 45–50.

MacKiernan, F. Mark, Alma R. Blair, and Paul M. Edwards, eds. *The Restoration Movement: Essays in Mormon History*. Lawrence, KS: Coronado Press, 1973.

Malmgren, Larry H. "A History of the WPA in Utah." Master's thesis, Utah State University, 1965.

Malone, Michael P. "Beyond the Last Frontier: Toward a New Approach to Western American History." In *Trails: Toward a New Western History*, edited by Patricia Nelson Limerick, Clyde A. Milner, and Charles E. Rankin, 139–60. Lawrence: University Press of Kansas, 1991.

Mangione, Jerre. *The Dream and the Deal: The Federal Writers' Project, 1935–1943*. 2nd ed. Philadelphia: University of Pennsylvania Press, 1983.

Marsden, George M. *Jonathan Edwards: A Life*. New Haven, CT: Yale University Press, 2003.

Marty, Martin E. "Two Integrities: An Address to the Crisis in Mormon Historiography." *Journal of Mormon History* 10 (1983): 3–19.

Maximilian, Prince Alexander Philipp. *The North American Journals of Prince Maximilian of Wied*. Edited by Stephen S. Witte and Marsha V. Gallagher. Translated by William J. Orr, Paul Schach, and Dieter Karch. Norman: University of Oklahoma Press, 2017.

McClure, George Morris. "On Being a Teacher of the Deaf." *American Annals of the Deaf* 92, no. 2 (March 1947): 133–41.

McGavin, E. Cecil. *The Mormon Pioneers*. Salt Lake City: Stevens & Wallis, 1947.

McKitterick, David. *A History of Cambridge University Press: New Worlds for Learning, 1873–1972*. Cambridge, UK: Cambridge University Press, 2004.

Mecklin, John. *The Story of American Dissent*. New York: Harcourt, Brace and Company, 1934.

Mettler, Suzanne. "The Creation of the GI Bill of Rights of 1944: Melding Social and Participatory Citizenship Ideals." *Journal of Policy History* 17, no. 4 (2005): 345–74.

Mitchell, Ross E. "How Many Deaf People are in the United States?: Estimates from the Survey of Income and Program Participation." *Journal of Deaf Studies and Deaf Education* 11, no. 1 (2006): 112–19.

Morgan, Dale L. *Dale Morgan on Early Mormonism: Correspondence and a New History*. Edited by John Philip Walker. Midvale, UT: Signature Books, 1986.

Morgan, Dale L. *Dale Morgan on the Mormons: Collected Works, 1939–1970*. 2 vols. Edited by Richard L. Saunders. Norman, OK: Arthur H. Clark Co., 2012–2013.

Morgan, Dale L. "GPH." In *GPH: An Informal Record of George P. Hammond and His Era in the Bancroft Library*, 1–20. Berkeley, CA: The Friends of The Bancroft Library, 1965.

Morgan, Dale L. Introduction to *A Mormon Bibliography, 1830–1930*, by Chad J. Flake, xv–xxvi. Salt Lake City: University of Utah Press, 1978.

Morgan, Dale L. "Literature in the History of the Church: The Importance of Involvement." *Dialogue: A Journal of Mormon Thought* 4, no. 3 (Autumn 1969): 26–32.

Morgan, Dale L. "Mormon Story Tellers." *Rocky Mountain Review* 7, no. 1 (Fall 1942): 1, 3–4, 7.

Morgan, Dale L. "Salt Lake City, City of the Saints." *Rocky Mountain Cities*. Edited by Ray B. West, Jr. New York: W. W. Norton, 1949.

Morgan, Dale L. *Shoshonean Peoples and the Overland Trail: Frontiers of the Utah Superintendency of Indian Affairs, 1849–1869*. Edited by Richard L. Saunders. Logan: Utah State University Press, 2007.

Morgan, Dale L. "The Significance and Value of the Overland Journal." In *Probing the American West: Papers from the Santa Fe Conference*. Edited by K. Ross Toole, John Alexander Carroll, Robert M. Utley, and A. R. Mortensen, 69–76. Santa Fe: Museum of New Mexico Press, 1962.

Morgan, Dale L. "Utah: A Viewpoint." *Rocky Mountain Review* 5, no. 2 (Winter 1941): 1, 4.

Mueller, Max Perry. *Race and the Making of the Mormon People*. Chapel Hill: University of North Carolina Press, 2017.

Mulder, William. "The Mormons in American History." Twenty-first Frederick Williams Reynolds Lecture, 14 January 1957. Salt Lake City: University of Utah Press, 1981. Also published in *Utah Historical Quarterly* 27, no. 1 (1959): 59–77.

Nam, Charles B. "Impact of the 'GI Bills' on the Educational Level of the Male Population." *Social Forces* 43, no. 1 (October 1964): 26–32.

National Center for Education Statistics. *The Condition of Education 1980, Statistical Report*. Washington, DC: Government Printing Office, 1980.

National Historical Publications Commission. *A National Program for the Publication of the Papers of American Leaders: A Preliminary Report to the President*. Washington, DC: General Services Administration, 1951.

National Institute of Diabetes and Digestive Diseases. "Definition and Facts for Colon Polyps." Accessed April 7, 2023. https://www.niddk.nih.gov/health -information/digestive-diseases/colon-polyps/definition-facts#.

National Society of the Sons of Utah Pioneers. "Mission and Activities." Accessed April 8, 2023. http://sup1847.com.

Neff, Andrew L. *The History of Utah, 1847–1869*. Edited by Leland Creer. Salt Lake City: Deseret News, 1940.

Neilson, Reid L., and Scott D. Marianno. "True and Faithful: Joseph Fielding Smith as Mormon Historian and Theologian." *BYU Studies Quarterly* 57, no. 1 (2018): 7–64.

Nelson, Josephus, and Judith Farley. *Full Circle: Ninety Years of Service in the Main Reading Room*. Washington, DC: Library of Congress, 1991.

"A New Decade, A New Director." *Bancroftiana,* no. 45 (July 1969): 1–2.

New York Public Library. "List of Works in the New York Public Library Relating to the Mormons." *Bulletin of the New York Public Library* 13, no. 3 (March 1909): 183–239.

Nibley, Preston W. *LDS Adventure Stories.* Salt Lake City: Bookcraft, 1953.

Nibley, Preston W. *Stalwarts of Mormonism.* Salt Lake City: Bookcraft, 1954.

Nimer, Cory. "The Old Guard and Rearguard Actions: Professionalization and the Church Historian's Office." *Journal of Mormon History* 45, no. 1 (January 2019): 110–38.

Nimer, Cory, and J. Gordon Daines III. "The Development and Professionalization of the Utah State Archives, 1897–1968," *Journal of Western Archives* 3, no. 1 (2012): 1–30.

Novak, Gary F. "'The Most Convenient Form of Error': Dale Morgan on Joseph Smith and the Book of Mormon." *FARMS Review of Books* 8, no. 1 (1996): 122–67.

Novick, Peter. *That Noble Dream: The "Objectivity Question" and the American Historical Profession.* New York: Cambridge University Press, 1988.

Office of Price Administration. *OPA Is Our Battle Line: Employee Handbook.* Region 7 ed. Washington, DC: Government Printing Office, 1943.

Parke-Bernet Galleries. *The Celebrated Collection of Americana Formed by the Late Thomas Winthrop Streeter.* 8 vols. New York: Parke-Bernet Galleries, 1966–1970.

Parke-Bernet Galleries. *Western Americana, Many of Great Rarity, Formed by W. J. Holliday.* New York: Parke-Bernet Galleries, 1954.

Paul, Rodman W. "The Mormons as a Theme in Western Historical Writing." *Journal of American History* 54, no. 3 (December 1967): 511–23.

Peeters, Paul J. H. L., Marloes T. Bazelier, Hubert G. M. Leufkens, Frank de Vries, and Marie L. DeBruin. "The Risk of Colorectal Cancer in Patients with Type 2 Diabetes: Associations with Treatment Stage and Obesity." *Diabetes Care* 38, no. 3 (March 2015): 495–502.

Pen Centennial. Salt Lake City: University Pen, 1950.

Penkower, Monty Noam. *The Federal Writers' Project: A Study in Government Patronage of the Arts.* Urbana: University of Illinois Press, 1977.

Peterson, Charles S. "Dale Morgan, Writers' Project, and Mormon History as a Regional Study." *Dialogue* 24, no. 2 (Summer 1994): 47–63.

Peterson, Charles S. Introduction to *Quicksand and Cactus: A Memoir of the Southern Mormon Frontier,* by Juanita Brooks, i–xxxvi. Logan: Utah State University Press, 1992.

Peterson, Charles S., and John A. Peterson. "Charles S. Peterson." In *Conversations with Mormon Historians.* Provo: Brigham Young University Religious Studies Center, 2015.

Peterson, Levi S. *Juanita Brooks: Mormon Woman Historian.* Salt Lake City: University of Utah Press, 1988.

Pole, Jack R. "Daniel J. Boorstin." In *Pastmasters: Some Essays on American Historians,* edited by Marcus Cunliffe and Robin W. Winks, 110–238. New York: Harper and Row, 1969.

Pole, Jack R. "Richard Hofstadter." In *Clio's Favorites: Leading Historians of the United States, 1945–2000,* edited by Robert Allen Rutland, 68–83. Columbia: University of Missouri Press, 2000.

Poll, Richard D. "The Swearing Elders: Some Reflections, a Response to Thomas Blakely." *Sunstone* 10, no. 9 (1985): 14–17.

Pomeroy, Earl. "Toward a Reorientation of Western History: Continuity and Environment." *Mississippi Valley Historical Review* 41, no. 4 (March 1955): 579–600.

Powell, H. M. T. *Santa Fe Trail to California, 1849–1852.* Edited by Douglas S. Watson. New York: Sol Lewis, 1981.

Pratt, Orson. *New and Easy Method of Solution of the Cubic and Biquadratic Equations, Embracing Several New Formulas, Greatly Simplifying this Department of Mathematical Science.* Liverpool, England: Longmans, Green, Reader, & Dyer, 1866.

Pratt, Parley P. *The Autobiography of Parley Parker Pratt, One of the Twelve Apostles of the Church of Jesus Christ of Latter-day Saints, Embracing His Life, Ministry, and Travels.* Chicago: Law, King & Law, 1888.

Price, David H. *Threatening Anthropology: McCarthyism and the FBI's Surveillance of Activist Anthropologists.* Durham, NC: Duke University Press, 2004.

Prince, Gregory. *Leonard Arrington and the Writing of Mormon History.* Salt Lake City: University of Utah Press, 2016.

Quinn, D. Michael. *The Mormon Hierarchy: Extensions of Power.* Salt Lake City, UT: Signature Books, 1997.

Quinn, D. Michael, ed. *The New Mormon History: Revisionist Essays on the Past.* Salt Lake City, UT: Signature Books, 1992.

Rasmussen, Alma Vernon. "The Government Work Relief Program in Utah, 1932–1940." Master's thesis, University of Utah, Salt Lake City, 1942.

Reeve, Paul W. *Religion of a Different Color: Race and the Mormon Struggle for Whiteness.* Oxford, UK: Oxford University Press, 2015.

Reilly, Charles, and Sen Qi. "Snapshot of Deaf and Hard of Hearing People, Postsecondary Attendance and Unemployment." Washington, DC: Gallaudet Research Institute, 2011. Accessed April 10, 2022. https://www.gallaudet.edu/office-of-international-affairs/demographics/deaf-employment-reports

Reinwand, Louis. "Andrew Jenson: Latter-day Saint Historian." *BYU Studies* 14, no. 1 (Autumn 1973): 29–46.

Ricoeur, Paul. *The Symbolism of Evil.* New York: Harper & Row, 1967.

Rischin, Moses. "The New Mormon History." *American West* 6, no. 2 (March 1969): 49.

Roberts, B. H. *Comprehensive History of the Church of Jesus Christ of Latter-day Saints.* 6 vols. Salt Lake City: Deseret News, 1930.

Roberts, B. H. "History of the 'Mormon' Church." *Americana* 4–10 (1909 July–1915 July).

Rollyson, Carl E. *A Higher Form of Cannibalism: Adventures in the Art and Politics of Biography.* New York: Ivan R. Dee, 2005.

Rubin, Joan Shelly. *The Making of Middle-Brow Culture.* Chapel Hill: University of North Carolina Press, 1992.

Saunders, Richard L. "Dear Dale, Dear Juanita: Two Friends and the Contest for Truth, Fact, and Perspective in Mormon History." 36th Juanita Brooks Lecture, Dixie State University, St. George, UT, 28 March 2019.

Saunders, Richard L. *Eloquence from a Silent World: A Bibliography of the Published Writings of Dale L. Morgan.* Salt Lake City: Caramon Press, 1990.

Saunders, Richard L. "Lost in Time: Dale L. Morgan and the Forty-niner Journal of William B. Lorton." *Southern California Quarterly* 98, no. 4 (2016): 457–86.

Saunders, Richard L. "Placing Juanita Brooks among the Heroes (Or Villains) of Mormon and Utah History." *Utah Historical Quarterly* 87, no. 3 (Summer 2019): 218–37.

Saunders, Richard L. "'The Strange Mixture of Emotion and Intellect:' A Social History of Dale L. Morgan 1933–1942." *Dialogue: A Journal of Mormon Thought* 28, no. 4 (Winter 1995): 39–58.

Saunders, Richard L. "The Utah Writers' Project and Writing of *Utah: A Guide to the State.*" *Utah Historical Quarterly* 70, no. 1 (Winter 2002): 21–38.

Schick, Frank L. *The Paperbound Book in America: The History of Paperbacks and Their European Background.* New York: R. R. Bowker, 1958.

Schoenberger, Dale T. "Interpretation of Western History: Academics versus Buffs." *Western Historical Quarterly* 2, no. 2 (April 1971): 232–33.

Schrader, Richard J. *The Hoosier House: Bobbs-Merrill and Its Predecessors, 1850–1985.* Farmington Hills, MI: Thomson Gale, 2004.

Schuster, Jack W., and Martin J. Finklestein. *The American Faculty: The Restructuring of Academic Work and Careers.* Baltimore, MD: Johns Hopkins University Press, 2006.

Serow, Robert C. "Policy as Symbol: Title II of the 1944 GI Bill." *Review of Higher Education* 27, no. 4 (2004): 481–99.

Shipps, Jan. "Richard Lyman Bushman: The Story of Joseph Smith and Mormonism, and the New Mormon History." *Journal of American History* 94, no. 2 (2007): 498–516.

Shugg, Roger W. "The Professors and their Publishers." *Daedalus* 92, no. 1 (Winter 1963): 68–77.

Simpson, Thomas W. *American Universities and the Birth of Modern Mormonism, 1867–1940.* Chapel Hill: University of North Carolina Press, 2016.

Smith, Joseph Fielding. *Essentials in Church History.* Salt Lake City: Deseret News, 1922.

Smith, Joseph Fielding. *The Origin of the Reorganized Church: The Question of Succession.* Salt Lake City: Skelton Publishing, 1907.

Stegner, Wallace E. *Beyond the Hundredth Meridian: John Wesley Powell and the Second Opening of the West.* New York: Penguin Books, 1992. First published 1954 by Houghton Mifflin Company.

Stegner, Wallace E. *The Gathering of Zion: The Story of the Mormon Trail.* New York: McGraw Hill, 1964.

Stenhouse, Fanny. *Exposé of Polygamy in Utah: A Lady's Life among the Mormons.* New York: American News Co., 1872.

Stenhouse, Fanny. *"Tell It All": The Story of a Life's Experience in Mormonism, an Autobiography.* Hartford, CT: A. D. Worthington, 1874.

Stenhouse, T. B. H. *Rocky Mountain Saints: A Full and Complete History of the Mormons from the First Vision of Joseph Smith to the Last Courtship of Brigham Young . . . and the Development of the Great Mineral Wealth of the Territory of Utah.* New York: D. Appleton & Co., 1873.

Stevens, Frank. "Is the Limited Edition the Solution to the Dollar Book Problem?" *Publishers Weekly,* 19 July 1930, 250–51.

Stott, William. *Documentary Expression and Thirties America.* New York: Oxford University Press, 1973.

Strach, Patricia. "Making Higher Education Affordable: Policy Design in Postwar America." *Journal of Policy History* 21, no. 1 (2008): 61–88.

Streeter, Thomas W. *Bibliography of Texas, 1795–1845.* 5 vols. Cambridge, MA: Harvard University Press, 1955–1960.

Sullivan, Tim. *No Communication with the Sea: Searching for an Urban Future in the Great Basin.* Tucson: University of Arizona Press, 2010.

Sutherland, Ian M. "Everybody Wins: Teaching Deaf and Hearing Students Together." In *Worlds Apart?: Disability and Foreign Language Learning,* edited by Tammy Berberi, Elizabeth C. Hamilton, and Ian M. Sutherland, 42–69. New Haven, CT: Yale University Press, 2008.

"A Symposium of Opinions: Certain Aspects of LDS. Education with Suggestions for Making It Less Theological and More Functional in Individual and Community Life." September 1950. Utah State University Special Collections and Archives, Logan.

Tabor, James D. "Do Historians of Religion Exclude the Supernatural?" *Huff-Post,* September 5, 2016. https://www.huffpost.com/entry/do-historians-of-religion-exclude-the-supernatural_b_57cda5cde4b06c750ddb3815.

Taylor, John. "The Organization of the Church." *Millennial Star,* 15 Nov 1851.

Tebbel, John. *A History of Book Publishing in the United States,* Volume 3: *The Golden Age between the Wars, 1920–1940.* New York: R. R. Bowker, 1975.

Tebbel, John. *A History of Book Publishing in the United States,* Volume 4: *The Great Change, 1940–1980.* New York: R. R. Bowker, 1978.

Thurston, Edwin Ross. "Teaching the Deaf." *Improvement Era* 49, no. 1 (January 1946): 24, 56.

Toland, John. *Captured by History: One Man's Vision of Our Tumultuous Century.* New York: St Martin's Press, 1997.

Toole, K. Ross, John Alexander Carroll, Robert M. Utley, and A. R. Mortensen, eds. *Probing the American West: Papers from the Santa Fe Conference.* Santa Fe: Museum of New Mexico Press, 1962.

Topping, Gary S. *D. Michael Quinn, Mormon Historian.* Salt Lake City, Utah: Signature Books, 2022.

Topping, Gary S. "Personality and Motivation in Utah Historiography." *Dialogue* 27, no. 1 (Spring 1994): 73–89.

Topping, Gary S. *Utah Historians and the Reconstruction of Western History.* Norman: University of Oklahoma Press, 2003.

Townsend, Robert B. *History's Babel: Scholarship, Professionalization, and the Historical Enterprise in the United States, 1880–1940.* Chicago: University of Chicago Press, 2013.

Toynbee, Arnold J. *Toynbee on Toynbee: A Conversation between Arnold J. Toynbee and G. R. Urban.* New York: Oxford University Press, 1974.

Turner, Frederick Jackson. *Rise of the New West, 1818–1829.* New York: Harper & Bros., 1906.

Turner, Frederick Jackson. "The Significance of the Frontier in American History." In *The Frontier in American History*, edited by Ray Allen Billington, 1–38. New York: Holt, Rinehart and Winston, 1962.

Turner, Frederick Jackson. *The United States, 1830–1850: The Nations and Its Sections.* New York: Peter Smith, 1950. First published 1935 by Henry Holt and Company.

Tyrell, Ian. *Historians in Public: The Practice of American History, 1890–1970.* Chicago: University of Chicago Press, 2005.

Underwood, Grant. "Re-visioning Mormon History." *Pacific Historical Review* 55, no. 3 (August 1986): 403–26.

United States Census Bureau. *The Blind and Deaf-mutes in the United States, 1930.* Washington, DC: Government Printing Office, 1931.

United States Census Bureau. *Fifteenth Census of the United States: 1930, Population,* vol. 3, pt. 2. Washington, DC: Government Printing Office, 1932.

Unruh, John D., Jr. *The Plains Across: Overland Emigrants and the Trans-Mississippi West, 1840–60.* Urbana: University of Illinois Press, 1978.

Utah Historical Records Survey. *WPA Historical Records Survey Project.* Ogden, UT: Works Progress Administration, 1940.

Utah Light and Traction Co. *Salt Lake City: Where to Go and How to Get There.* Salt Lake City: Utah Light and Traction Co., 1940.

Utley, Robert. *After Lewis and Clark: Mountain Men and the Paths to the Pacific.* Lincoln: University of Nebraska Press, 2004.

Utley, Robert. *A Life Wild and Perilous.* New York: Henry Holt & Company, 1997.

van Duym, A. A. "Where Is the Book Business Heading?" In "Strictly Personal," *Saturday Review of Literature,* 24 November 1945.

Veysey, Laurence R. *The Emergence of the American University.* Chicago: University of Chicago Press, 1965.

"Voice in Deseret," *Time,* 20 March 1950, 42.

Walker, Ronald W., David J. Whittaker, and James B. Allen. *Mormon History.* Urbana: University of Illinois Press, 2001.

Wallis, Wilson D. *Messiahs: Their Role in Civilization.* Washington, DC: American Council on Public Affairs, 1943.

Warfield, Ethel B. "Problems of Deafness." *American Annals of the Deaf* 83, no. 4 (September 1938): 300–305.

Washburn, Wilcomb E. "Anthropological Advocacy in the Hopi-Navajo Land Dispute." *American Anthropologist* 91, no. 3 (1989): 738–43.

Webb, Walter Prescott. "History as High Adventure." *American Historical Review* 64, no. 2 (January 1959): 265–81.

Werner, M. R. *Brigham Young.* New York: Harcourt, Brace and Company, 1925.

West, James L. W., III. *American Authors and the Literary Market Place since 1900.* Philadelphia: University of Pennsylvania Press, 1988.

West, James L. W., III. "The Divergent Paths of British and American Publishing." *Sewanee Review* 120, no. 4 (Fall 2012): 503–13.

Western Interstate Commission for Higher Education, Mental Health Program. *Information Gaps on the Deaf and Hard of Hearing Population: A Background Paper.* Boulder, CO: Western Interstate Commission for Higher Education, 2006, https://www.nasmhpd.org/sites/default/files /InformationGapsResearchPaper.pdf.

White, Hayden. "The Fictions of Factual Representation." In *Grasping the World: The Idea of the Museum,* edited by Donald Preziosi and Claire Farago, 22–34. London: Routledge, 2004.

Whiteley, Peter M., and David F. Aberle. "Can Anthropologists Be Neutral in Land Disputes? The Hopi-Navajo Case." *Man* 24, no. 2 (1989): 340–44.

Whittaker, David, ed. *Mormon Americana: A Guide to Sources and Collections in the United States.* Provo, Utah: Brigham Young University Studies, 1994.

Widtsoe, John A. *Joseph Smith: Seeker after Truth, Prophet of God.* Salt Lake City: Deseret News, 1952.

Widtsoe, John A. "On the Bookrack." *Improvement Era* 50, no. 4 (April 1947): 218.

Wilson, William A. Introduction to *The Roll-away Saloon: Cowboy Tales of the Arizona Strip,* ix–xii. By Rowland W. Rider. Edited by Deirdre Murray Paulsen. Logan: Utah State University Press, 1985.

Wilson, William Jerome. "Manuscripts in Microfilm: Problems of Librarian and Custodian." *Library Quarterly* 13, no. 3 (July 1943): 212–26.

Winther, Oscar Osburn. *A Classified Bibliography of the Periodical Literature of the Trans-Mississippi West, 1811–1957.* 2nd ed. Bloomington: Indiana University Press, 1961.

Withington, Mary. *A Catalogue of Manuscripts in the Collection of Western Americana Founded by William Robertson Coe, Yale University Library.* New Haven, CT: Yale University Press, 1952.

Works Division. *A Report of the Works Division.* Salt Lake City: Utah Emergency Relief Administration, 1935.

Wright, Doris Marian. *A Guide to the Mariano Guadalupe Vallejo Documentos para la Historia de California, 1780–1875.* Guides to the Manuscript Collections, no. 1. Berkeley: University of California Press, 1953.

Wunder, John R., ed. *Historians of the American Frontier: A Bio-bibliographical Sourcebook.* Westport, CT: Greenwood Press, 1988.

Young, Levi Edgar. *Chief Episodes in the History of Utah.* Chicago: Lakeside Press, 1912.

Young, Levi Edgar. *The Founding of Utah.* New York: Scribner, 1924.

Young, Levi Edgar. "The Great West in American History." *Bulletin of the University of Utah (new series)* 11, no. 9 (1920): 3–9.

Young, Levi Edgar. *The Story of Utah.* Danville, New York: Hall & McCreary, 1913.

Index